Davenport–Schinzel Sequences and Their Geometric Applications

Davenport–Schinzel sequences contain no pair of equal adjacent elements, and no alternating subsequence of specified length. These sequences arise in the analysis of the combinatorial complexity of the lower envelope of univariate functions, and are therefore a basic and important construct in many geometric applications, both combinatorial and algorithmic. They possess the surprising property that their maximum length is almost linear in the number of symbols.

This book presents a comprehensive treatment of Davenport–Schinzel sequences and their geometric applications. It begins by introducing the sequences and describing some of their basic properties. It then presents a detailed analysis of the maximum length of Davenport–Schinzel sequences, and describes two geometric realizations of sequences of nonlinear length in terms of lower envelopes of line segments in the plane. The book continues by presenting combinatorial and algorithmic applications of Davenport–Schinzel sequences to arrangements of curves in the plane. It then presents extensions of the Davenport–Schinzel theory to arrangements of hypersurfaces in higher dimensions. The book concludes with miscellaneous geometric applications of these sequences.

T0215715

To Irith, to my father and mother in memoriam,
and to my children Yoav and Uri

Micha

To my parents and grandparents

Pankaj

Davenport–Schinzel sequences and their geometric applications

MICHA SHARIR

Tel Aviv University

PANKAJ K. AGARWAL

Duke University

CAMBRIDGE
UNIVERSITY PRESS

CAMBRIDGE UNIVERSITY PRESS
Cambridge, New York, Melbourne, Madrid, Cape Town, Singapore,
São Paulo, Delhi, Dubai, Tokyo

Cambridge University Press
The Edinburgh Building, Cambridge CB2 8RU, UK

Published in the United States of America by Cambridge University Press, New York

www.cambridge.org
Information on this title: www.cambridge.org/9780521135115

First published 1995
This digitally printed version 2010

A catalogue record for this publication is available from the British Library

Library of Congress Cataloguing in Publication data
Sharir, Micha.
Davenport–Schinzel sequences and their geometric applications /
Micha Sharir, Pankaj K. Agarwal.
p. cm.
Includes bibliographical references and index.
ISBN 0–521–47025–0
1. Davenport–Schinzel sequences.   2. Envelopes (Geometry)
I. Agarwal, Pankaj K.   II. Title.
QA246.5.S53 1995
512′.72–dc20   94–30889
                                                          CIP

ISBN 978-0-521-47025-4 Hardback
ISBN 978-0-521-13511-5 Paperback

CONTENTS

PREFACE

Davenport–Schinzel sequences are interesting and powerful combinatorial structures that arise in the analysis and calculation of the lower or upper envelope
of collections of functions, and therefore have applications in many geometric problems that can be reduced to the calculation of such an envelope. In
addition, Davenport–Schinzel sequences play a central role in many related
geometric problems involving arrangements of curves and surfaces. For these
reasons, they have become one of the major tools in the analysis of combinatorial and algorithmic problems in geometry.

Roughly speaking, an (n, s) Davenport–Schinzel sequence, where n and s
are positive integers, is a sequence composed of n symbols with the properties that no two adjacent elements are equal and that it does not contain, as
a (possibly noncontiguous) subsequence, any alternation $\langle a \cdots b \cdots a \cdots b \cdots \rangle$
of length $s + 2$ between two distinct symbols a and b. Thus, for example,
an $(n, 3)$ sequence is not allowed to contain any subsequence of the form
$\langle a \cdots b \cdots a \cdots b \cdots a \rangle$. The first major goal in the analysis of these sequences,
which will occupy the first half of this book, is to estimate the maximum pos-
sible length of an (n, s) Davenport–Schinzel sequence, for any given values of
the parameters n and s, where usually s is regarded as a fixed constant and n
as a variable.

The importance of Davenport–Schinzel sequences lies in their relationship
to the combinatorial structure of the (lower or upper) envelope of a collection
of functions. Specifically, for any collection of n real-valued continuous functions, $f_1, \ldots, f_n$, defined on the real line and having the property that each pair
of them intersect in at most s points, the sequence of function indices i in the
order in which these functions attain their lower envelope (i.e., their pointwise
minimum $f(x) = \min_i f_i(x)$) from left to right is an (n, s) Davenport–Schinzel

sequence. Conversely, any (n, s) Davenport–Schinzel sequence can be realized
in this manner for an appropriate collection of n continuous univariate functions, each pair of which intersect in at most s points. Thus, the study of
problems that involve lower envelopes of collections of functions (and, as we
shall see in this book, there are many such important problems) is intimately
linked to the study of Davenport–Schinzel sequences.

Davenport–Schinzel sequences were originally introduced by H. Davenport
and A. Schinzel in the 1960s (motivated by a problem posed by Malanowski).
Curiously, their original papers were entitled 'On a combinatorial problem connected with differential equations,' because they were motivated by a particular
application that involved the pointwise maximum of a collection of independent
solutions of a linear differential equation. They established the connection between these sequences and upper or lower envelopes of functions, and obtained
several nontrivial bounds on the length of the sequences. The next significant
progress on the estimation of the length of Davenport–Schinzel sequences has
been made by E. Szemerédi in 1974, who derived improved bounds, close to
linear in n for any fixed s. The problem then lay dormant for nearly 10 years,
until M. Atallah, in 1983, rediscovered these sequences in a paper studying
problems in dynamic computational geometry. Atallah's work was the first to
emphasize the importance of Davenport–Schinzel sequences as a basic tool in
combinatorial and computational geometry, but it fell short of providing tight
bounds on their maximum length. (As we shall see in this book, this problem
is nontrivial for $s \geq 3$; the cases $s = 1$ and $s = 2$ are very easy.)

Such tight bounds have finally been obtained in 1984 by S. Hart and
M. Sharir, who showed that the maximum length of an $(n, 3)$ Davenport–
Schinzel sequence is within a constant factor of $n\alpha(n)$, where $\alpha(n)$ is the
extremely slowly growing inverse of Ackermann's function. Thus the length of
such a sequence is nearly linear in n, but can be (ever so slightly) superlinear.
This analysis has later been extended, by P. Agarwal, M. Sharir, and P. Shor
in 1989, to $s > 3$, and led to sharp, nearly tight, and nearly linear bounds for
all fixed s.

Hart and Sharir started their work without being aware of the history of the
problem, and proceeded for about half a year in frustration, splitting the time
between attempts to prove a linear upper bound and to construct a superlinear
lower bound. Then P. Erdős (to whom we are deeply grateful) communicated
to Hart and Sharir the earlier references. Szemerédi's upper bounds were
of the form $C_s n \log^* n$, for some constants C_s depending on s, where $\log^* n$
is the smallest height of an exponential 'tower' of 2's, $2^{2^{2^{\cdot^{\cdot^{\cdot}}}}}$ which is $\geq n$.
These bounds left little room for improvement, and, assuming at this point
that the true bound is superlinear, Hart and Sharir embarked on an attempt
to prove that the maximum length of $(n, 3)$ Davenport–Schinzel sequences is
proportional to $n\alpha(n)$, a rather natural choice for a function 'in between' linear
and Szemerédi's bound. They have borrowed ideas that R. Tarjan has used
in his analysis of the complexity of the union-find algorithm for maintaining

equivalence relations, which is also proportional to $n\alpha(n)$, and were fortunate enough to show that a slight modification of Tarjan's lower bound construction also applies to Davenport–Schinzel sequences. The proof of the upper bound, though, required a different approach.

This somewhat surprising property, that their length is nearly linear in n (for any fixed s), makes Davenport–Schinzel sequences a useful and powerful tool for solving numerous problems in discrete and computational geometry, usually by showing that the geometric structure being analyzed has smaller combinatorial complexity than what more naive considerations would have implied. Many such geometric applications have been obtained in the past decade, and the second half of this book presents most of these applications. A small sample of applications includes problems such as:

(i) Analysis of the combinatorial complexity of the boundary of any single face in an arrangement of segments or arcs in the plane.

(ii) Calculation of Euclidean shortest paths in 3-space amid polyhedral obstacles.

(iii) Analysis of the space of collision-free placements of a convex polygon in a 2-dimensional polygonal region.

(iv) Computing the minimum Hausdorff distance, under translation, between two point sets.

(v) Analysis of the visibility of a polyhedral terrain from a fixed or varying point lying above it.

(vi) Calculation of convex hulls of objects more general than points.

(vii) Analysis of certain geometric structures (convex hulls, nearest neighbors, Voronoi diagrams) defined by collections of time-varying points.

As noted above, Davenport–Schinzel sequences provide a complete combinatorial characterization of the lower envelope of certain collections of *univariate* functions. In many geometric problems (including some of those listed above), one faces the more difficult problem of calculating or analyzing the envelope of a collection of multivariate functions. Even for bivariate functions this problem appears to be considerably harder than the univariate case. Nevertheless, recent progress, starting in 1993, has been made on the multivariate case, leading to almost-tight bounds on the complexity of such envelopes. Chapter 7 of this book is devoted to the analysis of lower envelopes of multivariate functions and of related structures.

The material presented in this book is a mixture of the basic combinatorial analysis of Davenport–Schinzel sequences and of their geometric applications, both combinatorial and algorithmic. The first three chapters introduce the sequences, show their connection with lower envelopes, and are mostly devoted to the analysis of the maximum length of (n, s) Davenport–Schinzel sequences. Chapters 4–6 present basic geometric applications of Davenport–Schinzel sequences, and study in detail the role that these sequences play in various structures in arrangements of curves in the plane, including lower envelopes, single faces, and zones. Chapter 7 describes the analysis of lower envelopes and related structures in higher-dimensional spaces, and Chapter 8, the longest in the book, contains applications of Davenport–Schinzel sequences to a variety of specific problems in combinatorial and computational geometry. The applications in Chapter 8 are mostly independent from each other, and each of them can be studied in isolation, if the reader so wishes. The algorithmic portions of the book require some basic knowledge of computational geometry, while the purely combinatorial portions (Chapters 1–3) hardly require any specific prior knowledge.

In concluding the preface, we express our gratitude and appreciation to many colleagues and friends who contributed to the creation of this monograph through joint research, helpful discussions, providing useful information, and moral support. These include Boris Aronov, Mike Atallah, Paul Erdős, Danny Halperin, Sergiu Hart, Klara Kedem, János Pach, Ricky Pollack, Jack Schwartz, Peter Shor, Shmuel Sifrony, Boaz Tagansky, and Arik Tamir.

TEL AVIV AND DURHAM, 1995

1

INTRODUCTION

Definition 1.1 Let n, s be positive integers. A sequence $U = \langle u_1, \ldots, u_m \rangle$ of integers is an (n, s) *Davenport–Schinzel sequence* (a $DS(n, s)$-*sequence* for short), if it satisfies the following conditions:

(i) $1 \le u_i \le n$ for each i.

(ii) For each $i < m$ we have $u_i \ne u_{i+1}$.

(iii) There do not exist $s + 2$ indices $1 \le i_1 < i_2 < \cdots < i_{s+2} \le m$ such that $u_{i_1} = u_{i_3} = u_{i_5} = \cdots = a$, $u_{i_2} = u_{i_4} = u_{i_6} = \cdots = b$, and $a \ne b$.

In other words, this condition forbids the presence of long alternations of any pair of distinct symbols in a Davenport–Schinzel sequence.

We refer to s as the *order* of U and to n as the *number of symbols* composing U. We will write $|U| = m$ for the *length* of the sequence U. Define

$$\lambda_s(n) = \max\{\,|U| \mid U \text{ is a } DS(n, s)\text{-sequence}\,\}.$$

The estimation of $\lambda_s(n)$ is the major subject of the first part of the book.

This problem was first considered by Davenport and Schinzel (1965).[1] Their interest in it arose from its connection to the analysis of solutions of

---

[1] According to Davenport and Schinzel (1965), the problem was originally posed (in a

linear differential equations. Atallah (1985) raised it again independently, because of its significance for problems in dynamic computational geometry. These two applications are quite similar, and are two special cases of the following more general problem.

1.1   Davenport–Schinzel sequences and lower envelopes

Let $\mathcal{F} = \{f_1, \ldots, f_n\}$ be a collection of n real-valued continuous functions defined on a common interval I. Suppose that for each $i \neq j$ the functions f_i and f_j intersect in at most s points (this is the case for polynomials of fixed degree, Chebycheff systems, and so on). The *lower envelope* of $\mathcal{F}$ is defined as

$$E_{\mathcal{F}}(x) = \min_{1 \leq i \leq n} f_i(x), \quad x \in I$$

(i.e., $E_{\mathcal{F}}$ is the pointwise minimum of the functions f_i).[2] Let m be the smallest number of subintervals $I_1, \ldots, I_m$ of I such that for each k there exists an index u_k with $E_{\mathcal{F}}(x) = f_{u_k}(x)$ for all $x \in I_k$. In other words, m is the number of (maximal) connected portions of the graphs of the f_i's which constitute the graph of $E_{\mathcal{F}}$. The endpoints of the intervals I_k are called the *breakpoints* or the *transition points* of the envelope $E_{\mathcal{F}}$. Assuming that $I_1, \ldots, I_m$ are arranged in this order from left to right, put

$$U(f_1, \ldots, f_n) = \langle u_1, \ldots, u_m \rangle.$$

See Figure 1.1 for an illustration of this "lower envelope sequence."

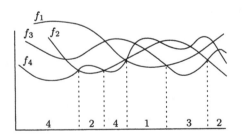

FIGURE 1.1. The lower envelope sequence.

The *upper envelope* of $\mathcal{F}$ is defined, in a fully symmetric manner, to be

$$E_{\mathcal{F}}^*(x) = \max_{1 \leq i \leq n} f_i(x), \quad x \in I.$$

---

slightly different form) by Malanowski. The term *Davenport–Schinzel sequence* was coined by Stanton and Roselle (1969).

[2] Abusing the definition slightly, we will also refer to the graph of the function $E_{\mathcal{F}}(x)$ as the *lower envelope*.

In this book we mostly consider lower envelopes. This choice is arbitrary, and all our results apply, of course, equally well to upper envelopes.

Lemma 1.2 $U(f_1, \ldots, f_n)$ *is a* $DS(n, s)$*-sequence. Conversely, for any given* $DS(n, s)$*-sequence* U *one can construct a collection* $f_1, \ldots, f_n$ *of functions as above for which* $U(f_1, \ldots, f_n) = U$.

Proof. For the first part, note that, by definition, $U = U(f_1, \ldots, f_n)$ does not contain a pair of adjacent identical elements. Suppose there exist two distinct indices $a \neq b$ so that U contains $s + 2$ indices $i_1 < i_2 < \cdots < i_{s+2}$ such that $u_{i_1} = u_{i_3} = \cdots = a$ and $u_{i_2} = u_{i_4} = \cdots = b$. By definition of the lower envelope, we must have $f_a(x) < f_b(x)$ for $x \in (int(I_{i_1}) \cup int(I_{i_3}) \cup \cdots)$ and $f_a(x) > f_b(x)$ for $x \in (int(I_{i_2}) \cup int(I_{i_4}) \cup \cdots)$, where $int(J)$ denotes the relative interior of the interval J. Since f_a and f_b are continuous, there must exist $s + 1$ distinct points $x_1, \ldots, x_{s+1}$ such that x_r lies between the intervals I_{i_r} and $I_{i_{r+1}}$ and $f_a(x_r) = f_b(x_r)$, for $r = 1, \ldots, s+1$. This, however, contradicts the fact that f_a and f_b intersect in at most s points (see Figure 1.2 for an illustration of the proof).

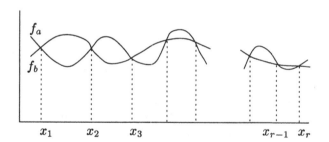

$$f_a$$
$$f_b$$
$$x_1 \qquad x_2 \qquad x_3 \qquad\qquad x_{r-1} \ \ x_r$$

FIGURE 1.2. Forbidden alternation along the lower envelope.

For the converse statement, let $U = \langle u_1, \ldots, u_m \rangle$ be a given $DS(n, s)$-sequence. Without loss of generality, suppose the symbols $1, 2, \ldots, n$ of which U is composed are ordered so that the leftmost appearance of symbol i in U precedes the leftmost appearance of symbol j in U if and only if $i < j$. We now define the required collection of functions $\mathcal{F} = \{f_1, \ldots, f_n\}$ as follows. We choose $m-1$ distinct "transition points" $x_2 < x_3 < \ldots < x_m$ on the x-axis, and $n+m-1$ distinct horizontal "levels," say, at $y = 1, 2, \ldots, n, -1, -2, \ldots, -(m-1)$. For each symbol $1 \leq a \leq n$ the graph of the corresponding function f_a is always horizontal at one of these levels, except at short intervals near some of the transition points, where it can drop very steeply from one level to a lower one. At each transition point exactly one function changes its level. More specifically:

(i) Before x_2, the function f_a is at the level $y = a$, for $a = 1, \ldots, n$.

(ii) At the transition point x_i, let $a = u_i$; then f_a drops down from its current level to the highest still "unused" level. See Figure 1.3 for an illustration.

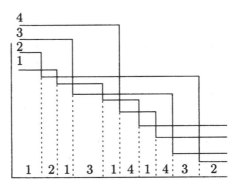

FIGURE 1.3. Realization of a sequence.

It is clear from this construction that $U(f_1, \ldots, f_n) = U$. It remains to show that each pair of functions intersect in at most s points. Let f_a and f_b be such a pair, with $a < b$, and suppose they intersect at $s + 1$ points. Note that by construction each of these intersections must occur at a transition point, when one of these two functions drops to the next minimum level. Moreover, to the left of all transition points we have $f_a < f_b$. Thus at the leftmost intersection point it is f_b that drops down, and immediately afterward appears along the lower envelope $E_{\mathcal{F}}$ of the functions; similarly, at the second intersection, f_a drops down and appears along $E_{\mathcal{F}}$, and so on. This gives us a subsequence V of U of length $s + 1$ of the form $\langle b \cdots a \cdots b \cdots a \cdots \rangle$, starting at b. But since $a < b$, the leftmost appearance of a in U lies to the left of the leftmost appearance of b in U. Thus, the subsequence consisting of the leftmost appearance of a followed by V is an alternation of a and b in U of length $s + 2$, contradicting the fact that U is a $DS(n, s)$-sequence. This contradiction completes the proof. $\square$

Corollary 1.3 *The maximum length of the sequence $U(f_1, \ldots, f_n)$ is $\lambda_s(n)$, where the maximum is taken over all collections of n continuous functions $\{f_1, \ldots, f_n\}$, where each pair of these functions intersect in at most s points.*

It is interesting to note that a similar equivalence exists between Davenport–Schinzel sequences and lower envelopes of *partially defined* functions. Specifically, let $f_1, \ldots, f_n$ be a collection of partially defined and continuous functions, so that the domain of definition of each function f_i is an interval I_i, and suppose further that each pair of these functions intersect in at most s points.

One can define the lower envelope sequence $U(f_1, \ldots, f_n)$ in much the same way as for totally defined functions; see Figure 1.4. In this case we have:

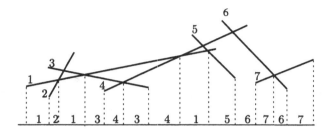

FIGURE 1.4. The lower envelope of a collection of (nonvertical) segments.

Lemma 1.4 *If $\{f_1, \ldots, f_n\}$ is a collection of partially defined functions as above, then the sequence $U(f_1, \ldots, f_n)$ is a $DS(n, s+2)$-sequence. Conversely, for any $DS(n, s+2)$-sequence U one can construct a collection $f_1, \ldots, f_n$ of partially defined and continuous functions, each defined over an interval, and each pair of which intersect in at most s points, such that $U(f_1, \ldots, f_n) = U$.*

Proof. The first assertion of the lemma is easily proved by transforming each f_i into a totally defined continuous function $f_i^\star$ by extending its graph by a steeply decreasing ray toward the left endpoint of the graph, and by a steeply increasing ray from the right endpoint of the graph. If we choose the absolute values of the slopes of all these rays to be equal and sufficiently large, then it is easily seen that the extended functions $f_1^\star, \ldots, f_n^\star$ are such that (i) each pair of them intersect in at most $s + 2$ points, and (ii) their lower envelope sequence $U(f_1^\star, \ldots, f_n^\star)$ is equal to the sequence $U(f_1, \ldots, f_n)$.

Conversely, given any $(n, s + 2)$ Davenport–Schinzel sequence U, we construct a collection of partial functions $f_1, \ldots, f_n$ with the desired properties, as follows. We carry out the construction given in the proof of Lemma 1.2, except for the following changes: For each symbol a in U, the graph of the corresponding function f_a starts immediately after the transition abscissa corresponding to the first (leftmost) appearance of a in U, at the appropriate currently lowest level. Similarly, the graph of f_a terminates on the lower envelope of the functions immediately after the transition corresponding to the last appearance of a in U. Arguing as in the preceding proof, it is easy to show that each pair of these partial functions intersect in at most s points, thus establishing the converse assertion, and completing the proof of the lemma. $\square$

Corollary 1.5 *The lower envelope sequence of n (nonvertical) line segments in the plane is an $(n, 3)$ Davenport–Schinzel sequence.*

Corollary 1.6 *If $f_1, \ldots, f_n$ are partially defined functions, with at most s intersection points between any pair, then the maximum length of the sequence $U(f_1, \ldots, f_n)$ is $\lambda_{s+2}(n)$.*

Remark 1.7 The functions constructed in Lemmas 1.2 and 1.4 to realize an arbitrary $DS(n, s)$-sequence have fairly irregular structure. A problem that arises naturally in this context is whether any $DS(n, s)$-sequence can be realized as the lower envelope sequence of a collection of n partial or total functions of some canonical special form. For example, can any $(n, 3)$ Davenport–Schinzel sequence be realized as the lower envelope sequence of a collection of n line segments? Some partially affirmative results on this kind of problem will be presented in Chapter 4.

Using an argument similar to that of Lemma 1.4, one can prove:

Lemma 1.8 *If $f_1, \ldots, f_n$ are partially defined functions, with at most s intersection points between any pair, such that there exists a vertical line that intersects all of their graphs, then the maximum length of $U(f_1, \ldots, f_n)$ is at most $2\lambda_{s+1}(n)$.*

As these last results show, Davenport–Schinzel sequences are strongly related to the problem of computing the (lower) envelope of a set of continuous functions, each pair of which intersect in at most some fixed number of points. This problem has many applications in discrete and computational geometry and related areas, and a considerable portion of this book will be devoted to the presentation of these applications.

1.2   Simple bounds on $\lambda_s(n)$

We begin our analysis of the quantities $\lambda_s(n)$ by "disposing" of the two simple cases $s = 1$ and $s = 2$, and by obtaining very simple (but weak) bounds for $s > 2$.

Theorem 1.9 (a) $\lambda_1(n) = n$.   (b) $\lambda_2(n) = 2n - 1$.

Proof. (a) Let U be an $(n, 1)$ Davenport–Schinzel sequence. Thus U does not contain any subsequence of the form $\langle a \cdots b \cdots a \rangle$ for $a \neq b$. Since adjacent elements of U cannot be equal, it follows that all elements of U are distinct, so $|U| \leq n$. Since $U = \langle 1\ 2\ 3 \cdots n \rangle$ is a $DS(n, 1)$-sequence, the bound is tight.

(b) The proof proceeds by induction on n. The case $n = 1$ is obvious. Suppose $\lambda_2(n - 1) = 2n - 3$, and let U be any $(n, 2)$ Davenport–Schinzel sequence. For each $1 \leq a \leq n$ let μ_a denote the smallest index such that $u_{\mu_a} = a$ (if μ_a is undefined for some a then U is an $(n - 1, 2)$ Davenport–Schinzel sequence, and the induction hypothesis implies $|U| \leq 2n - 1$). Let b be the symbol for which μ_b is largest. We claim that U contains only a single occurrence of b (at position μ_b). Indeed, suppose to the contrary that $u_k = b$ for some $k > \mu_b$. Then $c = u_{\mu_b+1}$ is different from b, and since U is a $DS(n,2)$-sequence, all appearances of c in U must occur between the positions μ_b and k, as is easily checked. Thus $\mu_c = \mu_b + 1$, contradicting the maximality of μ_b. Remove the single appearance of b from U, and, if $u_{\mu_b-1} = u_{\mu_b+1}$, remove also one of these newly adjacent equal elements from U. The resulting sequence is clearly an $(n-1,2)$ Davenport–Schinzel sequence, and is one or two elements shorter than U. The induction hypothesis then implies $|U| \leq 2n-3+2 = 2n-1$. Since the sequence $\langle 1\ 2\ 3 \cdots n-1\ n\ n-1 \cdots 3\ 2\ 1 \rangle$ is clearly a $DS(n,2)$-sequence of length $2n-1$, the bound is tight. $\qquad\square$

A cyclic sequence U will be called a $DS(n,2)$-*cycle* if no two adjacent symbols are the same and if U does not contain a subcycle of the form $\langle a \cdots b \cdots a \cdots b \rangle$, for $a \neq b$. Notice that the maximum length of a $DS(2,2)$-cycle is 2. Using the same argument as in Theorem 1.9 (b), one can show:

Corollary 1.10 *The maximum length of a $DS(n,2)$-cycle consisting of n symbols is $2n-2$.*

As we will see later, obtaining a sharp upper bound on the maximum length of a $DS(n,s)$-sequence, for $s \geq 3$, is not as simple. We will give tight or almost tight bounds on $\lambda_s(n)$, for $s \geq 3$, in the following two chapters. Here we give simple proofs of some weaker bounds.

Lemma 1.11 $\lambda_3(n) \leq 2n(\ln n + O(1))$.

Proof. Let U be any $(n,3)$ Davenport–Schinzel sequence. On the average, each symbol $1, 2, \ldots, n$ appears in the sequence $\frac{1}{n}|U| \leq \frac{1}{n}\lambda_3(n)$ times. Let a be a symbol whose number of appearances in U is smallest, and is thus at most $\frac{1}{n}\lambda_3(n)$. Remove a from U. It is possible that, after removal of a, some pairs of equal elements of U will become adjacent to one another, but we claim that this can happen at most twice, around the first and the last appearances of a in U. Indeed, if U contains a contiguous subsequence of the form $\langle xax \rangle$, where this appearance of a in U is neither the first nor the last one, then U contains a forbidden subsequence of the form $\langle a \cdots xax \cdots a \rangle$, which is impossible. Thus if we remove all appearances of a, and at most two additional elements, from U, we will obtain an $(n-1,3)$ Davenport–Schinzel sequence, whose length is at most $\lambda_3(n-1)$. We thus obtain the following recurrence relationship

$$\lambda_3(n) \leq \lambda_3(n-1) + \frac{\lambda_3(n)}{n} + 2,$$

for $n > 1$, and $\lambda_3(1) = 1$, as is easily checked. In other words, we have

$$\left(1 - \frac{1}{n}\right)\lambda_3(n) \leq \lambda_3(n-1) + 2,$$

or

$$\frac{\lambda_3(n)}{n} \leq \frac{\lambda_3(n-1)}{n-1} + \frac{2}{n-1}.$$

Summing these inequalities, we obtain

$$\lambda_3(n) \leq 2n\left(1 + \frac{1}{2} + \frac{1}{3} + \cdots + \frac{1}{n-1}\right) + n$$
$$= 2n(\ln n + O(1)). \qquad \square$$

We also have the following trivial upper bound, which at least shows that $\lambda_s(n)$ is always well defined.

Lemma 1.12 $\lambda_s(n) \leq \dfrac{sn(n-1)}{2} + 1.$

Proof. We use the equivalence, proved in Lemma 1.2, between Davenport–Schinzel sequences and lower envelopes of functions. Let $f_1, \ldots, f_n$ be n continuous functions, each pair of which intersects in at most s points. Then the total number of their intersection points is at most $sn(n-1)/2$, and the length of the corresponding lower envelope sequence $U(f_1, \ldots, f_n)$ is at most 1 more than the number of intersection points lying on the lower envelope. These observations clearly complete the proof. $\qquad \square$

Roselle and Stanton (1970, 1971) showed that, for $s \geq n$,

$$\lambda_s(n) \geq \frac{sn(n-1)}{2} - cn^3,$$

where $c < 1$ is a constant. Thus the bound of Lemma 1.12 is close to optimal if s is sufficiently larger than n, but it is far from being sharp if we assume s to be some fixed constant. Even the better bound in Lemma 1.11 for $\lambda_3(n)$ will be shown to be too large. Davenport and Schinzel proved in their original paper that $\lambda_s(n) = n \cdot 2^{O(\sqrt{\log n})}$, which was later improved by Szemerédi (1974) to $O(n \log^* n)$, with a constant of proportionality that is doubly exponential in s. Exact bounds for $\lambda_s(n)$ have also been obtained for some small values of s and n. Table 1.1 summarizes the known exact bounds.

We conclude this chapter by mentioning a variant of Davenport–Schinzel sequences that arises in a number of applications. Let

$$U = \langle u_1, u_2, \ldots, u_n \rangle$$

be a $DS(n, s)$-sequence. For $1 \leq j \leq m$, let $\mu(j)$ denote the number of symbols whose leftmost occurrences in U are either u_j or before u_j, and whose rightmost occurrences are after u_j. We define the *depth* of U to be the maximum value of $\mu(j)$ over all $j \leq m$. Define a $DS(n, s, t)$-sequence to be a $DS(n, s)$-sequence with depth at most t, and let $\lambda_{s,t}(n)$ denote the maximum length of a $DS(n, s, t)$-sequence.

TABLE 1.1. *Exact bounds on $\lambda_s(n)$ for small values of n and s.*

n	s									
	1	2	3	4	5	6	7	8	9	10
1	1	1	1	1	1	1	1	1	1	1
2	2	3	4	5	6	7	8	9	10	11
3	3	5	8	10	14	16	20	22	26	
4	4	7	12	16	23	28	35	40	47	
5	5	9	17	22	33	41	53	61	73	
6	6	11	22							
7	7	13	27							
8	8	15	32							
9	9	17								
10	10	19								

NOTE: The first two rows and first two columns extend regularly to all columns and all rows, respectively.

Theorem 1.13 $\lambda_{s,t}(n) \leq \left\lceil \dfrac{n}{t} \right\rceil \lambda_s(2t).$

Proof. Let $U = \langle u_1, \ldots, u_m \rangle$ be a $DS(n, s, t)$-sequence. We partition U from left to right into maximal contiguous subsequences $B_1, \ldots, B_q$ such that each B_i contains at most $2t$ distinct symbols, that is, if $B_j = \langle u_{i_j}, \ldots, u_{i_{j+1}-1} \rangle$ and $i_{j+1} \leq m$, then the subsequence $\langle u_{i_j}, \ldots, u_{i_{j+1}-1}, u_{i_{j+1}} \rangle$ has $2t + 1$ distinct symbols. By construction, $|B_j| \leq \lambda_s(2t)$ for each $1 \leq j \leq q$. We claim that each B_j, except for the last one, contains the leftmost occurrences of at least t distinct symbols (that is, there are at least t distinct symbols in B_j that do not occur in any of $B_1, \ldots, B_{j-1}$). The claim is obviously true for $j = 1$. Suppose, for the sake of contradiction, that the claim is false for some $j > 1$. Then there are at least $t+1$ distinct symbols that appear in B_j as well as to the left of u_{i_j}, which implies that $\mu(i_j - 1) > t$, thus contradicting the assumption that the depth of U is at most t. Hence, each B_j, for $j < q$, contains the leftmost occurrences of at least t distinct symbols, and therefore $q \leq \lceil n/t \rceil$. This completes the proof of the theorem. $\qquad\square$

An immediate corollary of the above theorem is

Corollary 1.14 *Let $\mathcal{F} = \{f_1, \ldots, f_t\}$ be a collection of t real-valued continuous piecewise-linear functions (i.e., the graph of each f_i is an x-monotone polygonal chain). Let n be the total number of edges in the graphs of the functions of $\mathcal{F}$. Then the lower envelope of $\mathcal{F}$ has at most $\lambda_{3,t}(n) \leq \lceil n/t \rceil \lambda_3(2t)$ breakpoints.*

Proof. Let E be the set of edges in the graphs of functions of $\mathcal{F}$. We can regard each edge $e_i \in E$ as the graph of a partially defined function g_i; let G

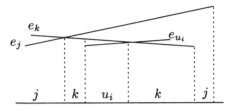

FIGURE 1.5. Edges corresponding to symbols that appear before as well as after u_i.

denote the resulting set of n partially defined functions. The lower envelope of G is the same as the lower envelope of $\mathcal{F}$, so it suffices to bound the number of breakpoints in the lower envelope of G. Let $U = \langle u_1, \ldots, u_m \rangle$ be the lower envelope sequence of G, as defined in Section 1.1. By Corollary 1.5, U is a $DS(n,3)$-sequence. If the depth of U is more than t, then $\mu(i) > t$ for some $i \le m$. This implies that there are two symbols j, k such that the edges e_j, e_k belong to the graph of the same function f_p of $\mathcal{F}$ and that j and k appear before or at u_i as well as after u_i in U. But then the x-projections of the edges e_j, e_k are not disjoint (see Figure 1.5), contradicting the x-monotonicity of f_p. Hence the depth of U is at most t, which implies that $|U| \le \lambda_{3,t}(n)$. $\square$

1.3 Bibliographic notes

The material presented in this chapter is mostly taken from Davenport and Schinzel (1965) and from Atallah (1985). It is worth providing a brief description of the evolution of the theory of Davenport–Schinzel sequences. The problem was originally posed by Malanowski, and was first studied by Davenport and Schinzel (1965). They were concerned with the analysis of the pointwise maximum of a system of independent solutions to linear differential equations, which is just a special case of the lower (or upper) envelope problem formulated in Section 1.1. The problem was studied in several early papers by Davenport and Schinzel (1965), Roselle and Stanton (1970, 1971), Stanton and Roselle (1969), Davenport (1971), Mullin and Stanton (1972), Mills (1973), Peterkin (1973), Dobson and Macdonald (1974), Roselle (1974), Rennie and Dobson (1975), and Stanton and Dirksen (1976) (see also the more recent paper of Gardy and Gouyou-Beauchamps (1990)), but no bounds really close to linear were obtained until Szemerédi (1974) showed that $\lambda_s(n) \le C(s)n \log^{\star} n$ for each $s \ge 3$ and for appropriate positive constants $C(s)$ (doubly exponential in s). The problem then lay dormant for about 10 years, until it was rediscovered by Atallah (1985), in connection with certain problems in "dynamic" computational geometry (see Section 8.6). He was not aware of the previous work on the problem, and again was not able to obtain nontrivial bounds on $\lambda_s(n)$. The first tight bounds on $\lambda_s(n)$ have been obtained by Hart and

Sharir (1986); improved upper and lower bounds on $\lambda_s(n)$, for $s > 3$, have been obtained by Sharir (1987, 1988a), and the best currently known bounds for $\lambda_s(n)$ have been obtained by Agarwal, Sharir, and Shor (1989). These bounds are presented in the next two chapters. A recent survey on Davenport–Schinzel sequences and their geometric applications is by Sharir (1988b).

The material in Section 1.1 is partly adapted from Atallah (1985), but includes some other results (e.g. Lemma 1.11). The upper bounds given in Section 1.2 are from Davenport and Schinzel (1965). Later Davenport (1971) proved that

$$\lambda_3(n) = O\left(n\frac{\log n}{\log\log n}\right).$$

Table 1.1 is taken from Stanton and Roselle (1969) and Roselle and Stanton (1970). They also proved bounds on $\lambda_s(n)$ for the case $s \geq n$. Theorem 1.13 is taken from Huttenlocher, Kedem, and Kleinberg (1992a). They used it to prove an upper bound on the number of combinatorial changes in the Voronoi diagram of a set of moving points; see Section 8.6.

Adamec, Klazar, and Valtr (1992) have studied some generalizations of Davenport–Schinzel sequences. In particular, they bound the length of sequences not containing more general forbidden subsequences, for example, subsequences consisting of more than two symbols. They also showed that the maximum length of a sequence not containing any forbidden subsequence $\langle a^{i_1}b^{i_2}a^{i_3}b^{i_4}\rangle$, where i_1, i_2, i_3, i_4 are some positive constants, is linear. See also Klazar (1992, 1993, 1994, 1995) and Klazar and Valtr (1994) for related results.

2

DAVENPORT–SCHINZEL SEQUENCES OF ORDER 3

In the previous chapter we presented a weak upper bound on $\lambda_3(n)$, showing that $\lambda_3(n) = O(n \log n)$. In this chapter we prove matching upper and lower bounds on $\lambda_3(n)$. We show that $\lambda_3(n) = \Theta(n\alpha(n))$, where $\alpha(n)$ is the functional inverse of the Ackermann's function. We also describe a relationship between $DS(n, 3)$-sequences and generalized path compression schemes, which was originally used in Hart and Sharir (1986) to obtain the asymptotically tight bound on $\lambda_3(n)$. In order to derive the upper and lower bounds for $\lambda_3(n)$ we first digress briefly and review the definition and basic properties of Ackermann's function.

2.1 Ackermann's function—A review

In this section we recall the definition of Ackermann's function and its functional inverse, which appears in the upper and lower bounds for $\lambda_s(n)$. Ackermann's function (also called "generalized exponentials") is an extremely fast growing function defined over the integers in the following recursive manner.

Let N denote the set of positive integers $1, 2, \ldots$. Given a function g from a set into itself, denote by $g^{(s)}$ the composition $g \circ g \circ \ldots \circ g$ of g with itself s times, for $s \in$ N. Define inductively a sequence $\{A_k\}_{k=1}^{\infty}$ of functions from N into itself as follows:

$$
\begin{aligned}
A_1(n) &= 2n, \\
A_k(n) &= A_{k-1}^{(n)}(1), \qquad k \geq 2
\end{aligned}
$$

for all $n \in \mathbb{N}$. Note that, for all $k \geq 2$, the function A_k satisfies

$$
\begin{aligned}
A_k(1) &= 2, \\
A_k(n) &= A_{k-1}(A_k(n-1)), \qquad n \geq 2.
\end{aligned}
$$

In particular, $A_2(n) = 2A_2(n-1)$, thus A_2 is the "power function"

$$
A_2(n) = 2^n, \qquad n \in \mathbb{N}.
$$

Then $A_3(n) = 2^{A_3(n-1)}$, thus A_3 is the "tower function"

$$
A_3(n) = 2^{2^{{\cdot}^{{\cdot}^{{\cdot}^2}}}},
$$

with n 2's in the exponential tower, for $n \in \mathbb{N}$. Finally, put

$$
A(n) = A_n(n).
$$

This is *Ackermann's function* (actually, there are several variants of this function; their orders of magnitude are essentially the same, and our results do not depend on which one we use; see for example Lemma 2.2 below). Ackermann's function A grows very fast; its first values are: $A(1) = 2$, $A(2) = 4$, $A(3) = 16$, and $A(4)$ is a tower of 65536 2's. For basic properties of the functions defined above, the reader is referred to Tarjan (1975).[1]

Given a strictly increasing function g from $\mathbb{N}$ into itself, its *functional inverse* is the function γ from $\mathbb{N}$ into itself given by

$$
\gamma(n) = \min\{s \geq 1 : g(s) \geq n\};
$$

thus, $\gamma(n) = s$ if and only if $g(s-1) < n \leq g(s)$. In particular, let α_k and α denote the functional inverses of A_k and A, respectively. Then, for all $n \in \mathbb{N}$,

$$
\begin{aligned}
\alpha_1(n) &= \left\lceil \frac{n}{2} \right\rceil, \\
\alpha_2(n) &= \lceil \log n \rceil.
\end{aligned}
$$

The functions α_k are easily seen to satisfy the following recursive formula:

$$
\alpha_k(n) = \min\{s \geq 1 : \alpha_{k-1}^{(s)}(n) = 1\};
$$

that is, $\alpha_k(n)$ is the number of iterations of α_{k-1} needed to go from n to 1. In particular, $\alpha_3(n)$ is commonly denoted by $\log^\star n$, and is equal to the smallest

---

[1] Note that his index k is one less than ours.

number of repeated (base 2) logarithms (each rounded to the nearest larger integer) one has to apply to n to obtain 1; alternatively, by definition, it is the length of the smallest tower $2^{2^{-2}}$ whose value is $\geq n$.

All the functions α_k are nondecreasing, and converge to infinity with their argument. The same holds for α too, which grows more slowly than any of the α_k. Note that $\alpha(n) \leq 4$ for all $n \leq A(4)$, which is a tower with 65536 2's, thus $\alpha(n) \leq 4$ for all practical values of n.

Remark 2.1 The inverse of Ackermann's function has also appeared in the analysis of the union-find algorithm in Tarjan (1975). The inverse function appearing there is, in our notations,

$$\alpha^T(n) = \min\{k \geq 1 : A_{k+1}(4) > \log n\}$$

(see Tarjan (1975), p. 221, for $m = n$); recall that our function is

$$\alpha(n) = \min\{k \geq 1 : A_k(k) \geq n\}.$$

However, the two functions are of the same order of magnitude:

Lemma 2.2 For all $n \geq 1$, $\frac{1}{4}\alpha(n) \leq \alpha^T(n) \leq 2\alpha(n)$.

To show this, we use the following

Lemma 2.3 For all $k \geq 1$ and $s \geq 3$, $A_k(s+1) \leq A_{k+1}(s)$.

Proof. It is easily checked that $A_k(s) \leq A_{k+1}(s)$ for all $k, s \geq 1$. Then

$$\begin{aligned} A_{k+1}(s) &= A_k(A_{k+1}(s-1)) \geq A_k(A_2(s-1)) \\ &= A_k(2^{s-1}) \geq A_k(s+1), \end{aligned}$$

for all $s \geq 3$. $\qquad\square$

Proof of Lemma 2.2. If $n \leq 16$, then $\alpha(n) \leq 3$ and $\alpha^T(n) = 1$. If $n > 16$, then $\alpha(n) \geq 4$, and, using Lemma 2.3, we obtain, for $k = \alpha(n)$

$$\log n < n \leq A_k(k) \leq A_{2k-4}(4),$$

thus $\alpha^T(n) \leq 2\alpha(n) - 5$.

For the converse, it is easily checked that if $\alpha^T(n) = 1$ or 2, then $\alpha(n) \leq 4$; if $\alpha^T(n) = 3$, then $\alpha(n) \leq 5$. Finally, if $k = \alpha^T(n) \geq 4$, then

$$\begin{aligned} n &< 2^{A_{k+1}(4)} = A_2(A_{k+1}(4)) \leq A_k(A_{k+1}(4)) \\ &= A_{k+1}(5) \leq A_{k+1}(k+1), \end{aligned}$$

thus $\alpha(n) \leq \alpha^T(n) + 1$. $\qquad\square$

Lemma 2.4 *For all $n \geq 1$,*

(a) $\alpha_{\alpha(n)}(n) \leq \alpha(n)$.

(b) $\alpha_{\alpha(n)+1}(n) \leq 4$.

Proof. Put $k = \alpha(n)$. By definition, $A_{k-1}(k-1) < n \leq A_k(k)$, which readily establishes (a). As to (b), note that $A_{k+1}(4) = A_k(A_{k+1}(3))$. By repeated applications of Lemma 2.3, we obtain

$$A_{k+1}(3) \geq A_k(4) \geq \cdots \geq A_1(k+3) > k.$$

Thus $A_{k+1}(4) \geq A_k(k) \geq n$, so, by definition, $\alpha_{k+1}(n) \leq 4$.   □

More properties of Ackermann's function and of several related functions will be presented in Chapter 3.

2.2   The upper bound

In this section we establish an almost linear upper bound on $\lambda_3(n)$. We first introduce some notation.

Let $U = \langle u_1, u_2, \ldots, u_m \rangle$ be a $DS(n, 3)$-sequence. Define, for each $i = 1, \ldots, n$,

$$\mu_i = \min \{\beta : u_\beta = i\},$$
$$\nu_i = \max \{\beta : u_\beta = i\};$$

that is, μ_i is the index of the first occurrence of i in U, and ν_i is the index of the last occurrence. Without loss of generality (permuting $1, \ldots, n$ if necessary), we may assume that $\mu_1 < \mu_2 < \cdots < \mu_n$.

Definition 2.5   A *block* $c = (u_\beta, \ldots, u_\gamma)$ is a maximal decreasing contiguous subsequence of U, that is,

$$(u_{\beta-1} <) u_\beta > u_{\beta+1} > \cdots > u_\gamma (< u_{\gamma+1}).$$

Blocks are obviously disjoint and their union is U.

Lemma 2.6 *Suppose that $i = u_{\beta-1} < u_\beta = j$. Then either $\beta - 1 = \nu_i$ or $\beta = \mu_j$.*

Proof. Suppose the contrary; then $\gamma = \mu_j < \beta - 1$ and $\delta = \nu_i > \beta$. Also, since $i < j$ we must have $\varepsilon = \mu_i < \mu_j = \gamma$. Overall, we obtain five indices $\varepsilon < \gamma < \beta - 1 < \beta < \delta$ such that $u_\varepsilon = u_{\beta-1} = u_\delta = i$ and $u_\gamma = u_\beta = j$, a contradiction which completes the proof.   □

Corollary 2.7 *There are at most $2n$ distinct blocks in U.*

Proof. By the preceding lemma, a block can end either at ν_i or at $\mu_i - 1$, for some $i = 1, \ldots, n$, and there are at most $2n$ such places. □

Remark 2.8 The correct upper bound on the number of blocks is actually $2n - 1$, since $\mu_1 - 1 = 0$; it is attained, for example, by the sequence (of length $5n - 8$)

$$\langle 1\ 2\ 1\ 3\ 1 \cdots 1\ n - 1\ 1\ n - 1\ n - 2 \cdots 3\ 2\ n\ 2\ n\ 3\ n \cdots n\ n - 1\ n \rangle.$$

A slightly weaker notion of a block is that of a chain. Specifically:

Definition 2.9 Let U be any $DS(n, 3)$-sequence. A *chain* (or 1-chain) c is a contiguous subsequence of U all of whose elements are distinct from one another.

Clearly each block in U is a chain but not vice versa (chains are required to be neither decreasing nor maximal). Thus, while the partitioning of U into blocks is unique and well defined, U can in general be partitioned into (pairwise disjoint) chains in many possible ways.

Lemma 2.10 *U can be partitioned into at most $2n - 1$ disjoint chains.*

Proof. Use the block partition of U and Corollary 2.7 (and Remark 2.8). □

Definition 2.11 Let $\Psi(m, n)$ denote the maximum length of an $(n, 3)$ Davenport–Schinzel sequence which is composed of m chains.

We begin by deriving a recurrence relation for the function Ψ.

Lemma 2.12 *Let $m, n \geq 1$, and let $b > 1$ be a divisor of m. Then there exist integers $n^\star, n_1, n_2, \ldots, n_b \geq 0$ such that*

$$n^\star + \sum_{i=1}^{b} n_i = n,$$

and

$$\Psi(m, n) \leq \Psi(b, n^\star) + 4m + 4n^\star + \sum_{i=1}^{b} \Psi\left(\frac{m}{b}, n_i\right). \tag{2.1}$$

Proof. Let U be a $DS(n, 3)$-sequence consisting of at most m chains $c_1, \ldots, c_m$ such that $|U| = \Psi(m, n)$, and let $b > 1$ be a divisor of m. Partition the sequence U into b *layers* (contiguous subsequences) $L_1, \ldots, L_b$, so that the layer L_i consists of the $p = m/b$ chains $c_{(i-1)p+1}, c_{(i-1)p+2}, \ldots, c_{ip}$. Call a symbol a *internal* to layer L_i if all the occurrences of a in U are within L_i. A symbol will be called *external* if it is not internal to any layer. Suppose that there are n_i internal symbols in layer L_i and $n^\star$ external symbols; thus $n^\star + \sum_{i=1}^{b} n_i = n$.

To estimate the total number of occurrences in U of symbols that are internal to L_i, we proceed as follows. Erase from L_i all external symbols. Next scan L_i from left to right and erase each element that has become equal to the element immediately preceding it. This leaves us with a sequence $L_i^\star$ which is clearly a $DS(n_i, 3)$-sequence consisting of at most m/b chains, and thus its length is at most $\Psi(m/b, n_i)$. Moreover, if two equal internal elements in L_i have become adjacent after erasing the external symbols, then these two elements must have belonged to two distinct chains, thus the total number of deletions of internal symbols is at most $(m/b) - 1$.

Hence, summing over all layers, we conclude that the total contribution of internal symbols to $|U|$ is at most

$$m - b + \sum_{i=1}^{b} \Psi\left(\frac{m}{b}, n_i\right).$$

Next, to estimate the contribution of external symbols to $|U|$, we argue as follows. For each L_i, call an external symbol a a *middle* symbol if none of its occurrences in L_i is the first or the last occurrence of a in U. Otherwise we call a a *nonmiddle* symbol. We will consider separately the contribution to the length of U of middle occurrences and of nonmiddle occurrences of external symbols.

Consider first middle symbols. To estimate their contribution to the length of L_i, we erase from L_i all other symbols occurring there, and, if necessary, also erase each occurrence of a middle symbol which has become equal to the element immediately preceding it. As above, at most $(m/b) - 1$ deletions of external middle symbols will be performed. Let $L_i^\star$ be the resulting subsequence, and suppose that it is composed of p_i distinct symbols.

We claim that $L_i^\star$ is a $DS(p_i, 1)$-sequence. Indeed, if this were not the case, $L_i^\star$ would contain an alternating subsequence W of two external middle symbols a, b, which has length 3 and which begins, say, with a. But since b is assumed to be middle, there must exist at least one occurrence of b to the left of L_i and one occurrence of b to the right of L_i, which, concatenated with W, yield a forbidden alternating subsequence of length 5 within U, contrary to assumptions.

Thus $L_i^\star$ is a $DS(p_i, 1)$-sequence, so that its length is at most p_i. Hence, summing over all layers, the total contribution of external middle symbols is at most

$$m - b + \sum_{i=1}^{b} p_i.$$

But $\sum_{i=1}^{b} p_i$ is the length of the sequence obtained by concatenating all the subsequences L_i^*. This concatenation can contain at most b pairs of adjacent equal elements, and if we erase each element that is equal to its predecessor, we obtain a sequence U^* which is clearly a $DS(n^*, 3)$-sequence composed of b chains (namely the subsequences L_i^*). Thus the length of U^* is at most $\Psi(b, n^*)$. Hence the contribution of middle external elements to the length of U is at most

$$m + \Psi(b, n^*).$$

Consider next the contribution of nonmiddle symbols. To estimate their contribution to the length of L_i we erase from L_i all symbols occurring there except for external symbols which make their first (leftmost) appearance, and, if necessary, also erase each occurrence of such a *starting* symbol which has become equal to the element immediately preceding it. As above, at most $\frac{m}{b} - 1$ deletions of external starting symbols will be performed. Let $L_i^{\#}$ be the resulting subsequence, and suppose that it is composed of p_i distinct symbols.

Note first that each external symbol can appear as a starting element in exactly one layer, thus $\sum_{i=1}^{b} p_i = n^*$. We claim that $L_i^{\#}$ is a $DS(p_i, 2)$-sequence. Indeed, if it contained an alternating subsequence of the form $\langle a \cdots b \cdots a \cdots b \rangle$, then, since a is external and starting at L_i, it must appear again at some succeeding layer, yielding a forbidden subsequence of the form $\langle a \cdots b \cdots a \cdots b \cdots a \rangle$ in U. Thus the length of $L_i^{\#}$ is at most $2p_i - 1$, and, summing over all layers, we conclude that the contribution of all external starting symbols to the length of U is at most

$$m - b + \sum_{i=1}^{b} (2p_i - 1) = m - 2b + 2n^*.$$

In a completely symmetric manner, the contribution of external *ending* symbols to the length of U is also at most $m - 2b + 2n^*$. Summing up all these contributions we finally obtain

$$\Psi(m, n) \;\leq\; m - b + \sum_{i=1}^{b} \Psi\left(\frac{m}{b}, n_i\right) + m + \Psi(b, n^*) + 2(m - 2b + 2n^*)$$

$$\leq\; 4m + 4n^* + \Psi(b, n^*) + \sum_{i=1}^{b} \Psi\left(\frac{m}{b}, n_i\right). \qquad \Box$$

Lemma 2.13 *Let $n, s \geq 1$, $k \geq 2$, and suppose that m divides $A_k(s)$. Then*

$$\Psi(m, n) \leq (4k - 4)ms + (4k - 2)n. \tag{2.2}$$

Proof. We will use (2.1) repeatedly to obtain the series of upper bounds on Ψ, stated in (2.2) for $k = 2, 3, \ldots$. At each step we choose b in an appropriate manner, and estimate $\Psi(b, n^*)$ using the bound obtained in the preceding step.

This yields a recurrence relation on Ψ which we solve to obtain a better upper bound on Ψ.

Specifically, we proceed by double induction on k and s. To start this iterative process with $k = 2$, suppose first that $m = A_2(s) = 2^s$. Choose $b = 2$ in (2.1); it is easily checked that $\Psi(b, n^\star) = \Psi(2, n^\star) = 2n^\star$ for all $n^\star$, so that (2.1) yields

$$\Psi(m, n) \leq 4m + 6n^\star + \Psi\left(\frac{m}{2}, n_1\right) + \Psi\left(\frac{m}{2}, n_2\right).$$

The solution to this recurrence relation, for m a power of 2 and $n = n^\star + n_1 + n_2$ arbitrary, is easily verified to be

$$\Psi(m, n) \leq 4m \log m + 6n.$$

To complete the argument for $k = 2$, note that if m divides $A_2(s) = 2^s$ then m is a power of 2 and $\log m \leq s$, thus

$$\Psi(m, n) \leq 4m \log m + 6n \leq 4ms + 6n.$$

In particular, we have for $m = 1, 2$

$$\Psi(m, n) \leq 4m + 6n \leq (4k - 4)m + (4k - 2)n$$

for all $k \geq 2$. Since $A_k(1) = 2$ it follows that (2.2) holds for each $k \geq 2$ and $s = 1$.

Suppose next that $k > 2$ and $s > 1$, and that the induction hypothesis is true for all $k' < k$ and $s' \geq 1$, and for $k' = k$ and all $s' < s$. Observe that $A_k(s-1)$ is a divisor of $A_k(s)$ because they are both powers of 2. Assume first that $m = A_k(s)$; let $t = A_k(s-1)$ and choose $b = m/t$, which is an integer dividing $m = A_k(s) = A_{k-1}(t)$. Hence, by the induction hypothesis (for $k-1$ and t), we have

$$\Psi(b, n^\star) \leq (4k - 8)bt + (4k - 6)n^\star = (4k - 8)m + (4k - 6)n^\star.$$

Then (2.1) becomes

$$\Psi(m, n) \leq (4k - 8)m + (4k - 6)n^\star + 4m + 4n^\star + \sum_{i=1}^{b} \Psi(t, n_i).$$

Using the induction hypothesis once more (for k and $s - 1$), we obtain

$$\begin{aligned}
\Psi(m, n) &\leq (4k - 4)m + (4k - 2)n^\star + \sum_{i=1}^{b}((4k - 4)t(s - 1) + (4k - 2)n_i) \\
&= (4k - 4)ms + (4k - 2)\left(n^\star + \sum_{i=1}^{b} n_i\right) \\
&= (4k - 4)ms + (4k - 2)n,
\end{aligned}$$

because $n^\star + \sum_{i=1}^{b} n_i = n$.

Finally, assume that m divides $A_k(s)$, say $A_k(s) = pm$. Let U be an $(n, 3)$ Davenport–Schinzel sequence composed of m chains whose length is $\Psi(m, n)$. Take p copies of U, having pairwise disjoint sets of symbols, and concatenate them to produce a new sequence U^*. Clearly U^* is a $(pn, 3)$ Davenport–Schinzel sequence composed of at most pm chains, and its length is $p\Psi(m, n)$. Thus

$$
\begin{aligned}
p\Psi(m, n) &\leq \Psi(pm, pn) \\
&= \Psi(A_k(s), pn) \\
&\leq (4k - 4)sA_k(s) + (4k - 2)pn,
\end{aligned}
$$

which, divided by p, yields the required inequality. This completes the proof of the lemma. □

Corollary 2.14 *For all $m, n \geq 1$ and $k \geq 2$,*

$$
\Psi(m, n) \leq (8k - 8)m\alpha_k(m) + (4k - 2)n,
$$

where α_k is the functional inverse of A_k as defined in Section 2.1.

Proof. Put $s = \alpha_k(m)$, so that $A_k(s - 1) < m \leq A_k(s)$. Let $p = \lfloor A_k(s)/m \rfloor \geq 1$, then $A_k(s) < (p + 1)m \leq 2pm$. As in the preceding proof, we have

$$
\begin{aligned}
p\Psi(m, n) &\leq \Psi(pm, pn) \\
&\leq \Psi(A_k(s), pn) \\
&\leq (4k - 4)sA_k(s) + (4k - 2)pn \\
&\leq (8k - 8)pms + (4k - 2)pn.
\end{aligned}
$$

Dividing by p, we obtain the desired inequality. □

Theorem 2.15 *For all $m, n \geq 1$,*

$$
\Psi(m, n) \leq 32m\alpha(m) + (4\alpha(m) + 2)n.
$$

Proof. Assume first $m > 4$ so that $\alpha(m) \geq 3$. Let $k = \alpha(m) + 1$, then $\alpha_k(m) \leq 4$ by Lemma 2.4. Using Corollary 2.14, we obtain

$$
\begin{aligned}
\Psi(m, n) &\leq 8\alpha(m) \cdot 4m + (4\alpha(m) + 2)n \\
&= 32m\alpha(m) + (4\alpha(m) + 2)n.
\end{aligned}
$$

For $m \leq 4$ the desired inequality holds trivially because $\Psi(m, n) \leq 4n$. □

Corollary 2.16 $\lambda_3(n) \leq (68n - 32)\alpha(n) + (70n - 32) = O(n\alpha(n))$.

Proof. Immediate from Theorem 2.15, Lemma 2.10, and the fact that

$$
\alpha(2n - 1) \leq \alpha(n) + 1.
$$

□

Corollary 2.17 *The lower envelope of a collection of n segments in the plane has $O(n\alpha(n))$ breakpoints.*

An immediate corollary of Corollaries 1.14 and 2.16 is

Corollary 2.18 *The lower envelope of a collection of t piecewise-linear functions with a total of n edges has $O(n\alpha(t))$ breakpoints.*

Remark 2.19 The constants appearing in the above corollaries are probably much too large, and are just a consequence of our (somewhat sloppy) analysis.

2.3   The lower bound

In this section we derive a lower bound for $\lambda_3(n)$ that matches, up to a multiplicative constant, the upper bound just derived, by providing an explicit inductive construction of $(n, 3)$ Davenport–Schinzel sequences whose length is $\Omega(n\alpha(n))$.

The construction proceeds by double induction, and produces a collection of sequences $S(k, m)$, defined in terms of two positive integer parameters k and m. Each sequence $S(k, m)$ is constructed from subsequences defined inductively for smaller values of k and m, which are then modified and merged to form $S(k, m)$.

2.3.1   Auxiliary functions

Define inductively a sequence $\{B_k\}_{k=1}^{\infty}$ of functions from the set $\mathbb{N}_0 = \mathbb{N} \cup \{0\}$ into itself as follows.

$$
\begin{aligned}
B_1(m) &= 0, & m \geq 0, & \\
B_k(0) &= 1, & k \geq 2, & \quad (2.3) \\
B_k(m) &= B_k(m-1) + B_{k-1}(2^{B_k(m-1)}), & k \geq 2, m \geq 1. &
\end{aligned}
$$

Here are some properties of the functions B_k. The proofs of the nontrivial properties are given in Appendix 2.1.

(B1) $B_2(m) = 1$, for $m \geq 0$.

(B2) $B_3(m) = m + 1$, for $m \geq 0$.

(B3) $B_4(m) \geq 2^{2^{\cdot^{\cdot^{2}}}}$, with m 2's in the exponential tower, for $m \geq 0$; i.e. $B_4(m) \geq A_3(m)$.

(B4) Each function $B_k(m)$ is strictly increasing in m, for all $k \geq 3$, and each sequence $\{B_k(m)\}_{k \geq 1}$ is strictly increasing, for all $m \geq 1$.

(B5) $B_k(m) \geq A_{k-1}(m)$, for $k \geq 4$, $m \geq 1$.

(B6) $2^{B_k(m)+2} \le A_k(m+3)$, for $k \ge 1$, $m \ge 0$.

(B7) $A_{k-1}(m) \le B_k(m) \le 2^{B_k(m)} \le A_k(m+3)$, for $k \ge 4$, $m \ge 1$,
so that the sequences of functions B_k and A_k have the same asymptotic order of growth.

Next we define another sequence of functions $\{C_k\}$ by putting $C_k(m) = 2^{B_k(m)}$, for all k and m. An explicit recursive definition of these functions, for positive k and m, is

$$
\begin{array}{lll}
C_1(m) & = & 1, & m \ge 1, \\
C_k(1) & = & 2C_{k-1}(2), & k \ge 2, \\
C_k(m) & = & C_k(m-1) \cdot C_{k-1}(C_k(m-1)), & k \ge 2, m \ge 2.
\end{array}
\tag{2.4}
$$

It follows easily from the preceding analysis that

(C1) $C_2(m) = 2$, for $m \ge 0$.

(C2) $C_3(m) = 2^{m+1}$, for $m \ge 0$.

(C3) $C_4(m) \ge 2^{2^{\cdot^{\cdot^{\cdot^2}}}}$, with $m+1$ 2's in the exponential tower.

(C4) $A_{k-1}(m) \le C_k(m) \le A_k(m+3)$, for $k \ge 4$, $m \ge 1$,
so that the growth of the sequences of functions $\{C_k\}$ and $\{A_k\}$ are also of the same asymptotic order of magnitude.

In what follows we will often use the shorthand notations

$$
\bar{\alpha} = C_k(m-1), \quad \bar{\beta} = C_{k-1}(C_k(m-1)) = C_{k-1}(\bar{\alpha})
$$

and $\bar{\gamma} = C_k(m) = \bar{\alpha} \cdot \bar{\beta}$ (by definition).

2.3.2   Generation of superlinear-size sequences

For each $k, m \ge 1$, the sequence $S(k, m)$ that we are going to construct will satisfy the following two properties:

(1) $S(k, m)$ is composed of $N_k(m) = m \cdot C_k(m)$ distinct symbols. (These symbols are named (d, γ), for $d = 1, \ldots, m$, $\gamma = 1, \ldots, \bar{\gamma}$, and are ordered in lexicographical order, so that $(d, \gamma) < (d', \gamma')$ if $\gamma < \gamma'$ or $\gamma = \gamma'$ and $d < d'$.)

(2) $S(k, m)$ contains $C_k(m)$ *fans* of size m, where each fan is a contiguous subsequence of the form

$$
\langle (1, \gamma)\, (2, \gamma) \, \cdots \, (m, \gamma) \rangle.
$$

Since fans are pairwise disjoint by definition, the naming scheme of the symbols of $S(k, m)$ can be interpreted as assigning to each symbol the index γ of the fan in which it appears, and its index d within that fan.

The construction proceeds by double induction on k and m, as follows.

1. $k = 1$: The sequence is a single fan of size m:

$$S(1, m) = \langle (1, 1)\, (2, 1)\, \cdots\, (m, 1) \rangle.$$

   Properties (1) and (2) clearly hold here ($C_1(m) = 1$).

2. $k = 2$: The sequence contains a pair of disjoint fans of size m, with a block following each of these fans. Specifically,

$$\begin{aligned}
S(2, m) \;=\; & \langle (1, 1)\, (2, 1)\, \cdots\, (m-1, 1)\, (m, 1)\, (m-1, 1)\, \cdots\, (1, 1) \\
& (1, 2)\, (2, 2)\, \cdots\, (m-1, 2)\, (m, 2)\, (m-1, 2)\, \cdots\, (1, 2) \rangle.
\end{aligned}$$

   Indeed, $S(2, m)$ contains $C_2(m) = 2$ fans and is composed of $2m$ symbols.

3. $k \geq 3, m = 1$: The sequence is identical to the sequence for $k' = k - 1$ and $m' = 2$, except for renaming of its symbols and fans: $S(k - 1, 2)$ contains $C_{k-1}(2) = \frac{1}{2} C_k(1)$ fans, each of which consists of two symbols; the symbol renaming in $S(k, 1)$ causes each of these two elements to become a 1-element fan. Properties (1) and (2) clearly hold.

4. The general case $k \geq 3, m > 1$:

   (i) Generate inductively the sequence $S' = S(k, m - 1)$; by induction, it contains $\bar{\alpha}$ fans of size $m - 1$ each and is composed of $(m - 1) \cdot \bar{\alpha}$ symbols.

   (ii) Create $\bar{\beta}$ copies of S' whose sets of symbols are pairwise disjoint. For each $\beta \leq \bar{\beta}$, rename the symbols in the βth copy S'_β of S' as (d, α, β) where $1 \leq d \leq m - 1$ is the index of the symbol in the fan of S'_β containing it, and $1 \leq \alpha \leq \bar{\alpha}$ is the index of this fan in S'_β.

   (iii) Generate inductively the sequence $S^\star = S(k - 1, \bar{\alpha})$ whose set of symbols is disjoint from that of any S'_β; by induction, it contains $\bar{\beta}$ fans of size $\bar{\alpha}$ each. Rename the symbols of $S^\star$ as (m, α, β) (where α is the index of that symbol within its fan, and β is the index of that fan in $S^\star$). Duplicate the last element $(m, \bar{\alpha}, \beta)$ in each of the $\bar{\beta}$ fans of $S^\star$.

   (iv) For each $1 \leq \alpha \leq \bar{\alpha}$, $1 \leq \beta \leq \bar{\beta}$, extend the αth fan of S'_β by duplicating its last element $(m - 1, \alpha, \beta)$, and by inserting the corresponding symbol (m, α, β) of $S^\star$ between these duplicated appearances of $(m - 1, \alpha, \beta)$. This process extends the $(m - 1)$-fans of S'_β into m-fans and adds a new element after each extended fan.

(v) Finally construct the desired sequence $S(k,m)$ by merging the $\bar{\beta}$ copies S'_β of S' with the sequence $S^\star$. This is done by replacing, for each $1 \leq \beta \leq \bar{\beta}$, the βth fan of $S^\star$ by the corresponding copy S'_β of S', as modified in (iv) above. Note that the duplicated copy of the last element in each fan of $S^\star$ (formed in step (iii) above) appears now after the copy S'_β that replaces this fan; see Figure 2.1 for an illustration of this process.

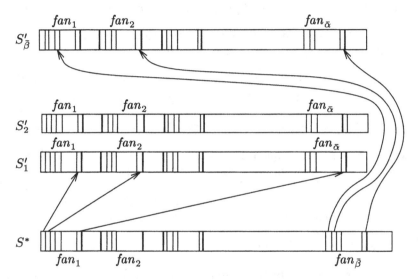

FIGURE 2.1. Merging the subsequences.

To establish property (1), note that $S(k,m)$ consists of

$$
\begin{aligned}
N_k(m) &= \bar{\beta} \cdot (m-1)\bar{\alpha} + \bar{\alpha}C_{k-1}(\bar{\alpha}) \\
&= (m-1)\bar{\alpha}\bar{\beta} + \bar{\alpha}\bar{\beta} \\
&= m\bar{\alpha}\bar{\beta} \\
&= mC_k(m)
\end{aligned}
$$

symbols. Property (2) is trivial, because the fans of $S(k,m)$ are precisely the extended fans of the copies S'_β of S', and their number is $C_k(m-1)\cdot\bar{\beta} = C_k(m)$.

We now establish several important properties of the sequences $S(k,m)$. For our present purpose, property (a) is all we need. However, later on in Chapter 4 we will be concerned with geometric realization of the sequences $S(k,m)$, and there we will need to use the other properties.

Theorem 2.20 *For each $k,m \geq 1$ the sequence $S = S(k,m)$ satisfies the following properties:*

(a) S is a $DS(N_k(m), 3)$-sequence.

(b) Each symbol of S appears in precisely one fan and makes its first (left-most) appearance in S.

(c) For $k \geq 2$ and for each $\gamma \leq \bar{\gamma}$, the last element (m, γ) of the γth fan of S forms the beginning of a contiguous subsequence that is the reverse of that fan:

$$\langle (m, \gamma)\, (m-1, \gamma)\, \cdots\, (2, \gamma)\, (1, \gamma) \rangle.$$

(Note that this sequence is the initial portion of a block of S.)

(d) For each block c of S, let f be the rightmost fan preceding or including c and let $c_1, c_2, \ldots, c_t$ be the blocks appearing in S between f and c, for some $t \geq 0$. Let a be the first (leftmost) element of c; then either this appearance of a is within f, or else a must also appear in one of the preceding blocks c_i.

Remark 2.21 (i) For each $\gamma \leq \bar{\gamma}$ and each $d < m$, the element (d, γ) in the γth fan of S forms a 1-element block. Note that property (d) is trivially correct for these singleton blocks.

(ii) Property (b) implies in particular that S starts with a fan.

(iii) Unless c is one of the singleton blocks mentioned in (i) above, the first block c_1 in property (d) is the block mentioned in (c) (whose initial portion is the reverse of the fan f). Note that property (d) clearly holds for the case $c = c_1$.

Proof. The proof proceeds by double induction on k and m. The base case $k = 1$ is trivial: $S(1, m)$ is plainly a $DS(m, 3)$-sequence, (b) and (d) are trivial, and (c) is vacuous in this case.

The case $k = 2$ is also easy. Here $\bar{\gamma} = 2$ and $S(2, m)$ is obviously a $DS(2m, 3)$-sequence, so (a) follows. Properties (b),(c), and (d) are also immediate.

Next consider the case $k > 2$, $m = 1$. Here $S(k, 1) = S(k - 1, 2)$ (with its symbols being renamed), so property (a) holds by induction. Property (b) is also trivial because the only change in the fan structure between $S(k - 1, 2)$ and $S(k, 1)$ is that each fan is split into two subfans. Since each fan is now of size 1, property (c) is trivial too. Finally, since the block structure in $S(k, 1)$ is identical to that in $S(k - 1, 2)$, (d) also follows immediately by induction.

Finally consider the general case $k > 2$, $m > 1$. We first prove property (a). First note that no two adjacent elements of $S = S(k, m)$ are equal: Indeed, by the induction hypothesis, no two adjacent elements either in S^* or in any S'_β are equal; all these sequences have pairwise disjoint sets of symbols, and the merging process clearly does not introduce any new duplication of adjacent elements in S.

Now suppose to the contrary that $S(k, m)$ contains a subsequence of the form

$$\langle a \quad \cdots \quad b \quad \cdots \quad a \quad \cdots \quad b \quad \cdots \quad a \rangle,$$

for some pair of distinct symbols a and b. By the induction hypothesis, it is clearly impossible for both a and b to belong to $S^\star$ or to belong to the same S'_β. Moreover, for each $\beta_1 < \beta_2$ the copy S'_{β_1} of S' lies in S wholly to the left of S'_{β_2}; thus a and b cannot belong to different copies S'_{β_1}, S'_{β_2} of S'.

Thus either a belongs to $S^\star$ and b to some S'_β or vice versa. However, in the first case, only the first appearance of a in (the appropriate fan of) $S^\star$ can appear in S between two elements of S'_β, so that the subsequence

$$\langle a \quad \cdots \quad b \quad \cdots \quad a \quad \cdots \quad b \quad \cdots \quad a \rangle$$

cannot appear in S. The same argument also rules out the second case in which b belongs to $S^\star$ and a to some S'_β.

Thus $S(k, m)$ is a $DS(m \cdot \bar\gamma, 3)$-sequence and property (a) holds.

Property (b) readily follows from the construction: All the symbols in each S'_β satisfy this property by the induction hypothesis. In addition, each symbol of $S^\star$ appears (in $S^\star$) in precisely one fan, where this appearance is its leftmost one in $S^\star$. Since each such first appearance in $S^\star$ is inserted into a fan of some S'_β, which then becomes a fan of S, property (b) holds also for the symbols of $S^\star$.

As to property (c), let f be the γth fan of S (where we write $\gamma = (\alpha, \beta)$). Then by construction f is the concatenation of the αth fan f' of S'_β and the corresponding element (m, α, β) of $S^\star$. By the induction hypothesis, the portion of S'_β starting at the last element of f' begins with the subsequence $\langle (m-1, \gamma) \cdots (1, \gamma) \rangle$. The construction then implies that the portion of S from the last element of f must begin with the extended subsequence $\langle (m, \gamma)(m - 1, \gamma) \cdots (1, \gamma) \rangle$, thus (c) holds for S.

To prove (d), note first that no block of $S^\star$ or of any S'_β was broken by the construction. Actually, it is easily checked that, by the way in which symbols of $S^\star$ and of the S'_β's are renumbered in S, the only changes in blocks caused by our construction are the extension of blocks immediately following fans of the copies S'_β by the corresponding element of $S^\star$ inserted at the end of such a fan, and the "detachment" of each block c of $S^\star$ that immediately follows a fan f of that sequence from f. (Note that c itself has not changed in this latter case, and that f is no longer a fan of S, but is distributed among the fans of some S'_β.)

Now let c be a block of S, and let $c_1, \ldots, c_t$ be the sequence of blocks lying in S between c and its preceding fan f. If c is not one of the special blocks mentioned above, then c must be a block of $S^\star$ or of some S'_β. In either case the (nonempty!) collection $c_1, \ldots, c_t$ of blocks must contain all blocks of $S^\star$

(resp. of S'_β) lying between c and the fan immediately preceding c in $S^\star$ (resp. in S'_β), where the first such block may have been extended in S. Thus in this case (d) follows by the induction hypothesis.

Next suppose c is an extended block of some S'_β. But then (d) is trivial, because the (new) first element of c is also the last element of the preceding fan in S.

Finally suppose c is a block of $S^\star$ that has been detached from its preceding fan f. Suppose f is the βth fan of $S^\star$. Then in this case the first element q of c is equal to the last element of f, which has been inserted into the *last* fan f' of S'_β. It thus follows from the construction that the fan of S immediately preceding c is f' extended by q, and that q belongs to the first block of S following that fan; thus (d) clearly holds for these blocks too.

This completes the induction step and thus proves the theorem.   □

Theorem 2.22 *For each $k, m \geq 1$ the length $\sigma(k, m)$ of $S(k, m)$ satisfies*

$$\sigma(k, m) > (km - 2) \cdot C_k(m) + 1.$$

Proof. The following recurrence formulas for $\sigma(k, m)$ follow easily from the inductive construction of $S(k, m)$:

$$
\begin{aligned}
\sigma(1, m) &= m, \\
\sigma(2, m) &= 4m - 2, \\
\sigma(k, 1) &= \sigma(k - 1, 2), & k > 2, \\
\sigma(k, m) &= \bar{\beta} \cdot \sigma(k, m - 1) + \sigma(k - 1, \bar{\alpha}) + \bar{\alpha} \cdot \bar{\beta} + \bar{\beta}, & k > 2, m > 1.
\end{aligned}
$$

To see the last equality, note that the first term on the right-hand side is the total length of the $\bar{\beta}$ copies S'_β of S', and that the second term is the length of the sequence $S^\star$. The third term is due to the fact that for each of the $\bar{\alpha} \cdot \bar{\beta}$ symbols (m, α, β) of $S^\star$, its first appearance in $S^\star$ is inserted into the αth fan of S'_β and causes the last element of that fan to be duplicated. Finally, the fourth term is due to the fact that the last element in each of the $\bar{\beta}$ fans of $S^\star$ is also duplicated in S.

The proof now follows from the following lemma.   □

Lemma 2.23 *Define $Z_k(m) = \dfrac{\sigma(k, m)}{C_k(m)}$. Then for each $k, m \geq 1$ we have:*

$$Z_k(m) > km - 2 + \frac{1}{C_k(m)}$$

(which clearly implies the lower bound on $\sigma(k, m)$ stated in Theorem 2.22).

Proof. We proceed by the standard double induction on k and m. For $k = 1$, we have

$$\begin{aligned} Z_1(m) \quad = \quad & m \; > \; 1 \cdot m - 2 + \frac{1}{C_1(m)} \\ = \quad & m - 1. \end{aligned}$$

For $k = 2$, we have

$$\begin{aligned} Z_2(m) \quad = \quad & \frac{4m-2}{2} = 2m - 1 \\ > \quad & 2 \cdot m - 2 + \frac{1}{C_2(m)} \\ = \quad & 2m - \frac{3}{2}. \end{aligned}$$

For $m = 1$, $C_k(1) = 2C_{k-1}(2)$ and thus, by the induction hypothesis,

$$\begin{aligned} Z_k(1) \quad = \quad & \frac{\sigma(k,1)}{C_k(1)} \\ = \quad & \frac{\sigma(k-1,2)}{2C_{k-1}(2)} = \frac{Z_{k-1}(2)}{2} \\ > \quad & \frac{2(k-1)-2}{2} + \frac{1}{2C_{k-1}(2)} \\ = \quad & k \cdot 1 - 2 + \frac{1}{C_k(1)}. \end{aligned}$$

Finally, for $k > 2$ and $m > 1$ we have

$$\begin{aligned} Z_k(m) \quad = \quad & \frac{\sigma(k,m)}{C_k(m)} \\ = \quad & \frac{\bar{\beta} \cdot \sigma(k,m-1) + \sigma(k-1,\bar{\alpha}) + \bar{\alpha} \cdot \bar{\beta} + \bar{\beta}}{\bar{\gamma}} \\ = \quad & \frac{\sigma(k,m-1)}{\bar{\alpha}} + \frac{\sigma(k-1,\bar{\alpha}) + \bar{\beta}}{\bar{\alpha} \cdot \bar{\beta}} + 1 \\ = \quad & Z_k(m-1) + \frac{Z_{k-1}(C_k(m-1)) + 1}{C_k(m-1)} + 1. \end{aligned}$$

Thus, by the induction hypothesis,

$$\begin{aligned} Z_k(m) \quad > \quad & k(m-1) - 2 + \frac{1}{C_k(m-1)} + \frac{(k-1)C_k(m-1) - 2}{C_k(m-1)} + \\ & \frac{1}{C_{k-1}(C_k(m-1)) \cdot C_k(m-1)} + \frac{1}{C_k(m-1)} + 1 \\ = \quad & \Big[k(m-1) + (k-1) + 1 \Big] - 2 + \frac{1}{C_k(m-1) \cdot C_{k-1}(C_k(m-1))} \\ = \quad & km - 2 + \frac{1}{C_k(m)}, \end{aligned}$$

and this proves the proposition.   □

Corollary 2.24 $\lambda_3(n) = \Omega(n\alpha(n))$.

Proof. For a given k, choose $m_k = C_{k+1}(k-3)$. Then

$$n_k = N_k(m_k) = C_{k+1}(k-2) \leq A_{k+1}(k+1)$$

by property (C4). This implies

$$\alpha(n_k) \leq k+1,$$

and

$$\lambda_3(n_k) \geq \sigma(k, m_k) \geq kn_k - 2C_k(m_k) \geq (k-2)n_k.$$

Now, given any n sufficiently large, choose k such that $n_{k-1} \leq n \leq n_k$, thus

$$\alpha(n) \leq \alpha(n_k) \leq k+1.$$

Let $t = \lfloor n/n_{k-1} \rfloor$. Then

$$n \leq (t+1)n_{k-1} \leq 2tn_{k-1},$$

and

$$\lambda_3(n) \geq t\lambda_3(n_{k-1})$$

(this latter inequality follows from the fact that the concatenation of t copies of $S(k-1, m_{k-1})$, having pairwise disjoint sets of symbols, is a $DS(n,3)$-sequence). Thus

$$
\begin{aligned}
\lambda_3(n) &\geq t\lambda_3(n_{k-1}) \\
&\geq tn_{k-1} \cdot (k-3) \\
&\geq \frac{1}{2}n(\alpha(n) - 4),
\end{aligned}
$$

which completes the proof.   □

In summary, we thus have

Theorem 2.25 $\lambda_3(n) = \Theta(n\alpha(n))$.

2.4   Path compressions on trees

In this section we establish an interesting relationship between Davenport–Schinzel sequences of order 3 and certain sequences of operations on rooted trees, which we call compression schemes.

2.4.1   Generalized path compressions

We begin with introducing some notations. Let T be an arbitrary rooted tree. It is given by a triple (V, r, ϕ), where V is a finite set of *vertices* (or, *nodes*), $r \in V$ is the *root* of T, and $\phi : V - \{r\} \rightarrow V$ is the *parenthood mapping*: for each $x \in V$, $x \neq r$, $\phi(x)$ is the *parent* of x, and x is a *child* of $\phi(x)$. The mapping ϕ has no cycles, so that by repeated applications of ϕ, every $x \in V$ is eventually mapped into r. A vertex is called a *leaf* if it has no children, and *inner* otherwise. We will use the following standard notations for $x, y \in V$: x is a *descendant* of y (and y is an *ancestor* of x) if there are $n \geq 1$ vertices $x_1, x_2, \ldots, x_n \in V$, such that $x_1 = x$, $x_n = y$, and $\phi(x_i) = x_{i+1}$ for $i = 1, \ldots, n-1$; x is a *proper* descendant of y if $n > 1$ (thus $x \neq y$), and *improper* otherwise (i.e., $x = y$).

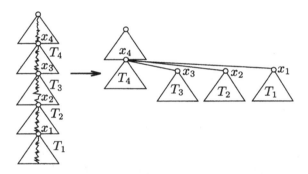

FIGURE 2.2. A generalized path compression.

We define an operation on T, called *generalized path compression* (GPC for short), as follows. Let $x_1, x_2, \ldots, x_k$ be a sequence of nodes of T such that each x_i is a proper descendant of x_{i+1}, for $i = 1, \ldots, k-1$. The generalized path compression $f = (x_1, x_2, \ldots, x_k)$ is an operation that modifies T so as to make each x_i, for $i = 1, \ldots, k-1$, a child of x_k. More precisely, f results in making $\phi(x_i) = x_k$ for $i = 1, \ldots, k-1$, and leaving $\phi(x)$ unchanged for all other x; see Figure 2.2.

This notion generalizes the notion of *standard* path compression, in that here the nodes $x_1, \ldots, x_k$ are *not* required to be adjacent along their present path. Standard compressions are used in the efficient implementation of the find operation in the set-union algorithm used for processing equivalence relationships (see Tarjan (1975) for an extensive analysis and earlier references).

For each GPC $f = (x_1, \ldots, x_k)$, call x_1 the *starting node* of f, and denote it by $\sigma(f)$; the *length* of f is $|f| = k - 1$; this is the number of *edges* $(x_1, x_2), \ldots, (x_{k-1}, x_k)$ in f (in general, these are not edges of T).

Another notion we need is that of a *postorder* on T. It is a linear order of the nodes of T obtained recursively as follows: Suppose the root r of T has l children $q_1, \ldots, q_l$. Then a postorder on T is obtained by concatenating postorders of the subtrees of T rooted at $q_1, \ldots, q_l$ and appending r at the end. (Thus T can have many postorders, depending on the order of the enumeration of the children of each of its nodes.) An example of a postordered tree is given in Figure 2.3.

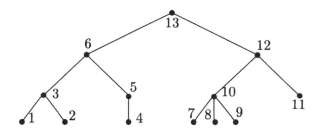

FIGURE 2.3. A postordered tree.

Finally, a sequence $F = (f_1, \ldots, f_n)$ of GPC's on a rooted tree T is *admissible* if

(i) it is *executable*, meaning that each f_i is a GPC on the tree T_i obtained from T after the compressions $f_1, \ldots, f_{i-1}$ have been executed ($T_1 \equiv T$);

(ii) it is *postordered*, meaning that there exists a postorder on T such that the starting nodes $\sigma(f_1), \ldots, \sigma(f_n)$ are arranged in (weak) postorder (thus more than one GPC may start at the same node; however, if $\sigma(f_i) \neq \sigma(f_{i+1})$ then $\sigma(f_{i+1})$ succeeds $\sigma(f_i)$ in the postorder).

The *length* $|F|$ of such a sequence is defined as $\sum_{i=1}^{n} |f_i|$. We are concerned here with the maximal possible value of $|F|$, or, more precisely, with the quantity

$$\chi(m, n) = \max\{\, |F| : F \text{ is an admissible sequence of } n$$
$$\text{GPC's on a tree } T \text{ with } m \text{ vertices} \,\}.$$

Note that $\chi(m, n)$ is well defined, e.g., $\chi(m, n) \leq (m - 1)n$, since $|f| \leq m - 1$ for any GPC f on T.

For our estimation of χ, it is useful to make the following simplifications: Let a tree T with m nodes and an admissible sequence F of n GPC's on T be given. For each $f = (x_1, \ldots, x_k) \in F$, we add to T a new leaf x_0, make it a child of x_1, and change f to $(x_0, x_1, \ldots, x_k)$. Furthermore, we extend the postorder on T so that all new leaves of some node x succeed all its original children, and are arranged according to the order of the GPC's they correspond to. Since we want to maximize $|F|$, we can assume, without loss of generality, that every node belongs to at least one GPC; otherwise, remove from the tree such a node (that does not appear at all in F), by connecting its children (if any) directly to its parent; add another node to the tree (so that it still has exactly m nodes) as a child of the starting point of the first GPC in F, and make it a leaf (the first in the postorder); finally, extend the first GPC so as to start from the new node; all these changes yield another tree with m nodes and an admissible sequence F' whose length is greater by 1 than that of F. In particular, each original leaf will now have at least one child (a new leaf).

All these modifications make T into a tree with $m + n$ vertices: m inner vertices and n leaves. Moreover, in the modified sequence F, each of the n GPC's starts at a different leaf. We will refer to such a T as an (m, n)-tree, and to the corresponding F as a *compression scheme* on T. Thus, a compression scheme on an (m, n)-tree consists of n GPC's, exactly one GPC starting at every one of the n leaves; moreover, the leaves attached to any node succeed all its inner children in postorder. In what follows we will aim at the estimation of the associated quantity

$$\chi^\star(m, n) = \max\{\, |F| : F \text{ is a compression scheme on an } (m, n)\text{-tree}\,\}.$$

Note that in the transformation above the length of each GPC is increased by 1, thus $|F|$ increases by n. Therefore $\chi^\star(m, n) = \chi(m, n) + n$ for all m, n.

It is known (see Fischer (1972), Tarjan (1975)) that if no restrictions on the order of the starting nodes of the GPC's or on the structure of T are imposed, then (even for standard path compressions) $\chi^\star(n, n) = \Theta(n \log n)$ (for easier comparison, we state all results in the case $m = n$; usually $m = \Theta(n)$, which of course yields the same asymptotic bounds). If the tree T is required to be *balanced* and one uses only standard path compressions, then $\chi^\star(n, n) = \Theta(n\alpha(n))$ (see Tarjan (1975)). We will show that, using *generalized* path compressions, and imposing no restrictions on the structure of T, but requiring that the GPC's be *postordered*, $\chi^\star(n, n)$ is also $\Theta(n\alpha(n))$. This result will follow from an equivalence between Davenport–Schinzel sequences of order 3 and compression schemes, to be established in the next subsection. Although the same bounds are obtained both for our compression schemes and for the union-find "schemes," there does not seem to be an obvious relation between the two problems, although the lower bound proved in the previous section, when interpreted as a compression scheme (as described in Section 2.4.3), is somewhat similar to the lower bound construction used in Tarjan (1975).

2.4.2   Linear equivalence between $\chi^\star$ and λ_3

In this section we show that the two functions $\chi^\star$ and λ_3 are of the same order of magnitude. This will follow by using two transformations, from $DS(n, 3)$-sequences to compression schemes and vice versa.

2.4.2.1 Transforming DS-sequences into compression schemes

Let $U = \langle u_1, u_2, \ldots, u_m \rangle$ be a $DS(n, 3)$-sequence. Enumerate the blocks of U in the order they occur as $c_1, c_2, \ldots, c_p$, where $p \leq 2n - 1$ (see Corollary 2.7). Let T be a (p, n)-tree, with the p inner nodes $1, \ldots, p$ corresponding to the blocks $c_1, \ldots, c_p$; they are arranged in a single path, where $q + 1$ is the parent of q, for $q = 1, \ldots, p - 1$; the n leaves $l_1, \ldots, l_n$ correspond to the symbols $1, \ldots, n$ appearing in the sequence U, and are attached to the p inner nodes as follows. For each i, let $t_1 < t_2 < \cdots < t_{q_i}$ be the indices of the blocks that contain i; we then attach the leaf l_i to the node t_1 in T. Define a GPC $f_i = (l_i, t_1, \ldots, t_{q_i})$ on T, and let $F = (f_1, \ldots, f_n)$. The total length of F is

$$|F| = \sum_{i=1}^{n} |f_i| = \sum_{i=1}^{n} q_i = \sum_{r=1}^{p} |c_r| = |U|.$$

As above, we assume that the symbols of U are numbered so that their leftmost appearances satisfy $\mu_i < \mu_j$ whenever $i < j$.

Lemma 2.26 *The sequence F is a compression scheme on T.*

Proof. For each $i = 1, \ldots, n$, let s_i be the index of the block containing the first occurrence of i in U (i.e. $\mu_i \in c_{s_i}$); since $\mu_1 < \mu_2 < \cdots < \mu_n$ and the blocks are decreasing sequences, we have $s_1 < s_2 < \ldots < s_n$, and thus the leaves $l_i = \sigma(f_i)$, whose parents are the nodes s_i, are indeed in postorder.

Suppose to the contrary that F is not executable, and let f_i be the first GPC in F which cannot be executed. Write $f_i = (l_i, t_1, \ldots, t_q)$ and suppose that when f_i is to be executed, t_k is no longer a descendant of t_{k+1} (note that the leaf l_i of t_1 has not yet been involved in any GPC, and is still a child of t_1). Then there had to exist a GPC f_j with $j < i$ which has separated t_k from t_{k+1}; thus f_j contains a node u with $t_k \leq u < t_{k+1}$, and its last node v is such that $t_{k+1} < v$. Since $j < i$, we also have $s_j < s_i = t_1 \leq t_k$. Therefore $j \in c_{s_j}$, c_u, c_v, and $i \in c_{t_k}$, $c_{t_{k+1}}$, implying that U contains a forbidden subsequence of the form $\langle j \cdots i \cdots j \cdots i \cdots j \rangle$, contrary to assumption (note that this occurs even if $t_k = u$, because, in the decreasing block c_u, the symbol i must precede the symbol j). □

Corollary 2.27 $\lambda_3(n) \leq \chi^*(2n - 1, n)$.

Proof. The transformation described above yields

$$\lambda_3(n) \leq \chi^*(p, n) \leq \chi^*(2n - 1, n),$$

since χ^* is monotone and $p \leq 2n - 1$. □

2.4.2.2 Transforming compression schemes into DS-sequences

Let T be an (m, n)-tree, and let $F = (f_1, f_2, \ldots, f_n)$ be a compression scheme on T. We will identify each GPC with the set of all vertices of T through which it passes, except for its last vertex. Specifically, for each $f_j = (x_1, \ldots, x_{k-1}, x_k)$, let $f_j^0 = \{x_1, \ldots, x_{k-1}\}$. Enumerate the $m + n$ nodes of T in the given postorder as $1, 2, \ldots, m + n$, and define, for each $\nu = 1, \ldots, m + n$, a sequence

$$U_\nu = \langle j : 1 \leq j \leq n \text{ and } \nu \in f_j^0 \rangle,$$

where the elements of each sequence U_ν are arranged in *decreasing* order. Let U be the concatenation

$$U = U_1 \| U_2 \| \cdots \| U_{m+n}.$$

To obtain a Davenport–Schinzel sequence V from U, we proceed through the subsequences U_ν in order, erasing the first element of U_ν whenever it equals the preceding nonerased element of U; in total, at most $m + n - 1$ elements are erased.

Lemma 2.28 *The sequence V is a $DS(n, 3)$-sequence of length*

$$|V| \geq |F| - (m + n - 1).$$

Proof. V is composed of n symbols; the erasing procedure and the fact that each sequence U_ν contains distinct elements imply that no two consecutive elements of V are equal. For each $f_j \in F$, its index j appears $|f_j|$ times in U (the last vertex of f_j is ignored), thus $|U| = |F|$ and $|V|$ satisfies the required inequality.

Finally, U—and thus V too—does not contain a subsequence of the form

$$\langle i \quad \cdots \quad j \quad \cdots \quad i \quad \cdots \quad j \quad \cdots \quad i \rangle.$$

Suppose the contrary; then there exist vertices

$$\beta \leq \gamma \leq \delta \leq \varepsilon \leq \theta$$

in T (with inequalities referring to the given postorder), and two distinct GPC's $f_i, f_j \in F$, such that

$$i \in U_\beta, U_\delta, U_\theta,$$
$$j \in U_\gamma, U_\varepsilon,$$

and moreover these five occurrences of i and j appear in U in the order $\langle i \cdots j \cdots i \cdots j \cdots i \rangle$. Let us denote this 'illegal' subsequence as Q.

 Without loss of generality, we can assume that Q is the (lexicographically) leftmost occurrence of such an illegal subsequence in U. In particular, no j

appears in U before the occurrence of i in U_β (for otherwise we would have an illegal subsequence of the form $\langle j \cdots i \cdots j \cdots i \cdots j \rangle$ lying left of Q). Moreover, we can assume, for similar reasons, that U_β contains the first occurrence of i in U and that U_γ contains the first occurrence of j in U. By definition, we must have $\beta = \sigma(f_i)$, $\gamma = \sigma(f_j)$, so that β and γ are *distinct* leaves of T. Thus $\beta < \gamma$ and so $i < j$ since the sequence F is postordered.

Furthermore, we also have $\delta \neq \varepsilon$, for otherwise U_δ would contain both i and j, and j would have to precede i in U_δ (since $i < j$). But then our subsequence Q would appear in U in the order $\langle i \cdots j \cdots j \cdots i \cdots j \rangle$, contrary to assumption. Moreover, γ is a leaf whereas δ is not (f_i starts at β and then passes through δ), so that we also have $\gamma \neq \delta$.

Now $\beta < \gamma < \delta$ and β is a proper descendant of δ (f_i contains both of them). Since the vertices of T are arranged in postorder, γ must also be a proper descendant of δ. By the same argument, δ must be a proper descendant of ε, and ε must be a (possibly improper) descendant of θ.

Let ζ be the lowest common ancestor of β and γ in T; then ζ is a descendant of δ. Since $\beta \neq \gamma$ are leaves, ζ is not a leaf, and so $\zeta \neq \beta, \gamma$. Let ξ be the child of ζ on the path from γ to ζ; see Figure 2.4.

FIGURE 2.4. The resulting compression scheme; solid edges denote proper ancestor relations, whereas dashed edges may represent improper ancestors also.

Since $\beta < \gamma$, we also have $\beta < \xi$, and in fact every leaf of the subtree T_ξ of T rooted at ξ succeeds β in postorder. Since the GPC's of F are executed in postorder, it follows that, by the time f_i is executed, no GPC has yet passed through any vertex of T_ξ; in particular γ is still a descendant of ζ at that time. Let η be the first vertex (i.e. furthest from the root of T) in f_i that is a (possibly improper) ancestor of ζ. Note that since $\delta \in f_i$, η must lie on the path between ζ and δ (including ζ, δ).

After f_i is executed, γ remains a descendant of ζ, and thus of η too. Let ρ be the last node of f_i (note that $\theta < \rho$). Execution of f_i has made η a *child* of ρ. Now ε lied originally strictly between η and ρ (strictly, because $\delta \neq \varepsilon$ and $\theta \neq \rho$). Thus, after execution of f_i, the node η, and hence *a fortiori* γ, will no longer be a descendant of ε. But this implies that f_j cannot be executed, a contradiction that completes the proof. $\square$

Corollary 2.29 $\chi^\star(m, n) \leq \lambda_3(n) + (m + n - 1)$.

Proof. Immediate from the above transformation. $\square$

Remark 2.30   (i) Various open problems arise in connection with compression schemes, such as that of finding other restricted classes of sequences of GPC's for which linear or almost linear upper bounds on their maximum length can be established. For example, suppose we allow only standard path compressions (i.e. path compressions whose nodes are adjacent to one another along their current path), and still require them to be executed in postorder. It has been recently shown by Loebl and Nešetřil (1988) that the maximal total length of such a sequence is linear in the number of nodes of the corresponding tree.

(ii) There is a similarity between the two problems studied here and in Tarjan (1975), in that they both involve path compressions on trees and they both attain similar upper and lower bounds. Is there some general problem of this kind, of which both our problem and that of Tarjan (1975) are special instances?

2.4.3   The lower bound revisited

In this section we will provide an interpretation of the lower bound construction for $DS(n, s)$-sequences, given in Section 2.3, as compression schemes on certain trees. The reason for doing so is twofold. First, this shows the similarity between our construction of superlinear Davenport–Schinzel sequences and Tarjan's construction of superlinear executions of the union-find algorithm. Second, the resulting compression scheme is highly symmetric and relatively easy to define, and it may provide the reader with more insight into the structure of these superlinear sequences.

In this derivation we use the sequence of functions B_k defined in Section 2.3.1.

The trees on which we want to define our compression schemes will be (essentially) symmetric binary trees, defined as follows. Let T be an arbitrary (m, n)-tree. Define a sequence of trees $T(i)$, for $i \geq 0$, as follows: $T(0) = T$; to construct $T(i + 1)$, take two disjoint copies of $T(i)$, introduce a new node r as the root of $T(i + 1)$, and make the roots of the two copies of $T(i)$ children of r (see Figure 2.5). Note that $T(i)$ is an (m_i, n_i)-tree, where

$$
\begin{aligned}
m_i &= (m+1)2^i - 1, \\
n_i &= n \cdot 2^i.
\end{aligned}
$$

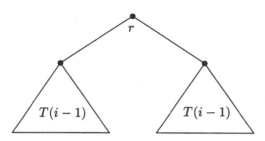

FIGURE 2.5. The tree $T(i)$.

Moreover, for any given postorder on T, we obtain inductively an *induced* postorder on $T(i+1)$ by taking in each of the two copies of $T(i)$ the same (induced) postorder. In the sequel, we always consider only such induced postorders on the trees $T(i)$.

Theorem 2.31 *Let T be a $(1, m)$-tree with $m \geq 1$, and let $k \geq 1$. Then, for each $i \geq B_k(m)$, there exists a compression scheme F on $T(i)$ such that each of the m_i GPC's in F is of length k.*

Proof. We use an argument similar to that in Tarjan (1975), based on double induction on k and m. Note that if the assertion of the theorem holds for some i, it also holds for all $j > i$; it thus suffices to prove it for $i = B_k(m)$. Moreover, we remark that the theorem holds for (n, m)-trees with arbitrary $n \geq 1$ as well; to reduce it to the case $n = 1$, ignore the inner structure of the tree, and assume that each leaf is connected directly to the root.

Suppose first that $k = 1$. Since $B_1(m) = 0$, it suffices to prove the assertion for T itself. Take F to be the sequence of GPC's $((l_1, r), \ldots, (l_m, r))$, where $l_1, \ldots, l_m$ are the leaves of T arranged in postorder, and r is the root of T.

Next suppose that $k = 2$ (this step is not essential to our inductive proof, but is given anyway to prepare for the following more complex steps). Consider $T(1) = T(B_2(m))$, and let r_0 denote its root. For each leaf l of $T(1)$ take the GPC (l, r, r_0) of length 2, where r is the root of the copy of T containing l, and let F be the postordered sequence of these GPC's.

Now suppose that $k \geq 3$. Assume that the assertion holds for all $k' < k$ and all $m' \geq 1$, and consider first the case $m = 1$. The tree T consists of just one leaf l and a root r (note that $l \neq r$). Let T^* be the subtree of $T(1)$ obtained by removing its (two) leaves; T^* is a $(1, 2)$-tree. Let $i_0 = B_{k-1}(2)$ and

$i = B_k(1)$; then, by definition, $i = 1 + i_0$. By the induction hypothesis, there exists a compression scheme $F^\star$ on $T^\star(i_0)$, all of whose GPC's are of length $k - 1$. Now $T^\star(i_0)$ may be regarded as a subtree of $(T(1))(i_0) = T(i)$, and we will extend each GPC $f^\star = (x_1, \ldots, x_k) \in F^\star$ to a GPC $f = (x_0, x_1, \ldots, x_k)$ in $T(i)$, by adding to $f^\star$ the leaf x_0 which is the unique child of x_1. The resulting sequence F is clearly postordered and executable in $T(i)$, and each of its GPC's has length k, thus F is the required compression scheme.

Finally, let $k \geq 3$ and $m > 1$, and assume that the assertion holds for all $k' < k$ and $m' \geq 1$, and for $k' = k$ and all $m' < m$. Let T be a $(1, m)$-tree, and let $l_1, \ldots, l_m$ be its leaves arranged in postorder. Let $T^\star$ be the $(1, m-1)$-tree obtained from T by removing its *last* leaf l_m. Put $i_0 = B_k(m - 1)$, $i_1 = B_{k-1}(2^{i_0})$, and $i = B_k(m)$; thus $i = i_0 + i_1$.

Consider $T(i_0)$ and its subtree $T^\star(i_0)$. By the induction hypothesis, there exists a compression scheme on $T^\star(i_0)$, all of whose GPC's have length k. Thus, starting at each leaf $l_1, \ldots, l_{m-1}$ in each copy of T in $T(i_0)$, we have a GPC of length k. Now $T(i) = (T(i_0))(i_1)$ contains 2^{i_1} copies of $T(i_0)$, and in each of these copies we have a corresponding compression scheme of the above form. Refer to the GPC's in all these schemes as GPC's of *type I*.

Next consider the subtree $T^{\star\star}$ of $T(i_0)$, obtained by removing all its $m \cdot 2^{i_0}$ leaves. Since T is a $(1, m)$-tree, the leaves of $T^{\star\star}$ are precisely the $p = 2^{i_0}$ copies (in $T(i_0)$) of the root of T. Regard $T^{\star\star}$ as a $(1, p)$-tree by ignoring its inner structure, and apply to it the induction hypothesis (recall the note at the beginning of this proof). We obtain a compression scheme $F^{\star\star}$ on $T^{\star\star}(i_1)$, consisting of GPC's of length $k - 1$ each, such that only the root and the leaves of each copy of $T^{\star\star}$ (but none of its intermediate nodes) participate in $F^{\star\star}$. Now $T^{\star\star}(i_1)$ is a subtree of $(T(i_0))(i_1) = T(i)$; we extend each GPC $f^{\star\star} = (x_1, \ldots, x_k) \in F^{\star\star}$ to a GPC $f = (x_0, x_1, \ldots, x_k)$ in $T(i)$ as follows: x_1 is the root of some copy of T, and we take x_0 to be the last leaf there (i.e., the copy of l_m). We will refer to these GPC's as being of *type II*.

We can now obtain a compression scheme on $T(i)$ by merging the GPC's of types I and II; namely, we proceed through the leaves of $T(i)$ in their induced postorder; for each leaf which is a copy of $l_1, \ldots, l_{m-1}$ (respectively, of l_m), we take the corresponding GPC of type I (respectively, type II) starting at that leaf.

The sequence F of GPC's obtained in this way is the required compression scheme on $T(i)$. It is clearly postordered, and its executability can be established by proceeding inductively through the sequence, and using the following arguments:

(a) All the postorders considered here (on $T(i)$, $T^\star(i_0)$, and $T^{\star\star}(i_1)$) are consistent with one another, since they are all induced by the original postorder on T. This implies the separate executability of the sequence of GPC's of type II, and also those of type I (in each copy of $T(i_0)$ separately, and also all together).

(b) Let $f = (l', \ldots, z)$ be a GPC of type I, where l' is a nonlast leaf, and let r' be the parent of l' (i.e. r' is the root of the copy of T containing l'). All the nodes of f are included in the same copy of $T(i_0)$; therefore, if g is any GPC of type II that contains a node on the path from l' to z (excluding z), then this node must be r', and g is thus executed only *after* f (since $\sigma(g)$ is the last leaf of r'). By (a), the other GPC's of type I also do not affect the executability of f.

(c) Let $f = (l', r', u, \ldots, z)$ be a GPC of type II, where l' is a last leaf and r' is its parent; let q' be the root of the copy of $T(i_0)$ that contains l' and r', then q' is a (possibly improper) descendant of u. The GPC f is executable at its turn, because: (i) l' belongs to no other GPC, thus it still is a child of r'. (ii) For any GPC g of type I, if it contains a node on the path from l' to z, then all its nodes lie in the copy of $T(i_0)$ with root q', thus g does not disconnect r' from q' and u, and of course does not affect the other nodes of f. (iii) Finally, the other GPC's of type II do not affect the executability of f (by (a)).

This establishes the assertion of the theorem for k and m too, and thus completes the proof.   □

We next claim that these compression schemes are nothing but the sequences $S(k, m)$ in disguise. That is:

Lemma 2.32 *For each $k, m \geq 1$, the compression scheme obtained in the preceding theorem, when transformed into a Davenport–Schinzel sequence as in the preceding subsection, yields the sequence $S(k, m)$ constructed in Section 2.3.*

Proof. By double induction that compares the two constructions used here and in Section 2.3. The interested reader should find it a good exercise in exploring the relationship between Davenport–Schinzel sequences and compression schemes, to work out the details of the proof.   □

2.5 Ackermann's functions and combinatorial problems

Although Ackermann's function A is very fast-growing, one can obtain functions that grow much faster than A by extending the recursive definitions from Section 2.1, as follows. For each countable ordinal γ we define a *generalized Ackermann's function* A_γ from the set N of positive integers into itself in the following transfinite inductive manner:

1. $A_1(n) = 2n$, $n \in$ N.

2. If γ is not a limit ordinal, say $\gamma = \beta + 1$, then $A_\gamma(n) = A_\beta^{(n)}(1)$, $n \in$ N.

3. If γ is a limit ordinal, we associate with γ some fixed increasing sequence $\{\gamma(n)\}$ of ordinals smaller than γ, whose limit is γ. Then $A_\gamma(n) = A_{\gamma(n)}(n)$, $n \in \mathbb{N}$.

Thus $A = A_\omega$ (if we put $\omega(n) = n$, for $n \in \mathbb{N}$).

The rate of growth of the functions A_γ increases with γ. For example, A_ω is not primitive recursive, and in fact grows faster than any primitive recursive function (see Rogers (1967)). The function A_{ε_0}, where ε_0 is the first *inaccessible* ordinal (it is the limit of the sequence ω, ω^ω, ω^{ω^ω}, ...), has the following remarkable property (see Kreisel (1952)): Consider statements Q of the form

$$\forall n \exists m \; P(n, m),$$

where $P(n, m)$ is a provably recursive first-order statement in Peano arithmetic with two free variables m, n (i.e., there is an algorithm for deciding if $P(n, m)$ is true for given n, m, and a proof—in Peano arithmetic—that the algorithm always terminates). Suppose that Q is a true statement, and associate with it a function $\phi_Q : \mathbb{N} \to \mathbb{N}$, so that, for each $n \in \mathbb{N}$, $\phi_Q(n)$ is the smallest m satisfying $P(n, m)$. Then Q is provable from the Peano axioms (i.e. is a theorem of first-order formal number theory) if and only if there exists an ordinal $\gamma < \varepsilon_0$ such that $\phi_Q(n) < A_\gamma(n)$ for all sufficiently large n. A recent result of Paris and Harrington (1977) yields a variant of Ramsey's Theorem that can be expressed in the above form Q, but for which the associated function ϕ_Q grows as fast as A_{ε_0}, so that Q is not provable from the Peano's axioms (see Graham et al. (1980) and Ketonen and Solovay (1981) for details).

As a matter of fact, even for the first infinite ordinal ω, there exist very few 'natural' statements Q of the form $\forall n \exists m P(n, m)$ whose associated function ϕ_Q grows like A_ω or faster. The bounds on $\lambda_3(n)$ may well be one of the most natural statements yet known that can be expressed in this form. Indeed, let

$$Q \equiv \forall k \exists m \; \lambda_3(m) \geq km.$$

The lower bound on λ_3 implies that Q is a true statement; moreover, both lower and upper bounds imply that ϕ_Q grows as fast as A_ω (note that for fixed k and m the statement $\lambda_3(m) \geq km$ is a provably recursive statement in Peano arithmetic: simply enumerate all sequences of length km composed of m symbols, and check each of them for being a $DS(m, 3)$-sequence). Tarjan's bounds (1975) on the complexity of the union-find algorithm can also be translated into such a statement Q with ϕ_Q growing as fast as A_ω.

Recently, Loebl and Nešetřil (1988) have introduced a very complicated extension of path compression schemes, for which the associated statement Q is such that φ_Q grows as fast as A_{ε_0} and is thus unprovable in Peano arithmetic.

2.6 Bibliographic notes

The material presented in this chapter is mostly taken from Hart and Sharir (1986), and Wiernik and Sharir (1988). Ackermann's functions have been introduced more than 65 years ago (Ackermann (1928)), and have been studied since then mainly in the theory of recursive functions (see Section 2.5), and, later, in the analysis of algorithms (as in Tarjan (1975)). The upper bound proof given in Section 2.2 is based on Lemma 2.12, whose proof deals explicitly with the sequences themselves rather than with compression schemes (as in Hart and Sharir (1986)), and is adapted from Sharir (1987); the remainder of the analysis in this section continues along the lines of the original proof in Hart and Sharir (1986). The lower bound construction given in Section 2.3 is taken from Wiernik and Sharir (1988), which was obtained by translating the original construction in Hart and Sharir (1986) into explicit sequence construction. See also Komjáth (1988) for a different lower bound construction. Section 2.4 is taken from Hart and Sharir (1986). The discussion in Section 2.5 is also taken from Hart and Sharir (1986).

Appendix 2.1

In this appendix, we provide the proofs of properties **(B3)**–**(B6)** of the functions $B_k(m)$.

(B3) $B_4(m) \geq 2^{2^{\cdot^{\cdot^2}}}$, with m 2's in the exponential tower, for $m \geq 0$; i.e., $B_4(m) \geq A_3(m)$.

Proof. Indeed, $B_4(0) \geq 1$, and

$$B_4(m) = B_4(m-1) + 2^{B_4(m-1)} \geq 2^{B_4(m-1)},$$

for $m \geq 1$. □

(B4) Each function $B_k(m)$ is strictly increasing in m, for all $k \geq 3$, and each sequence $\{B_k(m)\}_{k \geq 1}$ is strictly increasing, for all $m \geq 1$.

Proof. To see this, note first that $B_k(m) \geq 1$ for all $k \geq 2$ and $m \geq 0$. This implies, for $k \geq 3$ and $m \geq 0$, that

$$B_k(m+1) = B_k(m) + B_{k-1}(2^{B_k(m)}) \geq B_k(m) + 1,$$

hence also $B_k(m) \geq m + 1$. For the second part of (**B4**), we claim

$$B_{k+1}(m) \geq B_k(m) + 1, \quad k \geq 1, m \geq 1.$$

This is clear for $k = 1$. For $k > 1$, we have $2^{B_{k+1}(m-1)} \geq 2^m \geq m$, hence

$$B_{k+1}(m) = B_{k+1}(m-1) + B_k(2^{B_{k+1}(m-1)}) \geq 1 + B_k(m). \qquad \square$$

(B5) $B_k(m) \geq A_{k-1}(m)$, for $k \geq 4$, $m \geq 1$.

Proof. This is proven by double induction on k and m. (B5) holds for $k = 4$ by (B3), and holds for $m = 1$ since

$$B_k(1) = 1 + B_{k-1}(2) \geq 2 = A_{k-1}(1).$$

For $k > 4$ and $m > 1$, assume (B5) to hold for all $4 \leq k' < k$ and $m' \geq 1$, and for $k' = k$ and all $1 \leq m' < m$. Then we have

$$2^{B_k(m-1)} \geq B_k(m - 1) \geq A_{k-1}(m - 1),$$

hence

$$
\begin{aligned}
B_k(m) &\geq B_{k-1}(2^{B_k(m-1)}) \geq B_{k-1}(A_{k-1}(m - 1)) \\
&\geq A_{k-2}(A_{k-1}(m - 1)) = A_{k-1}(m).
\end{aligned}
$$
$\square$

(B6) $2^{B_k(m)+2} \leq A_k(m + 3)$, for $k \geq 1$, $m \geq 0$.

Proof. This is again proven by double induction on k and m. For $k = 1$ we have $2^{B_1(m)+2} = 4$ and $A_1(m + 3) \geq 2(m + 3) \geq 4$.

For $k = 2$, we have $2^{B_2(m)+2} = 8$ and $A_2(m + 3) = 2^{m+3} \geq 8$.

For $k \geq 3$ and $m = 0$, we have $2^{B_k(0)+2} = 8$ and

$$
\begin{aligned}
A_k(3) &= A_{k-1}(A_k(2)) = A_{k-1}(4) \\
&\geq A_1(4) = 8.
\end{aligned}
$$

Finally, for $k \geq 3$ and $m \geq 1$, put $t = B_k(m - 1)$; then

$$B_k(m) = t + B_{k-1}(2^t) \leq 3 \cdot (2^t - 1) + B_{k-1}(2^t),$$

which, by **(B4)**, implies

$$B_k(m) \leq B_{k-1}(2^t + 3 \cdot (2^t - 1)) \leq B_{k-1}(2^{t+2} - 3).$$

Thus

$$
\begin{aligned}
2^{B_k(m)+2} &\leq 2^{B_{k-1}(2^{t+2}-3)+2} \leq A_{k-1}(2^{t+2}) \\
&= A_{k-1}(2^{B_k(m-1)+2}) \leq A_{k-1}(A_k(m + 2)) \\
&= A_k(m + 3),
\end{aligned}
$$

where the last chain of inequalities follows by using the induction hypothesis twice.
$\square$

3

HIGHER-ORDER SEQUENCES

3.1 Introduction

In this chapter we first obtain optimal bounds for the maximal length $\lambda_4(n)$ of an $(n, 4)$ Davenport–Schinzel sequence, and then obtain improved and almost tight lower and upper bounds for $\lambda_s(n)$, $s > 4$.

The main results of this chapter are:

(i) The maximal length of a $DS(n, 4)$-sequence is
$$\lambda_4(n) = \Theta(n \cdot 2^{\alpha(n)}).$$

(ii) An upper bound on the maximal length of a $DS(n, s)$-sequence, for $s > 4$, is
$$\lambda_s(n) \leq \begin{cases} n \cdot 2^{\alpha(n)^{(s-2)/2} + C_s(n)} & \text{if } s \text{ is even,} \\ n \cdot 2^{\alpha(n)^{(s-3)/2} \log \alpha(n) + C_s(n)} & \text{if } s \text{ is odd,} \end{cases}$$
where $C_s(n)$ is a function of $\alpha(n)$ and s. For a fixed value of s, $C_s(n)$ is asymptotically smaller than the first term of the exponent and therefore, for sufficiently (and extremely) large values of n, the first term of the exponent dominates.

(iii) A lower bound on the maximal length of a $DS(n, s)$-sequence of an even order is
$$\lambda_s(n) = \Omega\left(n \cdot 2^{K_s \alpha(n)^{(s-2)/2} + Q_s(n)}\right),$$

where
$$K_s = 1 \bigg/ \left(\frac{s-2}{2} \right)!$$

and $Q_s(n)$ is a polynomial in $\alpha(n)$ of degree at most $(s-4)/2$.

Note that these lower and upper bounds, though generally 'tight,' still leave some gap for $s > 4$. For even s they are almost identical except for the constant K_s and the lower-order additive terms $C_s(n)$, $Q_s(n)$, appearing in the exponents. For odd s the gap is more "substantial."

The proofs are fairly complicated and involve many technical details. The upper bounds are derived in a manner that generally follows the proof of the upper bound for $\lambda_3(n)$ given in Chapter 2, but uses additional techniques, and also involves induction on s. For the sake of exposition, we first present the derivation of the tight bounds for $\lambda_4(n)$, which gives the general flavor of the techniques used in establishing the bounds, but is relatively simpler. Then we generalize these techniques for larger values of s. Another reason for considering $\lambda_4(n)$ separately is that we solve the recurrence relation that gives an upper bound for $\lambda_4(n)$ in a slightly more 'efficient' way, which enables us to get tight bounds, while for general values of s, where no such refinement could be obtained, the proofs are slightly different.

The chapter is organized as follows: In Section 3.2 we derive the upper bounds for $\lambda_4(n)$; in Section 3.3 we construct a class of $DS(n, 4)$-sequences and prove that their length is $\Omega(n \cdot 2^{\alpha(n)})$; in Section 3.4 we derive the upper bounds for general values of s and, finally, we establish in Section 3.5 our lower bounds for larger even values of s. As in Chapter 2, we will continue to exploit various properties of Ackermann's functions and of several of their variants. The proofs of these properties will be found in Appendixes 3.1–3.3.

3.2   An upper bound for $\lambda_4(n)$

In this section we establish the upper bound $\lambda_4(n) = O(n \cdot 2^{\alpha(n)})$. The next section will show that this bound is asymptotically tight.

3.2.1   Decomposition of DS-sequences into chains

We begin by extending some definitions and observations given in Chapter 2.

Definition 3.1   Let U be a $DS(n, s)$-sequence, and let $1 \leq t < s$. A t-chain c is a contiguous subsequence of U that is a Davenport–Schinzel sequence of order t.

Given n, s, t, and U as above, we partition U into disjoint t-chains, proceeding from left to right in the following inductive manner. Suppose that the initial portion $\langle u_1, \ldots, u_j \rangle$ of U has already been decomposed into t-chains.

The next t-chain in our partitioning is then the largest subsequence of U of the form $\langle u_{j+1}, \ldots, u_k \rangle$, which is still a Davenport–Schinzel sequence of order t. We refer to this partitioning as the *canonical decomposition* of U into t-chains, and let $m = m_t(U)$ denote the number of t-chains in this decomposition. (Note that 1-chains are the same as the chains of Definition 2.12.)

The problem of obtaining good upper bounds for the quantities

$$\mu_{s,t}(n) = \max \{ m_t(U) : U \text{ is a } DS(n, s)\text{-sequence} \}$$

seems quite hard for general s and t. However, for $t = s - 1, s - 2$ such bounds are easy to obtain. Specifically:

Lemma 3.2 $\mu_{s,s-1}(n) \leq n$ and $\mu_{s,s-2}(n) \leq 2n - 1$.

Proof. Consider first the case $t = s - 1$. Let c be an $(s - 1)$-chain in the canonical decomposition of U, and let x be the symbol immediately following c. Since $c \,\|\, \langle x \rangle$ is not a $DS(n, s - 1)$-sequence, it must contain an alternating subsequence $\langle \cdots y \cdots x \cdots y \cdots x \rangle$ of length $s + 1$ ending at x. It follows that the last occurrence of y in U must be within c, for otherwise U would have contained an alternation of length $s+2$. Hence each chain in our decomposition contains the last occurrence of at least one symbol, showing that $\mu_{s,s-1}(n) \leq n$.

The case $t = s - 2$ is similar. Let c be an $(s - 2)$-chain in the canonical decomposition, followed by a symbol x. Again, $c \,\|\, \langle x \rangle$ must contain an alternating subsequence of length s of the form $\langle \cdots y \cdots x \cdots y \cdots x \rangle$ ending at x. Suppose s is even, so this subsequence starts with y. Then, by an argument similar to that given above, c must contain either the last occurrence of y in U or the first occurrence of x in U. This implies $\mu_{s,s-2}(n) \leq 2n$, but since the first chain contains the first occurrences of at least two symbols, the bound reduces to $2n - 1$. If s is odd, the above subsequence starts and ends with x, so c must contain either the first or the last occurrence of y in U, and the conclusion follows as above. $\qquad\square$

The above result shows, in particular, that a $DS(n, 4)$-sequence can be decomposed into at most $2n - 1$ 2-chains.

Lemma 3.3 *Given a $DS(n, 4)$-sequence U composed of m 2-chains, we can construct another $DS(n, 4)$-sequence U' composed of m 1-chains such that*

$$|U'| \geq \frac{1}{2}(|U| - m).$$

Proof. Replace each 2-chain c by a 1-chain c' composed of the same symbols of c in the order of their leftmost appearances in c. Since $\lambda_2(k) = 2k - 1$, we have $|c'| \geq \frac{1}{2}|c| + \frac{1}{2}$. Take the concatenation of all these 1-chains, erasing any first element of a chain that is equal to its preceding element. The resulting sequence U' is clearly a $DS(n, 4)$-sequence composed of at most m 1-chains, whose length is

$$|U'| \geq \frac{1}{2}|U| + \frac{m}{2} - m = \frac{1}{2}(|U| - m). \qquad \square$$

Definition 3.4 Let n, m, and s be positive integers. We denote by $\Psi_s^t(m, n)$ the maximum length of a $DS(n, s)$-sequence composed of at most m t-chains. If $t = 1$, we denote this quantity also by $\Psi_s(m, n)$.

Corollary 3.5 $\lambda_4(n) \leq 2\Psi_4(2n - 1, n) + 2n - 1$.

Proof. The proof follows directly from Lemmas 3.2 and 3.3. $\qquad \square$

The main result of this section is that $\Psi_4(m, n) = O((m + n) \cdot 2^{\alpha(m)})$. This upper bound for $\Psi_4(m, n)$, in conjunction with Corollary 3.5, gives the desired upper bound for $\lambda_4(n)$.

3.2.2   More on Ackermann's function

Before proving the main result, we prove certain properties of Ackermann's function and of some auxiliary functions, which we need in establishing the desired upper bound. This extends the initial review of Ackermann's function given in Section 2.1. We delegate the proofs of some of the following properties to Appendix 3.1, since they are somewhat technical and the methods that they use are not required in the proofs of the main lemmas.

Lemma 3.6 For all $k \geq 4$ and $s \geq 3$,

$$2^{A_k(s)} \leq A_{k-1}(\log A_k(s)).$$

Lemma 3.7 Let $\xi_k(n) = 2^{\alpha_k(n)}$. Then, for $k \geq 3$, $n \geq A_{k+1}(4)$,

$$\min\{s' \geq 1 : \xi_k^{(s')}(n) \leq A_{k+1}(4)\} \leq 2\alpha_{k+1}(n) - 2.$$

We define a sequence of functions $\beta_k(n)$ that are related to the inverse Ackermann functions as follows:

$$\begin{aligned}
\beta_1(n) &\doteq \alpha_1(n), \\
\beta_2(n) &= \alpha_2(n), \\
\beta_k(n) &= \min\{s \geq 1 : (\alpha_{k-1} \cdot \beta_{k-1})^{(s)}(n) \leq 64\}.
\end{aligned}$$

The functions $\beta_k(n)$ are nondecreasing, and converge to infinity with their argument. Note that

$$\beta_3(n) = \min\left\{s \geq 1 : \left(\lceil \log \rceil^2\right)^{(s)}(n) \leq 64\right\}.$$

In the next lemma we give an upper bound on $\beta_k(n)$ that shows that these functions grow at the same asymptotic rate as the functions $\alpha_k(n)$:

Lemma 3.8 *For all $k \geq 1$, $n \geq 2$, we have $\beta_k(n) \leq 2\alpha_k(n)$.*

3.2.3   An upper bound for $\Psi_4(m,n)$

In this subsection we establish an upper bound on the maximal length $\Psi_4(m,n)$ of an $(n,4)$ Davenport–Schinzel sequence composed of at most m 1-chains. The first result extends Lemma 2.12.

Lemma 3.9 *Let $m, n \geq 1$, and $1 < b < m$ be integers. Then for any partitioning $m = \sum_{i=1}^{b} m_i$, with $m_1, \ldots, m_b \geq 1$, there exist nonnegative integers $n^{\star}, n_1, n_2, \ldots, n_b$ such that*

$$n^{\star} + \sum_{i=1}^{b} n_i = n,$$

and

$$\Psi_4(m,n) \leq \sum_{i=1}^{b} \Psi_4(m_i, n_i) + 2\Psi_4(b, n^{\star}) + \Psi_3(m, 2n^{\star}) + 3m. \qquad (3.1)$$

Proof. Let U be a $DS(n,4)$-sequence that consists of at most m 1-chains, $c_1, \ldots, c_m$, such that $|U| = \Psi_4(m,n)$, and let $m = \sum_{i=1}^{b} m_i$ be a partitioning of m as above. Partition the sequence U into b *layers* (i.e., contiguous subsequences) $L_1, \ldots, L_b$ so that the layer L_i consists of m_i 1-chains. Call a symbol a *internal* to layer L_i if all occurrences of a in U are within L_i. A symbol will be called *external* if it is not internal to any layer. Suppose there are n_i internal symbols in layer L_i and $n^{\star}$ external symbols (thus $n^{\star} + \sum_{i=1}^{b} n_i = n$).

To estimate the total number of occurrences in U of symbols that are internal to L_i, we proceed as follows. Erase from L_i all external symbols. Next scan L_i from left to right and erase each element that has become equal to the element immediately preceding it. This leaves us with a sequence $L_i^{\star}$ which is clearly a $DS(n_i, 4)$-sequence consisting of at most m_i 1-chains, and thus its length is at most $\Psi_4(m_i, n_i)$. Moreover, if two equal internal elements in L_i have become adjacent after erasing the external symbols, then these two elements must have belonged to two distinct 1-chains, thus the total number of deletions of internal symbols is at most $m_i - 1$.

Hence, summing over all layers, we conclude that the total contribution of internal symbols to $|U|$ is at most

$$m - b + \sum_{i=1}^{b} \Psi_4(m_i, n_i).$$

We estimate the total number of occurrences of external symbols in two parts. For each layer L_i, call an external symbol a a *middle symbol* if it neither starts in L_i nor ends in L_i. If an external symbol is not a middle symbol, call it an *end symbol*. An external symbol appears as an end symbol in exactly two layers. First we estimate the contribution of middle symbols. For each layer L_i, erase all internal symbols and end symbols, and, if necessary, also erase each occurrence of a middle symbol that has become equal to the element immediately preceding it. The above process deletes at most $m_i - 1$ middle symbols. Let us denote the resulting sequence by $L_i^\star$.

We claim that $L_i^\star$ is a $DS(p_i, 2)$-sequence, where p_i is the number of distinct symbols in $L_i^\star$. Suppose the contrary; then $L_i^\star$ contains a subsequence of the form

$$\langle a \ \cdots \ b \ \cdots \ a \ \cdots \ b \rangle,$$

where a and b are two distinct symbols of $L_i^\star$. Since a and b are middle symbols, each appears in a layer before $L_i^\star$ as well as in a layer after $L_i^\star$. This implies that U must contain a subsequence of the form

$$\langle (b \ \cdots \ a) \ \cdots \ a \ \cdots \ b \ \cdots \ a \ \cdots \ b \ \cdots \ (b \ \cdots \ a) \rangle,$$

in which each of the first and last pairs may appear in reverse order. But this alternation of length ≥ 6 contradicts the fact that U is a $DS(n, 4)$-sequence, showing that $L_i^\star$ is indeed a $DS(p_i, 2)$-sequence. Thus, the concatenation of all sequences $L_i^\star$, with the additional possible deletions of any first element of $L_i^\star$, which happens to be equal to the last element of $L_{i-1}^\star$, is a $DS(n^\star, 4)$-sequence V composed of b 2-chains, and it follows from Lemma 3.3 that we can replace this sequence by another $DS(n^\star, 4)$-sequence $V^\star$ composed of b 1-chains so that $|V| \leq 2|V^\star| + b$. Hence, the contribution of middle symbols to $|U|$ is at most

$$2\Psi_4(b, n^\star) + m + b.$$

Finally, we consider the contribution of end symbols. For each layer L_i, erase all internal symbols and middle symbols, and, if necessary, also erase each occurrence of an end symbol if it is equal to the element immediately preceding it. We erase at most $m_i - 1$ end symbols. Let us denote the resulting sequence by $L_i^\#$. Let q_i denote the number of distinct symbols in $L_i^\#$. We claim that $L_i^\#$ is a $DS(q_i, 3)$-sequence. Indeed, if this were not the case, $L_i^\#$ would have contained an alternating subsequence of the form

$$\langle a \ \cdots \ b \ \cdots \ a \ \cdots \ b \ \cdots \ a \rangle.$$

Since b is an external symbol, it also appears in a sequence $L_j^\#$ other than $L_i^\#$. But then U would have contained an alternation of length 6, which is impossible. Hence, $L_i^\#$ is a $DS(q_i, 3)$-sequence consisting of m_i 1-chains, so its length is at most $\Psi_3(m_i, q_i)$. Summing over all layers, the contribution of the end symbols is at most

$$m + \sum_{i=1}^{b} \Psi_3(m_i, q_i) \leq m + \Psi_3\left(m, \sum_{i=1}^{b} q_i\right).$$

But an external symbol appears as an end symbol only in two layers, thus $\sum_{i=1}^{b} q_i = 2n^\star$. Hence, the total contribution of external symbols is at most

$$2m + b + 2\Psi_4(b, n^\star) + \Psi_3(m, 2n^\star).$$

We thus obtain the asserted inequality:

$$\Psi_4(m, n) \leq \sum_{i=1}^{b} \Psi_4(m_i, n_i) + 3m + \Psi_3(m, 2n^\star) + 2\Psi_4(b, n^\star). \qquad \square$$

Lemma 3.10 Let $n, m \geq 1$, $k \geq 2$. Then

$$\Psi_4(m, n) \leq \left(\frac{19}{2} \cdot 2^k - 8k - 11\right) m \cdot \alpha_k(m) \cdot \beta_k(m) + \left(\frac{25}{2} \cdot 2^k - 8k - 12\right) n. \tag{3.2}$$

Proof. We use (3.1) repeatedly to obtain the above upper bounds for $k = 2, 3, \ldots$. At each step we choose b appropriately and estimate $\Psi_4(b, n^\star)$ using a technique similar to that of Section 2.2. At the kth step we refine the bound of $\Psi_3(m, 2n^\star)$ using the inequality

$$\Psi_3(m, n) \leq (8k - 8)m \cdot \alpha_k(m) + (4k - 2)n$$

obtained in Corollary 2.14.

We proceed by double induction on k and m. Initially $k = 2$, $m \geq 1$, and $\beta_k(m) = \alpha_k(m) = \lceil \log m \rceil$. Choose $b = 2$, $m_1 = \lfloor m/2 \rfloor$, $m_2 = \lceil m/2 \rceil$ in (3.1); then

$$\Psi_4(b, n^\star) = \Psi_4(2, n^\star) = 2n^\star$$

for all $n^\star$, and $\Psi_3(m, 2n^\star) \leq 8m \lceil \log m \rceil + 12n^\star$, so (3.1) becomes:

$$\begin{aligned} \Psi_4(m, n) &\leq \Psi_4\left(\left\lfloor \frac{m}{2} \right\rfloor, n_1\right) + \Psi_4\left(\left\lceil \frac{m}{2} \right\rceil, n_2\right) + 16n^\star + 3m + 8m \lceil \log m \rceil \\ &\leq \Psi_4\left(\left\lfloor \frac{m}{2} \right\rfloor, n_1\right) + \Psi_4\left(\left\lceil \frac{m}{2} \right\rceil, n_2\right) + 16n^\star + 11m \lceil \log m \rceil, \end{aligned}$$

where $n = n_1 + n_2 + n^\star$. The solution of the above recurrence is easily seen to be

$$\begin{aligned} \Psi_4(m, n) &\leq 11m(\lceil \log m \rceil)^2 + 16n \\ &= 11m \cdot \alpha_2(m) \cdot \beta_2(m) + 16n \\ &\leq \left(\frac{19}{2} \cdot 2^k - 8k - 11\right) \cdot m\alpha_k(m) \cdot \beta_k(m) + \\ &\quad \left(\frac{25}{2} \cdot 2^k - 8k - 12\right) \cdot n \end{aligned}$$

(for $k = 2$).

For $k > 2$ and $m \le 64$ the inequality holds because $\Psi_4(m, n) \le 64n$, which is less than the right-hand side of the inequality.

For $k > 2$ and $m > 64$, assume that the induction hypothesis is true for all $k' < k$ and $m' \ge 1$ and for $k' = k$ and $m' < m$; choose

$$t = \left\lceil \frac{\alpha_{k-1}(m) \cdot \beta_{k-1}(m)}{\alpha_k(m)} \right\rceil \text{ and } b = \left\lfloor \frac{m}{t} \right\rfloor .$$

For $m > 64$ and $k > 2$, $\alpha_k(m) > 2$ and $\alpha_{k-1}(m) \cdot \beta_{k-1}(m) \le \lceil \log m \rceil^2$; thus

$$t \le \left\lceil \frac{1}{2} \lceil \log m \rceil^2 \right\rceil < m - 1.$$

Suppose $m = b \cdot t + r$, then for the first r layers $L_1, \ldots, L_r$ choose $m_i = t + 1$, and for the remaining layers choose $m_i = t$; therefore $m_i \le t + 1 < m$ for all i.

By the induction hypothesis (for $k - 1$ and b) we have

$$\Psi_4(b, n^\star) \le \left(\frac{19}{2} \cdot 2^{k-1} - 8(k-1) - 11 \right) b \cdot \alpha_{k-1}(b) \cdot \beta_{k-1}(b) +$$
$$\left(\frac{25}{2} \cdot 2^{k-1} - 8(k-1) - 12 \right) n^\star.$$

However,

$$b \le \frac{m}{t} = m \left/ \left\lceil \frac{\alpha_{k-1}(m) \cdot \beta_{k-1}(m)}{\alpha_k(m)} \right\rceil \right. \le \frac{m \cdot \alpha_k(m)}{\alpha_{k-1}(m) \cdot \beta_{k-1}(m)}.$$

Since, clearly, $b \le m$, we have

$$\Psi_4(b, n^\star) \le \left(\frac{19}{2} \cdot 2^{k-1} - 8(k-1) - 11 \right) \cdot m\alpha_k(m) +$$
$$\left(\frac{25}{2} \cdot 2^{k-1} - 8(k-1) - 12 \right) \cdot n^\star.$$

Since each $m_i < m$, by the induction hypothesis (for k and m_i) (3.1) becomes

$$\Psi_4(m, n) \le 2 \cdot \left(\frac{19}{2} \cdot 2^{k-1} - 8(k-1) - 11 \right) \cdot m\alpha_k(m) +$$
$$2 \cdot \left(\frac{25}{2} \cdot 2^{k-1} - 8(k-1) - 12 \right) \cdot n^\star +$$
$$(8k - 8)m\alpha_k(m) + (8k - 4)n^\star + 3m +$$
$$\sum_{i=1}^{b} \left(\frac{19}{2} \cdot 2^k - 8k - 11 \right) \cdot m_i \cdot \alpha_k(m_i) \cdot \beta_k(m_i) +$$
$$\sum_{i=1}^{b} \left(\frac{25}{2} \cdot 2^k - 8k - 12 \right) n_i.$$

The value of $\beta_k(m_i)$ can be estimated as follows:

$$
\begin{aligned}
\beta_k(m_i) &\leq \beta_k(t+1) \\
&= \beta_k\left(\left\lceil \frac{\alpha_{k-1}(m) \cdot \beta_{k-1}(m)}{\alpha_k(m)} \right\rceil + 1\right) \\
&\leq \beta_k\left(\frac{\alpha_{k-1}(m) \cdot \beta_{k-1}(m)}{\alpha_k(m)} + 2\right).
\end{aligned}
$$

However, for all $m > 4$, $\alpha_k(m) \geq 3$ (and $\alpha_{k-1}(m) \cdot \beta_{k-1}(m) \geq 3$ too), and for $x \geq 3$, $y \geq 3$, we have $\frac{x}{y} + 2 \leq x$, therefore

$$
\beta_k(m_i) \leq \beta_k(\alpha_{k-1}(m) \cdot \beta_{k-1}(m)) = \beta_k(m) - 1,
$$

which implies

$$
\begin{aligned}
\Psi_4(m,n) &\leq \left(\frac{19}{2} \cdot 2^k - 8k - 11\right) \cdot \alpha_k(m) \cdot (\beta_k(m) - 1) \cdot \sum_{i=1}^{b} m_i + \\
&\quad \left(\frac{19}{2} \cdot 2^k - 8k - 11\right) \cdot m \cdot \alpha_k(m) + \\
&\quad \left(\frac{25}{2} \cdot 2^k - 8k - 12\right) \cdot \left(\sum_{i=1}^{b} n_i + n^\star\right) \\
&= \left(\frac{19}{2} \cdot 2^k - 8k - 11\right) m \alpha_k(m) \beta_k(m) + \left(\frac{25}{2} \cdot 2^k - 8k - 12\right) n,
\end{aligned}
$$

because $\sum_{i=1}^{b} m_i = m$ and $n^\star + \sum_{i=1}^{b} n_i = n$. $\square$

Theorem 3.11 $\Psi_4(m,n) = O((m+n) \cdot 2^{\alpha(m)})$.

Proof. By Lemma 3.8, $\beta_k(m) \leq 2\alpha_k(m)$, so that

$$
\Psi_4(m,n) \leq 2 \cdot \left(\frac{19}{2} \cdot 2^k - 8k - 11\right) m \cdot (\alpha_k(m))^2 + \left(\frac{25}{2} \cdot 2^k - 8k - 12\right) \cdot n.
$$

Choose $k = \alpha(m) + 1$. By Lemma 2.4(b), $\alpha_{\alpha(m)+1}(m) \leq 4$. Substituting this value of k in the above inequality, we get

$$
\begin{aligned}
\Psi_4(m,n) &\leq 2 \cdot \frac{19}{2} \cdot 2^{\alpha(m)+1} \cdot m \cdot 16 + \frac{25}{2} \cdot 2^{\alpha(m)+1} \cdot n \\
&= (608m + 25n) \cdot 2^{\alpha(m)} \quad\quad\quad\quad\quad\quad (3.3) \\
&= O((m+n) \cdot 2^{\alpha(m)}). \quad\quad\quad\quad\quad\quad \square
\end{aligned}
$$

Corollary 3.5 therefore yields:

Theorem 3.12 $\lambda_4(n) = O(n \cdot 2^{\alpha(n)})$.

3.3   A lower bound for $\lambda_4(n)$

In this section we establish the matching lower bound $\lambda_4(n) = \Omega(n \cdot 2^{\alpha(n)})$.

Our construction is based on a doubly inductive process that somewhat resembles that given in Section 2.3. In this construction we use a sequence of functions, $F_k(m)$, which grow faster than the functions $A_k(m)$, although asymptotically they grow at the same rate.

3.3.1   Auxiliary functions

Define inductively a sequence $\{F_k\}_{k=1}^{\infty}$ of functions from the set N to itself as follows:

$$
\begin{aligned}
F_1(m) &= 1, & m \geq 1, \\
F_k(1) &= (2^k - 1)F_{k-1}(2^{k-1}), & k \geq 2, \\
F_k(m) &= 2F_k(m-1) \cdot F_{k-1}(F_k(m-1)), & k \geq 2,\ m > 1.
\end{aligned}
$$

Here are some properties of the functions $F_k(m)$:

(F1) $F_2(m) = 3 \cdot 2^{m-1} \geq A_2(m)$.

(F2) Each function $F_k(m)$ is strictly increasing in m, for every $k \geq 2$. Thus $F_k(m) \geq m + 1$, for all $k \geq 2$, $m \geq 1$.
We also have $\rho F_k(m) \leq F_k(\rho m)$, for all $k \geq 2$, $m \geq 1$, $\rho \geq 1$.

(F3) $\{F_k(m)\}_{k \geq 1}^{\infty}$ is strictly increasing for any fixed $m \geq 1$.

(F4) $F_k(m) \geq A_k(m)$, for $k \geq 2$, $m \geq 1$.

(F5) $2^{F_k(m)} \leq A_k(m+4)$, for $k \geq 3$, $m \geq 1$.

(F6) Hence, $A_k(m) \leq F_k(m) \leq A_k(m+4)$ for all $k \geq 3$, $m \geq 1$.

Properties (F3)–(F5) are proved in Appendix 3.2 of this chapter.

We will also use an auxiliary sequence, $\{N_k\}_{k \geq 1}^{\infty}$, of functions defined on the integers, as follows:

$$
\begin{aligned}
N_1(m) &= m, & m \geq 1, \\
N_k(1) &= N_{k-1}(2^{k-1}), & k \geq 2, \\
N_k(m) &= 2N_k(m-1) \cdot F_{k-1}(F_k(m-1)) + N_{k-1}(F_k(m-1)), & \\
& & k \geq 2,\ m > 1.
\end{aligned}
$$

3.3.2   The sequences $S_4(k,m)$

We use a doubly inductive construction similar to that for $\lambda_3(n)$. For each pair of integers $k, m \geq 1$, we define a sequence $S_4(k,m)$ so that

(a) $S_4(k, m)$ is composed of $N_k(m)$ symbols;

(b) $S_4(k, m)$ is the concatenation of $F_k(m)$ *fans*, where each fan is composed of m distinct symbols $a_1, \ldots, a_m$ and has the form

$$\langle a_1\, a_2 \cdots a_{m-1}\, a_m\, a_{m-1} \cdots a_2\, a_1 \rangle,$$

so its length is $2m - 1$; we call m the *fan size*. Note the difference between this definition of a fan and that used in the lower bound construction for $\lambda_3(n)$. That is, now the sequence is composed *exclusively* of fans, and a symbol may (and does) appear in more than one fan. Also, the structure of a single fan is different.

(c) $S_4(k, m)$ is a Davenport–Schinzel sequence of order 4.

The doubly inductive construction of $S_4(k, m)$ proceeds as follows.

I. $S_4(1, m) = \langle 1\, 2 \cdots m - 1\, m\, m - 1 \cdots 2\, 1 \rangle$, for each $m \geq 1$.

II. $S_4(k, 1)$ is the sequence $S_4(k - 1, 2^{k-1})$; each fan (of length $2^k - 1$) in $S_4(k-1, 2^{k-1})$ is regarded in $S_4(k, 1)$ as $2^k - 1$ fans of size (and length) 1.

III. To obtain $S_4(k, m)$, for $k > 1$, $m > 1$, we proceed as follows.

(1) Construct $S' = S_4(k, m - 1)$. The sequence S' has $F_k(m - 1)$ fans, each of size $m - 1$.

(2) Create $2F_{k-1}(F_k(m - 1))$ distinct copies of S' (with pairwise disjoint sets of symbols). These copies have

$$2F_k(m - 1) \cdot F_{k-1}(F_k(m - 1)) = F_k(m)$$

fans altogether.

(3) Construct $S^\star = S_4(k-1, F_k(m-1))$. The sequence $S^\star$ has $F_{k-1}(F_k(m-1))$ fans, each of size $F_k(m - 1)$. Duplicate the middle element of each fan of $S^\star$. The total length of the modified $S^\star$ is

$$2F_k(m - 1) \cdot F_{k-1}(F_k(m - 1)) = F_k(m).$$

(4) For each $\beta \leq F_{k-1}(F_k(m - 1))$, merge the βth expanded fan of the modified $S^\star$ with the $(2\beta-1)$th and the (2β)th copies of S', by inserting the αth element of the first half (respectively, of the second half) of the fan into the middle place of the αth fan of the $(2\beta - 1)$th (respectively, the (2β)th) copy of S', for each $\alpha \leq F_k(m - 1)$, and by duplicating the former middle element of each of these fans (before and after the inserted element).

(5) $S_4(k, m)$ is just the concatenation of all these modified copies of S'.

Theorem 3.13 $S_4(k, m)$ *satisfies the properties (a)–(c) stated above.*

Proof. By double induction on k and m. Clearly, $S_4(1, m)$ satisfies these properties for each $m \geq 1$.

For arbitrary $k > 1$ and m, property (a) is a direct consequence of the inductive construction and of the definition of $N_k(m)$.

As to property (b), the inductive construction and the definition of $F_k(m)$ imply that $S_4(k, m)$ is the concatenation of $F_k(m)$ fans. That each fan consists of m distinct symbols and has the required form also follows from the inductive construction of the sequences.

As to property (c), we first observe that no pair of adjacent elements of $S_4(k, m)$ can be identical. Indeed, this is obvious for $k = 1$, and follows by induction for $k \geq 2$, $m = 1$. For general k and m, this property follows by the induction hypothesis for each copy of S' and for $S^\star$ (recall also that all these sequences are constructed on pairwise disjoint sets of symbols). The only duplications of adjacent elements that are generated by our construction are of the middle elements of all the fans of the copies of S' and of $S^\star$. However, in $S_4(k, m)$, an element of $S^\star$ is inserted between the two duplicated appearances of the middle element of each fan of any copy of S', and the two duplicated appearances of the middle element of a fan of $S^\star$ are inserted into two different fans in two different copies of S'. Thus $S_4(k, m)$ contains no pair of adjacent equal elements.

We next claim that $S_4(k, m)$ does not contain an alternation of the form

$$\langle a \cdots b \cdots a \cdots b \cdots a \cdots b \rangle,$$

for any pair of distinct symbols a and b. Indeed, the base cases are trivial. For the general case, the induction hypothesis implies that this property holds when both a and b belong to $S^\star$ or when both belong to the same copy of S'. If a and b belong to two different copies of S' then these two copies are not interspersed at all in $S_4(k, m)$. The only remaining cases are when a belongs to $S^\star$ and b to some copy S'_β of S' or vice versa. In the first case, only a single appearance of a (in the first or second half of the corresponding fan of $S^\star$) is inserted into S'_β, so the largest possible alternation between a and b in $S_4(k, m)$ is $a \cdots b \cdots a \cdots b \cdots a$. This same observation rules out the latter possibility (a belongs to S'_β and b to $S^\star$). Thus it follows by induction that $S_4(k, m)$ is a Davenport–Schinzel sequence of order 4. $\qquad\square$

It remains to estimate the length $|S_4(k, m)|$ of $S_4(k, m)$ as a function of its number of symbols $N_k(m)$. Clearly

$$\frac{|S_4(k, m)|}{N_k(m)} = \frac{(2m - 1)F_k(m)}{N_k(m)}.$$

To bound this from below, we will obtain an upper bound on $\dfrac{N_k(m)}{F_k(m)}$, as follows.

Theorem 3.14 $\dfrac{N_k(m)}{F_k(m)} \leq m \cdot D_k$, where $D_k = \displaystyle\prod_{j=1}^{k} c_j$, for $k \geq 1$, and

$$c_j = 1 \left/ \left(2 - \frac{1}{2^{j-1}} \right) \right. \qquad \text{for } j \geq 1.$$

Proof. For $k = 1$ we have $D_1 = c_1 = 1$ and $\dfrac{N_1(m)}{F_1(m)} = m = m \cdot D_1$, as required.

For $k > 1$ and $m = 1$ we have, by the induction hypothesis,

$$
\begin{aligned}
\frac{N_k(1)}{F_k(1)} &= \frac{N_{k-1}(2^{k-1})}{(2^k - 1)F_{k-1}(2^{k-1})} \\
&\leq \frac{2^{k-1}}{2^k - 1} \cdot D_{k-1} \\
&= c_k \cdot D_{k-1} = 1 \cdot D_k,
\end{aligned}
$$

as required.

For $k > 1$ and $m > 1$ we have, by the induction hypothesis,

$$
\begin{aligned}
\frac{N_k(m)}{F_k(m)} &= \frac{N_k(m-1)}{F_k(m-1)} + \frac{1}{2F_k(m-1)} \cdot \frac{N_{k-1}(F_k(m-1))}{F_{k-1}(F_k(m-1))} \\
&\leq (m-1) \cdot D_k + \frac{1}{2F_k(m-1)} \cdot F_k(m-1) \cdot D_{k-1} \\
&= (m-1)D_k + \frac{1}{2}D_{k-1} \\
&\leq m \cdot D_k \qquad \text{(because } \tfrac{1}{2} < c_k\text{).} \qquad \square
\end{aligned}
$$

Corollary 3.15 $\qquad \dfrac{|S_4(k,m)|}{N_k(m)} \geq \dfrac{2m-1}{m} \cdot 2^k \cdot \displaystyle\prod_{j=1}^{\infty} \left(1 - \frac{1}{2^j} \right).$

Proof. By Theorem 3.14,

$$
\begin{aligned}
\frac{|S_4(k,m)|}{N_k(m)} &\geq \frac{2m-1}{m \cdot D_k} = \frac{2m-1}{m} \cdot \prod_{j=1}^{k} \left(2\left(1 - \frac{1}{2^j}\right) \right) \\
&\geq \frac{2m-1}{m} \cdot 2^k \cdot \prod_{j=1}^{\infty} \left(1 - \frac{1}{2^j} \right)
\end{aligned}
$$

(the limit of the last infinite product is easily seen to be positive). $\qquad \square$

Theorem 3.16 $\lambda_4(n) = \Omega(n \cdot 2^{\alpha(n)})$.

Proof. Put

$$\beta = \prod_{j=1}^{\infty} \left(1 - \frac{1}{2^j}\right).$$

Clearly, $0 < \beta < 1$. Theorem 3.14 and property (F6) imply $N_k(1) \leq F_k(1) \leq A_k(5)$ for all $k \geq 3$. Hence, for each $k \geq 5$, we have

$$n_k \equiv N_k(1) \leq A_k(k) = A(k),$$

so that $\alpha(n_k) \leq k$. On the other hand, the sequence $\{n_k\}_{k \geq 1}$ is easily seen to converge to infinity. Thus, for any given n, we can find k such that $n_k \leq n < n_{k+1}$. Assume, without loss of generality, that $k \geq 4$. Put $t = \lfloor n/n_k \rfloor$ so that

$$tn_k \leq n < (t+1)n_k < 2tn_k.$$

Clearly,

$$
\begin{aligned}
\lambda_4(n) &\geq t\lambda_4(n_k) \geq t|S_4(k,1)| \\
&\geq \beta tn_k \cdot 2^k \qquad \text{(by Corollary 3.15)} \\
&> \frac{\beta}{2}n \cdot 2^k.
\end{aligned}
$$

However, $\alpha(n) \leq \alpha(n_{k+1}) \leq k+1$, so that $k \geq \alpha(n) - 1$, and we thus have

$$\lambda_4(n) \geq \frac{\beta}{4}n \cdot 2^{\alpha(n)}, \tag{3.4}$$

for all $n \geq N_4(1)$. For smaller values of n we have $\alpha(n) \leq 5$, $\beta < \frac{3}{8}$, so (3.4) will follow by showing that $\lambda_4(n) \geq 3n$, which is easily seen to hold for all $n \geq 3$. For $n = 1, 2$, the inequality (3.4) is trivial, thus we have for each $n \geq 1$

$$\lambda_4(n) \geq \frac{\beta}{4}n \cdot 2^{\alpha(n)} = \Omega(n \cdot 2^{\alpha(n)}). \qquad \square$$

Corollary 3.17 $\lambda_4(n) = \Theta(n \cdot 2^{\alpha(n)})$.

Proof. Immediate from the results of Theorems 3.12 and 3.16. $\square$

3.4   Upper bounds for $\lambda_s(n)$

In this section we extend the approach of Section 3.2 to obtain improved upper bounds for $\lambda_s(n)$. In particular, we show that

$$\lambda_s(n) \leq \begin{cases} n \cdot 2^{\alpha(n)^{\frac{s-2}{2}} + C_s(n)} & \text{if } s \text{ is even,} \\ n \cdot 2^{\alpha(n)^{\frac{s-3}{2}} \log \alpha(n) + C_s(n)} & \text{if } s \text{ is odd,} \end{cases} \tag{3.5}$$

where $C_s(n)$ satisfies the following bounds:

$$3 + s \leq C_s(n) = \begin{cases} 8 & \text{for } s = 3, \\ 12 & \text{for } s = 4, \\ O\left((\alpha(n))^{\frac{s-4}{2}} \cdot \log \alpha(n)\right) & \text{for even } s > 4, \\ O\left((\alpha(n))^{\frac{s-3}{2}}\right) & \text{for odd } s > 3. \end{cases} \tag{3.6}$$

A more precise definition of $C_s(n)$ is given in (3.8) below.

We have shown in Lemma 1.12 that

$$\lambda_s(n) \leq \frac{sn(n-1)}{2} + 1.$$

For $n \leq 4$ and $s \geq 3$, this directly implies that

$$\lambda_s(n) \leq n \cdot 2^{(\alpha(n))^{\frac{s-3}{2}} + C_s(n)}.$$

For $4 < n \leq 16$, we have $\alpha(n) \geq 2$ and

$$\begin{aligned} \lambda_s(n) &\leq 8sn \\ &= 2^{3 + \log s} n \\ &\leq n \cdot 2^{2^{\frac{s-3}{2}} + 3 + s} \\ &\leq n \cdot 2^{(\alpha(n))^{\frac{s-3}{2}} + C_s(n)}. \end{aligned}$$

Thus $\lambda_s(n)$ satisfies the desired inequality for $n \leq 16$. We can therefore restrict our attention to $n > 16$. It can be easily verified that (3.5) holds for $s = 3$ and for $s = 4$. Indeed, for $s = 3$, we have shown in Corollary 2.16 that

$$\begin{aligned} \lambda_3(n) &\leq 138n\alpha(n) \\ &= n \cdot 2^{\log 138 + \log(\alpha(n))} \\ &\leq n \cdot 2^{8 + \log(\alpha(n))} \\ &= n \cdot 2^{\log(\alpha(n)) + C_3(n)}. \end{aligned}$$

For $s = 4$, (3.3) actually gives, for $n > 16$,

$$\begin{aligned} \lambda_4(n) &\leq 2^{12} \cdot n \cdot 2^{\alpha(n)} \\ &= n \cdot 2^{\alpha(n) + C_4(n)}. \end{aligned}$$

For $s > 4$, we prove the desired upper bound (3.5) for $\lambda_s(n)$ by induction on s.   •

The analysis in this section makes use of several additional functions defined in terms of $\alpha(n)$. Let $\{\Gamma_s\}_{s\geq 2}$ be the sequence of functions defined on $\mathbb{N}$ by

$$\Gamma_s(n) = \begin{cases} (\alpha(n))^{\frac{s-2}{2}} & \text{if } s \text{ is even,} \\ (\alpha(n))^{\frac{s-3}{2}} \cdot \log \alpha(n) & \text{if } s \text{ is odd.} \end{cases} \tag{3.7}$$

Thus $\Gamma_2(n) = 1$, $\Gamma_3(n) = \log \alpha(n)$, and for all $s \geq 4$,

$$\Gamma_s(n) = \Gamma_{s-2}(n) \cdot \alpha(n).$$

We also define another sequence, $\{C_s(n)\}_{s\geq 3}$, of functions on $\mathbb{N}$ by

$$C_s(n) = \sum_{i=2}^{s-1} a_i^s \cdot \Gamma_i(n), \tag{3.8}$$

where the constant coefficients a_i^s are defined recursively as follows:

$$a_2^3 = 8, \qquad\qquad a_2^4 = 12, \qquad\qquad a_3^4 = 0,$$

and for $s > 4$

$$a_i^s = \begin{cases} a_{s-3}^{s-2} + 1 & \text{if } i = s - 1, \\ a_{i-2}^{s-2} + a_i^{s-1} & \text{if } 3 < i < s - 1, \\ a_i^{s-1} & \text{if } i \leq 3. \end{cases} \tag{3.9}$$

Finally, define the sequence of functions $\Pi_s(n)$ by

$$\Pi_s(n) = 2^{\Gamma_s(n) + C_s(n)} \qquad\qquad \text{for } s \geq 3. \tag{3.10}$$

Note that, for any fixed n, $\{\Pi_s(n)\}_{s\geq 3}$ is increasing, and that, for any fixed s, $\{\Pi_s(n)\}_{n\geq 1}$ is also increasing. The definition of $\Pi_s(n)$ implies that, to prove the desired upper bound for $\lambda_s(n)$, we have to show that

$$\lambda_s(n) \leq n \cdot \Pi_s(n). \tag{3.11}$$

3.4.1   Upper bounds for $\Psi_s(m, n)$

In this subsection we establish an upper bound on the maximal length $\Psi_s(m, n)$ of an (n, s) Davenport–Schinzel sequence composed of at most m 1-chains. The following lemma is a (somewhat modified) extension of Lemma 3.9.

Lemma 3.18 *Let $m, n \geq 1$ and $1 < b < m$ be integers. For any partitioning $m = \sum_{i=1}^b m_i$, with $m_1, \ldots, m_b \geq 1$, there exist integers $n^\star$, $n_1, n_2, \ldots, n_b \geq 0$ such that*

$$n^\star + \sum_{i=1}^b n_i = n$$

and

$$\Psi_s(m, n) \leq \Psi_s^{s-2}(b, n^\star) + 2\Psi_{s-1}(m, n^\star) + 4m + \sum_{i=1}^b \Psi_s(m_i, n_i). \tag{3.12}$$

Proof. We extend the proof given in Lemma 3.9 to handle the general case. Let U be a $DS(n, s)$-sequence consisting of at most m 1-chains, $c_1, \ldots, c_m$, such that $|U| = \Psi_s(m, n)$. Partition U into b layers (i.e. pairwise disjoint contiguous subsequences), $L_1, \ldots, L_b$, so that the layer L_i consists of m_i 1-chains. Call a symbol a *internal* (to a layer L_i) or *external* as in Lemma 3.9. Suppose there are n_i internal symbols in layer L_i, and $n^\star$ external symbols (thus $n^\star + \sum_{i=1}^b n_i = n$).

Using the same argument as in Lemma 3.9, we can show that the total contribution of internal symbols to $|U|$ is at most

$$m - b + \sum_{i=1}^b \Psi_s(m_i, n_i).$$

We bound the total number of occurrences of external symbols in three parts, instead of two as in Lemma 3.9. For each layer L_i, call an external symbol a a *starting symbol* if its first (i.e., leftmost) occurrence is in L_i, an *ending symbol* if its last (i.e., rightmost) occurrence is in L_i, and a *middle symbol* if it is neither a starting nor an ending symbol. An external symbol appears as a starting symbol or as an ending symbol in exactly one layer. We first estimate the total number of occurrences of middle symbols. For each layer L_i erase all internal symbols, starting symbols, and ending symbols. Also erase each occurrence of a middle symbol that has become equal to the element immediately preceding it (there are at most $m_i - 1$ such erasures). Let us denote the resulting sequence by $L_i^\star$.

By generalizing the argument given in the proof of Lemma 3.9, it can be easily shown that $L_i^\star$ is a $DS(n^\star, s - 2)$-sequence. Thus the concatenation of all sequences $L_i^\star$, with the additional possible deletions of any first element of a subsequence $L_i^\star$, which happens to be equal to the last element of the preceding subsequence $L_{i-1}^\star$, is a $DS(n^\star, s)$-sequence composed of b $(s - 2)$-chains, and therefore the contribution of the middle symbols is at most

$$\Psi_s^{s-2}(b, n^\star) + m.$$

Next consider the contribution of the starting external symbols. For each layer L_i, erase all internal symbols, middle symbols, and ending symbols, and, if necessary, also erase each occurrence of a starting symbol if it is equal to the element immediately preceding it. The above process deletes at most $m_i - 1$ starting symbols. Let us denote the resulting sequence by $L_i^\#$. Let q_i be the number of distinct symbols in $L_i^\#$. We claim that $L_i^\#$ is a $DS(q_i, s - 1)$-sequence. Indeed, if this were not the case, $L_i^\#$ would have contained an alternating subsequence of the form

$$\underbrace{\langle a \cdots b \cdots a \cdots \cdots a \cdots b \rangle}_{s+1}$$

if s is odd, or

$$\langle \underbrace{a \cdots b \cdots a \cdots \cdots b \cdots a}_{s+1} \rangle$$

if s is even. Since b and a are external symbols and their first appearance is in $L_i^\#$, they also appear in some layers after $L_i^\#$. But then U would have contained an alternation of a and b of length $s + 2$, which is impossible. Hence $L_i^\#$ is a $DS(q_i, s-1)$-sequence consisting of m_i 1-chains, so its length is at most $\Psi_{s-1}(m_i, q_i)$. Summing over all layers, the contribution of starting symbols is at most

$$m + \sum_{i=1}^{b} \Psi_{s-1}(m_i, q_i) \leq m + \Psi_{s-1}\left(m, \sum_{i=1}^{b} q_i\right).$$

However, an external symbol appears as a starting symbol only in one layer, therefore $\sum_{i=1}^{b} q_i = n^\star$. Hence the total contribution of starting symbols is bounded by

$$m + \Psi_{s-1}(m, n^\star).$$

The case of ending symbols is symmetric to that of starting symbols, so the same bound also holds for the number of appearances of ending symbols. Therefore the total contribution of external symbols is bounded by

$$3m + 2\Psi_{s-1}(m, n^\star) + \Psi_s^{s-2}(b, n^\star).$$

We thus obtain the desired inequality

$$\Psi_s(m, n) \leq \Psi_s^{s-2}(b, n^\star) + 2\Psi_{s-1}(m, n^\star) + 4m + \sum_{i=1}^{b} \Psi_s(m_i, n_i). \qquad \square$$

Remark 3.19 (i) Note that, in the above proof, we estimate the contribution of external symbols in three parts, instead of two as in Lemma 3.9. The reason is that while the treatment of starting and ending external symbols as a single case can be extended to *even* values of s, it fails for odd values, because the resulting sequence $L_i^\#$ might be of order s rather than $s - 1$; for instance, if a is a starting symbol and b is an ending symbol, then it is possible that a and b alternate $s + 1$ times in the layer L_i (starting with a and ending with b). That is why, in general, partitioning the external symbols into two parts does not suffice. Moreover, the improvement in the bounds that would have resulted for even values of s is not significant asymptotically, as will be indicated by our lower bounds.

(ii) In the above proof, each $L_i^\star$ is a $DS(n^\star, s - 2)$-sequence composed of at most m_i 1-chains, which implies that $|L_i^\star| \leq \Psi_{s-2}(m_i, n^\star)$. Hence, we also have the following inequality for $\Psi_s(m, n)$:

$$\Psi_s(m, n) \leq 2\Psi_{s-1}(m, n^\star) + 4m + \sum_{i=1}^{b}(\Psi_{s-2}(m_i, n^\star) + \Psi_s(m_i, n_i)). \qquad (3.13)$$

We need the following auxiliary lemma to prove an upper bound for $\lambda_s(n)$.

Lemma 3.20 *Let $m, n \geq 1$ and $3 \leq t < s$ be integers. Let $\{\varphi_t\}_{t \geq 1}$ be a sequence of functions defined on $\mathbb{N}$, such that $\lambda_t(n) \leq n \cdot \varphi_t(n)$. Then*

$$\Psi_s^t(m, n) \leq \varphi_t(n) \cdot (\Psi_s(m, n) + m - 1).$$

Proof. The lemma is a generalization of Lemma 3.3. Let U be a $DS(n, s)$-sequence composed of m t-chains and having maximum length. Replace each chain c_i of U by the 1-chain c_i' composed of the same symbols of c_i in the order of their leftmost appearances in c_i. Since $\lambda_t(n) \leq n \cdot \varphi_t(n)$, we have $|c_i| \leq |c_i'| \cdot \varphi_t(n)$. Construct another sequence U' by concatenating all the 1-chains c_i' and by erasing each first symbol of c_i' that is equal to the element immediately preceding it. It is clear that U' is a $DS(n, s)$-sequence composed of at most m 1-chains and that its length is at least $\sum_{i=1}^{m} |c_i'| - (m - 1)$. Therefore

$$\Psi_s(m, n) \geq \frac{1}{\varphi_t(n)} \cdot \sum_{i=1}^{m} |c_i| - (m - 1).$$

However, $\Psi_s^t(m, n) = \sum_{i=1}^{m} |c_i|$. Thus

$$\Psi_s^t(m, n) \leq \varphi_t(n) \cdot (\Psi_s(m, n) + m - 1). \qquad \square$$

Before obtaining the main result of this section, we prove a weaker but simpler upper bound on $\lambda_s(n)$.

Proposition 3.21 *For $s \geq 2$,*

$$\lambda_s(n) = O(n \log^{\gamma(s)} n),$$

where $\gamma(s) = \lfloor s/2 \rfloor (\lceil s/2 \rceil - 1)$.

Proof. We first prove, by a double induction on m and s, that for $s \geq 2$

$$\Psi_s(m, n) \leq C_s \cdot (m + n) \log^{s-2} m, \tag{3.14}$$

where $C_2 = 2$, and $C_s = 4(C_{s-1} + 1)$, for $s > 2$. Notice that (3.14) is obvious for $s = 2, m \geq 1$ and for $m = 1, s > 2$, because $\Psi_2(m, n) \leq \lambda_2(n) = 2n - 1$ and $\Psi_s(1, n) \leq n$. Assume that (3.14) is true for all $s' < s$, $m' \geq 1$, and for $s' = s$, $m' < m$, and consider the case of $s > 2$, $m > 1$. Substituting $b = 2$ and $m_1 = \lfloor m/2 \rfloor$ in (3.13), we obtain

$$
\begin{aligned}
\Psi_s(m, n) \;\leq\;& 2\Psi_{s-1}(m, n^*) + \Psi_{s-2}(\lfloor m/2 \rfloor, n^*) + \Psi_{s-2}(\lceil m/2 \rceil, n^*) \\
& + \Psi_s(\lfloor m/2 \rfloor, n_1) + \Psi_s(\lceil m/2 \rceil, n_2) + 4m \\
\leq\;& 4\Psi_{s-1}(m, n) + \Psi_s(\lfloor m/2 \rfloor, n_1) + \Psi_s(\lceil m/2 \rceil, n_2) + 4m \\
\leq\;& 4C_{s-1} \cdot (m + n) \log^{s-3} m + C_s \cdot (m + n) \log^{s-2} \left\lceil \frac{m}{2} \right\rceil + 4m \\
\leq\;& C_s \cdot (m + n) \log^{s-2} m,
\end{aligned}
$$

where the last inequality follows from the choice of the constants C_s. This completes the inductive proof of (3.14).

Next, by Lemmas 3.2 and 3.20,

$$
\begin{aligned}
\lambda_s(n) &\leq \Psi_s^{s-2}(2n-1, n) \\
&\leq \frac{\lambda_{s-2}(n)}{n} \cdot (\Psi_s(2n-1, n) + 2n - 2) \\
&\leq \frac{\lambda_{s-2}(n)}{n} \cdot (C_s(2n-1+n) \log^{s-2}(2n-1) + 2n - 2) \\
&\leq C_s' \log^{s-2} n \cdot \lambda_{s-2}(n),
\end{aligned}
$$

where C_s' is another constant depending only on s. By expanding the above recurrence and by using the fact that $\lambda_3(n) = O(n \log n)$, it can easily be verified that

$$
\lambda_s(n) = O(n \log^{\gamma(s)} n). \qquad \square
$$

We now prove the stronger upper bound on $\lambda_s(n)$, stated in (3.11), by induction on s. The base cases $s = 3$ and $s = 4$ have already been discussed above. Let $s > 4$, and suppose that the upper bound holds for each $t < s$, i.e., that $\lambda_t(n) \leq n \cdot \Pi_t(n)$. By Lemmas 3.2 and 3.20, we can deduce that, for $s \geq 4$,

$$
\lambda_s(n) \leq \Psi_s(2n-1, n) \cdot \Pi_{s-2}(n) + (2n-2) \cdot \Pi_{s-2}(n). \tag{3.15}
$$

Lemma 3.22 *Let $m, n \geq 1$, and $k \geq 2$. Then*

$$
\Psi_s(m, n) \leq \mathcal{F}_k(n) \cdot m\alpha_k(m) + \mathcal{G}_k(n) \cdot n, \tag{3.16}
$$

where $\mathcal{F}_k(n)$ and $\mathcal{G}_k(n)$ are defined recursively as follows:

$$
\begin{aligned}
\mathcal{F}_2(n) &= 4, \\
\mathcal{F}_k(n) &= 2\Pi_{s-2}(n) \cdot \mathcal{F}_{k-1}(n) + (\Pi_{s-2}(n) + 4), \tag{3.17} \\
\mathcal{G}_2(n) &= 5\Pi_{s-1}(n), \\
\mathcal{G}_k(n) &= \Pi_{s-2}(n) \cdot \mathcal{G}_{k-1}(n) + 2\Pi_{s-1}(n). \tag{3.18}
\end{aligned}
$$

Proof. $\Psi_s(m, n) \leq \lambda_s(n)$, therefore $\Psi_{s-1}(m, n^\star) \leq n^\star \cdot \Pi_{s-1}(n^\star)$. If we replace $\Psi_{s-1}(m, n^\star)$ by this bound in (3.12) and also replace $\Psi_s^{s-2}(b, n^\star)$ by the right-hand side of the bound of Lemma 3.20, we get:

$$
\begin{aligned}
\Psi_s(m, n) &\leq \Pi_{s-2}(n^\star) \cdot \Psi_s(b, n^\star) + (b-1) \cdot \Pi_{s-2}(n^\star) + 4m + \\
&\quad 2n^\star \cdot \Pi_{s-1}(n^\star) + \sum_{i=1}^{b} \Psi_s(m_i, n_i).
\end{aligned} \tag{3.19}
$$

We use (3.19) repeatedly to obtain the desired bound for $k = 2, 3, \ldots$. At each step we choose b appropriately and estimate $\Psi_s(b, n^\star)$ using a technique similar to that in Lemma 3.10.

We proceed by double induction on k and m. Initially $k = 2$, and $\alpha_k(m) = \lceil \log m \rceil$, for $m \geq 1$. Choose $b = 2$, $m_1 = \lfloor m/2 \rfloor$ and $m_2 = \lceil m/2 \rceil$ in (3.19); $\Psi_s(b, n^\star) = \Psi_s(2, n^\star) = 2n^\star$ for all $n^\star$, so (3.19) becomes

$$
\begin{aligned}
\Psi_s(m, n) \;\leq\; & \Psi_s\left(\left\lfloor \frac{m}{2} \right\rfloor, n_1\right) + \Psi_s\left(\left\lceil \frac{m}{2} \right\rceil, n_2\right) + \Pi_{s-2}(n^\star) + 4m + \\
& 2n^\star \cdot (\Pi_{s-1}(n^\star) + \Pi_{s-2}(n^\star)) \\
\leq\; & \Psi_s\left(\left\lfloor \frac{m}{2} \right\rfloor, n_1\right) + \Psi_s\left(\left\lceil \frac{m}{2} \right\rceil, n_2\right) + 4m + \\
& n^\star \cdot \left(2\Pi_{s-1}(n^\star) + 3\Pi_{s-2}(n^\star)\right),
\end{aligned}
$$

where $n = n_1 + n_2 + n^\star$. The solution of this recurrence is easily seen to be

$$
\Psi_s(m, n) \leq 4m \cdot \lceil \log m \rceil + n(2\Pi_{s-1}(n) + 3\Pi_{s-2}(n)).
$$

Since $\Pi_{s-1}(n) \geq \Pi_{s-2}(n)$, we have for $k = 2$

$$
\begin{aligned}
\Psi_s(m, n) \;\leq\; & 4m \cdot \lceil \log m \rceil + 5n \cdot \Pi_{s-1}(n) \\
=\; & m \cdot \mathcal{F}_2(n) \cdot \alpha_2(m) + n \cdot \mathcal{G}_2(n),
\end{aligned}
$$

as asserted.

For $k > 2$ and $m \leq 16$ the inequality (3.16) obviously holds, as $\Psi_s(m, n) \leq 16n$ and the right-hand side of (3.16) is $\geq 16n$. Now suppose that $k > 2$ and $m > 16$ and that the induction hypothesis holds for all $k' < k$ and $m' \geq 1$ and for $k' = k$ and for all $m' < m$. Choose $t = \lceil \frac{1}{2}\alpha_{k-1}(m) \rceil$, and $b = \lfloor m/t \rfloor$. For $k > 2$, $\alpha_{k-1}(m) \leq \lceil \log m \rceil$; thus

$$
t \leq \left\lceil \frac{\lceil \log m \rceil}{2} \right\rceil < m - 1.
$$

Suppose $m = b \cdot t + r$, then any $DS(n, s)$-sequence U composed of m 1-chains can be decomposed into b layers, $L_1, \ldots, L_b$ containing respectively $m_1, \ldots, m_b$ 1-chains, so that $m_i = t + 1$ for $i \leq r$ and $m_i = t$ for the remaining layers; therefore $m_i \leq t + 1 < m$ for all i. By the induction hypothesis (for $k - 1$ and b) we have

$$
\Psi_s(b, n^\star) \leq \mathcal{F}_{k-1}(n^\star) \cdot b\alpha_{k-1}(b) + \mathcal{G}_{k-1}(n^\star) \cdot n^\star.
$$

However,

$$
b \leq \frac{m}{t} = \frac{m}{\left\lceil \dfrac{\alpha_{k-1}(m)}{2} \right\rceil} \leq \frac{2m}{\alpha_{k-1}(m)}.
$$

Clearly, $b \leq m$, therefore $\alpha_{k-1}(b) \leq \alpha_{k-1}(m)$ and we have

$$
\Psi_s(b, n^\star) \leq \mathcal{F}_{k-1}(n^\star) \cdot 2m + \mathcal{G}_{k-1}(n^\star) \cdot n^\star.
$$

Since each $m_i < m$, we have, by the induction hypothesis,

$$\sum_{i=1}^{b} \Psi_s(m_i, n_i) \leq \sum_{i=1}^{b} (\mathcal{F}_k(n_i) \cdot m_i \alpha_k(m_i) + \mathcal{G}_k(n_i) \cdot n_i).$$

The value of $\alpha_k(m_i)$ can be estimated as follows:

$$\alpha_k(m_i) \leq \alpha_k(t+1) = \alpha_k\left(\left\lceil \frac{\alpha_{k-1}(m)}{2} \right\rceil + 1\right).$$

Now for $m \geq 16$, $\alpha_{k-1}(m) \geq 3$ so that

$$\left\lceil \frac{\alpha_{k-1}(m)}{2} \right\rceil + 1 \leq \alpha_{k-1}(m).$$

Thus

$$\alpha_k(m_i) \leq \alpha_k(\alpha_{k-1}(m)) = \alpha_k(m) - 1,$$

which implies

$$\sum_{i=1}^{b} \Psi_s(m_i, n_i) \leq \sum_{i=1}^{b}\left[\mathcal{F}_k(n_i) \cdot m_i(\alpha_k(m) - 1) + \mathcal{G}_k(n_i) \cdot n_i\right]$$

$$\leq m \cdot \mathcal{F}_k(n) \cdot (\alpha_k(m) - 1) + \mathcal{G}_k(n) \cdot \sum_{i=1}^{b} n_i.$$

If we substitute these values of $\Psi_s(b, n^\star)$ and $\sum_i^b \Psi_s(m_i, n_i)$ in (3.19) and use the fact that $b \leq m$, we obtain

$$\begin{aligned}
\Psi_s(m, n) \leq{}& \Pi_{s-2}(n) \cdot \left[\mathcal{F}_{k-1}(n) \cdot 2m + \mathcal{G}_{k-1}(n) \cdot n^\star\right] + \\
& (\Pi_{s-2}(n) + 4) \cdot m + 2n^\star \cdot \Pi_{s-1}(n) + \\
& \mathcal{F}_k(n) \cdot m(\alpha_k(m) - 1) + \mathcal{G}_k(n) \cdot \sum_{i=1}^{b} n_i \\
\leq{}& \left[2\Pi_{s-2}(n) \cdot \mathcal{F}_{k-1}(n) + (\Pi_{s-2}(n) + 4)\right] \cdot m + \\
& \left[\Pi_{s-2}(n) \cdot \mathcal{G}_{k-1}(n) + 2\Pi_{s-1}(n)\right] \cdot n^\star + \\
& \mathcal{F}_k(n) \cdot m(\alpha_k(m) - 1) + \mathcal{G}_k(n) \cdot \sum_{i=1}^{b} n_i,
\end{aligned}$$

which, by definition of $\mathcal{F}_k(n)$ and $\mathcal{G}_k(n)$, gives

$$\begin{aligned}
\Psi_s(m, n) &\leq \mathcal{F}_k(n) \cdot m\alpha_k(m) + \mathcal{G}_k(n) \cdot \left(n^\star + \sum_{i=1}^{b} n_i\right) \\
&= \mathcal{F}_k(n) \cdot m\alpha_k(m) + \mathcal{G}_k(n) \cdot n.
\end{aligned}$$

This completes the proof of the lemma. $\qquad\square$

Lemma 3.23 *For $k \geq 2$, $\mathcal{F}_k(n)$ and $\mathcal{G}_k(n)$ satisfy the following inequalities:*

$$\mathcal{F}_k(n) \leq 5 \cdot (2\Pi_{s-2}(n))^{k-2}, \tag{3.20}$$

$$\mathcal{G}_k(n) \leq 6\Pi_{s-1}(n) \cdot (\Pi_{s-2}(n))^{k-2}. \tag{3.21}$$

Proof. It is an easy exercise to verify that a recurrence relation of the form

$$T(2) = c$$
$$T(k) \leq aT(k-1) + b$$

has the following solution

$$T(k) \leq c \cdot a^{k-2} + \frac{a^{k-2} - 1}{a-1} \cdot b.$$

The recursive definition of $\mathcal{F}_k(n)$ given in (3.17) has the same form with $a = 2\Pi_{s-2}(n)$, $b = \Pi_{s-2}(n) + 4$, and $c = 4$. Therefore

$$\mathcal{F}_k(n) \leq 4 \cdot (2\Pi_{s-2}(n))^{k-2} + \frac{[(2\Pi_{s-2}(n))^{k-2} - 1]}{[2\Pi_{s-2}(n) - 1]} \cdot (\Pi_{s-2}(n) + 4).$$

However, for $x > 5$,

$$\frac{x+4}{2x-1} < 1.$$

Since $\Pi_{s-2}(n) > 5$, we get

$$\mathcal{F}_k(n) \leq 5 \cdot (2\Pi_{s-2}(n))^{k-2}.$$

Similarly, the recursive definition of $\mathcal{G}_k(n)$ given in (3.18) also has the above form with $a = \Pi_{s-2}(n)$, $b = 2\Pi_{s-1}(n)$, and $c = 5\Pi_{s-1}(n)$. Hence,

$$\mathcal{G}_k(n) \leq 5\Pi_{s-1}(n) \cdot (\Pi_{s-2}(n))^{k-2} + \frac{[(\Pi_{s-2}(n))^{k-2} - 1]}{[\Pi_{s-2}(n) - 1]} \cdot 2\Pi_{s-1}(n).$$

Since $\Pi_{s-2}(n) > 4$,

$$\frac{2}{[\Pi_{s-2}(n) - 1]} < 1,$$

and we obtain

$$\mathcal{G}_k(n) \leq 6\Pi_{s-1}(n) \cdot (\Pi_{s-2}(n))^{k-2}. \qquad \square$$

Theorem 3.24 *For $s \geq 2$, $n \geq 1$,*

$$\lambda_s(n) \leq n \cdot \Pi_s(n).$$

Proof. If we substitute $k = \alpha(n)$ in (3.16) we get

$$\Psi_s(m,n) \leq \mathcal{F}_{\alpha(n)}(n) \cdot m\alpha_{\alpha(n)}(m) + \mathcal{G}_{\alpha(n)}(n) \cdot n.$$

Substituting the above value of $\Psi_s(m,n)$ into (3.15), we obtain:

$$\lambda_s(n) \leq \Pi_{s-2}(n) \cdot \mathcal{F}_{\alpha(n)}(n) \cdot (2n-1)\alpha_{\alpha(n)}(2n-1) +$$
$$\Pi_{s-2}(n) \cdot \mathcal{G}_{\alpha(n)}(n) \cdot n + (2n-2) \cdot \Pi_{s-2}(n).$$

For $k \geq 2$, $\alpha_k(2n) \leq \alpha_k(n) + 1$ and $\alpha_{\alpha(n)}(n) \leq \alpha(n)$, so we have

$$\lambda_s(n) \leq n \cdot \Pi_{s-2}(n) \cdot \left[2\mathcal{F}_{\alpha(n)}(n) \cdot (\alpha(n)+1) + \mathcal{G}_{\alpha(n)}(n) + 2\right]$$
$$\leq n \cdot \Pi_{s-2}(n) \cdot \left[4\mathcal{F}_{\alpha(n)}(n) \cdot \alpha(n) + \mathcal{G}_{\alpha(n)}(n)\right].$$

After substituting the values of $\mathcal{F}_{\alpha(n)}$ and $\mathcal{G}_{\alpha(n)}$ from (3.20) and (3.21), the above inequality becomes

$$\lambda_s(n) \leq n \cdot \Pi_{s-2}(n) \cdot \left[4 \cdot 5(2\Pi_{s-2}(n))^{\alpha(n)-2} \cdot \alpha(n) + \right.$$
$$\left. 6(\Pi_{s-2}(n))^{\alpha(n)-2} \cdot \Pi_{s-1}(n)\right]$$
$$\leq n \cdot (\Pi_{s-2}(n))^{\alpha(n)-1} \cdot \left[5\alpha(n) \cdot 2^{\alpha(n)} + 6\Pi_{s-1}(n)\right].$$

Since for all $s > 4$,

$$\Pi_{s-1}(n) \geq \Pi_4(n) = 2^{\alpha(n)+12},$$

we get

$$\lambda_s(n) \leq n \cdot (\Pi_{s-2}(n))^{\alpha(n)} \cdot \frac{\Pi_{s-1}(n)}{\Pi_{s-2}(n)} \cdot \left[\frac{5\alpha(n)}{2^{12}} + 6\right].$$

However, for $n > 16$,

$$\Pi_{s-2}(n) \geq \Pi_3(n) = 2^8 \alpha(n),$$

thus

$$\lambda_s(n) \leq n \cdot (\Pi_{s-2}(n))^{\alpha(n)} \cdot \Pi_{s-1}(n) = n \cdot 2^{\vartheta}.$$

Substituting the values of Π_{s-1} and Π_{s-2} from (3.10), we obtain

$$\vartheta = \Gamma_{s-2}(n) \cdot \alpha(n) + \sum_{i=2}^{s-3} a_i^{s-2} \cdot \Gamma_i(n) \cdot \alpha(n) +$$
$$\Gamma_{s-1}(n) + \sum_{i=2}^{s-2} a_i^{s-1} \cdot \Gamma_i(n).$$

However, by definition, $\Gamma_i(n) \cdot \alpha(n) = \Gamma_{i+2}(n)$, so that

$$
\begin{aligned}
\vartheta &= \Gamma_s(n) + \sum_{i=2}^{s-3} a_i^{s-2} \cdot \Gamma_{i+2}(n) + \Gamma_{s-1}(n) + \sum_{i=2}^{s-2} a_i^{s-1} \cdot \Gamma_i(n) \\
&= \Gamma_s(n) + (1 + a_{s-3}^{s-2}) \cdot \Gamma_{s-1}(n) + \sum_{i=4}^{s-2}(a_{i-2}^{s-2} + a_i^{s-1}) \cdot \Gamma_i(n) + \\
&\qquad a_3^{s-1} \cdot \Gamma_3(n) + a_2^{s-1} \cdot \Gamma_2(n) \\
&= \Gamma_s(n) + \sum_{i=2}^{s-1} a_i^s \cdot \Gamma_i(n) \\
&= \Gamma_s(n) + C_s(n).
\end{aligned}
$$

Thus, we get the desired upper bound for $\lambda_s(n)$.   □

Corollary 3.25 *For $s \geq 2$ and for sufficiently large n*

$$\lambda_s(n) = n \cdot 2^{\Gamma_s(n) \cdot (1+o(1))}.$$

Proof. We have already shown that the above equality holds for $s \leq 4$. Assume that $s > 4$. By definition of Γ_s, for all $i < s$

$$\lim_{n \to \infty} \frac{\Gamma_i(n)}{\Gamma_s(n)} = 0.$$

Thus

$$\lim_{n \to \infty} \frac{C_s(n)}{\Gamma_s(n)} = 0,$$

so that

$$
\begin{aligned}
\lambda_s(n) &\leq n \cdot 2^{\Gamma_s(n) \cdot \left(1 + \frac{C_s(n)}{\Gamma_s(n)}\right)} \\
&= n \cdot 2^{\Gamma_s(n)(1+o(1))}.
\end{aligned}
$$
□

Remark 3.26 Note that in (3.19) we approximate $\Psi_{s-1}(m,n)$ by $\lambda_{s-1}(n)$ instead of substituting the bound achieved from (3.19) inductively, as we did in the case of $s = 4$. If we were to estimate $\Psi_{s-1}(m,n)$ using (3.19) instead of approximating it by $\lambda_{s-1}(n)$, we could have obtained a slightly improved upper bound for $\lambda_s(n)$ involving a smaller polynomial $C_s(n)$. However, this would not have affected the leading term and also, as we will see in the next section, even then the bounds we obtain still do not fully match our lower bounds. In addition, the proof would have become much more complicated.

3.5   Lower bounds for $\lambda_s(n)$

In this section we establish the lower bounds for $\lambda_s(n)$ mentioned in the introduction. We show that for $n \geq A(4)$ and even $s \geq 6$,

$$\lambda_s(n) \geq n \cdot 2^{K_s \alpha(n)^{\frac{s-2}{2}} + Q_s(n)},$$

where $K_s = 1/\left(\frac{s-2}{2}\right)!$ and Q_s is a polynomial in $\alpha(n)$ of degree at most $(s - 4)/2$, defined later in this section. These bounds almost match the upper bounds given in the previous section for even values of s.

The proof of these bounds is quite similar to, though more complex than, the proof of the lower bound for $s = 4$. Before we give the proof, we will need to define several new functions which behave similarly to the Ackermann function, and prove certain properties about them. We will then define a collection of Davenport–Schinzel sequences of order s that realize our lower bounds.

3.5.1 Auxiliary functions

The derivation of the lower bounds makes use of two classes of functions that grow faster than Ackermann's functions, though still at the same asymptotic rate. These functions, $F_k^s(m)$ and $N_k^s(m)$, are defined for integral $k \geq 1$, integral $m \geq 1$, and even $s \geq 2$. $N_k^s(m)$ gives the number of symbols composing the sequence $S_s(k, m)$, and $F_k^s(m)$ gives the number of fans in $S_s(k, m)$ (see below for more details). These functions are defined inductively by the following equations.

$$
\begin{aligned}
F_1^s(m) &= 1 & m \geq 1, s \geq 2, \\
F_k^2(m) &= 1 & m \geq 1, k \geq 1, \\
F_k^s(1) &= (2^k - 1) \cdot F_{k-1}^{s-2}(2^{k-1}) \cdot F_{k-1}^s(N_{k-1}^{s-2}(2^{k-1})) & k \geq 2, s \geq 4, \\
F_k^s(m) &= 2F_k^s(m-1) \cdot F_{k-1}^{s-2}(F_k^s(m-1)) \cdot F_{k-1}^s(N_{k-1}^{s-2}(F_k^s(m-1))) \\
& & m \geq 2, k \geq 2, s \geq 4.
\end{aligned}
$$

$$
\begin{aligned}
N_1^s(m) &= m & m \geq 1, s \geq 2, \\
N_k^2(m) &= m & m \geq 1, k \geq 1, \\
N_k^s(1) &= N_{k-1}^s(N_{k-1}^{s-2}(2^{k-1})) & k \geq 2, s \geq 4, \\
N_k^s(m) &= N_{k-1}^s(N_{k-1}^{s-2}(F_k^s(m-1)))+ \\
& \quad 2N_k^s(m-1) \cdot F_{k-1}^{s-2}(F_k^s(m-1)) \cdot F_{k-1}^s(N_{k-1}^{s-2}(F_k^s(m-1))) \\
& & m \geq 2, k \geq 2, s \geq 4.
\end{aligned}
$$

For $s = 4$, these formulas define the functions $F_k(m)$ and $N_k(m)$ that were used in the lower bounds for $\lambda_4(n)$.

We next state several lemmas about the functions $F_k^s(m)$ and $N_k^s(m)$. Their proofs are given in Appendix 3.3. Notice that it is clear from the definitions that these functions are always positive integers.

Lemma 3.27 For $m \geq 2$, $F_k^s(m) \geq F_k^s(m - 1)$.

Lemma 3.28 For $m \geq 2$, $N_k^s(m) \geq N_k^s(m - 1)$.

These lemmas are trivially true when $k = 1$ or $s = 2$. For $k > 1$ we see that $F_k^s(m) \geq 2F_k^s(m - 1)$ and $N_k^s(m) \geq 2N_k^s(m - 1)$.

We will again make use of the product D_k that was used in the lower bound proof for $s = 4$. We recall its definition:

$$D_k = \prod_{j=1}^{k} \frac{2^{j-1}}{2^j - 1}.$$

We need the following properties of D_k:

Lemma 3.29 For $k \geq 2$, $D_k \leq 2^{-(k-2)}$.

Proof. See Appendix 3.3.   □

Another function that we will use is $P(k, s)$, defined for positive integers k and even positive integers s, as follows:

$$P(k, s) = \sum_{i=1}^{(s/2)-1} \binom{k - 2}{i},$$

where we define the binomial coefficient $\binom{a}{b}$ to be 0 if $a < b$.

Lemma 3.30 For $k \geq 2$,

$$P(k, s) = \sum_{i=1}^{k-1} P(i, s - 2) + k - 2.$$

Proof. See Appendix 3.3.   □

Lemma 3.31
$$\frac{N_k^s(m)}{F_k^s(m)} \leq m \cdot 2^{-P(k,s)}. \tag{3.22}$$

Proof. We will actually show that

$$\frac{N_k^s(m)}{F_k^s(m)} \leq m \cdot D_k \cdot 2^{-\sum_{i=1}^{k-1} P(i,s-2)}. \tag{3.23}$$

Lemmas 3.29 and 3.30 show that (3.23) implies (3.22). The proof of (3.23) will be by induction. During the induction, we use both inequalities (3.22), (3.23) for *smaller* values of s, k, and m.

We prove that (3.23) holds for m, k, and s, assuming that it holds for m', k', and s', whenever $s' < s$, or $k' < k$ and $s' = s$, or $m' < m$, $k' = k$ and $s' = s$.

Case 1: $s = 4$. In this case $P(i, s - 2) = 0$ for $i \geq 1$, so we have to show

$$\frac{N_k^4(m)}{F_k^4(m)} \leq m \cdot D_k,$$

which is what we have shown in Theorem 3.14.

Case 2: $k = 1$. In this case

$$\frac{N_1^s(m)}{F_1^s(m)} = m = m \cdot 1 = m \cdot D_1 = m \cdot 2^{-P(1,s)}.$$

Case 3: $m = 1$, $k > 1$. We have

$$
\begin{aligned}
\frac{N_k^s(1)}{F_k^s(1)} &= \frac{N_{k-1}^s(N_{k-1}^{s-2}(2^{k-1}))}{(2^k - 1) \cdot F_{k-1}^{s-2}(2^{k-1}) \cdot F_{k-1}^s(N_{k-1}^{s-2}(2^{k-1}))} \\
&\leq \frac{N_{k-1}^{s-2}(2^{k-1})}{(2^k - 1) \cdot F_{k-1}^{s-2}(2^{k-1})} \cdot D_{k-1} \cdot 2^{-\sum_{i=1}^{k-2} P(i,s-2)} \\
&\qquad \text{(using (3.23))} \\
&\leq \frac{2^{k-1}}{2^k - 1} \cdot D_{k-1} \cdot 2^{-P(k-1,s-2)} \cdot 2^{-\sum_{i=1}^{k-2} P(i,s-2)} \\
&\qquad \text{(using (3.22))} \\
&= D_k \cdot 2^{-\sum_{i=1}^{k-1} P(i,s-2)}.
\end{aligned}
$$

Case 4: $m > 1$, $k > 1$. We have

$$
\begin{aligned}
\frac{N_k^s(m)}{F_k^s(m)} &= \frac{N_{k-1}^s(N_{k-1}^{s-2}(F_k^s(m-1)))}{2F_k^s(m-1) \cdot F_{k-1}^{s-2}(F_k^s(m-1)) \cdot F_{k-1}^s(N_{k-1}^{s-2}(F_k^s(m-1)))} + \\
&\qquad \frac{N_k^s(m-1)}{F_k^s(m-1)} \\
&\leq \frac{N_{k-1}^{s-2}(F_k^s(m-1))}{2F_k^s(m-1) \cdot F_{k-1}^{s-2}(F_k^s(m-1))} \cdot D_{k-1} \cdot 2^{-\sum_{i=1}^{k-2} P(i,s-2)} + \\
&\qquad (m-1) \cdot D_k \cdot 2^{-\sum_{i=1}^{k-1} P(i,s-2)} \\
&\qquad \text{(using (3.23))} \\
&\leq \frac{D_{k-1}}{2} \cdot 2^{-P(k-1,s-2)} \cdot 2^{-\sum_{i=1}^{k-2} P(i,s-2)} + \\
&\qquad (m-1) \cdot D_k \cdot 2^{-\sum_{i=1}^{k-1} P(i,s-2)} \\
&\qquad \text{(using (3.22))} \\
&\leq m \cdot D_k \cdot 2^{-\sum_{i=1}^{k-1} P(i,s-2)},
\end{aligned}
$$

since $D_{k-1}/2 < D_k$.   □

For the lower bound proof, we must also relate the functions F_k^s to the Ackermann's function. We do this by using a new collection of 'limit functions,' $F_k^\omega(m)$, satisfying $F_k^\omega(m) \geq F_k^s(m)$ for all s. We define the limit function $F_k^\omega(m)$ by

$$
\begin{aligned}
F_1^\omega(m) &= 1, & m \geq 1, \\
F_k^\omega(1) &= (2^k - 1) \cdot F_{k-1}^\omega(2^{k-1}) \cdot F_{k-1}^\omega(2^{k-1} \cdot F_{k-1}^\omega(2^{k-1})), & k \geq 2, \\
F_k^\omega(m) &= 2 \cdot F_k^\omega(m - 1) \cdot F_{k-1}^\omega(F_k^\omega(m - 1)) \cdot \\
& \quad F_{k-1}^\omega(F_k^\omega(m - 1) \cdot F_{k-1}^\omega(F_k^\omega(m - 1))), & m \geq 2, k \geq 2.
\end{aligned}
$$

Lemma 3.32 *For all* s, $F_k^\omega(m) \geq F_k^s(m)$.

Proof. See Appendix 3.3. $\qquad\qquad\square$

We next prove various lemmas about the functions F^ω.

Lemma 3.33 $F_2^\omega(m) = 3 \cdot 2^{m-1}$.

This follows from the definition: substituting $F_1^\omega(m) = 1$ in the recursive definition, we get $F_2^\omega(m) = 2 \cdot F_2^\omega(m - 1)$ and $F_2^\omega(1) = 3$.

Lemma 3.34 *For* $k \geq 2$ *and* $a \geq 0$,

$$2^a \cdot F_k^\omega(m) \leq F_k^\omega(m + a).$$

This follows from $F_k^\omega(m) \geq 2 \cdot F_k^\omega(m - 1)$, which is immediate from the definition of F_k^ω. Since $2^a > a$ for $a \geq 1$, Lemma 3.34 implies:

Lemma 3.35 *For* $k \geq 2$ *and* $a \geq 0$,

$$a \cdot F_k^\omega(m) \leq F_k^\omega(m + a).$$

Finally, we show:

Lemma 3.36 *For* $k \geq 2$, $A_k(m + 1) \geq 2A_k(m)$.

Proof. See Appendix 3.3. $\qquad\qquad\square$

These lemmas imply:

Lemma 3.37 $\qquad F_k^\omega(m) \leq A_k(7m)$.

Proof. See Appendix 3.3. $\qquad\qquad\square$

3.5.2 The sequences $S_s(k, m)$

We now define a collection of Davenport–Schinzel sequences of order s that participate in our lower bound construction. For technical reasons, we first construct an auxiliary collection of sequences, where each sequence is indexed by two integer variables, k and m, and denoted $S_s(k, m)$. The sequences $S_s(k, m)$ are 'almost' Davenport–Schinzel sequences of order s, except that they can contain equal adjacent elements. After trimming these sequences, erasing each element that is equal to its predecessor, we obtain the desired collection of Davenport–Schinzel sequences of order s, and, as will be shown, the trimming does not substantially reduce the length of the sequences.

Similar to the case $s = 4$, the sequence $S_s(k, m)$ will be composed of $N_k^s(m)$ symbols, and will be a concatenation of $F_k^s(m)$ fans of size m, where such a fan is composed of m distinct symbols, $a_1, a_2, \ldots, a_m$, and has the form

$$\langle a_1 a_2 \cdots a_{m-1} a_m a_{m-1} \cdots a_2 a_1 \rangle,$$

so its length is $2m - 1$. In our construction, we will be replacing fans in certain subsequences by sequences of the form $S_{s-2}(k, m)$. When we replace a fan by a sequence, the sequence will contain the same symbols as in the replaced fan, and the first (leftmost) appearances of these symbols in the sequence will be in the same order as in the fan.

We define $S_s(k, m)$, for even $s \geq 2$, and integral $k \geq 1$, $m \geq 1$, in the following inductive manner.

I. $S_s(1, m) = \langle 1\ 2\ \cdots\ m - 1\ m\ m - 1\ \cdots\ 2\ 1 \rangle$, for $s \geq 2$, and $m \geq 1$.

II. $S_2(k, m) = \langle 1\ 2\ \cdots\ m - 1\ m\ m - 1\ \cdots\ 2\ 1 \rangle$, for $k, m \geq 1$.

III. To obtain $S_s(k, 1)$, for $k > 1$, $s > 2$, proceed as follows:

    (a) Construct the sequence

$$S' = S_s(k - 1, N_{k-1}^{s-2}(2^{k-1})).$$

    S' has $F_{k-1}^s(N_{k-1}^{s-2}(2^{k-1}))$ fans, each of size $N_{k-1}^{s-2}(2^{k-1})$.

    (b) Replace each fan of S' by the sequence $S_{s-2}(k - 1, 2^{k-1})$, using the same set of $N_{k-1}^{s-2}(2^{k-1})$ symbols as in the replaced fan, with the first appearances of symbols occurring in the same order.

    (c) Regard each element of the resulting sequence as its own singleton fan.

IV. To obtain $S_s(k, m)$, for $k > 1$, $s > 2$, $m > 1$, proceed as follows:

(a) First construct the sequence $S_s(k, m-1)$. It has $F_k^s(m-1)$ fans, each of size $m-1$.

(b) Create $2 \cdot F_{k-1}^{s-2}(F_k^s(m-1)) \cdot F_{k-1}^s(N_{k-1}^{s-2}(F_k^s(m-1)))$ distinct copies of $S_s(k, m-1)$, having pairwise disjoint sets of symbols. Duplicate the middle element of each fan in these copies of $S_s(k, m-1)$, and concatenate all these copies into one long sequence. Call this sequence S'. These copies have

$$2 \cdot F_k^s(m-1) \cdot F_{k-1}^{s-2}(F_k^s(m-1)) \cdot F_{k-1}^s(N_{k-1}^{s-2}(F_k^s(m-1))) = F_k^s(m)$$

fans altogether.

(c) Now construct the sequence $S_s(k-1, N_{k-1}^{s-2}(F_k^s(m-1)))$. It has $F_{k-1}^s(N_{k-1}^{s-2}(F_k^s(m-1)))$ fans, each of size $N_{k-1}^{s-2}(F_k^s(m-1))$.

(d) Replace each fan of this sequence by the sequence $S_{s-2}(k-1, F_k^s(m-1))$, using the same set of $N_{k-1}^{s-2}(F_k^s(m-1))$ symbols as in the replaced fan, which make their first appearances in the same order as in the fan. Duplicate the middle element of each fan of this sequence; these fans come from the sequences $S_{s-2}(k-1, F_k^s(m-1))$ and thus have size $F_k^s(m-1)$. Call the resulting sequence $S^\star$.

(e) Notice that the sequence $S^\star$ has

$$2 \cdot F_k^s(m-1) \cdot F_{k-1}^{s-2}(F_k^s(m-1)) \cdot F_{k-1}^s(N_{k-1}^{s-2}(F_k^s(m-1))) = F_k^s(m)$$

elements, which is the same as the number of fans in S'.

To obtain $S_s(k, m)$, insert the sequence $S^\star$ into the sequence S', with each element of $S^\star$ going into the middle of a corresponding fan of S'. The fans of $S_s(k, m)$ are the fans of S', with the extra symbol from $S^\star$ added in the middle.

Theorem 3.38 $S_s(k, m)$ *satisfies the following properties:*

(i) $S_s(k, m)$ *is composed of* $N_k^s(m)$ *symbols.*

(ii) $S_s(k, m)$ *is the concatenation of* $F_k^s(m)$ *fans of size* m, *as defined above (each fan is composed of* m *distinct symbols).*

(iii) $S_s(k, m)$ *does not contain any alternating subsequence* $\langle a \cdots b \cdots a \cdots b \cdots \rangle$ *of length* $s + 2$, *for any pair of distinct symbols* a, b.

(iv) *If every fan* f *in* $S_s(k, m)$ *is replaced by some sequence* $S^{(f)}$ *on the same* m *symbols, with their first appearances occurring in the same order as in the fan, such that none of the sequences* $S^{(f)}$ *contain any alternating subsequence* $\langle a \cdots b \cdots a \cdots b \cdots \rangle$ *of length* s, *then the resulting sequence still satisfies property* (iii).

Proof. By induction on s, k, and m. Assume that these properties hold for $S_{s'}(k', m')$, for $s' < s$, for $s' = s$ and $k' < k$, and for $s' = s$, $k' = k$, and $m' < m$. Properties (i) and (ii) for $S_s(k, m)$ follow from the construction, the induction hypothesis, and the definition of the functions $N_k^s(m)$ and $F_k^s(m)$. The only subtle issue here is to show that each fan of $S_s(k, m)$ consists of m distinct symbols. This is trivial when $S_s(k, m)$ is generated by one of the rules I–III (in the case of rule III, each fan is of size 1), and is also easy to verify by induction when $S_s(k, m)$ is generated by rule IV. Properties (iii) and (iv) obviously hold when

$$S_s(k, m) = \langle 1\ 2\ \cdots\ m - 1\ m\ m - 1\ \cdots\ 2\ 1 \rangle,$$

which is the case when $S_s(k, m)$ is generated by rule I or rule II in our construction. We must then prove that (iii) and (iv) hold when $S_s(k, m)$ is generated by rule III or by rule IV.

Consider first the case where $S_s(k, 1)$ is obtained by rule III. We must first show that $S_s(k, 1)$ does not contain an alternating subsequence of length $s + 2$. This is true because, by the induction hypothesis, property (iv) holds for the sequence $S' = S_s(k - 1, N_{k-1}^{s-2}(2^{k-1}))$, and the sequence $S_s(k, 1)$ is obtained by replacing every fan of S' by an S_{s-2} sequence, which, by the induction hypothesis, does not contain an alternating subsequence of length s. Property (iv) for $S_s(k, 1)$ follows trivially from property (iii), since all fans have size 1.

Consider next the case where $S_s(k, m)$ is obtained by rule IV. We first show that $S_s(k, m)$ does not contain an alternating subsequence of the form

$$\underbrace{\langle a\ \cdots\ b\ \cdots\ a\ \cdots\ b\ \cdots \rangle}_{s+2}$$

of length $s+2$, for $a \neq b$. If a and b are both from $S^\star$ then there is no such alternating subsequence, because, by induction hypothesis, $S_s(k - 1, N_{k-1}^{s-2}(F_k^s(m - 1)))$ satisfies property (iv). If a and b are both from S', there is no alternating subsequence of length $s + 2$ because S' is the concatenation of sequences on pairwise disjoint sets of symbols, where each sequence satisfies property (iii). This leaves the case where a belongs to S' and b to $S^\star$ (or vice versa – the proof for both cases is the same). We are safe here too because, for each copy of $S_s(k, m - 1)$ contained in S', we have only inserted into that copy either the *ascending* or the *descending* half of a fan of $S^\star$, and all the symbols in half of a fan are distinct. Thus, between two a's from the sequence S', there can only be one occurrence of b, so at worst we get the alternating subsequence

$$\langle b\ \cdots\ a\ \cdots\ b\ \cdots\ a\ \cdots\ b \rangle.$$

Finally, we establish property (iv)—that if every fan in $S_s(k, m)$ is replaced by some sequence on the same m symbols, with their first appearances remaining in the same order, so that none of these sequences contains an alternating

subsequence of length s, then the resulting sequence still contains no alternating subsequence

$$\langle a \cdots b \cdots a \cdots b \cdots \rangle$$

of length $s + 2$. Suppose to the contrary that such a sequence did appear
among the elements of S'. It must have appeared within one copy of $S_s(k, m -
1)$, because different copies contain distinct symbols and do not interleave.
If we delete the symbols of $S^\star$ from this copy of $S_s(k, m - 1)$, we obtain
a copy of $S_s(k, m - 1)$ where each fan has been replaced by some sequence
with no alternating subsequence of length s, whose symbols make their first
appearances in the proper order. Such an expanded copy of $S_s(k, m-1)$ cannot
contain an alternating subsequence of length $s + 2$, as follows from property
(iv) applied to $S_s(k, m - 1)$.

When each fan of $S_s(k, m)$ is replaced by another sequence, as above, a
subsequence

$$\langle a \cdots b \cdots a \cdots b \cdots \rangle$$

of length $s + 2$ cannot appear among the elements of $S^\star$, because each fan of
$S_s(k, m)$ contains only one element of $S^\star$. Thus, replacing each fan by a subsequence containing the same symbols cannot introduce any new alternations
among the elements of $S^\star$.

We must still show that we cannot have a 'bad' subsequence

$$\langle a \cdots b \cdots a \cdots b \cdots \rangle$$

of length $s + 2$, when a belongs to S' and b to $S^\star$ (the argument for the
reverse situation is identical). Recall that for each copy of $S_s(k, m - 1)$ in S',
a different symbol of $S^\star$ is added to each fan. Since the only appearances of a
are in a single copy of $S_s(k, m - 1)$, we can restrict our attention to this copy
and assume (in the worst case) that b's also occur on both sides of it. The
symbol b can appear in only one fan, f, of this copy. After f is replaced by a
sequence $S^{(f)}$, as above, $S^{(f)}$ will contain at worst a subsequence

$$\langle \underbrace{a \cdots b \cdots a \cdots \cdots b \cdots a}_{s-1} \rangle$$

of length $s - 1$ (a appears first because b was the middle element of f). There
may be a's before and after f within the copy of $S_s(k, m - 1)$, and b's before
and after this copy of $S_s(k, m - 1)$. We thus get, at worst, the alternating
subsequence

$$\langle b \cdots a \cdots \underbrace{(a \cdots b \cdots a \cdots \cdots b \cdots a)}_{s-1} \cdots a \cdots b \rangle$$

of length $s + 1$. Property (iv) thus holds for $S_s(k, m)$. $\square$

We now complete the construction. For each s, k, and m, as above, we
construct a new sequence, $\bar{S}_s(k, m)$, by erasing from $S_s(k, m)$ every element
that is equal to the element preceding it.

Lemma 3.39 *For each even* s, $k \geq 1$, *and* $m > 1$, $\bar{S}_s(k, m)$ *is a Davenport–Schinzel sequence of order* s *composed of* $N_k^s(m)$ *symbols, whose length is at least* $(2m - 2)F_k^s(m)$.

Proof. That $\bar{S}_s(k, m)$ is a Davenport–Schinzel sequence of order s composed of $N_k^s(m)$ symbols, follows from the above construction, and from properties (i) and (iii) of Theorem 3.38. By property (ii) of that theorem, only the first element of any fan of $S_s(k, m)$ may have to be erased, so the length of each truncated fan in $\bar{S}_s(k, m)$ is at least $2m - 2$. This completes the proof of the lemma.   □

Remark 3.40 The above proof fails for odd values of s. In particular, the last argument depends crucially on s being even, so that the alternating sequence of length $s - 1$ starts and ends with a.

Theorem 3.41 *When* $n \geq A(4)$,

$$\lambda_s(n) \geq n \cdot 2^{K_s \alpha(n)^{\frac{s-2}{2}} + Q_s(n)},$$

where $K_s = 1/\left(\frac{s-2}{2}\right)!$ *and* $Q_s(n)$ *is a polynomial in* $\alpha(n)$ *of degree at most* $(s - 4)/2$.

Proof. Let $n_k^s = N_k^s(2)$. Then, for $k \geq 3$, we have, by Lemmas 3.32, 3.34, and 3.37,

$$n_k^s = N_k^s(2) \leq 2F_k^s(2) \leq 2F_k^\omega(2) \leq F_k^\omega(3) \leq A_k(21) \leq A(k+1) \quad (3.24)$$

(where the last inequality is easy to verify for $k \geq 3$), so we have $k + 1 \geq \alpha(n_k^s)$. We next observe that

$$N_k^s(2) > N_{k-1}^s(N_{k-1}^{s-2}(2^{k-1})) > N_{k-1}^s(2),$$

for $k > 1$. Thus, for any n, we can find k such that

$$n_k^s \leq n < n_{k+1}^s.$$

Put $t = \lfloor n/n_k^s \rfloor$, so

$$t \cdot n_k^s \leq n < (t+1) \cdot n_k^s < 2t \cdot n_k^s.$$

Now, using Lemmas 3.31 and 3.39,

$$
\begin{aligned}
\lambda_s(n) &\geq t \cdot \lambda_s(n_k^s) \geq t \cdot |\bar{S}_s(k, 2)| \\
&\geq 2t \cdot F_k^s(2) \\
&\geq t \cdot N_k^s(2) \cdot 2^{P(k,s)} \\
&> n \cdot 2^{P(k,s)-1}.
\end{aligned}
$$

The definition of $P(k,s)$ gives

$$P(\alpha(n) - 2, s) - 1 = K_s \cdot \alpha(n)^{\frac{s-2}{2}} + Q_s(n),$$

where Q_s is a polynomial in $\alpha(n)$ of degree at most $(s-4)/2$ and $K_s = 1/(\frac{s-2}{2})!$.

If $n \geq A(4)$, then $n \geq n_3^s$, so the above k is at least 3, and (3.24) yields

$$\alpha(n) \leq \alpha(n_{k+1}^s) \leq k + 2.$$

Since P is an increasing function of k, this gives

$$\begin{aligned}
\lambda_s(n) &\geq n \cdot 2^{P(\alpha(n)-2,s)-1} \\
&= n \cdot 2^{K_s \alpha(n)^{\frac{s-2}{2}} + Q_s(n)}.
\end{aligned}$$

$\square$

3.6   Bibliographic notes

The material in this chapter is taken from Agarwal, Sharir, and Shor (1989). The first nontrivial upper bound on $\lambda_s(n)$ was proved by Davenport and Schinzel (1965) in their original paper, where they showed that $\lambda_s(n) \leq n \cdot 2^{C_s \sqrt{\log n}}$ for some suitable constant C_s depending on s. This bound was later improved by Szemerédi (1974) to $O(n \log^\star n)$ (with the constant of proportionality being doubly exponential in s). In 1987, Sharir generalized the proof of the upper bound on $\lambda_3(n)$ and proved that $\lambda_s(n) = n\alpha(n)^{O(\alpha(n)^{s-3})}$, for $s \geq 4$. Sharir (1988a) also proved that $\lambda_{2s+1}(n) = \Omega(n(\alpha(n))^s)$, by extending the construction described in Section 2.3.

Although Agarwal, Sharir, and Shor (1989) almost succeeded in closing the gap between the upper and lower bounds on $\lambda_s(n)$, the bounds are not asymptotically tight for $s > 4$, particularly for odd values of s. The most intriguing issue is that the best known asymptotic lower bound for $\lambda_{2s+1}(n)$ is the same as that for $\lambda_{2s}(n)$, although one would expect the former to be larger.

Appendix 3.1

In this appendix, we give the proofs of Lemmas 3.6–3.8.

Lemma 3.6 *For all $k \geq 4$ and $s \geq 3$,*

$$2^{A_k(s)} \leq A_{k-1}(\log(A_k(s))).$$

Proof.

$$A_{k-1}(\log(A_k(s))) = A_{k-2}(A_{k-1}(\log(A_k(s)) - 1))$$

$$\begin{aligned}
&= A_{k-2}(A_{k-2}(A_{k-1}(\log(A_k(s)) - 2)))\\
&\geq A_2(A_2(2^{\log(A_k(s))-2}))\\
&= A_2(2^{\frac{1}{4}A_k(s)}).
\end{aligned}$$

For $x \geq 16$, $2^{\frac{x}{4}} \geq x$. For $k \geq 3$ and $s \geq 3$, $A_k(s) \geq 2^{2^2} = 16$. Therefore

$$A_{k-1}(\log(A_k(s))) \geq A_2(A_k(s)) = 2^{A_k(s)}. \qquad \qquad \square$$

Lemma 3.7 *Let $\xi_k(n) = 2^{\alpha_k(n)}$. Then, for $k \geq 3$, $n \geq A_{k+1}(4)$*

$$\min\{\, s' \geq 1 : \xi_k^{(s')}(n) \leq A_{k+1}(4)\,\} \leq 2 \cdot \alpha_{k+1}(n) - 2.$$

Proof. We first prove the lemma for n having the form $n = A_{k+1}(q)$, by induction on q. It is obvious for $n = A_{k+1}(4)$, as the left-hand side is 1. Let us assume that the inequality is true for all $q' \leq q$. Now consider $n = A_{k+1}(q+1)$:

$$\begin{aligned}
&\min\{\, s' \geq 1 : \xi_k^{(s')}(A_{k+1}(q+1)) \leq A_{k+1}(4)\,\}\\
&= \min\{\, s' \geq 1 : \xi_k^{(s')}(A_k(A_{k+1}(q))) \leq A_{k+1}(4)\,\}\\
&= \min\{\, s' \geq 1 : \xi_k^{(s')}(2^{A_{k+1}(q)}) \leq A_{k+1}(4)\,\} + 1\\
&\leq \min\{\, s' \geq 1 : \xi_k^{(s')}(A_k(\log(A_{k+1}(q)))) \leq A_{k+1}(4)\,\} + 1\\
&\quad \text{(using Lemma 3.6)}\\
&= \min\{\, s' \geq 1 : \xi_k^{(s')}(A_{k+1}(q)) \leq A_{k+1}(4)\,\} + 2\\
&\leq 2 \cdot \alpha_{k+1}(A_{k+1}(q)) - 2 + 2\\
&\quad \text{(by the induction hypothesis)}\\
&= 2q - 2 + 2 = 2 \cdot (q+1) - 2\\
&= 2 \cdot \alpha_{k+1}(A_{k+1}(q+1)) - 2.
\end{aligned}$$

For general values of n,

$$A_{k+1}(\alpha_{k+1}(n) - 1) < n \leq A_{k+1}(\alpha_{k+1}(n))$$

and also $\alpha_{k+1}(n) = \alpha_{k+1}(A_{k+1}(\alpha_{k+1}(n)))$. Thus

$$\begin{aligned}
&\min\{\, s' \geq 1 : \xi_k^{(s')}(n) \leq A_{k+1}(4)\,\}\\
&\leq \min\{\, s' \geq 1 : \xi_k^{(s')}(A_{k+1}(\alpha_{k+1}(n))) \leq A_{k+1}(4)\,\}\\
&= 2 \cdot \alpha_{k+1}(A_{k+1}(\alpha_{k+1}(n))) - 2\\
&= 2 \cdot \alpha_{k+1}(n) - 2. \qquad\qquad \square
\end{aligned}$$

Lemma 3.8 *For all $k \geq 1$, $n \geq 2$, $\beta_k(n) \leq 2\alpha_k(n)$.*

Proof. For $k \leq 2$, this follows directly from the definition of $\beta_k(n)$. For $k = 3$,

$$\beta_3(n) = \min\{\, s' \geq 1 : (\alpha_2 \cdot \alpha_2)^{(s')}(n) \leq 64\,\}.$$

We first prove the claim for n of the form $A_3(q)$. For $n = A_3(2) = 4$, and for $n = A_3(3) = 16$, the claim follows as $\beta_3(n)$ is simply 1. Assume that it is true for some $q \geq 3$; then

$$
\begin{aligned}
\beta_3(A_3(q+1)) &= \min\{\, s' \geq 1 : (\log^2)^{(s')}(A_3(q+1)) \leq 64 \,\} \\
&= \min\{\, s' \geq 1 : (\log^2)^{(s')}(A_2(A_3(q))) \leq 64 \,\} \\
&= \min\{\, s' \geq 1 : (\log^2)^{(s')}(A_3(q) \cdot A_3(q)) \leq 64\} + 1 \\
&= \min\{\, s' \geq 1 : (\log^2)^{(s')}(4\log^2 A_3(q)) \leq 64\} + 2.
\end{aligned}
$$

For $q = 3$, $A_3(q) = 16$ and thus $4\log^2 A_3(q) = 64$, which implies

$$
\beta_3(A_3(q+1)) = 3 \leq 2 \cdot \alpha_3(A_3(q+1)).
$$

For $q > 3$, $\log A_3(q) \geq 16$ and for $x \geq 16$, $4x^2 \leq 2^x$; therefore

$$
\begin{aligned}
\beta_3(A_3(q+1)) &\leq \min\{\, s' \geq 1 : (\log^2)^{(s')}(A_3(q)) \leq 64\} + 2 \\
&= \beta_3(A_3(q)) + 2 \\
&\leq 2\alpha_3(A_3(q)) + 2 \\
&= 2\alpha_3(A_3(q+1)).
\end{aligned}
$$

For general values of n,

$$
A_3(\alpha_3(n) - 1) < n \leq A_3(\alpha_3(n))
$$

and $\alpha_3(n) = \alpha_3(A_3(\alpha_3(n)))$. Using the same argument as in the previous lemma, we can show that $\beta_3(n) \leq 2\alpha_3(n)$.

For $k > 3$, $n \leq A_k(4) = A_{k-1}(A_k(3))$, we have $\alpha_{k-1}(n) \leq A_k(3)$, and, by the induction hypothesis, $\beta_{k-1}(n) \leq 2A_k(3)$. Hence

$$
\alpha_{k-1}(n) \cdot \beta_{k-1}(n) \leq 2A_k^2(3).
$$

However, for $k > 3$, $A_k(3) \geq 8$, and for $x \geq 8$, $2x^2 \leq 2^x$; hence

$$
\begin{aligned}
q &\equiv \alpha_{k-1}(n) \cdot \beta_{k-1}(n) \\
&\leq 2^{A_k(3)} \\
&= 2^{A_{k-1}(A_k(2))} \\
&= 2^{A_{k-1}(4)} \\
&\leq A_{k-2}(A_{k-1}(4)) \\
&= A_{k-1}(5),
\end{aligned}
$$

and thus

$$
\alpha_{k-1}(q) \cdot \beta_{k-1}(q) \leq 5 \times 10 < 64.
$$

Thus, for $n \leq A_k(4)$, $\beta_k(n) \leq 2$, which clearly implies the assertion. For $n > A_k(4) = A_{k-1}(A_k(3))$, we have

$$
\begin{aligned}
\beta_k(n) &= \min \{ s' \geq 1 : (\alpha_{k-1} \cdot \beta_{k-1})^{(s')}(n) \leq 64 \} \\
&= \min \{ s' \geq 1 : q \equiv (\alpha_{k-1} \cdot \beta_{k-1})^{(s')}(n) \leq A_k(4) \} + \\
&\quad \min \{ t \geq 1 : (\alpha_{k-1} \cdot \beta_{k-1})^{(t)}(q) \leq 64 \}.
\end{aligned}
$$

By the induction hypothesis,

$$
\alpha_{k-1}(n') \cdot \beta_{k-1}(n') \leq \alpha_{k-1}(n') \cdot 2\alpha_{k-1}(n').
$$

But, as long as $n' > A_k(4)$, we have $\alpha_{k-1}(n') \geq A_k(3) \geq 8$, so that

$$
\begin{aligned}
\alpha_{k-1}(n') \cdot \beta_{k-1}(n') &\leq 2\alpha_{k-1}^2(n') \\
&\leq 2^{\alpha_{k-1}(n')} \\
&= \xi_{k-1}(n').
\end{aligned}
$$

Therefore

$$
\begin{aligned}
\beta_k(n) &\leq \min \{ s' \geq 1 : q' \equiv \xi_{k-1}^{(s')}(n) \leq A_k(4) \} + \\
&\quad \min \{ t \geq 1 : (\alpha_{k-1} \cdot \beta_{k-1})^{(t)}(q') \leq 64 \} \\
&\leq 2 \cdot \alpha_k(n) - 2 + \beta_k(A_k(4)) \\
&\leq 2 \cdot \alpha_k(n) - 2 + 2 \\
&= 2\alpha_k(n). \qquad \square
\end{aligned}
$$

Appendix 3.2

In this appendix, we provide the proofs of properties (F3)–(F5) of the functions $F_k(m)$.

(F3) $\{F_k(m)\}_{k\geq 1}^{\infty}$ is strictly increasing for any fixed $m \geq 1$.

Proof. Indeed, for $k = 2$, $F_2(m) = 3 \cdot 2^{m-1} \geq 1 = F_1(m)$. For $k > 2$ and $m = 1$,

$$
\begin{aligned}
F_k(1) &= (2^k - 1) \cdot F_{k-1}(2^{k-1}) \\
&> F_{k-1}(2^{k-1}) \\
&> F_{k-1}(1).
\end{aligned}
$$

For $k > 2$, $m \geq 1$, assume the assertion is true for all $k' < k$ and for $k' = k$ and $m' < m$. Then we have

$$
\begin{aligned}
F_k(m) &= 2F_k(m - 1) \cdot F_{k-1}(F_k(m - 1)) \\
&\geq 2F_k(m - 1) \cdot F_{k-1}(m) \\
&> F_{k-1}(m). \qquad \square
\end{aligned}
$$

(F4) $F_k(m) \geq A_k(m)$ for $k \geq 2$, $m \geq 1$.

Proof. Indeed, for $k = 2$, the assertion is true by (F1). For $k > 2$, $m = 1$,

$$
\begin{aligned}
F_k(1) &= (2^k - 1) \cdot F_{k-1}(2^{k-1}) \geq 2 \\
&= A_k(1).
\end{aligned}
$$

For $k \geq 2$, $m \geq 1$, assume that the assertion is true for all $k' < k$, and for all $k' = k$ and $m' < m$. We have

$$
\begin{aligned}
F_k(m) &= 2F_k(m - 1) \cdot F_{k-1}(F_k(m - 1)) \\
&\geq F_{k-1}(F_k(m - 1)) \\
&\geq A_{k-1}(A_k(m - 1)) \\
&= A_k(m).
\end{aligned}
$$
□

(F5) $2^{F_k(m)} \leq A_k(m + 4)$ for $k \geq 3$, $m \geq 1$.

Proof. For $k = 3$ we prove the stronger inequality $F_3(m) \leq \frac{1}{2}A_3(m+3)$, which implies

$$
2^{F_3(m)} \leq 2^{A_3(m+3)} = A_3(m + 4).
$$

Indeed,

$$
\begin{aligned}
F_3(1) &= (2^3 - 1) \cdot F_2(2^2) \\
&\leq 2^3 \times 3 \times 2^4 \\
&\leq 2^{3+2+4} \leq \frac{1}{2} \cdot 2^{16} \\
&= \frac{1}{2}A_3(4).
\end{aligned}
$$

For $k = 3$ and $m > 1$, assume the assertion is true for all $m' < m$, then

$$
\begin{aligned}
F_3(m) &= 2F_3(m - 1) \cdot F_2(F_3(m - 1)) \\
&= 3F_3(m - 1) \cdot 2^{F_3(m-1)} \\
&\leq \frac{3}{2}A_3(m + 2) \cdot 2^{A_3(m+2)/2} \\
&\leq \frac{1}{2} \cdot 2^{A_3(m+2)} \\
&= \frac{1}{2}A_3(m + 3).
\end{aligned}
$$

The last inequality holds, because $3x \leq 2^{x/2}$ for $x = A_3(m + 2) \geq 10$.

Now, for $k > 3$ and $m = 1$,

$$
\begin{aligned}
F_k(1) &= (2^k - 1) \cdot F_{k-1}(2^{k-1}) \\
&\leq 2^k \cdot F_{k-1}(2^{k-1}) \\
&\leq F_{k-1}(2^k \cdot 2^k) \\
&\leq F_{k-1}(2^{2k}).
\end{aligned}
$$

Therefore,

$$2^{F_k(1)} \leq 2^{F_{k-1}(2^{2k})} \leq A_{k-1}(2^{2k} + 4).$$

But for $k \geq 4$,

$$
\begin{aligned}
A_k(4) &\geq A_3(A_k(3)) \geq A_3(2k) \\
&= A_2(A_3(2k - 1)) \geq A_2(2(2k - 1)).
\end{aligned}
$$

For $k \geq 4$, $2(2k - 1) > 2k + 1$, so

$$A_k(4) \geq A_2(2k + 1) = 2^{2k+1} \geq 2^{2k} + 4,$$

and thus

$$2^{F_k(1)} \leq A_{k-1}(A_k(4)) \leq A_k(5).$$

Finally, for $k > 3$ and $m > 1$, assume the assertion is true for all $k' < k$ and $m \geq 1$, and for $k' = k$ and $m' < m$; then

$$
\begin{aligned}
F_k(m) &= 2F_k(m - 1) \cdot F_{k-1}(F_k(m - 1)) \\
&\leq F_{k-1}(2F_k(m - 1) \cdot F_k(m - 1)).
\end{aligned}
$$

Thus

$$
\begin{aligned}
2^{F_k(m)} &\leq 2^{F_{k-1}(2F_k(m-1)\cdot F_k(m-1))} \\
&\leq A_{k-1}(2F_k(m - 1) \cdot F_k(m - 1) + 4) \\
&\leq A_{k-1}(2^{F_k(m-1)}) \\
&\quad \text{(because } F_k(m - 1) \geq F_4(1) \geq 15) \\
&\leq A_{k-1}(A_k(m + 3)) \\
&= A_k(m + 4). \qquad \qquad \Box
\end{aligned}
$$

Appendix 3.3

In this appendix, we provide proofs of some properties of the auxiliary functions used in obtaining the lower bounds for $\lambda_s(n)$.

Lemma 3.29   For $k \geq 2$, $D_k \leq 2^{-(k-2)}$.

Proof.

$$
\begin{aligned}
D_k &= \prod_{j=1}^{k} \frac{2^{j-1}}{2^j - 1} \\
&\leq 1 \cdot \prod_{j=2}^{k} \frac{2^j - 1}{2^{j+1} - 4}
\end{aligned}
$$

$$= \frac{\prod_{j=2}^{k}(2^j - 1)}{\prod_{j=2}^{k}(2^{j+1} - 4)}$$

$$= \frac{\prod_{j=2}^{k}(2^j - 1)}{4^{k-1} \cdot \prod_{j=1}^{k-1}(2^j - 1)}$$

$$= \frac{2^k - 1}{4^{k-1}}$$

$$\leq 2^{-k+2}. \qquad \square$$

Lemma 3.30   For $k \geq 2$,

$$P(k, s) = \sum_{i=1}^{k-1} P(i, s - 2) + k - 2.$$

Proof. We prove this equality by induction. It is clearly true when $k = 2$, since all terms in the summation are zero. Now, assume this is true for all $k' < k$. Then

$$
\begin{aligned}
\sum_{i=1}^{k-1} P(i, s-2) + k - 2 &= 1 + P(k-1, s-2) + \sum_{i=1}^{k-2} P(i, s-2) + k - 3 \\
&= 1 + P(k-1, s-2) + P(k-1, s) \\
&= 1 + \sum_{i=1}^{(s/2)-2} \binom{k-3}{i} + \sum_{i=1}^{(s/2)-1} \binom{k-3}{i} \\
&= \sum_{i=1}^{(s/2)-1} \left(\binom{k-3}{i-1} + \binom{k-3}{i} \right) \\
&= \sum_{i=1}^{(s/2)-1} \binom{k-2}{i} \\
&= P(k, s),
\end{aligned}
$$

which is what we wanted to prove. $\qquad \square$

Lemma 3.32 *For all s, $F_k^\omega(m) \geq F_k^s(m)$.*

Proof. We proceed using induction, Lemmas 3.27 and 3.28, and the inequality $m \cdot F_k^s(m) \geq N_k^s(m)$, which follows from Lemma 3.31.

For $k = 1$ or $s = 2$, the claim is trivial since $F_1^s(m) = F_k^2(m) = 1$.

Suppose that the claim is true for smaller s, for smaller k with the same s, and for smaller m with the same k and s. For $m = 1$, we have

$$
\begin{aligned}
F_k^s(1) &= (2^k - 1) \cdot F_{k-1}^{s-2}(2^{k-1}) \cdot F_{k-1}^s(N_{k-1}^{s-2}(2^{k-1})) \\
&\leq (2^k - 1) \cdot F_{k-1}^\omega(2^{k-1}) \cdot F_{k-1}^s(2^{k-1} \cdot F_{k-1}^\omega(2^{k-1}))
\end{aligned}
$$

$$\leq \quad (2^k - 1) \cdot F_{k-1}^{\omega}(2^{k-1}) \cdot F_{k-1}^{\omega}(2^{k-1} \cdot F_{k-1}^{\omega}(2^{k-1}))$$
$$= \quad F_k^{\omega}(1).$$

Similarly, for $k, m > 1$, we have

$$F_k^s(m)$$
$$= \quad 2F_k^s(m-1) \cdot F_{k-1}^{s-2}(F_k^s(m-1)) \cdot F_{k-1}^s(N_{k-1}^{s-2}(F_k^s(m-1)))$$
$$\leq \quad 2F_k^{\omega}(m-1) \cdot F_{k-1}^{s-2}(F_k^{\omega}(m-1)) \cdot F_{k-1}^s(N_{k-1}^{s-2}(F_k^{\omega}(m-1)))$$
$$\leq \quad 2F_k^{\omega}(m-1) \cdot F_{k-1}^{\omega}(F_k^{\omega}(m-1)) \cdot F_{k-1}^s(F_k^{\omega}(m-1) \cdot F_{k-1}^{s-2}(F_k^{\omega}(m-1)))$$
$$\leq \quad 2F_k^{\omega}(m-1) \cdot F_{k-1}^{\omega}(F_k^{\omega}(m-1)) \cdot F_{k-1}^{\omega}(F_k^{\omega}(m-1) \cdot F_{k-1}^{\omega}(F_k^{\omega}(m-1)))$$
$$= \quad F_k^{\omega}(m). \qquad \qquad \square$$

Lemma 3.33   For $k \geq 2$, $A_k(m+1) \geq 2A_k(m)$.

Proof. We use induction on k. This is clear for $k = 2$. For $k \geq 3$, we assume this to be true for smaller k. This gives

$$A_k(m+1) \quad = \quad A_{k-1}(A_k(m))$$
$$\geq \quad 2A_{k-1}(A_k(m) - 1)$$
$$\geq \quad 2A_{k-1}(A_k(m-1))$$
$$= \quad 2A_k(m). \qquad \qquad \square$$

Lemma 3.37 $F_k^{\omega}(m) \leq A_k(7m)$.

Proof. We first show several 'horrible' inequalities involving F^{ω}. Using Lemmas 3.33–3.35 extensively, we see that, for $k \geq 3$,

$$F_k^{\omega}(1) \quad = \quad (2^k - 1) \cdot F_{k-1}^{\omega}(2^{k-1}) \cdot F_{k-1}^{\omega}(2^{k-1} \cdot F_{k-1}^{\omega}(2^{k-1}))$$
$$\leq \quad F_{k-1}^{\omega}(k + 2^{k-1}) \cdot F_{k-1}^{\omega}(F_{k-1}^{\omega}(k - 1 + 2^{k-1}))$$
$$\leq \quad F_{k-1}^{\omega}(2 \cdot F_{k-1}^{\omega}(k + 2^{k-1}))$$
$$\leq \quad F_{k-1}^{\omega}(F_{k-1}^{\omega}(k + 1 + 2^{k-1}))$$
$$\leq \quad F_{k-1}^{\omega}(F_{k-1}^{\omega}(2^k))$$
$$\leq \quad F_{k-1}^{\omega}(F_{k-1}^{\omega}(F_{k-1}^{\omega}(k)))$$
$$\leq \quad F_{k-1}^{\omega}(F_{k-1}^{\omega}(F_{k-1}^{\omega}(F_{k-1}^{\omega}(1)))).$$

The last step follows since

$$F_{k-1}^{\omega}(1) \geq 2^{k-1} - 1 \geq k \qquad \text{for } k \geq 3.$$

Similarly, for $k \geq 3$,

$$F_k^{\omega}(m) \quad = \quad 2 \cdot F_k^{\omega}(m-1) \cdot F_{k-1}^{\omega}(F_k^{\omega}(m-1)) \cdot$$
$$F_{k-1}^{\omega}(F_k^{\omega}(m-1) \cdot F_{k-1}^{\omega}(F_k^{\omega}(m-1)))$$

$$
\begin{aligned}
&\leq\ 2 \cdot F_{k-1}^{\omega}(2 \cdot F_k^{\omega}(m-1)) \cdot F_{k-1}^{\omega}(F_{k-1}^{\omega}(2 \cdot F_k^{\omega}(m-1))) \\
&\leq\ 2 \cdot F_{k-1}^{\omega}(2 \cdot F_{k-1}^{\omega}(2 \cdot F_k^{\omega}(m-1))) \\
&\leq\ F_{k-1}^{\omega}(1 + 2 \cdot F_{k-1}^{\omega}(2 \cdot F_k^{\omega}(m-1))) \\
&\leq\ F_{k-1}^{\omega}(4 \cdot F_{k-1}^{\omega}(2 \cdot F_k^{\omega}(m-1))) \\
&\leq\ F_{k-1}^{\omega}(F_{k-1}^{\omega}(2 + 2 \cdot F_k^{\omega}(m-1))) \\
&\leq\ F_{k-1}^{\omega}(F_{k-1}^{\omega}(4 \cdot F_k^{\omega}(m-1))) \\
&\leq\ F_{k-1}^{\omega}(F_{k-1}^{\omega}(F_{k-1}^{\omega}(F_k^{\omega}(m-1)))).
\end{aligned}
$$

The last step follows from the inequalities $F_{k-1}^{\omega}(x) \geq 2^x \geq 4x$ when $x \geq 4$, $k \geq 3$, and $F_k^{\omega}(x) \geq 2^k - 1 \geq 4$ when $k \geq 3$.

We will now show $F_k^{\omega}(m) \leq A_k(7m)$. This is easy for $k = 1$ and $k = 2$. For $k \geq 3$, we assume that the inequality is true for k', m', when $k' < k$, and when $k' = k$ and $m' < m$. This gives

$$
\begin{aligned}
F_k^{\omega}(1) &\leq\ F_{k-1}^{\omega}(F_{k-1}^{\omega}(F_{k-1}^{\omega}(F_{k-1}^{\omega}(1)))) \\
&\leq\ A_{k-1}(7 \cdot A_{k-1}(7 \cdot A_{k-1}(7 \cdot A_{k-1}(7)))) \\
&\leq\ A_{k-1}(8 \cdot A_{k-1}(7 \cdot A_{k-1}(7 \cdot A_{k-1}(7)))) \\
&\leq\ A_{k-1}(A_{k-1}(3 + 7 \cdot A_{k-1}(7 \cdot A_{k-1}(7)))) \\
&\leq\ A_{k-1}(A_{k-1}(16 \cdot A_{k-1}(7 \cdot A_{k-1}(7)))) \\
&\leq\ A_{k-1}(A_{k-1}(A_{k-1}(4 + 7 \cdot A_{k-1}(7)))) \\
&\leq\ A_{k-1}(A_{k-1}(A_{k-1}(A_{k-1}(11)))) \\
&\leq\ A_{k-1}(A_{k-1}(A_{k-1}(A_{k-1}(A_{k-1}(A_{k-1}(2)))))) \\
&=\ A_k(7).
\end{aligned}
$$

Similarly, for $m > 1$, we get

$$
\begin{aligned}
F_k^{\omega}(m) &\leq\ F_{k-1}^{\omega}(F_{k-1}^{\omega}(F_{k-1}^{\omega}(F_k^{\omega}(m-1)))) \\
&\leq\ A_{k-1}(7 \cdot A_{k-1}(7 \cdot A_{k-1}(7 \cdot A_k(7m-7)))) \\
&\leq\ A_{k-1}(A_{k-1}(3 + 7 \cdot A_{k-1}(7 \cdot A_k(7m-7)))) \\
&\leq\ A_{k-1}(A_{k-1}(A_{k-1}(4 + 7 \cdot A_k(7m-7)))) \\
&\leq\ A_{k-1}(A_{k-1}(A_{k-1}(A_k(7m-3)))) \\
&=\ A_k(7m). \qquad\qquad\qquad\qquad\qquad\qquad \square
\end{aligned}
$$

4

GEOMETRIC REALIZATION

4.1   Introduction

In the previous chapter we proved that there exist $DS(n, 3)$-sequences U of length $\Omega(n\alpha(n))$. Moreover, the construction given in Lemma 1.2 shows that any such sequence U can be realized as the lower envelope sequence of a collection of n 'pseudo-segments,' that is, partially defined continuous functions, each pair of which intersect at most once. However, this construction generally yields rather irregularly shaped functions (see Figure 1.3), so the question arises whether a $DS(n, 3)$-sequences of length $\Omega(n\alpha(n))$ can be realized by collections of functions of simple shape, in particular, by collections of segments.

In this chapter we show that this is indeed possible. Specifically, we show that each of the sequences $S(k, m)$, constructed in Section 2.3, can be realized as the lower envelope sequence of a collection of segments. The construction is fairly involved, and is based on a doubly inductive scheme, which follows the inductive pattern in the construction of the sequences $S(k, m)$. We then present an alternative construction, which is somewhat simpler, and whose resulting lower envelope sequences are different (but still of length $\Omega(n\alpha(n))$).

4.2   Realizing the sequences $S(k, m)$ by segments

4.2.1   Basic definitions and notations

The following definitions refer to a collection $G = G(k, m)$ of closed line segments in the plane, none of which is vertical (in fact, in our construction all segments in G have positive slope), which will be used to realize $S(k, m)$. We further assume, and will enforce it in our construction, that no endpoint of any segment in G lies on any other segment in G. Using the notation of Section 2.3, we write

$$G(k, m) = \{l_{d, \gamma} \mid 1 \leq d \leq m, 1 \leq \gamma \leq \bar{\gamma}\},$$

so that the segment $l_{d, \gamma}$ will realize the symbol (d, γ) of $S(k, m)$.

For each nonvertical segment, its *starting point* is its left endpoint and its *ending point* is its right endpoint.

A point p is *hidden* by a segment l if the vertical line passing through p intersects l at a point lying below p. A segment is *hidden* by l if all its points are hidden by l.

A point p is *seen* (below G) if it is not hidden by any segment of G. A segment is *seen* if one of its points is seen.

The lower envelope E_G of G is a piecewise linear function consisting of subsegments of the segments in G; E_G is not necessarily continuous.

G is *contiguous* if the domain of definition of E_G is some closed interval. Thus G is contiguous iff no vertical line can separate G into two parts without crossing some segment of G. Note that if G_1 and G_2 are two contiguous sets of segments that are both crossed by the same vertical line, then $G_1 \cup G_2$ is contiguous as well.

Let U_G denote the lower envelope sequence of G. As shown in Corollary 1.5, U_G is a $DS(n, 3)$-sequence, so its length is always $O(n\alpha(n))$, for any collection G of n segments.

The 'transition' points in which the current segment in E_G changes, as we trace E_G from left to right, are of three possible types:

Starting points: E_G changes because of the appearance of the starting endpoint of a new segment below any other segment. These points will be denoted as *S-points*.

Crossing points: E_G changes because the presently lowest segment of G crosses another segment (which will thus become lowest). These points are denoted as *C-points*.

Ending points: E_G changes because the presently lowest segment of G reaches its ending point when there is no segment below it. These points are denoted as *E-points*.

The set $\Pi_X(G)$ (where X is any combination of S, C, and E) is the set of the x-coordinates of the transition points of type in X. For example, $\Pi_{CE}(G)$ is the set of all x-coordinates of ending and crossing points in E_G.

A *graph fan* in $G(k,m)$ is the subset of m line segments $\{l_{d,\gamma}\}_{d=1}^m$ for some γ (these m line segments will be used to represent the γth fan of $S(k,m)$).

A *tube* $T = (x_L, x_H, y_L, y_H, \{t_i\}_{i=1}^r)$ is a set of relatively open line segments t_i, with left endpoints (x_i^1, y_i^1) and right endpoints (x_i^2, y_i^2), all having positive slopes and contained in the open rectangle $(x_L, x_H) \times (y_L, y_H)$ (so $x_L < x_i^1 < x_i^2 < x_H$ and $y_L < y_i^1 < y_i^2 < y_H$, for each $1 \leq i \leq r$). The rectangle is called the *frame* of the tube.

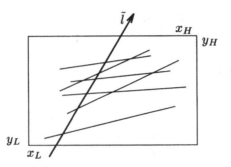

FIGURE 4.1. A line passing through a tube.

A straight line $\tilde{l}$ defined by $y = ax + b$ is said to *pass through* a tube T (written $\tilde{l} \bar{\in} T$), if $\tilde{l}$ crosses each $t_i \in T$ from below, so that $y_i^1 > ax_i^1 + b$ and $y_i^2 < ax_i^2 + b$ (see Figure 4.1). The slope of $\tilde{l}$ is obviously greater than that of any t_i in T (and is thus positive). The segments (t_i) *are not* part of G, and are used only to control the lines that pass through T, so that they pass in a specific range of positions in the plane.

A segment l is said to *pass through* T when the line containing l passes through T (even though l itself need not cross any t_i in T). A line $\tilde{l}$ passing through a tube can cross the outer frame in any two sides, excluding combinations that force $\tilde{l}$ to have negative slope.

A tube T is *valid* if there exists at least one line $\tilde{l} \bar{\in} T$.

Two lines $\tilde{l}_1$ and $\tilde{l}_2$ that pass through a tube T *cross inside* the tube T if their crossing point is contained inside the frame of the tube but not on its boundary (see Figure 4.2).

A line $\tilde{l}_1$ is *above* a line $\tilde{l}_2$ *relative to* a tube T if both lines pass through T, they cross inside it, and the slope of $\tilde{l}_1$ is greater than that of $\tilde{l}_2$. It is obvious that, for any $x > x_H$, one has $\tilde{l}_1(x) > \tilde{l}_2(x)$ (regarding the $\tilde{l}_i$ as linear functions). We also say that $\tilde{l}_1$ is *above* $\tilde{l}_2$ for $x > x_0$, if $\tilde{l}_1(x) > \tilde{l}_2(x)$ for $x > x_0$ (again, regarding $\tilde{l}_i$ as linear functions).

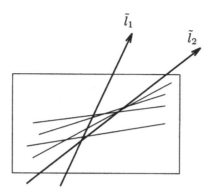

FIGURE 4.2. Two lines crossing inside a tube.

If two lines $\tilde{l}_1$ and $\tilde{l}_2$ pass through a tube T and cross inside it, the tube can be *limited* by $\tilde{l}_1$ and $\tilde{l}_2$ to produce a modified tube T'. The modification is done by adding to the set of segments of T two new segments (inside the frame boundary) so that any line passing through the modified tube will fall between $\tilde{l}_1$ and $\tilde{l}_2$ (in the sense defined above; see Figure 4.3).

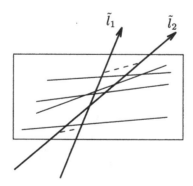

FIGURE 4.3. Two lines limiting a tube; the dashed segments are added to the limited tube.

It can easily be shown that the resulting tube T' is valid, that every line $\tilde{l} \bar{\in} T'$ also passes through the original tube T and falls between $\tilde{l}_1$ and $\tilde{l}_2$ outside the frame, and that the slope of every line $\tilde{l} \bar{\in} T'$ is between the slopes of $\tilde{l}_1$ and of $\tilde{l}_2$. Note that not every line passing between $\tilde{l}_1$ and $\tilde{l}_2$ necessarily passes through T'.

The limiting operation is not uniquely defined—any resulting tube T' that constrains lines passing through it to be between $\tilde{l}_1$ and $\tilde{l}_2$ (and to pass through the original T) is acceptable.

Note that, since the segments $\{t_i\}$ defining a tube are relatively open, a tube defines an open domain of lines passing through it. In particular, there is no line with maximal or minimal slope among these lines, although the appropriate supremum and infimum of slopes do exist.

A tube corresponds to an open convex structure of lines in the dual plane— if $\tilde{l}_1, \tilde{l}_2 \bar{\in} T$ then any line incident to their crossing point and having a slope between those of the two lines also passes through T. In particular, for any pair $\tilde{l}_1, \tilde{l}_2 \bar{\in} T$ of lines that cross inside T, there is always a line $\tilde{l} \bar{\in} T$ that lies between them.

A tube T can thus be associated with a pair of convex polygons so that any line $\tilde{l} \bar{\in} T$ must pass between (i.e., separate) them, and vice versa. These polygons are, respectively, the convex hulls of the right and of the left endpoints of the segments t_i, and are thus contained in the frame of T. If a tube is valid, these polygons will be disjoint and arranged so that any line separating them has positive slope (any line passing through the tube can serve as a separator between them).

Adding constraint segments to the tube while keeping it valid (e.g., when limiting a tube) is equivalent to enlarging the two corresponding polygons while keeping them convex and disjoint.

Two tubes, T_1, T_2, are called *parallel* (written $T_1 \parallel T_2$), if T_2 is a planar translate of T_1 by some vector u. Thus for every $\tilde{l}_1 \bar{\in} T_1$ there is a *matching* parallel line $\tilde{l}_2 \bar{\in} T_2$ formed by translating $\tilde{l}_1$ by the same vector u.

A tube T_1 is *steeper* than T_2 (written $T_1 \succ T_2$) if, for every $\tilde{l}_1 \bar{\in} T_1$ and $\tilde{l}_2 \bar{\in} T_2$, the slope of $\tilde{l}_1$ is greater than that of $\tilde{l}_2$.

4.2.2   Valid constraints

We next introduce the notion of a *valid constraint* $C(k, m)$, parametrized by the same two indices used to parametrize $S(k, m)$, and show that for any such constraint one can construct a corresponding set of line segments $G(k, m)$ that satisfies it. We will recursively construct $G(k, m)$ from $G(k, m - 1)$ and $G(k - 1, \bar{\alpha})$, where $\bar{\alpha} = C_k(m - 1)$, following the way in which $S(k, m)$ is constructed from $S(k, m - 1)$ and $S(k - 1, \bar{\alpha})$. In particular, $G(k, m)$, which corresponds to the set of symbols of $S(k, m)$, will simply be the union of $G(k - 1, \bar{\alpha})$ and of $\bar{\beta} = C_{k-1}(\bar{\alpha})$ disjoint and translated copies of $G(k, m - 1)$. However, to guarantee that the union of all these subcollections does have $S(k, m)$ as its lower envelope sequence, we need to impose geometric constraints on $G(k, m-1)$ and on $G(k-1, \bar{\alpha})$ that will make them fit together in the manner desired. This will be achieved by generating induced constraints $C(k, m - 1)$ and $C(k - 1, \bar{\alpha})$ from $C(k, m)$, and require $G(k, m - 1)$ and $G(k - 1, \bar{\alpha})$ to satisfy these respective constraints. This is an intricate feature of our construction, into which geometry enters in a significant way.

Specifically, A *valid constraint* $C(k, m) = (\mathcal{T}, x_L, x_H, y_L, y_H)$ over the m segments in a single graph fan of $G(k, m)$ consists of a rectangular *outer frame* $[x_L, x_H] \times [y_L, y_H]$ and of a set of m valid tubes $\mathcal{T} = \{T_j\}_{j=1}^{m}$, which satisfy the following properties:

V1) The tube frames are ordered 'from northwest to southeast' (herein referred to as 'NW to SE' order) inside the outer frame, so that:

$$
\begin{array}{rcl}
x_L & < & x_L(T_1) \\
x_H(T_i) & < & x_L(T_{i+1}) \qquad \text{for } 1 \le i \le m - 1 \\
x_H(T_m) & < & x_H \\
y_H & > & y_H(T_1) \\
y_L(T_i) & > & y_H(T_{i+1}) \qquad \text{for } 1 \le i \le m - 1 \\
y_L(T_m) & > & y_L.
\end{array}
$$

In particular, all the segments defining each of the tubes are contained in the outer frame.

V2) $T_j \,\|\, T_p$, for any $1 \le j, p \le m - 1$.

V3) $T_m \succ T_{m-1}$.

V4) There exist lines $u \widetilde{\in} T_{m-1}$ and $v \widetilde{\in} T_m$ that cross each other at a point to the right of x_H.

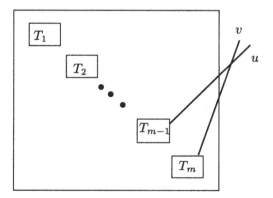

FIGURE 4.4. A valid constraint.

Remark 4.1 (i) See Figure 4.4 for an illustration of a valid constraint.

(ii) Conditions (V1)–(V4) are actually independent of k. The dependence of $C(k, m)$ on k is implicit in the recursive construction given below, and is reflected in the inner structure of the tubes T_j.

Lemma 4.2 *Let $\mathcal{C} = \mathcal{C}(k, m)$ be a valid constraint and let $M = \{l_i \bar{\in} T_i\}_{i=1}^m$ be any set of m segments such that the starting point of each l_i is inside the frame of its corresponding tube T_i. Furthermore, assume that $\Pi_{CE}(M)$ is outside $[x_L, x_H]$. Take the portions of these segments lying inside the x-range $[x_L, x_H]$ to create a set $M^\#$ of truncated segments. Then the lower envelope sequence $R = U_{M^\#}$ (in which each appearance of l_i is encoded as i) is $\langle 1\,2\,\cdots\,m \rangle$.*

Proof. For each $1 \leq i < j \leq m$, the tube T_i lies northwest to T_j. Thus l_i cannot pass below the starting point of l_j and hide it, as this would force l_i to have a negative slope. Thus R contains the (not necessarily contiguous) subsequence $\langle 1\,2\,\cdots\,m \rangle$. Furthermore, if R contains a subsequence of the form $\langle x\,\cdots\,y\,\cdots\,x \rangle$ then there must exist a point in $\Pi_{CE}(M)$ inside $[x_L, x_H]$, contrary to assumption. Thus $R = \langle 1\,2\,\cdots\,m \rangle$.   □

4.2.3   The induction scheme

In order to convert the sequence of symbols $S(k, m)$ into the corresponding collection of segments $G(k, m)$, we use a doubly inductive scheme that follows the inductive construction of $S(k, m)$. Our construction shows that, given a valid constraint $\mathcal{C} = \mathcal{C}(k, m)$, there exists a set $G(k, m)$ of segments satisfying certain properties (P1–P5 below), related to the constraint $\mathcal{C}$; the most important of these properties is $U_{G(k,m)} = S(k, m)$. Before presenting the formal (and rather complex) construction, we offer an intuitive description of the inductive step for the general case ($k \geq 3, m > 1$); the other base cases are considerably simpler.

Here is a brief summary of the properties $G = G(k, m)$ has to satisfy. This set has to consist of $\bar{\gamma}$ disjoint subsets (fans) of m segments each (property P2) and each fan has to meet the constraints imposed on G by an appropriate translated copy of $\mathcal{C}$, where these $\bar{\gamma}$ copies of $\mathcal{C}$ are placed in the plane from NW to SE (property P1). Specifically, for each $1 \leq d \leq m, 1 \leq \gamma \leq \bar{\gamma}$, the segment $l_{d,\gamma}$ in G (the dth segment in the γth fan) corresponds to the dth tube T_d in the γth copy of $\mathcal{C}$, in the sense that the starting point of $l_{d,\gamma}$ is inside the tube frame of T_d (property P2A) and the segment passes through the tube (property P2B; this property forces all segments of G to have positive slope).

The transition points along E_G—S-, C-, and E-points—have to satisfy the following properties. The starting points of the segments of G must all be S-points (i.e., each segment starts below all other segments in G). (This, in fact, will follow from the properties that each segment starts inside a tube frame, that there is a NW to SE order among the tube frames and among the outer frames of copies of $\mathcal{C}$, and that all the segments of G have positive slope.) We furthermore require that all other transition points (in $\Pi_{CE}(G)$) lie outside the x-ranges of the outer frames of the copies of $\mathcal{C}$ (property P3A).

These properties are used in the inductive merging process described below. Some additional properties (P3B, P4A, and P5) are used to establish the correctness of our inductive process. Finally, property P4B states that $G(k,m)$ has indeed the desired property: $U_{G(k,m)} = S(k,m)$.

The inductive pattern of our construction for the general case is as follows:

1. We construct from $C(k,m)$ a modified constraint $C' = C(k, m-1)$ by discarding the last tube T_m and a few additional modifications.

2. Based on this constraint C', we build inductively a set of segments $G' = G(k, m-1)$. This construction duplicates the original constraint C $\bar{\alpha}$ times (one for each fan of G').

3. We use these copies of C to construct a new constraint $C^\star = C(k-1, \bar{\alpha})$. This $C^\star$ involves the $\bar{\alpha}$ copies of the discarded tubes T_m (one in each of the $\bar{\alpha}$ copies of C).

4. We then construct inductively another set of segments $G^\star = G(k-1, \bar{\alpha})$ satisfying the constraint $C^\star$. This construction creates $\bar{\beta}$ copies of $C^\star$ (one for each fan of $G^\star$).

5. G is then constructed as the union of $G^\star$ with $\bar{\beta}$ translated copies of G', each lying within a corresponding copy of the constraint $C^\star$ (by construction, each copy of $C^\star$ will encompass a single copy of G').

The intuitive reason why the constraints $C(k,m)$ are needed is that, when we construct $G^\star$ inductively, we already have a set G', which constrains $G^\star$ by requiring that each of its segments 'pierce' an appropriate copy of G' at exactly one place, i.e., at the 'end' of an appropriate fan. The tubes serve this purpose in a twofold manner; first, they constrain the location for the starting points of the segments of $G^\star$ (at which the required piercing has to take place), and, second, they constrain the slopes of the segments of $G^\star$ so as to ensure that none of them appear again after this initial piercing below any of the copies of G', thus ensuring that adding the segments of $G^\star$ has no effect on the lower envelope sequences $U_{G'}$ other than the piercings just described.

4.2.4 The realization theorem

Having presented this 'bird's eye' overview of our construction, we next proceed to describe it formally and in detail. For our construction to work, $G(k,m)$ needs to satisfy the following conditions:

P1) $\bar{\gamma} = C_k(m)$ disjoint translates of C are created and placed in the plane so that their outer frames are ordered from NW to SE.

P2) $G(k,m)$ consists of $\bar{\gamma} \cdot m$ segments $l_{d,\gamma}$, for $1 \leq d \leq m, 1 \leq \gamma \leq \bar{\gamma}$; these segments are grouped into $\bar{\gamma}$ disjoint subsets, $(l_{1,\gamma}, \ldots, l_{m,\gamma})_{\gamma=1}^{\bar{\gamma}}$, each forming a fan of size m, with the following properties:

P2A) The starting point of each $l_{d,\gamma}$ is inside the corresponding dth tube, $T_{d,\gamma}$, in the γth copy of $\mathcal{C}$.

P2B) The segment $l_{d,\gamma}$ passes through the tube $T_{d,\gamma}$.

P3) Segment properties:

P3A) The set $\Pi_{CE}(G(k,m))$ is disjoint from the x-range $[x_L, x_H]$ of the outer frame of any copy of $\mathcal{C}$.

P3B) Any other crossing or ending point of segments in $G(k,m)$ (i.e., not on the lower envelope) may have x-coordinate lying inside an x-range $[x_L, x_H]$ of some outer frame, but then the point must lie above this frame (i.e., above y_H).

P4) General properties:

P4A) $G(k,m)$ is contiguous.

P4B) $U_{G(k,m)} = S(k,m)$.

P5) In each portion of E_G representing a block c of $S(k,m)$ of more than one element, each segment l has a slope lower than that of the segment l' preceding it in c, and l crosses l' from above (at a point in $\Pi_C(G)$). (In other words, c is represented by a 'downward-convex' portion of E_G; see Figure 4.5.)

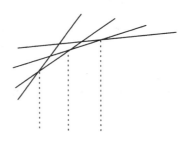

FIGURE 4.5. Condition P5—the realization of a block.

Theorem 4.3 *Given integers $k, m \geq 1$ and a valid constraint $C = \mathcal{C}(k,m)$, one can construct a set $G(k,m)$ of segments that satisfies the conditions P1–P5 described above.*

Remark 4.4 (i) In our inductive construction, we will follow the notations of Chapter 2 and re-index each segment $l_{d,\gamma}$ of $G(k,m)$ as $l_{d,\alpha,\beta}$, where $1 \leq \alpha \leq \bar{\alpha}$, $1 \leq \beta \leq \bar{\beta}$, and $\gamma = \alpha + \bar{\alpha}(\beta - 1)$.

(ii) Note that properties P1 and P2 imply that, after leaving the outer frame in which it starts, a segment of G can never enter another outer frame or pass below it.

4.2.5 Proof of Theorem 4.3

4.2.5.1 The case $k = 1$

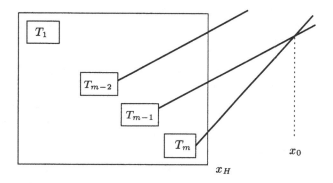

FIGURE 4.6. The case $k = 1$.

See Figure 4.6. The sequence $S(1, m)$ to be realized is:

$$\langle (1, 1)\,(2, 1)\,\cdots\,(m, 1)\rangle.$$

In this case $\bar{\gamma} = 1$ and thus no additional copies of $\mathcal{C}(1, m)$ need be created. Take $u \bar{\in} T_{m-1}$ and $v \bar{\in} T_m$ as given by (V4), and let x_0 be the x-coordinate of their crossing point. For each $i < m$, take $l_{i,1}$ to be a segment contained in the line passing through T_i that matches the line containing u, so that l_i starts inside the tube frame of T_i and ends at some $x \in (x_H, x_0)$. Take $l_{m,1}$ to be a segment contained in v, starting inside the frame of T_m and ending at $x = x_0$.

The properties asserted in the theorem clearly hold for $G(1, m) = \{l_{i,1}\}_{i=1}^m$:

P1) Trivial ($\bar{\gamma} = 1$).

P2) Both P2A and P2B are trivial.

P3) To prove P3A, note that, except for the crossings of $l_{m-1,1}$ and $l_{m,1}$, the segments do not cross at all, since all the segments $l_{i,1}$, for $i = 1, \ldots, m - 1$, are parallel and end before crossing $l_{m,1}$. Their ending points all lie to the right of x_H. Thus all points in $\Pi_{CE}(G)$ lie to the right of $[x_L, x_H]$. P3B is trivial.

P4) P4A is trivial, and P4B is a direct consequence of Lemma 4.2.

P5) Inapplicable—there are no multielement blocks.

4.2.5.2   The case $k > 2$ and $m = 1$

In this case $S(k,1) = S(k-1,2)$, so we will obtain $G(k,1)$ as an appropriate collection $G(k-1,2)$ that satisfies certain constraints derived from the given valid constraint $C = C(k,1)$. This constraint has a single tube T_1 inside an outer frame (note that in this case the conditions V1–V4 of the constraint are mostly vacuous).

Construct a new constraint $C' = C(k-1,2)$ from C as follows: Create a translate C_1 of C far enough in the SE direction so that the outer frames of both copies have disjoint x-ranges and disjoint y-ranges. Take a line $w \bar{\in} T_1(C)$ and its corresponding translate $w' \bar{\in} T_1(C_1)$ in C_1. Limit the tube of C to lines passing below the line w and limit the tube of C_1 to lines passing above the line w'. Rename the limited tubes T_1' and T_2', respectively, and use them as the two tubes of C'. For an outer frame of C', take any rectangle that contains the outer frames of both C and C_1.

C' is clearly valid: V1–V3 are trivially true and V4 is true since we can always choose lines $u \bar{\in} T_1'$ and $v \bar{\in} T_2'$ sufficiently close to w and w', respectively, so that their crossing point lies as far to the right as desired.

By the induction hypothesis, there exists a set $G' = G(k-1,2)$, based on $\bar{\gamma}' = C_{k-1}(2) = C_k(1)/2$ copies of C' and consisting of $\bar{\gamma}' \cdot 2 = \bar{\gamma}$ segments, satisfying properties P1–P5 for $(k-1,2)$. We now take $G = G(k,1)$ to be this set, renaming each segment $l_{d,\gamma}$ $(d = 1,2)$ as $l_{1,2\gamma+d-2}$, and, indeed, P1–P5 (for $(k,1)$) hold for G:

P1) As noted above, $\bar{\gamma} = \bar{\gamma}' \cdot 2$; the NW to SE order follows immediately from our construction and from property P1 of G'.

P2) Both P2A and P2B are trivial from property P2 of G'.

P3) Both P3A and P3B are direct consequences of properties P3A and P3B of G'.

P4) P4A is trivial by induction. P4B is a consequence of property P4B of G', because $U_{G(k,1)} = U_{G(k-1,2)} = S(k-1,2) = S(k,1)$.

P5) Trivial from property P5 of G' (the renaming did not change the block structure of G').

Thus the properties of the theorem hold for $(k,1)$.

4.2.5.3   The general case: $k > 2$ and $m > 1$

We first construct a modified valid constraint $C' = C(k, m-1)$, as follows (see Figure 4.7). By V4, there exist lines $u \bar{\in} T_{m-1}$ and $v \bar{\in} T_m$, which cross each other at a point to the right of x_H (call it A). Since $T_{m-2} \| T_{m-1}$, there is a line $w \bar{\in} T_{m-2}$ that is a matching translate of u. This line is above u and thus B, its crossing point with v, is to the right of, and above, A.

Take two lines, $u_1, u_2 \bar{\in} T_{m-1}$, so that the slope of u_2 is slightly greater than the slope of u_1, which is slightly greater than that of u, and such that u_2 is slightly above u_1 which is slightly above u (relative to T_{m-1}). These lines cross v at points A_1, A_2, respectively, which are ordered along v between A and B. The lines u_1 and u_2 cross w at two respective points, B_1, B_2, ordered along w in the order B, B_2, B_1.

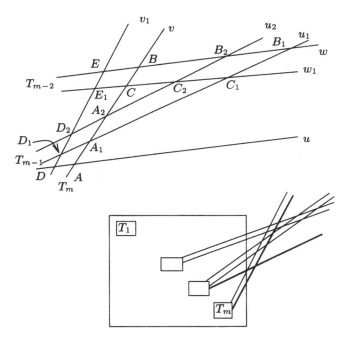

FIGURE 4.7. The general case.

Take a line $w_1 \bar{\in} T_{m-2}$ (below w and with slightly smaller slope), which crosses v at C, u_2 at C_2, and u_1 at C_1 (in that order). The line w_1 should be close enough to w so that C_2 is to the right of B and C lies between A_2 and B.

Take a line $v_1 \bar{\in} T_m$ which lies slightly above v and has slope slightly greater than that of v. This line should cross the vertical line $x = x_H$ and then u, u_1, u_2, w_1, w in that order. Call these crossing points, from left to right, D, D_1, D_2, E_1, E. These points are adjacent along their lines to the points A, A_1, A_2, C, B, respectively.

First induction over $k, m - 1$: Define $\mathcal{C}'$ (over $(k, m - 1)$) as follows:

1. The set of tubes $\mathcal{T}'$ of $\mathcal{C}'$ consists of $m - 1$ tubes T_i'. For each $i < m - 1$,

T_i' is the tube T_i, limited by the two lines that are the corresponding translates of w and of w_1 in T_{m-2}. The tube T_{m-1}' is defined as T_{m-1} limited by u_1 and u_2. We also limit the tube T_m by v and v_1 to create T_m'. This last limiting is used only later, in the second induction step.

2. Any pair of lines passing through T_{m-2}' and T_{m-1}' will thus have to cross inside the quadrangle $B_1B_2C_2C_1$. Any pair of lines passing through T_{m-1}' and T_m' will have to cross inside the quadrangle $A_1A_2D_2D_1$.

3. The outer frame of C' has the same left lower corner (x_L, y_L) as that of C, but its right upper corner has coordinates $x_H' = x(B)$ and $y_H' = \max(y(B), y_H)$ (i.e., the outer frame is extended so as to include B too).

C' is valid for $(k, m-1)$, since:

V1) The $m-1$ tubes T_i' are clearly contained in the outer frame of C' and are ordered there from NW to SE, by the original condition V1 for C.

V2) All tubes T_i', for $i < m-1$, are parallel, since the original tubes T_i (for $i < m-1$) are parallel and matching limitations were added to each.

V3) $T_{m-1}' \succ T_{m-2}'$ because the slopes of u_1, u_2 are greater than those of w, w_1.

V4) There exist $u' \bar{\in} T_{m-2}'$ and $v' \bar{\in} T_{m-1}'$ crossing to the right of the new x_H'; indeed, by construction, any pair of lines $u' \bar{\in} T_{m-2}', v' \bar{\in} T_{m-1}'$ cross inside the region $B_1B_2C_2C_1$, which lies to the right of B.

By the induction hypothesis, there exists a set of segments $G' = G(k, m-1)$ based on $\bar{\alpha}$ copies of C' and satisfying properties P1–P5 for k and $m-1$. By property P4 of G', the sequence $U_{G'}$ is the sequence $S' = S(k, m-1)$, as defined in Chapter 2. In S', the fans do not include the 'last' segments l_m and have the form

$$\langle (1, \alpha)(2, \alpha) \cdots (m-2, \alpha)(m-1, \alpha) \rangle.$$

The lower envelope sequence associated with the part of G' inside the x-range of the outer frame of any copy C_α' of C' (for $1 \leq \alpha \leq \bar{\alpha}$) coincides with the corresponding fan in S' (by properties P1–P3 and Lemma 4.2).

Second induction over $k-1, \bar{\alpha}$:   Next define a valid constraint $C^\star(k-1, \bar{\alpha})$ as follows:

1. The induction step over C' has created $\bar{\alpha}$ copies of the original C, which are ordered in the plane from NW to SE. Let C_α' denote the αth copy of C'. Each of these copies contains a copy of T_m'. The set of tubes $\mathcal{T}^\star$ for $C^\star$ then consists of these $\bar{\alpha}$ copies of T_m', each limited further by taking any line $w^\star \bar{\in} T_{\bar{\alpha}}^\star$ (the $\bar{\alpha}$th copy of T_m'), by generating the corresponding translates w_α of $w^\star$ in each $T_\alpha^\star$, by limiting $T_\alpha^\star$, for $\alpha < \bar{\alpha}$, to admit only lines below w_α, and by limiting $T_{\bar{\alpha}}^\star$ to admit only lines above $w^\star$.

2. The outer frame of $C^\star$ can be taken to be any sufficiently large rectangle $[x_L, x_H] \times [y_L, y_H]$ that contains all the outer frames of all copies of C' and all the segments of G'.

$C^\star$ is valid since:

V1) The $\bar{\alpha}$ tubes of $C^\star$ are properly ordered, as each $T_\alpha^\star$ is contained in the outer frame of the corresponding C_α' and these outer frames are ordered NW to SE by property P1 of G'. These tubes are contained in the outer frame of $C^\star$ by construction.

V2) All tubes $T_\alpha^\star$, for $\alpha < \bar{\alpha}$, are parallel by construction (because of the matching limitations added to each).

V3) $T_{\bar{\alpha}}^\star \succ T_{\bar{\alpha}-1}^\star$ because of the $w^\star$-limitations in the above construction.

V4) We can always choose lines $w' \bar{\in} T_{\bar{\alpha}-1}^\star$, $w'' \bar{\in} T_{\bar{\alpha}}^\star$ sufficiently close to $w_{\bar{\alpha}-1}$ and to $w^\star$, respectively, so that their crossing point lies as far to the right as desired, so V4 follows immediately.

Again, by the induction hypothesis, there exists a set $G^\star$, based on $\bar{\beta}$ copies of $C^\star$ and consisting of $\bar{\gamma} = \bar{\alpha} \cdot \bar{\beta}$ segments, that satisfies properties P1–P5 for $k - 1$ and $\bar{\alpha}$.

The merging step: We now construct the desired set G as follows. For each $1 \le \beta \le \bar{\beta}$, let G_β' denote the translated copy of G' inside the βth copy of $C^\star$, created by the construction of $G^\star$. The collection G is then defined as the union of $G^\star$ and of all these copies G_β' of G', for $1 \le \beta \le \bar{\beta}$. We also number the segments of $G^\star$ and of the G_β's, using the same renumbering as in the construction of $S(k, m)$ given in Chapter 2.

The following lemma is a consequence of Theorem 2.20, and establishes the crucial property of the merged set G, namely that the interaction of $G^\star$ with each G_β' matches exactly the interaction between $S^\star$ and the corresponding copy S_β' of S', as described in Chapter 2.

Lemma 4.5 *Let $1 \le \beta \le \bar{\beta}$. For each $1 \le \alpha \le \bar{\alpha}$, the segment $l_\alpha^\star = l_{m,\alpha,\beta}$ of $G^\star$ appears below $E_{G_\beta'}$ in exactly one interval, which is contained in the interior of the range corresponding to the first appearance of $l_{m-1,\alpha,\beta}$ in $E_{G_\beta'}$.*

Proof. First we claim that the slope of $l_\alpha^\star$ is larger than the slope of any segment in G_β'. Indeed, $l_\alpha^\star$ lies on a line that passes through a limited version of a copy of the original mth tube T_m of C; similarly, any segment of G_β' lies on a line that passes through a copy of some original tube T_d, for $d < m$. Thus conditions V3 and V4 for C imply that the slope of $l_\alpha^\star$ is larger than that of any segment of G_β'.

Let $\bar{S}$ be the portion of the sequence $U_{G_\beta'} = S_\beta'$ realized by the portion of $E_{G_\beta'}$ lying to the right of the starting point of $l_\alpha^\star$. Let x_1 be the x-coordinate of this starting point, and let x_2 be the x-coordinate of the crossing point of $l_\alpha^\star$ and of $l_{m-1,\alpha,\beta}$ (recall that, by our construction, this crossing point lies inside the outer frame of C_α'). Associate with $\bar{S}$ a sequence $\bar{I}$ of intervals on the x-axis, so that the jth interval I_j is the projection of the portion of $E_{G_\beta'}$ corresponding to the jth element of $\bar{S}$, with the exception that the first interval I_1 of $\bar{I}$ starts at x_2.

For $x_1 \leq x \leq x_2$, the segment $l_\alpha^\star$ lies below $l_{m-1,\alpha,\beta}$ and $l_{m-1,\alpha,\beta}$ is the lowest segment of G_β' there. Indeed each preceding segment l of G_β' either starts inside a preceding copy C_{α_1}' of C' or starts at the present copy $\bar{C}_\alpha'$ of C'. In the first case C_{α_1}' lies NW to $\bar{C}_\alpha'$ and since l has positive slope it must pass above the outer frame of C_α' and thus above $l_{m-1,\alpha,\beta}$. In the second case l must also be above $l_{m-1,\alpha,\beta}$ because their crossing point must be to the right of C_α' (by property P3A of G').

Thus, immediately after x_2, the lower envelope $E_{G_\beta' \cup \{l_\alpha^\star\}}$ is attained by $l_{m-1,\alpha,\beta}$ and $l_\alpha^\star$ lies above it. The proof now proceeds by induction on the elements in the sequence $\bar{S}$ (the first of which is clearly $(m-1,\alpha,\beta)$), and shows that, for each element s_j in $\bar{S}$, the segment l_{s_j} of G_β' lies below $l_\alpha^\star$ over the corresponding interval I_j. The base case $j = 1$ has just been observed, because $s_1 = (m-1,\alpha,\beta)$ and I_1 starts at x_2. Suppose the claim holds for all elements in $\bar{S}$ preceding the jth one, and let the jth element of $\bar{S}$ be the index σ of some segment l_σ of G_β'. $\bar{S}$ is the tail of $S' = S(k, m-1)$, and the proof depends on the place in S' in which the current appearance of σ takes place.

1. If this appearance is at a fan of S' then it comes after the αth fan, and by construction and by the NW to SE order of the frames of C_α', l_σ must appear below $l_\alpha^\star$ over the corresponding interval I_j (because l_σ starts at a point lying SE to the starting point of $l_\alpha^\star$, and $l_\alpha^\star$ has a slope greater than that of l_σ).

2. If this appearance of σ is at some later block of S', such that σ is not the first symbol of that block, then let the preceding symbol in that block be σ'. By the induction hypothesis, $l_{\sigma'}$ lies below $l_\alpha^\star$ over the corresponding interval I_{j-1}, and since $l_{\sigma'}$ crosses l_σ from below (by property P5 of G'), and the slopes of both $l_{\sigma'}$ and l_σ are smaller than the slope of $l_\alpha^\star$, it follows that l_σ must lie below $l_\alpha^\star$ over I_j.

3. Finally, suppose that the present appearance of σ is as the first symbol of some later block, which is not contained in a fan of S'. Then, by Theorem 2.20(d), σ also appears in S' before its current appearance so that no fan of S' lies between these two occurrences. In particular, σ has a preceding appearance in $\bar{S}$ as its ith element, for some $i < j$. By induction, l_σ lies below $l_\alpha^\star$ over I_i, and since $l_\alpha^\star$ has slope greater than that of l_σ, it continues to lie above l_σ also over I_j.

This completes the inductive proof of the lemma. □

We can now establish properties P1–P5 for G:

P1) $\bar{\gamma} = \bar{\alpha} \cdot \bar{\beta}$ copies of $\mathcal{C}$ are created in the double induction process. They are ordered NW to SE because each of the copies of $\mathcal{C}$ is ordered NW to SE inside each copy of $\mathcal{C}^\star$, which are themselves ordered NW to SE by property P1 of $G^\star$.

P2) G consists of

$$\bar{\beta} \cdot (m - 1)\bar{\alpha} + \bar{\alpha} C_{k-1}(\bar{\alpha}) = m \cdot C_k(m)$$

segments (as in the construction of $S(k, m)$), which are grouped into $\bar{\alpha} \cdot \bar{\beta} = \bar{\gamma}$ fans.

P2A) By induction, the starting point of each of the segments of G is inside its corresponding tube frame—the first induction substep implies this property for segments $l_{d,\gamma}$, for $d < m$; the second substep implies it for segments $l_{m,\gamma}$. Note that the construction did not change the tube frames in the original $\mathcal{C}(k, m)$.

P2B) Each segment $l_{d,\gamma}$, for $d < m$, lies on a line that passes through the corresponding tube, by the first induction substep, and each segment $l_{m,\gamma}$ lies on a line that passes through its corresponding tube, by the second induction substep. These tubes are just limited versions of the tubes in $\mathcal{C}(k, m)$, so all these segments lie on lines that pass through the corresponding original tubes.

P3) By property P3 of G'_β, all points in $\Pi_{CE}(G'_\beta)$ lie outside the x-range of any of the $\bar{\alpha}$ copies of the extended outer frame of $\mathcal{C}'$, and other crossing/ending points of segments of G'_β lie either above these extended frames or outside their x-ranges. Thus, in particular, property P3 also holds for the points in each $\Pi_{CE}(G'_\beta)$ with respect to the outer frames of the copies of $\mathcal{C}$.

By property P3 of $G^\star$, all points in $\Pi_{CE}(G^\star)$ lie outside the $\bar{\beta}$ copies of the outer frame of $\mathcal{C}^\star$, and any other crossing/ending points of segments of $G^\star$ lie either above these outer frames or outside their x-ranges. Thus again, these properties also hold for the outer frames of the copies of $\mathcal{C}$.

Thus the only type of points that still need to be considered are points on the envelope at which segments in $G^\star$ cross segments in some G'_β (call these X-points). However, by construction of $\mathcal{C}^\star$ and of G', there is only one such X-point inside the outer frame of each $\mathcal{C}'_\alpha$—namely the point in which $l_{m,\alpha,\beta}$ crosses $l_{m-1,\alpha,\beta}$. However, this point lies inside the corresponding quadrangle $A_1 A_2 D_2 D_1$ and thus outside the frame of the copy of $\mathcal{C}(k, m)$ from which this $\mathcal{C}'_\alpha$ is constructed (see Figure 4.7).

From this point on, the segment $l_{m,\alpha,\beta}$ of $G^\star$ does not cross $E_{G'_\beta}$ again (because of Lemma 4.5), and thus $l_{m,\alpha,\beta}$ does not pass below $E_{G'_\beta}$. Also, since $l_{m,\alpha,\beta}$ lies outside the outer frame of any copy of C^* other than the βth copy, and lies above all such subsequent copies, $l_{m,\alpha,\beta}$ cannot cross segments from any other G'_{β_1} (each contained inside one such frame).

P4) General properties:

P4A) G is contiguous since G^* is contiguous (by property P4A of G^*), each G'_β is contiguous (by property P4A of G'), and each G'_β has points common to G^*, e.g., the crossing point of $l_{m,\alpha,\beta}$ with $l_{m-1,\alpha,\beta}$, for any α.

P4B) $U_{G(k,m)} = S(k,m)$: Note that $U_{G'} = S'$ by property P4B of G', and $U_{G^*} = S^*$ by property P4B of G^*. By Lemma 4.5 and the construction of G^*, for each $1 \leq \beta \leq \bar{\beta}$, the parts of G^* seen inside the x-range of $E_{G'_\beta}$ are only the segments $l_{m,\alpha,\beta}$ (for $1 \leq \alpha \leq \bar{\alpha}$), each making a single appearance over an interval 'inserted into' the interior of the range of the initial appearance of its corresponding segment $l_{m-1,\alpha,\beta}$ (in the fan containing $l_{m-1,\alpha,\beta}$).

Thus, it is easily checked that the lower envelope $E_{G(k,m)}$ is such that:

1. Outside the outer frames of the copies of C^* (more precisely, outside the x-ranges of the copies G'_β of G'), E_G coincides with E_{G^*}.

2. Within the x-range of a copy G'_β of G', Lemma 4.5 implies that E_G is equal to $E_{G'_\beta}$, with each of the additional segments $l_{m,\alpha,\beta}$ making a single appearance at the 'end' of the corresponding fan, thereby splitting the range of the first appearance of the corresponding segment $l_{m-1,\alpha,\beta}$ into two subintervals. It is also easily checked, using property P3 of G^*, that the segment of G^* seen immediately to the right of the x-range of G'_β is the segment $l_{m,\bar{\alpha},\beta}$. Similarly, the segment of G^* seen immediately to the left of the x-range of G'_β is the segment immediately preceding (in E_{G^*}) the βth fan of G^* (in particular, no other segment of G^* has a lower y-value at the x-coordinate of the left edge of the outer frame of the βth copy C^*_β of C^*, and G'_β is still not defined for this value of x).

It therefore follows that $U_{G(k,m)}$ is constructed from $U_{G'} = S'$ and from $U_{G^*} = S^*$ in exactly the same way in which $S(k,m)$ is constructed from S' and from S^*, as described in Chapter 2. Hence $U_{G(k,m)} = S(k,m)$.

P5) In the first block after each fan of G, the slopes of the segments from $l_{m-1,\alpha,\beta}$ to $l_{1,\alpha,\beta}$ are arranged in decreasing order (by property P5 of G'). The segment $l_{m,\alpha,\beta}$ has a slope larger than that of $l_{m-1,\alpha,\beta}$, as has already been observed.

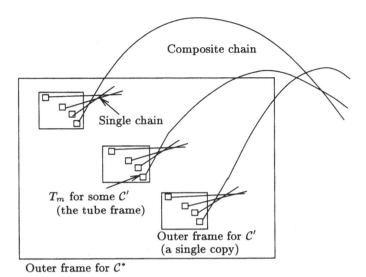

FIGURE 4.8. Overall construction.

The envelope E_G can be partitioned into modified copies $E_{G'_\beta}$ of $E_{G'}$ (in which the left endpoints of the segments in an appropriate fan of $G^\star$ pierce through the envelope), and into blocks of $G^\star$. By Lemma 4.5, the only change in the block structure of the various G'_β is the extension of each block immediately succeeding each of their fans. The preceding argument establishes property P5 for such blocks, and the induction hypothesis establishes property P5 for each of the remaining blocks of G. See Figure 4.8 for an illustration of the argument.

This completes the proof of the Realization Theorem 4.3.

4.2.6   Actual realizations

In order to actually create $G(k, m)$ we need to start the above inductive construction with some initial valid base constraint of size m. It is quite easy to construct such an initial constraint C (as in Figure 4.4), and we leave the details to the reader. Theorem 4.3 then implies the existence of a collection $G(k, m)$ of segments built on top of appropriate copies of C, which satisfies, among other properties, the desired equality $U_{G(k,m)} = S(k, m)$.

It is rather easy to modify the construction so that the starting points of the segments all lie on the line $\ell(x) = -x$ (or for that matter, an arbitrary line ℓ). We will call this construction an *anchored realization* of the sequence using the *anchor* ℓ.

To do this, for $\ell(x) = -x$, the definition of a valid constraint has to be slightly modified so that ℓ will have to cross the tubes of $C(k, m)$. The segments will be selected so as to start on the anchor ℓ. This is trivial to do for $k = 1$. We just have to modify the construction for the case $m = 1$, so as to ensure that the two copies of C created in the inductive generation of $G(k-1, 2)$ will be placed in the plane so that ℓ will cross the tubes in both constraints. The general case needs no modification—if each of the two steps in the inductive construction ensures that ℓ crosses all the tubes in all the copies of the respective induced constraints, it follows that the same holds for the resulting copies of the original constraint $C(k, m)$. For an arbitrary anchor line ℓ, take the construction just described and apply to it an appropriate affine transformation that will carry the anchor to ℓ.

This modified construction will also work for any segment or ray (half-line) ℓ—after creating the anchored realization whose anchor is the line ℓ' containing ℓ, we can apply an affine mapping to 'pack' $G(k, m)$ into the x-range of ℓ.

Once this is done, we can construct a realization of $S(k, m)$ whose anchor is an arbitrary curve $y = f(x)$ provided that the curve can be enclosed in the strip between two parallel nonvertical lines. This is done by first applying an affine transformation to 'squash' the curve so that it is contained in an ε-wide strip around a segment, ray, or line ℓ, by constructing a realization of $S(k, m)$ anchored on ℓ, by trimming the resulting segments so as to have their starting points lie on the image of $y = f(x)$, and finally by applying the inverse affine transformation to the resulting collection. This construction is feasible provided ε is small enough compared to the size of the tubes.

4.3   An alternative construction

In this section we construct another family of collections $G = G(k, m, r)$ of segments, so that the lower envelope of each G has $\Omega(|G|\alpha(|G|))$ subsegments. Here k and m are positive integers, and $r \geq 2$ is a real number. The sequence realized by the lower envelope of $G(k, m, r)$ is somewhat different from $S(k, m)$, but its length is also superlinear, as asserted.

The new construction uses a slightly different notion of a fan.

Definition 4.6 A *fan* of size m is a set of m segments with positive slopes and with a common left endpoint (see Figure 4.9). The common left endpoint will be referred to as the *fan point*.

The collection $G(k, m, r)$ will consist of $N_k(m)$ segments and will have $C_k(m)$ fans, where $C_k(m)$ and $N_k(m)$ are the functions defined in Section 2.3. We also denote by $\tilde{\sigma}_k(m)$ the number of subsegments forming the lower envelope of $G(k, m, r)$. Each fan in $G(k, m, r)$ will have size m, and every segment of $G(k, m, r)$ will be contained in a unique fan; thus $N_k(m) = mC_k(m)$, as

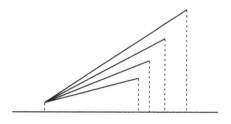

FIGURE 4.9. $G(1, 4, r)$.

in Section 2.3. The parameter r plays here a role similar to that of a valid constraint in the preceding construction: it is only used to enforce certain geometric properties on G, and does not affect the combinatorial properties of the lower envelope of G. That is why r does not appear in the expressions $C_k(m), N_k(m)$, and $\tilde{\sigma}_k(m)$.

For the construction to work, $G(k, m, r)$ has to satisfy the following three properties:

(a) The lower envelope of $G(k, m, r)$ is contiguous.

(b) The ratio between the slopes of any two adjacent segments in each fan is at least r.

(c) There exists a sufficiently small $0 < \varepsilon < 1$ (that depends on G), such that, if each segment of G is translated by some distance $\leq \varepsilon$, then the only changes in the lower envelope sequence of G occur in the immediate neighborhoods of fan points, and the only new elements that appear in the sequence over such a neighborhood are segments from the corresponding fan.

$G(k, m, r)$ is constructed by the usual double induction on k and m, as follows:

I. $k = 1$: $G(1, m, r)$ is a single fan of m segments. The lengths of the segments are chosen so that the right endpoint of the ith segment appears to the left of that of the $(i + 1)$st segment (as in Figure 4.9), and the slopes of the segments are chosen so as to satisfy condition (b). Condition (a) trivially holds, and condition (c) is also easily seen to hold if ε is chosen sufficiently small.

$G(1, m, r)$ has only $C_1(m) = 1$ fan of size m, it consists of $N_1(m) = m$ segments, and its lower envelope is composed of $\tilde{\sigma}_1(m) = m$ subsegments.

II. $k \geq 2, m = 1$: Construct inductively $G(k - 1, 2, r)$, and assume that it satisfies properties (a)–(c). Translate the second segment of each fan to the right by some small distance, not exceeding the ε provided by (c) for $G(k-1,2,r)$, so that both segments of each fan appear on the lower envelope near the former fan point (see Figure 4.10). By property (c) of $G(k-1,2,r)$, there is no other change in the lower envelope sequence of $G(k-1,2,r)$. The collection $G(k,1,r)$ is the modified $G(k-1,2,r)$, in which we treat each segment as a fan of size 1. Thus $G(k,1,r)$ has $2C_{k-1}(2) = C_k(1)$ fans, and consists of $N_{k-1}(2) = N_k(1)$ segments.

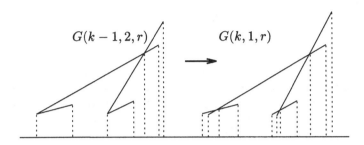

FIGURE 4.10. Alternative construction: the case $m = 1$.

For each fan of $G(k-1,2,r)$, the translation of its second segment creates two new subsegments in the lower envelope. Since $G(k-1,2,r)$ has $C_{k-1}(2)$ fans, the length of $G(k,1,r)$ is

$$\tilde{\sigma}_k(1) = \tilde{\sigma}_{k-1}(2) + 2C_{k-1}(2) = \tilde{\sigma}_{k-1}(2) + C_k(1).$$

It is easily checked that properties (a)–(c) hold for $G(k,1,r)$.

III. The general case $k > 1, m > 1$:

1. We inductively construct $G'(r) = G(k, m-1, r)$. It contains $\bar{\alpha} = C_k(m-1)$ fans of size $m-1$ and consists of $(m-1)\bar{\alpha}$ segments.

2. We apply an affine transformation $y \to cy$ on $G'(r)$, so that the transformed $G'(r)$ satisfies the following three conditions:

    (i) Any ray of slope ≥ 1 starting at a fan point of $G'(r)$ is not seen below $E_{G'(r)}$ in the x-range of this collection. (Note that if the lower envelope of $G'(r)$ were not contiguous, we could not have satisfied this condition.)

    (ii) Let (x_α, y_α) denote the coordinates of the fan point of the αth fan of $G'(r)$; then, for all $\alpha = 1, \ldots, \bar{\alpha}$,

    $$10|y_\alpha| < \min\{x_\alpha - x_{\alpha-1}, x_{\alpha+1} - x_\alpha\}. \qquad (4.1)$$

    (iii) The slope of every segment in $G'(r)$ is at most $1/r$.

    It is easily seen that these conditions will be satisfied if c is chosen sufficiently small.

3. Choose

$$r^* = \max \left\{ 2 + \max_{2 \leq \alpha \leq \bar{\alpha}-1} \frac{11}{9} \cdot \frac{x_{\alpha+1} - x_\alpha}{x_\alpha - x_{\alpha-1}}, \frac{10}{9} \cdot \frac{1}{x_{\bar{\alpha}} - x_{\bar{\alpha}-1}} \right\},$$
(4.2)

and construct inductively $G^*(r^*) = G(k - 1, \bar{\alpha}, r^*)$. The collection $G^*(r^*)$ has $\bar{\beta} = C_{k-1}(\bar{\alpha})$ fans of size $\bar{\alpha}$ and consists of $N_{k-1}(\bar{\alpha})$ segments.

4. Flatten $G^*(r^*)$ so that the maximum slope of a segment in $G^*(r^*)$ is at most $1/r^*$, and then apply the transformation $y \to x + y$ to make the slopes of all segments of $G^*(r^*)$ lie between 1 and $1+1/r^*$.

5. We now scale down $G'(r)$ so as to obtain a homothetic copy for which the length of the x-range of its lower envelope becomes shorter than $\varepsilon^*/2$, where ε^* is the value of ε provided by property (c) of $G^*(r^*)$. For each fan f of $G^*(r^*)$, we place this 'microscopic' copy of $G'(r)$ so that its leftmost point coincides with the fan point of f. Finally, we translate each segment of f (by some appropriate distance $\leq \varepsilon^*/2$) so that the left endpoint of the αth segment of f coincides with the fan point of the αth fan of the corresponding copy of $G'(r)$. See Figure 4.11.

6. $G(k, m, r)$ is the union of $G^*(r^*)$ and of the $\bar{\beta}$ copies of $G'(r)$, with the modifications described above.

Thus each fan of $G(k, m, r)$ comes from a fan of a copy of $G'(r)$ (extended by one segment of $G^*(r^*)$) and each segment of $G(k, m, r)$ comes either from $G^*(r^*)$ or from some copy of $G'(r)$. Since there are $\bar{\beta}$ copies of $G'(r)$, it follows that $G(k, m, r)$ has $\bar{\alpha} \cdot \bar{\beta} = C_k(m)$ fans, and consists of $N_{k-1}(\bar{\alpha}) + \bar{\beta} \cdot N_k(m - 1) = N_k(m)$ segments.

Lemma 4.7 $G(k, m, r)$ *satisfies properties (a)–(c).*

Proof. We use the same double induction on k and m. The base cases $G(1, m, r)$ and $G(k, 1, r)$ have been handled above, so it suffices to consider the general case $k > 1, m > 1$. Since the lower envelopes of $G'(r)$ and of $G^*(r^*)$ are contiguous, by induction, and for each copy of $G'(r)$ there is a vertical line intersecting both envelopes of this copy and of $G^*(r^*)$, the lower envelope of $G(k, m, r)$ is also contiguous.

The affine transformation of Step 2 does not change the ratios between slopes of the segments of $G'(r)$; since every segment of the transformed $G'(r)$ has slope $\leq 1/r$ and every segment of $G^*(r^*)$ has slope ≥ 1, the induction hypothesis clearly implies that property (b) holds for $G(k, m, r)$.

Observe that, even after Steps 1–5, there is an ε' for which every microscopic copy of $G'(r)$ satisfies property (c). Similarly, there is an ε^* for which $G^*(r^*)$ satisfies property (c). This, and the manner in which the segments of

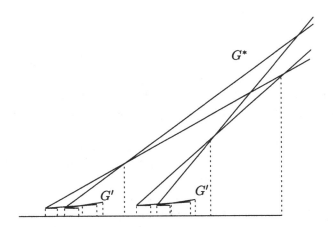

FIGURE 4.11. Alternative construction: The general case.

$G^*(r^*)$ are moved in Step 5, are easily seen to imply that $G(k, m, r)$ satisfies property (c) with $\varepsilon < \min\{\varepsilon', \varepsilon^*/2\}$.

Hence, $G(k, m, r)$ satisfies properties (a)–(c) for all k and m. $\qquad\square$

Before estimating the value of $\tilde{\sigma}_k(m)$, we need to prove the following lemma.

Lemma 4.8 *In $G(k, m, r)$, after every copy of $G'(r)$, the shifted segments of the corresponding fan of $G^*(r^*)$ appear in the lower envelope in the reverse order.*

Proof. The proof of this lemma follows from the following two claims, for each fan f of $G^*(r^*)$:

(i) After translating the segments of f in step 5 of the construction, the intersection point of the αth and $(\alpha + 1)$st segments of f appears to the left of the intersection of the αth and $(\alpha - 1)$st segments of f, for $\alpha = 2, 3, \ldots, \bar{\alpha} - 1$.

(ii) The last segment of f appears in the lower envelope immediately after the corresponding copy of $G'(r)$.

Consider the first claim, and let us denote the $(\alpha - 1)$st, αth, and $(\alpha + 1)$st segments of f as $\ell_{\alpha-1}, \ell_\alpha$, and $\ell_{\alpha+1}$, respectively. Let s_j denote the slope of ℓ_j, and let d_j be the horizontal distance between the left endpoints of ℓ_{j+1} and ℓ_j. Assume, without loss of generality, that the left endpoint of ℓ_α is the origin. By our construction, the left endpoints of $\ell_{\alpha-1}$ and $\ell_{\alpha+1}$ are very close to the x-axis (see (4.1)). Let ζ (respectively, η) be the intersection point of

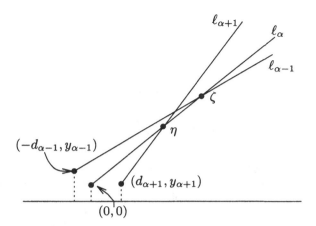

FIGURE 4.12. Illustration of Lemma 4.8.

$l_{\alpha-1}$ and l_α (respectively, of l_α and $l_{\alpha+1}$); see Figure 4.12. Then

$$\begin{aligned}
y_\zeta &= x_\zeta \cdot s_\alpha = (x_\zeta + d_{\alpha-1}) \cdot s_{\alpha-1} + y_{\alpha-1} \\
y_\eta &= x_\eta \cdot s_\alpha = (x_\eta - d_\alpha) \cdot s_{\alpha+1} + y_{\alpha+1},
\end{aligned}$$

which implies

$$x_\zeta = \frac{d_{\alpha-1}s_{\alpha-1} + y_{\alpha-1}}{s_\alpha - s_{\alpha-1}}, \quad x_\eta = \frac{d_\alpha s_{\alpha+1} - y_{\alpha+1}}{s_{\alpha+1} - s_\alpha}. \tag{4.3}$$

Since $x_\zeta, x_\eta > 0$, it suffices to show that $x_\zeta/x_\eta > 1$. We have

$$\frac{x_\zeta}{x_\eta} = \frac{d_{\alpha-1}s_{\alpha-1} + y_{\alpha-1}}{d_\alpha s_{\alpha+1} - y_{\alpha+1}} \cdot \frac{s_{\alpha+1} - s_\alpha}{s_\alpha - s_{\alpha-1}}.$$

Let s'_j be the slope of l_j before applying the transformation $y \to x + y$; then $s_j = 1 + s'_j$ and $s'_j/s'_{j-1} \geq r^*$, which implies

$$\frac{s_{\alpha+1} - s_\alpha}{s_\alpha - s_{\alpha-1}} = \frac{s'_{\alpha+1} - s'_\alpha}{s'_\alpha - s'_{\alpha-1}} > \frac{s'_{\alpha+1} - s'_\alpha}{s'_\alpha} \geq r^* - 1.$$

By (4.1) and the fact that $1 \leq s_j \leq 1 + \frac{1}{r^*}$, we obtain

$$\begin{aligned}
\frac{d_{\alpha-1}s_{\alpha-1} + y_{\alpha-1}}{d_\alpha s_{\alpha+1} - y_{\alpha+1}} &\geq \frac{d_{\alpha-1}s_{\alpha-1} - d_{\alpha-1}/10}{d_\alpha s_{\alpha+1} + d_\alpha/10} \\
&\geq \frac{d_{\alpha-1}}{d_\alpha} \cdot \frac{9/10}{11/10 + 1/r^*}.
\end{aligned}$$

Furthermore, by (4.2),

$$\frac{d_{\alpha-1}}{d_\alpha} \geq \frac{11}{9(r^* - 2)}.$$

Hence

$$\frac{x_\zeta}{x_\eta} > \frac{11}{9(r^* - 2)} \cdot \frac{9}{11 + 10/r^*} \cdot (r^* - 1)$$

$$= \frac{11r^*(r^* - 1)}{(11r^* + 10)(r^* - 2)} > 1.$$

This completes the proof of the first claim. We now prove the second claim, i.e., that the $\bar{\alpha}$th segment of f appears in the lower envelope immediately after the corresponding copy of $G'(r)$. Following the same notation as above and setting $\alpha = \bar{\alpha} - 1$, it suffices to show that $x_\eta > \varepsilon^*$, because the length of the x-range of the lower envelope of $G'(r)$ is at most $\varepsilon^*/2$. By (4.3),

$$x_\eta = \frac{d_{\bar{\alpha}-1}s_{\bar{\alpha}} - y_{\bar{\alpha}}}{s_{\bar{\alpha}} - s_{\bar{\alpha}-1}} \geq \frac{9}{10}d_{\bar{\alpha}-1} \cdot r^*,$$

because $1 \leq s_{\bar{\alpha}-1} < s_{\bar{\alpha}} \leq 1 + 1/r*$ and $|y_{\bar{\alpha}}| \leq d_{\bar{\alpha}-1}/10$. By (4.2), we have $x_\eta \geq 1 > \varepsilon^*$. $\square$

We now analyze the combinatorial complexity of the lower envelope of $G(k, m, r)$.

Theorem 4.9 *For* $k, m \geq 1$,

$$\tilde{\sigma}_k(m) \geq \frac{1}{2}km \cdot C_k(m).$$

Proof. The above construction gives the following recurrence for $\tilde{\sigma}_k(m)$:

$$\begin{aligned}
\tilde{\sigma}_1(m) &= m, & m \geq 1, \\
\tilde{\sigma}_k(1) &= \tilde{\sigma}_{k-1}(2) + C_k(1), & k > 1, \\
\tilde{\sigma}_k(m) &= \tilde{\sigma}_{k-1}(\bar{\alpha}) + \tilde{\sigma}_k(m-1) \cdot \bar{\beta} + \frac{1}{2}C_k(m), & k > 1, m > 1.
\end{aligned}$$

The first two equations have already been noted. To see the third equation, condition (c) for $G^*(r^*)$ implies that all transition points of the lower envelope of $G^*(r^*)$ appear in the lower envelope of $G(k, m, r)$, and condition (i) of Step 1 implies that all transition points of the lower envelope of each copy of $G'(r)$ also appear in the lower envelope of $G(k, m, r)$. By Lemma 4.8, each fan of $G^*(r^*)$ contributes $\bar{\alpha} - 1$ additional transition points, so the total number of new transition points is $(\bar{\alpha} - 1)\bar{\beta} \geq C_k(m)/2$. The third equation is now immediate. The proof now follows from the following lemma, which is a variant of Lemma 2.23. $\square$

Lemma 4.10 *Let* $\tilde{Z}_k(m) = \dfrac{\tilde{\sigma}_k(m)}{C_k(m)}$. *Then, for* $k, m \geq 1$, *we have*

$$\tilde{Z}_k(m) \geq \frac{1}{2}km.$$

Proof. By double induction on k and m. For $k = 1$, we have

$$\tilde{Z}_1(m) \;=\; \frac{\tilde{\sigma}_1(m)}{C_1(m)} \;=\; m \;\geq\; \frac{1}{2} \cdot m.$$

For $k > 1, m = 1$, we have

$$
\begin{aligned}
\tilde{Z}_k(1) \;&=\; \frac{\tilde{\sigma}_k(1)}{C_k(1)} \\
&=\; \frac{\tilde{\sigma}_{k-1}(2) + C_k(1)}{C_k(1)} \\
&=\; \frac{\tilde{\sigma}_{k-1}(2)}{2C_{k-1}(2)} + 1 \\
&\geq\; \frac{1}{2} \cdot \frac{1}{2} \cdot 2(k-1) + 1 \\
&\qquad \text{(by the induction hypothesis)} \\
&\geq\; \frac{1}{2} \cdot k.
\end{aligned}
$$

Finally, for $k, m > 1$, we have

$$
\begin{aligned}
\tilde{Z}_k(m) \;&=\; \frac{\tilde{\sigma}_k(m)}{C_k(m)} \\
&=\; \frac{\tilde{\sigma}_{k-1}(\bar{\alpha}) + \bar{\beta}\tilde{\sigma}_k(m-1) + \frac{1}{2}\bar{\alpha} \cdot \bar{\beta}}{\bar{\alpha}\bar{\beta}} \\
&=\; \frac{\tilde{\sigma}_k(m-1)}{C_k(m-1)} + \frac{\tilde{\sigma}_{k-1}(\bar{\alpha})}{\bar{\alpha}C_{k-1}(\bar{\alpha})} + \frac{1}{2} \\
&=\; \tilde{Z}_k(m-1) + \frac{\tilde{Z}_{k-1}(\bar{\alpha})}{\bar{\alpha}} + \frac{1}{2} \\
&\geq\; \frac{1}{2} \cdot k(m-1) + \frac{1}{2\bar{\alpha}} \cdot (k-1)\bar{\alpha} + \frac{1}{2} \\
&\qquad \text{(by the induction hypothesis)} \\
&=\; \frac{1}{2}\Big[k(m-1) + (k-1) + 1\Big] \\
&=\; \frac{1}{2} \cdot km.
\end{aligned}
$$

This completes the proof.   □

Following the same argument as in Theorem 2.22 and Corollary 2.24, we thus conclude:

Theorem 4.11 *For any integer n, we can obtain, using the new construction, a collection of n line segments in the plane, whose lower envelope consists of $\Omega(n\alpha(n))$ subsegments.*

4.4   Discussion

The result established in this chapter, that superlinear Davenport–Schinzel sequences of order 3 can be realized as lower envelope sequences of collections of line segments, is perhaps the most surprising and intriguing property of these sequences. Among other things, it provides a natural construction of simple geometric objects that give rise to the inverse Ackermann's function $\alpha(n)$. Philosophically speaking, one can regard it as evidence that the inverse Ackermann's function does "exist in nature," and is not just a technical tool used in logic and in the analysis of certain algorithms.

The results of this chapter provide superlinear lower bounds (which are often tight) for a variety of problems in combinatorial geometry. Several of these problems will be presented in the following chapters.

Our results still leave many challenging open problems. First of all, we have only shown that certain superlinear $DS(n,3)$-sequences can be realized by segments. Can every such sequence arise as the lower envelope sequence of an appropriate collection of segments? We suspect that this is not true, intuitively because there appears to be too much freedom in generating such sequences.

Another open problem is to construct geometric realization of higher-order Davenport–Schinzel sequences by collections of arcs or curves having simple shape. For example, can one realize $DS(n,4)$-sequences of length $\Theta(n \cdot 2^{\alpha(n)})$ as the lower envelope sequences of collections of n circular arcs? of n parabolic arcs? of n full quartic curves (namely graphs of functions $y = P(x)$, where P is a fourth-degree polynomial)? Our constructions fall short of achieving this.

Another line of further research is to find conditions on a given collection of line segments that will ensure that its lower envelope sequence has only linear size, or has complexity that is smaller than $\Theta(n\alpha(n))$. We mention here three examples of this kind.

1. If instead of segments we are given a collection of rays, then it is easy to show that the lower envelope has only linear complexity. In fact, this also holds for the complexity of any single face in an arrangement of rays—see Chapter 5 for more details.

2. Suppose we require that all given segments have both their endpoints lie on some fixed convex curve γ, for example, on a lower semicircle. What is the complexity of their lower envelope? The anchored construction mentioned at the end of Section 4.2 can only enforce the left endpoint

of each segment to lie on γ. Can the construction be modified so as to make both endpoints lie on γ?

3. Suppose that the n given segments compose the graphs of $t \ll n$ piecewise linear functions. Corollary 1.14 implies that the complexity of their lower envelope is $O(n\alpha(t))$. The constructions of this chapter show that this bound is tight in the worst case: Let $G = \{e_1, \ldots, e_t\}$ be a set of t segments, whose lower envelope has complexity $\Omega(t\alpha(t))$. Create $\lfloor n/t \rfloor$ translated copies, $G_1, \ldots, G_{n/t}$, of G, having pairwise-disjoint x-ranges; denote by e_{ij} the translated copy of e_i in G_j, for $i = 1, \ldots, t$, $j = 1, \ldots, \lfloor n/t \rfloor$. For each $i = 1, \ldots, t$, define a piecewise-linear function f_i, whose graph is $\bigcup_{j=1}^{n/t} e_{ij}$. We have a collection of t piecewise-linear functions, whose graphs consist of a total of at most n segments, and the complexity of their lower envelope is clearly

$$\lfloor n/t \rfloor \cdot \Omega(t\alpha(t)) = \Omega(n\alpha(t)) \ .$$

(The functions f_i are not continuous, but, if so desired, we can make each of them continuous by connecting between the segments within a single graph by sufficiently steep additional segments; this increases the overall number of segments by only a constant factor, and does not decrease the complexity of their lower envelope.)

We conclude with the following beautiful open problem posed by Tamir (1988). Let $\mathcal{L} = \{\ell_1, \ldots, \ell_n\}$ be a collection of n lines in the plane. With each $\ell_i \in \mathcal{L}$ we associate a time interval $[s_i, t_i]$. We maintain dynamically, over time, the lower envelope of the lines in $\mathcal{L}$, as follows. We proceed through the time axis from left to right. We start the process with an empty collection of lines. When we reach the left endpoint s_i of the interval of ℓ_i we add ℓ_i to the current collection, and when we reach t_i we remove ℓ_i. At any time t we maintain the lower envelope of the lines in the current collection. The problem is to obtain tight bounds for the maximum number of pairs (ℓ_i, ℓ_j) whose intersection point appears along the lower envelope at some time t (we count such an intersection only once, even if it appears and disappears from the envelope several times). Tamir has shown that the complexity in question lies between $O(n \log n)$ and $\Omega(n\alpha(n))$. The lower bound is a consequence of the constructions in this chapter. Specifically, if we take each segment l of $G(k, m)$, extend it to a full line $\tilde{l}$, and associate with $\tilde{l}$ the time interval $[s, t]$, where s and t are the x-coordinates of the endpoints of l, then it can be shown that every vertex of $E_{G(k,m)}$, excluding segment endpoints, also appears as a vertex in the dynamic lower envelope of the lines $\tilde{l}$. What is the true asymptotic growth of the complexity in question?

4.5   Bibliographic notes

The construction given in Section 4.2 is due to Wiernik and Sharir (1988). It was the first geometric realization of superlinear Davenport–Schinzel sequences. The simpler construction described in Section 4.3 is by Shor (1990). Shor (1994) has also produced realizations of superlinear $DS(n, 3)$-sequences as lower envelopes of other kinds of curves, such as parabolic arcs or full quartic curves. However, these results are less exciting, since the upper bound for the complexity of the envelopes of such curves is $\lambda_4(n)$, so the lower bound $\lambda_3(n)$ that Shor's extended construction provides is not tight.

5

PLANAR ARRANGEMENTS

5.1 Introduction

In this chapter we consider certain topological extensions of the lower envelope problem, where Davenport–Schinzel sequences still play a major role in their analysis. Specifically, let $\Gamma = \{\gamma_1, \ldots, \gamma_n\}$ be a collection of n Jordan arcs in the plane, with the property that each pair of them intersect in at most s points, for some fixed constant s.[1]

Definition 5.1 The *arrangement* $\mathcal{A}(\Gamma)$ of Γ is the planar subdivision induced by the arcs of Γ; that is, $\mathcal{A}(\Gamma)$ is a planar map whose *vertices* are the endpoints of the arcs of Γ and their pairwise intersection points, whose *edges* are maximal (open) connected portions of the γ_i's that do not contain a vertex, and whose *faces* are the connected components of $\mathbb{R}^2 - \bigcup \Gamma$.

The total combinatorial complexity of $\mathcal{A}(\Gamma)$ (i.e., the number of vertices, edges, and faces of $\mathcal{A}(\Gamma)$) is clearly at most $O(sn^2)$, and this bound is generally tight, but, as will be shown in this chapter, the combinatorial complexity of any single face f of $\mathcal{A}(\Gamma)$ (that is, the total number of vertices and edges of

---

[1] A *Jordan arc* is an image of the closed unit interval under a continuous bijective mapping. Similarly, a *closed Jordan curve* is an image of the unit circle under a similar mapping, and an *unbounded Jordan curve* is an image of the open unit interval (or of the entire real line) that separates the plane.

$\mathcal{A}(\Gamma)$ along the boundary of f) is only $O(\lambda_{s+2}(n))$. This result plainly extends Corollary 1.6; indeed, if all the given arcs are x–monotone, then their lower envelope is a portion of the boundary of the unbounded face of $\mathcal{A}(\Gamma)$, so Corollary 1.6 follows easily from this result. If the γ_i's are closed (or unbounded) Jordan curves then we show that the complexity of a single face of $\mathcal{A}$ is only $\lambda_s(n)$. This latter result constitutes a similar extension of Corollary 1.3.

The proofs of these topological generalizations are more complicated, due to the potentially more complex structure of the boundary of a face of $\mathcal{A}(\Gamma)$, as compared with the structure of the lower envelope of monotone arcs. Still, the main idea in the proofs is quite simple; that is, we show that the sequence in which the given arcs appear along the face boundary is a Davenport–Schinzel sequence of an appropriate order, although certain transformations have to be applied to facilitate this property.

The second result derived in this chapter is a bound on the complexity of a *zone* in an arrangement of Jordan arcs.

Definition 5.2   Given a collection Γ as above, and another curve γ_0, the *zone* of γ_0 in $\mathcal{A}(\Gamma)$ is the set of all faces of $\mathcal{A}(\Gamma)$ that are crossed by γ_0. The complexity of the zone is the sum of the complexities of all the faces in the zone.

Zones have been studied extensively for arrangements of lines (see Edelsbrunner (1987)) but have only recently been extended to arrangements of arcs. We will show that the complexity of a zone of a curve γ_0 in $\mathcal{A}(\Gamma)$ is also $O(\lambda_{s+2}(n))$, where s is the maximum number of intersection points between any two arcs of Γ, provided that γ_0 intersects each arc of Γ in a constant number of points (possibly larger than s).

The third result derived in this chapter concerns *levels* in an arrangement of Jordan curves. The level of a point in such an arrangement is the number of curves that lie below it. Using a probabilistic analysis technique, we show that the maximum number of vertices of $\mathcal{A}(\Gamma)$, with Γ as above, that lie at level $\leq k$ is $O((k+1)^2 \lambda_s(n/(k+1)))$.

5.2   Complexity of a single face

In this section we obtain an almost-linear upper bound on the combinatorial complexity of a single face of $\mathcal{A}(\Gamma)$, where Γ is a collection of n Jordan arcs in the plane, as in the previous section. We first consider the case of Jordan arcs, and in the following subsection we obtain a slightly improved bound for the case of closed or unbounded Jordan curves.

5.2.1   The case of Jordan arcs

Theorem 5.3 *Under the assumptions made in the beginning of the chapter, the combinatorial complexity of any single face of $\mathcal{A}(\Gamma)$ is $O(\lambda_{s+2}(n))$.*

Proof. Let f be the given face, and let C be a connected component of its boundary. It suffices to show that, if k arcs of Γ appear along C, then the number of subarcs of these arcs that constitute C is $O(\lambda_{s+2}(k))$. This follows from the easy observation that an arc cannot appear along two disjoint boundary components of the same face. Thus, without loss of generality, we can assume that all n arcs of Γ appear along C. For each γ_i, let u_i, v_i be its endpoints. Let γ_i^+ (respectively, γ_i^-) be the directed arc γ_i oriented from u_i to v_i (respectively, from v_i to u_i).

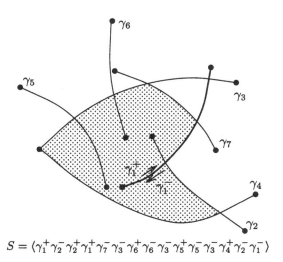

$$S = \langle \gamma_1^+ \gamma_2^- \gamma_2^+ \gamma_1^+ \gamma_7^- \gamma_3^- \gamma_6^+ \gamma_6^- \gamma_3^- \gamma_5^+ \gamma_5^- \gamma_3^- \gamma_4^+ \gamma_2^- \gamma_1^- \rangle$$

FIGURE 5.1. A single face and its associated boundary sequence; all arcs are positively oriented from left to right.

Without loss of generality, assume C is the exterior boundary component of f. Traverse C in counterclockwise direction (so that f lies to our left) and let $S = \langle s_1, s_2, \ldots, s_t \rangle$ be the circular sequence of oriented curves in Γ in the order in which they appear along C (if C is unbounded, S is a linear, rather than circular, sequence). More precisely, if during our traversal of C we encounter a curve γ_i and follow it in the direction from u_i to v_i (respectively, from v_i to u_i) then we add γ_i^+ (respectively, γ_i^-) to S. As an example, if the endpoint u_i of γ_i is on C and is not incident to any other arc, then traversing C past u_i will add the pair of elements γ_i^-, γ_i^+ to S, and symmetrically for v_i. See Figure 5.1 for an illustration. Note that in this example *both* sides of an arc γ_i might belong to our connected component.

In the analysis we will use the following notation. We denote the oriented arcs of Γ as $\xi_1, \ldots, \xi_{2n}$. For each ξ_i we denote by $|\xi_i|$ the nonoriented arc γ_j coinciding with ξ_i. For the purpose of the proof we transform each arc γ_i into a very thin closed Jordan curve $\gamma_i^\star$ by taking two nonintersecting copies of γ_i lying very close to one another, and by joining them at their endpoints. This will perturb the face f slightly but can always be done in such a way that the combinatorial complexity of C does not decrease. Note that this transformation allows a natural identification of one of the two sides of $\gamma_i^\star$ with γ_i^+ and the other side with γ_i^-.

The proof now follows from the next two lemmas, which imply that $|S| = O(\lambda_{s+2}(4n)) = O(\lambda_{s+2}(n))$. $\qquad\qquad\qquad\qquad\qquad\qquad\qquad\qquad\qquad\qquad\qquad\qquad\qquad$ $\square$

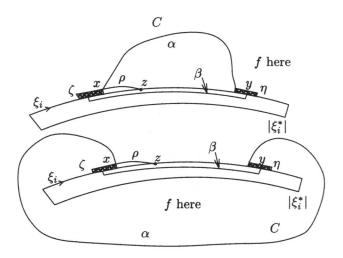

FIGURE 5.2. Proof of the Consistency Lemma.

Lemma 5.4 (Consistency Lemma) *The portions of each arc ξ_i appear in S in a circular order that is consistent with their order along the oriented ξ_i. That is, there exists a starting point in S (which depends on ξ_i) such that if we read S in circular order starting from that point, we encounter these portions in their order along ξ_i.*

Proof. Let ζ, η be two portions of ξ_i that appear consecutively along C in this order (i.e., no other portion of ξ_i appears along C between ζ and η). Choose two points $x \in \zeta$ and $y \in \eta$ and connect them by the portion α of C traversed from x to y, and by another arc β within the interior of $|\xi_i|^\star$; see Figure 5.2. Clearly, α and β do not intersect (except at their endpoints) and they are both contained in the complement of (the interior of) f. Thus their union $\alpha \cup \beta$ is a closed Jordan curve and f is fully contained either in its exterior or in its interior. We claim that any point on ξ_i between ζ and η is contained in the side of $\alpha \cup \beta$ that does not contain f. Indeed, connect such a point z to x along an arc ρ that proceeds very near ξ_i along the exterior of $|\xi_i|^*$ (see Figure 5.2). Clearly, ρ and β are disjoint, and, deforming α slightly as necessary, we can assume that ρ intersects α transversally and exactly once, which is easily seen to imply our claim. This claim completes the proof of the lemma. $\square$

For each directed arc ξ_i, consider the linear sequence V_i of all appearances of ξ_i in S, arranged in the order they appear along ξ_i. Let μ_i and ν_i denote respectively the index in S of the first and of the last element of V_i. Consider $S = \langle s_1, \ldots, s_t \rangle$ as a linear, rather than a circular, sequence (this change is not needed if C is unbounded). For each arc ξ_i, if $\mu_i > \nu_i$ we split the symbol ξ_i into two distinct symbols ξ_{i1}, ξ_{i2}, and replace all appearances of ξ_i in S between the places μ_i and t (respectively, between 1 and ν_i) by ξ_{i1} (respectively, by ξ_{i2}). (Note that Lemma 5.4 implies that we can actually split the arc ξ_i into two connected subarcs, so that all appearances of ξ_{i1} in the resulting sequence represent portions of the first subarc, whereas all appearances of ξ_{i2} represent portions of the second subarc.) This splitting produces a sequence S^*, of the same length as S, composed of at most $4n$ symbols.

Lemma 5.5 S^* *is a* $(4n, s + 2)$ *Davenport–Schinzel sequence.*

Proof. Since it is clear that no two adjacent elements of S^* can be equal, it remains to show that S^* does not contain an alternating subsequence of the form $\langle \zeta \cdots \eta \cdots \zeta \cdots \eta \cdots \rangle$ of length $s + 4$. Suppose to the contrary that S^* does contain such an alternation, and consider any four consecutive elements of this alternation, which, without loss of generality, can be assumed to be $\langle \zeta \cdots \eta \cdots \zeta \cdots \eta \rangle$. Choose points $x, y \in \zeta$ and points $z, w \in \eta$ so that C passes through these points in the order x, z, y, w. Consider the following six Jordan arcs (see Figure 5.3):

$\beta_{xy} = $ an arc within the interior of $|\zeta|^*$ connecting x to y;

$\beta_{zw} = $ an arc within the interior of $|\eta|^*$ connecting z to w;

$\beta_{xz} = $ the portion of C traversed in counterclockwise direction from x to z;

$\beta_{zy} = $ the portion of C traversed in counterclockwise direction from z to y;

$\beta_{yw} = $ the portion of C traversed in counterclockwise direction from y to w.

$\beta_{wx} = $ the portion of C traversed in counterclockwise direction from w to x.

Note that, except for common endpoints, $\beta_{xz}, \beta_{zy}, \beta_{yw}, \beta_{wx}$ are pairwise nonintersecting and also that they do not intersect β_{xy}, β_{zw}. We claim that β_{xy} and β_{zw} must intersect one another. Suppose the contrary, and consider the planar graph composed of these six arcs as edges. Choose a point u in the interior of f and connect it to x, y, z, w by four arcs having pairwise disjoint relative interiors which are contained in f. The resulting graph is a plane embedding of K_5, a contradiction that implies that β_{xy} and β_{zw} do indeed intersect. (The argument given here assumes that C is bounded, but an appropriate modification of the proof works in the unbounded case as well.)

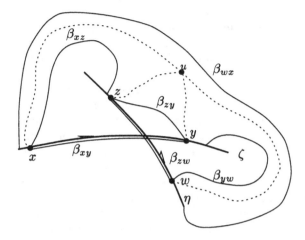

FIGURE 5.3. The structure of an alternation $\langle \zeta \cdots \eta \cdots \zeta \cdots \eta \rangle$.

This shows that each quadruple of consecutive elements in our alternation induces at least one intersection point between the corresponding arcs $\beta_{xy} \subset \zeta$ and $\beta_{zw} \subset \eta$. Moreover, it easily follows from the Consistency Lemma that for any pair of distinct quadruples of this type, either the two corresponding subarcs of the form β_{xy} along ζ are disjoint, or the two subarcs β_{zw} along η are disjoint. Thus all these intersections between ζ and η must be distinct. Since the number of such quadruples is $s + 4 - 3 = s + 1$, we obtain $s + 1$ points of intersection between ζ and η, a contradiction that completes the proof of the lemma, and thus also of Theorem 5.3. □

Remark 5.6 Applying our theorem to the case where each γ_i is a line segment, we obtain an upper bound of $O(\lambda_3(n)) = O(n\alpha(n))$ on the complexity of a single face of $\mathcal{A}(\Gamma)$. The results described in the previous chapter imply that this bound is tight in the worst case.

5.2.2 The case of Jordan curves

If the given arcs γ_i are actually closed (or unbounded) Jordan curves, we can obtain a slight improvement of the above bound. That is:

Theorem 5.7 *The combinatorial complexity of a single face in an arrangement of n closed (or unbounded) Jordan curves in the plane, each pair of which intersect in at most s points, is at most $\lambda_s(n)$.*

Proof. We will give the proof for the case of closed Jordan curves, and then comment on the modifications needed for the more general case. In the case of closed curves, we may assume that s is even, if we exclude degenerate configurations in which curves meet nontransversally. Such degeneracies can be handled by slightly perturbing the curves so as to remove any nontransversal intersection in a manner that does not decrease the combinatorial complexity of the given face.

Consider the circular sequence S of arcs appearing along a component C of the boundary of the given face f, as defined above; here we do not orient the arcs of Γ, so S is composed of at most n symbols. We claim that, for each i and j, the maximum length of any alternating subsequence $\langle \gamma_i \cdots \gamma_j \cdots \gamma_i \cdots \gamma_j \cdots \rangle$ of S is $s + 1$, from which the theorem follows by definition of Davenport–Schinzel sequences.

Clearly, there exists some simple arc π lying along the union $\bigcup_{k \neq i,j} \gamma_k$ that connects γ_i and γ_j and that has no points other than its endpoints in common with γ_i or γ_j; if γ_i and γ_j have any intersection, π is simply taken to be null. Let Δ be the component of $\mathbb{R}^2 - (\gamma_i \cup \gamma_j \cup \pi)$ that contains f. Since the boundary of Δ is connected, Δ is simply connected. Let S_0 denote the circular sequence composed of the three symbols γ_i, γ_j, π, obtained as we trace the boundary of Δ in counterclockwise order. Note that if π is nonnull, S_0 has at most one occurrence of γ_i (respectively, of γ_j), whereas if π is null, S_0 has at most s elements, alternating between γ_i and γ_j.

Plainly, any portion of γ_i or of γ_j that appears along C must also appear along $\partial\Delta$, and the Consistency Lemma implies that the (circular) order of these portions along C coincides with their circular order along $\partial\Delta$. Suppose to the contrary that S contains an alternation of γ_i, γ_j of length $s + 2$. Then this alternation must correspond to a similar alternation occurring along $\partial\Delta$. This, however, is impossible, because S_0 has at most s elements and s is even. (Note that an (odd) alternation of $s + 1$ elements along $\partial\Delta$ is possible, as the first and last elements of such an alternation could lie on the same arc of $\partial\Delta$.) This contradiction completes the proof for the case of closed Jordan curves.

If some (or all) of the curves in Γ are unbounded, then s can be either even or odd, and S_0 may consist of $s + 1$, rather than s, elements. However, if S_0 does consist of $s + 1$ elements then it is easily verified that $\partial\Delta$ must be unbounded, in which case an alternation of γ_i and γ_j of length $s + 2$ along $\partial\Delta$ is still impossible. With these observations, the proof proceeds in much the same way as above. $\square$

As a corollary, we obtain:

Theorem 5.8 *Let* $\gamma_1, \ldots, \gamma_n$ *be* n *closed Jordan curves in the plane such that any pair of them have at most* s *intersection points, for some* $s \geq 2$, *all transversal. Let* $K = \text{conv}(\gamma_1 \cup \cdots \cup \gamma_n)$ *be the convex hull of the arcs in* Γ, *that is, the smallest convex set that contains all arcs of* Γ. *Divide the boundary* *of K into disjoint maximal subarcs, $\alpha_1, \alpha_2, \ldots, \alpha_m$, such that the interior of each α_i has a nonempty intersection with exactly one of the curves γ_j. Then the number m of such arcs is at most $\lambda_s(n)$.*

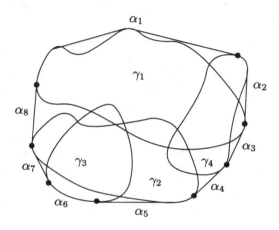

FIGURE 5.4. Illustration to the proof of Theorem 5.8.

Proof. It is easily checked that such a decomposition of the boundary of K is always possible. Label each of the arcs α_i by the curve γ_j that it intersects, and consider the circular sequence S of labels that we encounter by tracing ∂K in, say, a clockwise direction (see Figure 5.4). By definition, S has no adjacent equal elements. We claim that S contains no alternation of the form $\langle \gamma_i \ldots \gamma_j \ldots \gamma_i \ldots \gamma_j \ldots \rangle$ of length $s + 2$ (with $\gamma_i \neq \gamma_j$). Indeed, connect γ_i to γ_j by an arc π within K, as in the proof of Theorem 5.7, and let Δ be the unbounded component of $\mathbb{R}^2 - (\gamma_i \cup \gamma_j \cup \pi)$. Clearly γ_i and γ_j alternate at most s times along $\partial \Delta$. A close inspection of the proof of the Consistency Lemma shows that the same holds for ∂K too. This easily implies the theorem. □

5.3   Zones in arrangements

After studying the complexity of a single face in an arrangement of Jordan arcs, we next consider the problem of analyzing the maximum possible combinatorial complexity of the zone of a curve in an arrangement of Jordan arcs, which is defined as the sum of the complexities of all the faces of the zone.

As will be shown below, this problem is intimately related to that involving the complexity of a single face. As a warm-up exercise we first study the special case of lines.

5.3.1   Zones in arrangements of lines

Let $\mathcal{L} = \{\ell_1, \ell_2, \ldots, \ell_n\}$ be a collection of n lines in the plane, and let ℓ be another line, which, without loss of generality, is assumed to be the x-axis. Consider the edges of the zone of ℓ in $\mathcal{A}(\mathcal{L})$ that lie above ℓ. We truncate each line ℓ_i to its portion ρ_i lying in that half-plane, which is simply a half-line emerging from some point on the x-axis. We also expand each ρ_i to a narrow angular wedge $\rho_i^\star$ from that point, and distinguish between the left side ρ_i^- and the right side ρ_i^+ of $\rho_i^\star$. We need to bound the number of edges in the bottom unbounded face f of the arrangement $\mathcal{A}(\{\rho_1^+, \ldots, \rho_n^+, \rho_1^-, \ldots, \rho_n^-\})$. This will bound the complexity of the portion of the zone lying above ℓ, and a symmetric argument will handle the other portion of the zone. As in Section 5.2, we pick some connected component C of ∂f. It is easily checked that in this case C must be an unbounded Jordan arc, and we traverse it so that f lies to our right (this is equivalent to a clockwise, left-to-right traversal of the top portions of (some of) the faces of $\mathcal{A}(\mathcal{L})$ crossed by ℓ). We now write down the sequence S of half-lines in the order they appear along C, but we split this sequence into two subsequences, S^- and S^+, so that S^- (respectively, S^+) contains only the appearances of the left half-lines ρ_i^- (respectively, the right half-lines ρ_i^+). See Figure 5.5.

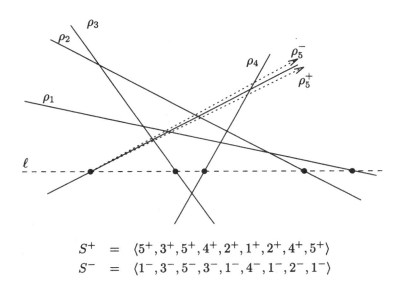

$$S^+ = \langle 5^+, 3^+, 5^+, 4^+, 2^+, 1^+, 2^+, 4^+, 5^+ \rangle$$
$$S^- = \langle 1^-, 3^-, 5^-, 3^-, 1^-, 4^-, 1^-, 2^-, 1^- \rangle$$

FIGURE 5.5. The sequences S^- and S^+ in the zone of a line.

We claim that S^- and S^+ are both $DS(n, 2)$-sequences, and we will prove this for S^-. First note that S^- does not contain a pair of equal adjacent elements. Indeed, suppose to the contrary that S^- contains an adjacent pair $\rho_i^- \rho_i^-$. Clearly, these two appearances of ρ_i^- must occur in two different faces of $\mathcal{A}(\mathcal{L})$, and let z be the rightmost intersection point of ℓ with the leftmost of these two faces. Clearly, C passes through z in between these two appearances of ρ_i^-. If $z \notin \rho_i^-$ then, just before reaching z, C traverses a left half-line different from ρ_i^-, so these appearances of ρ_i^- cannot be adjacent in S^-. If $z \in \rho_i^-$ then an easy application of the Consistency Lemma implies that this must be the last appearance of ρ_i^- along C, so the second assumed appearance of ρ_i^- cannot occur. These contradictions imply the asserted claim.

Next we show that S^- does not contain any alternating quadruple of the form

$$\langle \rho_i^- \ \cdots \ \rho_j^- \ \cdots \ \rho_i^- \ \cdots \ \rho_j^- \rangle,$$

for any pair of distinct rays ρ_i^-, ρ_j^-. Indeed, suppose to the contrary that S^- does contain such a quadruple. Let $x, y \in \rho_i^- \cap C$, $z, w \in \rho_j^- \cap C$ be four points appearing along C in the order x, z, y, w. Using the same arguments as in the proof of Lemma 5.5, one can show that the segments xy and zw must intersect (at the unique point q of intersection of ρ_i^- and ρ_j^-). But then it is easily checked that the angular wedge xqw must be disjoint from the zone, and that ρ_j^- cannot appear along C in the vicinity of w (see Figure 5.6).

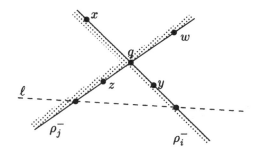

FIGURE 5.6. Two rays ρ_i^- and ρ_j^- in the zone.

Thus each of the lengths of S^- and of S^+ is at most $2n_C - 1$, where n_C is the number of half-lines appearing in C. Hence the total number of edges in C is at most $4n_C - 2$. Summing over all components C, it follows that the total complexity of the "upper zone" of ℓ is at most $4n - 2$, which matches the bounds obtained by Edelsbrunner, O'Rourke, and Seidel (1986) and by Chazelle, Guibas, and Lee (1985). It is also known, and easy to show, that there exist arrangements in which this bound is attained (the arrangement in Figure 5.5 is such an example).

We summarize this result in the following theorem.

Theorem 5.9 *The number of edges bounding the faces in the "upper zone" of a line in an arrangement of n other lines is at most $4n - 2$. This bound is tight in the worst case.*

Remark 5.10 If we repeat this argument for the "lower zone" of ℓ and add up the bounds, we obtain $8n - 4$, but, as easily checked, we have doubly counted each edge of the zone that crosses ℓ. Since there are $2n$ such edges (one on the left and one on the right of each line), we conclude that the overall complexity of the zone of ℓ is at most $6n - 4$. However, this bound is not tight. A more complex analysis by Bern et al. (1991) gives an upper bound of roughly $5.5n$, which is shown to be tight in the worst case.

5.3.2   Zones in arrangements of Jordan arcs

Next we consider the general zone problem as stated in the beginning of this section. For each intersection point, z, of γ_0 with an arc $\gamma_i \in \Gamma$ we split γ_i at z into two subarcs, and we leave an arbitrarily small gap between these pieces. In this manner all faces in the zone of γ_0 are merged into one face, at the cost of increasing the number of arcs from n to at most $(t + 1)n$, where t is the maximum number of intersection points between γ_0 and an arc of Γ. Now we can apply Theorem 5.3 to conclude immediately the following result:

Theorem 5.11 *The complexity of the zone of a curve γ_0 in an arrangement of n Jordan arcs, each pair of which intersect in at most s points, is*

$$O(\lambda_{s+2}((t + 1)n)) = O(\lambda_{s+2}(n)),$$

where t is the maximum number of intersections between γ_0 and any of the given arcs, and is assumed to be constant.

Remark 5.12 (i) If Γ consists of closed or unbounded Jordan curves, the order of the resulting Davenport–Schinzel sequence may still be $s + 2$, and not s as in Theorem 5.7. The reason is that the proof splits each curve that crosses γ_0 into two or more subarcs which are bounded Jordan arcs. For example, the zone of a 'well-behaving' curve γ_0 in an arrangement of n lines is transformed into a single face in an arrangement of lines, half-lines, and segments, and the best upper bound we can offer for its complexity is $O(n\alpha(n))$. If γ_0 is a closed convex curve, then this bound is not known to be tight; see also the discussion in Section 4.5.

(ii) Since the zone of γ_0 consists of $O(n)$ faces of $\mathcal{A}(\Gamma)$, one might be tempted to deduce that the complexity of any n faces in such an arrangement is close to linear. However, this is not true. It is known that, for instance, there exist arrangements of n lines that contain n faces whose overall complexity is $\Theta(n^{4/3})$ (Szemerédi and Trotter (1983), Clarkson et al. (1990)). Similar bounds hold for other types of curves. The proof of Theorem 5.11 for a zone indicates that the complexity of n faces is close to linear if the faces are "close" to one another in the arrangement.

Curiously though, our Zone Theorem 5.11 can be used to obtain an upper bound on the complexity of any m faces in an arrangement of n Jordan arcs. Specifically, let $\Gamma = \{\gamma_1, \gamma_2, \ldots, \gamma_n\}$ be a collection of n Jordan arcs as above, consider the zone of γ_i in $\mathcal{A}(\Gamma - \{\gamma_i\})$, for $1 \leq i \leq n$, and sum up the complexities of all these zones. By Theorem 5.11, the sum is bounded by $O(n\lambda_{s+2}(n))$. Let f be a face in $\mathcal{A}(\Gamma)$, let k_f be the number of curves contributing edges to f, and let n_f be the number of edges bounding f. Observe that the edges of f are counted in the zone of every one of the k_f curves. More precisely, when we consider the zone of γ_i, which contributes $j_i > 0$ edges to f, then we add $n_f - 2j_i$ to the total sum (we do not count the j_i edges of f that lie on γ_i and each edge of f adjacent to such an edge is counted as one together with the edge on the other side of γ_i). Thus, the total contribution of f to the above sum is

$$n_f k_f - 2n_f = n_f(k_f - 2).$$

Hence,

$$\sum_{f \in \mathcal{A}(\Gamma)} n_f k_f = \sum_f n_f(k_f - 2) + 2\sum_f n_f$$

$$= O(n\lambda_{s+2}(n)) + O(sn^2) = O(n\lambda_{s+2}(n)).$$

As shown in Theorem 5.3, $n_f = O(\lambda_{s+2}(k_f))$, which implies

$$\sum_{f \in \mathcal{A}(\Gamma)} n_f^2 = O\left(\sum_f n_f \lambda_{s+2}(k_f)\right)$$

$$= O\left(\sum_f n_f k_f \frac{\lambda_{s+2}(k_f)}{k_f}\right)$$

$$= O\left(\frac{\lambda_{s+2}(n)}{n} \cdot \sum_f n_f k_f\right)$$

$$= O(\lambda_{s+2}^2(n)).$$

We have thus shown

Theorem 5.13 *The sum of squares of cell complexities in an arrangement of n Jordan arcs as above is $O(\lambda_{s+2}^2(n))$.*

Suppose we are now interested in the maximum number of edges bounding some m distinct faces, $f_1, \ldots, f_m$, of $\mathcal{A}(\Gamma)$. Using the Cauchy–Schwarz inequality, we get

$$
\sum_{i=1}^{m} n_{f_i} = \sum_{i=1}^{m} 1 \cdot n_{f_i} \le m^{1/2} \left(\sum_i n_{f_i}^2 \right)^{1/2}
$$

$$
\le m^{1/2} \left(\sum_{f \in \mathcal{A}(\Gamma)} n_f^2 \right)^{1/2}
$$

$$
= O(m^{1/2} \lambda_{s+2}(n)).
$$

We formulate this result as a theorem. It is weaker than bounds known for several special types of arcs, such as lines, line segments, and circles (see Canham (1969), Clarkson et al. (1990), Edelsbrunner, Guibas, and Sharir (1990), and Aronov et al. (1992)), but applies to more general arcs.

Theorem 5.14 *Let Γ be a set of n curves satisfying the conditions stated earlier. The maximum number of edges bounding m distinct faces of $\mathcal{A}(\Gamma)$ is $O(m^{1/2} \lambda_{s+2}(n))$.*

Another useful application of the zone theorem, which we discuss in the next chapter, is that it facilitates an efficient incremental construction of arrangements, in which we insert the given arcs one at a time in any order, and update the arrangement after each insertion.

5.4   Levels in arrangements

Definition 5.15   Let $\Gamma = \{\gamma_1, \ldots, \gamma_n\}$ be a collection of x-monotone unbounded Jordan curves in the plane. The *level* of a point $p \in \mathbb{R}^2$ in $\mathcal{A}(\Gamma)$ is the number of curves of Γ lying strictly below p, and the level of an edge $e \in \mathcal{A}(\Gamma)$ is the common level of all the points lying in the relative interior of e. For a nonnegative integer $k < n$, the *k-level* (respectively, *$(\le k)$-level*) of $\mathcal{A}(\Gamma)$ is the set of (the closures of) all edges in $\mathcal{A}(\Gamma)$ whose level is k (respectively, at most k); see Figure 5.7.

Let $g_k(\Gamma)$ denote the number of edges in the $(\le k)$-level of $\mathcal{A}(\Gamma)$, and let

$$
g_k(n, s) = \max g_k(\Gamma),
$$

where the maximum is taken over all collections Γ of n curves, as above, in which any pair of curves intersect in at most s points. The lower envelope of Γ is the 0-level of $\mathcal{A}(\Gamma)$, therefore $g_0(n, s) = \lambda_s(n)$.

Theorem 5.16 *For $n, s > 0$ and for an integer $0 \le k < n$,*

$$
g_k(n, s) = O\left((k+1)^2 \lambda_s \left(\left\lfloor \frac{n}{k+1} \right\rfloor \right) \right).
$$

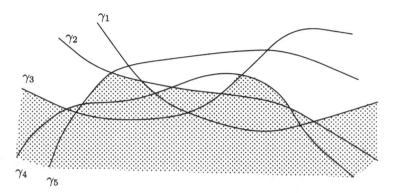

FIGURE 5.7. An arrangement of Jordan curves; edges of the (≤ 2)-level lie in the closed shaded region.

Proof. As noted, the theorem holds for $k = 0$, so assume $k \geq 1$. Let Γ be a collection of n x-monotone Jordan curves in the plane with at most s intersection points between any pair. For a subset $X \subseteq \Gamma$, let $V(X)$ denote the set of vertices in $\mathcal{A}(X)$, and let $V_j(X)$, for $0 \leq j \leq n - 2$, denote the set of vertices in $\mathcal{A}(X)$ whose level is j. The theorem essentially asserts that

$$\sum_{j=0}^{k} |V_j(\Gamma)| = O\left((k+1)^2 \lambda_s \left(\left\lfloor \frac{n}{k+1} \right\rfloor\right)\right).$$

Let $r \leq n$ be a parameter to be chosen later. We randomly choose a subset $R \subseteq \Gamma$ of r curves, where each subset of size r is chosen with equal probability. Clearly, the expected number of vertices in $V_0(R)$ is (where $\Pr\{A\}$ denotes the probability of an event A)

$$
\begin{aligned}
\mathbf{E}\big[|V_0(R)|\big] &= \sum_{v \in V(\Gamma)} \Pr\{v \in V_0(R)\} \\
&= \sum_{j=0}^{n-2} \sum_{v \in V_j(\Gamma)} \Pr\{v \in V_0(R)\} \\
&\geq \sum_{j=0}^{k} \sum_{v \in V_j(\Gamma)} \Pr\{v \in V_0(R)\}.
\end{aligned}
\tag{5.1}
$$

Suppose an intersection point $v = \gamma \cap \gamma'$, for $\gamma, \gamma' \in \Gamma$, is a vertex in $V_j(\Gamma)$. The vertex v appears on the lower envelope of R (the 0-level of $\mathcal{A}(R)$) if and only if the following two conditions are satisfied:

(i) both γ, γ' are chosen in R, and

(ii) none of the j arcs of Γ lying below v are chosen in R.

Since there are $\binom{n-j-2}{r-2}$ subsets of Γ that satisfy the above two conditions, we obtain, for $v \in V_j(\Gamma)$ and $j \le k$,

$$
\begin{aligned}
\Pr\{v \in V_0(R)\} &= \binom{n-j-2}{r-2} \bigg/ \binom{n}{r} \\
&= \frac{r(r-1)}{n(n-1)} \cdot \frac{(n-r)(n-r-1)\cdots(n-j-r+1)}{(n-2)(n-3)\cdots(n-j-1)} \\
&\ge \frac{r(r-1)}{n(n-1)} \cdot \left(\frac{n-r-k+1}{n-k-1}\right)^k.
\end{aligned}
$$

Set $r = \lfloor n/(k+1) \rfloor$; then, as is easily checked,

$$
\frac{n-r-k+1}{n-k-1} \ge 1 - \frac{1}{k+1}
$$

for $k \ge 0$. Thus, for $k \ge 1$,

$$
\left(\frac{n-r-k+1}{n-k-1}\right)^k \ge \left(1 - \frac{1}{k+1}\right)^k \ge \frac{1}{e}.
$$

Therefore

$$
\mathbf{E}\big[|V_0(R)|\big] \ge \sum_{j=0}^{k} |V_j(\Gamma)| \cdot \frac{r(r-1)}{en(n-1)}.
$$

On the other hand, $|V_0(R)| \le \lambda_s(r)$, so

$$
\begin{aligned}
\sum_{j=0}^{k} |V_j(\Gamma)| &\le \lambda_s\left(\left\lfloor \frac{n}{k+1} \right\rfloor\right) \cdot \frac{en(n-1)}{\left\lfloor \frac{n}{k+1} \right\rfloor \left(\left\lfloor \frac{n}{k+1} \right\rfloor - 1\right)} \\
&= O\left((k+1)^2 \lambda_s\left(\left\lfloor \frac{n}{k+1} \right\rfloor\right)\right).
\end{aligned}
$$

This completes the proof of the theorem. $\square$

An immediate corollary of the above theorem is:

Corollary 5.17 *The number of edges in the $(\le k)$-level of an arrangement of n lines in the plane is $O(n(k+1))$.*

If Γ is a collection of x-monotone *bounded* Jordan arcs, points on the same edge of $\mathcal{A}(\Gamma)$ may have different levels, which makes Definition 5.16 problematic. In this case, the k-level of the arrangement will denote just the set of vertices at level k, and similarly for the $(\le k)$-level. A straightforward modification of the proof of Theorem 5.16 yields:

Corollary 5.18 *The number of vertices in the ($\leq k$)-level of an arrangement of n x-monotone Jordan arcs, each pair of which intersect in at most s points, is*

$$O\left((k+1)^2\lambda_{s+2}\left(\left\lfloor\frac{n}{k+1}\right\rfloor\right)\right).$$

Theorem 5.16 can be extended to another more general setting. Let $\Gamma = \{\gamma_1, \ldots, \gamma_n\}$ be a given collection of (closed or unbounded) Jordan curves. For each γ_i, let K_i be one of the two open regions separated by γ_i, and let $\mathcal{K} = \{K_i \mid 1 \leq i \leq n\}$ be the resulting collection of regions. For an integer $0 \leq k \leq n-2$, we define $S_{\leq k}(\mathcal{K})$ to be the set of vertices in $\mathcal{A}(\Gamma)$ that lie in the relative interior of at most k regions of $\mathcal{K}$. Suppose that the expected size of $S_{\leq 0}(R)$, for a random subset $R \subseteq \mathcal{K}$ of size r, is at most $f(r)$; then, following the proof of Theorem 5.16, one can easily show:

Corollary 5.19 *Let $\mathcal{K}$ be a set of n Jordan regions as defined above, and let $0 \leq k \leq n-2$ be an integer. Then, in the above notations,*

$$|S_{\leq k}(\mathcal{K})| = O\left((k+1)^2 f\left(\left\lfloor\frac{n}{k+1}\right\rfloor\right)\right).$$

For example, if Γ is a set of n x-monotone Jordan curves with at most s intersections per pair, and $\mathcal{K}$ is the same as defined above, then, for any $r \leq n$, $f(r) = O(\lambda_s(r))$. Indeed, let $R \subseteq \Gamma$ be a subset of size r and let $R^+ \subseteq R$ (respectively, $R^- \subseteq R$) denote the set of Jordan curves $\gamma_i \in R$ such that K_i lies above (respectively, below) γ_i. A vertex in $S_{\leq 0}(R)$ is a vertex of the lower envelope of R^+, or a vertex of the upper envelope of R^-, or an intersection point of an edge of the lower envelope of R^+ and an edge of the upper envelope of R^-. The number of vertices of the lower and upper envelopes is at most $\lambda_s(r)$, and, since these envelopes are x-monotone Jordan curves, it is easily seen that the number of intersection points between the envelopes is $O(\lambda_s(r))$, which implies that $|S_{\leq 0}(R)| = O(\lambda_s(r))$. Hence, we can conclude:

Corollary 5.20 *Let Γ be a collection of n x-monotone Jordan curves, let $\mathcal{K}$ be as defined above, and let $0 \leq k \leq n-2$ be an integer. Then $|S_{\leq k}(\mathcal{K})| = O((k+1)^2\lambda_s(\lfloor n/(k+1)\rfloor))$, where s is the maximum number of intersection points between any pair of curves of Γ.*

5.5   Bibliographic notes

Tight bounds on the maximum complexity of a single cell in an arrangement of n hyperplanes in $\mathbb{R}^d$, for any $d \geq 2$, have been obtained about 25 years ago (see, e.g., Grünbaum (1967), McMullen and Shepard (1971), and Brønsted (1983)). The bounds are $\Theta(n^{\lfloor d/2 \rfloor})$, with a constant of proportionality depending on d. In fact, an exact upper bound on this maximum complexity is known; this is the dual version of the celebrated 'Upper Bound Theorem' in the theory of convex polytopes. However, for general surfaces, the problem was open, even in two dimensions, until recently. Pollack, Sharir, and Sifrony (1988) proved that the complexity of a single face in an arrangement of line segments is $O(n\alpha(n))$, which, in view of Theorem 4.11, is tight in the worst case. A result of Alevizos, Boissonnat, and Preparata (1990) shows that the complexity of a single face in an arrangement of rays is linear. Theorem 5.3 is due to Guibas, Sharir, and Sifrony (1989), and Theorem 5.7 is due to Schwartz and Sharir (1990). As in the case of lower envelopes, no matching lower bound is known for the complexity of a single face in an arrangement of Jordan arcs, each pair of which intersects in at most $s > 1$ points, if we insist that the arcs have 'simple shape', e.g., be algebraic of constant degree. We also refer the reader to recent surveys on arrangements by Guibas and Sharir (1993), and by Halperin and Sharir (1994a).

The result of Guibas, Sharir, and Sifrony (1989) almost settles the question concerning the complexity of a single face in two-dimensional arrangements, but the problem is still open for $d \geq 3$ dimensions, in spite of some recent progress. Chapter 7 presents some of these recent advances and contains more details concerning the higher-dimensional variants of the problem.

Theorem 5.9 was first proved by Edelsbrunner, O'Rourke, and Seidel (1986). A simpler proof appears in Chazelle, Guibas, and Lee (1985), which is a variant of the proof given in Section 5.3. Chazelle and Lee (1986) showed that the 'outer' zone of a circle (the portion of the zone lying outside the circle) in an arrangement of n unit circles has linear complexity. The result of Alevizos et al. (1990) mentioned above is also easily seen to imply that the outer zone of a convex curve in an arrangement of n lines has linear complexity. In both cases, no tight bounds are known for the complexity of the complementary 'inner zone.' Theorems 5.11–5.14 were first observed in Edelsbrunner et al. (1992). Again, Chapter 7 presents extensions of the zone theorem to higher dimensions.

A tight bound of $O(n^{\lfloor d/2 \rfloor}(k+1)^{\lceil d/2 \rceil})$ on the combinatorial complexity of the ($\leq k$)-level in arrangements of n hyperplanes in $\mathbb{R}^d$ was proved by Clarkson and Shor (1989); thus Corollary 5.17 is a special case of their result. The use of probabilistic techniques in the analysis of combinatorial and algorithmic problems in geometry has become very popular recently, and the work of Clarkson and Shor (1989) is one of the cornerstones in this development. Theorem 5.16 is taken from Sharir (1991), where the proof technique is an adaptation of the Clarkson–Shor technique. In Chapter 7 we extend the proof of Theorem 5.16 to higher dimensions. Additional applications of probabilistic techniques will be presented in all three subsequent chapters.

We conclude by mentioning a classical open problem in combinatorial geometry: What is the maximum number of edges in a k-level of an arrangement of n lines in the plane? More than 20 years ago, Lovász (1971) proved an upper bound of $O(n\sqrt{k})$ (see also Erdős et al. (1973)), which has been slightly improved by Pach, Steiger, and Szemerédi (1992) to $O(n\sqrt{k}/\log^\star k)$. However, the best known lower bound is $\Omega(n \log k)$, due to Edelsbrunner and Welzl (1985). See Bárány, Füredi, and Lovász (1990), Aronov et al. (1991), Dey and Edelsbrunner (1994), and Živaljević and Vrećica (1992) for upper bounds on the complexity of a single level of an arrangement of planes or hyperplanes in three and higher dimensions.

6

ALGORITHMS FOR ARRANGEMENTS

6.1   Introduction

In the previous chapter we showed that Davenport–Schinzel sequences play a vital role in solving some basic combinatorial problems related to arrangements of Jordan arcs in the plane. We now turn our attention to algorithmic problems involving such arrangements. We consider three problems—computing the lower envelope, computing a single or several faces of the arrangement, and computing the entire arrangement. Even though most of the material in this chapter is algorithmic in nature, it also contains some useful combinatorial results. Of particular interest is the 'Combination Lemma 6.7' given in Section 6.3.1.

Let Γ be a collection of n Jordan arcs in the plane. We assume that the shape of each arc in Γ is relatively simple and not too 'wiggly.' Specifically, we assume that each pair of arcs intersect in at most s points, for some fixed constant s, and that each arc in Γ has at most t points of vertical tangency, for some fixed constant t, so that we can break it into at most $t + 1$ Jordan arcs that are monotone in the x-direction (this additional condition is satisfied in most applications; in particular, it holds for arcs that are algebraic of a fixed maximal degree). Thus, in the remainder of this chapter, we will assume each $\gamma \in \Gamma$ to be x-monotone. Also, we assume that the arcs in Γ are in general position, so that each intersection of a pair of these arcs is either at a common endpoint, or a transversal intersection at a point in the relative interior of both arcs. We also assume that no two intersection points or endpoints lie on the same vertical line, so as to simplify the description of our algorithms. (None of these latter assumptions are essential, and simple modifications of our algorithms will also make them work in the presence of degeneracies of this kind.)

We assume a model of computation allowing infinite-precision real arithmetic, in which certain primitive operations involving one or two arcs are assumed to take constant time; typical such operations are:

(i) finding the intersection points of a pair of arcs;

(ii) finding the points of vertical tangency of a given arc;

(iii) finding the intersections of an arc with a vertical line.

All these assumptions are reasonable if the arcs γ_i have reasonably simple shape, for example, if they are all algebraic of low bounded degree.

This chapter is organized as follows. We first present algorithms for computing the lower envelope in an arrangement of Jordan arcs or curves. Next we describe several algorithms—both deterministic and randomized—for computing a single face in an arrangement of arcs. The deterministic algorithm requires $O(\lambda_{s+2}(n) \log^2 n)$ time. It is based on a divide-and-conquer approach, whose merge step requires a sophisticated sweep-line technique. In Sections 6.4 and 6.5 we show that if we allow randomization, the (expected) running time can be improved to $O(\lambda_{s+2}(n) \log n)$. We first describe a very simple randomized divide-and-conquer algorithm, and then present a randomized incremental algorithm. Finally, we present two incremental algorithms for computing the entire arrangement $\mathcal{A}(\Gamma)$—one of them is a randomized algorithm, whose expected running time is proportional to the size of the output, and the other is a deterministic algorithm that is close to optimal in the worst case.

6.2   Computing lower envelopes

Let Γ be a collection of n (unbounded, x-monotone) Jordan curves, and let s be the maximum number of intersection points between any pair of curves of Γ. We first present a very simple divide-and-conquer algorithm that computes the lower envelope of Γ in time $O(\lambda_s(n) \log n)$. If Γ is a collection of (x-monotone) Jordan arcs, the running time becomes $O(\lambda_{s+2}(n) \log n)$. We also present a more involved algorithm for computing the lower envelope of a set of Jordan arcs, whose running time is $O(\lambda_{s+1}(n) \log n)$.

6.2.1   A divide-and-conquer algorithm

Let Γ be a collection of n unbounded x-monotone Jordan curves. Let E_Γ denote the lower envelope of Γ. We partition Γ into two subsets, Γ_1, Γ_2, each of size at most $\lceil n/2 \rceil$, compute the lower envelopes of each of them recursively, and then merge these subenvelopes to obtain the overall lower envelope E_Γ. We represent the lower envelopes $E_{\Gamma_1}, E_{\Gamma_2}$ by the lists of their transition points, including a virtual point at $x = -\infty$, sorted from left to right. For each transition point, we also store the curve that appears on the lower envelope immediately to its right. The length of each list is $O(\lambda_s(n/2)) = O(\lambda_s(n))$.

To merge the two lower envelopes, we sweep a vertical line from left to right. At each point t, the sweep line intersects one curve $\gamma_1 \in E_{\Gamma_1}$ and one curve $\gamma_2 \in E_{\Gamma_2}$. Let σ_1 (respectively, σ_2) be the next transition point of E_{Γ_1} (respectively, E_{Γ_2}), and let ξ be the leftmost intersection point of γ_1 and γ_2 lying to the right of t. If there is no such point, we set ξ to $+\infty$. The sweep line moves to the leftmost point, t', among ξ, σ_1, σ_2. If $t' = \xi$, we add t' to the list of transition points of E_Γ; if γ_1 lies below γ_2 immediately to the right of t', then we associate γ_1 with t', otherwise we associate γ_2 with t'. If $t' = \sigma_1$ and γ_2 lies above γ_1 at t', then we add t' to the transition points of E_Γ, and associate with it the curve γ_1' that was associated with it in E_{Γ_1}. If γ_2 lies below γ_1 at t', then t' is not a transition point of E_Γ; we replace γ_1 by γ_1' as the current curve attaining E_{Γ_1}. Symmetric actions are taken if $t' = \sigma_2$.

Thus the sweep line advances in discrete steps over the intervals determined by the transition points of E_{Γ_1}, E_{Γ_2} and by the intersection points of the two lower envelopes. Since every intersection point of E_{Γ_1} and E_{Γ_2} is a transition point of E_Γ, and we spend $O(1)$ time at each step, the merge step requires $O(\lambda_s(n))$ time. Let $T(n)$ denote the maximum running time of the algorithm for a collection of n curves as above. We obtain the following recurrence:

$$T(n) = \begin{cases} O(1) & \text{if } n = 1, \\ 2T(n/2) + O(\lambda_s(n)) & \text{if } n > 1. \end{cases}$$

The solution of the above recurrence is $O(\lambda_s(n) \log n)$. Hence, we obtain:

Theorem 6.1 *Given a set of n (unbounded x-monotone) Jordan curves with at most s intersections between any pair of curves, its lower envelope can be computed in time $O(\lambda_s(n) \log n)$.*

If Γ is a collection of bounded x-monotone Jordan arcs, then the same algorithm applies, except that some transition points in the envelope may have no arc attaining the envelope immediately to their right. This requires a few obvious modifications, which are not detailed here. Since the number of transition points of E_Γ (and of $E_{\Gamma_1}, E_{\Gamma_2}$) is $O(\lambda_{s+2}(n))$, the merge step takes $O(\lambda_{s+2}(n))$ time. Hence, we have:

Corollary 6.2 *Given a set of n x-monotone Jordan arcs with at most s intersections between any pair of arcs, its lower envelope can be computed in $O(\lambda_{s+2}(n) \log n)$ time.*

If Γ is a collection of m piecewise-linear functions, whose graphs are composed of a total of n segments, then the running time of the above divide-and-conquer algorithm can be slightly improved, as follows. At each step of the algorithm, partition Γ into two subsets Γ_1, Γ_2, each of size at most $\lceil m/2 \rceil$, compute their envelopes recursively, and then merge the resulting envelopes, using the same technique as above. We stop the recursion when $|\Gamma| = 1$. Following the same analysis as above, and using Corollary 2.18, we easily obtain:

Corollary 6.3 *The lower envelope of a collection of m piecewise-linear functions, whose graphs are composed of a total of n segments, can be computed in time $O(n\alpha(m)\log m)$.*

6.2.2   An improved algorithm

We now describe a faster algorithm that computes the lower envelope of a set of n x-monotone Jordan arcs, as above, in time $O(\lambda_{s+1}(n)\log n)$. This algorithm works in three phases: In the first phase, we partition Γ into $k \le \lceil \log n \rceil$ subsets $\Gamma_1, \ldots, \Gamma_k$, such that for each i, E_{Γ_i} has $O(\lambda_{s+1}(n_i))$ transition points, where $n_i = |\Gamma_i|$. In the second phase, we compute the lower envelopes of each Γ_i using the algorithm of Corollary 6.2, and, finally, in the third phase, we merge all k lower envelopes $E_{\Gamma_1}, \ldots, E_{\Gamma_k}$ to obtain the overall lower envelope E_Γ.

For an arc $\gamma \in \Gamma$, let I_γ denote the x-projection of γ. Let L be the list of endpoints of these intervals sorted from left to right. Intervals between two consecutive points of L are called *atomic intervals*; L has at most $2n - 1$ atomic intervals. We construct a minimum-height binary tree $\mathcal{T}$ on these atomic intervals. The i-th leftmost leaf of $\mathcal{T}$ is associated with the i-th leftmost atomic interval. With each interior node v we associate: (i) an interval δ_v, the union of the atomic intervals stored at the leaves of the subtree rooted at v, and (ii) a point σ_v, the right endpoint of the interval associated with the left child of v (it is the same as the left endpoint of the interval associated with the right child of v).

For an arc γ, if I_γ is an atomic interval, γ is stored at the corresponding leaf of $\mathcal{T}$; otherwise γ is stored at the highest node v for which σ_v lies in the interior of I_γ (clearly, such a node is unique).[1] Let Γ_v be the set of segments stored at v. Our scheme ensures that, for every $\gamma \in \Gamma_v$, (i) $I_\gamma \subseteq \delta_v$, and (ii) $\sigma_v \in I_\gamma$. Let Γ_i denote the set of arcs stored at nodes of $\mathcal{T}$ at level i. The collection $\{\Gamma_1, \ldots, \Gamma_k\}$ ($k \le \lceil \log n \rceil$) is the desired partition of Γ. It is easily seen that this partition can be obtained in $O(n \log n)$ time, because each interval can be stored at the appropriate node of $\mathcal{T}$ in $O(\log n)$ time. Put $n_i = |\Gamma_i|$, for $i = 1, \ldots, k$.

Lemma 6.4 *For every $i \le k$, the lower envelope of Γ_i has $O(\lambda_{s+1}(n_i))$ transition points.*

---

[1] Such a tree is known as an *interval tree*; see Preparata and Shamos (1985) for details.

Proof. Since all arcs stored at a node v intersect the vertical line $x = \sigma_v$, the lower envelope of Γ_v has $O(\lambda_{s+1}(|\Gamma_v|))$ transition points (see Lemma 1.8). For any two nodes, u, v, of the same level, δ_u and δ_v are disjoint, therefore, by property (i), E_{Γ_u} and E_{Γ_v} have disjoint x-projections, which implies

$$|E_{\Gamma_u \cup \Gamma_v}| = |E_{\Gamma_u}| + |E_{\Gamma_v}| = O(\lambda_{s+1}(|\Gamma_u| + |\Gamma_v|)).$$

Hence, $|E_{\Gamma_i}| = O(\lambda_{s+1}(n_i))$. $\square$

We compute the lower envelope of each Γ_i using Corollary 6.2. In view of the above lemma, E_{Γ_i} can be computed in $O(\lambda_{s+1}(n_i) \log n_i)$ time, because Lemma 6.4 holds not only for Γ_i but also for every subset Γ_i' of Γ_i. The total time spent in the second phase is thus $\sum_i O(\lambda_{s+1}(n_i) \log n_i)$, where $\sum_i n_i = n$. Since $\lambda_s(n)$ is a superadditive function,

$$\sum_i O(\lambda_{s+1}(n_i) \log n_i) = O(\lambda_{s+1}(n) \log n).$$

Finally, we merge the k envelopes $E_{\Gamma_1}, \ldots, E_{\Gamma_k}$ using a divide-and-conquer approach. That is, we partition them into two subcollections, each consisting of at most $\lceil k/2 \rceil$ envelopes, merge the envelopes of each subcollection recursively, and then merge the resulting two envelopes using the same technique as in the merge step of the previous algorithm. Again, the merge step can be accomplished in time $O(\lambda_{s+2}(n))$. Let $T(n, k)$ denote the maximum time spent in merging the k lower envelopes of a total of n functions as above, then

$$T(n, k) = T(n_1, \lceil k/2 \rceil) + T(n_2, \lfloor k/2 \rfloor) + O(\lambda_{s+2}(n)),$$

where $n_1 + n_2 = n$. The solution of the above recurrence is $O(\lambda_{s+2}(n) \log k)$. Since $k = O(\log n)$, this bound is clearly dominated by $O(\lambda_{s+1}(n) \log n)$, so we obtain:

Theorem 6.5 *Given a collection Γ of n x-monotone Jordan arcs, each pair of which intersect in at most s points, the lower envelope of Γ can be computed in $O(\lambda_{s+1}(n) \log n)$ time.*

Corollary 6.6 *The lower envelope of a collection of n line segments can be computed in optimal $O(n \log n)$ time.*

6.3 Computing a single face: Deterministic construction

In this section we present a deterministic algorithm for computing a single face in an arrangement of a collection Γ of n Jordan arcs (or closed, or unbounded Jordan curves) with the properties described in the beginning of the chapter. The input to the algorithm is such a collection Γ and a point x not lying on any arc of Γ. The output of the algorithm is a discrete representation of the face f of the arrangement $\mathcal{A}(\Gamma)$ containing x. The representation that we will use is the collection of the connected components of the boundary of f, each given as a circular (or, in case of an unbounded component, a linear) list of subarcs and vertices appearing along that component in counterclockwise order.

The high-level description of our algorithm is quite simple. We use the following divide-and-conquer technique. We split Γ into two subcollections Γ_1, Γ_2, of roughly $n/2$ curves each, calculate recursively the faces, f_1, f_2, of $\mathcal{A}(\Gamma_1)$, $\mathcal{A}(\Gamma_2)$, respectively, that contain x, and then 'merge' these two faces to obtain the desired face f. Note that f is the connected component of $f_1 \cap f_2$ containing x. However, it is generally too expensive to calculate this intersection in its entirety, and then select the component containing x, because the boundaries of f_1 and f_2 might intersect in many (in the worst case, quadratically many) points that do not belong to the boundary of f, and we cannot afford to find all of them. We therefore need a more clever way of performing the merge, which we now describe.

The setup for the merge step is as follows. We are given two connected (but not necessarily simply connected) regions in the plane, which we denote, respectively, as the red region R and the blue region B. Both regions contain the point x in their interior, and our task is to calculate the connected component f of $R \cap B$ that contains x. The boundaries of R and B are composed of (maximal connected) portions of the given curves in Γ, each of which will be denoted in what follows as an *arc segment* (or 'subarc').

For technical reasons that will be explained below, we extend this task as follows. Let P be the set containing x and all endpoints of the arcs of Γ that lie on the boundary of either R or B. Clearly, P contains at most $2n + 1$ points. For each $w \in P$, let f_w denote the connected component of $R \cap B$ that contains w (these components are not necessarily distinct, and some may be empty). Our task is now to calculate all these components (but produce each distinct component just once, even if it contains several points of P). We will refer to this task as the *red–blue merge*. (The algorithm given below actually works in more generality—R and B can be the union of several connected regions, and P can be an arbitrary (finite) collection of points, as long as it contains all the endpoints of the arcs in Γ that lie inside B, R, as above.) We call the resulting components f_w *purple regions*, as each of them is covered by both the red and the blue regions. An illustration of this merge is shown below in Figure 6.1.

The major technical result on which our algorithm relies is that the overall complexity of these purple regions is small, so that it is not expensive to produce all of them. This will be a consequence of the following 'Combination Lemma.'

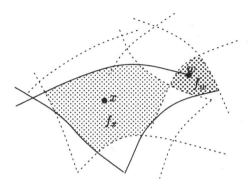

FIGURE 6.1. The red–blue merge; the solid arcs are the blue arcs, and the dashed arcs are red.

6.3.1 Combination Lemma

The Combination Lemma that we will establish in this subsection is somewhat stronger than the version needed for our red–blue merge. We first introduce a few notations. Let $R_1, \ldots, R_m$ be a collection of m distinct faces in an arrangement of a set Γ_r of 'red' Jordan arcs, and let $B_1, \ldots, B_n$ be a similar collection of faces in an arrangement of a set Γ_b of 'blue' Jordan arcs (where, again, each pair of arcs from $\Gamma_r \cup \Gamma_b$ are assumed to intersect in at most some fixed number, s, of points). Let $P = \{p_1, \ldots, p_k\}$ be a collection of points, so that each $p_i \in P$ belongs to one red face R_{m_i} and to one blue face B_{n_i}. Let E_i be the connected component of $R_{m_i} \cap B_{n_i}$ containing p_i (i.e., E_i is the face of the combined arrangement of $\Gamma_r \cup \Gamma_b$ containing p_i). Then we have:

Lemma 6.7 (Combination Lemma) *The total combinatorial complexity of all the regions E_i is at most $O(r + b + k)$, where r and b are the total number of arc segments composing the boundaries of the red faces and of the blue faces, respectively.*

Proof. We assume that the red and blue arrangements are in general position, so as to avoid degeneracies in the structure of R_i, B_i, and E_i, such as tangencies or points of triple intersection of curves along the boundaries of these regions. This assumption is made for the sake of exposition; a more refined version of the analysis given below can handle these degeneracies.

The first step in the proof is to consider the special case of a single red face, R, a single blue face, B, and a single point p belonging to $B \cap R$. Let E be the connected component of $B \cap R$ containing p. Let u (respectively, v) denote the number of connected components of ∂R (respectively, ∂B), and let r (respectively, b) denote the total complexity (that is, number of arc segments composing the boundary) of R (respectively, B).

We claim that, under the nondegeneracy assumptions made above, the complexity of E is at most $(s+2)(b+r+2u+2v-4t)$, where t is the number of connected components of ∂E.

This is the major step in our analysis; it is fairly complex, so we first describe the general outline of the proof of this claim, and then fill in the details of each substep. We analyze each component ζ of the boundary of E separately, by tracing the sequence of red arc segments and the sequence of blue arc segments in the order that they appear along ζ. An extension of the Consistency Lemma 5.4 shows that the sequence of red arc segments along ζ is consistent with the sequences of red arc segments along each of the components of the boundary of R, and similarly for the blue sequence. Notice that a single red arc segment from R can be repeated several times along ζ. However, these repetitions must be interspersed with blue arc segments that 'advance' along the boundary of B. Although it is possible for a single red arc segment to be interspersed with a single blue arc segment for a while, after at most $s+3$ alternations at least one of them has to be replaced by another, as in the proof of Lemma 5.5. Another complication that can arise is that ζ may visit several components of the boundary of R or of B, so that some of them are visited more than once. We show that the duplication of arc segments along ζ that may result from this effect is only linear in the number of components. Altogether, these arguments imply that the complexity of E is linear in the input size, as asserted in the lemma.

To begin a detailed presentation of the proof, let us fix a single component ζ of ∂E, and assume, without loss of generality, that it is the exterior component. Trace ζ in, say, counterclockwise direction (with E lying to the left), and let $S = S_\zeta = \langle s_1, \ldots, s_m \rangle$ be the (circular) sequence of the arc segments of ∂R, ∂B as they appear along ζ. Clearly, the sum of the lengths of S_ζ, over all connected portions ζ of ∂E, is the complexity of E. (We assume here that E is bounded; the same analysis, with minor and obvious modifications, applies to unbounded faces.)

The proof consists of the following steps:

Step 1: Let a be an arc segment of, say, ∂R, which appears along ζ. Let a_1, a_2 be two connected portions of $a \cap \zeta$, consecutive along a, such that when a is traversed with R lying to its left, a_1 precedes a_2. It follows from the Consistency Lemma that a_1 and a_2 are also adjacent along ζ, in the strong sense that the portion of ζ between a_1 and a_2 does not intersect the connected component of ∂R containing a.

In what follows, we will use the notation 'the portion of S between s_i and s_j' to mean the subsequence $\langle s_{i+1}, \ldots, s_{j-1} \rangle$ if $i < j$, or the subsequence $\langle s_{i+1}, \ldots, s_m, s_1, \ldots, s_{j-1} \rangle$ if $j < i$. The property stated above then amounts to saying that if $s_i = s_j$ are two appearances of some red arc segment a in S, with the first appearance preceding the second one along a and with no other portion of a between a_1 and a_2 appearing along ζ, then either the portion of

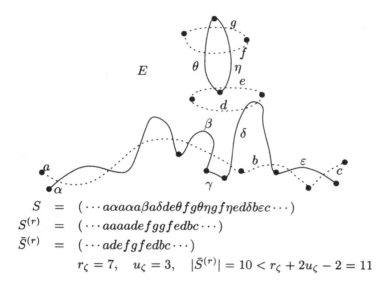

$$S = (\cdots a\alpha a\alpha a\beta a\delta de\theta f g\theta \eta g f \eta ed\delta b\varepsilon c \cdots)$$
$$S^{(r)} = (\cdots aaaadef gg fedbc \cdots)$$
$$\bar{S}^{(r)} = (\cdots adef g fedbc \cdots)$$
$$r_\zeta = 7, \quad u_\zeta = 3, \quad |\bar{S}^{(r)}| = 10 < r_\zeta + 2u_\zeta - 2 = 11$$

FIGURE 6.2. The sequences $S, S^{(r)}, \bar{S}^{(r)}$.

S between s_i and s_j consists of blue arc segments exclusively or, if it contains red arcs at all, they must all belong to other components of ∂R.

Step 2: Let $S^{(r)}$ be the (circular) subsequence of S obtained by deleting from S all the blue arc segments, and let $\bar{S}^{(r)}$ be the sequence obtained from $S^{(r)}$ by further deleting, in circular fashion, each element that becomes equal to the element immediately preceding it. The sequences $S^{(b)}$ and $\bar{S}^{(b)}$ are defined symmetrically for the blue parts of S. See Figure 6.2 for an illustration.

We claim that $\bar{S}^{(r)}$ is of length at most $r_\zeta + 2u_\zeta - 2$, where u_ζ is the number of distinct connected components of ∂R appearing along ζ, and r_ζ is the total number of red arc segments composing these u_ζ components.

(Note that $\sum_\zeta u_\zeta \leq u$, and $\sum_\zeta r_\zeta \leq r$, since no component of ∂R can appear along two distinct components of ∂E.)

To prove the claim, suppose a is a red arc segment appearing more than once in $\bar{S}^{(r)}$. By the argument in Step 1, all elements of $\bar{S}^{(r)}$ lying between two consecutive appearances, $\bar{s}_i^{(r)}$, $\bar{s}_j^{(r)}$, of a (appearing consecutively in this order along a) must belong to other components of ∂R. We charge the second appearance of a to the component of ∂R containing $\bar{s}_{i+1}^{(r)}$. Let $\sigma^{(r)}$ be the (circular) sequence of the connected components of ∂R in the order they appear along ζ (so that no two adjacent elements of $\sigma^{(r)}$ are equal). As in the proof of Theorem 5.8, it can be shown that $\sigma^{(r)}$ is a circular $(u_\zeta, 2)$ Davenport–Schinzel cycle. Hence, by Corollary 1.10, its length is at most $2u_\zeta - 2$. Moreover, it is easily checked that the charging scheme described above never charges an element of $\sigma^{(r)}$ more than once. Hence the total number of duplications of elements in $\bar{S}^{(r)}$ is at most $2u_\zeta - 2$, from which the claim follows.

In a fully symmetric manner, it follows that the length of $\bar{S}^{(b)}$ is at most $b_\zeta + 2v_\zeta - 2$, where v_ζ, b_ζ are defined analogously as the number of connected components of ∂B appearing along ζ, and the number of blue arc segments composing these components.

Step 3:   We now have to account for duplications of adjacent elements in $S^{(r)}$, $S^{(b)}$, which have been erased in $\bar{S}^{(r)}$, $\bar{S}^{(b)}$, respectively. Consider $S^{(r)}$; it consists of (maximal) *runs*, where each run is a contiguous subsequence of identical elements, which is represented as a single element in $\bar{S}^{(r)}$. Let us mark the first element of each run, as a representative of the corresponding element of $\bar{S}^{(r)}$. Similarly mark the first element of each run of $S^{(b)}$. The total number of marked elements of S is thus

$$|\bar{S}^{(r)}| + |\bar{S}^{(b)}| \le r_\zeta + b_\zeta + 2u_\zeta + 2v_\zeta - 4.$$

Consider a portion S^* of S between two consecutive marked elements. Clearly, S^* is a 'blending' of a portion of a single run of $S^{(r)}$ with a portion of a single run of $S^{(b)}$, excluding the first element of each run. Let a and b denote the red and blue arc segments, respectively, which form these runs. As in Lemma 5.5, the number of alternations of a and b along ζ is at most $s + 3$, of which $s + 1$ can occur in S^*.

In other words, we have shown that the excess of $S^{(r)}$ and $S^{(b)}$ over $\bar{S}^{(r)}$ and $\bar{S}^{(b)}$, between any two adjacent marked elements, is at most $s + 1$. Since the number of marked elements is at most $r_\zeta + b_\zeta + 2u_\zeta + 2v_\zeta - 4$, it follows that the total length of S is at most $(s+2)(r_\zeta + b_\zeta + 2u_\zeta + 2v_\zeta - 4)$. Summing over all components ζ of ∂E, we obtain that its total complexity is at most $(s+2)(r + b + 2u + 2v - 4t)$, as asserted.

Remark 6.8   A stronger combination lemma has been obtained by Edelsbrunner, Guibas, and Sharir (1990) for the case of line segments, where the complexity of E is bounded by $r + b + O(u + v)$; that is, r and b appear in the bound without any multiplicative factor. It therefore appears that the bound just derived is not the best possible, at least for the case of straight segments. It would be nice to sharpen our bound, which we strongly believe to be possible. However, our result implies that the complexity of E is $O(r + b)$, which is sufficient for our purposes.

We now continue with the proof of the general combination lemma. Fix a blue face $B = B_j$ which contains k_j of the given points, say $p_1, \ldots, p_{k_j}$. Let $\zeta_1, \ldots, \zeta_{l_j}$ be the distinct connected components of ∂B. For each p_i, let E_i denote the connected component of $B \cap R_{m_i}$ that contains p_i, as defined above. For each E_i, we choose only one point $p_i \in E_i$ and ignore all other such points. Traverse each ζ_ℓ and partition it into connected portions δ, so that each such portion intersects the boundary of only a single region E_i (and so that two adjacent portions intersect distinct such regions); note that, in general, the (endpoints of the) portions δ are not uniquely defined. We define a plane embedding of a planar graph $\mathcal{G}$ as follows. The vertices of $\mathcal{G}$ are the points $p_1, \ldots, p_{k_j}$ and l_j additional points, $q_1, \ldots, q_{l_j}$, so that q_i lies inside the connected component H_i of $\mathbb{R}^2 - B$ whose common boundary with B is ζ_i. For each portion δ lying on some ζ_ℓ and intersecting some ∂E_i, we add the edge (q_ℓ, p_i) to $\mathcal{G}$, and draw it by taking an arbitrary point in $\delta \cap \partial E_i$ and by connecting it to p_i within E_i and to q_ℓ within H_ℓ. The connectedness of each E_i and each H_ℓ is easily seen to imply that we can draw all edges of $\mathcal{G}$ so that they do not cross one another. See Figure 6.3 for an illustration. It follows from the definition of the portions δ and from the fact that $\mathcal{G}$ is bipartite, that in this embedding of $\mathcal{G}$ each face is bounded by at least four edges (note, however, that $\mathcal{G}$ can have multiple edges between a pair of vertices). Thus, by Euler's formula, the number of edges in $\mathcal{G}$, and thus the number of portions δ, is at most $2(k_j + l_j)$.

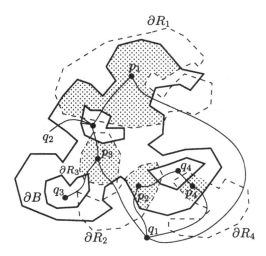

FIGURE 6.3. Bounding the number of boundary portions.

We next define, for each p_i, a modified 'blue-red' region $B_i^\star$ containing p_i, as follows. If $R = R_{m_i}$ does not intersect ∂B at all, then we take $B_i^\star = R$. Otherwise we start at some point z on $\partial B \cap \partial E_i$, and traverse the corresponding portion δ of ∂B with B lying to the left until its last intersection with ∂E_i. Then we turn along ∂R into B and follow ∂R until its next intersection with ∂B. Since this intersection necessarily lies in ∂E_i, we have landed on another portion δ' of ∂B that intersects ∂E_i, and we follow δ' in the direction that keeps B to our left, until its last intersection with ∂E_i, and continue this way until we get back to the starting point z. This yields one component of the boundary of the desired red–blue region $B_i^\star$. If in this process we have not encountered all portions δ of ∂B intersecting ∂E_i, we pick another starting point on one of the portions we have missed, and repeat the tracing from that point. Finally, we add as components of $B_i^\star$ all components of ∂R that bound E_i but that are not intersected by ∂B at all. Tracing all components of the boundary of $\partial B_i^\star$ in this way yields a well-defined connected region bounded between these boundaries.

It is easily checked that $B_i^\star$ contains E_i and is contained in B. We define, in a completely symmetric manner, a modified 'red–blue' region $R_i^\star$ around each p_i. It follows that the connected component of $B_i^\star \cap R_i^\star$ that contains p_i is exactly E_i. Moreover, since we have assumed that no two points p_i, p_j give rise to the same intersection face E, it is easy to check that $\partial B_i^\star \cap E_j = \partial R_i^\star \cap E_j = \emptyset$ for any $i \neq j$. In other words, no arc of $B_i^\star$ or of $R_i^\star$ can appear on the boundary of another E_j (with E_j lying on the same side of that arc).

We are now in a position to apply the bound derived above for the special case of a single point. Let

$b_i = $ the number of blue arc segments of $B_i^\star$,

$r_i = $ the number of red arc segments of $R_i^\star$,

$u_i = $ the number of connected components of $\partial B_i^\star$, and

$v_i = $ the number of connected components of $\partial R_i^\star$.

(By construction, all such components actually appear along ∂E_i.) Since each arc of ∂E_i is either a (portion of a) blue arc of $B_i^\star$ or a (portion of a) red arc of $R_i^\star$, a slight modification of the proof step for a single point (in which we only need to account for duplications of blue arcs of $B_i^\star$ and of red arcs of $R_i^\star$) implies that the complexity of E_i is at most $O(b_i + r_i + u_i + v_i)$. Summing these inequalities over all points p_i, we conclude that the overall complexity of the regions E_i is at most

$$O\left(\sum_i b_i + \sum_i r_i + \sum_i (u_i + v_i)\right). \qquad (6.1)$$

To bound $\sum_i b_i$, consider all blue-red regions $B_i^\star$ contained in one original blue region B_j. Then $\sum_{p_i \in B_j} b_i$ is bounded by the number of arcs of B_j plus a term proportional to the number of pieces δ into which ∂B_j is partitioned. By the preceding argument, this additional term is $O(k_j + l_j)$, where k_j is the number of points p_i in B_j, and l_j is the number of connected components of ∂B_j. We thus obtain, summing over all blue faces B_j,

$$\sum_i b_i = O\left(b + \sum_{j=1}^n k_j + \sum_{j=1}^n l_j\right).$$

But $\sum_j k_j = k$, and the total number of components of the blue faces is clearly bounded by their total complexity b. Hence

$$\sum_i b_i = O(b + k). \tag{6.2}$$

Repeating this counting for the red–blue faces, we obtain

$$\sum_i r_i = O(r + k). \tag{6.3}$$

Finally, $\sum_i u_i$ (and $\sum_i v_i$) can be bounded in a similar manner, noting that for each original blue face B_j, the sum $\sum_{p_i \in B_j} u_i$ is bounded by l_j plus the number of pieces δ along ∂B_j, so that

$$\sum_i u_i = O\left(\sum_{j=1}^n k_j + \sum_{j=1}^n l_j\right) = O(b + k), \tag{6.4}$$

and similarly

$$\sum_i v_i = O(r + k). \tag{6.5}$$

Combining inequalities (6.1)–(6.5) completes the proof of the lemma. $\square$

The Combination Lemma has a useful application to the case in which we want to bound the complexity of a single face (containing a marking point p) in an arrangement $\mathcal{A}(\Gamma)$ of a set of n Jordan curves or arcs, with the following properties:

(i) $\Gamma = \Gamma_1 \cup \Gamma_2 \cup \cdots \cup \Gamma_t$, for some constant t.

(ii) For each $i = 1, \ldots, t$, any pair of curves in Γ_i intersect in at most s_i points.

(iii) Any pair of curves of Γ intersect in at most s points.

A naive application of Theorem 5.3 (or Theorem 5.7) gives a bound of $O(\lambda_{s+2}(n))$ (or $\lambda_s(n)$) for the complexity of the face. However, using the Combination Lemma, we can do better: For each $i = 1, \ldots, t$, let F_i be the face containing p in $\mathcal{A}(\Gamma_i)$. Assume for now that Γ consists of Jordan arcs. Then the complexity of F_i is $O(\lambda_{s_i+2}(n))$. Now merge the faces $F_1, \ldots, F_t$ in a binary-tree fashion (merging them in pairs, then in pairs of pairs, etc.). By the Combination Lemma, the complexity of the output face (containing p) of each merge step is proportional to the sum of the complexities of the two input faces. Since the merge is executed only a constant number of times, it easily follows that the complexity of the final face containing p in $\mathcal{A}(\Gamma)$ is $O(\sum_{i=1}^t \lambda_{s_i+2}(n_i))$, where $n_i = |\Gamma_i|, i = 1, \ldots, t$; this sum is clearly bounded by $O(\lambda_{s^*+2}(n))$, where $s^* = \max_i s_i$. (The constant of proportionality depends on s and t—it is bounded by $O(s)^{\log t}$, as is easily checked.) An analogous analysis applies to the case of closed Jordan curves, leading to the following result:

Corollary 6.9 *The complexity of a single face in an arrangement of Jordan arcs (respectively, curves) satisfying the conditions (i)–(iii) listed above is $O(\lambda_{s^*+2}(n))$ (respectively, $O(\lambda_{s^*}(n))$), where $s^* = \max_{1 \le i \le t} s_i$.*

As an illustration, suppose that Γ consists of n parabolas of the form $y = a_i x^2 + b_i x + c_i$, for $1 \le i \le n$, and of n other parabolas of the form $x = \alpha_i y^2 + \beta_i y + \gamma_i$, for $n < i \le 2n$. The above corollary implies that the complexity of a single cell in $\mathcal{A}(\Gamma)$ is only $O(\lambda_2(n)) = O(n)$, as opposed to the naive bound of $O(\lambda_4(n))$, if all curves in Γ are lumped together.

6.3.2   The red–blue merge

We now continue the description of our red–blue merge. Let π be the total number of vertices in the purple regions. The Combination Lemma 6.7 implies that $\pi = O(b + r + n) = O(b + r)$.

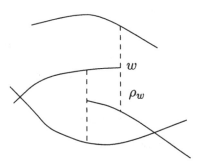

FIGURE 6.4. Vertical dividers.

To facilitate our merge, we require certain information to be precomputed and available for each collection. Specifically, we require that the red region R be subdivided into x-monotone subregions by drawing vertical segments up and down from each point w in $P \cap R$, extended till they meet an edge of R. We call the resulting vertical segment through w the red *vertical divider* at w, and denote it by $\rho(w)$ (see Figure 6.4). It is easily checked that this does produce a decomposition of R as desired. Similar partitioning is required for the blue region, using blue vertical dividers (denoted as $\beta(w)$), thereby obtaining a similar collection of blue x-monotone subregions.

These monotone decompositions of the red and blue regions are easy to obtain using a straightforward vertical line sweeping, in time $O((b + r) \log(b +$

r)). Note that a particular monotone subregion may terminate on the left or on the right either because of a point of P, or because of a locally x-extremal vertex of the corresponding region. Our algorithm will produce a similar partitioning of the purple regions into monotone subregions, which we call the *purple subregions.*

We calculate the purple subregions by sweeping with a straight vertical line. Notice that purple subregions start or end at x-coordinates associated with a point of P, an x-extremum of the red or the blue regions, or a red–blue intersection. In a left-to-right sweep we will discover the portion of each purple subregion that is to the right of the leftmost point in P giving rise to it. Then afterward, in a right-to-left sweep, we will get the portion of each purple subregion to the left of the rightmost point in P giving rise to it. Together, the two sweeps discover all the purple subregions.

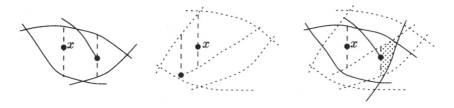

FIGURE 6.5. A spurious purple subregion (the shaded region).

Our algorithm will thus also attempt to construct purple regions incident to each blue or red endpoint (provided that the endpoint is also contained in the opposite-colored region, otherwise no such purple region is to be generated), even though such a purple region might not belong to the desired purple component $f = f_x$. That is, some of these purple subregions might be disconnected from f (see Figure 6.5 for an example). However, we will be able to detect this at the end of the algorithm, as follows. Consider the graph whose nodes are the final purple subregions, and whose edges connect pairs of purple subregions adjacent along some vertical divider. Then a simple breadth-first search on this graph, starting from the purple subregion that contains x, will yield the desired component f; all the unreachable purple subregions will simply be discarded. (As noted above, Lemma 6.7 implies that the size of the additional 'fake' purple regions is at most $O(b + r)$.)

We describe below only the left-to-right sweeping step; the right-to-left step is symmetric. We start this sweep by constructing a priority queue, ordered by x-coordinates, which contains all the vertices appearing along the boundaries of the given red and blue regions, together with the point x. We will be sweeping over the red and blue subregions separately, and at the same time will also be sweeping over the purple subregions, and construct (portions of) them as we sweep. We will speak of the red, blue, and purple planes, respectively.

The purpose of these separate sweeps is to avoid having to process too many 'uninteresting' red–blue intersections, that is, intersections that do not occur along the boundary of a purple region.

Every time we encounter a point p of P, we start one or two new purple subregions in the purple plane. For each new purple subregion, we create two new purple 'scouts': the upper scout, and the lower scout. It is the job of these two scouts to walk, respectively, along the upper and lower boundaries of a new purple subregion. We describe the behavior of the upper scout u of one such region; the lower scouts behave symmetrically.

The upper scout u starts on a red or blue arc, as determined by the closest of the upper endpoints of the vertical dividers $\rho(p)$, $\beta(p)$. The scout u will move right along that arc following the sweep line, but it needs to watch out for certain events that might influence the upper purple boundary of its subregion. Without loss of generality, we assume that u currently sits on a red arc.

The scout u has first of all to look up to the nearest blue arc β (note that, since u is 'purple,' the entire vertical segment between u and β must be contained in B). The reason is that the blue boundary above u might at some future point drop below the red boundary the scout is currently following. If this were to occur, then u would have to follow the blue boundary, because now it delimits (from above) the purple subregion. However, there might be another scout v already 'watching' that blue arc β from below. In that case only the highest of u and v needs to watch β from below: the other scout can rest, since it is certain that the higher scout is 'protecting' it from β.

In more technical detail, watching a blue arc β means that u has to determine whether the arc ρ it lies on and β intersect to the right of the sweep-line, and, if so, insert the leftmost such intersection as an event into the priority queue of the sweep (each of these operations, except for the priority queue insertion, is assumed to take constant time in our model of computation). In addition, if the sweeping process reaches the right endpoint c of either ρ or β, which is not an endpoint of the whole curve (from Γ) containing that subarc, u has to retest for a potential intersection between the new pair of arcs (in which the arc terminating at c is replaced by a new arc that starts there), and, if it exists, add the leftmost such intersection to the queue. When such a red–blue intersection is eventually swept across, u has to move to the blue arc β, and to begin to watch the red boundary above it (starting with ρ). Note that the blue boundary above u, or the red boundary it currently follows, may also change discontinuously, when the sweep reaches the endpoint of the corresponding full curve. When this happens, one of the additional things we have to do is to check whether the watching assignment of some purple scout has to change, and to inform the scout of this change. See below for more details.

The scout u has also to look down to its lower partner and check for their (leftmost) possible intersection (to the right of the sweep-line), because when the two of them meet the current purple subregion must end. This might happen earlier too, if another point of P is encountered between these scouts.

The key property here is that each blue or red arc is watched (at any given time) by at most one upper scout and by at most one lower scout, who sit on arcs of the opposite color. This is crucial to the efficiency of the algorithm, because it implies that when a watched arc is to be replaced by another, only a constant number of updates of watching assignments are required.

The need to update these assignments of who watches over whom can arise in several cases. One such case is when a purple region ends at a point where its two purple scouts come together. This will occur, for instance, when the rightmost vertex of a red subregion lies inside a blue subregion. In this event, the two purple scouts of that purple subregion are eliminated. However, some transfer of watching responsibility may now be indicated. If the upper scout u was watching a blue arc β, then we must consult the next upper purple scout down from u, say, v. If v is currently idle, because the next higher blue arc above v is the same arc β watched by u, then u transfers to v the responsibility of watching β. However, if v is already watching another blue arc, then we leave it undisturbed, as its blue arc must be below β; in that case, β stops (for now) being watched from below.

Another way the two purple partner scouts can come together is when a purple region ends at a red–blue crossing. Any transfers of watching responsibility that need to happen now can be dealt with in an entirely analogous way. If a purple region ends because another point p of P appears between the scouts, then again the two scouts are eliminated, but in this case they will generally be replaced by new scouts spawned by p.

The reassignment of watching responsibility that occurs when we sweep through a point p of P is, in more detail, as follows. At this time, zero, one, or two new purple subregions are created. Suppose for simplicity that only one new subregion arises, and let u be its top scout. This scout u finds the opposite-colored arc e it has to watch by a binary search through the list of arcs of that color currently intersecting the sweepline. But then u also has to consult the upper purple scout u^+ (respectively, u^-) lying directly above u (respectively, below u). If u^+ is watching the same e (more precisely, if u^+ lies below e) then u remains idle. Otherwise u begins to watch e and checks whether u^- is also watching e, in which case u^- becomes idle. Similar but somewhat modified actions are taken when two new purple regions are spawned at p.

In further detail, suppose p is an endpoint of a red original curve; then we check whether p also lies in the blue region B. If so, we start one or two new purple regions incident to p (and lying to its right), and proceed with scout creation and watching reassignments as above; otherwise no new purple region is to be generated at p. In either case, if the vertical divider $\rho(p)$ extends both up and down from p (i.e., p is a point of 'vertical tangency' on the boundary of its region), then some red boundaries currently watched by a purple scout may change discontinuously. For example, if two red arcs, e_1, e_2, incident to p, extend to the right of p (with e_1 lying below e_2), then we search through the list of purple regions along the sweepline to find the upper scout u lying directly below p, and, if it lies on a blue arc, tell u to start watching e_1, unless it is watching a red arc lying below p. If u lies on a red arc, then if it is idle we leave it undisturbed; if it is watching a blue arc lying below p we again leave it undisturbed; however, if u watches a blue arc β above p, then it is easily checked that p must also lie within the blue region B, and, consequently, two new purple regions will be created at p, new purple scouts will be spawned along e_1, e_2, and the (upper) scout along e_2 will relieve u from the responsibility of watching β, as explained above. Similar or symmetric actions are taken in all the other subcases.

Finally, some transfer of watching may be required at a red–blue crossing lying, say, on the top boundary of some purple subregion. Suppose the corresponding upper purple scout u was lying on a red arc ρ just before the intersection, and afterward it moves along a blue arc β. As noted above, u now has to start watching ρ, but we also need to check whether the upper purple scout v lying directly below u has to change the arc it is watching, or become idle. Details are similar to those in the cases considered above, and can be easily worked out by the reader.

Note that this procedure produces not only the purple regions, but also their x-monotone decompositions into purple subregions, which will be handy for further processing. However, some preprocessing might still be required before subsequent merges (call them purple-violet) can be performed. This is because an endpoint p of some purple original curve may also lie within the violet region, in which case we will need to find the violet vertical divider at p, and this information in general is neither part of the 'purple' data nor part of the 'violet' data, and can be obtained only by combining information from these two collections prior to their merge.

Let us now analyze the complexity of this process. The purple scouts simply trace the boundaries of the purple regions. Each such scout needs to schedule into the priority queue possible intersection events between the arc it is currently sitting on, and the arc it is watching (including the possible intersection between the current upper and lower arcs of the same purple subregion). Note that new events are scheduled when we sweep through a point in P, through a blue vertex, through a red vertex, or through a red–blue crossing (which is a vertex of a purple subregion). Moreover, at each such point only a constant number of new events are scheduled. Thus the total number of events ever scheduled is proportional to the total input and output size, which, by Lemma 6.7, is $O(b + r)$. Thus each event costs $O(\log(b + r))$ time to insert into (and delete from) the priority queue. The additional operations of our procedure involve updating the red, blue, and purple lists along the sweepline, creating and eliminating scouts (i.e., purple subregions), and reassigning watching responsibilities. It is plain that we need to perform only $O(b+r)$ such operations (making use of the crucial fact that no arc is ever watched by more than a constant number of scouts at a time), and that each operation can be carried out in $O(\log(b+r))$ time (because the maximum size of the red, blue, and purple lists along the sweepline is at most $O(b+r)$). The final step of detecting 'true' purple subregions (those that are connected to the 'anchor' point x), and of eliminating the other subregions, can be done by a simple graph searching (as explained earlier) in time linear in the number of purple subregions produced by the algorithm, that is, in $O(b+r)$ time. Thus our procedure runs in overall time $O((b+r)\log(b+r))$.

We have thus shown:

Theorem 6.10 *Given two connected 'red' and 'blue' regions R, B, both containing a given point x, whose boundaries are composed respectively of r and b subarcs of some collection of Jordan arcs (or curves), no pair of which intersect at more than a constant number, s, of points, one can calculate the connected component f of the intersection $R \cap B$ that contains x, in time $O((r+b)\log(r+b))$, under the assumptions made at the beginning of the section concerning the given curves and the model of computation.*

Moreover, in our application, each of the regions R and B is a single connected component in an arrangement of at most $\lceil n/2 \rceil$ Jordan arcs (or curves), each pair of which intersect in at most s points. The time bounds given above are for the merge step of our overall algorithm. Using Theorem 5.3, we thus obtain, by straightforward calculation,

Theorem 6.11 *Given a collection Γ of n Jordan arcs (or curves), having the property that no pair of them intersect in more than s points, and also satisfying the conditions made above, one can calculate the face of $\mathcal{A}(\Gamma)$ containing a specified point x, in time $O(\lambda_{s+2}(n)\log^2 n)$ (or in time $O(\lambda_s(n)\log^2 n)$ for closed or unbounded Jordan curves).*

Remark 6.12 Concerning lower bounds, it is easy to establish an $\Omega(n\log n)$ bound, by a linear-time reduction from the problem of sorting n real numbers. We do not know of any larger lower bound. In particular, we pose it as an open problem whether a face of $\mathcal{A}(\Gamma)$ can be computed by a deterministic algorithm in time $O(\lambda_{s+2}(n)\log n)$, which will then be comparable to the algorithm given in Section 6.2 for the calculation of lower envelopes. As we will see next, this time bound can be achieved if we allow randomization.

6.4 Randomized divide-and-conquer construction

In this section we present a rather simple randomized divide-and-conquer algorithm for computing a single face in an arrangement $\mathcal{A}(\Gamma)$ of n Jordan arcs in the plane, where Γ is, as above, a collection of n Jordan arcs (or curves) satisfying the conditions stated earlier. Many randomized algorithms have been recently designed in computational geometry. They are often much simpler than their deterministic counterparts, and are sometimes even more efficient, as the current case demonstrates.

The basic idea of the algorithm is as follows: Randomly choose a subset $\Gamma_1 \subseteq \Gamma$ of $\lfloor n/2 \rfloor$ arcs; recursively compute the faces f_1, f_2 in $\mathcal{A}(\Gamma_1)$ and in $\mathcal{A}(\Gamma - \Gamma_1)$, respectively, that contain the point x; and then merge f_1 and f_2 to compute the face of $\mathcal{A}(\Gamma)$ that contains x. The merge step is different from the red–blue merge described above, and appears to be much less efficient. However, because of the random nature of the divide step, we can show that the *expected* cost of the merge, under the random choice of Γ_1, is only $O(\lambda_{s+2}(n))$. This will result in an overall algorithm with expected running time $O(\lambda_{s+2}(n) \log n)$. We emphasize that in this algorithm, as well as in all other randomized algorithms presented later in the book, the expectation of the cost of the algorithm is with respect to the internal randomization performed by the algorithm, and holds for *any* input collection Γ. We also note that all the randomized algorithms that we will be presenting are of the type known as 'Las Vegas': They always terminate, and always produce the correct output, but their running time is a random variable (over the internal randomizations); we will mainly be concerned with obtaining upper bounds for its expected value.

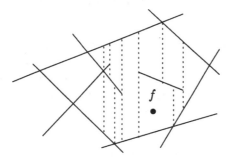

FIGURE 6.6. Vertical decomposition of a face (in an arrangement of line segments; here each cell is indeed a trapezoid, or a triangle).

In order to facilitate the merge step, we need to have available the *vertical decomposition* f^* of f, obtained by drawing, through each vertex v of f, a maximal vertical line segment whose relative interior does not meet ∂f at a point other than v (see also Figure 6.6). This decomposes f into *pseudo-trapezoidal cells* (or *cells* for brevity). A typical cell τ of f^* is bounded by two vertical edges, called the *left* and *right* edges of τ, and by (portions of) two arcs of Γ, called the *top* and *bottom* edges of τ (recall that the arcs of Γ are assumed to be x-monotone). Some of the cells may be unbounded and some of them may have fewer than four edges. Without loss of generality, we assume that no two vertices in $\mathcal{A}(\Gamma)$ (i.e., endpoints of arcs in Γ and intersection points of arcs) have the same x-coordinate. Therefore a cell τ shares its vertical boundaries with at most four other cells, referred to as the vertical neighbors of τ. The data structure that we will use to represent f^* consists of the cells τ constituting f^*, arranged in a *vertical adjacency graph*, whose edges connect pairs of vertical neighboring cells. In addition, the cell of f^* containing the face-marking point x is also assumed to be known.

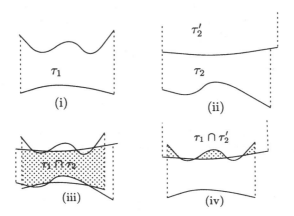

FIGURE 6.7. Intersection cells: (iii) $\tau_1 \cap \tau_2$ is connected; (iv) $\tau_1 \cap \tau_2'$ consists of three connected components.

Assume that we have already computed recursively the decomposed faces f_1^* and f_2^* (as defined above). We now want to merge f_1^* and f_2^* to produce f^*. We call a connected component of a (nonempty) intersection $\tau_1 \cap \tau_2$, for $\tau_1 \in f_1^*$, $\tau_2 \in f_2^*$, an *intersection cell* of $f_1^* \cap f_2^*$; τ is also a 'trapezoid-like' cell, in the sense that it is bounded by at most two (possibly unbounded) vertical segments, and by an x-monotone top boundary and an x-monotone bottom boundary. If the left (respectively, right) vertical edge of τ is nonempty, then it is a portion of the left (respectively, right) edge of τ_1 or of τ_2. The top boundary of τ is a portion of the lower envelope of the top edges of τ_1 and of τ_2, and the bottom boundary is a portion of the upper envelope of the bottom edges of τ_1 and of τ_2; these boundaries may contain new vertices of $\mathcal{A}(\Gamma)$ (see Figure 6.7 (iii)). If $\tau_1 \cap \tau_2$ consists of more than one connected component, then these components have nonoverlapping x-projections, and at most two of them have vertical edges: The leftmost component has a left vertical edge, and the rightmost component has a right vertical edge (see Figure 6.7 (iv)). If x lies in an intersection cell τ that does not have any vertical edge, then $f = \tau$. Otherwise, for any pair of overlapping cells $\tau_1 \in f_1^*$, $\tau_2 \in f_2^*$, only those intersection cells of $\tau_1 \cap \tau_2$ that have vertical edges can possibly lie in f. Hence, at most two connected components of $\tau_1 \cap \tau_2$ lie in f.

As mentioned in the previous section, we cannot afford in general to compute all intersection cells in $f_1^* \cap f_2^*$, so we construct only those intersection cells that lie in f. An intersection cell τ in $f_1^* \cap f_2^*$ lies in f if and only if there is a path π from x to a point $y \in \tau$, such that π intersects only vertical edges (and does not meet any top or bottom edge) of intersection cells in $f_1^* \cap f_2^*$. Therefore, the desired intersection cells τ can be computed by traversing the intersection cells of $f_1^* \cap f_2^*$ in a, say, depth-first manner, starting from the intersection cell τ_x that contains the point x (which is the connected component containing x of the intersection of the two corresponding cells in f_1^* and f_2^*), and moving from each visited intersection cell τ to other intersection cells adjacent to τ along vertical edges.

In more detail, suppose that, during the search, we have reached, for the first time, an intersection cell $\tau \subseteq \tau_1 \cap \tau_2$, for $\tau_1 \in f_1^*, \tau_2 \in f_2^*$. If τ has a left vertical edge, e_L, and if this edge is a portion of the left edge of τ_1 (respectively, of τ_2), then, for each vertical neighbor τ_1' of τ_1 (respectively, τ_2' of τ_2), whose right edge overlaps e_L, we visit the rightmost intersection cell of $\tau_1' \cap \tau_2$ (respectively, $\tau_1 \cap \tau_2'$), if such an intersection cell exists. If τ has a right vertical edge, we perform a symmetric step for that edge.

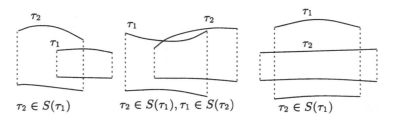

FIGURE 6.8. Different types of intersection cells.

For each cell $\tau_1 \in f_1^*$, we maintain a set $S(\tau_1)$ of certain intersection cells τ in the overlay of f_1^* and f_2^*, such that $\tau \subseteq \tau_1$, and τ has already been visited. Note that a cell $\tau_2 \in f_2^*$ may generate at most two elements of $S(\tau_1)$ (namely, the leftmost and rightmost components of $\tau_1 \cap \tau_2$). A similar list $S(\tau_2)$ is maintained for each cell $\tau_2 \in f_2^*$. These lists are constructed as follows. If the two cells $\tau_1 \in f_1^*, \tau_2 \in f_2^*$ intersect, then one of the following cases must arise (see Figure 6.8):

(i) One of the cells, say, τ_2, contains a vertex of the other. In this case we put (the relevant leftmost or rightmost component of) $\tau_1 \cap \tau_2$ in $S(\tau_1)$, after (this component of) $\tau_1 \cap \tau_2$ has been visited.

(ii) A top or bottom edge of τ_1 intersects a top or bottom edge of τ_2. In this case we put (the relevant component of) $\tau_1 \cap \tau_2$ in $S(\tau_1)$ and in $S(\tau_2)$, after this component has been visited.

(iii) The two vertical sides of, say, τ_1, intersect both the top and the bottom edges of τ_2, but the top and bottom edges of τ_1 are disjoint from τ_2. In this case we put (the relevant component of) $\tau_1 \cap \tau_2$ in $S(\tau_1)$, after this component has been visited.

Hence, if an intersection cell $\tau \subseteq \tau_1 \cap \tau_2$ has already been visited, then it is stored in at least one of the lists $S(\tau_1)$, $S(\tau_2)$, so scanning these two lists allows us to determine whether τ has already been visited. (Note that it always suffices to scan just one of these lists, depending on which of the three patterns of intersection between τ_1 and τ_2, as listed above, occurs; in cases (i), (iii), the list to be searched is uniquely defined, whereas in case (ii) any of the two lists will do.)

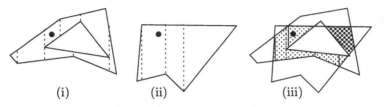

FIGURE 6.9. Merging two faces: (i) f_1^*, (ii) f_2^*, (iii) $f_1^* \cap f_2^*$; the darkly shaded portion of $f_1^* \cap f_2^*$ is not in f^*; the solid vertical segments are new vertical edges in $f_1^* \cap f_2^*$.

After the search is exhausted, we obtain all intersection cells that constitute f. The algorithm also calculates the vertical adjacency of these intersection cells. Note that each intersection cell τ is still bounded by two vertical segments and by two x-monotone top and bottom boundaries. However, these boundaries may contain new vertices of $\mathcal{A}(\Gamma)$, in which case we need to further partition τ into (a constant number of) pseudo-trapezoidal cells by drawing vertical segments through each such vertex within τ. In addition, the left or right vertical edge of τ may now be redundant (as in the first and last cases of Figure 6.8), in which case we need to erase such an edge, and merge the two pseudo-trapezoidal cells that it bounds into a single cell. This cleanup phase yields the vertical decomposition f^* in the required format. This completes the description of the algorithm.

We now analyze the running time of the algorithm. Let F_1 (respectively, F_2) denote the collection of cells of f_1^* (respectively, f_2^*) that intersect f; these are the cells in f_1^* (respectively, f_2^*) that have been visited by the algorithm. For a cell τ of f_1^* or of f_2^*, let $|S(\tau)|$ denote the cardinality of the list $S(\tau)$ at the end of the merge step. Each time we visit an intersection cell $\tau \subseteq \tau_1 \cap \tau_2$, we spend either $O(|S(\tau_1)|)$ or $O(|S(\tau_2)|)$ time to determine whether τ has already been visited (depending on the pattern of intersection between τ_1 and τ_2). Moreover, τ is visited only when a neighboring intersection cell is newly constructed. Since τ has only $O(1)$ such neighbors, it is visited only a constant number of times. Finally, after τ is visited, it belongs to the list $S(\tau_1)$ or $S(\tau_2)$ that we have searched through. For each cell $\tau_1 \in f_1^*$, define $\tilde{S}(\tau_1)$ to be the set of cells $\tau_2 \in f_2^*$ whose intersections with τ_1 define cells stored at $S(\tau_1)$, and define $\tilde{S}(\tau_2)$, for cells $\tau_2 \in f_2^*$, in a symmetric manner. Since the algorithm visits at most two connected components of any intersection $\tau_1 \cap \tau_2$, it follows that $|S(\tau_1)| \leq 2|\tilde{S}(\tau_1)|$ and $|S(\tau_2)| \leq 2|\tilde{S}(\tau_2)|$, for any $\tau_1 \in f_1^*$, $\tau_2 \in f_2^*$. Hence, the total running time of the algorithm is bounded by

$$O\left(\sum_{\substack{\tau_1 \in F_1 \\ \tau_2 \in \tilde{S}(\tau_1)}} |\tilde{S}(\tau_1)| + \sum_{\substack{\tau_2 \in F_2 \\ \tau_1 \in \tilde{S}(\tau_2)}} |\tilde{S}(\tau_2)| \right) = O\left(\sum_{\tau_1 \in F_1} |S(\tau_1)|^2 + \sum_{\tau_2 \in F_2} |S(\tau_2)|^2 \right),$$

where the sets $S(\tau_1)$, $\tilde{S}(\tau_1)$, $S(\tau_2)$, and $\tilde{S}(\tau_1)$ assume their final (largest) value. We will bound the expected value of the first sum. A symmetric argument gives the same bound for the second sum.

Let n_τ denote the number of arcs in $\Gamma_2 = \Gamma - \Gamma_1$ that intersect a cell τ of F_1. Recall that a cell $\tau_2 \in F_2$ is in $\tilde{S}(\tau_1)$ if either τ_2 contains a vertex of τ_1, or a nonvertical boundary of τ_2 intersects a nonvertical boundary of τ_1, or both nonvertical boundaries of τ_2 cross τ_1. The number of cells τ_2 of the first type is at most 4. The number of cells τ_2 of the second type is clearly proportional to n_{τ_1} (because each of the n_{τ_1} arcs intersecting τ_1 can intersect the top and bottom edges of τ_1 in only a constant number of times). The same bound is also easily seen to hold for cells τ_2 of the third type. Hence,

$$\begin{aligned}
\sum_{\tau \in F_1} |S(\tau)|^2 &= O\left(\sum_{\tau \in F_1} (1 + n_\tau)^2 \right) = \sum_{\tau \in F_1} O\left(1 + \binom{n_\tau}{2} \right) \\
&= O(|F_1|) + O\left(\sum_{\tau \in F_1} \binom{n_\tau}{2} \right) \\
&= O(\lambda_{s+2}(n)) + O\left(\sum_{\tau \in F_1} \binom{n_\tau}{2} \right).
\end{aligned}$$

Each cell τ of f^* is 'defined' by at most four arcs of Γ, in the sense that there is a subset $\Gamma(\tau) \subseteq \Gamma$, $|\Gamma(\tau)| \leq 4$, such that τ is a cell in the vertical decomposition of $\mathcal{A}(\Gamma(\tau))$ (see Figure 6.10). Let $\mathcal{F}(\Gamma)$ denote the set of all cells that intersect f and are defined by at most four arcs of Γ. Since all cells of f_1^* are defined by at most four arcs of $\Gamma_1 \subseteq \Gamma$ and all cells in F_1 intersect f, we have $F_1 \subseteq \mathcal{F}(\Gamma)$.

Lemma 6.13 $\mathbf{E}\left[\sum_{\tau \in F_1} \binom{n_\tau}{2} \right] = O(\lambda_{s+2}(n))$ *(where $\mathbf{E}$ denotes expectation)*.

Proof. For a cell $\tau \in \mathcal{F}(\Gamma)$, let

$$P_\tau = \Pr\{\tau \in F_1\},$$

FIGURE 6.10. Some types of cells defined by at most four arcs.

where $\Pr\{A\}$ denotes the probability of an event A. Then we have

$$\mathbf{E}\left[\sum_{\tau \in F_1} \binom{n_\tau}{2}\right] = \sum_{\tau \in \mathcal{F}(\Gamma)} \binom{n_\tau}{2} P_\tau.$$

We next estimate the value of P_τ. A cell $\tau \in \mathcal{F}(\Gamma)$ is in F_1 if and only if the following two conditions hold:

(i) The set $\Gamma(\tau)$ of the $k_\tau \le 4$ arcs defining τ is a subset of Γ_1.

(ii) None of the n_τ arcs of Γ intersecting the interior of τ are in Γ_1.

Put $r = |\Gamma_1| = \lfloor n/2 \rfloor$. To satisfy these two conditions, we must choose all k_τ arcs defining τ in Γ_1, and choose the remaining $r - k_\tau$ arcs of Γ_1 from the $n - n_\tau - k_\tau$ arcs that neither define nor cross τ. There are $\binom{n}{r}$ ways of selecting r arcs from Γ, so we have

$$P_\tau = \binom{n - n_\tau - k_\tau}{r - k_\tau} \Big/ \binom{n}{r}.$$

Since

$$\binom{n - n_\tau - k_\tau}{r - k_\tau} = O\left(\frac{n^2}{r^2}\right) \cdot \binom{n - n_\tau - k_\tau}{r - k_\tau - 2},$$

we have

$$\sum_{\tau \in \mathcal{F}(\Gamma)} \binom{n_\tau}{2} P_\tau = O\left(\frac{n^2}{r^2}\right) \sum_{\tau \in \mathcal{F}(\Gamma)} \binom{n_\tau}{2}\binom{n - n_\tau - k_\tau}{r - k_\tau - 2} \Big/ \binom{n}{r}$$

$$= O\left[\sum_{\tau \in \mathcal{F}(\Gamma)} \binom{n_\tau}{2}\binom{n - n_\tau - k_\tau}{r - k_\tau - 2} \Big/ \binom{n}{r}\right]$$

(because $r = \lfloor n/2 \rfloor$.)

The proof is now completed by the following lemma.   □

Lemma 6.14 $\displaystyle \sum_{\tau \in \mathcal{F}(\Gamma)} \binom{n_\tau}{2}\binom{n - n_\tau - k_\tau}{r - k_\tau - 2} \Big/ \binom{n}{r} = O(\lambda_{s+2}(n)).$

Proof. Let $\mathcal{F}^2(\Gamma_1) \subseteq \mathcal{F}(\Gamma)$ denote the set of all cells that (a) are defined by at most four arcs of Γ_1, (b) intersect the face f of $\mathcal{A}(\Gamma)$, and (c) are crossed by exactly two arcs of Γ_1.

Using a similar argument to the one given above, it is easily checked that a cell $\tau \in \mathcal{F}(\Gamma)$ is in $\mathcal{F}^2(\Gamma_1)$ if and only if (i) the k_τ arcs defining τ and exactly two arcs crossing τ are chosen in Γ_1, and (ii) the remaining $r - k_\tau - 2$ arcs of Γ_1 are chosen from the $n - n_\tau - k_\tau$ arcs that neither define nor cross τ. Since there are $\binom{n_\tau}{2}$ ways of choosing two of the n_τ arcs that cross τ, the probability P'_τ of $\tau \in \mathcal{F}(\Gamma)$ being in $\mathcal{F}^2(\Gamma_1)$ is

$$P'_\tau = \binom{n_\tau}{2}\binom{n - n_\tau - k_\tau}{r - k_\tau - 2} \Big/ \binom{n}{r}.$$

Therefore,

$$\mathbf{E}[|\mathcal{F}^2(\Gamma_1)|] = \sum_{\tau \in \mathcal{F}(\Gamma)} \binom{n_\tau}{2}\binom{n - n_\tau - k_\tau}{r - k_\tau - 2} \Big/ \binom{n}{r},$$

which is the same as the left-hand side of the equation asserted by the lemma. It thus suffices to show that $\mathbf{E}[|\mathcal{F}^2(\Gamma_1)|] = O(\lambda_{s+2}(n))$.

Let $\Gamma'_1 \subseteq \Gamma_1$ be a random subset of size $r' = \lfloor r/2 \rfloor$, where each such subset is chosen with equal probability. Let $F(\Gamma'_1)$ denote the set of pseudo-trapezoidal cells in the vertical decomposition of the face f' of $\mathcal{A}(\Gamma'_1)$ that contains f. Then

$$\begin{aligned}
\mathbf{E}[|F(\Gamma'_1)|] &= \sum_{\tau \in \mathcal{F}(\Gamma_1)} \Pr\{\tau \in F(\Gamma'_1)\} \\
&\geq \sum_{\tau \in \mathcal{F}^2(\Gamma_1)} \Pr\{\tau \in F(\Gamma'_1)\}
\end{aligned}$$

(where Γ_1 is considered as fixed, and the probability is taken only with respect to the choice of Γ'_1).

A cell $\tau \in \mathcal{F}^2(\Gamma_1)$ is in $F(\Gamma'_1)$ if and only if its k_τ defining arcs are in Γ'_1 and neither of the two arcs of Γ_1 that intersect τ is chosen in Γ'_1. Using the same argument as above, we have

$$\begin{aligned}
\Pr\{\tau \in F(\Gamma'_1)\} &= \binom{r - 2 - k_\tau}{r' - k_\tau} \Big/ \binom{r}{r'} \\
&= \frac{(r - r')(r - r' - 1) \cdot r'(r' - 1) \cdots (r' - k_\tau + 1)}{r(r - 1) \cdots (r - k_\tau - 1)}.
\end{aligned}$$

The last right-hand side is bounded from below by some suitable absolute constant $c > 0$, because $r' \geq r/2 - 1$ and $k_\tau \leq 4$. Hence, if we also take expectation with respect to the choice of Γ_1, we obtain:

$$\mathbf{E}[|F(\Gamma'_1)|] \geq c\mathbf{E}[|\mathcal{F}^2(\Gamma_1)|].$$

Each cell of $F(\Gamma'_1)$ appears in f'^*, the vertical decomposition of f'. Theorem 5.3 implies that f'^* has only $O(\lambda_{s+2}(r'))$ cells, so $|F(\Gamma'_1)| = O(\lambda_{s+2}(r'))$. Hence,

$$\mathbf{E}[|\mathcal{F}^2(\Gamma_1)|] \leq \frac{1}{c}O(\lambda_{s+2}(r')) = O(\lambda_{s+2}(n)),$$

which completes the proof of the lemma.   □

Theorem 6.15 *Given a set Γ of n Jordan arcs, each pair of which intersect in at most s points, and a point x not lying on any arc, the face of $\mathcal{A}(\Gamma)$ containing x can be computed by a randomized divide-and-conquer algorithm in $O(\lambda_{s+2}(n)\log n)$ expected time, in an appropriate model of computation.*

6.5 Randomized incremental construction

In this section we describe a randomized incremental algorithm for constructing the face of $\mathcal{A}(\Gamma)$ that contains a given point x. Again, without loss of generality, we assume that the arcs in Γ are x-monotone and that no two endpoints of arcs in Γ have the same x-coordinate. Unlike the previous two algorithms, which were based on the divide-and-conquer approach, the new algorithm constructs the face containing x incrementally, by adding the arcs of Γ one by one in a random order. The only randomized step in our algorithm is the choice of the order in which we add arcs, where each permutation of Γ is chosen with equal probability. While the worst-case running time of this algorithm is quadratic, we show that, if the arcs are added in a random order, then the expected running time of the algorithm is only $O(\lambda_{s+2}(n)\log n)$. An advantage of this approach is that it can be extended to compute efficiently the entire arrangement $\mathcal{A}(\Gamma)$, as will be described in the next section.

Let $\langle \gamma_1, \gamma_2, \ldots, \gamma_n \rangle$ denote the insertion sequence, and let f_i denote the face in the arrangement of $\gamma_1, \ldots, \gamma_i$ that contains x. As in the previous section, we will actually compute the vertical decomposition, f_i^*, of f_i. Recall that f_i^* decomposes f_i into pseudo-trapezoidal cells, each defined by at most four arcs. In the $(i+1)$st step, we add γ_{i+1} and compute f_{i+1}^* from f_i^*. As we add γ_{i+1}, it may chop off a part of f_i by separating it from the point x, so some of the cells of f_i^* may not appear in f_{i+1}^*, and some of them, which are crossed by γ_{i+1}, may have to be replaced by new cells, for which γ_{i+1} is a defining arc. See Figure 6.11 for an illustration. Thus, adding γ_{i+1} requires the following steps:

1. Compute the set of cells in f_i^* that γ_{i+1} intersects.

2. Determine the set of new cells that (may) appear in f_{i+1}^*.

3. Determine the portion of f_i that is chopped off by γ_{i+1}.

4. Discard the cells of f_i^* that do not appear in f_{i+1}^*.

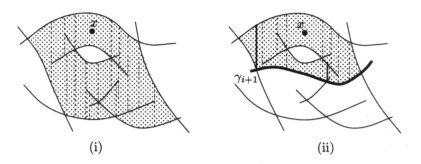

FIGURE 6.11. Adding a new arc: (i) f_i^*; (ii) f_{i+1}^*—the bold vertical segments are the new vertical edges in f_{i+1}^*, some old dashed vertical edges have been truncated or eliminated in f_{i+1}^*.

6.5.1   Data structures

In order to perform the above four steps efficiently, we maintain three data structures. After the ith step, they store the following information. The first data structure stores f_i^* as a vertical adjacency graph whose edges connect pairs of cells sharing a vertical edge (more precisely, having overlapping vertical edges); for each cell in f_i^* we store the list of the (at most four) cells that are its vertical neighbors.

The boundary ∂f_i of f_i is not necessarily connected, and the topology of ∂f_i may change as we add arcs—some of the connected components of ∂f_i may merge into a single component when we add an arc. To keep track of these changes, we maintain a second data structure, which is a union-find data structure, representing the partitioning of $\{\gamma_1, \ldots, \gamma_i\}$ into sets, each consisting of all arcs appearing along a single connected component of ∂f_i (clearly, an arc cannot appear along two such components). This is not an exact definition of the partitioning (for example, some arcs may not show up at all along ∂f_i); a more precise description is given below. Each set in the partitioning is stored as a separate linked list along with some additional pointers, so that one can merge two lists in time proportional to the size of the smaller list and so that, given an arc γ_j, one can find in $O(1)$ time the connected component of ∂f_i in which γ_j appears. See any textbook on data structures, for example, Coreman, Leiserson, and Rivest (1990), for details.

Finally, we maintain a directed acyclic graph (dag) G, which we call the *history dag*. The nodes of G, at the ith insertion stage, correspond to the cells that appeared in at least one f_j^*, for $j \leq i$. For each such cell τ, we associate with its corresponding node v the set of (at most) four arcs of Γ defining τ; the root of the dag corresponds to the entire plane, and no arc is associated with the root. If a cell τ is still *active* at the current insertion stage (i.e., τ is a cell in the vertical decomposition of the current face), then it is stored as a leaf of G (has no successors in G). Otherwise, τ is not part of the current face, which can happen if one of the following two situations arises:

(i) τ was crossed by an arc γ, inserted after τ had been created. The first time this happens, γ creates several new subcells that overlap τ, and G contains directed edges from τ to all these subcells.

(ii) τ was cut off the face by the insertion of an arc γ, but γ did not cross τ. In this case τ remains an *inactive* leaf of G, and no successor of τ will ever be created in G.

If s is the maximum number of intersection points between any pair of arcs in Γ, then the out-degree of a node in G is at most $6 \lfloor s/2 \rfloor + 4$. See Figure 6.12 for an example in which the out-degree of a node is $6 \lfloor s/2 \rfloor + 4$. After the ith step, the internal nodes and inactive leaves of G essentially correspond to cells that appeared in f_j^*, for some $j < i$, but no longer appear in f_i^*. The active leaves correspond to the cells that constitute f_i^*. Once a leaf is marked inactive, it remains inactive, i.e., it can no longer become either an internal node or an active leaf. More details on the construction of G are given below.

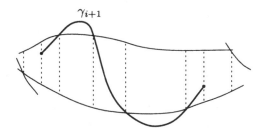

FIGURE 6.12. γ_{i+1} decomposes a cell into $6 \lfloor s/2 \rfloor + 4$ subcells (here s=2).

6.5.2 Adding an arc

After having described the data structures, we can now explain in detail how f_{i+1}^* is obtained from f_i^*, and how the data structures are updated.

First, initialization of the structures is easy: f_0^* is the entire plane (regarded as a single cell); the adjacency graph has the single node f_0^* and no edges; the union-find structure is empty, and the history dag contains f_0^* as a single node (which is an active leaf).

We use the history dag G to determine the cells of f_i^* that γ_{i+1} intersects. To this end, we compute the decomposition of $\gamma_{i+1} \cap f_i$ into a sequence of maximal connected subarcs, sorted from left to right, such that each subarc is a maximal portion of γ_{i+1} lying in a single cell of f_i^*. Starting from the root of

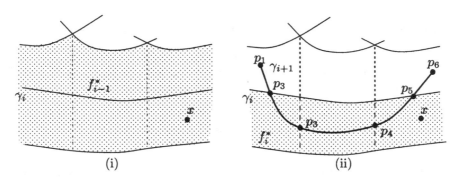

FIGURE 6.13. (i) Adding γ_i to f_{i-1}^*; (ii) adding γ_{i+1} to f_i^*. The search through G partitions γ_{i+1} into fives subarcs, but p_3 and p_4 are redundant points, since the dashed portions of the vertical segments do not appear in f_i^*.

G, γ_{i+1} is propagated downward to all active leaves corresponding to cells that intersect γ_{i+1}. Each recursive step involves processing a node v of G and a portion γ' of γ_{i+1}. If the pair (γ', v) has already been processed, we do nothing; otherwise, for all children w of v that are not inactive leaves, we compute the constant number of connected components, γ'', of $\gamma' \cap \tau_w$, where τ_w is the cell associated with w. We sort all the components γ'', over all children w, from left to right, and recursively process the pairs (γ'', τ_w) of the resulting list, in the sorted order. (As will become clear in a moment, the number of children of v, and thus the number of pairs (γ'', τ_w), is constant.) At the end of this process we obtain a decomposition of $f_i \cap \gamma_{i+1}$, sorted from left to right, such that each subarc lies in a single cell of f_i^*. However, these subarcs may not be maximal, because there may exist pairs of adjacent subarcs lying in the same cell of f_i^*, whose common endpoint lies on a vertical edge of some 'history' cell τ' that does not appear in f_i^*; see Figure 6.13. By making an additional pass through this sequence, we can easily merge such pairs of subarcs. Since the out-degree of each node of G is constant (as already argued), and since $\gamma_{i+1} \cap \tau$, for any cell τ, consists of at most $6 \lfloor s/2 \rfloor + 4$ connected components, the total time spent by the above procedure is proportional to the number of nodes of G that are visited.

By making yet another pass through the resulting decomposition of γ_{i+1}—merging each pair of adjacent subarcs if their common endpoint lies on a vertical edge of a cell in f_i^*—we obtain the connected components, $\gamma_{i+1}^1, \ldots, \gamma_{i+1}^t$, of $\gamma_{i+1} \cap f_i$, sorted from left to right. For each $j = 1, \ldots, t$, let l_j, r_j denote the left and right endpoints of γ_{i+1}^j, respectively, let $f_i(j)$ denote the face containing x after adding $\gamma_1, \ldots, \gamma_i, \gamma_{i+1}^1, \ldots, \gamma_{i+1}^j$, and let $f_i^*(j)$ denote the vertical decomposition of $f_i(j)$; we have $f_i^*(0) = f_i^*$ and $f_i^*(t) = f_{i+1}^*$. We will add the connected components γ_{i+1}^j one by one from left to right, and maintain the incremental versions $f_i^*(j)$ of the face. After adding each γ_{i+1}^j, we will update the vertical adjacency graph and the union-find structure, but will not update the dag G; it will be updated only after inserting all connected components of $\gamma_{i+1} \cap f_i$. In addition, for each cell τ in $f_i^*(j)$, which is not in f_i^* (i.e., created while inserting one of the components of γ_{i+1}), we store the set of cells of f_i^* that intersect τ.

Suppose that we have already added $\gamma_{i+1}^1, \ldots, \gamma_{i+1}^{j-1}$ and have computed $f_i^*(j-1)$, and we want to add γ_{i+1}^j to $f_i^*(j-1)$. We update the cells of $f_i^*(j-1)$ intersected by γ_{i+1}^j and create new cells of $f_i^*(j)$ that did not exist in $f_i^*(j-1)$. Since γ_{i+1} is x-monotone, all cells of $f_i^*(j-1)$ intersected by γ_{i+1}^j, except possibly for the leftmost cell, also appear as cells of f_i^* (intersected by γ_{i+1}). Since the cells of f_i^* intersected by γ_{i+1}^j were computed while tracing γ_{i+1} through G, we easily have at our disposal all the cells of $f_i^*(j-1)$ intersected by γ_{i+1}^j. Let $\tau_1, \ldots, \tau_k$ denote these cells, in their left-to-right order (a cell may appear more than once in this sequence).

We begin by drawing a vertical segment e through l_j in both directions until it meets the top and bottom edges of τ_1 (if l_j lies on an arc of Γ_i, which must be the case when $j > 1$, then one of the endpoints of e is l_j itself). The left edge of τ_1 and e, together with the arcs bounding the top and bottom edges of τ_1, form a new cell, which we denote by $\bar{\tau}_0$. Similarly, we draw a vertical segment through r_j, and obtain a new cell, denoted $\bar{\tau}_{k+2}$.

Next, we process $\tau_1, \ldots, \tau_k$ from left to right, and maintain a pair of 'candidate' cells τ^+, τ^- above and below γ_{i+1}^j. The top cell τ^+ is bounded on the left by a vertical edge descending from some vertex of f_i lying above γ_{i+1}^j, or, initially, by the top portion of e; τ^+ is bounded from above by an arc of Γ_i and from below by γ_{i+1}. The bottom cell τ^- satisfies symmetric properties. When we process τ_ℓ, we distinguish between two cases. If the vertex defining the right edge e_ℓ of τ_ℓ lies above γ_{i+1}^j, we 'close' the top cell τ^+, with the portion of e_ℓ above γ_{i+1}^j as its right edge, and 'open' a new top cell with this portion of e_ℓ as its left edge, and with the new top arc of $\tau_{\ell+1}$ as its upper arc. The bottom cell τ^- remains unchanged. Symmetric actions are taken if the vertex defining e_ℓ lies below γ_{i+1}^j. When τ_k is reached, both τ^+ and τ^- are closed (by the vertical segment through r_j), and one or both of them become neighbors of $\bar{\tau}_{k+2}$. (It is easily checked that the number of new cells is indeed $k+3$.) See Figure 6.14 for an illustration. As this process is performed, we maintain and update vertical adjacency pointers between the new cells. In addition, we store, for each newly created cell of $f_i^*(j)$, the cells of f_i^* that overlap it. Since each cell has at most four vertical neighbors, the total time spent is easily seen to be $O(k)$.

Next, we need to determine whether the drawing of γ_{i+1}^j has caused a portion of $f_i(j-1)$ to be removed from $f_i^*(j)$. To this end, we compute the (at most two) connected components of $\partial f_i(j-1)$ that contain the endpoints l_j, r_j of γ_{i+1}^j. This can be done by querying the union-find structure with the arcs of f_i^* that contain the points l_j, r_j. (An arc of Γ_i can appear in at most one connected component of $\partial f_i(j-1)$, and stores a pointer, in the union-find structure, that points to that component.) If these endpoints lie in different connected components of $\partial f_i(j-1)$, all of the newly created cells appear in $f_i^*(j)$, as is easily checked. Furthermore, these two connected components merge into a single component of $\partial f_i(j)$, so we have to merge, in the union-find structure, the two corresponding lists that store the arcs of these components (and we have to add γ_{i+1} to the merged list).

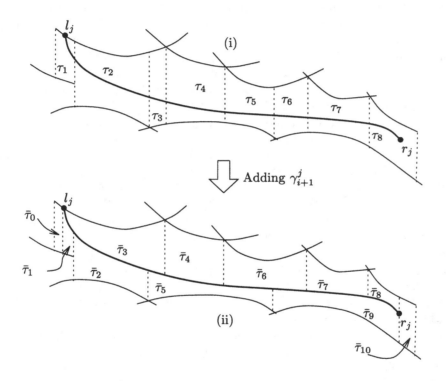

FIGURE 6.14. Updating the set of cells intersected by γ_{i+1}^j.

If l_j and r_j lie on the same connected component of $\partial f_i(j-1)$, say c, then γ_{i+1}^j splits $f_i(j-1)$ into two connected regions, one of which is not part of $f_i(j)$. This portion cannot be determined by a local test. Instead, we perform two graph traversals in lock-step, starting, say, at the two leftmost cells lying above and below γ_{i+1}^j, and find all cells that are reachable from them by crossing only vertical edges of cells. These traversals use the vertical adjacency information and advance in a strictly alternating fashion, one cell at a time. The traversal stops when either one region is exhausted without finding the cell that contains x, or when the cell containing x is found. We then delete the cells of the region not in $f_i^*(j)$. Notice that this lock-step strategy ensures that the time spent in this step is at most proportional to the number of cells deleted.

We repeat the above procedure for all portions of γ_{i+1}^j of γ_{i+1}. After having inserted all of them, we update G. We add a new node for each new cell created while inserting the γ_{i+1}^j's. Since for each such cell τ we have stored the set of cells of f_i^* that intersect τ, we can easily add to G the corresponding new pointers from these cells to τ. If a cell of f_i^* not intersecting γ_{i+1}, or a newly created cell, was deleted after one of the graph traversals (i.e., it is not in f_{i+1}^*), we mark the corresponding leaf of G as inactive. After all arcs of Γ are added, the active leaves of G, together with the vertical adjacency pointers between them, yield the vertical decomposition of the face of $\mathcal{A}(\Gamma)$ containing x. This concludes the description of the algorithm.

Remark 6.16 In the above description, we have assumed that the arcs of Γ are bounded. Nevertheless, the algorithm will also work for unbounded arcs, with a few simple and obvious modifications.

6.5.3 Analysis

The algorithm presented in the previous subsection is a purely on-line algorithm (with the exception of the initial choice of the insertion order). Its correctness is easy to establish, regardless of the order in which the arcs of Γ are inserted. In this subsection we show that, if the arcs are inserted in a random order, the expected behavior of the algorithm is quite good in terms of both running time and storage.

Recall that the main data structures used in our algorithm are a union-find structure, an adjacency graph that stores vertical adjacency pointers between cells, and a history dag. The size of the first structure is $O(n)$, and the size of the adjacency graph and of the dag is proportional to the number of cells constructed during the course of the algorithm. We will show below that the expected number of cells that are constructed by the algorithm is always $O(\lambda_{s+2}(n))$.

The activities performed by the algorithm can be classified into union-find operations, constructing cells, searching for cells to be deleted, and propagating newly inserted arcs down the dag. Since we always merge the smaller list into the bigger one in the union-find structure, the total time spent in merging the connected components is $O(n \log n)$. It is a consequence of Lemma 6.17, proven below, that the expected number of find operations is $O(\lambda_{s+2}(n))$, so these operations take expected time $O(\lambda_{s+2}(n))$.

The time spent in updating f_{i+1}^* is proportional to the number of cells created in this step, plus the number of cells deleted. Each cell is deleted only once, and the number of cells created in the $(i+1)$st step is proportional to the number of cells in f_i^* that intersect γ_{i+1}, because each cell of f_i^* intersecting γ_{i+1} can cause at most $6 \lfloor s/2 \rfloor + 4$ new cells to be created. Since any cell of

f_i^* intersecting γ_{i+1} does not appear in f_{i+1}^*, the total time spent in updating the face, over all n steps, is proportional to the number of distinct cells that appear in some f_j^*, for $j = 1, \ldots, n$.

To understand the cost of propagating an arc down the history dag, let us define the *weight* of a cell τ (of some f_j^*), denoted $w(\tau)$, as the number of arcs (from the entire set Γ) that intersect τ. The total cost of these propagations is then proportional to $\sum_\tau w(\tau)$, where the sum is taken over all cells τ constructed by the algorithm as cells of some f_j^*. Indeed, each of these arcs is added only after τ has been created (or else τ will not be created), and thus will be propagated through τ in the dag. We will show, in Lemma 6.18 below, that the expectation of this sum of weights is $O(\lambda_{s+2}(n) \log n)$.

Lemma 6.17 *The expected number of cells constructed by the algorithm is* $O(\lambda_{s+2}(n))$.

Proof. Fix a cell τ (i.e., a region bounded above and below by portions of a pair, γ_i, γ_j, of arcs of Γ, and by two vertical segments on the left and right sides, each passing either through a vertex of $\mathcal{A}(\Gamma)$ lying either on γ_i or on γ_j, or through an endpoint of a third arc lying between γ_i and γ_j), and define the following two events:

$X_{q,\tau}$: τ is a cell in f_q^*, the vertical decomposition of the face containing x after adding the first q arcs.

$Z_{q,\tau}$: τ is a cell in some f_i^*, for $0 \le i \le q$.

Clearly $Z_{n,\tau} = \bigcup_{q=0}^{n} X_{q,\tau}$, and $\sum_\tau \Pr\{Z_{n,\tau}\}$ is the expected number of cells that appear in some f_i^*, where the sum is taken over all cells τ defined above.

Notice that a cell τ can be constructed only once, thus $\overline{X}_{q-1,\tau} \cap X_{q,\tau}$ is nonempty for at most one q, namely the q for which τ is constructed at the time the qth arc is added. Therefore, $Z_{n,\tau}$ is the *disjoint* union of the events $\overline{X}_{q-1,\tau} \cap X_{q,\tau}$, for $1 \le q \le n$. This is true for all cells τ, except for the unique cell of f_0^*, which is the entire plane, by definition. It follows that

$$\sum_\tau \Pr\{Z_{n,\tau}\} = 1 + \sum_\tau \sum_{q=1}^{n} \Pr\{\overline{X}_{q-1,\tau} \cap X_{q,\tau}\}.$$

By the definition of conditional probability, we have

$$\Pr\{\overline{X}_{q-1,\tau} \cap X_{q,\tau}\} = \Pr\{\overline{X}_{q-1,\tau} | X_{q,\tau}\} \cdot \Pr\{X_{q,\tau}\}.$$

To estimate the conditional probability, we note that τ is defined by a collection Γ_τ of at most four arcs and, assuming that τ is in f_q^*, then it was also in f_{q-1}^* if and only if the qth arc to be added is not one of the arcs of Γ_τ. This implies

$$\Pr\{\overline{X}_{q-1,\tau}|X_{q,\tau}\} \leq \frac{4}{q}.$$

The above equations thus imply

$$\sum_\tau \Pr\{Z_{n,\tau}\} \leq 1 + \sum_\tau \sum_{q=1}^n \frac{4}{q} \Pr\{X_{q,\tau}\} = 1 + \sum_{q=1}^n \frac{4}{q} \sum_\tau \Pr\{X_{q,\tau}\}. \quad (6.6)$$

However, $\sum_\tau \Pr\{X_{q,\tau}\}$ is the expected number of cells in the face f_q^*, after q arcs have been added. By Theorem 5.3, f_q can have at most $O(\lambda_{s+2}(q))$ edges, and therefore at most $O(\lambda_{s+2}(q))$ cells. This finally gives

$$\sum_\tau \Pr\{Z_{n,\tau}\} = \sum_{q=1}^n O\left(\frac{\lambda_{s+2}(q)}{q}\right) = O(\lambda_{s+2}(n)). \qquad \square$$

Next, we bound the expected value of the sum of weights of cells. Recall that the weight $w(\tau)$ of a cell τ is defined as the number of arcs of Γ that intersect τ (excluding the (at most four) arcs defining τ).

Lemma 6.18 *The expected sum of weights of all cells constructed by the algorithm is* $O(\lambda_{s+2}(n) \log n)$.

Proof. Using the notations in the proof of Lemma 6.17, the expected sum of weights, over all cells constructed by the algorithm, is $\sum_\tau w(\tau) \Pr\{Z_{n,\tau}\}$. In addition to the events $Z_{q,\tau}$ and $X_{q,\tau}$, we define

$Y_{q,\tau}$: τ is a cell of f_q^*, and γ_{q+1}, the arc added at the next stage, is one of the $w(\tau)$ arcs that intersect τ.

Note that if τ is a cell of f_q^* then none of the arcs intersecting τ was chosen in the first q steps. So for $Y_{q,\tau}$ to occur, given that $X_{q,\tau}$ has occurred, we have to choose at the $(q+1)$st step one of these $w(\tau)$ arcs out of the remaining $n-q$ arcs. Hence,

$$\Pr\{Y_{q,\tau}\} = \Pr\{X_{q,\tau}\} \cdot \frac{w(\tau)}{n-q}.$$

Observe that

$$Y_{q,\tau} \subseteq X_{q,\tau} \cap \overline{X}_{q+1,\tau}, \quad (6.7)$$

and in general we may have proper inclusion, because τ can also be removed from the face by an arc that does not intersect τ. Independent of whether we have proper or improper inclusion, (6.7) implies that

$$\sum_\tau \sum_{i=1}^q \Pr\{Y_{i,\tau}\} \leq \sum_\tau \sum_{i=1}^q \Pr\{X_{i,\tau} \cap \overline{X}_{i+1,\tau}\}$$
$$\leq \sum_\tau \Pr\{Z_{q,\tau}\} = O(\lambda_{s+2}(q)). \quad (6.8)$$

(The last equality follows by a trivial modification of the proof of Lemma 6.17.) In other words, the expected number of cells that become internal nodes of the dag G during the first $q + 1$ insertions is $O(\lambda_{s+2}(q))$, which is clear because these cells have to be constructed first, and the expected number of such cells, over the course of the first q insertions, is $O(\lambda_{s+2}(q))$, as is implied by Lemma 6.17. Now fix τ and recall from the proof of Lemma 6.17 that

$$\Pr\{Z_{n,\tau}\} = \sum_{q=1}^{n} \Pr\{\overline{X}_{q-1,\tau}|X_{q,\tau}\} \cdot \Pr\{X_{q,\tau}\} \le \sum_{q=1}^{n} \frac{4}{q} \Pr\{X_{q,\tau}\}.$$

This implies that

$$\begin{aligned}
w(\tau)\Pr\{Z_{n,\tau}\} &\le 4\sum_{q=1}^{n} \frac{n-q}{n-q} \cdot \frac{w(\tau)}{q} \Pr\{X_{q,\tau}\} \\
&= 4\sum_{q=1}^{n} \frac{n-q}{q} \Pr\{Y_{q,\tau}\}.
\end{aligned}$$

To simplify the notation, we set $D_q = \sum_{\tau} \Pr\{Y_{q,\tau}\}$, and can now write

$$\begin{aligned}
\sum_{\tau} w(\tau)\Pr\{Z_{n,\tau}\} &\le 4\sum_{q=1}^{n-1} \frac{n-q}{q} D_q \\
&= 4\sum_{q=1}^{n-1} \left(\frac{n-q}{q} - \frac{n-q-1}{q+1}\right) \sum_{i=1}^{q} D_i.
\end{aligned} \tag{6.9}$$

However, we have shown that

$$\sum_{i=1}^{q} D_i = \sum_{\tau} \sum_{i=1}^{q} \Pr\{Y_{i,\tau}\} = O(\lambda_{s+2}(q)).$$

Hence, we finally obtain

$$\begin{aligned}
\sum_{\tau} w(\tau)\Pr\{Z_{n,\tau}\} &\le 4\sum_{q=1}^{n-1} \frac{n}{q(q+1)} O(\lambda_{s+2}(q)) \\
&= O(\lambda_{s+2}(n)\log n),
\end{aligned}$$

as is easily verified. $\square$

In conclusion, we have shown:

Theorem 6.19 *Given a collection Γ of n Jordan arcs, each pair of which intersect in at most s points, and a point x not lying on any arc, the face of $\mathcal{A}(\Gamma)$ containing x can be computed by a randomized incremental algorithm with expected running time $O(\lambda_{s+2}(n)\log n)$, in an appropriate model of computation.*

6.6 Incremental construction of arrangements

In this section we describe two incremental algorithms for computing the entire arrangement $\mathcal{A}(\Gamma)$ of a given collection Γ of n arcs in the plane. The first algorithm is randomized, with expected running time $O(n \log n + k)$, where k is the number of vertices of $\mathcal{A}(\Gamma)$, and the second one is a deterministic algorithm with worst case running time $O(n\lambda_{s+2}(n))$, where s is the maximum number of intersection points between any pair of arcs of Γ.

6.6.1 A randomized algorithm

A variant of the algorithm described in the previous section for computing a single face can be used to compute the entire arrangement $\mathcal{A}(\Gamma)$. Again, we compute the vertical decomposition $\mathcal{A}^*(\Gamma)$ of $\mathcal{A}(\Gamma)$. We add the arcs of Γ one by one in a random order, and maintain the vertical decomposition of the arrangement of the arcs added so far. Let Γ_i be the set of arcs added in the first i steps. For each cell $\tau \in \mathcal{A}^*(\Gamma_i)$, we store its (at most 4) vertical neighbors. We also maintain the history dag G as described in Section 6.5. Since we are maintaining the entire arrangement, all leaves of G are now active. Moreover, we do not need the union-find structure, because all cells of $\mathcal{A}^*(\Gamma_i)$ that are not intersected by γ_{i+1} appear in $\mathcal{A}^*(\Gamma_{i+1})$.

In the $(i+1)$st step, we add γ_{i+1} to $\mathcal{A}^*(\Gamma_i)$, compute $\mathcal{A}^*(\Gamma_{i+1})$, and update the data structures. We first compute, using G, the decomposition of γ_{i+1} into a sequence $\gamma_{i+1}^1, \ldots, \gamma_{i+1}^t$ of maximal connected subarcs, sorted from left to right, so that each subarc lies within a single cell of $\mathcal{A}(\Gamma_i)$. Let

$$\Gamma_i^{(j)} = \Gamma_i \cup \{\gamma_{i+1}^1, \ldots, \gamma_{i+1}^j\},$$

for $j = 1, \ldots, t$. We add the subarcs from left to right. Suppose we have already added $\gamma_{i+1}^1, \ldots, \gamma_{i+1}^{j-1}$, and have computed $\mathcal{A}^*(\Gamma_i^{(j-1)})$. We now add γ_{i+1}^j to $\mathcal{A}^*(\Gamma_i^{(j-1)})$, compute $\mathcal{A}^*(\Gamma_i^{(j)})$, and update the dag G and the relevant vertical adjacency pointers. To be more precise, we split the cells of $\mathcal{A}^*(\Gamma_i^{(j-1)})$ containing the endpoints of γ_{i+1}^j and shrink the vertical boundaries of other cells of $\mathcal{A}^*(\Gamma_i^{(j-1)})$ that intersect γ_{i+1}^j, as in Section 6.5 (see Figure 6.14). Next, we create a leaf in G for each new cell τ in $\mathcal{A}^*(\Gamma_i^{(j)})$, and connect it to all nodes of G corresponding to the cells of $\mathcal{A}^*(\Gamma_i^{(j-1)})$ that intersect τ.

The analysis of the expected running time of this algorithm proceeds exactly as in Section 6.5.3. Let k be the total number of intersection points between the arcs of Γ. Such an intersection point p appears as a vertex of $\mathcal{A}(\Gamma_i)$ if and only if both the arcs forming p are in Γ_i, so the expected number of vertices of $\mathcal{A}(\Gamma_i)$ is $O(i + ki^2/n^2)$, which also bounds the expected number of cells in $\mathcal{A}^*(\Gamma_i)$. Hence, (6.6) implies that the expected number, $S(r)$, of cells created by the first r steps of the algorithm is

$$S(r) = \sum_{i=1}^{r} \frac{1}{i} \cdot O\left(i + k\frac{i^2}{n^2}\right) = O\left(r + k\frac{r^2}{n^2}\right).$$

Hence, the total number of cells created by the algorithm, and thus the total space required by the algorithm, is $S(n) = O(n + k)$. Next, the expected running time of the algorithm, $T(n)$, is bounded by the expected value of the sum of 'weights' of all the cells ever created by the algorithm, where the weight of a cell τ is the number of arcs that intersect τ. By (6.8) in Lemma 6.18, we have

$$
\begin{aligned}
T(n) &\leq \sum_{r=1}^{n-1} \frac{4n}{r(r+1)} S(r) \\
&= \sum_{r=1}^{n-1} \frac{4n}{r(r+1)} \cdot O\left(r + k\frac{r^2}{n^2}\right) \\
&= \sum_{r=1}^{n-1} O\left(\frac{n}{r} + \frac{k}{n}\right) \\
&= O(n \log n + k).
\end{aligned}
$$

Hence, we can conclude:

Theorem 6.20 *Given a collection Γ of n Jordan arcs, one can construct the arrangement $\mathcal{A}(\Gamma)$ by a randomized incremental algorithm with expected running time $O(n \log n + k)$, where k is the number of intersection points between the arcs of Γ. The expected storage of the algorithm is $O(n + k)$.*

6.6.2   A deterministic algorithm

We now present a deterministic incremental algorithm to compute $\mathcal{A}(\Gamma)$. This algorithm is simpler and slightly faster (if the number of intersection points is quadratic) than the sweep-line algorithm by Bentley and Ottmann (1979). The algorithm is rather similar to the one given in the previous subsection, except that we use a simpler procedure to determine the cells intersected by a newly added arc, because we allow more time for that task. In more detail, we add the arcs of Γ one by one in an arbitrary order and maintain $\mathcal{A}^*(\Gamma_i)$, where Γ_i is, as above, the set of the first i added arcs. We do not need the history dag G for this algorithm. Instead, for each edge e of every cell in $\mathcal{A}^*(\Gamma_i)$, we store the list, $L(e)$, of cells in $\mathcal{A}^*(\Gamma_i)$ that are adjacent to e on its other side; see Figure 6.15. It suffices to describe how to compute the cells of $\mathcal{A}^*(\Gamma_i)$ intersected by γ_{i+1}, because, once we have computed these cells, $\mathcal{A}^*(\Gamma_{i+1})$ can be constructed in much the same way as above.

Let z_0 be the leftmost point of γ_{i+1}, if it exists; otherwise, we can choose $z_0 \in \gamma_{i+1}$ to be a point lying to the left of all intersection points between γ_{i+1}

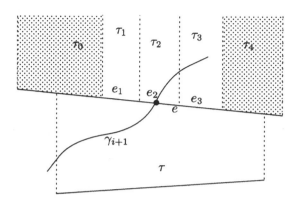

FIGURE 6.15. Charging scheme for cells in $L(e) = [\tau_0, \tau_1, \tau_2, \tau_3, \tau_4]$; here τ_0, τ_4 are charged to e and τ_1, τ_2, τ_3 are charged to e_1, e_2, e_3, respectively.

and the arcs in Γ_i. By drawing a vertical line through z_0 and by determining its two nearest intersection points with the arcs in Γ_i, we can compute the cell of $\mathcal{A}^*(\Gamma_i)$ containing z_0, in $O(i)$ time. Next we trace γ_{i+1} from z_0 to its right, stopping at every vertex of $\mathcal{A}^*(\Gamma_{i+1})$ lying on γ_{i+1} until we reach the right endpoint of γ_{i+1}; each of these vertices is either an endpoint of γ_{i+1}, or an intersection point of γ_{i+1} and an edge of $\mathcal{A}^*(\Gamma_i)$. Suppose we are at a vertex σ_j. If σ_j is the right endpoint of γ_{i+1}, we are done. Otherwise, let τ_{j-1} be the cell of $\mathcal{A}^*(\Gamma_i)$ that γ_{i+1} intersects immediately to the left of σ_j. If σ_j lies in the interior of τ_{j-1}, then it must be the right endpoint of γ_{i+1}. We draw a vertical edge through σ_j, partition τ_{j-1} into subcells as appropriate, and terminate this insertion stage. If σ_j lies on an edge e of τ_{j-1}, we search through the list $L(e)$ and determine the cell τ_j. (Note that this takes $O(1)$ time if e is a vertical edge, but may be rather time consuming if e is a portion of an arc of Γ_i.) After having computed τ_j, σ_{j+1} can be computed in $O(1)$ time, because τ_j has at most four edges. This completes the description of a single insertion stage, and thus also of the entire algorithm.

We now analyze the running time of the algorithm. By the zone theorem for Jordan arcs (see Theorem 5.11), γ_{i+1} intersects at most $O(\lambda_{s+2}(i))$ cells of $\mathcal{A}^*(\Gamma_i)$. Therefore, once we have found the cells of $\mathcal{A}^*(\Gamma_i)$ that intersect γ_{i+1}, they can be manipulated and updated in time $O(\lambda_{s+2}(i))$. As for tracing γ_{i+1}, we spend $O(|L(e)|)$ time at each step to compute τ_j, where e is the edge of τ_{j-1} containing σ_j. We spend another $O(1)$ time to compute σ_{j+1}. If e is a vertical edge, then $|L(e)| \leq 2$, and the total number of such edges is $O(\lambda_{s+2}(i))$. Thus it suffices to consider the case when e is a nonvertical edge. Let E_i denote the set of nonvertical edges in $\mathcal{A}^*(\Gamma_i)$ that intersect γ_{i+1}. Since γ_{i+1} intersects an edge of $\mathcal{A}^*(\Gamma_i)$ at most s times, the total time spent in tracing γ_{i+1} is

$$O(\lambda_{s+2}(i)) + \sum_{e \in E_i} s|L(e)|.$$

We bound the second term by using the following charging scheme. For each edge $e \in E_i$, we charge the leftmost and rightmost cells of $L(e)$ to e itself, and we charge any other cell $\tau \in L(e)$ to the edge e' of τ that overlaps e. Notice that if a cell $\tau' \in L(e)$ is not the leftmost or the rightmost cell of $L(e)$, then the edge e' of τ' overlapping e is actually contained in e, so each such edge is charged in this manner only once. Furthermore, all cells in $L(e)$ lie in the same face f of $\mathcal{A}(\Gamma)$ and if γ_{i+1} intersects e then it also intersects f, so all charged edges lie in the zone of γ_{i+1} in $\mathcal{A}^*(\Gamma_i)$. Since the number of cells in that zone is $O(\lambda_{s+2}(i))$, it is easily seen that the number of charged edges is also $O(\lambda_{s+2}(i))$. Hence,

$$\sum_{e \in E_i} |L(e)| = O(\lambda_{s+2}(i)),$$

which implies that γ_{i+1} can be added to $\mathcal{A}^*(\Gamma_i)$ in overall time $O(\lambda_{s+2}(i))$. Summing these bounds over all arcs in Γ, we obtain

Theorem 6.21 *The arrangement of a given collection of n Jordan arcs in the plane, each pair of which intersect in at most s points, can be computed deterministically in time $O(n\lambda_{s+2}(n))$.*

6.7   Bibliographic notes

The divide-and-conquer algorithm for computing lower envelopes, described in Section 6.2.1, is due to Atallah (1985), and the improved algorithm of Section 6.2.2 is by Hershberger (1989). It is an open problem whether the lower envelope of a collection of n Jordan curves in $\mathbb{R}^2$, with at most $2s$ intersections per pair, $s > 1$, can be computed in $O(n \log n)$ time. (If the maximum number of intersection points between two curves is at most 2, then Theorem 6.1 gives such an algorithm.) Goodrich (1991) gave a parallel algorithm, in Valiant's comparison model, for computing the lower envelope of n Jordan curves or arcs. His algorithm basically parallelizes the divide-and-conquer algorithm of Atallah. It computes the lower envelope in $O(\log n)$ time using $O(\lambda_s(n))$ or $O(\lambda_{s+2}(n))$ processors, where s is the maximum number of intersection points between any pair of curves or arcs.

A single face in an arrangement of lines can be computed in $O(n \log n)$ time by modifying any of the known optimal convex hull algorithms; see, e.g., Preparata and Shamos (1985). However, in general, computing a single face in an arrangement of Jordan curves seems to be a harder problem than computing the lower envelope. Alevizos, Boissonnat, and Preparata (1990) presented an $O(n \log n)$-time algorithm to compute a face in an arrangement of n rays. Pollack, Sharir, and Sifrony (1988) developed a rather complicated $O(n \log^2 n)$ time algorithm for computing the unbounded face in an arrangement of segments, in the special case where the segments can be decomposed into two subsets (of roughly equal size), so that the boundary of the unbounded face in the arrangement of each subset is connected, and the condition holds recursively for each of the two subsets. The first algorithm for computing a single face in an arrangement of arbitrary segments was developed by Edelsbrunner et al. (1990) (see also Agarwal (1990)). As a matter of fact their algorithm can be extended to compute efficiently all faces in an arrangement of segments that contain a given set of points. The Combination Lemma and the red–blue merge procedure were first used in this paper. Guibas, Sharir, and Sifrony (1989) extended the Combination Lemma to the case of general arcs and developed the $O(\lambda_{s+2}(n) \log^2 n)$ time algorithm, presented in Section 6.3, for computing a single face in an arrangement of n Jordan arcs. Their algorithm, however, does not extend to computing many faces in such an arrangement of arcs. Corollary 6.9 is due to Sifrony (1989). A recent result of Har Peled (1993) extends the Combination Lemma to the case of overlaying more than two arrangements. This 'multicolor' Combination Lemma has been used by Aronov and Sharir (1994c) to show that the maximum complexity of a single face in the common exterior of k convex polygons, with a total of n edges, is $\Theta(n\alpha(k))$.

The randomized divide-and-conquer algorithm for computing a single face is due to Clarkson (1990). The analysis of this algorithm is a special case of fairly general probabilistic results obtained by Clarkson and Shor (1989). The randomized incremental algorithm for computing a single face was developed by Chazelle et al. (1993). Miller and Sharir (1991) present extensions of this algorithm for computing the union of 'fat' triangles (see Section 8.10.1) and of 'pseudo-disks' (planar regions having the property that the boundaries of any pair of them intersect in at most two points).

In the last few years, randomized algorithms have been developed for a wide variety of geometric problems, including the vertical decomposition of an arrangement of segments (Clarkson and Shor (1989), Mulmuley (1990, 1991b)), intersection of spheres in three dimensions (Clarkson and Shor (1989)), convex hull in higher dimensions (Seidel (1991, 1993)), Delaunay triangulation (Guibas, Knuth, and Sharir (1992), Boissonnat et al. (1992)), and ($\leq k$)-levels (Mulmuley (1991c), Agarwal, de Berg, et al. (1994)). See also the survey papers by Seidel (1993) and by Clarkson (1992), and the recent textbook of Mulmuley (1993) for some other results in this direction. De Berg, Dobrint, and Schwarzkopf (1994) have developed a variant of the randomized incremental technique, which also yields an $O(n\alpha(n) \log n)$ expected-time algorithm for computing a single face in an arrangement of segments. Agarwal, Matoušek, and Schwarzkopf (1994) have obtained an efficient randomized algorithm for computing many faces in an arrangement of lines or of line segments.

Chazelle (1993b) and Brönnimann, Chazelle, and Matoušek (1993) have shown that some of the randomized incremental algorithms can be derandomized without increasing their asymptotic time complexity, but their technique does not seem to work for computing a single face in an arrangement of Jordan arcs. We also note that the analysis of randomized algorithms given in this chapter deals mainly with the expected running time and storage of these algorithms. However, it is also important to analyze other statistical parameters of the performance of randomized algorithms, for example, to obtain *tail estimates* on the distribution of their running time and storage. (An ideal algorithm of this kind should not only have good expected performance; we also want the probability that it deviates significantly from this expectation to be very small.) Such estimates have recently been obtained by Mehlhorn, Sharir, and Welzl (1993).

The deterministic incremental algorithm, presented in Section 6.6, for computing the entire arrangement of arcs is a simplified version of the algorithm described by Edelsbrunner et al. (1992).

7

ARRANGEMENTS IN HIGHER DIMENSIONS

7.1 Introduction

In Chapter 1 we studied lower envelopes of univariate functions and showed the relationship between such envelopes and Davenport–Schinzel sequences, which eventually led to the derivation of tight or almost tight bounds on their complexity. In this chapter we extend our results to multivariate functions. Let $\mathcal{F} = \{f_1, \ldots, f_n\}$ be a collection of (partially defined) d-variate functions. The *lower envelope* of $\mathcal{F}$, denoted $E_{\mathcal{F}}$ (or E for brevity), is defined as

$$E_{\mathcal{F}}(\bar{\mathbf{x}}) = \min_{1 \le i \le n} f_i(\bar{\mathbf{x}}), \quad \bar{\mathbf{x}} \in \mathbb{R}^d.$$

(If a function $f_i \in \mathcal{F}$ is only partially defined, then $f_i(\bar{\mathbf{x}})$ is set to $+\infty$ at points $\bar{\mathbf{x}}$ where it is not defined.) The *upper envelope* $E_{\mathcal{F}}^*$ of $\mathcal{F}$ is defined in a symmetric manner.

$E_{\mathcal{F}}$ induces a partition of $\mathbb{R}^d$ into maximal connected (d-dimensional) regions such that $E_{\mathcal{F}}$ is attained by a single function f_i (or by no function at all) over the interior of each such region. The boundary of such a region consists of points at which $E_{\mathcal{F}}$ is attained by at least two of the functions, or by the relative boundary of the graph of at least one of the (partially defined) functions. Let $M_{\mathcal{F}}$ denote this subdivision of $\mathbb{R}^d$, which we call the *minimization* *diagram* for the collection $\mathcal{F}$. A *face* of $M_{\mathcal{F}}$ is a maximal connected region over which $E_{\mathcal{F}}$ is defined by the same set of functions and/or relative boundaries of function graphs in $\mathcal{F}$. The *combinatorial complexity* of $E_{\mathcal{F}}$, denoted $\kappa(\mathcal{F})$, is the number of faces of all dimensions in $M_{\mathcal{F}}$. The *maximization diagram* is defined as the subdivision of $\mathbb{R}^d$ induced, in the same manner, by the upper envelope $E^*_{\mathcal{F}}$ of $\mathcal{F}$.

As in Chapter 1, we assume that the functions in $\mathcal{F}$ are of reasonably simple shape. In most of the cases studied here, we assume that the given functions (and their relative boundaries, if any) are all algebraic, of constant maximum degree; see below for a more precise definition. Then an easy upper bound on $\kappa(\mathcal{F})$ is $O(n^{d+1})$ (which is an upper bound on the complexity of the entire arrangement $\mathcal{A}(\mathcal{F})$ of the given function graphs in $\mathbb{R}^{d+1}$).[1] However, motivated by the analysis for the case $d = 1$, as given in earlier chapters, it has been conjectured that, for collections $\mathcal{F}$ of well-behaved functions (including collections of algebraic functions of constant maximum degree), $\kappa(\mathcal{F}) = O(n^{d-1}\lambda_s(n))$, where s is some constant depending on the intersection pattern of the functions of $\mathcal{F}$. In other words, the conjecture asserts that the complexity of the lower envelope is roughly one order of magnitude smaller than the complexity of the entire arrangement of the given functions. Matching lower bounds are known for certain collections $\mathcal{F}$ (see, e.g., Theorem 7.1), so the asserted bound, if established, would be optimal, or close to optimal, in the worst case.

Unlike the univariate case, the problem in higher dimensions appears to be considerably more difficult, and this conjecture is still largely open, even in $\mathbb{R}^3$ ($d = 2$), although the results of this chapter get very close to the conjectured bound. Before discussing this further, we note that much better bounds can be obtained for certain special kinds of functions. For example, if the functions in $\mathcal{F}$ are linear (and everywhere defined), then the (graph of the) lower envelope of $\mathcal{F}$ is a convex polyhedron in $\mathbb{R}^{d+1}$, defined as the intersection of n half-spaces. Therefore, by the so-called Upper Bound Theorem, $\kappa(\mathcal{F}) = O(n^{\lceil d/2 \rceil})$ (see McMullen and Shepard (1971), and Edelsbrunner (1987)). Also, if the graphs of the functions in $\mathcal{F}$ are d-spheres (or, more precisely, lower d-hemispheres), then, using a standard 'lifting' transformation to $(d + 2)$-space, it is easy to show that $\kappa(\mathcal{F}) = O(n^{\lfloor d/2 \rfloor + 1})$; see also Section 7.5.4.

The conjecture has been proved for several special cases, some of which will be described in this chapter. A decisive step toward the establishment of the conjecture in a general setting was made by Halperin and Sharir (1994c) and by Sharir (1994a), who have shown that, for d-variate functions, one has $\kappa(\mathcal{F}) = O(n^{d+\varepsilon})$, for any $\varepsilon > 0$ (where the constant of proportionality depends on ε and on the intersection pattern of the given function graphs). This bound is within a multiplicative factor of $O(n^\varepsilon)$ off the conjectured bound.

---

[1] In this bound, and in other bounds derived in this chapter, we regard the dimension d (and the maximum algebraic degree b) as constant, and are mainly interested in the dependence of these bounds on n, the number of functions. Further dependence on d and b is usually hidden in the constants of proportionality.

The chapter begins with Section 7.2, where we show that, if $\mathcal{F}$ is a collection of piecewise-linear functions (i.e., functions whose graphs consist of an overall finite number, n, of d-simplices in $\mathbb{R}^{d+1}$), then the complexity of $M_{\mathcal{F}}$ is $O(n^d \alpha(n))$, which is asymptotically tight in the worst case (thus, in this special case, our conjecture is fully established). The proof of this bound is based on an inductive scheme, introduced by Edelsbrunner, Seidel, and Sharir (1993) for obtaining an upper bound on the zone of a hyperplane in hyperplane arrangements. We also present, in Section 7.2.2, an efficient algorithm for constructing the lower envelope of piecewise-linear functions in any dimension.

We continue the chapter with the derivation of its central result. We show that the combinatorial complexity of the minimization diagram $M_{\mathcal{F}}$ of a set $\mathcal{F}$ of n (possibly partially defined) d-variate functions having a 'simple shape' is $O(n^{d+\varepsilon})$, for any $\varepsilon > 0$. By 'simple shape' we mean that $\mathcal{F}$ is a collection of totally or partially defined d-variate algebraic functions of constant maximum degree, and, in case of partial functions, that the boundary of each function graph is defined by a constant number of polynomial equalities or inequalities of constant maximum degree. The proof is by induction on d; for this reason, and for the sake of clarity of exposition, we first give, in Section 7.3, the proof for the case $d = 2$, and then present, in Section 7.4, the generalization to higher dimensions. In Section 7.3.3 we also prove that if we superimpose the minimization diagrams of two collections of simply shaped bivariate functions, with a total of n functions, the complexity of the resulting planar map is also $O(n^{2+\varepsilon})$, i.e., it is asymptotically no worse than the complexity of a single diagram. This yields a simple divide-and-conquer algorithm for computing the lower envelope of n bivariate functions in time $O(n^{2+\varepsilon})$, under an appropriate model of computation. This divide-and-conquer algorithm, described in Section 7.3.4, does not extend to higher dimensions. Nevertheless, we present, in Section 7.4.2, a randomized incremental algorithm for computing the vertices, edges, and two-dimensional faces of the minimization diagram in higher dimensions, which is sufficient for many applications. We apply this algorithm, in Section 7.4.3, to obtain an efficient randomized algorithm for computing lower envelopes in $\mathbb{R}^4$ ($d = 3$). No similarly efficient algorithms are currently known in higher dimensions.

For the sake of simplicity, we assume that the functions in $\mathcal{F}$ are in *general position*. Formally, if we assume that the given functions are polynomials of constant maximum degree b, and that their relative boundaries (if any) are also defined by polynomials of degree at most b, the functions are said to be in general position if the coefficients of these polynomials are algebraically independent over the rationals. This assumption is easily seen to exclude all kinds of degenerate configurations, such as more than $d + 1$ functions meeting at a single point (or, in general, more than $k + 1$ functions meeting in a $(d - k)$-dimensional surface patch), or two functions becoming tangent to each other, etc. We will show that no generality is lost by assuming general position, because the asymptotic bounds that we will establish for collections of functions in general position will also apply to degenerate collections. Moreover, if the functions of $\mathcal{F}$ are in general position, then the combinatorial complexity of $M_{\mathcal{F}}$ is proportional to the number of vertices in $M_{\mathcal{F}}$ plus an additive $O(n^{d-1})$ term. Indeed, under our assumptions, the number of faces in $M_{\mathcal{F}}$ that are not incident to any vertex is $O(n^{d-1})$. Also, by the general position assumption, no more than $d+1$ function graphs meet at any vertex of $E_{\mathcal{F}}$, so it easily follows that the number of faces of $M_{\mathcal{F}}$ incident to some vertex is proportional to the number of vertices of $M_{\mathcal{F}}$. For this reason, our analysis will focus on establishing upper bounds for the number of vertices of $M_{\mathcal{F}}$.

After having proved the general result, we obtain improved bounds on the complexity of lower envelopes in some special cases. We begin with a few special cases of *bivariate* functions. In Section 7.5.1 we study the case of 'pseudo-planes.' We show that if every triple of functions in $\mathcal{F}$ intersect in at most one point and if the intersection curves $\gamma_{ij}\colon \{\,(x,y) \mid f_i(x,y) = f_j(x,y)\,\}$ satisfy certain mild properties, then $\kappa(\mathcal{F}) = O(n)$. Next, in Section 7.5.2, we consider the case in which every triple of functions intersect in at most two points and the intersection curves γ_{ij} are all (closed or unbounded) Jordan curves (see Chapter 5 for the definition). We show that $\kappa(\mathcal{F}) = O(n^2)$ in this case. Section 7.5.3 mentions a specific result involving bivariate functions with 'favorable' cross sections. In Section 7.5.4 we present a general scheme, called *linearization*, that yields improved bounds on the complexity of the lower envelope of certain classes of functions, by lifting them to hyperplanes in higher dimensions.

Finally, we study the related structures of *single cells* and *zones* in arrangements of surfaces in higher dimensions. We derive in Section 7.6 an almost tight upper bound for the combinatorial complexity of a single cell in an arrangement of d-simplices in $\mathbb{R}^{d+1}$. The proof of this bound follows the same induction scheme of Section 7.2. For the sake of completeness, we also provide in Section 7.7 an analysis of the complexity of the zone of a hyperplane in an arrangement of hyperplanes, following the original proof of Edelsbrunner, Seidel, and Sharir (1993). We conclude the chapter, in Section 7.8, with a 'sneak preview' of several recent and related results, the most significant of which is a near-quadratic upper bound on the complexity of a single cell in an arrangement of algebraic surfaces in $\mathbb{R}^3$.

7.2   Lower envelopes of piecewise-linear functions

In this section we obtain tight bounds on the combinatorial complexity of the lower envelope of piecewise-linear d-variate functions and present an efficient algorithm for computing the lower envelope.

7.2.1   Combinatorial complexity

Let $\mathcal{F}$ be a collection of piecewise-linear d-variate functions. By partitioning the graph of every $f_i \in \mathcal{F}$ into simplices, we may assume that the graph of each (now only partially defined) function is a d-dimensional simplex. Hence, we have a set $\boldsymbol{\Delta} = \{\Delta_1, \ldots, \Delta_n\}$ of n d-simplices in $\mathbb{R}^{d+1}$ and we want to bound the complexity of their lower envelope $E_{\boldsymbol{\Delta}}$, where each simplex is regarded as the graph of a partially defined linear d-variate function. Abusing the notation slightly, we will use Δ_i to denote the simplex as well as its corresponding function. See Figure 7.1 for an example of the lower envelope of triangles in $\mathbb{R}^3$. The lower envelope of n d-simplices in $\mathbb{R}^{d+1}$ is also a piecewise-linear function, and the main result of this subsection is:

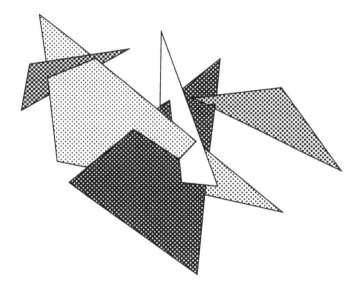

FIGURE 7.1. The lower envelope of triangles in $\mathbb{R}^3$ (a view from below).

Theorem 7.1 *The maximum combinatorial complexity of the lower envelope of n d-simplices in $\mathbb{R}^{d+1}$ is $\Theta(n^d \alpha(n))$.*

With no loss of generality, we may assume that the simplices of $\boldsymbol{\Delta}$ are in general position; otherwise, we can perturb slightly the simplices so as to put them in general position, without losing any feature of their lower envelope (see also Section 7.3.1 for a discussion of the issue of general position in more general situations). We will prove an upper bound on the complexity of a subdivision which is a refinement of $M_{\boldsymbol{\Delta}}$. For a simplex $\Delta \in \boldsymbol{\Delta}$, let Δ^* denote its projection on the hyperplane $x_{d+1} = 0$. Let $\boldsymbol{\Delta}^* = \{\Delta^* | \Delta \in \boldsymbol{\Delta}\}$, and let H

denote the set of $(d-1)$-hyperplanes in $\mathbb{R}^d$ (that is, in the hyperplane $x_{d+1} = 0$) supporting the simplices in Δ^* (note that there are $n(d+1)$ hyperplanes in H). Let M'_Δ denote the subdivision of $\mathbb{R}^d$ obtained by superimposing the arrangement of the hyperplanes of H with M_Δ. We will prove:

Theorem 7.2 *The number of faces of all dimensions in M'_Δ, for a set Δ of n d-simplices in $\mathbb{R}^{d+1}$, is $O(n^d \alpha(n))$.*

An immediate corollary of Theorem 7.2 is:

Corollary 7.3 *Let Δ be a set of n d-simplices in $\mathbb{R}^{d+1}$ and let Γ be a set of m $(d-1)$-hyperplanes lying in the hyperplane $x_{d+1} = 0$. Then the complexity of $M'_{(\Delta,\Gamma)}$, the subdivision of $x_{d+1} = 0$ obtained by superimposing Γ on M'_Δ, is $O((m+n)^d \alpha(m+n))$.*

We will prove Theorem 7.2 and Corollary 7.3 simultaneously, using induction on d. For the proof we need the following lemma.

Lemma 7.4 *Let H be a finite collection of hyperplanes in $\mathbb{R}^d$. Let $1 \leq k \leq d$, and let f be a convex set of affine dimension k, lying in general position with respect to the hyperplanes of H. Then the hyperplanes of H split f into m convex subsets of affine dimension k if and only if there are m distinct subsets (including the empty set) $A \subseteq H$ such that $(\bigcap_{h \in A} h)$ intersects f.*

Before we prove the lemma, we refer the reader to Figure 7.2 for an illustration of the lemma in the two-dimensional case. Notice that ℓ_1 and ℓ_2 intersect f in both (iii) and (iv), but in (iii) f is split into three subsets (rather than four as in (iv)), because the intersection point $\ell_1 \cap \ell_2$ does not lie in f. Note that the case $m = 1$ means (in any dimension) that no hyperplane of H intersects f.

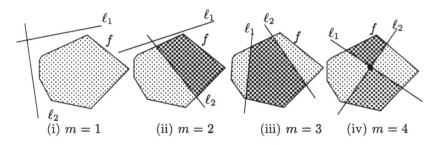

(i) $m = 1$ (ii) $m = 2$ (iii) $m = 3$ (iv) $m = 4$

FIGURE 7.2. An illustration of Lemma 7.4.

Proof. The proof proceeds by induction on $n = |H|$ and on k. The case $k = 1$ is trivial: in this case f is a line segment, and the general position assumption implies that a hyperplane of H can intersect f only at a point, and no two hyperplanes of H can intersect f at a common point. The lemma thus asserts that f is split into m subsegments if and only if exactly $m - 1$ hyperplanes of H intersect f, which is obvious (the m subsets in the lemma are the empty set and the $m - 1$ singleton subsets whose elements are the hyperplanes that intersect f).

Suppose the lemma is true for all $k' < k$, and let us prove it for k by induction on n. The case $n = 0$ is trivial (one may also start the induction with $n = 1$, which is equally trivial). Suppose the claim is true for k and for all $n' < n$, and consider the case of n hyperplanes. Suppose there are m distinct subsets A of H so that the intersection of each subset, $\bigcap_{h \in A} h$, meets f. Fix one hyperplane $h \in H$, let m' denote the number of subsets that do not contain h, and let m'' denote the number of subsets that contain h; thus $m = m' + m''$. If we remove h from H, we are left with only m' subsets of $H - \{h\}$, such that the intersection of each subset meets f. By the induction hypothesis, f is split by the hyperplanes of $H - \{h\}$ into m' subsets of affine dimension k. If we add h back, some of these subsets may be further split by h, each into two subsets. If f' is one of these subsets, its split can be charged uniquely to the set $f' \cap h$, which is a subset of $f \cap h$ (both of affine dimension $k - 1$). Thus the increase in the number of subsets of affine dimension k, caused by the reinsertion of h, is equal to the number of subsets of affine dimension $k - 1$ into which $f \cap h$ is split by the collection $H - \{h\}$. By the induction hypothesis, this number is equal to the number of distinct subsets of $H - \{h\}$ with the property that the intersection of each subset meets $f \cap h$. But if we add h to each such subset, we obtain exactly the m'' subsets of H that contain h and have the property that the intersection of each of them meets f. Thus the number of these subsets, and thus also the number of additional splits of f caused by h, is m'', so f is split into a total of $m' + m'' = m$ subsets, as asserted. This completes the induction step, and thus also completes the proof of the lemma.   □

Proof of Theorem 7.2. We prove the theorem (and, at the same time, Corollary 7.3) by induction on d. In the base case $d = 1$, the theorem is the same as Corollary 2.17, and the corollary is a trivial extension of it. Assume that the theorem holds for all $d' < d$, and consider the lower envelope of a collection Δ of n d-simplices in $\mathbb{R}^{d+1}$. Let $0 \le k \le d$ be fixed. We pick some simplex $\Delta \in \Delta$, and count the number of k-faces f in M'_Δ such that

(i) f is not contained in any hyperplane supporting Δ^*; and

(ii) Δ is not one of the lowest simplices of Δ over f (that is, the lower envelope of Δ over f is not realized by Δ).

If we remove Δ from Δ (and, with it, the set H_Δ of the $d + 1$ supporting hyperplanes of Δ^*), then it is easily seen that any such face f is contained in a k-face of $M'_{\Delta-\{\Delta\}}$. Our strategy is thus to consider the collection of k-faces of $M'_{\Delta-\{\Delta\}}$ and to estimate the increase in the number of faces (that satisfy conditions (i) and (ii)) when Δ (and the set H_Δ) are added back to Δ. We will first add H_Δ and then add Δ itself; see Figure 7.3.

Let f be a (necessarily convex) k-face of $M'_{\Delta-\{\Delta\}}$. Suppose that the insertion of the hyperplanes in H_Δ splits f into $m+1$ k-faces, say $f_0, f_1, \ldots, f_m$. Then, by Lemma 7.4, there are m faces of various dimensions, $g_1, \ldots, g_m$, of Δ^* (none equal to Δ^*), such that $\text{aff}(g_i)$ intersects f, where $\text{aff}(g)$ is the affine hull of g. Thus the increase in the number of k-faces within f, which is m, is equal to the number of faces g_i of Δ^* whose affine hull intersects f.

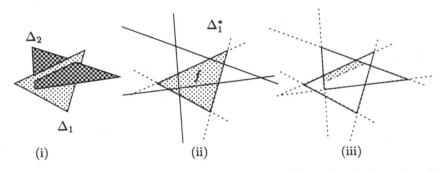

FIGURE 7.3. (i) The lower envelope of two triangles; (ii) adding the lines bounding Δ_2 to $M'_{\{\Delta_1\}}$, the triangle Δ_1^* splits into 5 2-faces; (iii) adding Δ_2, the face f is split into two faces, so that Δ_2 appears over only one of them in the overall lower envelope..

Let g be a j-face of Δ^* with that property. Define $\widehat{g}$ to be the vertical $(j+1)$-hyperplane erected on $\text{aff}(g)$, that is,

$$\widehat{g} = \{(\mathbf{x}, z) \mid \mathbf{x} \in \text{aff}(g), \; z \in \mathbb{R}\}.$$

Let us now intersect each simplex Δ_i of $\Delta - \{\Delta\}$ with $\widehat{g}$. The intersection, denoted Δ_i^g, is not necessarily a simplex, but, if not empty, it is a j-dimensional convex polytope whose number of faces is at most some constant (depending on d). Let $E^g = E^g_{\Delta-\{\Delta\}}$ denote the lower envelope of the polyhedra Δ_i^g within $\widehat{g}$. Project E_g on $\text{aff}(g)$. In addition, intersect each hyperplane in $H - H_\Delta$ (that is, each hyperplane supporting the projection of some simplex of $\Delta - \{\Delta\}$) with $\text{aff}(g)$, and superimpose these intersections on the projected lower envelope. Clearly, $f \cap \text{aff}(g)$ is a face, or a union of several faces, of the resulting partition of $\text{aff}(g)$, which we denote by $M'^g_{(\Delta-\{\Delta\}, H-H_\Delta)}$.

In other words, if we repeat this analysis for all faces f of $M'_{\Delta-\{\Delta\}}$, the increase in the number of faces of $M'_{\Delta-\{\Delta\}}$ that satisfy (i) and (ii), caused by adding the hyperplanes of H_Δ, is bounded by the overall complexity of the partitions $M'^g_{(\Delta-\{\Delta\},H-H_\Delta)}$, where g ranges over all faces of Δ^*. Consider such a face g, and observe that the complexity of $M'^g_{(\Delta-\{\Delta\},H-H_\Delta)}$ can only increase if we replace it by the partition $M'^g_{(T,H-H_\Delta)}$, where each polyhedron Δ^g_i is replaced by a constant number of simplices that form a triangulation of Δ^g_i, and where T is the collection of all such simplices. The number of simplices forming T and the number of hyperplanes in $H - H_\Delta$ are $O(n)$, and since the dimension of $\hat{g}$ is at most d, it follows, by the induction hypothesis (for both the theorem and Corollary 7.3), that the complexity of $M'^g_{(T,H-H_\Delta)}$, and thus also the complexity of $M'^g_{(\Delta-\{\Delta\},H-H_\Delta)}$, is at most $O(n^{d-1}\alpha(n))$. Since the number of faces g is a constant (depending on d), it follows that the increase in the number of faces of $M'_{\Delta-\{\Delta\}}$ that satisfy (i) and (ii), caused by adding the hyperplanes of H_Δ, is bounded by $O(n^{d-1}\alpha(n))$.

Next we reinsert Δ itself. Let M'' denote the partition of $\mathbb{R}^d$ obtained after adding the hyperplanes of H_Δ to $M'_{\Delta-\{\Delta\}}$, and let f be a k-face of M'' that does not lie in any hyperplane of H_Δ. Let Δ' be a simplex of $\Delta - \{\Delta\}$ that attains the lower envelope over f, and let $\hat{f}$ denote the portion of Δ' whose vertical projection is f. By construction, either f is disjoint from Δ^* or is fully contained in it. In the former case, f contributes exactly one k-face to M'_Δ, namely f itself. In the latter case, if we consider only the portion of E_Δ restricted to f, then inserting Δ has the same effect as inserting the hyperplane γ containing Δ. Since f, and thus also $\hat{f}$, are convex (which is a consequence of having superimposed the hyperplanes of H on M_Δ), the insertion of γ may split $\hat{f}$ into at most two subsets, and at most one of those can appear on the envelope E_Δ. Thus f can contribute at most one k-face to M'_Δ, namely the projection of the subface of $\hat{f}$ that lies below γ (if it exists). Hence, inserting Δ does not cause any additional increase in the number of k-faces that satisfy (i) and (ii).

Let $\tau_k(\Delta)$ denote the number of k-faces in M'_Δ, for $k = 0, 1, \ldots, d$, and let

$$\tau_k(n,d) = \max_{|\Delta|=n} \tau_k(\Delta),$$

where the maximum is taken over all collections Δ of n d-simplices in $\mathbb{R}^{d+1}$. Then the total number of faces in M'_Δ that satisfy (i) and (ii) is at most

$$\tau_k(n-1,d) + O(n^{d-1}\alpha(n)).$$

We repeat the above analysis for all simplices $\Delta \in \Delta$, and sum up the resulting bounds. We observe that each k-face is counted in this manner at least $n-d+k-1$ times. Indeed, any k-face f of M'_Δ is formed by intersecting the hyperplanes supporting some j simplices of Δ with several vertical flats $\hat{g}$, for faces g of some other simplices of Δ^*, so that the sum of co-dimensions of the g's in $\mathbb{R}^d$ is $d+1-j-k$. In particular, the number of g's is $\leq d+1-j-k$. In other words, the number of simplices of Δ for which either condition (i) or condition (ii) can be violated is at most $d + 1 - k$. We thus obtain the recurrence

$$\tau_k(n, d) \leq \frac{n}{n - d + k - 1}\left(\tau_k(n - 1, d) + O(n^{d-1}\alpha(n))\right).$$

We claim that, for $k \geq 2$, the solution of this recurrence is

$$\tau_k(n, d) = O(n^d\alpha(n)).$$

To see this, assume $n \geq d + 1$, and substitute

$$\tau_k(n, d) = \frac{n!}{(n - d + k - 1)!}\psi_k(n, d + 1).$$

The recurrence then becomes

$$\psi_k(n, d + 1) \leq \psi_k(n - 1, d + 1) + O(n^{k-2}\alpha(n)).$$

Since $k \geq 2$, it is easily seen that $\psi_k(n, d + 1) = O(n^{k-1}\alpha(n))$, which implies that

$$\tau_k(n, d) = O(n^d\alpha(n)).$$

For $k = 0, 1$, observe that the faces of M'_Δ are convex; therefore, by a well-known property of Euler's characteristic function of cell complexes in $\mathbb{R}^d$,

$$\sum_{k=0}^{d}(-1)^k\tau_k(\Delta) = 1 + (-1)^d.$$

See, for example, Greenberg (1967). Since we have already shown that $\tau_k(n, d) = O(n^d\alpha(n))$, for $k \geq 2$, we obtain

$$\mid \tau_1(\Delta) - \tau_0(\Delta) \mid = O(n^d\alpha(n)).$$

By the general position assumption on Δ, each vertex is incident to at least $d + 1$ and to at most $2d$ edges of M'_Δ. Hence,

$$\frac{d + 1}{2}\tau_0(\Delta) \leq \tau_1(\Delta) \leq d\tau_0(\Delta),$$

which implies that $\tau_k(n, d) = O(n^d\alpha(n))$ for $k = 0, 1$ too.

This establishes the assertion of the theorem in d dimensions, and thus also of Corollary 7.3. This completes the inductive step, and thus also the entire proof.

To complete the proof of Theorem 7.1, we next show that there is a set Δ of n d-simplices in $\mathbb{R}^{d+1}$ such that the complexity of E_Δ is $\Omega(n^d\alpha(n))$. For the sake of clarity, we will first describe the construction for $d = 2$, and then briefly mention how to extend it to higher dimensions.

Take a set Γ of $n/4$ segments in the yz-plane whose lower envelope has $\Omega(n\alpha(n))$ vertices; Theorem 4.11 of Chapter 4 implies the existence of such a set of segments. By taking the Cartesian product of each segment with the interval $[0, n/4 + 1]$ on the x-axis, we obtain a collection of $n/4$ rectangles. Each vertex of the lower envelope of Γ becomes an edge in the lower envelope of these rectangles. We divide each rectangle into two triangles; let Δ_1 denote the set of the $n/2$ resulting triangles. Let γ be a rectangle in the yz-plane that contains all segments of Γ in its interior. We place $n/4$ copies of the rectangle γ by translating it, parallel to the x-axis, to each of the vertical planes $x = i$, for $i = 1, \ldots, n/4$. If we divide each of these rectangles into two triangles, we obtain a collection Δ_2 of $n/2$ additional triangles. By construction, the intersection point of a triangle in Δ_2 with an edge of the lower envelope of Δ_1 is a vertex on the lower envelope of $\Delta = \Delta_1 \cup \Delta_2$. Since there are $\Omega(n\alpha(n))$ edges in the lower envelope of Δ_1 and each edge of this envelope is intersected by $n/4$ triangles of Δ_2, the total number of vertices in the lower envelope of Δ is $\Omega(n^2\alpha(n))$. (The triangles in Δ_2 are vertical, so they are not graphs of partially defined functions. To overcome this technical difficulty, simply tilt each triangle of Δ_2 slightly—this will only increase the asymptotic complexity of the envelope.)

In higher dimensions, we take, using induction on d, a collection of $\frac{n}{2d}$ $(d-1)$-simplices in the hyperplane $x_1 = 0$, whose lower envelope has $\Omega(n^{d-1}\alpha(n))$ vertices. By taking the Cartesian product with the interval $[0, \frac{n}{2d!} + 1]$ on the x_1-axis, we obtain a set of $\frac{n}{2d}$ d-prisms. We divide each prism into d d-simplices, obtaining a set Δ_1 of $n/2$ simplices. Next, we take a hyperrectangle in the plane $x_1 = 0$ that contains all of the original $(d-1)$-simplices. We make $\frac{n}{2d!}$ translated copies of this hyperrectangle, where the i-th copy is placed in the hyperplane $x_1 = i$, so that each hyperrectangle intersects all the edges of the lower envelope of Δ_1. We divide each hyperrectangle into $d!$ simplices, and let Δ_2 denote the set of (appropriately slightly tilted copies of) the resulting $n/2$ simplices. It is easy to verify that the lower envelope of $\Delta_1 \cup \Delta_2$ has $\Omega(n^d\alpha(n))$ vertices.

This completes the proof of Theorem 7.1. $\qquad\square$

7.2.2 Computing lower envelopes

We now describe a deterministic divide-and-conquer algorithm for computing the lower envelope of a collection Δ of n d-simplices in $\mathbb{R}^{d+1}$. In fact, we will compute the convex subdivision M'_Δ of $\mathbb{R}^d$ (i.e., of the hyperplane $x_{d+1} = 0$) defined in the previous subsection. Once we have M'_Δ, the subdivision M_Δ can be easily obtained, if so desired, by spending an additional $O(n^d\alpha(n))$ time. The algorithm is based on the recent theory of ε-nets as developed by Haussler and Welzl (1987), Clarkson (1987b), Chazelle and Friedman (1990), Chazelle (1993a), and Matoušek (1991); for the sake of the reader's convenience, we provide an appendix at the end of the chapter (Appendix 7.2), containing basic details on ε-nets and related concepts that are also used here and later in this book.

Let Π be the set of all semi-unbounded vertical prisms in $\mathbb{R}^{d+1}$ of the form

$$\tau_\Delta = \{\, (\mathbf{x}, x_{d+1}) \mid \mathbf{x} \in \Delta^*, x_{d+1} < \Delta(\mathbf{x}) \,\},$$

where Δ is any d-simplex, Δ^* is its projection on the hyperplane $x_{d+1} = 0$, and $\Delta(\mathbf{x})$ is the x_{d+1}-coordinate of the point on Δ whose projection on $x_{d+1} = 0$ is $\mathbf{x}$. Consider the *range space*

$$\Sigma_\Pi = (\Delta, \ \{\{\Delta \mid \Delta \text{ intersects } \tau\} \mid \tau \in \Pi\})$$

(see Appendix 7.2 for the definition of range spaces and related concepts). Let r be a sufficiently large constant. Corollary 7.70 in Appendix 7.2 implies that Σ_Π admits a $(1/r)$-net of size $O(r \log r)$, and, by Theorem 7.64 in Appendix 7.2, a $(1/r)$-net $R \subseteq \Delta$ of size $O(r \log r)$ can be computed in linear time. By definition of $(1/r)$-nets, any prism $\tau \in \Pi$ that does not intersect any simplex of R is intersected by at most n/r simplices of Δ. We construct the convex subdivision M'_R of $\mathbb{R}^d$, and then triangulate each face of M'_R, in increasing order of the face dimensions, as follows. Assume that we have triangulated all faces of dimension less than k, and let f be a k-face of M'_R. Choose a vertex v of f, say the bottommost vertex (in the x_d-direction), and form a k-simplex by connecting v to each $(k-1)$-simplex in the triangulation of every $(k-1)$-face of f not incident to v (this scheme can also be easily extended to unbounded faces). Let Ξ be the set of all d-simplices in the resulting triangulation. Since the combinatorial complexity of M'_R is at most $O((r \log r)^d \alpha(r))$ (see Theorem 7.2), the total number of simplices in Ξ is also $O((r \log r)^d \alpha(r))$. For a simplex τ in $\mathbb{R}^d$, let $\hat{\tau}$ denote the prism in $\mathbb{R}^{d+1}$

$$\hat{\tau} = \{\, (\mathbf{x}, x_{d+1}) \mid \mathbf{x} \in \tau, x_{d+1} < E_R(\mathbf{x}) \,\}.$$

For each simplex $\tau \in \Xi$, let Δ_τ denote the set of simplices of Δ that intersect the prism $\hat{\tau}$ (including the simplex of R that attains E_R over τ). Since R is a $(1/r)$-net of Δ and since no simplex of R cuts $\hat{\tau}$, by construction, we have,

$$n_\tau = |\Delta_\tau| \leq \frac{n}{r} + 1.$$

We recursively compute the convex subdivision M'_{Δ_τ} for each prism $\hat{\tau}$, and clip it within τ. The recursion stops when the number of simplices in Δ_τ falls below some prespecified constant, in which case we compute M'_{Δ_τ} by any brute-force method. Finally, we glue all the subdivisions M'_{Δ_τ} together by matching the faces appearing on the boundary of adjacent prisms. We omit here the easy details. It is easily seen that the total time spent in the merge step is bounded by the total complexity of the subdivision M'_{Δ_τ}, over all prisms $\hat{\tau}$, which is

$$\sum_{\tau \in \Xi} O(n_\tau^d \alpha(n_\tau)) = O(r^d \alpha(r) \log^d r) \cdot O\left((n/r)^d \alpha(n/r)\right) = O(n^d \alpha(n)).$$

(The last equality follows from the assumption that r is a constant.) Let $T(n)$ be the maximum time spent in computing M'_Δ, over all collections Δ of n d-simplices in $\mathbb{R}^{d+1}$; we get the following recurrence:

$$T(n) \leq \begin{cases} c_0 & \text{for } n \leq n_0, \\ c_1 r^d \alpha(r) \log^d r \cdot T\left(\dfrac{n}{r} + 1\right) + c_2 n^d \alpha(n) & \text{for } n > n_0, \end{cases}$$

where c, c_0, c_1, c_2, n_0 are some appropriate constants, and c_2 depends on r. The solution of the above recurrence is

$$T(n) \leq A n^{d+\varepsilon}, \tag{7.1}$$

for any $\varepsilon > 0$, where $A = A(\varepsilon)$ is a sufficiently large constant depending on ε. Indeed, (7.1) holds for $n \leq n_0$ if A is sufficiently large. For $n > n_0$ we have, using induction,

$$\begin{aligned} T(n) &\leq c_1 r^d \alpha(r) \log^d r \cdot T\left(\frac{n}{r} + 1\right) + c_2 n^d \alpha(n) \\ &\leq c_1 A r^d \alpha(r) \log^d r \cdot \left(\frac{n}{r} + 1\right)^{d+\varepsilon} + c_2 n^d \alpha(n) \\ &\leq A n^{d+\varepsilon} \left(\frac{c_1 \alpha(r) \log^d r}{r^\varepsilon}\left(1 + \frac{r}{n}\right)^{d+\varepsilon} + \frac{c_2 \alpha(n)}{A n^\varepsilon}\right) \\ &\leq A n^{d+\varepsilon}, \end{aligned}$$

provided that the constants n_0, A, and r are chosen sufficiently large. Hence, we can conclude:

Theorem 7.5 *The lower envelope of a set of n d-simplices in $\mathbb{R}^{d+1}$ can be computed in time $O(n^{d+\varepsilon})$, for any $\varepsilon > 0$ (with the constant of proportionality depending on ε).*

Remark 7.6 Using a randomized incremental algorithm, similar to the one described in Section 6.5 for computing a single face in an arrangement of segments, the lower envelope of a set of n d-simplices in $\mathbb{R}^{d+1}$, for $d \geq 2$, can be computed in expected time $O(n^d \alpha(n))$. Such an algorithm for $d = 2$ is given by Boissonnat and Dobrindt (1992, 1993). See also de Berg, Dobrindt, and Schwarzkopf (1994).

7.3 Lower envelopes in three dimensions

In this section and the following one we prove the main result of this chapter, deriving an almost tight upper bound on the complexity of lower envelopes of collections of rather general functions in arbitrary dimension. In this section we consider the three-dimensional case, and then extend the results to higher dimensions in the following section.

ASSUMPTIONS 7.1. Assumptions on bivariate functions.

(i) Each f_i is a portion of an algebraic surface of constant maximum degree b. That is, f_i is a set of the form $P(x_1, \ldots, x_d) = 0$ for some polynomial P of degree at most b.

(ii) The vertical projection of each f_i onto the xy-plane is a planar region bounded by a constant number of algebraic arcs of constant maximum degree (say, b too).

(iii) The relative interiors of any triple of the given surfaces intersect in at most s points (by Bezout's theorem (see, e.g., Hartshorne (1977)) and by Property (iv) below, we always have $s \leq b^3$).

(iv) The functions in $\mathcal{F}$ are in *general position*, in the sense defined in the introduction of this chapter.

Let $\mathcal{F} = \{f_1, \ldots, f_n\}$ be a collection of n partially defined bivariate functions in $\mathbb{R}^3$; with a slight abuse of notation, we denote by f_i both the function and its graph. We assume that the functions f_i satisfy Assumptions 7.1. We assume in this chapter some familiarity of the reader with basic structural and algorithmic properties involving real algebraic and semialgebraic sets (see Definition 7.72). Details can be found, for example, in Bochnak, Coste, and Roy (1987), and in Heintz, Recio, and Roy (1991).

We remark that requiring the f_i's to be graphs of (partially defined) functions is not essential, because we can partition any algebraic surface of constant degree into a constant number of xy-monotone patches (which also satisfy condition (ii)) by cutting it along the locus of points that have vertical tangency. Condition (iii) is, as noted, also not essential; we state it because the constants of proportionality in the bounds that we will derive depend on s in a much more significant manner than on the maximum degree of the surfaces. Finally, we will argue in the following subsection that condition (iv) is also not essential. Hence the results obtained in this section also hold in more general settings, involving arbitrary algebraic surfaces (or surface patches) of constant degree, not necessarily in general position. Nevertheless, for convenience, we will state and prove our results for collections of functions satisfying Assumptions 7.1.

7.3.1 The issue of general position

As claimed above, the assumption that the functions in $\mathcal{F}$ are in general position involves no real loss of generality. This is because, roughly speaking, the complexity of the envelope of n partial algebraic functions with a fixed maximum algebraic degree and a fixed maximum degree of their boundary curves, if any, attains its maximum value, at least up to some constant factor, when the functions are in general position. Here is a more precise way of stating and proving this claim. Suppose $\mathcal{F}$ is not in general position, and consider a slight perturbation of the functions in $\mathcal{F}$, obtained by replacing each polynomial $P_i(x, y, z) = 0$ defining these functions by the polynomial

$$P_i((1 - \varepsilon_{i1})x + \varepsilon_{i1}, (1 - \varepsilon_{i2})y + \varepsilon_{i2}, (1 - \varepsilon_{i3})z + \varepsilon_{i3}) = 0,$$

where the ε_{ij}'s are arbitrarily small, algebraically independent transcendentals. (For partially defined functions, we also apply a similar perturbation to the polynomials defining the boundaries of the graphs of the functions.) Let $\mathcal{F}'$ denote the resulting collection of perturbed functions, which now lie in general position. If v is an *inner vertex* of $E_{\mathcal{F}}$, formed by the *transversal* intersection of the relative interiors of the graphs of three or more functions of $\mathcal{F}$, then, as is easily checked, v will be replaced in $E_{\mathcal{F}'}$ by one or more vertices (provided the ε_{ij}'s are sufficiently small, which we assume anyway). Thus the number of such vertices can only grow when we pass from $\mathcal{F}$ to $\mathcal{F}'$.

There are several other kinds of vertices for which this argument does not apply:

(a) *Boundary vertices*, namely vertices formed by the intersection of a boundary of one surface with another surface. The number of such vertices is clearly only $O(n^2)$. If a portion of the boundary of one surface lies on another surface, this portion may constitute an edge of $E_{\mathcal{F}}$; the number of such edges is also easily seen to be $O(n^2)$.

(b) *Boundary-visible vertices*, namely vertices that lie along the boundary of the graph of one function of $\mathcal{F}$, and directly below the intersection curve of two other surfaces (or below the boundary of another surface). Let $f \in \mathcal{F}$, let γ be one of the (constant number of) algebraic arcs that form the boundary of the graph of f, and let V be the vertical surface formed by the union of all vertical rays whose bottom endpoints lie on γ. For each function $f_i \neq f$ in $\mathcal{F}$, let $\zeta_i = f_i \cap V$. The properties that the functions of $\mathcal{F}$ satisfy imply that each ζ_i is the union of a constant number of connected arcs, and that each pair of such arcs intersect in at most some constant number, q, of points (or, more generally, connected arcs). Note that all boundary-visible vertices w that lie on γ are vertical projections onto γ of vertices of the lower envelope, within V, of the arcs ζ_i. Since the number of these arcs is $O(n)$ and each pair of them intersect in at most q points (or connected arcs), it follows that the number of vertices of their envelope is at most $O(\lambda_{q+2}(n))$ (see Corollary 1.6). Repeating this analysis for each f and γ, we conclude that the number of boundary-visible vertices is at most $O(n\lambda_{q+2}(n))$. See also Section 8.3 in the next chapter, where a similar argument is applied in the analysis of a different problem.

(c) *Singular inner vertices*, namely inner vertices that are singular[2] on at least one of their incident function graphs. Since the locus of all singular points along each graph is an algebraic curve of constant maximum degree, one can argue, as in case (a) above, that the total number of such vertices is $O(n^2)$.

(d) *Nontransversal inner vertices*, namely inner vertices v incident to (the relative interior of) a triple of function graphs, such that v is a nonsingular point on each of these graphs, but the three tangent planes to the graphs at v are not linearly independent. (We can ignore cases where v is a point of tangency between just two surfaces, because the number of such vertices is, again, only $O(n^2)$.) The difficulty in this case is that a small perturbation of these functions in the 'wrong' direction may cause v to disappear. However, suppose we choose the ε_{ij}'s randomly and independently from a sufficiently small neighborhood of 0. Then, as is easily checked, there is a constant probability that v will show up on the perturbed envelope as one or more vertices. This implies that an appropriate random choice of the ε_{ij}'s will cause at least a fixed fraction of these vertices to show up on the perturbed envelope.

To sum up, an appropriate random perturbation of the functions will result in a collection of functions in general position, and the (expected) number N' of vertices on its envelope satisfies $N' \geq cN - K$, where c is some absolute positive fraction, N is the number of vertices on the original envelope, and $K = O(n\lambda_{q+2}(n))$, for some constant q that depends on the maximum degree b. Since the bounds that we will establish will be asymptotically (slightly) larger than K, this argument implies that it suffices to bound the number of envelope vertices for collections of functions in general position.

Concerning higher-dimensional faces of $E_{\mathcal{F}}$, we can argue as follows. A random perturbation, as above, will cause at least some constant fraction of the number of such faces to appear on the perturbed envelope. If such a face F has an incident vertex, charge F to any such vertex. Since the perturbed collection is in general position, each vertex will be charged in this manner only a constant number of times. It is also easy to show that the number of faces with no incident vertex is only $O(n^2)$. For example, any edge of $E_{\mathcal{F}}$ not incident to a vertex must be a full connected component of the intersection curve of a pair of functions, and the number of such components is easily seen to be $O(n^2)$ (each intersection curve has only a constant number of components).

In conclusion, it suffices to establish our bounds for collections of functions in general position, since these bounds will also apply, up to some constant factor, in degenerate configurations. Finally, this argument concerning general

---

[2] A point v is *singular* on an algebraic surface, defined by $P = 0$ for some polynomial P, if all the partial derivatives $\partial P/\partial x_i$, for $i = 1, \ldots, d$, vanish at v; see Bochnak, Coste, and Roy (1987) and Hartshorne (1977).

position can be extended to higher dimensions, but we omit the (fairly routine) details (see Sharir (1994a)).

7.3.2 Combinatorial complexity of the envelope

Theorem 7.7 *The combinatorial complexity $\kappa(\mathcal{F})$ of the lower envelope of a collection $\mathcal{F}$ of n (partially defined) functions that satisfy Assumptions 7.1 is $O(n^{2+\varepsilon})$, for any $\varepsilon > 0$, where the constant of proportionality depends on ε, s, and the shape and degree of the function graphs and of their boundaries.*[3]

The following is an immediate corollary of Theorem 7.7; we state it here because its proof technique will be needed in the proof of Theorem 7.7.

Corollary 7.8 *Let $\mathcal{F}$ be a collection of n bivariate functions that satisfy Assumptions 7.1. For $1 \le k < n$, the number of vertices in the $(\le k)$-level of the arrangement $\mathcal{A}(\mathcal{F})$ is $O(n^{2+\varepsilon}(k+1)^{1-\varepsilon})$, for any $\varepsilon > 0$, where the constant of proportionality depends on ε, s, and the shape and degree of the function graphs and of their boundaries.*[4]

Proof. For a subset $X \subseteq \mathcal{F}$ and an integer $0 \le k \le |X| - 3$, let $V_k(X)$ denote the set of vertices at level k in $\mathcal{A}(\mathcal{F})$. We thus need to bound $\sum_{j=0}^{k} |V_j(\mathcal{F})|$. We bound below only the number of inner vertices in the first k levels; the other types of vertices are easier to analyze, and the same bound applies to them as well. Following the same approach as in Theorem 5.16, we choose a random subset $R \subseteq \mathcal{F}$ of size $r = \lfloor n/(k+1) \rfloor$ and bound the expected number of vertices in $V_0(R)$. A vertex $v \in V_j(\mathcal{F})$ is in $V_0(R)$ if and only if the three functions defining v are in R and none of the j functions of $\mathcal{F}$ lying below v are chosen in R, so the probability that $v \in V_0(R)$ is $\binom{n-j-3}{r-3}/\binom{n}{r}$. Hence,

$$
\begin{aligned}
\mathbf{E}\big[|V_0(R)|\big] &= \sum_{j=0}^{n-3} |V_j(\mathcal{F})| \frac{\binom{n-j-3}{r-3}}{\binom{n}{r}} \\
&\ge \sum_{j=0}^{k} |V_j(\mathcal{F})| \frac{\binom{n-j-3}{r-3}}{\binom{n}{r}} \\
&= \Omega\left(\frac{1}{(k+1)^3}\right) \sum_{j=0}^{k} |V_j(\mathcal{F})|,
\end{aligned}
$$

---

[3]The term 'shape' refers to additional properties that the given functions might possess, which restrict the patterns of intersections and other interactions between the functions, more than what follows only from the fact that the functions are algebraic of constant degree. For example, the shape of the graphs might imply that the maximum number s of intersections between any three of them is much smaller than b^3.

[4]A vertex p is in the k-level (respectively, $(\le k)$-level) of a d-dimensional arrangement $\mathcal{A}(\mathcal{F})$ if, as in the planar case, there are exactly k (respectively, at most k) function graphs of $\mathcal{F}$ passing vertically below p.

where the last inequality follows from the same argument as in the proof of Theorem 5.16. Thus

$$\sum_{j=0}^{k} |V_j(\mathcal{F})| \le c(k+1)^3 \mathbf{E}\big[|V_0(R)|\big], \qquad (7.2)$$

for some constant c. Since every vertex in $V_0(R)$ lies on the lower envelope of R, the corollary now follows from Theorem 7.7.   □

Proof of Theorem 7.7. Let $\phi(\mathcal{F})$ denote the number of *inner vertices* of $E_{\mathcal{F}}$, as defined in the previous subsection; namely, these are points of intersection of (the relative interiors of graphs of) three functions of $\mathcal{F}$ that lie on the envelope. Thus we do not count boundary vertices and boundary-visible vertices, as defined in the preceding subsection. This will not affect our bounds, because, as noted above, the number of boundary and boundary-visible vertices on $E_{\mathcal{F}}$ is only $O(n\lambda_{q+2}(n))$, for an appropriate constant q. We also denote by $\phi(n)$ the maximum of $\phi(\mathcal{F})$, taken over all collections $\mathcal{F}$ of n functions that satisfy Assumptions 7.1, with the same b and s. Finally, we denote by $\phi^*(\mathcal{F})$ the total number of vertices of $E_{\mathcal{F}}$ of all types (including boundary vertices and boundary-visible vertices, as enumerated in the preceding subsection), and by $\phi^*(n)$ the maximum of $\phi^*(\mathcal{F})$, taken over all collections $\mathcal{F}$ as above. The discussion in the preceding subsection easily implies that $\phi^*(n) = \phi(n) + O(n\lambda_{q_0+2}(n))$, where q_0 is a constant (depending on b), equal to the maximum of the values that q can assume in case (b) of the analysis in the preceding subsection.

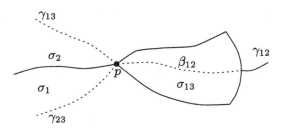

FIGURE 7.4. An inner vertex; solid edges lie on the envelope, and dashed edges are hidden.

Let p be an inner vertex of $E_{\mathcal{F}}$, formed by the intersection of the graphs of three functions f_1, f_2, $f_3 \in \mathcal{F}$. Let us denote by γ_{ij} the curve of intersection between f_i and f_j, for $1 \le i < j \le 3$. Let $\beta_{ij}(p)$ denote the maximal relatively open connected x-monotone subarc of γ_{ij} that contains no singular point, has p as an endpoint, and is disjoint from $E_{\mathcal{F}}$ (see Figure 7.4). Note that, since each γ_{ij} is algebraic of constant maximum degree, and we have assumed general position, one can partition γ_{ij} into a constant number of connected x-monotone subarcs with no singular points; the total number of such subarcs, over all intersection curves of the surfaces, is thus $O(n^2)$, and each $\beta_{ij}(p)$ is fully contained in such a subarc.

By our assumption on general position, we may assume that the point p is a point of transversal intersection between these functions, and that none of these functions is singular at p. Thus we can assume that the three surfaces are smooth at p, so $E_{\mathcal{F}}$ can be approximated, at a neighborhood of p, by the lower envelope of the three tangent planes to these surfaces at p, which is easily seen to imply that the three tangent directions of $\beta_{12}(p)$, $\beta_{13}(p)$, $\beta_{23}(p)$ at p, all pointing from p along their respective arcs, are such that the positive span of their xy-projections is the entire xy-plane; indeed, the three vectors oppositely oriented to these directions lie along the edges, emerging from p, of the lower envelope of the three tangent planes to the surfaces at p, and the xy-projections of these vectors cannot lie in a single half-plane, as is easily checked. In particular, at least one of these arcs, say, $\beta_{12}(p)$, emanates from p in the positive x-direction (and at least one arc emanates in the negative x-direction).

We define the *index* $j = j(p)$ of p to be the number of intersection points of f_1, f_2, f_3 that lie in the half-space $x > x(p)$; note that $0 \le j \le s - 1$. We define $\phi^{(j)}(\mathcal{F})$, for $j = 0, \ldots, s - 1$, to be the number of inner vertices of $E_{\mathcal{F}}$ having an index at most j. We also define $\phi^{(j)}(n)$ to be the maximum possible value for $\phi^{(j)}(\mathcal{F})$, over all collections $\mathcal{F}$ of n bivariate functions satisfying Assumptions 7.1 (with the same b and s).

Our method is to derive a recurrence relationship for $\phi^*(n)$, by bounding each of the functions $\phi^{(j)}$ in terms of $\phi^{(j-1)}$, and by using the resulting inequality for $\phi^{(s-1)}$ to obtain a similar inequality for ϕ^*; the solution to this recurrence will yield the asserted bound.

Let p be an inner vertex of index at most j, formed by the intersection of three function graphs, f_1, f_2, f_3. Suppose, with no loss of generality, that the arc $\beta_{12}(p)$ emanates from p in the positive x-direction, and let u denote its other endpoint. Several cases can arise:

(a) u is an endpoint of a maximal connected x-monotone piece, with no singular points, of the whole intersection curve γ_{12} (Figure 7.5 (i)). In this case, we charge p to u. Each such u can be charged in this manner at most a constant number of times: there are only a constant number of intersection curves ending at u, and u can be charged along each of them at most once—the vertex p charging u along β_{12} must be the *first* point on $E_{\mathcal{F}}$ encountered as we traverse β_{12} from u to the left. Since there are only $O(n^2)$ such points u, over the entire collection of intersection curves, the number of vertices p of this kind is $O(n^2)$.

(b) u is a point on $E_{\mathcal{F}}$ (Figure 7.5 (ii)) and $\beta_{12}(p) \cup \{u\}$ does not intersect f_3. Hence either u lies below f_3, or f_3 does not meet at all the vertical

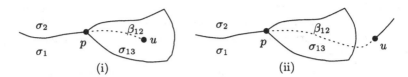

FIGURE 7.5. (i) u is an endpoint of γ_{12}; (ii) u is a point on $E_{\mathcal{F}}$.

line through u. On the other hand, when we start tracing $\beta_{12}(p)$ from p, we move along points hidden from $E_{\mathcal{F}}$ by f_3, which thus lies below the curve. Since f_3 does not intersect $\beta_{12}(p)$, it follows that $\beta_{12}(p)$ must contain a point w that lies vertically above the boundary of f_3, and we charge p to the point w.

Let w' be the point on ∂f_3 that lies vertically below w, and let t denote the number of graphs that either cross the portion pw of $\beta_{12}(p)$ or have a point on their boundary that lies vertically below pw. We fix some threshold parameter $k = k_j$, to be determined below, and consider the following two subcases:

(b.i) $t > k$: Extend each graph $f \in \mathcal{F}$ to a surface f^* by erecting an upward-directed vertical ray from each point on the boundary of f. Let $\mathcal{F}^*$ denote the collection of these extended surfaces, and let $\mathcal{A}(\mathcal{F}^*)$ denote their arrangement. By assumption, $\beta_{12}(p)$ contains at least t vertices of $\mathcal{A}(\mathcal{F}^*)$, and we will charge p to the block of the first k of these vertices in their order from p to w along $\beta_{12}(p)$. Clearly, arguing as in case (a) above, each vertex of $\mathcal{A}(\mathcal{F}^*)$ can be charged in this manner only a constant number of times, and the level in $\mathcal{A}(\mathcal{F}^*)$ of each charged vertex is at most k (note that, in the definition of the level of a point u in $\mathcal{A}(\mathcal{F}^*)$, we do not count surfaces whose vertical extensions pass through u).

By (7.2), the number of vertices of $\mathcal{A}(\mathcal{F}^*)$ at level $\leq k$ is at most $O(k^3 \phi^*(n/k))$, which in turn implies that the number of inner vertices p of $E_{\mathcal{F}}$ in this subcase is $O(k^2 \phi^*(n/k))$. Strictly speaking, we should write this bound as $O(k^2 \phi^*(\lfloor n/(k+1) \rfloor))$. We use the above more sloppy notation to avoid more complicated expressions in the recurrences that follow, and we will continue to use a similar style below. Nevertheless, the resulting analysis is not affected by this sloppy notation, as the reader can easily verify.

(b.ii) $t \leq k$: Let γ be the algebraic arc that forms part of the boundary of f_3 and contains w', and let V be the vertical surface formed by the union of all vertical rays whose bottom endpoints lie on γ. For each surface $f_i \neq f_3$ in $\mathcal{F}$, let $\zeta_i = f_i \cap V$. As argued in the preceding subsection, each ζ_i is the union of a constant number of connected arcs, and each pair of such arcs intersect in at most q points, for some constant q. Note also that w is a vertex of the two-dimensional arrangement $\mathcal{A}_\gamma$ of the curves ζ_i, whose level in $\mathcal{A}_\gamma$ is at most k. Hence, by Theorem 5.16, the number of points w in this subcase, over all choices of f_1, f_2, but with a fixed f_3, is $O(k^2 \lambda_{q+2}(n/k))$, so the overall number of vertices p in this subcase is

$$O(nk^2 \lambda_{q+2}(n/k)) = O(nk\lambda_{q+2}(n)).$$

(c) u is a point on $E_\mathcal{F}$ and f_3 intersects $\beta_{12}(p) \cup \{u\}$ (this case arises only when the index $j(p) \geq 1$). Let w be the point of intersection of f_3 with $\beta_{12}(p)$ that lies nearest to p along that curve. Clearly, the index of w is at most $j - 1$. Let δ denote the portion of $\beta_{12}(p)$ between p and w, and let t denote the number of extended surfaces of $\mathcal{F}^*$ that cross δ. We consider the following two subcases:

(c.i) $t > k$: As in case (b.i) above, we conclude that δ contains at least k vertices of $\mathcal{A}(\mathcal{F}^*)$, and we charge p to the first k of these vertices, in their order along δ from p to w. As argued above, all these vertices are at level at most k in $\mathcal{A}(\mathcal{F}^*)$, and each of them can be charged in this way only a constant number of times. Repeating the random-sampling argument given in case (b.i) above, we conclude that the number of inner vertices p that are charged in this manner is $O(k^2 \phi^*(n/k))$.

(c.ii) $t \leq k$: Here we observe, arguing as above, that w lies at level at most t in $\mathcal{A}(\mathcal{F}^*)$. Hence, if we remove the $\xi \leq t$ surfaces that hide w from $E_\mathcal{F}$, w becomes an inner vertex of the envelope of the remaining functions. To exploit this observation, we apply the following variant of Corollary 7.8. Draw a random sample R of $r = \lfloor n/(k+1) \rfloor$ surfaces from $\mathcal{F}$. By definition, the expected number of inner vertices of E_R with index at most $j - 1$ is

$$\phi^{(j-1)}(R) \leq \phi^{(j-1)}(r).$$

Let G_ξ be the number of inner vertices w of $E_\mathcal{F}$, as above, with exactly ξ surfaces passing below them. Arguing, as in Corollary 7.8, that the probability that our w will show up as such a vertex of E_R is $\binom{n-\xi-3}{r-3}/\binom{n}{r}$, we obtain

$$\sum_{\xi=0}^{k} \frac{\binom{n-\xi-3}{r-3}}{\binom{n}{r}} G_\xi \leq \phi^{(j-1)}(r).$$

Therefore (using again our sloppy notation),

$$\sum_{\xi=0}^{k} G_\xi = O(k^3 \phi^{(j-1)}(n/k));$$

in other words, if we charge each of the inner vertices p in this sub-case to the corresponding point w, and observe that each such point w can be charged only a constant number of times, we conclude that the number of vertices p in this subcase is $O(k^3 \phi^{(j-1)}(n/k))$.

Thus, summing up these bounds, we obtain the following recurrence (where, for $j = 0$, we put in the right-hand side $\phi^{(-1)} = 0$):

$$\phi^{(j)}(\mathcal{F}) = O(k^2 \phi^*(n/k) + k^3 \phi^{(j-1)}(n/k) + nk\lambda_{q+2}(n)). \qquad (7.3)$$

We now unfold the recurrence (7.3), using a different parameter $k = k_j$ at each stage. We then obtain, as is easily verified:

$$
\begin{aligned}
\phi^{(j)}(\mathcal{F}) \;\leq\;\; & C_j k_j^2 \phi^* \left(\frac{n}{k_j} \right) + C_{j-1} k_j^3 k_{j-1}^2 \phi^* \left(\frac{n}{k_j k_{j-1}} \right) + \\
& C_{j-2} k_j^3 k_{j-1}^3 k_{j-2}^2 \phi^* \left(\frac{n}{k_j k_{j-1} k_{j-2}} \right) + \cdots + \\
& C_0 k_j^3 k_{j-1}^3 \cdots k_1^3 k_0^2 \phi^* \left(\frac{n}{k_j k_{j-1} \cdots k_0} \right) + \\
& C k_j k_{j-1} \cdots k_0 n \lambda_{q+2}(n), \qquad (7.4)
\end{aligned}
$$

where $C, C_0, C_1, \ldots, C_j$ are appropriate constants.

If we now take the inequality (7.4) for $j = s - 1$, and add the nearly quadratic bound for the number of boundary and boundary-visible vertices of $E_{\mathcal{F}}$, we obtain the final recurrence that we are aiming at:

$$
\begin{aligned}
\phi^*(n) \;\leq\;\; & C_{s-1} k_{s-1}^2 \phi^* \left(\frac{n}{k_{s-1}} \right) + C_{s-2} k_{s-1}^3 k_{s-2}^2 \phi^* \left(\frac{n}{k_{s-1} k_{s-2}} \right) + \\
& C_{s-3} k_{s-1}^3 k_{s-2}^3 k_{s-3}^2 \phi^* \left(\frac{n}{k_{s-1} k_{s-2} k_{s-3}} \right) + \cdots + \\
& C_0 k_{s-1}^3 k_{s-2}^3 \cdots k_1^3 k_0^2 \phi^* \left(\frac{n}{k_{s-1} k_{s-2} \cdots k_0} \right) + \\
& C k_{s-1} k_{s-2} \cdots k_0 n \lambda_{q+2}(n). \qquad (7.5)
\end{aligned}
$$

We claim that the solution to (7.5) is

$$\phi^*(n) \leq A n^{2+\varepsilon}, \qquad (7.6)$$

for any $\varepsilon > 0$, where A is a constant that depends on ε and on the constants $C, C_0, C_1, \ldots, C_{s-1}$. This is proved by holding ε fixed, and by using induction on n. By choosing A sufficiently large, we can assume that (7.6) holds for all $n \leq n_0$, for some constant threshold value n_0 for which $\lambda_{q+2}(n) < n^{1+\varepsilon}$ for all $n > n_0$.

For $n > n_0$, we choose

$$k_1 = k_0^\varepsilon, \quad k_2 = k_1^\varepsilon, \quad k_3 = k_2^\varepsilon, \quad \cdots \quad k_{s-1} = k_{s-2}^\varepsilon,$$

and choose k_0 to be sufficiently large; this yields

$$
\phi^*(n) \;\leq\; C_{s-1}k_{s-1}^2 \phi^*\left(\frac{n}{k_{s-1}}\right) + C_{s-2}k_{s-2}^{2+3\varepsilon}\phi^*\left(\frac{n}{k_{s-2}^{1+\varepsilon}}\right) +
$$

$$
C_{s-3}k_{s-3}^{2+3\varepsilon+3\varepsilon^2}\phi^*\left(\frac{n}{k_{s-3}^{1+\varepsilon+\varepsilon^2}}\right) + \cdots +
$$

$$
C_0 k_0^{2+3\varepsilon+3\varepsilon^2+\cdots+3\varepsilon^{s-1}}\phi^*\left(\frac{n}{k_0^{1+\varepsilon+\varepsilon^2+\cdots+\varepsilon^{s-1}}}\right) +
$$

$$
Ck_0^{1+\varepsilon+\varepsilon^2+\cdots+\varepsilon^{s-1}}n\lambda_{q+2}(n).
$$

By the induction hypothesis and by the choice of n_0, we have, as is easily verified:

$$
\phi^*(n) \leq An^{2+\varepsilon} \cdot \left[\frac{C_{s-1}+C_{s-2}+C_{s-3}+\cdots+C_0}{k_0^{\varepsilon^s}} + \frac{C}{A}k_0^{1+\varepsilon+\varepsilon^2+\cdots+\varepsilon^{s-1}}\right],
$$

which can be made smaller than $An^{2+\varepsilon}$, provided k_0 and A are chosen to be sufficiently large. This completes the proof of the theorem. $\qquad\square$

Remark 7.9 A closer inspection of our analysis shows that A grows, as a function of s, at least as fast as $c^{(s-1)/\varepsilon^{s-1}}$, for some absolute constant c. The dependence of A on the maximum degree of the functions and of their boundaries (ignoring the effect of s) is much milder. However, we strongly suspect that the upper bound (7.6) is not tight, so the actual dependence of A on ε is probably much milder.

7.3.3   Overlay of two envelopes

In this subsection we prove that the combinatorial complexity of the overlay of the minimization diagrams of two families of a total of n bivariate functions satisfying Assumptions 7.1, is only $O(n^{2+\varepsilon})$, for any $\varepsilon > 0$. This is a considerably stronger result than Theorem 7.7, and has several interesting applications, including a simple algorithm for computing lower envelopes of bivariate functions. Let $\mathcal{F}$ and $\mathcal{G}$ be two given families of a total of n bivariate functions, satisfying Assumptions 7.1. Let $\mathcal{M}$ denote the planar map obtained by superimposing the minimization diagrams $M_{\mathcal{F}}$ and $M_{\mathcal{G}}$. We refer to $\mathcal{M}$ as the *overlay* of $M_{\mathcal{F}}$ and of $M_{\mathcal{G}}$.

Theorem 7.10 *The combinatorial complexity of the overlay of the minimization diagrams of two collections of a total of n bivariate functions satisfying Assumptions 7.1 is $O(n^{2+\varepsilon})$, for any $\varepsilon > 0$, where the constant of proportionality depends on ε, s, and b.*

Proof. For simplicity of exposition, we prove the theorem in detail only for the case of totally defined functions. We then comment briefly on the modifications of the proof required when these functions are only partially defined.

We use a two-stage counting argument to obtain a recurrence for the complexity of the overlay. As in Theorem 7.7, it suffices to bound the number of vertices of $\mathcal{M}$. There are two types of vertices in $\mathcal{M}$: (i) the vertices of $M_{\mathcal{F}}$ or of $M_{\mathcal{G}}$, and (ii) the intersection points of edges of $M_{\mathcal{F}}$ with edges of $M_{\mathcal{G}}$. We will refer to vertices of the second type as *crossings* in $\mathcal{M}$. Clearly, we only have to obtain an upper bound on the number of crossings in $\mathcal{M}$, because, by Theorem 7.7, the number of vertices of type (i) is $O(n^{2+\varepsilon})$.

For the purpose of analysis, we generalize the notion of a crossing, as follows.

Definition 7.11 Let e be an edge of $\mathcal{A}(\mathcal{F})$ at level ξ,[5] and let e' be an edge of $\mathcal{A}(\mathcal{G})$ at level ξ', such that the xy-projections of e and e' cross each other at a point σ. Then we say that (e, e', σ) is an *edge-crossing* in $(\mathcal{A}(\mathcal{F}), \mathcal{A}(\mathcal{G}))$ at *level* (ξ, ξ'). If the point σ is not important or is clear from the context, we just use (e, e') to denote (e, e', σ).

Note that the original crossings in $\mathcal{M}$ correspond to edge-crossings at level $(0, 0)$. Let $C_{p,q}(\mathcal{F}, \mathcal{G})$ denote the number of edge crossings in $(\mathcal{A}(\mathcal{F}), \mathcal{A}(\mathcal{G}))$ whose level is (p', q'), for any $p' \le p$, $q' \le q$, and let

$$C_{p,q}(n) = \max C_{p,q}(\mathcal{F}, \mathcal{G}),$$

where the maximum is taken over all collections $\mathcal{F}$ and $\mathcal{G}$ as above, such that $|\mathcal{F}| + |\mathcal{G}| = n$. The goal is thus to obtain a near-quadratic upper bound for $C_{0,0}(n)$.

Let e be an edge of $M_{\mathcal{F}}$, and let V_e be the vertical 2-manifold obtained as the union of all z-vertical lines passing through points of e. The intersection of the graph of each function $g \in \mathcal{G}$ with V_e is an algebraic arc of constant maximum degree, so each pair of these arcs intersect in at most some constant number, u, of points. Let $\mathcal{A}^{(e)}(\mathcal{G})$ denote the cross-section of $\mathcal{A}(\mathcal{G})$ within V_e (see Figure 7.6; for clarity, we have drawn e in that figure to lie below all arcs of $\mathcal{A}^{(e)}(\mathcal{G})$, but in general e can cross this arrangement in a fairly arbitrary fashion), and let $C_{0,q}(e, \mathcal{G})$ denote the number of edge-crossings of the form (e, e', σ), whose level is $(0, q')$, for any $q' \le q$. A simple but crucial observation is:

Lemma 7.12 *Let e' be an edge of $\mathcal{A}(\mathcal{G})$. Then (e, e', σ) is an edge-crossing in $(\mathcal{A}(\mathcal{F}), \mathcal{A}(\mathcal{G}))$ at level $(0, \xi)$ if and only if the point of $e' \cap V_e$ that lies on the z-vertical line through σ is a vertex of level ξ in $\mathcal{A}^{(e)}(\mathcal{G})$.*

---

[5]Recall that, since the functions are assumed to be totally defined, the level of an edge of $\mathcal{A}(\mathcal{F})$ is well-defined: it is equal to the level of any point on the edge.

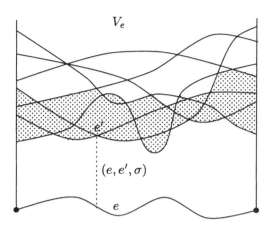

FIGURE 7.6. The vertical manifold V_e, the arrangement $\mathcal{A}^{(e)}(\mathcal{G})$, and the lower envelope $E_{\mathcal{F}}^{(e)}$; the shaded region is the (≤ 3)-level of $\mathcal{A}^{(e)}(\mathcal{G})$; here $t = 5$.

This lemma implies that each crossing of e in $\mathcal{M}$ corresponds to a vertex in the cross-section $E_{\mathcal{G}}^{(e)}$ of the lower envelope $E_{\mathcal{G}}$ within V_e. Let $\mathcal{G}^{(e)} \subseteq \mathcal{G}$ be the subset of functions of $\mathcal{G}$ that appear on $E_{\mathcal{G}}^{(e)}$, and let $t = |\mathcal{G}^{(e)}|$. By Corollary 1.3,

$$C_{0,0}(e, \mathcal{G}) \leq \lambda_u(t).$$

Let k be a threshold parameter, whose value will be specified later on. Suppose first that $t \leq k$. Then there are at most $\lambda_u(k)$ edge-crossings at level $(0,0)$ involving e. Since the number of edges in $M_{\mathcal{F}}$ is $O(n^{2+\varepsilon})$ (see Theorem 7.7), the overall number of crossings involving such edges is at most $O(\lambda_u(k)n^{2+\varepsilon})$. Thus, assume that $t > k$.

Let g, g' be a pair of distinct functions in $\mathcal{G}^{(e)}$. Since we assume the functions of $\mathcal{G}$ to be totally defined, g and g' are also totally defined within V_e. Hence, by continuity, g and g' must intersect within V_e at least once. Thus each function $g \in \mathcal{G}^{(e)}$ must cross at least $t - 1$ other functions of $\mathcal{G}$ within V_e, that is, each function $g \in \mathcal{G}^{(e)}$ is incident to at least $t - 1$ vertices of $\mathcal{A}^{(e)}(\mathcal{G})$, and since the graph of g contains points at level 0 in this cross section, it follows that g is incident to at least k vertices of $\mathcal{A}^{(e)}(\mathcal{G})$ at level $\leq k$ (see Figure 7.6), so the number of vertices of $\mathcal{A}^{(e)}(\mathcal{G})$ at level $\leq k$ is $\Omega(tk)$, which, by Lemma 7.12, implies

$$C_{0,k}(e, \mathcal{G}) = \Omega(tk) = \Omega\left(k\frac{t}{\lambda_u(t)} \cdot C_{0,0}(e, \mathcal{G})\right) \geq \frac{k}{\beta(n)} \cdot C_{0,0}(e, \mathcal{G}), \qquad (7.7)$$

where $\beta(n) = \lambda_u(n)/n$ is an extremely slowly growing function of n.

Summing (7.7) over all edges e of $M_{\mathcal{F}}$ for which $t > k$, adding the bound for the other edges of $M_{\mathcal{F}}$, and observing that each edge-crossing in $C_{0,k}(\mathcal{F}, \mathcal{G})$ is counted in this manner exactly once, we obtain:

$$C_{0,0}(\mathcal{F}, \mathcal{G}) = \sum_{e \in M_{\mathcal{F}}} C_{0,0}(e, \mathcal{G}) \le \frac{\beta(n)}{k} C_{0,k}(\mathcal{F}, \mathcal{G}) + O(\lambda_u(k) n^{2+\varepsilon}),$$

or

$$C_{0,0}(n) \le \frac{\beta(n)}{k} C_{0,k}(n) + O(\lambda_u(k) n^{2+\varepsilon}). \tag{7.8}$$

We next bound $C_{0,k}(n)$ in terms of $C_{k,k}(n)$, using a similar analysis. Let e' be an edge of $\mathcal{A}(\mathcal{G})$ at some level $\xi \le k$, let $V_{e'}$ be the vertical 2-manifold erected from e', defined as above, and consider the cross section $\mathcal{A}^{(e')}(\mathcal{F})$ of $\mathcal{A}(\mathcal{F})$ within $V_{e'}$. Let $E_{\mathcal{F}}^{(e')}$ denote the lower envelope of $\mathcal{A}^{(e')}(\mathcal{F})$, let $\mathcal{F}^{(e')}$ denote the subset of functions of $\mathcal{F}$ that appear along $E_{\mathcal{F}}^{(e')}$, and let $t = |\mathcal{F}^{(e')}|$. If $t \le k$ then e' contributes at most $\lambda_u(k)$ edge-crossings to $C_{0,k}(\mathcal{F}, G)$. By Corollary 7.8, there are only $O(k^{1-\varepsilon} n^{2+\varepsilon})$ edges of $\mathcal{A}(\mathcal{G})$ at level at most k, so the overall number of edge-crossings in this subcase is $O(\lambda_u(k) k^{1-\varepsilon} n^{2+\varepsilon}) = O(k^2 n^{2+\varepsilon})$. We can thus assume that $t > k$. We can then repeat, within $V_{e'}$, the preceding analysis, replacing $\mathcal{G}$ by $\mathcal{F}$, so as to conclude that the number of edge-crossings of the form (e, e') at level (p, ξ), for any $p \le k$, is $\Omega(tk)$. Following the same analysis as above, and noting that each such crossing (e, e') is counted in this manner at most once, we conclude that

$$C_{0,k}(n) \le \frac{\beta(n)}{k} C_{k,k}(n) + O(k^2 n^{2+\varepsilon}). \tag{7.9}$$

Next, we estimate $C_{k,k}(n)$, using the same probabilistic technique as in Theorem 5.16 and Corollary 7.8. If we choose a random subset $R \subseteq \mathcal{F}$ of size $\lfloor |\mathcal{F}|/(k+1) \rfloor$ and another random subset $S \subseteq \mathcal{G}$ of size $\lfloor |\mathcal{G}|/(k+1) \rfloor$, then an edge-crossing (e, e') at level (ξ, ξ') is a crossing in the overlay of M_R and M_S if and only if (i) the two functions of $\mathcal{F}$ (respectively, $\mathcal{G}$) whose intersection curve contains e (respectively, e') are in R (respectively, in S), and (ii) none of the ξ (respectively, ξ') functions of $\mathcal{F}$ (respectively, $\mathcal{G}$) that lie below e (respectively, e') are chosen in R (respectively, in S). Hence, following the same analysis as in Theorem 5.16 and Corollary 7.8, we obtain (using once again a sloppy notation):

$$C_{k,k}(n) = O((k+1)^4) \cdot C_{0,0}\left(\frac{n}{k}\right). \tag{7.10}$$

(Intuitively, the exponent 4 comes from the fact that we need to choose four functions in $R \cup S$—two in R and two in S—to ensure that the crossing (e, e') materializes in the sample configuration.) Combining (7.8), (7.9), and (7.10), we thus obtain:

$$\begin{aligned} C_{0,0}(n) &= O((\lambda_u(k) + k\beta(n)) n^{2+\varepsilon}) + \frac{\beta^2(n)}{k^2} \cdot O((k+1)^4) \cdot C_{0,0}\left(\frac{n}{k}\right) \\ &= O(k\beta(n) n^{2+\varepsilon}) + O(k^2 \beta^2(n)) \cdot C_{0,0}\left(\frac{n}{k}\right). \end{aligned}$$

The solution of this recurrence is easily seen to be

$$C_{0,0}(n) = O(n^{2+\delta}),$$

for any $\delta > \varepsilon$. This can be shown by induction on n, choosing $k = c\beta^{2/\delta}(n)$, for an appropriate constant c, and using the fact that $\beta(n)$ is an extremely slowly growing function of n.

If the functions of $\mathcal{F}$ and $\mathcal{G}$ are only partially defined, some modifications are required in the proof. Consider, for example, the first counting scheme, applied to an edge e of $M_{\mathcal{F}}$. The difficulty is that a pair of functions in $\mathcal{G}^{(e)}$ may now fail to intersect within V_e, so (7.7) may fail to hold. We overcome this difficulty as follows. Let g be any function in $\mathcal{G}^{(e)}$. If g meets at least k other functions within V_e at vertices that lie in the $(\leq k)$-level of $\mathcal{A}^{(e)}(\mathcal{G})$, then g contributes 'its share' to the term $\Omega(tk)$ in (7.7). If this is not the case, then it is easily seen that either the graph of g within V_e has an endpoint that lies in the $(\leq k)$-level of $\mathcal{A}^{(e)}(\mathcal{G})$, or else g passes above such an endpoint w of another function graph, so that both w and the point on g above w lie in the $(\leq k)$-level of $\mathcal{A}^{(e)}(\mathcal{G})$. It follows that the number of functions g of the latter kind is at most k times the number, $\Xi_k(e)$, of graph endpoints in the $(\leq k)$-level of $\mathcal{A}^{(e)}(\mathcal{G})$. Any such endpoint necessarily lies on the boundary of the corresponding function graph in $\mathcal{G}$. It follows that $\sum_e \Xi_k(e)$, summed over all edges e of $M_{\mathcal{F}}$, is bounded from above by the number of edge-crossings between the edges of $M_{\mathcal{F}}$ and the boundaries of the function graphs in $\mathcal{G}$. Arguing exactly as in case (b) in Section 7.3.1, this number is $O(n\lambda_{u'}(n))$, for an appropriate constant u'. The preceding arguments imply that we can rewrite (7.7) as

$$C_{0,k}(e,\mathcal{G}) = \Omega(tk - k^2 \cdot \Xi_k(e)), \qquad (7.11)$$

and, when we sum (7.11) over all edges e of $M_{\mathcal{F}}$, we obtain the following revised form of (7.8):

$$C_{0,0}(n) \leq \frac{\beta(n)}{k}C_{0,k}(n) + O(kn^{2+\varepsilon}) + O(k^2 n\lambda_{u'}(n)).$$

A similar adjustment has to be made in the second counting scheme, when we derive (7.9). This results in a modified inequality with an extra term of the form $O(k^4 n\lambda_{u'}(n/k))$ (this term is k^2 times the number of crossings between the boundaries of the graphs in $\mathcal{F}$ and the edges of the $(\leq k)$-level of $\mathcal{A}(\mathcal{G})$; this number can be bounded by the same technique used in case (b.ii) of the proof of Theorem 7.7). These extra terms do not change the asymptotic behavior of $C_{0,0}(n)$, as is easily verified.

This concludes the proof of Theorem 7.10. □

Remark 7.13 An obvious modification of the above proof yields a bound of $O(n^{2+\varepsilon})$ for the complexity of the overlay of the minimization diagram of $\mathcal{F}$ and of the maximization diagram of $\mathcal{G}$ (i.e., the xy-projection of the upper envelope of $\mathcal{G}$).

The following theorem is an immediate consequence of Theorem 7.10:

Theorem 7.14 *Let $\mathcal{T}$ and $\mathcal{B}$ be two given families of a total of n, possibly partially defined, bivariate functions satisfying Assumptions 7.1. Let K be the region lying between the lower envelope $E_{\mathcal{T}}$ of $\mathcal{T}$ and the upper envelope $E_{\mathcal{B}}^*$ of $\mathcal{B}$, i.e.,*

$$K = \{(x, y, z) \mid E_{\mathcal{B}}^*(x, y) \leq z \leq E_{\mathcal{T}}(x, y)\}.$$

Then the complexity of K is $O(n^{2+\varepsilon})$, for any $\varepsilon > 0$, where the constant of proportionality depends on ε, s, and b.

Proof. Let $M_{\mathcal{B}}^*$ denote the maximization diagram of the upper envelope $E_{\mathcal{B}}^*$. Theorem 7.10 and Remark 7.13 imply that the combinatorial complexity of the overlay $\mathcal{M}$ of the two planar maps $M_{\mathcal{T}}$ and $M_{\mathcal{B}}^*$ is $O(n^{2+\varepsilon})$, for any $\varepsilon > 0$. Next, construct the vertical decomposition $\mathcal{M}^*$ of $\mathcal{M}$ (as in Section 6.4). The number of pseudo-trapezoidal cells in $\mathcal{M}^*$ is clearly $O(n^{2+\varepsilon})$. Furthermore, for each of these cells τ, there is a single function $f \in \mathcal{T}$ and a single function $g \in \mathcal{B}$ such that $E_{\mathcal{T}} \equiv f$ and $E_{\mathcal{B}}^* \equiv g$ over τ (if the given functions are only partially defined, then either f or g or both may not exist at all, in which case the corresponding envelope(s) are undefined over τ). This implies that the portion of K that projects into τ has constant complexity—it is defined by the interaction between f, g, and the functions defining the (at most four) edges of τ. Since the number of cells τ is $O(n^{2+\varepsilon})$, the theorem follows. $\square$

Remark 7.15 The proof of Theorem 7.14 implies the stronger result that the (three-dimensional) vertical decomposition of K consists of $O(n^{2+\varepsilon})$ cells. Vertical decompositions of are analyzed in detail in Section 8.3.

7.3.4   Computing lower envelopes

We now present an efficient divide-and-conquer algorithm for computing the lower envelope $E_{\mathcal{F}}$ of a set $\mathcal{F}$ of n bivariate functions, satisfying Assumptions 7.1. This is equivalent to constructing the minimization diagram $M_{\mathcal{F}}$, with each face φ of $M_{\mathcal{F}}$ labeled by the unique function of $\mathcal{F}$ (if any) appearing on $E_{\mathcal{F}}$ over φ. The algorithm partitions $\mathcal{F}$ into two subcollections, $\mathcal{F}_1$, $\mathcal{F}_2$, of roughly $n/2$ functions each, constructs recursively the minimization diagrams $M_{\mathcal{F}_1}$, $M_{\mathcal{F}_2}$, and then merges these diagrams to obtain the final minimization diagram $M_{\mathcal{F}}$.

The merge step is done as follows. We first compute the overlay $\mathcal{M}$ of $M_{\mathcal{F}_1}$ and $M_{\mathcal{F}_2}$. This can be done, for example, by applying a standard sweep-line procedure (see Preparata and Shamos (1985)), whose running time is

$$O((|M_{\mathcal{F}_1}| + |M_{\mathcal{F}_2}| + |\mathcal{M}|) \log n) = O(n^{2+\varepsilon}),$$

for any $\varepsilon > 0$. We next compute the vertical decomposition $\mathcal{M}^*$ of $\mathcal{M}$; actually, this can be achieved as a by-product of the preceding sweeping procedure. The number of the pseudo-trapezoidal cells in $\mathcal{M}^*$ is $O(n^{2+\varepsilon})$.

Let c be a cell in this vertical decomposition. Note that, over c, the envelope $E_{\mathcal{F}_1}$ is attained by a single function $f_1 \in \mathcal{F}_1$ (or by no function at all), and $E_{\mathcal{F}_2}$ is attained by a single function $f_2 \in \mathcal{F}_2$ (or by no function at all). Hence, the envelope $E_{\mathcal{F}}$ is equal, over c, to $\min\{f_1, f_2\}$ if both functions exist; if only one of them exists, $E_{\mathcal{F}}$ is equal over c to that function, and if none of them exists, $E_{\mathcal{F}}$ is undefined over c. In any case, $E_{\mathcal{F}}$ over c can be computed in constant time.

As in Chapter 6, we have to assume here an appropriate model of computation, in which such a computation of $\min\{f_1, f_2\}$, as well as various primitive operations used in the sweep over $M_{\mathcal{F}_1}$ and $M_{\mathcal{F}_2}$, can each be performed in constant time. In general, we can either assume an infinite-precision real arithmetic model, in which the roots of any polynomial of constant degree can be computed exactly in constant time, or the more realistic model of precise rational arithmetic used in computational real algebraic geometry; see Collins (1975) and Heintz, Recio, and Roy (1991) for details.

We repeat this computation over all cells of $\mathcal{M}$, in overall $O(n^{2+\varepsilon})$ time, and thus obtain the entire envelope $E_{\mathcal{F}}$. We still need to apply a final clean-up stage, in which the computed portions of $E_{\mathcal{F}}$ are properly glued together, removing, as appropriate, any redundant data concerning the behavior of $E_{\mathcal{F}}$ over edges of the cells of $\mathcal{M}$. This stage also produces the final minimization diagram $M_{\mathcal{F}}$, with its faces labeled in the required manner. We omit the routine details of this step, and note that it also takes only $O(n^{2+\varepsilon})$ time. It follows that the cost of the entire divide-and-conquer process is also $O(n^{2+\varepsilon})$. In conclusion, we thus have:

Theorem 7.16 *The lower envelope of a set of n bivariate functions that satisfy Assumptions 7.1 can be computed, in an appropriate model of computation, in time $O(n^{2+\varepsilon})$, for any $\varepsilon > 0$, where the constant of proportionality depends on ε, s, and b.*

7.4 Lower envelopes in higher dimensions

In this section we extend the analysis technique of Section 7.3 to obtain sharp upper bounds on the combinatorial complexity of lower envelopes of d-variate functions, for $d > 2$. The analysis given in this section is very similar to that of Section 7.3. However, since there are several technical differences between the three-dimensional case and the general case, we prefer to present the arguments in detail.

Let $\mathcal{F} = \{f_1, \ldots, f_n\}$ be a given collection of n d-variate (possibly partially defined) functions. Again we will denote by f_i both the function and its graph in $\mathbb{R}^{d+1}$. We assume that these functions satisfy Assumptions 7.2, which are an appropriate generalization of Assumptions 7.1 (we denote the coordinates by $x_1, \ldots, x_{d+1}$, where x_{d+1} is the direction relative to which the lower envelope

ASSUMPTIONS 7.2. Assumptions on d-variate functions.

(i) Each f_i is a portion of a d-dimensional algebraic surface of constant maximum degree b.

(ii) The projection of each f_i in the x_{d+1}-direction onto the hyperplane $h : x_{d+1} = 0$ is a semialgebraic set defined in terms of a constant number of d-variate polynomials of constant maximum degree (say, b too).

(iii) The relative interiors of any $d + 1$ of the given function graphs intersect in at most s points, for some constant parameter s (by Bezout's theorem (Hartshorne (1977)) and by Property (iv) below, we always have $s \leq b^{d+1}$).

(iv) The functions in $\mathcal{F}$ are in *general position*, in the sense defined in the introduction of this chapter.

is defined). As in the preceding section, some of these assumptions can be relaxed, but we will state and prove our results under these assumptions only.

For each $\mathbf{x} \in h$, let $V(\mathbf{x})$ denote the maximal closed segment contained in the x_{d+1}-parallel line through $\mathbf{x}$, whose bottom endpoint lies on the envelope $E_{\mathcal{F}}$ and which does not cross the relative interior of any function graph in $\mathcal{F}$ (if $E_{\mathcal{F}}$ is undefined at $\mathbf{x}$, the segment $V(\mathbf{x})$ is also undefined). We say that the envelope is *attained* over $\mathbf{x}$ by all functions whose graphs touch that segment; if the envelope point does not lie on any graph boundary, then $V(\mathbf{x})$ is a singleton, and we say that the envelope is attained at $\mathbf{x}$ by all the functions whose graphs are incident to that point.

To simplify the subsequent analysis, we extend, as in Section 7.3, each $f_i \in \mathcal{F}$ to a surface f_i^* by drawing all rays emanating in the positive x_{d+1}-direction from each point on the boundary of f_i. Let $\mathcal{F}^*$ denote the resulting collection of extended surfaces.

For the sake of brevity, we omit here the appropriate extension of the arguments given in Section 7.3.1, concerning the issue of general position. Since the bound that is asserted below is sufficiently large, it can be shown, as above, that, once we establish that bound for collections of surfaces in general position, it will also hold, up to some constant of proportionality, for degenerate collections as well.

7.4.1 Combinatorial complexity of the envelope

Theorem 7.17 *The combinatorial complexity $\kappa(\mathcal{F})$ of the lower envelope of a collection of n (partially defined) d-variate functions that satisfy Assump-*

tions 7.2 is $O(n^{d+\varepsilon})$, for any $\varepsilon > 0$, where the constant of proportionality depends on ε, d, s, and the maximum degree b and the shape of the given function graphs and of their boundaries.

As in the previous section, an immediate corollary of Theorem 7.17 is:

Corollary 7.18 *The number of vertices of the $(\leq k)$-level of the arrangement $\mathcal{A}(\mathcal{F})$, for a collection $\mathcal{F}$ of n d-variate functions that satisfy Assumptions 7.2, is $O(n^{d+\varepsilon}(k+1)^{1-\varepsilon})$, for any $\varepsilon > 0$.*

Proof. For a subset $X \subseteq \mathcal{F}$ and for an integer $0 \leq j < |X|$, let $V_j(X)$ denote the set of vertices in $\mathcal{A}(\mathcal{F})$ of level j. Let $R \subseteq \mathcal{F}$ be a random subset of $\mathcal{F}$ of size $r = \lfloor n/(k+1) \rfloor$. The probability that a vertex in $V_j(\mathcal{F})$ appears in $V_0(R)$ is, in complete analogy to the argument in the proof of Corollary 7.8, at least $\binom{n-j-d-1}{r-d-1}/\binom{n}{r}$ (we count here both 'inner' and 'outer' vertices; any vertex is defined by at most $d+1$ function graphs, which implies the asserted inequality). Hence, the same argument as in the proofs of Theorem 5.16 and Corollary 7.8 implies that

$$\sum_{j=0}^{k} |V_j(\mathcal{F})| \leq c(k+1)^{d+1} \mathbf{E}\big[|V_0(R)|\big], \tag{7.12}$$

for some constant c. The claim now follows from Theorem 7.17. □

Proof of Theorem 7.17. The proof is based on induction on d, and follows closely the analysis given in the proof of Theorem 7.7. The base case $d = 2$ has already been proven (and the simpler case $d = 1$ is immediate from the results of earlier chapters). Let $d > 2$ and suppose that the theorem is true for all $d' < d$. Let $\mathcal{F}$ be a collection of n partially defined d-variate functions that satisfy the above assumptions.

As in the case of bivariate functions, it can be shown that it suffices to bound the number of vertices (0-dimensional cells) of $M_{\mathcal{F}}$, because the number of all other features is proportional to the number of vertices, plus an 'overhead' term that is at most $O(n^d)$. As above, we call a vertex *inner* if it is formed by the intersection of the relative interiors of $d+1$ function graphs in $\mathcal{F}$, and *outer* otherwise.

Consider first outer vertices. Fix a function $f \in \mathcal{F}$, and let c denote the orthogonal projection of the boundary of f onto h. By assumption, c is a semialgebraic set defined in terms of a constant number of polynomials of constant maximum degree. Let V_c denote the union of all rays that emanate in the positive x_{d+1}-direction from all points on the boundary of f. For each function graph $f_i \in \mathcal{F}$, $f_i \neq f$, let $\psi_i = f_i \cap V_c$. We can parametrize c using $d-1$ real parameters, so as to embed c in $(d-1)$-dimensional Euclidean space. Hence, if we add the coordinate x_{d+1}, we obtain an embedding of the functions ψ_i over c into d-dimensional Euclidean space, in such a way that they become graphs of partially defined $(d-1)$-variate functions that satisfy Assumptions 7.2, where the maximum degree of the functions and of their boundaries is some constant (depending on b but possibly much larger than b).[6] Each outer vertex of $E_{\mathcal{F}}$ whose projection lies in c must also be an (inner or outer) vertex of the lower envelope of the ψ_i's. By the induction hypothesis, the complexity of the lower envelope of these surfaces is $O(n^{d-1+\varepsilon})$, for any $\varepsilon > 0$ (with an appropriate constant of proportionality). Hence, if we repeat the analysis for all functions $f \in \mathcal{F}$, we conclude that the total number of outer vertices of $E_{\mathcal{F}}$ is $O(n \cdot n^{d-1+\varepsilon}) = O(n^{d+\varepsilon})$, for any $\varepsilon > 0$.

Let $\phi(\mathcal{F})$ denote the number of inner vertices of $E_{\mathcal{F}}$. We also denote by $\phi(n)$ the maximum of $\phi(\mathcal{F})$, taken over all collections $\mathcal{F}$ of n d-variate functions that satisfy Assumptions 7.2, with the same b and s. Finally, we denote by $\phi^*(\mathcal{F})$ the total number of vertices of $E_{\mathcal{F}}$, both inner and outer, and by $\phi^*(n)$ the maximum of $\phi^*(\mathcal{F})$, taken over all collections $\mathcal{F}$ as above. The preceding analysis implies that $\phi^*(n) = \phi(n) + O(n^{d+\varepsilon})$, for any $\varepsilon > 0$.

Let p be an inner vertex of $E_{\mathcal{F}}$, formed by the intersection of $d+1$ function graphs $f_1, \ldots, f_{d+1} \in \mathcal{F}$. Let us denote by γ_i the curve of intersection between all these graphs except f_i, for $i = 1, \ldots, d+1$. Let $\beta_i(p)$ denote the maximal relatively open connected x_1-monotone subarc of γ_i that contains no singular point on any graph, has p as an endpoint, and is disjoint from $E_{\mathcal{F}}$. Note that, since each γ_i is algebraic of constant maximum degree, one can partition γ_i into a constant number of connected x_1-monotone subarcs with no singular points; the total number of such subarcs, over all intersection curves of the surfaces, is thus $O(n^d)$. Each $\beta_i(p)$ is fully contained in a single subarc of this form.

As in the case of bivariate functions, we may assume that the point p is a point of transversal intersection between these function graphs, and that none of these graphs is singular at p. Thus we can assume that these $d+1$ graphs are smooth at p, so $E_{\mathcal{F}}$ can be approximated at a neighborhood of p by the lower envelope of the $d+1$ tangent hyperplanes to these function graphs at p, which is easily seen to imply, in complete analogy to the three-dimensional case, that the $d+1$ tangent directions of $\beta_1(p), \ldots, \beta_{d+1}(p)$ at p, all pointing from p along their respective arcs, are such that the positive span of their orthogonal projections onto h is the entire hyperplane h. Thus at least one of these arcs emanates from p in the positive x_1-direction, and at least one arc emanates in the negative x_1-direction.

We define the *index* $j = j(p)$ of p to be the number of intersection points of $f_1, \ldots, f_{d+1}$ that lie in the half-space $x_1 > x_1(p)$; note that $0 \le j(p) \le s - 1$. Let $\phi^{(j)}(\mathcal{F})$, for $j = 0, \ldots, s-1$, be the number of inner vertices of $E_{\mathcal{F}}$ whose index is at most j. As above, we will derive a recurrence relationship for $\phi^*(n)$, by bounding each of the functions $\phi^{(j)}$ in terms of $\phi^{(j-1)}$ (with a special handling of $\phi^{(0)}$); the solution to this recurrence will yield the asserted bound.

Let p be a nonsingular inner vertex of index at most j, formed by the

---

[6]This follows from algebraic elimination theory; see, for example, van der Waerden (1970).

transversal intersection of $d+1$ function graphs, $f_1, \ldots, f_{d+1}$; we continue to use the notations introduced above. Suppose, with no loss of generality, that $\beta_1(p)$ emanates from p in the positive x_1-direction, and let u denote its other endpoint. Several cases can arise:

(a) u is an endpoint of a maximal connected x_1-monotone piece, with no singular points, of the whole intersection curve γ_1. In this case, we charge p to u. Since each such u can be charged in this manner at most a constant number of times, and since there are only $O(n^d)$ such points, over the entire collection of intersection curves, the number of vertices p of this kind is $O(n^d)$.

(b) u is a point on $E_{\mathcal{F}}$ and $\beta_1(p) \cup \{u\}$ does not intersect f_1. If we start tracing $\beta_1(p)$ from p, we move initially along points hidden from $E_{\mathcal{F}}$ by f_1, which thus lies below the curve. It follows that $\beta_1(p)$ must contain a point w that lies directly above the boundary of f_1, and we charge p to the point w.

Let w' be the point on ∂f_1 that lies directly below w, and let t denote the number of functions $f_i \in \mathcal{F}$ whose graphs either cross the portion pw of $\beta_1(p)$ or have a point on their boundary which lies directly below pw (in other words, the corresponding extended surfaces f_i^* cross pw). We fix some threshold parameter $k = k_j$, to be determined below, and consider the following two subcases:

(b.i) $t > k$: By assumption, $\beta_1(p)$ contains at least t vertices of the arrangement $\mathcal{A}(\mathcal{F}^*)$ of the collection $\mathcal{F}^*$ of extended surfaces, and we will charge p to the block of the first k of these vertices in their order from p to w along $\beta_1(p)$. Clearly, each vertex of $\mathcal{A}(\mathcal{F}^*)$ can be charged in this manner only a constant number of times, and the level of each such vertex is at most k. By (7.12), the number of vertices of $\mathcal{A}(\mathcal{F}^*)$ at level $\leq k$ is $O(k^{d+1}\phi^*(n/k))$, which in turn implies that the number of inner vertices p of $E_{\mathcal{F}}$ in this subcase is $O(k^d\phi^*(n/k))$. (We use here and below the same sloppy notation, of writing n/k instead of $\lfloor n/(k+1) \rfloor$, as in the case of bivariate functions. This does not affect the bounds obtained in the analysis.)

(b.ii) $t \leq k$: Let c be the projection of ∂f_1 onto h, as described above, and let V_c be the vertical surface formed by the union of all x_{d+1}-parallel rays whose bottom endpoints lie on the boundary of f_1. For each surface $f_i \neq f_1$ in $\mathcal{F}$, let $\psi_i = f_i \cap V_c$. As argued above, an appropriate parametrization of c makes the surfaces ψ_i graphs of partially defined $(d-1)$-variate functions that satisfy Assumptions 7.2, for appropriate constant maximum degree and constant maximum number of d-wise intersection points. Moreover, w is a vertex of the arrangement $\mathcal{A}_c$ of the surfaces ψ_i over c, and w lies at level $\leq k$ in that arrangement. By the induction hypothesis and by Corollary 7.18, the number of vertices of $\mathcal{A}_c$ at level $\leq k$ is

$$O(k^d(n/k)^{d-1+\varepsilon}) = O(k^{1-\varepsilon}n^{d-1+\varepsilon}).$$

Summing this bound over the boundaries of all function graphs in $\mathcal{F}$, we conclude that the overall number of vertices p that are charged in this subcase is $O(k^{1-\varepsilon}n^{d+\varepsilon})$, for any $\varepsilon > 0$.

(c) u is a point on $E_{\mathcal{F}}$ and f_1 intersects $\beta_1(p) \cup \{u\}$ (this case arises only when $j(p) \geq 1$). Let w be the intersection point of f_1 and $\beta_1(p) \cup \{u\}$ that lies nearest to p along that curve. Clearly, the index of w is at most $j - 1$. Let δ denote the portion of $\beta_1(p)$ between p and w, and let t denote the number of extended surfaces in $\mathcal{F}^*$ that cross δ. We consider the following two subcases:

(c.i) $t > k$: As in case (b.i) above, we conclude that δ contains at least k vertices of $\mathcal{A}(\mathcal{F}^*)$, and we charge p to the first k of these vertices, in their order along δ from p to w. As argued above, all these vertices are at level at most k in $\mathcal{A}(\mathcal{F}^*)$, and each of them can be charged in this way only a constant number of times. Repeating the random-sampling argument given above, we conclude that the number of inner vertices p that are charged in this manner is $O(k^d\phi^*(n/k))$.

(c.ii) $t \leq k$: Here we observe, arguing as above, that w lies at level at most t in $\mathcal{A}(\mathcal{F}^*)$. Hence, if we remove the $t' \leq t$ surfaces that hide w from $E_{\mathcal{F}}$, w becomes an inner vertex of the envelope of the remaining functions. Following the same arguments as in Section 7.3 and Corollary 7.18, we can obtain:

$$\sum_{\xi=0}^{k} G_\xi = O(k^{d+1}\phi^{(j-1)}(n/k)),$$

where G_ξ is the number of inner vertices w of $E_{\mathcal{F}}$ as above, with exactly ξ surfaces passing below them. In other words, if we charge each of the inner vertices p in this subcase to the corresponding point w, and observe that each such point can be charged only a constant number of times, we conclude that the number of vertices p in this subcase is $O(k^{d+1}\phi^{(j-1)}(n/k))$.

Thus, summing up these bounds, we obtain the following recurrence (where, for $j = 0$, we put in the right-hand side $\phi^{(-1)} = 0$):

$$\phi^{(j)}(\mathcal{F}) = O(k^d\phi^*(n/k) + k^{d+1}\phi^{(j-1)}(n/k) + k^{1-\varepsilon}n^{d+\varepsilon}). \tag{7.13}$$

We now unfold the recurrence (7.13), using a different parameter $k = k_j$ at each stage. We then obtain, as above:

$$\phi^{(j)}(\mathcal{F}) \leq C_j k_j^d \phi^* \left(\frac{n}{k_j} \right) + C_{j-1} k_j^{d+1} k_{j-1}^d \phi^* \left(\frac{n}{k_j k_{j-1}} \right) +$$

$$C_{j-2}k_j^{d+1}k_{j-1}^{d+1}k_{j-2}^d\phi^*\left(\frac{n}{k_jk_{j-1}k_{j-2}}\right)+\cdots+$$

$$C_0k_j^{d+1}k_{j-1}^{d+1}\cdots k_1^{d+1}k_0^d\phi^*\left(\frac{n}{k_jk_{j-1}\cdots k_0}\right)+$$

$$C(k_jk_{j-1}\cdots k_0)^{1-\varepsilon}n^{d+\varepsilon}, \tag{7.14}$$

where $C,C_0,C_1,\ldots,C_j$ are appropriate constants (and C depends also on ε).

If we now take the last inequality (7.14) for $j=s-1$, and add the already established bound for the number of outer vertices, we obtain the following final recurrence:

$$\begin{aligned}
\phi^*(n) \;\le\; & C_{s-1}k_{s-1}^d\phi^*\left(\frac{n}{k_{s-1}}\right)+C_{s-2}k_{s-1}^{d+1}k_{s-2}^d\phi^*\left(\frac{n}{k_{s-1}k_{s-2}}\right)+ \\
& C_{s-3}k_{s-1}^{d+1}k_{s-2}^{d+1}k_{s-3}^d\phi^*\left(\frac{n}{k_{s-1}k_{s-2}k_{s-3}}\right)+\cdots+ \\
& C_0k_{s-1}^{d+1}k_{s-2}^{d+1}\cdots k_1^{d+1}k_0^d\phi^*\left(\frac{n}{k_{s-1}k_{s-2}\cdots k_0}\right)+ \\
& C(k_{s-1}k_{s-2}\cdots k_0)^{1-\varepsilon}n^{d+\varepsilon}. \tag{7.15}
\end{aligned}$$

Arguing as in Section 7.3, one can easily show that the solution to this recurrence is

$$\phi^*(n)\le An^{d+\varepsilon}, \tag{7.16}$$

for any $\varepsilon>0$, where A is a constant that depends on ε and on the constants $C,C_0,C_1,\ldots,C_{s-1}$. We leave it to the reader to work out the details of the proof of this claim. As in the case of bivariate functions, one can show that the number of all other features of $E_{\mathcal{F}}$ is at most proportional to the number of vertices plus $O(n^d)$. This completes the proof of the theorem. $\qquad\square$

Remark 7.19 (i) One of the intriguing open problems concerning lower envelopes in higher dimensions is to tighten the upper bounds obtained in Theorems 7.7 and 7.17, replacing the $O(n^\varepsilon)$ factors in these bounds by smaller factors (polylogarithmic, or, ideally, factors of the form $\lambda_q(n)/n$, for some constant q). The current proof, which relates the number of vertices on the envelope to the number of vertices at level $\le k$ in a sample of n/k functions, does not seem to yield such an improvement.

(ii) As a useful exercise, the reader may wish to redo the proofs of Theorems 7.7 and 7.17 for the univariate case $d=1$. This will yield the weak bound $\lambda_s(n)\le cn^{1+\varepsilon}$, for any $\varepsilon>0$, where c depends on s and ε. One merit of this proof is that it uses a purely geometric approach. It is an interesting open problem to come up with a similar geometric proof that yields the sharper bounds on $\lambda_s(n)$ derived in Chapters 2 and 3.

7.4.2   Computing lower envelopes

In this subsection we consider the problem of computing lower envelopes in higher dimensions. We have seen so far two approaches to this problem. Section 7.2.2 describes an efficient algorithm for computing the lower envelope of a collection of simplices. However, this approach requires the existence of a decomposition of the region that lies below the lower envelope of a sample of r d-variate functions, into $O(r^{d+\varepsilon})$ cells of constant description complexity. As we have seen, such a decomposition exists for $d = 2$ and for piecewise-linear functions in any dimension, but no such decomposition is known to exist for arrangements of more general (algebraic) surfaces in higher dimensions. (See also Section 8.3 for a study of related problems.) The other approach, described in Section 7.3.4, requires a bound on the complexity of the overlay of two minimization diagrams. Currently, it is not known whether Theorem 7.10 can be extended to higher dimensions, to yield a bound of $O(n^{d+\varepsilon})$ on the complexity of such an overlay. Hence, none of these approaches seems usable, at the present state of the art, for computing minimization diagrams of d-variate functions, for $d \geq 3$.

In this subsection we present a randomized incremental algorithm for computing the vertices, edges, and 2-faces of the minimization diagram of a collection of n d-variate functions satisfying Assumptions 7.2, for any $d \geq 2$; its expected running time is $O(n^{d+\varepsilon})$, for any $\varepsilon > 0$. Thus it provides only a partial solution to our problem, which is nevertheless sufficient for some applications, e.g., for finding the lowest or highest vertex of $E_{\mathcal{F}}$. Moreover, this algorithm will be used, in Section 7.4.3 below, as a major component of an algorithm that computes lower envelopes in four dimensions (i.e., for $d = 3$).

Let $\mathcal{F} = \{f_1, \ldots, f_n\}$ be a collection of (partial) d-variate functions satisfying Assumptions 7.2. To compute the lower envelope $E_{\mathcal{F}}$ of $\mathcal{F}$, in the above incomplete sense, we proceed as follows. Let Σ be the family of all $(d-1)$-subsets of $\mathcal{F}$. We fix a subset $\sigma = \{f_1, \ldots, f_{d-1}\} \in \Sigma$, and let

$$\Pi^\sigma = \{\mathbf{x} \in \mathbb{R}^d \mid f_1(\mathbf{x}) = \cdots = f_{d-1}(\mathbf{x})\}.$$

Since the f_i's are assumed to be in general position, Π^σ is a (possibly empty) two-dimensional surface (or surface patch). For the sake of simplicity, we assume that Π^σ is an $x_1 x_2$-monotone surface (otherwise, we decompose it into a constant number of pieces, so that each piece is an $x_1 x_2$-monotone two-dimensional surface, and work with each piece separately). For each $i \geq d$, let

$$\gamma_i = \{\mathbf{x} \in \Pi^\sigma \mid f_i(\mathbf{x}) = f_1(\mathbf{x}) = \cdots = f_{d-1}(\mathbf{x})\};$$

γ_i is a one-dimensional curve, which partitions Π^σ into two (not necessarily connected) regions, K_i^+, K_i^-, where

$$
\begin{aligned}
K_i^+ &= \{\mathbf{x} \in \Pi^\sigma \mid f_i(\mathbf{x}) > f_1(\mathbf{x}) = \cdots = f_{d-1}(\mathbf{x})\}, \\
K_i^- &= \{\mathbf{x} \in \Pi^\sigma \mid f_i(\mathbf{x}) < f_1(\mathbf{x}) = \cdots = f_{d-1}(\mathbf{x})\}.
\end{aligned}
$$

Then the intersection $Q^\sigma = \bigcap_{i>d} K_i^+$ is the portion of Π^σ over which the envelope $E_{\mathcal{F}}$ is attained by the functions of σ. The algorithm will compute the regions Q^σ, over all choices of $(d-1)$-tuples σ of functions, thereby yielding all the vertices, edges, and 2-faces of $M_{\mathcal{F}}$ (because of general position, any such feature must show up as a feature of at least one of the regions Q^σ).

We compute Q^σ using a randomized incremental approach, similar to the one described in Section 6.5. Since the basic idea is the same, we give only a brief overview of the algorithm. Let

$$\Gamma^\sigma = \{\gamma_i \mid d \le i \le n\}.$$

We first compute the set Γ^σ. (As above, we assume an appropriate model of computation, in which any of the various primitive operations required by the algorithm can be performed in constant time.) Next, we add the curves γ_j one by one in a random order, and maintain the intersection of the regions K_j^+ for the curves added so far. Let $\langle \gamma_d, \gamma_{d+1}, \ldots, \gamma_n \rangle$ be the (random) insertion sequence, and let Q_i^σ denote the intersection of $K_d^+, K_{d+1}^+, \ldots, K_i^+$, for $i = d, d+1, \ldots, n$. We construct and maintain the 'vertical decomposition' $\tilde{Q}_i^\sigma$ of Q_i^σ, defined as the partitioning of each 2-face ϕ of Q_i^σ into 'pseudo-trapezoidal' cells, obtained by drawing, from each vertex of ϕ and from each locally x_1-extreme point on $\partial\phi$, a curve orthogonal to the x_1-axis within Π^σ, and extend it till it hits $\partial\phi$ again. Each cell is defined by at most four curves of Γ^σ; conversely, any four or fewer curves of Γ^σ define a constant number of pseudo-trapezoidal cells (those formed along Π^σ when only these curves are inserted). (Note that this construction is well-defined, since Π^σ is an $x_1 x_2$-monotone surface.) In the $(i+1)$st step we add K_{i+1}^+ and compute $\tilde{Q}_{i+1}^\sigma$ from $\tilde{Q}_i^\sigma$, using a technique similar to the one described in Section 6.5. (Some modifications in the algorithm are required, because we now construct a region that is not necessarily connected, so the maintenance of the topology of the intersection is somewhat more complicated. These modifications are not difficult, and are detailed, e.g., in Miller and Sharir (1991).)

The analysis of the expected running time of the algorithm proceeds along the same lines as described in Section 6.5.3. We define the *weight*, $w(\tau)$, of a pseudo-trapezoidal cell τ, defined by the arcs of Γ^σ, to be the number of functions f_i (excluding the functions of σ itself, and the up-to-four functions whose intersections with Π^σ *define* τ), such that $f_i(\mathbf{x}) \le f_1(\mathbf{x}) = \cdots = f_{d-1}(\mathbf{x})$ for at least some point $\mathbf{x} \in \tau$.

As in Section 6.5.3, the cost of the above procedure can be shown to be proportional to the number of cells that are created during the execution of the algorithm, plus the sum of their weights, plus an overhead term of $O(n^d)$, needed to prepare the collections of curves γ_i and regions K_i^+, over all two-dimensional intersection surfaces Π^σ. The analysis given below deals only with cells that are defined by exactly four such curves, and easy and obvious modifications are necessary to handle all other types of cells.

Let T^σ denote the set of cells defined by four arcs of Γ^σ, and let $T =$

$\bigcup_{\sigma \in \Sigma} T^{\sigma}$. Each cell of T is defined by $d - 1 + 4 = d + 3$ functions of $\mathcal{F}$. In what follows we implicitly assume that the specification of a cell $\tau \in T$ includes the $d+3$ functions defining τ, where there is a clear distinction between the first $d - 1$ functions (constituting the set σ), and the last four functions (defining the four curves that generate τ along Π^{σ}). For an integer $k \geq 0$ and a subset $R \subseteq \mathcal{F}$, let $T_k(R) \subseteq T$ (respectively, $T_{\leq k}(R)$) denote the set of cells, defined by $d + 3$ functions of R, and having weight k (respectively, at most k). Let $N_k(R) = |T_k(R)|$ and $N_k(r) = \max N_k(R)$, where the maximum is taken over all subsets R of $\mathcal{F}$ of size r. Similarly, we define $N_{\leq k}(R)$ and $N_{\leq k}(r)$. Since each cell of $T_0(R)$ lies on the lower envelope of R, it follows that $N_0(r) = O(r^{d+\varepsilon})$, for any $\varepsilon > 0$.

Lemma 7.20 *The probability that a pseudo-trapezoidal cell $\tau \in T_k(\mathcal{F})$ is created during the incremental construction of Q^{σ}, where $\sigma \in \Sigma$ is the tuple for which Π^{σ} contains τ, is $1/\binom{k+4}{4}$.*

Proof. For τ to be created, it is necessary and sufficient that the four curves of Γ^{σ} defining τ will appear in the random insertion order before any of the k functions that contribute to the weight of τ, and this probability is easily seen to be $1/\binom{k+4}{4}$. $\square$

Adapting the analysis technique of Theorem 5.16, we also have:

Lemma 7.21 *For any $0 \leq k \leq n$ and for any $\varepsilon > 0$,*

$$N_{\leq k}(n) = O((k + 1)^{3-\varepsilon} n^{d+\varepsilon}).$$

Proof. We use a variant of the probabilistic analysis technique described in Theorem 5.16 and in Corollaries 7.8 and 7.18. If we choose a random sample $R \subseteq \mathcal{F}$ of $r = \lfloor n/(k + 1) \rfloor$ functions of $\mathcal{F}$, then a cell $\tau \in T_k(\mathcal{F})$ is in $T_0(R)$ if all $d + 3$ functions $f_1, \ldots, f_{d+3}$ defining τ are chosen in R, and none of the remaining k functions f_i, such that $f_i(\mathbf{x}) \leq f_1(\mathbf{x})$ for some $\mathbf{x} \in \tau$, are chosen in R. The same analysis as above implies

$$
\begin{aligned}
N_{\leq k}(n) &= O((k + 1)^{d+3} N_0(\lfloor n/(k + 1) \rfloor)) \\
&= O((k + 1)^{d+3} (n/(k + 1))^{d+\varepsilon}) \\
&= O((k + 1)^{3-\varepsilon} n^{d+\varepsilon}).
\end{aligned}
$$
                                                                                $\square$

For a cell $\tau \in T$, let A_τ be the event that $\tau \in \tilde{Q}_i^{\sigma}$, for the tuple $\sigma \in \Sigma$ for which Π^{σ} contains τ, and for some $d \leq i \leq n$. The expected running time of the algorithm, over all choices of $(d - 1)$-tuples σ of functions, is thus proportional to

$$
\begin{aligned}
O(n^d) + \sum_{\tau \in T} (w(\tau) + 1) \cdot \Pr\{A_\tau\} &= O(n^d) + \sum_{k \geq 0} \sum_{\tau \in T_k(\mathcal{F})} (k + 1) \cdot \Pr\{A_\tau\} \\
&= O\left(\sum_{k=0}^{n-d-3} \frac{(k + 1) N_k(\mathcal{F})}{\binom{k+4}{4}} + n^d \right),
\end{aligned}
$$

where the last inequality follows from Lemmas 7.20 and 7.21. Since

$$N_k(\mathcal{F}) = N_{\leq k}(\mathcal{F}) - N_{\leq (k-1)}(\mathcal{F}),$$

we obtain

$$
\begin{aligned}
& \sum_{k=0}^{n-d-3} \frac{(k+1)N_k(\mathcal{F})}{\binom{k+4}{4}} \\
= \; & N_0(\mathcal{F}) + 24 \sum_{k=1}^{n-d-3} \frac{N_{\leq k}(\mathcal{F}) - N_{\leq (k-1)}(\mathcal{F})}{(k+4)(k+3)(k+2)} \\
= \; & O(n^{d+\varepsilon}) + 24 \sum_{k=1}^{n-d-4} N_{\leq k}(n) \left[\frac{1}{(k+4)(k+3)(k+2)} - \frac{1}{(k+5)(k+4)(k+3)} \right] \\
= \; & O\!\left(n^{d+\varepsilon} + \sum_{k=1}^{n-d-4} \frac{k^{3-\varepsilon} n^{d+\varepsilon}}{(k+5)(k+4)(k+3)(k+2)} \right) \\
= \; & O\!\left(n^{d+\varepsilon} \cdot \sum_{k=1}^{n-d-4} \frac{1}{k^{1+\varepsilon}} \right) \\
= \; & O(n^{d+\varepsilon}).
\end{aligned}
$$

We thus conclude:

Theorem 7.22 *The vertices, edges, and 2-faces of the lower envelope of n (partial) d-variate functions, satisfying Assumptions 7.2, can be computed, in an appropriate model of computation, in randomized expected time $O(n^{d+\varepsilon})$, for any $\varepsilon > 0$.*

Remark 7.23   We can also use an alternative technique, based on a randomized divide-and-conquer approach, for computing the vertices, edges, and 2-faces of the lower envelope. As above, we compute the 2-manifolds Π^σ, and, within each fixed manifold Π^σ, consider the regions K_i^+, as defined above. We next partition the collection of these regions into two subcollections of roughly equal size, compute recursively the intersection of each subcollection, and then compute the intersection of the two resulting intersection regions, using the same approach as in Section 6.4. It can be shown that the expected running time of this algorithm is also $O(n^{d+\varepsilon})$, for any $\varepsilon > 0$.

7.4.3   Computing lower envelopes in 4-space

Theorem 7.22 can be applied to compute the lower envelope $E_{\mathcal{F}}$ of a set $\mathcal{F}$ of trivariate functions, satisfying Assumptions 7.2, in the following strong sense: One can preprocess $\mathcal{F}$ into an efficient data structure that supports fast queries of the form: given a point $w \in \mathbb{R}^3$, compute the function(s) attaining $E_{\mathcal{F}}$ at

w. The algorithm summarized in Theorem 7.22 computes the vertices, edges, and 2-faces of the minimization diagram $M_{\mathcal{F}}$ of $\mathcal{F}$. Since $M_{\mathcal{F}}$ is a three-dimensional subdivision, this information is essentially sufficient to provide a complete representation of $M_{\mathcal{F}}$. We first partition the cells of $M_{\mathcal{F}}$ into 'monotone' subcells, in the sense of Lemma 7.24 below, to obtain a refinement $M'_{\mathcal{F}}$ of $M_{\mathcal{F}}$. We then use the point-location data structure of Preparata and Tamassia (1992) to produce the desired structure for answering queries of the above type.

We define and construct $M'_{\mathcal{F}}$ as follows. We mark, along each 2-face F of $M_{\mathcal{F}}$, the locus γ_F of all points of F having a vertical tangency (in the z-direction). The arcs γ_F, for all 2-faces F, lie along $O(n^2)$ curves in $\mathbb{R}^3$, each being the xyz-projection of the locus of all points with z-vertical tangency along some two-dimensional surface $f_i = f_j$, for a pair of indices $i \neq j$, or along the boundary of some f_i. We consider below only the former case; the latter case can be handled in almost the same (and, actually, simpler) manner. Let δ be one of these curves. We consider the two-dimensional surface V_δ, within the xyz-space, obtained as the union of all lines passing through points of δ and parallel to the z-axis; let V_δ^+, V_δ^- denote the portions of V_δ that lie, respectively, above and below δ. (Note that V_δ may have self-intersections along some vertical lines, along which V_δ^+ and V_δ^- are not well-defined; we omit here details of the (rather easy) handling of such cases.) Let δ_0 be the portion of δ over which the functions f_i and f_j attain the envelope $E_{\mathcal{F}}$. Clearly, δ_0 is the union of all arcs γ_F that are contained in δ, so the overall number of connected components of δ_0, over all curves δ, is $O(n^{3+\varepsilon})$ (as easily follows from Theorem 7.17).

Let w be a point in δ_0. Then the cell c of $M_{\mathcal{F}}$ lying immediately above w is such that, within c, the envelope $E_{\mathcal{F}}$ is attained by either f_i or f_j. Thus the upward-directed z-vertical ray emanating from w leaves c (if at all) at a point that lies on a two-dimensional surface of either the form $f_i = f_k$ or $f_j = f_k$ or the boundary of some f_k. For fixed i and j, there are only $O(n)$ possible two-dimensional surfaces of this kind. Next, we compute the lower envelope $E^{(\delta)}$ of these $O(n)$ two-dimensional surfaces, restricted to V_δ^+. As argued in earlier proofs, it is easily seen that the complexity of $E^{(\delta)}$ is $O(\lambda_q(n))$, for some constant q depending on the maximum degree and shape of these two-dimensional surfaces (and thus also on the maximum degree b of the functions in $\mathcal{F}$). We next take the portions of the graph of $E^{(\delta)}$ that lie over δ_0, and "etch" them along the corresponding 2-faces of $M_{\mathcal{F}}$. We apply a fully symmetric procedure within V_δ^-, for all curves δ. The overall combinatorial complexity of all the added curves is thus $O(n^2 \lambda_q(n)) = O(n^{3+\varepsilon})$, and they can be computed in $O(n^2 \lambda_q(n) \log n) = O(n^{3+\varepsilon})$ time, as is easily verified.

Let $M'_{\mathcal{F}}$ denote the refined cell decomposition of $\mathbb{R}^3$, obtained by adding to $M_{\mathcal{F}}$ the arcs γ_F, the etched arcs of the upper and lower envelopes in the vertical surfaces V_δ, and the z-vertical walls (i.e., union of all z-vertical segments) connecting between δ_0 and these arcs in V_δ, for all arcs δ. As just argued, the combinatorial complexity of $M'_{\mathcal{F}}$ is still $O(n^{3+\varepsilon})$, and $M'_{\mathcal{F}}$ has the following crucial property:

Lemma 7.24 *For each 3-cell c of $M'_{\mathcal{F}}$, every connected component of a cross section of c by a plane parallel to the xz-plane is x-monotone.*

Proof. Suppose π is a plane parallel to the xz-plane, for which there exists a connected component c' of $c \cap \pi$ that is not x-monotone. Then there is a point $w \in \partial c'$ so that the z-vertical line passing through w meets $c \cap \pi$ both slightly above and slightly below w. But then w is a point with z-vertical tangency on one of the curves γ_F, so, by construction, $M'_{\mathcal{F}}$ must contain the vertical segment passing through w and contained in c, as part of some vertical wall, a contradiction, which completes the proof of the lemma. $\qquad\square$

We are now in a position to apply the point-location technique of Preparata and Tamassia (1992). They show that a three-dimensional subdivision of combinatorial complexity N satisfying certain monotonicity properties can be preprocessed, in time $O(N \log^2 N)$, into a data structure of size $O(N \log^2 N)$, so that any point-location query in the subdivision can be answered in $O(\log^2 N)$ time. As shown by Agarwal, Aronov, and Sharir (1994), $M'_{\mathcal{F}}$ satisfies the desired properties. Omitting further details, which are rather technical and are given in the paper just cited, we can obtain the following result:

Theorem 7.25 *Let $\mathcal{F}$ be a given collection of n trivariate, possibly partially defined, functions, satisfying Assumptions 7.2. Then, for any $\varepsilon > 0$, $\mathcal{F}$ can be preprocessed, in randomized expected time $O(n^{3+\varepsilon})$, into a data structure of size $O(n^{3+\varepsilon})$, so that, given any query point $w \in \mathbb{R}^3$, we can compute $E_{\mathcal{F}}(w)$, as well as the function(s) attaining $E_{\mathcal{F}}$ at w, in $O(\log^2 n)$ time.*

7.5 Lower envelopes in some special cases

In this section we obtain improved upper bounds on the combinatorial complexity of lower envelopes in a few special cases. We first obtain a linear upper bound on the complexity of the lower envelope of a collection of 'pseudo-planes' in $\mathbb{R}^3$, and then prove a quadratic upper bound on the complexity of the lower envelope of 'pseudo-spheres' in $\mathbb{R}^3$. We next mention briefly another special 'favorable' case of bivariate functions. Finally, we describe a general scheme that maps the lower envelope of a set of d-variate functions to the intersection of a fixed-degree algebraic surface with the lower envelope of a collection of hyperplanes in some dimension $> d$. This scheme, called *linearization*, yields improved bounds for the envelope complexity in several useful special cases.

ASSUMPTIONS 7.3. Assumptions on pseudo-planes.

(i) Each triple f_i, f_j, f_k of distinct functions in $\mathcal{F}$ intersect in at most one point.

(ii) For each pair f_i, f_j of distinct functions in $\mathcal{F}$, the plane curve $f_i(x,y) = f_j(x,y)$ is either empty or a (closed or unbounded) Jordan curve. (Condition (i) implies that two intersection curves of the same surface intersect in at most one point. Moreover, the general position assumption (iii) on our functions allows us to assume that such intersections are always transversal.)

(iii) The functions of $\mathcal{F}$ are in general position.

7.5.1 Pseudo-planes

In this section we consider a collection $\mathcal{F} = \{f_1(x,y), \ldots, f_n(x,y)\}$ of n bivariate continuous functions, defined over the entire plane, which satisfy Assumptions 7.3. We refer to the graphs of such a collection of functions as a family of *pseudo-planes*. Our definition of pseudo-planes is somewhat different from the standard definition (see Björner et al. (1993) and Mandel (1981)), in the sense that we also allow an intersection curve to be empty or a closed Jordan curve.

Theorem 7.26 *If $\mathcal{F}$ is a collection of n bivariate functions satisfying Assumptions 7.3, then $\kappa(\mathcal{F}) = O(n)$, and this bound is tight in the worst case.*

In order to prove the theorem, we need the following lemma.

Lemma 7.27 *Let $\Gamma = \{\gamma_1, \gamma_2, \ldots, \gamma_n\}$ be a collection of Jordan curves in $\mathbb{R}^2$, and let R_i be one of the regions into which γ_i divides $\mathbb{R}^2$, for $i = 1, \ldots, n$. If any pair of curves in Γ intersect in at most one point, then $R = \bigcap_{i=1}^{n} R_i$, the common intersection of all regions R_i, is (possibly empty but) connected.*

Proof. We prove the lemma by induction on n, the number of curves in Γ. The lemma follows for $n = 1$ from the Jordan curve theorem. Assume that the lemma holds for any subcollection of Γ of at most $n - 1$ curves, so, in particular, $R' = \bigcap_{i=1}^{n-1} R_i$ is connected.

If γ_n is a closed curve, then it cannot intersect any other curve of Γ, because a closed Jordan curve intersects another Jordan curve in at least two points (under the general position assumption). In this case R is easily seen to be (possibly empty but) connected (at worst, R_n adds one more boundary component to R). Similarly, if γ_n does not intersect R', then R is connected as well.

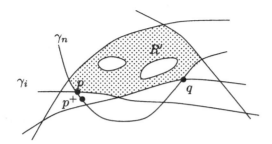

FIGURE 7.7. Illustration of Lemma 7.27; the shaded region is $\bigcap_{i=1}^{n-1} R_i$.

Thus we can assume that γ_n is an open unbounded Jordan curve and that it intersects R'. We claim that $R' \cap \gamma_n$ is a single connected arc. Indeed, if $R' \cap \gamma_n$ were not connected, then there would exist two intersection points, p and q, of γ_n and $\partial R'$, such that the portion of γ_n between p and q (excluding p, q), denoted δ, does not lie in R'; see Figure 7.7. Let γ_i (for some $i \neq n$) be the other arc containing p. Since γ_i and γ_n can intersect in at most one point, $q \notin \gamma_i$, which implies $q \in R_i$. Let $p^+ \in \delta$ be a point sufficiently close to p such that γ_n does not intersect any arc at any point between p and p^+; then $p^+ \notin R_i$. Since $p^+ \notin R_i$ and $q \in R_i$, the arc δ intersects γ_i, which contradicts the assumption that γ_i and γ_n intersect in at most one point. $R' \cap \gamma_n$ is thus a single connected arc. But then it is easily seen that γ_n must separate R' into exactly two connected regions, only one of which is contained in R_n. Hence $R = R' \cap R_n$ is connected. $\square$

Proof of Theorem 7.26. Fix one of the functions f_i of the given collection $\mathcal{F}$, let f_j be any other function of $\mathcal{F}$, and let R_{ij} be the region in the xy-plane over which $f_i < f_j$. By our assumptions, each R_{ij} is empty, or is the entire plane, or is bounded by a closed or unbounded Jordan curve. If any R_{ij} is empty, f_i does not appear in the lower envelope at all. Otherwise, conditions (i) and (ii) and Lemma 7.27 imply that the intersection of all the regions R_{ij} (with i remaining fixed) is connected. That is, the region over which f_i appears in the lower envelope $E_{\mathcal{F}}$ is connected. Thus, the number of two-dimensional faces in the minimization diagram $M_{\mathcal{F}}$ is at most n. Euler's relation now implies that $\kappa(\mathcal{F}) = O(n)$. This bound is clearly tight in the worst case; in fact, it can be attained by a collection of planes. $\square$

7.5.2   Pseudo-spheres

Let $\mathcal{F} = \{f_1(x,y), ..., f_n(x,y)\}$ be a collection of n bivariate continuous functions, defined over the entire plane and satisfying Assumptions 7.4. We will refer to the graphs of functions in such a collection as a family of *pseudo-spheres*.

ASSUMPTIONS 7.4. Assumptions on pseudo-spheres.

(i) Each triple f_i, f_j, f_k of distinct functions in $\mathcal{F}$ intersect in at most two points.

(ii) For each $i \neq j$, the plane curve $f_i(x,y) = f_j(x,y)$ is either empty or a (closed or unbounded) Jordan curve.

(iii) The functions of $\mathcal{F}$ are in general position.

Theorem 7.28 *The complexity $\kappa(\mathcal{F})$ of the minimization diagram of a collection $\mathcal{F}$ of n pseudo-spheres in $\mathbb{R}^3$ is $O(n^2)$, and this bound is tight in the worst case.*

To prepare for the proof of Theorem 7.28, we first introduce some terminology and recall the result of Kedem et al. (1986) (see also Livne and Sharir (1985)). Let $\Gamma = \{\gamma_1, ..., \gamma_n\}$ be a collection of n closed Jordan curves in the plane. Call Γ 2-*intersecting* if every pair of curves $\gamma_i, \gamma_j \in \Gamma$ intersect in at most two points, and if each such intersection is transversal. For each curve γ_i, let $K(\gamma_i)$ denote the closure of one of the regions into which γ_i partitions the plane. We refer to these regions as *pseudo-disks*. Let $K(\Gamma) = \bigcup_{i=1}^{n} K(\gamma_i)$. Denote by $I(\Gamma)$ the set of all intersection points of pairs of the curves in Γ, and let $B(\Gamma) = I(\Gamma) \cap \partial K(\Gamma)$. Even though $|I(\Gamma)|$ is $\Omega(n^2)$ in the worst case, we nevertheless have:

Theorem 7.29 (Kedem et al. (1986)) *If Γ is a 2-intersecting collection of $n \geq 3$ (closed) Jordan curves, then $|B(\Gamma)| \leq 6n - 12$, and the bound is tight in the worst case.*

The above linear bound on $|B(\Gamma)|$ fails to hold if pairs of curves in Γ are allowed to intersect in more than two points. If pairs of curves are allowed to intersect in as many as four points per pair, $|B(\Gamma)|$ can easily become $\Omega(n^2)$ (see Figure 7.8). An interesting 'intermediate' result, detailed in Section 8.10, is that, if pairs of curves in Γ (which can now be either closed or unbounded) are allowed to intersect in at most three points, then, with some additional mild assumptions on Γ, one has $|B(\Gamma)| = O(n\alpha(n))$.

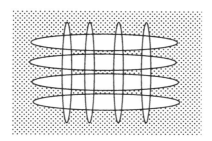

FIGURE 7.8. Union of Jordan regions, where each pair of curves may intersect in up to four points.

Note that Theorem 7.29 allows each of the $K(\gamma_i)$'s to be *either* of the two regions into which γ_i partitions the plane. For our application, we need to allow some of the γ_i's to be unbounded, which requires the following technical enhancement of the results of Kedem et al. (1986):

Theorem 7.30 *If* Γ *is a 2-intersecting collection of* $n \geq 3$ *closed or unbounded Jordan curves, then* $|B(\Gamma)| \leq 6n - 12$, *and the bound is tight in the worst case.*

We provide a brief outline of this enhancement and omit most of the rather straightforward technical details.

Sketch of Proof. Compactify the plane onto the sphere $\mathbb{S}^2$ by adding a point p_∞ at infinity. The curves γ_i now become closed Jordan curves on $\mathbb{S}^2$, each pair of which intersect in at most two points other than p_∞. Next, enclose p_∞ by a sufficiently small cap C so that all (finite) intersection points between the curves γ_i lie outside C, and such that all intersections that lie along the same curve γ_j are contained in a connected portion of that curve that is disjoint from C. Replace each curve γ_i that passes through p_∞ by a modified curve γ_i^*,

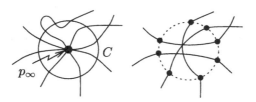

FIGURE 7.9. Extension of Theorem 7.29.

obtained by taking the connected portion of $\gamma_i - C$ that contains all intersection points of γ_i with the other curves, and by connecting its endpoints by a great circular chord within C (if γ_i does not intersect any other curve, we can simply discard it, because its presence can only decrease $|B(\Gamma)|$). It is now easy to check that the collection Γ^* of all resulting curves γ_i^* satisfies the assumptions of Theorem 7.29 (a pair of modified curves can intersect at most once within C, and, if they do intersect within C, they can have only one other intersection point outside C, as is easily checked). Hence $|B(\Gamma^*)|$, which clearly dominates $|B(\Gamma)|$, is at most $6n - 12$. $\qquad\square$

With this extension of Kedem et al.'s theorem, we now prove Theorem 7.28.

Proof of Theorem 7.28. For each $i = 1, \ldots, n$, let σ_i denote the graph of $z = f_i(x, y)$. Fix such a σ_i, and, for each $j \neq i$, let γ_{ij} denote the vertical projection of the curve $\sigma_i \cap \sigma_j$ onto the xy-plane. Let Γ_i denote the set of resulting curves in $\mathbb{R}^2$. By our assumptions, each γ_{ij} is either empty or a simple closed or unbounded Jordan curve, and, furthermore, each pair γ_{ij}, γ_{ik} of these curves intersect in at most two points. For each $j \neq i$, define $K(\gamma_{ij})$ to be the portion of the plane over which $f_j < f_i$. Theorem 7.30 implies that the number of intersections of the curves γ_{ij} that lie on the boundary of $\bigcup_{j \neq i} K(\gamma_{ij})$ is at most $6(n - 1) - 12 = 6n - 18$ (assuming $n \geq 4$). These intersection points stand in a one-to-one correspondence with the points of triple intersection of the functions in $\mathcal{F}$ that lie on the intersection of σ_i with the graph of the lower envelope $E_{\mathcal{F}}$.

Repeating the above analysis for each σ_i, and observing that each triple intersection point on the envelope is counted by this process three times, we conclude that the number of envelope vertices is at most $\frac{1}{3}n(6n - 18) < 2n^2$, which completes the proof of the upper bound of Theorem 7.28.

It is also easy to give examples of collections $\mathcal{F}$ of n bivariate functions satisfying Assumptions 7.4, for which $\kappa(\mathcal{F}) = \Omega(n^2)$. For example, one can take $\mathcal{F} = \{f_1, \ldots, f_{n/2}, g_1, \ldots, g_{n/2}\}$ such that

$$f_i(x, y) = (x - i)^2 \quad \text{and} \quad g_i(x, y) = a_i y + b_i,$$

for $i = 1, \ldots, n/2$, where the a_i, b_i are chosen so that each g_i appears along the lower envelope of the functions g_k, and so that each intersection point of two functions, g_i, g_j, that lies on the lower envelope has a z-coordinate between 0 and $1/4$. It is easy to see that $\mathcal{F}$ satisfies Assumptions 7.4, and that $\kappa(\mathcal{F}) = \Omega(n^2)$. This completes the proof of Theorem 7.28. $\qquad\square$

Remark 7.31 Another proof of Theorem 7.28 can be obtained by adapting the proof of Theorem 7.7. The idea is that, in the notations of that proof, any inner vertex p of $E_{\mathcal{F}}$ (there are no outer vertices in this case) can be uniquely charged to an endpoint or to a local x-maximum or minimum of some curve γ_{ij} incident to p. We leave it to the reader to work out the details of this proof.

7.5.3   Functions with favorable cross sections

Let $\mathcal{F} = \{f_1, \ldots, f_n\}$ be a collection of n totally defined continuous bivariate functions, so that each pair of functions intersect in a curve with at most t points of y-vertical tangency, each triple of functions intersect in at most s points (where s and t are constants), and, for each $i \neq j$ and each x_0, the equation $f_i(x_0, y) = f_j(x_0, y)$ has at most *two* roots, $r_{ij}^-(x_0)$ and $r_{ij}^+(x_0)$.

Although the above extra condition seems quite artificial, it arises in a number of interesting applications; see Schwartz and Sharir (1990), and also a note in Section 8.6, for some of these applications. The following theorem, which gives an upper bound on the complexity $\kappa(\mathcal{F})$ for such a set of functions, is taken from Schwartz and Sharir (1990); its proof is rather technical, and we omit it here.

Theorem 7.32 (Schwartz and Sharir (1990)) *For a collection $\mathcal{F}$ of n bivariate functions satisfying the above assumptions, $\kappa(\mathcal{F}) = O(n\lambda_{s+2}(n))$, where the constant of proportionality depends on s and t.*

7.5.4   Linearization

Let $\mathcal{F} = \{f_1, \ldots, f_n\}$ be a collection of n (totally defined) d-variate polynomials of constant maximum degree b. In this subsection we describe a general scheme that yields improved upper bounds (better than $O(n^{d+\varepsilon})$) on $\kappa(\mathcal{F})$ in certain special cases.

We say that $\mathcal{F}$ admits a *linearization* of dimension k if, for some $p > 0$, there exists a $(d + p)$-variate polynomial

$$g(\mathbf{x}, \mathbf{a}) = \psi_0(\mathbf{a}) + \psi_1(\mathbf{a})\varphi_1(\mathbf{x}) + \psi_2(\mathbf{a})\varphi_2(\mathbf{x}) + \cdots + \psi_k(\mathbf{a})\varphi_k(\mathbf{x}) + \varphi_{k+1}(\mathbf{x}),$$

for $\mathbf{x} \in \mathbb{R}^d$, $\mathbf{a} \in \mathbb{R}^p$, such that, for each $1 \leq i \leq n$, we have $f_i(\mathbf{x}) = g(\mathbf{x}, \mathbf{a}_i)$ for some $\mathbf{a}_i \in \mathbb{R}^p$. Here each $\psi_j(\mathbf{a})$, for $0 \leq j \leq k$, is a p-variate polynomial, and each $\varphi_j(\mathbf{x})$, for $1 \leq j \leq k+1$, is a d-variate polynomial. It is easily seen that such a polynomial always exists for $p \leq d^{b+1}$—let the φ's be the monomials that appear in at least one of the polynomials of $\mathcal{F}$, and let $\psi_j(\mathbf{a}) = a_j$.

We define a transform $\varphi : \mathbb{R}^d \longrightarrow \mathbb{R}^k$ that maps each point in $\mathbb{R}^d$ to the point

$$\varphi(\mathbf{x}) = (\varphi_1(\mathbf{x}), \varphi_2(\mathbf{x}), \ldots, \varphi_k(\mathbf{x}));$$

the image $\varphi(\mathbb{R}^d)$ is a d-dimensional algebraic surface Γ in $\mathbb{R}^k$. For each function $f_i(\mathbf{x}) = g(\mathbf{x}, \mathbf{a}_i)$, we define a k-variate linear function

$$h_i(\mathbf{y}) = \psi_0(\mathbf{a}_i) + \psi_1(\mathbf{a}_i)y_1 + \cdots \psi_k(\mathbf{a}_i)y_k.$$

Let $H = \{h_i \mid 1 \leq i \leq n\}$. By definition,

$$E_{\mathcal{F}}(\mathbf{x}) = \min_{1 \leq i \leq n} f_i(\mathbf{x}) = \varphi_{k+1}(\mathbf{x}) + \min_{1 \leq i \leq n} h_i(\varphi(\mathbf{x})).$$

Thus, each vertex $(\mathbf{x}, x_{d+1})$ of $E_{\mathcal{F}}$ maps to a vertex $(\varphi(\mathbf{x}), x_{d+1} - \varphi_{k+1}(\mathbf{x}))$ of $(\Gamma \times \mathbb{R}) \cap E_H$. Since each h_i is a k-variate linear function and the degree of Γ depends only on d and b, the Upper Bound Theorem for convex polyhedra (see McMullen and Shepard (1971) and Edelsbrunner (1987)) is easily seen to imply that the number of vertices in $(\Gamma \times \mathbb{R}) \cap E_H$ is $O(n^{\lceil k/2 \rceil})$. Hence, we can conclude:

Theorem 7.33 *Let $\mathcal{F}$ be a collection of n (totally defined) d-variate polynomials of constant maximum degree b. If $\mathcal{F}$ admits a linearization of dimension k, then the combinatorial complexity of the lower envelope of $\mathcal{F}$ is $O(n^{\lceil k/2 \rceil})$, where the constant of proportionality depends on k, d, and b.*

We also have the following extension:

Theorem 7.34 *Let Σ be a collection of n regions of $\mathbb{R}^d$, each of the form $K_i : f_i(\mathbf{x}) \geq 0$, where the f_i's are d-variate polynomials of constant maximum degree b. If these polynomials admit a linearization of dimension k, then the combinatorial complexity of the union $\bigcup_{i=1}^n K_i$ is $O(n^{\lceil k/2 \rceil})$. A similar bound applies to the intersection $\bigcap_{i=1}^n K_i$.*

Proof. For $i = 1, \ldots, n$, let $\hat{h}_i$ denote the k-variate linear function $y_{k+1} = h_i(\mathbf{y})$, obtained by linearizing f_i in the above manner, and let $\left(\hat{h}_i\right)^+$ denote the half-space $y_{k+1} \geq h_i(\mathbf{y})$ in $\mathbb{R}^{k+1}$. It is easily seen that a point $\mathbf{x} \in \mathbb{R}^d$ lies on the boundary of $\bigcup_{i=1}^n K_i$ if and only if $(\varphi(\mathbf{x}), -\varphi_{k+1}(\mathbf{x}))$ lies on the boundary of $\bigcap_{i=1}^n \left(\hat{h}_i\right)^+$. Hence, the complexity of the union is dominated by the complexity of (the intersection of the surface $\Gamma \times \mathbb{R}$ with) a convex polyhedron formed by the intersection of n half-spaces in $\mathbb{R}^{k+1}$, so the claim follows from the Upper Bound Theorem. A similar argument applies to the intersection $\bigcap_{i=1}^n K_i$. □

We now describe some examples where these results yield an improved bound on $\kappa(\mathcal{F})$. Additional examples will be given in the next chapter. A sphere in $\mathbb{R}^d$ with center $\mathbf{a} = (a_1, \ldots, a_d)$ and radius a_{d+1} can be regarded as the set $g(\mathbf{x}, \mathbf{a}) = 0$, where

$$g(\mathbf{x}, a_1, \ldots, a_{d+1}) = [a_1^2 + \cdots + a_d^2 - a_{d+1}^2] - [2a_1 \cdot x_1] - [2a_2 \cdot x_2] - \cdots - [2a_d \cdot x_d] + [x_1^2 + \cdots + x_d^2].$$

Therefore a collection of spheres admits a linearization of dimension d, which implies, by Theorems 7.33 and 7.34,

Corollary 7.35 *The combinatorial complexity of the union of a collection of n balls, or the lower envelope of a collection of n spheres, in $\mathbb{R}^d$ is $O(n^{\lceil d/2 \rceil})$.*

Remark 7.36 The application of Theorem 7.33 to the case of spheres requires some technical modifications, because spheres are not graphs of totally defined functions. These modifications are fairly routine, and we omit them here.

We end this subsection by giving another example, where Theorem 7.33 yields an improved bound. Consider a set $\mathcal{F} = \{f_1, \ldots, f_n\}$ of n trivariate functions, where each f_i is of the form

$$f_i(x_1, x_2, x_3) = (x_1 - u_i - w_i x_3)^2 + \left(x_2 - v_i - \sqrt{1 - w_i^2} \cdot x_3\right)^2, \quad (7.17)$$

for appropriate real parameters u_i, v_i, w_i, with $|w_i| \leq 1$. These functions have the following geometric interpretation (see also Section 8.6.3). Let $p_1, \ldots, p_n$ be n points in the plane, each moving along some straight line at unit speed. Suppose that the initial position (i.e., at $t = 0$) of p_i is (u_i, v_i) and that p_i moves parallel to the unit vector $(w_i, \sqrt{1 - w_i^2})$. Then $f_i(x_1, x_2, x_3)$ is the square of the distance of a point (x_1, x_2) from point p_i at time $t = x_3$. Thus the lower envelope of the f_i's can be used to find out which point p_i is nearest to any point in the plane at any given time; for more details, see Section 8.6.3.

By Theorem 7.17, $\kappa(\mathcal{F}) = O(n^{3+\varepsilon})$, for any $\varepsilon > 0$, but we can get a slightly improved bound using Theorem 7.33. Let

$$g(x_1, x_2, x_3, a_1, a_2, a_3, a_4) =$$
$$[a_1^2 + a_2^2] - [2a_1 \cdot x_1] - [2a_2 \cdot x_2] + [2(a_1 a_3 + a_2 a_4) \cdot x_3] -$$
$$[2a_3 \cdot x_1 x_3] - [2a_4 \cdot x_2 x_3] + [x_1^2 + x_2^2 + x_3^2].$$

It is easily seen that, for each $i = 1, \ldots, n$,

$$f_i(\mathbf{x}) = g\left(\mathbf{x}, u_i, v_i, w_i, \sqrt{1 - w_i^2}\right).$$

Hence, $\mathcal{F}$ admits a linearization of dimension 5, and we obtain:

Corollary 7.37 *The combinatorial complexity of the lower envelope of a collection $\mathcal{F}$ of n trivariate functions of the form (7.17) is $O(n^3)$.*

7.6 Single cells in simplex arrangements

In this section we study the combinatorial complexity of a single cell in an arrangement of n d-simplices in $\mathbb{R}^{d+1}$. In Chapter 5 we showed that the maximum combinatorial complexity of a single cell in arrangements of Jordan arcs in the plane is asymptotically the same as the maximum combinatorial complexity of the lower envelope of such a collection of arcs. We now derive a similar, albeit not quite as tight, result for arrangements of simplices in higher dimensions:

Theorem 7.38 *The combinatorial complexity (that is, the number of faces of all dimensions on the boundary) of a single cell in an arrangement of n d-simplices in $\mathbb{R}^{d+1}$ is $O(n^d \log n)$.*

The proof of Theorem 7.38, due to Aronov and Sharir (1994a), proceeds along the same lines as the proof of Theorem 7.1, but is more involved because the topology of a single cell can be considerably more complicated than that of the lower envelope. The proof of Theorem 7.38 is rather technical, and, for the sake of brevity, we give here only the first part of the proof of Aronov and Sharir (1994a), which yields a somewhat weaker bound, namely:

Theorem 7.39 *The combinatorial complexity of a single cell in an arrangement of n d-simplices in $\mathbb{R}^{d+1}$ is $O(n^d \log^d n)$.*

In order to prove the above theorem, we first have to introduce some definitions and notation, and prove some technical auxiliary results. Let Δ denote a collection of n d-simplices in $\mathbb{R}^{d+1}$, which we assume to be in general position. We view each d-simplex as the disjoint union of its relative interior and of the relatively open faces of its boundary, whose dimensions range between 0 and $d - 1$. The relative interior of a simplex is regarded as a d-face of the simplex. We say that two faces of the arrangement are *incident* to each other if one is contained in the closure of the other.

We distinguish between two types of faces in $\mathcal{A}(\Delta)$—an *outer* face is contained in the relative boundary of some simplex of Δ, while an *inner* k-face, for $k = 0, 1, \ldots, d + 1$, lies in the intersection of exactly $d + 1 - k$ simplex interiors and avoids simplex boundaries. Note that only k-faces with $k < d$ can be outer. It is easy to verify that the total number of outer faces is $O(n^d)$. Consider, for example, the case of outer vertices. Since an outer vertex is contained in the boundary of at least one simplex, it is a vertex of the intersection of at most d simplices, an observation that easily yields the claimed bound. Thus it suffices to consider only inner faces.

For technical reasons, we distinguish between different *sides* of an inner face. For example, the arrangement consisting of one simplex has a single d-face with two "sides." More formally, let f be an inner k-face ($0 \le k \le d + 1$) contained in the relative interiors of $d + 1 - k$ simplices. The hyperplanes spanning these simplices subdivide space into 2^{d+1-k} open regions. A *side* of f is simply a pair (f, R) where R is one of these regions. Note that if f is a full-dimensional cell (avoiding all simplices), then f has only one side, namely $(f, \mathbb{R}^{d+1})$. Thus a cell has exactly one side, an inner d-face (*facet*) has two sides, an inner $(d - 1)$-face has four sides, and so on.

Definition 7.40 A side (f, R) is called a *k-border* of a cell C if either $f = C$ and $k = d + 1$, or f is an inner k-face on the boundary of C and some open neighborhood of f in $R \cup f$ is contained in $C \cup f$. Intuitively, this means that f is on the boundary of C and C touches f on the side of R.

We define the (*inner-face*) *complexity* of a cell in $\mathcal{A}(\Delta)$ to be the total number of its k-borders, for all k. As already noted, since this quantity omits outer faces, it is less than the count of all faces (or, rather, borders) bounding C by at most $O(n^d)$. Note that we count inner faces f on the boundary of C with multiplicity—once for every side of f that lies locally near f in C. (For example, consider two segments in the plane, crossing each other at a point q. Their arrangement has a single cell, and its complexity counts q four times, and each of the four subsegments incident to q is counted twice.)

Definition 7.41 For $0 \le k \le i \le d+1$, we define a (k,i)-*border* of a cell C to be a pair $((f,R),(g,Q))$ of borders of C of dimensions k and i, respectively, with $f \subset \bar{g}$ (here $\bar{g}$ denotes the closure of g) and $R \subset Q$.

Note that, once f, g, and R are specified, the side Q is uniquely defined. A $(k,d+1)$-border is a pair $((f,R),(C,\mathbb{R}^{d+1}))$, where (f,R) is a k-border of C. Intuitively, a (k,i)-border is a pair of oriented inner faces of C, with the first face incident to the second, so that their orientations agree. (For an illustration, in the arrangement formed in the plane by the two coordinate axes, the northeast side of the origin together with the upper side of the positive x-axis form a $(0,1)$-border of the northeast quadrant.)

Definition 7.42 For a fixed cell C of $\mathcal{A}(\Delta)$, we call an inner k-face f of C *popular* if, for each of the 2^{d+1-k} sides, R, of f, the border (f,R) is a k-border of C. For example, a popular (in fact, the only popular) cell is C, and a popular facet is one that touches C on both sides. A (k,i)-border $((f,R),(g,Q))$ of C is *popular* if g is a popular i-face.

Let $\tau_k^{(i)}(p;\Delta)$ denote the number of popular (k,i)-borders of the cell $C_p = C(\Delta,p)$ of $\mathcal{A}(\Delta)$ containing a specified point p (not lying on any simplex). Notice that the problem of bounding the complexity of C_p reduces to bounding the quantities $\tau_k^{(d+1)}(p;\Delta)$, for all $0 \le k \le d+1$, as they denote the total number of borders of various dimensions bounding C_p. We put

$$\tau_k^{(i)}(n) = \max \tau_k^{(i)}(p;\Delta),$$

with the maximum taken over all collections Δ of n d-simplices in $\mathbb{R}^{d+1}$ and over all choices of a point p not on any simplex (that is, of a cell of $\mathcal{A}(\Delta)$).

Theorem 7.43 $\tau_k^{(i)}(n) = O(n^d \log^{i-1} n)$, *for* $0 \le k \le i \le d+1$.

Notice that this theorem immediately implies Theorem 7.39, because the maximum combinatorial complexity of a single cell in $\mathcal{A}(\Delta)$ is at most

$$\sum_{k=0}^{d+1} \tau_k^{(d+1)}(n) = O(n^d \log^d n).$$

To prove Theorem 7.43, we first need to establish the following theorem and lemma.

Theorem 7.44 (Chopping Theorem) *Let* $\Delta = \{\Delta_1, \ldots, \Delta_n\}$ *be a collection of n d-simplices in $\mathbb{R}^{d+1}$. Let $\mathcal{C}$ be any collection of m cells in the arrangement of these simplices. Then there exists a decomposition of the cells of $\mathcal{C}$ into $m + O(n^d)$ convex polyhedra, i.e., a collection of $m + O(n^d)$ open pairwise-disjoint convex polyhedra, each fully contained in some cell of $\mathcal{C}$, so that their closures cover (the union of) $\mathcal{C}$.*

Proof. Clearly, we can ignore all convex cells of $\mathcal{C}$. We will subdivide *all* nonconvex cells in $\mathcal{A} = \mathcal{A}(\Delta)$ into $O(n^d)$ convex subcells, as follows. We assume, without loss of generality, that no simplex is parallel to the x_{d+1} axis. Intuitively, the only nonconvexities present in cells of $\mathcal{A}$ are caused by relative boundaries of the simplices protruding into a cell. We will erect vertical "walls," each fully contained in the interior of a cell, extending from each such boundary, thereby eliminating any nonconvex features. Let Δ be one of the given simplices, and let Δ_1 be one of the $d + 1$ $(d - 1)$-simplices bounding Δ; throughout the proof we will refer to such a $(d - 1)$-simplex as a "subsimplex" of Δ. Construct the hyperplane h_1 passing through Δ_1 and parallel to the x_{d+1} axis (we refer to h_1 as the *vertical hyperplane spanned by* Δ_1) and consider the d-dimensional arrangement $\mathcal{A}_1$ obtained by intersecting $\mathcal{A}$ with h_1; note that Δ_1 itself is a simplex in $\mathcal{A}_1$. We take all the cells of $\mathcal{A}_1$ whose boundary meets Δ_1 in a $(d - 1)$-face (these cells constitute the *zone* of Δ_1 in $\mathcal{A}_1$), and add them to the arrangement $\mathcal{A}$. We refer to these cells (d-faces) as the *vertical walls erected from* Δ_1. Intuitively, we have drawn a vertical hyperplane through Δ_1, "flooded" all faces that touch Δ_1, and added them to the arrangement $\mathcal{A}$.

We now repeat this process in an incremental fashion, for each of the d remaining subsimplices Δ_j bounding Δ and for each subsimplex bounding the remaining simplices in Δ. Whenever we process such a subsimplex, the walls erected from it become part of $\mathcal{A}$. Thus when we process a subsimplex Δ', the vertical hyperplane that it spans has to be intersected with the original arrangement $\mathcal{A}$ as well as with all the vertical walls erected from previously processed subsimplices. Note that the resulting decomposition may depend on the order in which subsimplices are being processed, so it is not necessarily unique. It is easy to check that the introduction of the walls erected from a subsimplex Δ' eliminates Δ' as a source of local nonconvexity and does not create any further points of local nonconvexity. It follows that the end result is a decomposition of the cells of $\mathcal{A}$ into open pairwise-disjoint convex polyhedra.

Next, we bound the number of subcells created by the above process (from the nonconvex cells of $\mathcal{A}$). Recall that a wall is a d-face, so its addition to the arrangement increases the cell count by at most one—either it splits the cell in which it is contained into two subcells, or it does not affect the number of cells at all, if it cuts the cell without splitting it in two; in the latter case the wall alters the topology of the cell. In any case, it suffices to show that the number of walls created during our construction is at most $O(n^d)$. This will be established by arguing that no subsimplex Δ' has more than $O(n^{d-1})$ walls erected from it.

The claim is immediate for the first subsimplex, Δ_1. A wall is a full-dimensional cell in the arrangement $\mathcal{A}_1 = \mathcal{A} \cap h_1$ whose boundary meets Δ_1 in a $(d-1)$-face. Thus the number of walls is at most twice the number of full-dimensional cells in the $(d-1)$-dimensional arrangement $\mathcal{A}_1 \cap \Delta_1 = \mathcal{A} \cap \Delta_1$. Since this arrangement is formed by a collection of at most n polytopes, $\{\Delta \cap \Delta_1 \mid \Delta \in \boldsymbol{\Delta}\}$, each of small constant complexity, it has $O(n^{d-1})$ faces altogether, which implies our assertion for Δ_1.

The situation is more complicated for walls constructed later in the process, as the d-dimensional cross-sectional arrangements, in which new walls are constructed, consist of not only (cross sections of) original simplices but also previously constructed walls. We treat this case in the following indirect manner.

Suppose we are currently processing a subsimplex Δ' of some simplex $\Delta \in \boldsymbol{\Delta}$. Let h' be the vertical hyperplane spanned by Δ', and consider the arrangement $\mathcal{A}'$ formed in h' by its intersections with all the simplices of $\boldsymbol{\Delta}$ and with the vertical hyperplanes spanned by all the subsimplices bounding the simplices of $\boldsymbol{\Delta}$. Clearly, $\mathcal{A}'$ is a refinement of the intersection of h' and the current version $\mathcal{A}_c$ of $\mathcal{A}$. It is easy to see that the number of faces of $\mathcal{A}'$ touching Δ' in a $(d-1)$-dimensional set is at least as large as the number of such faces in the coarser arrangement $\mathcal{A}_c \cap h'$. Moreover, as argued above, the former quantity is bounded by twice the number of full-dimensional cells in the $(d-1)$-dimensional arrangement $\mathcal{A}' \cap \Delta'$. Since this arrangement is formed by at most n polytopes of small constant complexity and by $(d+1)n$ additional hyperplanes, the number of its cells is clearly $O(n^{d-1})$.

This inductive argument completes the proof of the Chopping Theorem. $\square$

Corollary 7.45 *A single cell in an arrangement of n d-simplices in $\mathbb{R}^{d+1}$ can be decomposed into $O(n^d)$ convex polyhedra (with pairwise-disjoint interiors).*

Lemma 7.46 $\tau_i^{(i)}(p; \boldsymbol{\Delta}) = O(n^d)$, *for* $i = 0, 1, \ldots, d$, *and* $\tau_{d+1}^{(d+1)}(p; \boldsymbol{\Delta}) = 1$.

Proof. First of all, observe that, since C_p is the only popular cell and has only one side, $\tau_{d+1}^{(d+1)}(p; \boldsymbol{\Delta}) = 1$. Now let $i = 0, 1, \ldots, d$. Recall that $\tau_i^{(i)}(p; \boldsymbol{\Delta})$ is simply the number of popular i-borders of C_p, i.e., 2^{d+1-i} times the number of inner i-faces, all of whose 2^{d+1-i} sides are contained in C_p locally near the face. To prove our claim, we associate each such face with a vertex of C_p and argue that (1) no vertex is charged more than a constant number of times, and (2) the number of charged vertices is $O(n^d)$.

We set up the correspondence as follows: Rotate the arrangement, if necessary, in such a fashion that every inner i-face has a unique lowest vertex, where the height of a vertex is its x_{d+1}-coordinate. Let f be an inner popular i-face and let v_f be its lowest vertex. We claim that v_f is either an outer vertex of C_p, or a locally lowest vertex of C_p (meaning that there is a side R of v_f so that R lies fully above v_f and (v_f, R) is a border of C_p). Indeed, if v_f lies in the interior of $d + 1$ simplices, the hyperplanes spanning them partition space into 2^{d+1} orthants, and exactly one of these orthants, call it O, has v_f as its lowest point. In a neighborhood of v_f, the i-face f appears as the intersection of $d + 1 - i$ of these hyperplanes with the upper halfspaces bounded by the remaining i hyperplanes. Since f is popular, all 2^{d+1-i} of its sides touch C_p, and it is clear that O must be contained in one of these sides. Hence O, locally near f, lies in C_p, so v_f is indeed a locally lowest vertex of C_p.

We have assigned each popular i-face to its lowest vertex. The above argument implies that no vertex is charged by more than $\binom{d+1}{i}$ popular i-faces, since we assume general position.

As already noted, the number of outer vertices in the entire arrangement is $O(n^d)$. Thus it remains to show that the number of locally lowest inner vertices of C_p is also $O(n^d)$. The Chopping Theorem implies that C_p can be decomposed into a collection of $O(n^d)$ pairwise-disjoint open convex polyhedra, the union of whose closures covers C_p. Then a locally lowest vertex of C_p is necessarily a lowest vertex of one of these polyhedra. Applying an appropriate rotation as necessary, we can assume that each of these convex polyhedra has at most one lowest vertex. Hence, the number of locally lowest vertices of C_p is also $O(n^d)$, which completes the proof of the lemma.   □

Remark 7.47 As will be seen shortly, the proof of Theorem 7.43 uses the preceding lemma only in the special case $i = 1$.

Proof of Theorem 7.43. First of all, observe that, for any i,

$$\tau_0^{(i)}(p; \mathbf{\Delta}) \le 2\tau_1^{(i)}(p; \mathbf{\Delta}),$$

since any face has at most twice as many vertices as edges. Next, for $k > 1$, we "charge" a popular (k, i)-border $((f, R), (g, Q))$ to one of the edges e of f, regarded as the $(1, i)$-border $((e, R'), (g, Q))$, for an appropriate side R' (clearly, this is a popular $(1, i)$-border). By the assumption of general position, such a $(1, i)$-border cannot be charged by more than $\binom{d}{d+1-k}$ (k, i)-borders, which implies that $\tau_k^{(i)}(p; \mathbf{\Delta}) = O(\tau_1^{(i)}(p; \mathbf{\Delta}))$. Hence it suffices to prove that $\tau_1^{(i)}(n) = O(n^d \log^{i-1} n)$.

Next, proceeding by induction on i and using an approach similar to that used in the proof of Theorem 7.1, we derive a recurrence for $\tau_1^{(i)}(p; \mathbf{\Delta})$, for $i = 2, \ldots, d + 1$. Fix a simplex $\Delta \in \mathbf{\Delta}$ and consider a popular $(1, i)$-border $((f_0, R), (g_0, Q))$ of $C_p(\mathbf{\Delta})$ with $f_0 \not\subseteq \Delta$. When we remove Δ, the face g_0 becomes part of a possibly larger inner i-face g, which is clearly also popular. Moreover, f_0 (respectively, (f_0, R)) is a part of some inner edge (respectively, 1-border) of g.

So let $((f, R), (g, Q))$ be a popular $(1, i)$-border of $C_p(\mathbf{\Delta} - \{\Delta\})$, and consider what happens to it when Δ is reinserted into the arrangement. Let (g, Q_ℓ), for $\ell = 1, \ldots, 2^{d+1-i}$, be the sides of g in $\mathcal{A}(\mathbf{\Delta} - \{\Delta\})$ (note that (g, Q) is one of these sides). The following cases may occur:

$\Delta \cap g = \emptyset$: In this case g may or may not occur on the boundary of $C_p(\mathbf{\Delta})$, but $((f, R), (g, Q))$ contributes at most one popular $(1, i)$-border to $\tau_1^{(i)}(p; \mathbf{\Delta})$, namely itself.

$\Delta \cap g \neq \emptyset$ and $\Delta \cap f = \emptyset$: Insertion of Δ may leave g connected (but alter its topology), or may split g into two or more pieces, more than one of which may contain f on its boundary. It is easily checked, however, that only one component, g^+, of $g - \Delta$ has the property that $((f, R), (g^+, Q))$ is a $(1, i)$-border of some cell in $\mathcal{A}$. Thus $((f, R), (g, Q))$ can contribute at most one popular $(1, i)$-border to $C_p(\mathbf{\Delta})$, namely $((f, R), (g^+, Q))$.

$\Delta \cap g \neq \emptyset$ and $\Delta \cap f \neq \emptyset$: Let h^+, h^- denote the two open halfspaces bounded by the hyperplane spanned by Δ. Since f is a 1-face, Δ splits f into two subedges, $f^+ = f \cap h^+$, $f^- = f \cap h^-$. As above, let g^+ (respectively, g^-) be the unique subface of g in $\mathcal{A}(\Delta)$ that is incident to f^+ (respectively, to f^-) on the correct side of f; it may be that $g^+ = g^-$. Let $g^\star$ be the unique subface of $g \cap \Delta$ that is incident to the point $f \cap \Delta$ and is contained in R near that point. Consider the two $(1, i)$-borders $((f^+, R), (g^+, Q))$ and $((f^-, R), (g^-, Q))$. We are interested only in cases where both of them become popular borders in $C_p(\mathbf{\Delta})$, for only then will our count go up. Let $Q_\ell^+ = Q_\ell \cap h^+$, $Q_\ell^- = Q_\ell \cap h^-$, for $\ell = 1, \ldots, 2^{d+1-i}$. Thus we are interested in situations where C_p meets all 2^{d+2-i} orthants Q_ℓ^+, Q_ℓ^- locally near g. Note that all these orthants are incident to $g^\star$, an $(i-1)$-face in $\mathcal{A}$. Hence $g^\star$ is a popular $(i-1)$-face of C_p and $((f \cap \Delta, R \cap h^+), (g^\star, Q \cap h^+))$ and $((f \cap \Delta, R \cap h^-), (g^\star, Q \cap h^-))$ are popular $(0, i-1)$-borders of $C_p(\mathbf{\Delta})$.

To sum up, the number of popular $(1, i)$-borders in $C_p(\mathbf{\Delta})$ that are not contained in Δ is bounded by

$$\tau_1^{(i)}(p; \mathbf{\Delta} - \{\Delta\}) + \frac{1}{2}\rho_\Delta,$$

where ρ_Δ is the number of popular $(0, i-1)$-borders $((f', R'), (g', Q'))$ with $g' \subset \Delta$. A factor of $\frac{1}{2}$ appears because an increase of 1 in $\tau_1^{(i)}$ is charged to two popular $(0, i-1)$-borders. Summing these bounds over all simplices $\Delta \in \mathbf{\Delta}$, and observing that every popular $(1, i)$-border in $C(\mathbf{\Delta}, p)$ is counted exactly $n - d$ times (it is not counted if and only if Δ is one of the d simplices containing the 1-face of the border), we obtain:

$$(n - d)\tau_1^{(i)}(p; \mathbf{\Delta}) \leq \sum_{\Delta \in \mathbf{\Delta}} \tau_1^{(i)}(p; \mathbf{\Delta} - \{\Delta\}) + \frac{d + 2 - i}{2}\tau_0^{(i-1)}(p; \mathbf{\Delta}),$$

where the factor $(d + 2 - i)$ comes from the fact that a popular $(0, i - 1)$-border is charged at most $d + 2 - i$ times, once for each simplex Δ containing its $(i - 1)$-face.

Passing to the maximum quantities $\tau_k^{(i)}(n)$, we thus obtain:

$$\tau_1^{(1)}(n) = O(n^d),$$

and

$$\tau_1^{(i)}(n) \leq \frac{n}{n - d}\tau_1^{(i)}(n - 1) + \frac{d + 2 - i}{n - d}\tau_1^{(i-1)}(n), \quad i = 2, \ldots, d + 1,$$

where we have used an earlier observation that $\tau_0^{(i)}(n) \leq 2\tau_1^{(i)}(n)$, for $1 \leq i \leq d$.

We first transform these equations into simpler ones, by assuming that $n > d$ and by substituting

$$\tau_1^{(i)}(n) = \frac{n!}{(n - d)!}\psi_1^{(i)}(n).$$

This yields the following relations, as is easily verified:

$$\psi_1^{(1)}(n) = O(1), \tag{7.18}$$

and

$$\psi_1^{(i)}(n) \leq \psi_1^{(i)}(n - 1) + \frac{d + 2 - i}{n - d}\psi_1^{(i-1)}(n), \quad i = 2, \ldots, d + 1. \tag{7.19}$$

We claim that, for $i = 1, 2, \ldots, d + 1$, $\psi_1^{(i)}(n) = O(\log^{i-1} n)$, with the constant of proportionality depending on i and d. This easily follows from (7.18) and (7.19) by induction on i. By definition of ψ, this yields

$$\tau_1^{(i)}(n) = O(n^d \log^{i-1} n).$$

This completes the proof of the theorem. $\square$

Remark 7.48 (i) The proof of Theorem 7.38 proceeds along the same lines, and first establishes Theorem 7.39 as a preparatory result. It then derives bounds on $\tau_2^{(i)}(p; \Delta)$ rather than $\tau_1^{(i)}(p; \Delta)$, using a more careful analysis of the changes that can occur to a 2-face f when a simplex Δ is reinserted into the arrangement. See Aronov and Sharir (1994a) for more details.

(ii) These results raise the problem of efficient construction of a single cell in an arrangement of simplices. The only known algorithm of this kind is due to Aronov and Sharir (1990, 1994a), which applies only to triangles in $\mathbb{R}^3$. It is a variant of the algorithm described in Section 7.2.2, and runs in $O(n^{2+\varepsilon})$ time, for any $\varepsilon > 0$.

(iii) A major application of these bounds is to *motion planning* problems. See Section 8.9 in the next chapter for details.

7.7 Zones

In Chapter 5 we obtained sharp bounds on the combinatorial complexity of zones in arrangements of Jordan arcs in $\mathbb{R}^2$. We now study the complexity of zones in arrangements of hyperplanes and simplices in higher dimensions.

Definition 7.49 Let H be a set of n hyperplanes in $\mathbb{R}^{d+1}$. The *zone* of a hyperplane b (not belonging to H), denoted as $zone(b; H)$, is defined to be the set of cells ($(d+1)$-dimensional faces) in $\mathcal{A}(H)$ whose closures intersect b. The complexity of $zone(b; H)$ is defined to be the sum of complexities of the cells of $\mathcal{A}(H)$ that belong to $zone(b; H)$, where the complexity of a cell in $\mathcal{A}(H)$ is the number of faces of all dimensions that are contained in the closure of the cell. The zone of a hyperplane in an arrangement of simplices can be defined in a similar manner.

The main result of this section is:

Theorem 7.50 *The maximum complexity of the zone of a hyperplane in an arrangement of n hyperplanes in $\mathbb{R}^{d+1}$ is $\Theta(n^d)$.*

We have already proved this result in Section 5.3 for $d = 1$. For $d \geq 2$, the proof of Theorem 7.50 proceeds along the same lines as the proof of Theorem 7.1. For a set H of n hyperplanes in $\mathbb{R}^{d+1}$ and another hyperplane b, let $\tau_k(b; H)$ denote the total number of k-faces contained in the (closure of) cells in $zone(b; H)$ (where each such k-face is counted once for each cell that it bounds), and let

$$\tau_k(n, d) = \max \tau_k(b; H),$$

where the maximum is taken over all hyperplanes b and all sets H of n hyperplanes in $\mathbb{R}^{d+1}$. The maximum complexity of $zone(b; H)$ is at most $\sum_{k=0}^{d+1} \tau_k(n, d)$. Thus the following lemma immediately implies Theorem 7.50.

Lemma 7.51 *For each d and $0 \leq k \leq d+1$,*

$$\tau_k(n, d) = O(n^d),$$

where the constants of proportionality depend on d (and on k).

Proof. We use induction on d. As just noted, the claim holds for $d = 1$. Assume that the claim holds for all $d' < d$, let H be a set of n hyperplanes in $\mathbb{R}^{d+1}$, and let b be some other hyperplane. Without loss of generality, we can assume that the hyperplanes in $H \cup \{b\}$ are in general position. We define a *k-border* to be a pair (f, C), where f is a k-face incident to a (full-dimensional) cell C of $\mathcal{A}(H)$. Thus $\tau_k(b; H)$ is the total number of k-borders (f, C) for which $C \in zone(b; H)$.

As in the proof of Theorem 7.1, we pick a hyperplane $h \in H$ and count the number of all k-borders (f, C) in $zone(b; H)$ such that f is not contained in

h. If we remove h from H, then any such k-border is contained in a k-border (f', C') of $zone(b; H - \{h\})$ (i.e., $f \subseteq f'$ and $C \subseteq C'$). Our strategy is thus to consider the collection of k-borders in $zone(b; H - \{h\})$ and to estimate the increase in the number of k-borders as we add h back to H (not counting k-borders that lie in h).

Let $H/h = \{h' \cap h \mid h' \in H - \{h\}\}$; the set H/h forms a d-dimensional arrangement of $n - 1$ hyperplanes contained in h. Let (f, C) be a k-border of $zone(b; H - \{h\})$, and consider what happens to it when we reinsert h. The following cases may occur:

$h \cap C = \emptyset$: In this case the k-border (f, C) gives rise to exactly one k-border in $zone(b; H)$, namely itself.

$h \cap C \neq \emptyset$, $h \cap f = \emptyset$: Let h^+ be the open half-space bounded by h that contains f, and let $C^+ = C \cap h^+$. If C^+ intersects b, then (f, C) gives rise to one k-border in $zone(b; H)$, namely (f, C^+) (this is the case for the edge $f = e_3$ in Figure 7.10); otherwise it gives rise to no border in $zone(b; H)$.

$h \cap f \neq \emptyset$: Let h^+ and h^- be the two open half-spaces bounded by h and let $C^+ = C \cap h^+$ and $C^- = C \cap h^-$. If (the closure of) only one of C^+ and C^- intersects b, say, C^+, then (f, C) gives rise to only one k-border in $zone(b; H)$, namely $(f \cap h^+, C^+)$ (this is the case for the edge $f = e_2$ in Figure 7.10). If both C^+ and C^- intersect b, then (f, C) gives rise to two k-borders in $zone(b; H)$, namely $(f \cap h^+, C^+)$ and $(f \cap h^-, C^-)$ (this is the case for the edge $f = e_1$ in Figure 7.10). In this case, however, we can charge this increase in the number of k-borders to $(f \cap h, C \cap h)$, which, as easily seen, is a $(k - 1)$-border in $zone(b \cap h; H/h)$.

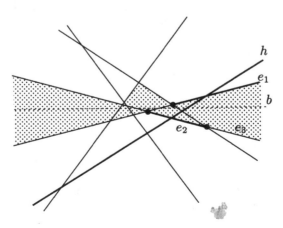

FIGURE 7.10. Inserting h into $zone(b; H - \{h\})$.

If we repeat this process over all k-borders of $zone(b; H - \{h\})$, we obtain that the total number of k-borders (f, C) in $zone(b; H)$, for f not contained in h, is at most

$$
\begin{aligned}
\tau_k(b; H - \{h\}) + \tau_k(b \cap h; H/h) &\leq \tau_k(n-1, d) + \tau_{k-1}(n-1, d-1) \\
&= \tau_k(n-1, d) + O(n^{d-1}),
\end{aligned}
$$

where the last inequality follows from the induction hypothesis. Repeating this analysis for all hyperplanes $h \in H$, summing up the resulting bounds, and observing that each k-border of $zone(b; H)$ is counted exactly $n - d + k - 1$ times, we obtain

$$
\tau_k(n, d) \leq \frac{n}{n - d + k - 1} \left(\tau_k(n-1, d) + O(n^{d-1}) \right).
$$

If we substitute (assuming $n > d$)

$$
\tau_k(n, d) = \frac{n!}{(n - d + k - 1)!} \psi_k(n, d),
$$

then the above recurrence becomes

$$
\psi_k(n, d) \leq \psi_k(n-1, d) + O(n^{k-2}).
$$

The solution of this recurrence, for $k \geq 2$, is easily seen to be

$$
\psi_k(n, d) = O(n^{k-1}),
$$

which implies that $\tau_k(n, d) = O(n^d)$, for $k \geq 2$. Using Euler's formula for cell complexes, as in the proof of Theorem 7.1, we can show that $\tau_k(n, d) = O(n^d)$ for $k = 0, 1$ as well. This completes the proof of the theorem. (For the lower bound, it is easily checked that the complexity of the zone of a hyperplane b in an arrangement of n hyperplanes in $\mathbb{R}^{d+1}$ in general position is $\Omega(n^d)$. In fact, the complexity of the cross-section of the arrangement within b is already $\Omega(n^d)$.) $\square$

The same idea as in Section 5.3.2 can be used to bound the complexity of the zone of a hyperplane in an arrangement of simplices. Let $\boldsymbol{\Delta}$ be a set of n d-simplices in $\mathbb{R}^{d+1}$, and let h be a hyperplane. We split each $\Delta \in \boldsymbol{\Delta}$ into two polytopes at the intersection of Δ and h (if the intersection is nonempty), push these two polytopes slightly away from each other, and, if necessary, retriangulate each polytope into a constant number of simplices. In this manner, we obtain a collection $\boldsymbol{\Delta}'$ of $O(n)$ simplices, and all cells of the zone of b in $\mathcal{A}(\boldsymbol{\Delta})$ now fuse into a single cell of $\mathcal{A}(\boldsymbol{\Delta}')$. Moreover, by the general position assumption, the complexity of the zone of h in $\boldsymbol{\Delta}$ is easily seen to be dominated by the complexity of the new single cell of $\mathcal{A}(\boldsymbol{\Delta}')$. Hence, by Theorem 7.38, we obtain:

Theorem 7.52 *The complexity of the zone of a hyperplane in an arrangement of n d-simplices in $\mathbb{R}^{d+1}$ is $O(n^d \log n)$.*

7.8   Other related results

In this section we briefly review, without proof, several recent related results that involve arrangements in higher dimensions.

7.8.1   Single cells in three dimensions

Halperin and Sharir (1994b) have recently shown the following:

Theorem 7.53 *Let Σ be a collection of n algebraic surface patches in $\mathbb{R}^3$, satisfying Assumptions 7.1. The combinatorial complexity of any single cell C of $\mathcal{A}(\Sigma)$ is $O(n^{2+\varepsilon})$, for any $\varepsilon > 0$, where the constant of proportionality depends on ε and on the maximum degree and shape of the given surfaces and of their boundaries.*

(Assumptions 7.1 require the surfaces to be graphs of functions, but this condition can be relaxed in Theorem 7.53.) The proof of this theorem borrows ideas from the proof of Theorem 7.7, which bounds the complexity of the lower envelope of such a collection. However, to 'bootstrap' the desired recurrences, two additional results need to be established, extending the approach used in the proof of Theorem 7.39:

(a) There are only $O(n^2)$ vertices v of C that are locally x-extreme (that is, there is a neighborhood N of v and a connected component C' of the intersection of N with the interior of C, such that v lies to the left (in the x-direction) of all points of C', or v lies to the right of all these points).

(b) There are only $O(n^{2+\varepsilon})$ vertices on *popular faces* of C, that is, faces f for which C lies locally near f on both sides of f (this is defined in complete analogy to the definition of popular faces in the case of simplices, as given in Section 7.6).

Property (a) is proved by an appropriate decomposition of C into $O(n^2)$ subcells, each being 'x-monotone' in a certain sense, which implies that each subcell has at most two points that are locally x-extreme. Property (b) is proved by applying the same machinery of the proof of Theorem 7.7, where the quantity to be analyzed is the number of vertices of popular faces of C, rather than all inner vertices. Once these two results are available, the proof of Theorem 7.7 can be carried through, with appropriate modifications, to yield a recurrence for the number of vertices of C, whose solution is $O(n^{2+\varepsilon})$. We refer the reader to Halperin and Sharir (1994b) for more details.

It appears that this proof can be extended to higher dimensions, to yield a bound of $O(n^{d+\varepsilon})$ on the complexity of a single cell in an arrangement of n surfaces in $\mathbb{R}^{d+1}$ satisfying Assumptions 7.2. For this, appropriate extensions of both properties (a) and (b) have to be established. The extension of (a) appears to require topological considerations related to Morse theory, and the extension of (b) requires an inductive argument, in which bounds on the number of vertices of popular faces of all dimensions need to be derived, using induction on the dimension of the faces.

The result reported above is only combinatorial, and at present no similarly efficient algorithm (with running time $O(n^{2+\varepsilon})$) for constructing a single cell in such a three-dimensional arrangement is known. Halperin and Sharir (1993) obtained a near-quadratic algorithm for the special case of arrangements of surfaces that arise in the motion planning problem for a rigid polygonal object moving (translating and rotating) in a two-dimensional polygonal environment. This result will be reviewed later, and in more detail, in Section 8.9.

7.8.2   More on zones

The zone theorem for hyperplane arrangements, as given in Section 7.7, can be extended as follows. Let H be a collection of n hyperplanes in $\mathbb{R}^{d+1}$, and let σ be a p-dimensional algebraic surface of some fixed degree, or the relative boundary of any convex set with affine dimension $p + 1$, for $0 \le p \le d$. The zone of σ in $\mathcal{A}(H)$, denoted $zone(\sigma; H)$, is the collection of all cells of $\mathcal{A}(H)$ whose closures intersect σ. Aronov, Pellegrini, and Sharir (1993) have shown:

Theorem 7.54 *The complexity of the zone of σ in $\mathcal{A}(H)$, as defined above, is $O(n^{\lfloor (d+1+p)/2 \rfloor} \log^{\gamma} n)$, where $\gamma = (d + p + 1)$ (mod 2), and the bound is almost tight (up to the logarithmic factor) in the worst case.*

In particular, for $p = d$, the complexity of the zone is $O(n^d \log n)$, which is almost the same as the complexity of the zone of a hyperplane in such an arrangement.

The proof proceeds along the same lines of the inductive proof of Theorem 7.50. However, when a hyperplane $h \in H$ is removed and then reinserted, and splits a face f of $zone(\sigma; H - \{h\})$ into two subfaces, both lying in $zone(\sigma; H)$, the charging scheme used in the proof of Theorem 7.50 becomes inadequate, because $f \cap h$ need not belong to the zone of $\sigma \cap h$ in the d-dimensional cross-section of $\mathcal{A}(H)$ along h. What is true, however, is that $f \cap h$ is a face incident to a *popular facet* of $zone(\sigma; H)$ along h, that is, a facet $g \subseteq h$ whose two incident cells belong to the zone. Thus the induction proceeds not by decreasing the dimension of the arrangement (as was done in the proof of Theorem 7.50), but by reapplying the same machinery to bound the number of vertices of popular facets of the original $zone(\sigma; H)$. This in turn requires similar bounds on the number of vertices of lower-dimensional popular faces, defined in complete analogy to the case of arrangements of simplices in Section 7.6. We refer the reader to Aronov, Pellegrini, and Sharir (1993) for more details.

We can also define, in complete analogy to the above definitions, the zone of a surface in an arrangement of a collection Σ of n surfaces in $\mathbb{R}^3$, satisfying conditions similar to Assumptions 7.1. Using Theorem 7.53 and the same argument as in the proof of Theorem 7.52, one can prove (see Halperin and Sharir (1994b)):

Theorem 7.55 *Let Σ be a collection of n algebraic surface patches in $\mathbb{R}^3$, satisfying Assumptions 7.1. The combinatorial complexity of the zone in $\mathcal{A}(\Sigma)$ of an algebraic surface σ of some fixed degree is $O(n^{2+\varepsilon})$, for any $\varepsilon > 0$, where the constant of proportionality depends on ε, on the maximum degree and shape of the given surfaces and their boundaries, and on the degree and shape of σ.*

7.8.3 The sum of squares of cell complexities

Let H be a collection of n hyperplanes in $\mathbb{R}^{d+1}$. For each cell c of $\mathcal{A}(H)$, let N_c denote the complexity of c (that is, the total number of faces of all dimensions on the boundary of c). We are interested in obtaining a sharp bound for the quantity $\sum_c N_c^2$, where the sum extends over all cells of $\mathcal{A}(H)$.

For $d = 1$ and $d = 2$, an easy application of the zone theorem (see Edelsbrunner (1987)) implies that $\sum_c N_c^2 = O(n^{d+1})$, and this bound is obviously tight if the lines or planes of H are in general position. For $d \geq 3$, the same application of the zone theorem yields only $\sum_c n_c N_c = O(n^{d+1})$, where n_c is the number of hyperplanes of H appearing on the boundary of c. Using the same induction scheme as in the proof of the Zone Theorem 7.50, Aronov, Matoušek, and Sharir (1994) have shown:

Theorem 7.56 $\sum_c N_c^2 = O(n^{d+1} \log^{\lfloor \frac{d+1}{2} \rfloor - 1} n)$.

This result has applications in bounding the overall complexity of many cells in an arrangement of hyperplanes, and in obtaining a sharp bound on the complexity of the vertical decomposition of an arrangement of hyperplanes in $\mathbb{R}^4$ (see Section 8.3).

7.8.4 Union of convex polyhedra

Let $\mathcal{P}$ be a collection of k convex polyhedra in $\mathbb{R}^3$ with a total of n faces, and let U denote their union. The combinatorial complexity of U is the number of vertices, edges, and faces forming its boundary. Using a somewhat more involved variant of the inductive scheme of Section 7.7, Aronov and Sharir (1993, 1994d) have shown:

Theorem 7.57 *The combinatorial complexity of the union of a collection of k convex polyhedra in $\mathbb{R}^3$, with a total of n faces, is $O(k^3 + kn \log^2 k)$. The bound is almost tight in the worst case, as there are examples where the complexity is $\Omega(k^3 + kn\alpha(k))$. The boundary of the union can be constructed by a randomized algorithm whose expected running time is $O(k^3 + kn \log^3 k)$.*

An important special case of this result is the case where the polyhedra of $\mathcal{P}$ are obtained as Minkowski sums of pairwise openly disjoint convex polyhedra. More precisely, let $A_1, \ldots, A_k$ be k convex polyhedra in $\mathbb{R}^3$ having pairwise-disjoint interiors, and let B be another convex polyhedron. Define, for each $i = 1, \ldots, k$,

$$P_i = A_i \oplus B \equiv \{x + y \mid x \in A_i, \, y \in B\}\,;$$

P_i is called the *Minkowski sum* of A_i and B. Let n denote the total number of faces of the P_i's. Aronov and Sharir (1994b) have recently shown:

Theorem 7.58 *The combinatorial complexity of the union U of k Minkowski sums, as above, is $O(kn \log^2 k)$. The bound is almost tight in the worst case, as there are examples where the complexity is $\Omega(kn\alpha(k))$. The boundary of the union of such polyhedra can be constructed by a randomized algorithm whose expected running time is $O(kn \log^3 k)$.*

This result has interesting applications to translational motion planning in three dimensions, as will be described in Section 8.9.

7.9 Bibliographic notes

The tight bounds on the complexity of the lower envelope of triangles in $\mathbb{R}^3$ were first obtained by Pach and Sharir (1989). Their approach also yields an $O(n^d \alpha(n))$ upper bound on the number of d-faces in the lower envelope of n d-simplices in $\mathbb{R}^{d+1}$, but it fails to give a similar bound on the number of lower-dimensional faces on the envelope. The proof of Pach and Sharir is based on a divide-and-conquer approach, and uses a higher-dimensional variant of the Combination Lemma (see Section 6.3). Later, Edelsbrunner (1989) proved that the number of faces of all dimensions on the envelope is also $O(n^d \alpha(n))$. See also Edelsbrunner, Guibas, and Sharir (1989) for related work. The proof presented in Section 7.2 is based on the recent technique of Edelsbrunner, Seidel, and Sharir (1993) for bounding the complexity of the zone of a hyperplane in an arrangement of hyperplanes, as presented in Section 7.7. The proof presented here is simpler than the original proof of Edelsbrunner (1989).

Sections 7.3 and 7.4 are taken from Halperin and Sharir (1994c) and from Sharir (1994a). As noted there, it remains an open problem to tighten the upper bound on the complexity of the lower envelope of a collection of n partially defined d-variate functions, satisfying Assumptions 7.2, to $O(n^{d-1}\lambda_q(n))$, where q is some constant.

The divide-and-conquer algorithm described in Section 7.2.2 is based on the theory of ε-nets, and is typical of a class of similar algorithms that were recently developed; see Edelsbrunner, Guibas, and Sharir (1990), Agarwal (1991), Agarwal, Pellegrini, and Sharir (1993), and Mulmuley (1993). A randomized incremental algorithm for computing the lower envelopes of simplices, similar to the one described in Section 6.5 for computing a single face in arrangements of segments, is proposed by Boissonnat and Dobrindt (1992, 1993). They present the algorithm only in $\mathbb{R}^3$, but it can be extended to higher dimensions as well. See also the recent work of de Berg, Dobrindt, and Schwarzkopf (1994), for another approach to the problem, also based on a randomized incremental construction. The divide-and-conquer algorithm described in Section 7.3.4 is due to Agarwal, Schwarzkopf, and Sharir (1994), and the randomized algorithms given in Section 7.4.2 and in Section 7.4.3 are due to Agarwal, Aronov, and Sharir (1994). The algorithms of Boissonnat and Dobrindt (1993) and of de Berg, Dobrindt, and Schwarzkopf (1994) can also be used to compute lower envelopes of surface patches in $\mathbb{R}^3$.

Sections 7.5.1 and 7.5.2 are taken from Schwartz and Sharir (1990). They also give divide-and-conquer algorithms for computing lower envelopes in these special cases; the time complexity of their algorithms is within a logarithmic factor of the maximum size of the corresponding lower envelope. Using the theory of oriented matroids, one can show that the lower envelope of n pseudo-hyperplanes in $\mathbb{R}^{d+1}$ (defined by an appropriate generalization of the definition of pseudo-planes) is $O(n^{\lceil d/2 \rceil})$, which is asymptotically the same as the complexity of the lower envelope of n hyperplanes in $\mathbb{R}^{d+1}$. However, it is not known whether the complexity of the lower envelope of n pseudo-spheres in $\mathbb{R}^{d+1}$ is the same as that of spheres, i.e., $O(n^{\lfloor d/2 \rfloor +1})$. Cappell et al. (1990) attempted to obtain such a bound, but it turned out that their argument had technical difficulties.

The linearization technique of Section 7.5.4 has been used by several researchers in a wide variety of problems. Yao and Yao (1985) were probably the first to apply it to range searching with semialgebraic ranges (i.e., to the problem of preprocessing a set S of points in $\mathbb{R}^d$, so that, for a query semialgebraic set τ, one can report $S \cap \tau$ efficiently). Chazelle et al. (1989b) used linearization via Plücker coordinates to represent a line in $\mathbb{R}^3$ as a hyperplane or as a point in $\mathbb{R}^5$, and reduced a number of problems involving lines in $\mathbb{R}^3$ to the problem of computing and searching in the lower envelope of a collection of hyperplanes in $\mathbb{R}^5$. See Agarwal and Matoušek (1994) for a detailed discussion on linearization. They give a very simple algorithm for constructing a linearization of the smallest possible dimension.

The bound given in Section 7.6 on the combinatorial complexity of a single cell in an arrangement of simplices was obtained by Aronov and Sharir (1994a). No efficient algorithm is known for computing a single cell in arrangements of simplices for $d > 2$, because the Chopping Theorem (see Theorem 7.44) only gives a bound on the number of convex polyhedra into which a single cell can be decomposed, but fails to give a similarly sharp bound on the total combinatorial complexity of these polyhedra. A close-to-$O(n^d)$ bound on the complexity of these polyhedra will yield an efficient algorithm for computing a single cell in such an arrangement. For $d = 2$, where such a complexity bound is known, an efficient algorithm for constructing a single cell is described in Aronov and Sharir (1990). It remains an open problem whether the techniques used in Sections 7.3 and 7.4 can be extended to obtain a similar upper bound on the combinatorial complexity of a single cell in arrangements of surface patches in $\mathbb{R}^d$, and on the time complexity of computing such a cell. Nevertheless, significant progress on this problem was recently made, as reported in Section 7.8.1.

Section 7.7 is taken from Edelsbrunner, Seidel, and Sharir (1993). Their result corrected a previous erroneous proof of the Zone Theorem, given by Edelsbrunner, O'Rourke, and Seidel (1986).

Appendix 7.1: Voronoi diagrams and lower envelopes

The *Voronoi diagram* of a set of geometric objects is one of the central constructs in discrete and computational geometry, and arises in many applications. It was introduced by Voronoi (1907,1908) nearly 90 years ago, and has been a topic of extensive research in computational geometry during the past 20 years. The purpose of this appendix is to highlight the strong connection between Voronoi diagrams and lower envelopes in higher dimensions, and to exploit this connection in deriving bounds on the complexity of Voronoi diagrams. Comprehensive surveys of Voronoi diagrams can be found, for example, in Aurenhammer (1991), Fortune (1992), and Leven and Sharir (1987c).

In rather full generality, let S be a collection of n pairwise-disjoint compact convex sets in $\mathbb{R}^d$. We refer to the sets in S as *sites*, and assume, for simplicity of exposition, that each set in S is defined as a Boolean combination of a constant number of polynomial equalities and inequalities of constant maximum degree. (The simplest case is when S is a set of points.) Let $\rho(\cdot,\cdot)$ denote a metric in $\mathbb{R}^d$ (in the simplest case, $\rho(\cdot,\cdot)$ is the Euclidean distance). The Voronoi diagram of S, denoted $Vor(S)$, under the metric ρ is a subdivision of $\mathbb{R}^d$ into cells $V(s)$, for $s \in S$, where

$$V(s) = \{\mathbf{x} \in \mathbb{R}^d \mid \rho(\mathbf{x}, s) \le \rho(\mathbf{x}, s') \text{ for all } s' \in S\},$$

and where $\rho(\mathbf{x}, s) = \min \{\rho(\mathbf{x}, \mathbf{y}) \mid \mathbf{y} \in s\}$.

Let us illustrate this definition for a set S of n points in the plane under the Euclidean metric. For each pair s, s' of distinct points in S, the constraint $\rho(\mathbf{x}, s) \le \rho(\mathbf{x}, s')$ defines a half-plane bounded by the perpendicular bisector line of the segment ss' and containing s. Hence, $V(s)$ is the intersection of $n-1$ such half-planes, and is therefore a convex (possibly unbounded) polygon that contains s and has at most $n-1$ edges. Thus, in this case, $Vor(S)$ is a convex subdivision of $\mathbb{R}^2$ with n faces; Euler's formula for planar maps implies that the overall complexity of the diagram in this case is $O(n)$. See Figure 7.11 for an illustration.

It has taken some time for researchers to realize that Voronoi diagrams are nothing but minimization diagrams of appropriate collections of 'distance functions'; this was first observed by Edelsbrunner and Seidel (1986). To

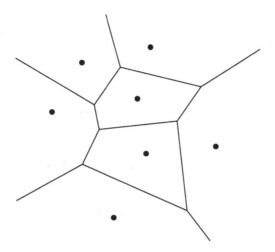

FIGURE 7.11. The Euclidean Voronoi diagram of a planar point set.

see this, define a collection $\mathcal{F}_S = \{\rho_s \mid s \in S\}$ of n d-variate functions, where $\rho_s(\mathbf{x}) = \rho(\mathbf{x}, s)$, for $s \in S$. The claim that $Vor(S)$ is the minimization diagram of $\mathcal{F}_S$ is immediate from the definition. Hence the whole machinery developed in this chapter can be applied to obtain combinatorial complexity bounds and efficient algorithms for constructing Voronoi diagrams.

Let us illustrate this for the case of the Voronoi diagram of a set S of n points in $\mathbb{R}^d$, under the Euclidean metric. In this case, we have, for each point $s \in S$:

$$\rho_s(\mathbf{x}) = \|\mathbf{x} - s\| = \sqrt{\|\mathbf{x}\|^2 + \|s\|^2 - 2\mathbf{x} \cdot s}.$$

Clearly, the minimization diagram will not change if we replace each function ρ_s by its square

$$\rho_s^2(\mathbf{x}) = \|\mathbf{x}\|^2 + \|s\|^2 - 2\mathbf{x} \cdot s,$$

and will also not change if we subtract the common term $\|\mathbf{x}\|^2$ from all these squared functions. Thus, $Vor(S)$ is the minimization diagram of the set $\mathcal{F}$ consisting of the functions

$$f_s(\mathbf{x}) = \|s\|^2 - 2\mathbf{x} \cdot s,$$

for $s \in S$. Each function f_s is linear in $\mathbf{x}$, so $E_{\mathcal{F}}$ is the boundary of a convex polyhedron in $\mathbb{R}^{d+1}$ bounded by at most n hyperplanes. By the Upper Bound Theorem (see McMullen and Shepard (1971)), the combinatorial complexity of $E_{\mathcal{F}}$ is $O(n^{\lceil d/2 \rceil})$ (where the constant of proportionality depends on d). Hence $Vor(S) = M_{\mathcal{F}}$ is a convex subdivision of $\mathbb{R}^d$ with the same combinatorial complexity.

This special case, involving point sets under the Euclidean metric, is 'too simple' and does not require the more sophisticated machinery developed in this chapter. However, if we consider cases involving sites with more complex shape, or other metrics, or both, then the above reduction to the case of lower envelopes of hyperplanes does not apply, and we need to analyze lower envelopes of functions with more complex structure. Still, by our assumption concerning the shape of the sites of S, and by making a similar assumption that the metric $\rho(\cdot, \cdot)$ is also defined in terms of a constant number of polynomials of constant degree, the resulting functions ρ_s are all piecewise-algebraic, and their algebraic pieces satisfy Assumptions 7.2. We can thus apply Theorem 7.17, to conclude:

Theorem 7.59 *Under the assumptions made above, the combinatorial complexity of the Voronoi diagram $Vor(S)$ is $O(n^{d+\varepsilon})$, for any $\varepsilon > 0$, where the constant of proportionality depends on ε, d, and the maximum degree of the polynomials defining the sites in S and the metric ρ.*

Similarly, applying Theorems 7.16, 7.22, and 7.25, we obtain:

Theorem 7.60 *For $d = 2, 3$, the Voronoi diagram of a set S of n sites in $\mathbb{R}^d$, as above, can be computed, in an appropriate model of computation, in time $O(n^{d+\varepsilon})$, for any $\varepsilon > 0$. (For $d = 3$, the algorithm is randomized, and this bounds its expected running time.) For an arbitrary d, the vertices, edges, and 2-faces of the Voronoi diagram can be computed in randomized expected time $O(n^{d+\varepsilon})$, for any $\varepsilon > 0$.*

We also note that in the case of point sites under the Euclidean metric, we need to compute the intersection of n halfspaces in $\mathbb{R}^{d+1}$, bounded by n respective hyperplanes. This problem is dual to the problem of computing the convex hull of a set of n points in $\mathbb{R}^{d+1}$, which can be done in worst-case optimal time $O(n^{\lceil d/2 \rceil} + n \log n)$; see Clarkson and Shor (1989), Seidel (1991), and Chazelle (1993b).

In spite of these results, there is a prevailing conjecture that the complexity of general Voronoi diagrams, as above, ought to be significantly smaller than the bound asserted in Theorem 7.59. The feeling is that the functions ρ_s have special structural properties that should lead to improved bounds (as in the case of point sites under the Euclidean metric). In particular, the conjecture asserts that the complexity of general Voronoi diagrams in 3-space, under the above assumptions, should be $O(n^{2+\varepsilon})$, for any $\varepsilon > 0$. This is still open, although recent progress has been made by Chew et al. (1995), where this bound has been established for Voronoi diagrams of n lines in 3-space, under a metric induced by a convex polytope with a fixed number of faces (see this paper for more details; we note that this case includes the L_1 and L_∞ metrics). However, no similar near-quadratic bound is known for the complexity of the diagram of n lines in 3-space under the Euclidean metric. The best known upper bound for this complexity is only $O(n^{3+\varepsilon})$, as implied by Theorem 7.59.

In the following chapter we will study several other problems involving Voronoi diagrams, where lower envelopes and Davenport–Schinzel sequences play an important role in their analysis.

Appendix 7.2: Range Spaces and ε-Nets

In this appendix we give a brief overview of range spaces, ε-nets, and other related concepts. A more comprehensive survey of these concepts and their applications can be found in Matoušek (1993a) and in Agarwal (1991).

A *range space* is a pair $\Sigma = (X, \mathcal{R})$, where X is a (possibly infinite) set and $\mathcal{R}$ is a set of subsets of X. The elements of X are generally called *objects* and the elements of $\mathcal{R}$ are called *ranges*. Σ is called a *finite range space* if X is finite. For a subset $Y \subseteq X$, the subspace of Σ induced by Y is the range space $(Y, \{R \cap Y \mid R \in \mathcal{R}\})$. For a given range space $\Sigma = (X, \mathcal{R})$, a subset $A \subset X$ is said to be *shattered* by $\mathcal{R}$ if $\{A \cap R \mid R \in \mathcal{R}\} = 2^A$.

Definition 7.61 The *Vapnik-Chervonenkis dimension* (or VC-dimension) of a range space Σ, denoted as VC-dim (Σ), is the maximum size of a shattered subset of X. If no such maximum size exists, Σ is said to have *infinite* VC-dimension.

Definition 7.62 Let $\Sigma = (X, \mathcal{R})$ be a finite range space, and let $0 < \varepsilon < 1$. A subset $S \subseteq X$ is called an ε-*net* if $S \cap R \neq \emptyset$ for every range $R \in \mathcal{R}$ with $|R| > \varepsilon |X|$.

The notion of ε-nets was introduced by Haussler and Welzl (1987); see also Vapnik and Chervonenkis (1971). They proved that a range space of finite VC-dimension d has an ε-net whose size depends only on d and on ε, not on the size of the range space. Specifically, Haussler and Welzl showed:

Theorem 7.63 *For any range space* $(X, \mathcal{R})$ *of finite VC-dimension d and for* $0 < \varepsilon, \delta < 1$, *if S is a subset of X obtained by*

$$\max \left\{ \frac{4}{\varepsilon} \log \frac{2}{\delta}, \frac{8d}{\varepsilon} \log \frac{8d}{\varepsilon} \right\}$$

random independent draws, then, with probability at least $1 - \delta$, S is an ε-net of Σ.

This theorem implies that range spaces of VC-dimension d admit ε-nets of size at most $\frac{8d}{\varepsilon} \log \frac{8d}{\varepsilon}$. The upper bound on the size of an ε-net was improved by Komlós, Pach, and Woeginger (1992) to $(1 + o(1)) \frac{d}{\varepsilon} \log \frac{d}{\varepsilon}$; see also Blumer et al. (1989).

Another consequence of Theorem 7.63 is that for a range space $\Sigma = (X, \mathcal{R})$ of VC-dimension d and for a parameter $r > 1$, a random subset $N \subseteq X$ of size $\Theta(dr \log dr)$ is a $(1/r)$-net of Σ with high probability. In the past few years much work has been done on computing deterministically a $(1/r)$-net of size $O(dr \log dr)$; see Matoušek (1991) and Brönnimann, Chazelle, and Matoušek (1993). The best known result to date, due to Brönnimann, Chazelle, and Matoušek (1993), is:

Theorem 7.64 *Let $\Sigma = (X, \mathcal{R})$ be a finite range space of VC-dimension d. For a given parameter $r > 1$, one can compute, in time $O(d)^{3d} r^d \log^d(dr) \cdot |X|$, a $(1/r)$-net of size $O(dr \log(dr))$ of Σ, provided there is an algorithm that, given any subset $Y \subseteq X$, produces the ranges of the subspace induced by Y in time $O(|Y|^{d+1})$.*

We now give, without proof, some (geometric) examples of range spaces of finite VC-dimension. Proofs of these results can be found in Anthony and Biggs (1992) and Blumer et al. (1989).

Lemma 7.65 *Let S be a finite set of points in $\mathbb{R}^d$. The VC-dimension of the range space*

$$H_d = (S, \ \{S \cap h \mid h \text{ is a half-space in } \mathbb{R}^d\}).$$

is $d + 1$.

Lemma 7.66 *Let H be a set of n hyperplanes in $\mathbb{R}^d$. The VC-dimension of the range space*

$$\Gamma_d = (H, \ \{\{h \in H \mid h \cap \gamma \neq \emptyset\} \mid \gamma \text{ is a segment in } \mathbb{R}^d\})$$

is $O(d)$.

Lemma 7.67 *Let Δ be a set of n $(d-1)$-simplices in $\mathbb{R}^d$. The VC-dimension of the range space*

$$\Lambda_d = (\Delta, \ \{\{\Delta \in \Delta \mid \Delta \cap \gamma \neq \emptyset\} \mid \gamma \text{ is a segment in } \mathbb{R}^d\})$$

is $O(d \log d)$.

Lemma 7.68 *Let $\mathcal{F}(d, b)$ be the set of all d-variate polynomials of maximum degree b, and let $F \subset \mathcal{F}(d, b)$ be a finite subset. The VC-dimension of the range space*

$$F_{d,b} = (F, \ \{\{f \in F \mid \exists \mathbf{x} \in \mathbb{R}^d \ s.t. \ f(\mathbf{x}) = 0 \ and \ g(\mathbf{x}) > 0\} \mid g \in \mathcal{F}(d, b)\})$$

is $O(d^b)$.

An important property of range spaces of finite VC-dimension is that they are closed under set-theoretic operations. In particular, Haussler and Welzl (1987) (see also Dudley (1978) and Wenocur and Dudley (1981)) proved:

Lemma 7.69 *Let $\Sigma = (X, R)$ be a range space with VC-dim $(\Sigma) = d$. Consider a new range space $\Sigma' = (X, R')$, where each range in R' is defined as $\varphi(R_1, \ldots, R_k)$ and where φ is a set-theoretic formula (involving unions, intersections, and complementations) and $R_1, \ldots, R_k \in R$. Then VC-dim $(\Sigma') = O(dk \log(dk))$.*

An immediate corollary of Lemmas 7.66 and 7.69 is:

Corollary 7.70 *Let H be a finite set of hyperplanes in $\mathbb{R}^d$. The VC-dimension of the range space Δ_d*

$$\Delta_d = (H, \ \{ \{h \mid h \cap \Delta \neq \emptyset\} \mid \Delta \text{ is an open simplex in } \mathbb{R}^d \})$$

is $O(d^2 \log d)$. If H is a set of $(d-1)$-simplices in $\mathbb{R}^d$ and Δ_d is defined as above, then the VC-dimension of Δ_d is finite (and depends only on d).

Proof. For the case of hyperplanes, let Δ be an open simplex in $\mathbb{R}^d$, and let v be a vertex of Δ. Any hyperplane intersecting Δ has to intersect at least one of the d edges incident to v. Therefore, a range in Δ_d can be written as a union of d ranges of Γ_d.

The proof for the case of simplices is similar, although somewhat more complicated. $\qquad\square$

Corollary 7.70 implies that if we triangulate the arrangement of an ε-net N of the range-space Δ_d, then each (open) simplex τ of the triangulated arrangement intersects at most $\varepsilon|H|$ hyperplanes (or simplices) of H, because τ does not intersect any hyperplane (simplex) of N.

Definition 7.71 A subset of $\mathbb{R}^d$ is called a *real semialgebraic set* if it is obtained as a finite Boolean combination of sets of the form $\{f = 0\}$ or $\{f > 0\}$ for d-variate polynomials f. A semialgebraic set has *constant description complexity* if it can be described in terms of a constant number of such sets, with a constant bound on the degrees of the corresponding polynomials.

For given constants $d, b, k > 0$, let $\Psi(d, b, k)$ denote the family of all semialgebraic sets formed by the Boolean combination of at most k d-variate polynomials of maximum degree b. A corollary of Lemmas 7.68 and 7.69 is:

Corollary 7.72 *Let F be a finite set of d-variate polynomials with maximum degree b. Then the VC-dimension of the range space*

$$\mathcal{F}_{d,b}^k = (F, \ \{\{f \in F \mid \exists \mathbf{x} \in \psi \text{ such that } f(\mathbf{x}) = 0\} \mid \psi \in \Psi(d, b, k)\})$$

is $O(d^b k \log(d^b k))$.

The results presented so far in the Appendix can be intuitively interpreted as saying that, for a 'geometric' range space $(X, \mathcal{R})$, if X is a set of geometric objects, each having constant description complexity (points, hyperplanes, disks, simplices, and even general semialgebraic sets with constant description complexity), and if each range of $\mathcal{R}$ is the subset of X consisting of all objects that meet some given object (a segment, a simplex, or a semialgebraic set) of constant description complexity, then $(X, \mathcal{R})$ has finite VC-dimension.

To illustrate the significance of the condition of constant description complexity, we conclude the Appendix with the following example of a geometric range space that has infinite VC-dimension. Let $S \subset \mathbb{R}^2$ be a finite set of points lying on a circle. The VC-dimension of the range space

$$(S, \quad \{ S \cap C \mid C \text{ is a convex set} \})$$

is infinite, because for any subset $N \subseteq S$, one can find a convex set C such that $C \cap S = N$ (e.g., take C to be the convex hull of N). Thus any subset can be shattered in this case.

8

GEOMETRIC APPLICATIONS

Chapters 5 and 6 presented basic applications of Davenport–Schinzel sequences to the combinatorial and algorithmic analysis of arrangements of curves in the plane. However, there are many other geometric applications of Davenport–Schinzel sequences, including also applications of the results of Chapter 7 concerning envelopes in higher dimensions. These applications are quite diverse, and many of them require the introduction of problem-specific and rather sophisticated geometric machinery. This chapter presents some of these applications. It is beyond the scope of this book to present all of them in full detail. Instead, we describe in detail only a few applications, which we deem to be either of basic significance or easy to present, and then give a list of other known applications, presented in a much sketchier manner.

8.1 Applications of $DS(n, 2)$-sequences

We begin by describing some applications of Davenport–Schinzel sequences of order 2. In Chapter 5 we proved an upper bound on the complexity of the zone of a line in an arrangement of lines in the plane, using $DS(n, 2)$-sequences (see Section 5.3), and we also applied $DS(n, 2)$ sequences in the analysis of the complexity of the convex hull of a collection of Jordan regions (see Section 5.2). In this section we present three more applications of $DS(n, 2)$-sequences. We first present a sweep-line algorithm for computing the Voronoi diagram of a set of points in the plane, and analyze its time complexity using the bound on $\lambda_2(n)$ proved in Chapter 1. Next, we show a close relationship between $DS(n,2)$-sequences and triangulations of convex polygons. Finally, we show that $DS(n,2)$-sequences arise in the analysis of patterns in which a collection of pairwise disjoint Jordan regions can touch a Jordan curve that encloses all of them. Additional applications of $DS(n,2)$ sequences are also given later in the chapter, for example, in Theorem 8.12 on geometric permutations.

8.1.1 Voronoi diagrams

Let $P = \{p_1, \ldots, p_n\}$ be a set of n points in the plane. Let $Vor(P)$ denote the *Voronoi diagram* of P under the Euclidean distance, as defined in Appendix 7.1. Recall that $Vor(P)$ is a straight-line planar map with n faces, one face for each point $p_i \in P$, so it has $O(n)$ edges and vertices; see Figure 7.11 for an example. As mentioned in Appendix 7.1, there are several known optimal algorithms (requiring $O(n \log n)$ time) for constructing the Voronoi diagram of a set of n points in the plane. We present here one of these algorithms, due to Fortune (1987), which exploits $DS(n,2)$-sequences in its analysis.

For a point $p = (x(p), y(p))$, let C_p denote the cone in $\mathbb{R}^3$ defined as

$$C_p = \{ (x, y, z) \mid (x - x(p))^2 + (y - y(p))^2 = z^2; z \geq 0 \},$$

and let $\mathcal{C} = \{C_p \mid p \in P\}$ be the set of n cones corresponding to the points of P. Then, by definition, $Vor(P)$ is the minimization diagram of $\mathcal{C}$ (regarding each cone C_p as a bivariate function of x and y). For a given $t \in \mathbb{R}$, let $h(t)$ be the plane $x + z = t$; $h(t)$ intersects a cone C_p if and only if $x(p) \leq t$ and $h(t)$ is tangent to C_p if $t = x(p)$; see Figure 8.1.

The intersection of $h(t)$ and the xy-plane (i.e., $z = 0$) is a vertical line $\ell(t)$ parallel to the y-axis at $x = t$. Our approach is to compute the minimization diagram of $\mathcal{C}$ by sweeping the xy-plane with the line $\ell(t)$ from left to right (by varying t from $-\infty$ to $+\infty$), and by maintaining the xy-projection of the intersection of $h(t)$ and the lower envelope of $\mathcal{C}$.

The xy-projection, $\hat{p}(t)$, of $C_p \cap h(t)$ is a parabola with directrix $\ell(t)$ and focus p, that is,

$$\hat{p}(t) = \{ q = (x(q), y(q)) \mid d(q, p) = t - x(q) \},$$

where $d(\cdot, \cdot)$ is the Euclidean distance; this parabola is defined only when $t > x(p)$ and degenerates to a ray

$$\{ q = (x(q), y(q)) \mid y(q) = y(p), x(q) \leq x(p) \}$$

when $t = x(p)$.

Let $\hat{P}(t) = \{\hat{p}(t) \mid p \in P, x(p) < t\}$. For a given t, let $M(t)$ denote the 'right envelope' of $\hat{P}(t)$, where each parabola is regarded as a univariate function of y and

$$M(t)(y) = \max \{ \hat{p}(t)(y) \mid p \in P, x(p) < t \};$$

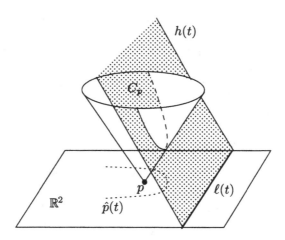

FIGURE 8.1. Illustration of $C_p, h(t), \ell(t)$, and $\hat{p}(t)$.

$M(t)$ will be referred to as the *parabolic front* of P at time t. It is easily seen that $M(t)$ is the xy-projection of the intersection between $h(t)$ and the lower envelope of C. The front $M(t)$ consists of a sequence of parabolic arcs delimited by breakpoints. (If t is equal to the x-coordinate of some point(s) $p \in P$, we add to $M(t)$ the horizontal segment extended from p in the negative x-direction until it hits a parabola of $\hat{P}(t)$.) We will label each breakpoint of $M(t)$ by the ordered pair (p, q), where $\hat{p}(t), \hat{q}(t)$ are the parabolas containing arcs lying, respectively, above and below the breakpoint (in the y-direction). Each arc of $M(t)$ lies in a single Voronoi region, and each breakpoint (p, q) lies on the common edge of the Voronoi regions of p and q. Since the axis of every parabola is parallel to the x-axis, any two of them intersect in at most two points, so, by Lemma 1.2 and Theorem 1.9(b), $M(t)$ has at most $2n - 1$ breakpoints.

As we sweep the line $\ell(t)$ to the right, $M(t)$ moves continuously, and each breakpoint (p, q) moves along the bisector of p and q. The loci of the breakpoints thus give the edges of $Vor(P)$. Although $M(t)$ changes continuously, the combinatorial structure of $M(t)$ changes only at certain discrete values of t, called *event points*, where one of the following two events occurs:

1. *Site event:* A site event occurs when the sweep-line $\ell(t)$ meets a point of P, that is, $t = x(p)$ for some $p \in P$. In this case, a new parabolic arc, initially appearing as a ray emanating leftward from p and then growing into a very thin parabola encircling p, and at most two new breakpoints, appear on the parabolic front (see Figure 8.2 (i)).

2. *Circle event:* A circle event occurs when two (consecutive) breakpoints along $M(t)$ collide with each other. This occurs at a vertex v of $Vor(P)$; v is

equidistant from the sweep-line $\ell(t)$ and from the three points of P that determine v. In this case, a parabolic arc and at most two breakpoints disappear from the front, and one new breakpoint appears on the front (see Figure 8.2 (ii)).

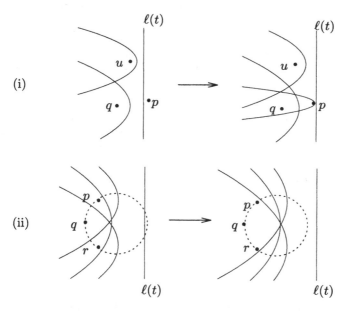

FIGURE 8.2. Examples of event points: (i) a site event, and (ii) a circle event.

It is easily verified that new arcs appear on the parabolic front only at site events, and arcs disappear from the front only at circle events.

We sweep the xy-plane by $\ell(t)$, stopping at every event point. To facilitate the sweep, we store the breakpoints of the front in a height-balanced binary search tree T, sorted in increasing y-order. (See any textbook on algorithms, for example, Coreman, Leiserson, and Rivest (1990), for details on height-balanced binary search trees. A set A of ordered elements can be stored in a height-balanced binary search tree, so that an element can be inserted into or deleted from it in $O(\log|A|)$ time, and, for a query element x, the successor (or the predecessor) of x in A can be determined in $O(\log|A|)$ time; see also Section 6.3.2. In order to determine the next event point, we also store a superset of event points in a priority queue Q, ordered by their x-coordinates. The minimum element of Q always gives the next actual event point. For a given t, Q stores the x-coordinates of points in P that lie to the right of $\ell(t)$, and, for each pair $(p,q),(q,r)$ of consecutive breakpoints in $M(t)$, the x-coordinate of the rightmost point ξ of the circle passing through p,q,r. Notice that some circle events stored in Q may be spurious, and may not correspond to vertices of the Voronoi diagram; however, spurious events will always be deleted from Q before the sweep-line reaches them. We also store the portion of the Voronoi diagram lying to the left of $M(t)$ in an appropriate data structure (this is the portion of the diagram that has already been computed by the algorithm).

At a site event corresponding to a point $p \in P$, we search T with the y-coordinate of p, and determine the breakpoints (u,q) and (q,v) that lie immediately above and below p, respectively. We add two new breakpoints (q,p) and (p,q) to T (in between (u,q) and (q,v)). We add new circle events to Q, if appropriate, corresponding to the circumcircles of $\{u,q,p\}$ and of $\{p,q,v\}$, and delete the circle event corresponding to $\{u,q,v\}$. A similar procedure updates the data structure at each circle event.

We perform $O(1)$ updates in T and Q at each event point, so we spend $O(\log n)$ time at each event point. Since $Vor(P)$ has $O(n)$ vertices, the front has $O(n)$ vertices, and each circle event corresponds to a vertex of $Vor(P)$, the total number of event points is $O(n)$. Hence, the total running time of the algorithm is $O(n \log n)$.

Theorem 8.1 *The Voronoi diagram of a set of n points in the plane can be computed in $O(n \log n)$ time by the sweep-line algorithm described above.*

8.1.2   Triangulations

A convex polygon with $n+1$ vertices can be triangulated into $n-1$ triangles by drawing $n-2$ noncrossing diagonals (i.e., chords that connect pairs of vertices; see Figure 8.3). Assuming that the vertices are labeled $1, 2, \ldots, n+1$ in counterclockwise direction, we can represent a triangulation T of the polygon by the set (which we also denote by T) of diagonals (i,j), $1 \le i < j \le n+1$, forming the triangulation. For the sake of uniformity, we also add the sides of the polygon to T, that is, $(i, i+1) \in T$, for every $1 \le i \le n$, and $(1, n+1) \in T$. Let Δ_{n+1} denote the set of all possible triangulations of a convex $(n+1)$-gon. We define a function

$$\varphi : \Delta_{n+1} \longrightarrow \{1, \ldots, n\}^{2n-1},$$

which maps every triangulation in Δ_{n+1} to a $DS(n,2)$-sequence of length $2n-1$, as follows. Let $T \in \Delta_{n+1}$. For each vertex i of the polygon, let $\xi(i)$ be the sequence whose elements are all the indices $j < i$ for which $(j,i) \in T$, sorted in decreasing order. The resulting sequence $\varphi(T)$ is then defined as

$$\varphi(T) = \xi(2) \, \| \, \xi(3) \, \| \, \cdots \, \| \, \xi(n+1).$$

See Figure 8.3 for an example.

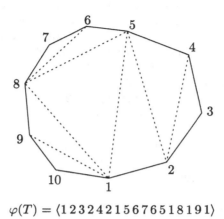

$$\varphi(T) = \langle 1\,2\,3\,2\,4\,2\,1\,5\,6\,7\,6\,5\,1\,8\,1\,9\,1 \rangle$$

FIGURE 8.3. Triangulation of a convex polygon and the corresponding $DS(n, 2)$-sequence.

Lemma 8.2 *Let T be a triangulation of a convex $(n + 1)$-gon. Then the sequence $\varphi(T)$ is a $DS(n, 2)$-sequence of length $2n - 1$. Conversely, let σ be a $DS(n, 2)$-sequence of length $2n - 1$, whose symbols are numbered so that the leftmost appearance of i precedes the leftmost appearance of j whenever $i < j$. Then σ is the image $\varphi(T)$ of some triangulation T of a convex $(n + 1)$-gon.*

Proof. For the first part of the lemma, note that, by construction, no two adjacent symbols in $\varphi(T)$ are the same—this clearly holds within each block $\xi(i)$, and the first element of a block $\xi(i)$, namely $i - 1$, cannot be equal to the last element of $\xi(i - 1)$ (which is always nonempty for $i \geq 2$). Thus, if $\varphi(T)$ were not a $DS(n, 2)$-sequence, then there would have to exist a subsequence $\langle u_{i_1} \ldots u_{i_2} \ldots u_{i_3} \ldots u_{i_4} \rangle$ of $\varphi(T)$ such that $u_{i_1} = u_{i_3} = a$ and $u_{i_2} = u_{i_4} = b$ for some $1 \leq a \neq b \leq n$. Without loss of generality, assume that this is the lexicographically leftmost subsequence of this form. That is, u_{i_1} and u_{i_2} are, respectively, the leftmost occurrences of a and of b, there is no occurrence of a between u_{i_2} and u_{i_3}, and there is no occurrence of b between u_{i_3} and u_{i_4}. Since the leftmost occurrence of a is before the leftmost occurrence of b, it is easily verified that $a < b$. Let us assume that $u_{i_3} = a \in \xi(k)$ and $u_{i_4} = b \in \xi(l)$. Since the vertices in each block are enumerated in decreasing order and $u_{i_3} = a < u_{i_4} = b$, we must have $k < l$. But then $a < b < k < l$, so the diagonals (a, k) and (b, l), which belong to T by definition of $\varphi(T)$, will have to cross each other. This contradicts the fact that T is a triangulation. Hence, $\varphi(T)$ does not contain an alternation of length 4, and is thus a $DS(n, 2)$-sequence.

The length of $\varphi(T)$ is $2n - 1$, because P has $n + 1$ sides and $n - 2$ diagonals, and each of them contributes exactly one element to $\varphi(T)$.

Next, we show that every $DS(n,2)$-sequence σ of length $2n-1$, whose symbols are numbered as in the second part of the lemma, is the image of a triangulation of a convex $(n+1)$-gon. Let P be any convex $(n+1)$-gon. Draw a diagonal (b,k) in P if b appears in σ between the leftmost appearance of $k-1$ and the leftmost appearance of k (note that b must be smaller than k). Using an argument similar to that in the first part of the lemma, we can show that no two diagonals cross each other. Since $|\sigma| = 2n-1$, the resulting subdivision is a triangulation T of P. It is easy to verify that indeed $\varphi(T) = \sigma$.   □

The above relationship between $DS(n,2)$-sequences and triangulations of convex polygons has an interesting consequence. It is well-known that a convex $(n+1)$-gon can be triangulated in $\frac{1}{n}\binom{2n-2}{n-1}$ different ways; see, for example, Polya (1956). We call two sequences $U_1, U_2 \in \{1,\ldots,n\}^*$ *distinct* if U_2 cannot be obtained from U_1 by renumbering its symbols. Since φ is a bijective function, we obtain:

Theorem 8.3 *For any $n \geq 1$, there are $\frac{1}{n}\binom{2n-2}{n-1}$ distinct $DS(n,2)$-sequences of length $2n-1$.*

8.1.3   A topological application

We next consider the following simple application of $DS(n,2)$-sequences, which is somewhat similar in nature to the application in the proof of Theorem 5.8. Let $\Gamma = \{\gamma_1,\ldots,\gamma_n\}$ be a collection of n closed Jordan curves in the plane, and let γ be another closed Jordan curve. Denote by $K(\gamma')$ the closed bounded region enclosed by a closed Jordan curve γ'. Assume that the regions $K(\gamma_i)$, for $\gamma_i \in \Gamma$, are pairwise disjoint and are all contained in $K(\gamma)$ (possibly touching γ). Trace the curve γ in, say, counterclockwise direction, and partition it into a cyclic sequence σ of pairwise openly disjoint arcs, $\langle \delta_1,\ldots,\delta_m \rangle$, so that each δ_j meets a single curve of Γ, and so that no two adjacent arcs meet the same curve. (We assume that at least one of the curves of Γ partially overlaps γ, otherwise the ongoing analysis is vacuous.) We label each arc of σ by the index of the curve of Γ that it meets, thus obtaining a cycle σ^* composed of n distinct symbols. See Figure 8.4 for an illustration of this setup.

Lemma 8.4 *Under the above assumptions, σ^* is a $DS(n,2)$-cycle, hence its length m is at most $2n-2$.*

Proof. By construction, σ^* does not contain two equal adjacent elements. Suppose to the contrary that σ^* contains a subcycle of the form $\langle a \cdots b \cdots a \cdots b \rangle$, for two distinct symbols a and b. Then γ contains four points, x, y, z, w, arranged in this order in counterclockwise direction along γ, so that $x, z \in \gamma_a$ and $y, w \in \gamma_b$. Then one can construct two arcs $\lambda_a \subseteq K(\gamma_a)$, $\lambda_b \subseteq K(\gamma_b)$, so that λ_a connects x and z and λ_b connects y and w. But then, as is easily

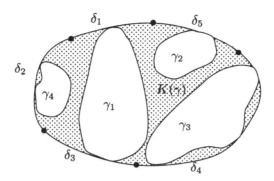

FIGURE 8.4. Illustration of the setup; $\sigma^* = \langle 1, 4, 1, 3, 2 \rangle$.

checked, λ_a and λ_b must cross each other, which is impossible. This contradiction completes the proof of the lemma. □

The assumptions of the preceding lemma can be relaxed, by requiring only that the regions $K(\gamma_i)$, for $\gamma_i \in \Gamma$, have pairwise disjoint interiors. An interesting application of this result is to triangulations of simple polygons: Let P be a simple polygon in the plane with $n \geq 3$ vertices. Any triangulation T of P is obtained by drawing $n - 3$ pairwise openly disjoint diagonals within P (each connecting a pair of nonadjacent vertices of P), which partition P into $n - 2$ triangles, $\Delta_1, \ldots, \Delta_{n-2}$, having pairwise disjoint interiors. Regard ∂P as γ and let Γ consist of the $n - 2$ boundaries of the triangles in such a triangulation of P. By adapting the analysis in the proof of the preceding lemma, we easily obtain the following result.

Go around the boundary of P in, say, counterclockwise direction, and construct a sequence σ, as follows. When reaching a new vertex v of P, add to σ all triangles incident to v in clockwise order about v, except for the triangle incident to the edge of P that led us to v. Then the preceding analysis implies that σ is a $DS(n - 2, 2)$-cycle, and thus consists of at most $2n - 6$ elements. See Figure 8.5 for an illustration of this construction. Note that a triangle Δ can appear in σ once, if Δ shares two edges with ∂P, or twice, if Δ shares just one edge with ∂P, or three times, if Δ is only bounded by diagonals. Let n_i denote the number of triangles Δ that appear i times in σ, for $i = 1, 2, 3$. Then we have

$$n_1 + n_2 + n_3 = n - 2,$$

$$n_1 + 2n_2 + 3n_3 \leq 2n - 6.$$

By subtracting the second equation from twice the first equation, we obtain

$$n_1 - n_3 \geq 2,$$

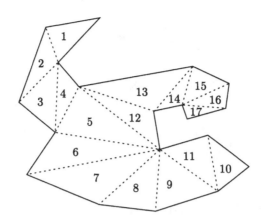

$$\sigma \;=\; \langle 2\,3\,4\,5\,6\,7\,8\,9\,11\,10\,11\,9\,8\,7\,6\,5\,12\,13\,14\,15\,16$$
$$17\,16\,15\,14\,13\,12\,5\,4\,3\,2\,1 \rangle$$

FIGURE 8.5. Triangulation of a simple polygon.

which, in particular, implies that $n_1 \geq 2$. That is, we have shown that every triangulation of P has at least 2 'ears,' namely triangles that share two edges with P. (This is a well-known result that can also be established by other much more elementary arguments; see O'Rourke (1987).)

8.2   Transversals of a set of objects

Let $\mathcal{S} = \{\, S_1, S_2, \ldots, S_n \,\}$ be a collection of n compact convex sets in the plane. A directed (or undirected) line that intersects all sets of $\mathcal{S}$ is called a *transversal* (or a *stabber*) of $\mathcal{S}$. Note that a line intersects a set if and only if it intersects its convex hull, so convexity is not a real restriction. A line is called *tangent* to a convex set R if R lies fully in one of the closed half-planes bounded by ℓ and ℓ intersects R. If the sets in $\mathcal{S}$ are pairwise disjoint, a transversal intersects these sets in a well-defined order. For undirected lines, such an order can be described by a pair of permutations, one being the reversal of the other. Such a pair is called a *geometric permutation* of $\mathcal{S}$.

In this section, we will study various problems related to transversals and to geometric permutations, such as what is the complexity of the space of all transversals of $\mathcal{S}$ (see below for a precise definition), how to determine efficiently whether a given line is a transversal of $\mathcal{S}$, what is the maximum number of geometric permutations of $\mathcal{S}$, etc. We will show that Davenport–Schinzel sequences play an important role in the solutions to these problems.

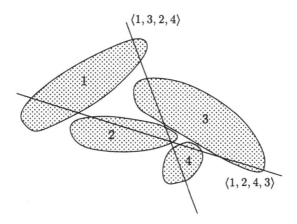

FIGURE 8.6. Stabbing lines and their corresponding geometric permutations.

8.2.1 *Complexity of the space of transversals*

It is convenient to study transversals by applying a standard form of geometric duality, in which the *dual* of a point (a, b) is the line $y = ax + b$ and the dual of a line $y = \alpha x + \beta$ is the point $(-\alpha, \beta)$. We will denote the dual of an object γ by γ^*. An important property of this duality transform is that it preserves the above-below relationship between points and (nonvertical) lines, that is, if a point p lies above (respectively, below, on) a line ℓ, then the line p^* lies above (respectively, below, on) the point ℓ^*; see Figure 8.7. (Note that this duality is undefined for vertical lines; thus our analysis will handle only nonvertical transversals.) For a compact convex set R, we define its *stabbing region* R^* to be the set of points dual to the lines that intersect R. The boundary ∂R^* of R^* is the set of points dual to the tangents to R. It is easily checked that R^* is bounded from above by a convex x-monotone curve and from below by a concave x-monotone curve; they will be referred to as the *upper* and *lower* boundaries of R^*, respectively. The dual of a point ℓ^* lying on the upper (respectively, lower) boundary of R^* is a tangent ℓ to R such that R lies in the closed half-plane lying below (respectively, above) ℓ. The dual of a point lying on the upper (respectively, lower) boundary of R^* will be called an *upper* (respectively, *lower*) *tangent* of R. The *stabbing region* (or the *space of all transversals*) of S is the intersection $S^* = \bigcap_{i=1}^{n} S_i^*$. By definition, the lines dual to any point in S^* are precisely all the nonvertical transversals of S. The combinatorial complexity of S^* is defined to be the number of vertices of S^*, where a vertex is an intersection point between the boundaries of two stabbing regions S_i^*, S_j^* that lies on ∂S^* (i.e., it is dual to a common tangent of the two corresponding sets S_i, S_j).

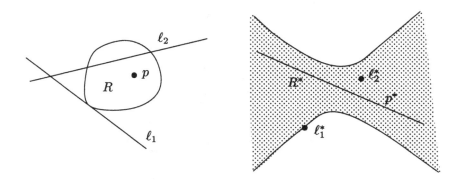

FIGURE 8.7. A convex set and its stabbing region.

Theorem 8.5 *Let S be a collection of n (possibly intersecting) compact convex sets in the plane, such that any two sets have at most s upper common tangents and at most s lower common tangents. Then the combinatorial complexity of the space of transversals of S is $O(\lambda_s(n))$.*

Proof. For each set $S_i \in \mathcal{S}$, let U_i and L_i denote the upper and lower boundary of S_i^*, respectively. By definition, S^* lies below U_i and above L_i, for each $1 \leq i \leq n$. Consequently, every vertex of $\mathcal{S}^*$ is a vertex of the lower envelope $E_{\mathcal{U}}$ of $\mathcal{U} = \{U_1, \ldots, U_n\}$, a vertex of the upper envelope $E_{\mathcal{L}}^*$ of $\mathcal{L} = \{L_1, \ldots, L_n\}$, or an intersection point of an arc of $E_{\mathcal{U}}$ and an arc of $E_{\mathcal{L}}^*$. An intersection point of U_i and U_j is the dual of a common upper tangent of S_i and S_j, so U_i and U_j intersect in at most s points. Hence $E_{\mathcal{U}}$ has at most $\lambda_s(n)$ vertices. Similarly, $E_{\mathcal{L}}^*$ also has at most $\lambda_s(n)$ vertices. An intersection between an upper boundary U_i and a lower boundary L_j is the dual of a common tangent ℓ to S_i and S_j such that S_i lies below ℓ and S_j lies above ℓ. Such common tangents exist if and only if S_i and S_j are either disjoint or intersect at a single point, and the number of such common tangents is then only 2 or 1, respectively. Hence, an argument similar to that given in Section 6.2 implies that the number of intersection points between the upper envelope of $\mathcal{L}$ and the lower envelope of $\mathcal{U}$ is $O(\lambda_s(n))$. This completes the proof of the theorem. $\qquad\square$

Remark 8.6 The assumption that the sets in $\mathcal{S}$ are convex is not essential, since we can replace each set in $\mathcal{S}$ by its convex hull, without affecting the transversality of any line, and without changing the parameter s.

The above theorem assumes that any two sets in $\mathcal{S}$ have at most some constant number of common tangents. But in certain cases this assumption may not hold. For example, two convex k-gons may have up to $2k$ common tangents. However, for a convex polygon P, it is easily checked that the upper and lower boundaries of P^* are polygonal chains whose edges are portions of lines dual to the vertices of P. Therefore, if $\mathcal{S}$ is a set of m convex polygons with a total of n vertices, then the lower envelope of the corresponding collection $\mathcal{U}$ is the lower envelope of m piecewise-linear functions whose graphs consist of at most n segments, so, by Corollary 2.18, it has $O(n\alpha(m))$ vertices. The same holds for the upper envelope of the collection $\mathcal{L}$. Hence, we can conclude:

Corollary 8.7 *The combinatorial complexity of the stabbing region of a set $\mathcal{S}$ of m convex polygons with a total of n vertices is $O(n\alpha(m))$.*

Remark 8.8 The above corollary can be extended to show that if $\mathcal{S}$ is a collection of m convex 'splinegons' with a total of n spline-edges (see Dobkin and Souvaine (1990) for a precise definition of splinegons), such that any two edges intersect in at most s points, then $\mathcal{S}^*$ has $O((n/m)\lambda_{s+2}(m))$ vertices.

Another interesting case occurs when the sets of $\mathcal{S}$ are pairwise disjoint, because then $s = 2$, as is easily verified. This case will be studied in Section 8.2.2 below.

The stabbing region $\mathcal{S}^*$ can be computed using the algorithms described in Section 6.2. To facilitate the algorithms we need to assume a model of computation similar to that of Section 6.1. When translated into the primal plane, this requires that we can compute in constant time the set of all common tangents to a pair of sets in $\mathcal{S}$, and that, given a query line ℓ and a set $S_i \in \mathcal{S}$, we can test in constant time whether ℓ passes above S_i, intersects S_i, or passes below S_i. (The model of computation when $\mathcal{S}$ is a set of convex polygons is even simpler, as the reader may easily check.)

$\mathcal{S}^*$ may consist of several connected components, but they have a special structure; namely:

(i) The x-projections of the connected components of S^* are pairwise disjoint.

(ii) The boundary of each connected component c consists of two x-monotone chains. The upper chain is a portion of the lower envelope of $\mathcal{U}$ and the lower chain is a portion of the upper envelope of $\mathcal{L}$.

Once $\mathcal{S}^*$ has been computed, it can be preprocessed into a data structure, so that one can quickly determine whether a query line ℓ is a stabbing line. As discussed above, it suffices to determine whether the point ℓ^* lies in $\mathcal{S}^*$. Let C be the set of all endpoints of the x-projections of the components of S^*, sorted in increasing x-order. For a connected component c of $\mathcal{S}^*$, let U_c, L_c denote the upper and lower chains of ∂c, respectively. Given a query point ℓ^*, we can determine in $O(\log n)$ time whether ℓ^* lies in $\mathcal{S}^*$: Let x^* be the x-coordinate of ℓ^*. First, by a binary search in C, we determine the connected component

c of S^* whose x-projection contains x^*. If there is no such component, we can conclude that $\ell^* \notin S^*$. Otherwise, by another binary search through the vertices of U_c, we determine the edge e_U of U_c whose projection contains x^*. Similarly, we determine the edge e_L of L_c whose projection contains x^*. The point ℓ^* lies in c if and only if it lies above e_L and below e_U. The total time spent in answering a query, in an appropriate model of computation, is $O(\log n)$. Hence, we can conclude:

Theorem 8.9 *Let S be a set of n convex sets in the plane, each pair of which having at most s upper common tangents and at most s lower common tangents. Under the model of computation assumed above, we can preprocess S into a data structure of size $O(\lambda_s(n))$, in time $O(\lambda_s(n) \log n)$, so that we can determine in $O(\log n)$ time whether a query line is a transversal of S. If S is a set of m convex polygons with a total of n vertices, the space and preprocessing time become $O(n\alpha(m))$ and $O(n\alpha(m) \log m)$, respectively.*

The notion of transversals can be extended to partial transversals, that is, lines that intersect most of the sets in S. Formally, a line is called a k-transversal of S if it intersects at least $n - k$ sets of S. A natural question to ask is what is the combinatorial complexity of the space of k-transversals of S. The combinatorial complexity is defined as the number of intersection points of the pairs of boundaries ∂S_i^*, which lie on the boundary of the dual space of all k-transversals of S. The dual of such an intersection point is a line that is tangent to two sets in S and that intersects the interior of $n - k - 2$ other sets in S.

Theorem 8.10 *Let S be a collection of n compact convex sets such that any two sets in S have at most s upper common tangents and at most s lower common tangents. For any nonnegative integer $k \leq n$, the overall combinatorial complexity of the spaces of j-transversals of S, for $0 \leq j \leq k$, is $O((k+1)^2 \lambda_s(\lfloor n/(k+1) \rfloor))$.*

Proof. For each $S_i \in S$ let U_i and L_i denote the upper and lower boundaries of S_i^*, respectively, and let K_{2i-1} (respectively, K_{2i}) denote the (open) region lying above U_i (respectively, below L_i). Let $\mathcal{K}$ denote the set of the resulting $2n$ open regions. A line ℓ intersects a set S_i if and only if the point dual to ℓ lies neither in K_{2i-1} nor in K_{2i}, so each vertex on the boundary of the space of j-transversals of S lies in the interior of at most $2j - 2$ regions of $\mathcal{K}$. Since each U_i, L_i is an x-monotone Jordan curve, and since any pair of these curves intersect in at most s points, Corollary 5.20 implies that the number of such vertices is $O((k+1)^2 \lambda_s(\lfloor n/(k+1) \rfloor))$. $\square$

If S is a collection of m convex polygons with a total of n edges, then the above analysis yields the following result. The proof is a little tricky, and we leave it as an exercise for the reader.

Corollary 8.11 *For any $k \leq m$, the overall combinatorial complexity of the space of all j-transversals of a collection of m convex polygons with a total of n edges, over all $0 \leq j \leq k$, is $O(n(k+1)\alpha(\lfloor m/(k+1) \rfloor))$.*

8.2.2 Geometric permutations

Let S be a collection of n pairwise-disjoint compact convex sets in the plane. Assume that the sets in S are labeled from 1 to n. We say that a directed line transversal $\vec{\ell}$ induces a permutation $(i_1, \ldots, i_n)$ if $\vec{\ell}$ intersects the sets of S in this order. An undirected line transversal ℓ induces a *geometric permutation* consisting of $(i_1, \ldots, i_n)$ and its reverse, if one of the two directed lines coinciding with ℓ intersects the sets of S in the order $(i_1, \ldots, i_n)$. In this subsection, we will obtain bounds on the number of geometric permutations for S.

Since the sets in S are pairwise disjoint, a simple continuity argument shows that all lines dual to points lying in a single connected component of the space S^* of transversals of S induce the same geometric permutation. Hence, the number of geometric permutations is bounded by the number of connected components in S^*, which in turn is bounded by the combinatorial complexity of S^*. The number of common upper (or lower) tangents between two disjoint convex sets is at most two, which, by Theorem 8.5, gives a linear upper bound on the number of geometric permutations of S. Using a more careful analysis, we next derive an exact worst-case upper bound on the number of these geometric permutations.

Theorem 8.12 *For $n \geq 4$, the maximum number of geometric permutations for a set of n pairwise-disjoint compact convex sets in the plane is $2n - 2$. This bound is tight in the worst case. The maximum number of geometric permutations is $1, 1$, and 3, for $n = 1, 2, 3$, respectively.*

In order to prove the theorem, we first introduce some notations. A non-vertical directed line $\vec{\ell}$ is called a *left tangent* to a set i if $\vec{\ell}$ is tangent to i, and i is contained in the closed half-plane lying to the left of $\vec{\ell}$. For an angle $\theta \in [0, 2\pi)$, let $\vec{\ell}(\theta)$ denote the unique directed line that satisfies the following three properties:

(i) The orientation of e, that is, the angle between the positive x-axis and $\vec{\ell}$ in the counterclockwise direction, is θ.

(ii) No set of S is contained in the open half-space to the left of $\vec{\ell}(\theta)$.

(iii) $\vec{\ell}(\theta)$ is a left tangent to at least one set in S.

These conditions imply that if there is a transversal of S with orientation θ then $\vec{\ell}(\theta)$ is the rightmost transversal with this orientation, that is, $\vec{\ell}(\theta)$ is a transversal of S, and there is no transversal with orientation θ contained in the open half-plane lying to the right of $\vec{\ell}(\theta)$. A line is called *extremal* if it is a left tangent to two sets of S.

Lemma 8.13 *For every geometric permutation t, there is an extremal line that induces t.*

Proof. Let θ_0 and $\theta_1 = \theta_0 + \pi$ be the orientations of two oppositely directed lines that induce the geometric permutation t. Then $\vec{\ell}_0 = \vec{\ell}(\theta_0)$ and $\vec{\ell}_1 = \vec{\ell}(\theta_1)$ also induce t. Let $i_0, i_1 \in S$ be the sets contained in the left closed half-planes of $\vec{\ell}_0$ and $\vec{\ell}_1$, respectively. If i_0 or i_1 is not unique, we are done, so assume that they are unique.

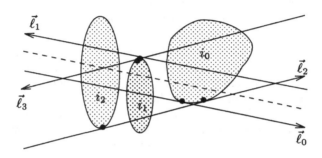

FIGURE 8.8. Illustration of Lemma 8.13.

First consider the case when $i_0 \neq i_1$ and $\vec{\ell}_0$ meets i_1 *before* i_0. Simultaneously rotate $\vec{\ell}_0$ around i_0 and $\vec{\ell}_1$ around i_1 in the counterclockwise direction, keeping $\vec{\ell}_0$ and $\vec{\ell}_1$ parallel to each other, until $\vec{\ell}_0$ becomes tangent to a set other than i_0, or $\vec{\ell}_1$ becomes tangent to a set other than i_1. Let $\vec{\ell}_2, \vec{\ell}_3$ be the lines resulting from these rotations of $\vec{\ell}_0$ and $\vec{\ell}_1$, respectively (see Figure 8.8 for an illustration). It is easy to check, using the fact that $\vec{\ell}_0$ meets i_1 before i_0, that $\vec{\ell}_2$ and $\vec{\ell}_3$ cannot coincide. Without loss of generality, assume that $\vec{\ell}_2$ is tangent to another set i_2 (possibly equal to i_1). Then $\vec{\ell}_2$ must be a left tangent to i_2, because $\vec{\ell}_3$ lies to the left of $\vec{\ell}_2$ and must intersect i_2. Thus, $\vec{\ell}_2$ is an extremal line, which induces the same geometric permutation t.

If $i_0 \neq i_1$ but $\vec{\ell}_0$ meets i_1 *after* i_0, then simultaneously rotate $\vec{\ell}_0$ around i_0 and $\vec{\ell}_1$ around i_1 in the clockwise direction, keeping $\vec{\ell}_0$ and $\vec{\ell}_1$ parallel to each other, until $\vec{\ell}_0$ becomes tangent to a set other than i_0, or $\vec{\ell}_1$ becomes tangent to a set other than i_1. Using the same argument as above, it can be shown that one of the lines resulting from the rotation is an extremal line that induces t.

Finally, if $i_0 = i_1$, then it does not matter in which direction the lines $\vec{\ell}_0, \vec{\ell}_1$ are rotated for the above analysis to apply. $\square$

Proof of Theorem 8.12. In view of Lemma 8.13, it suffices to bound the number of extremal lines. Divide the circle of orientations into maximal intervals such that, for each interval δ, $\vec{\ell}(\theta)$ is a left tangent to some fixed set $S \in \mathcal{S}$ for all orientations θ in the interior of the interval. The endpoints of these intervals correspond to extremal lines. We label each interval δ with the corresponding set S, and let C denote the resulting cyclic sequence of labels. We claim that C is a $DS(n, 2)$-cycle. Indeed, by construction, C has no pair of equal adjacent elements. If the sequence contained a cyclic subsequence of the form $\langle a \ldots b \ldots a \ldots b \rangle$ with $a \neq b$, then there would exist four orientations, $\theta_1 < \theta_2 < \theta_3 < \theta_4$, such that $\vec{\ell}(\theta_1)$ and $\vec{\ell}(\theta_3)$ are left tangents to a and $\vec{\ell}(\theta_2)$ and $\vec{\ell}(\theta_4)$ are left tangents to b. But then, by a continuity argument, a and b would have a common left tangent $\vec{\ell}(\theta)$ for some θ in each of the intervals (θ_1, θ_2), (θ_2, θ_3), (θ_3, θ_4), and (θ_4, θ_1). However, since a and b are disjoint, they have only two common left tangents, a contradiction. Hence, C is a $DS(n, 2)$-cycle. The upper bound of Theorem 8.12 now follows from Corollary 1.10.

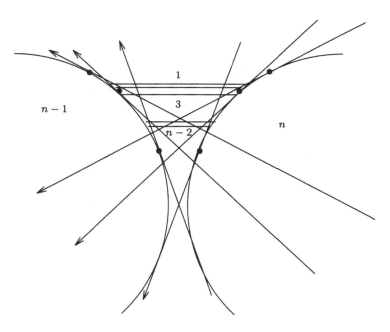

FIGURE 8.9. Lower bound construction for geometric permutations.

Concerning the lower bound, Figure 8.9 shows a set $\mathcal{S}$ of n disjoint convex sets that has $2n - 2$ geometric permutations. $\mathcal{S}$ consists of two large discs labeled $n - 1, n$, and of $n - 2$ horizontal segments between the discs labeled from 1 to $n - 2$ in decreasing order of their y-coordinates. The centers of the discs lie on a horizontal line and the endpoints of the segments all lie sufficiently close to the discs.

The geometric permutations of S are

$$(1, 2, \ldots, i, n, i+1, \ldots, n-2, n-1), \quad \text{for } i = 0, 1, \ldots, n-2,$$

and

$$(n, n-2, n-3, \ldots, i+1, n-1, i, i-1, \ldots, 1), \quad \text{for } i = 0, 1, \ldots, n-2.$$

Finally, it is easily checked that, for $n = 1, 2, 3$, the maximum number of geometric permutations is $1, 1$, and 3, respectively.   □

Remark 8.14 If S is a set of n pairwise-disjoint segments, then the maximum number of geometric permutations is only $n-1$ (see Edelsbrunner et al. (1982)), and if S is a set of n disjoint translates, then the maximum number of geometric permutations is 3 (see Katchalski, Lewis, and Liu (1987, 1992)).

8.2.3   Transversals in 3-space

In this subsection we extend Theorem 8.5 to $\mathbb{R}^3$. Let $S = \{S_1, \ldots, S_n\}$ be a collection of n compact convex sets in $\mathbb{R}^3$. A plane π is a *transversal* of S if it intersects every set of S.

As in two dimensions, it is more convenient to study plane transversals in dual space, where each nonvertical plane $z = \xi x + \eta y + \zeta$ is mapped to a point (ξ, η, ζ), and each point (u, v, w) is mapped to a plane $z = -ux - vy + w$. Note that a plane $z = \xi x + \eta y + \zeta$ intersects a compact convex set S if and only if $\phi_S(\xi, \eta) \leq \zeta \leq \psi_S(\xi, \eta)$, where $\phi_S(\xi, \eta)$, $\psi_S(\xi, \eta)$ are defined so that the plane $z = \xi x + \eta y + \phi_S(\xi, \eta)$ (respectively, $z = \xi x + \eta y + \psi_S(\xi, \eta)$) is tangent to S from below (respectively, from above). Thus, in dual space, the set of all planes that intersect S is the set

$$S^* = \{ (\xi, \eta, \zeta) \mid \phi_S(\xi, \eta) \leq \zeta \leq \psi_S(\xi, \eta) \}.$$

Let $\mathcal{S}^* = \bigcap_{S \in \mathcal{S}} S^*$; $\mathcal{S}^*$ is the set of points dual to transversals of $\mathcal{S}$. By definition,

$$\mathcal{S}^* = \left\{ (\xi, \eta, \zeta) \mid \max_{S \in \mathcal{S}} \phi_S(\xi, \eta) \leq \zeta \leq \min_{S \in \mathcal{S}} \psi_S(\xi, \eta) \right\}.$$

That is, $\mathcal{S}^*$ is the region lying between the lower envelope and the upper envelope of two respective collections of functions. The combinatorial complexity of $\mathcal{S}^*$ is defined as the total number of vertices, edges, and faces (of the arrangement of the union of these two collections) on the boundary of $\mathcal{S}^*$. If we assume that each $S \in \mathcal{S}$ has constant description complexity (i.e., it is defined by a constant number of algebraic equalities and inequalities of constant maximum degree), then it is easy to show that the functions ϕ_S and ψ_S satisfy Assumptions 7.1, so we can apply Theorem 7.14.[1] We thus have:

Theorem 8.15 *The complexity of the space of common plane transversals of a collection of n compact convex sets in 3-space, each of constant description complexity, is $O(n^{2+\varepsilon})$, for any $\varepsilon > 0$.*

Remark 8.16 (i) Convexity is not essential here, since we can replace each set in S by its convex hull, without affecting the transversality of any plane.

(ii) If the sets in S are not each of constant description complexity, the complexity of S^* can be arbitrarily large. However, if one assumes, in addition, that the sets are *separated*, in the sense that no three of them are met by a common line, then it is shown by Cappell et al. (1990) that the combinatorial complexity of S^* is $O(n^2)$. This bound, in this restricted case, is slightly better than the bound derived above. The result of Cappell et al. can also be extended to higher dimensions.

(iii) An open problem is to extend Theorem 8.15 to bound the complexity of the space of common hyperplane transversals of n compact convex sets in $\mathbb{R}^d$. This space, and its combinatorial complexity, is defined in a complete analogy to the two- and three-dimensional cases. However, no appropriate generalization of Theorem 7.10 is known in higher dimensions.

8.3 Decomposing arrangements of surfaces

Let $\Gamma = \{\gamma_1, \gamma_2, \dots, \gamma_n\}$ be a collection of surfaces in $\mathbb{R}^d$. We assume that each γ_i is a real algebraic surface $V(f_i) \equiv \{f_i = 0\}$ for some polynomial f_i, and that the maximum degree of the f_i's is some (relatively small) constant b. We wish to decompose $\mathcal{A}(\Gamma)$ into (relatively open) *elementary* cells of dimensions ranging from 0 to d. By an elementary cell we mean a connected real semialgebraic set that has a constant description complexity (that is, defined in terms of a constant number of polynomial equalities and inequalities of constant maximum degree). (See Appendix 7.2 for the definition of semialgebraic sets and of related concepts.) More formally, we want to decompose $\mathbb{R}^d$ into cells of constant description complexity so that each f_i has constant sign (positive, zero, or negative) over each cell. It is well-known that $\mathcal{A}(\Gamma)$ has a maximum of $\Theta(n^d)$ d-dimensional cells (see, e.g., Warren (1968) or Pollack and Roy (1993)), so the number of elementary cells has to be $\Omega(n^d)$. Each f_i has constant sign within each cell c of $\mathcal{A}(\Gamma)$, but c can have arbitrarily large

---

[1]Actually, ϕ_S and ψ_S may only be piecewise-algebraic, so we may have to replace them by a constant number of appropriate partially defined algebraic functions, which do satisfy Assumptions 7.1, and apply Theorem 7.14 to the resulting new collection of functions.

complexity. For example, even for a collection of n hyperplanes (that is, where each f_i is a linear function), the combinatorial complexity of a cell can be as large as $\Omega(n^{\lfloor d/2 \rfloor})$. Therefore, we cannot use the cells of $\mathcal{A}(\Gamma)$ themselves as elementary cells. The goal is to construct a cell decomposition of $\mathcal{A}(\Gamma)$ of the desired form with a small number of elementary cells.

Before describing the decomposition scheme, let us give some motivation for the need for such a decomposition. A major application is *point location* in arrangements of surfaces. That is, we wish to preprocess $\mathcal{A}(\Gamma)$ into a data structure so that, for a query point p, we can efficiently determine whether p lies on any surface of Γ. In several applications, more information than a mere 'yes/no' answer is required. For example, if p lies on a surface, then one may want to return an index i such that $p \in \gamma_i$. Similarly if p does not lie on any surface of Γ, that is, it lies in some d-dimensional cell τ of $\mathcal{A}(\Gamma)$, one may want to return some information related to τ, for example, a precomputed representative point of τ, or the surface lying immediately above p in the x_d-direction, or the number of surfaces γ_i such that $f_i(p) > 0$, etc. The generalized point location problem is quite powerful and several geometric problems can be reduced to it. It is beyond the scope of this book to describe these applications; interested readers can refer to Chazelle and Sharir (1990), Chazelle et al. (1993), Agarwal, Pellegrini, and Sharir (1993), and Agarwal, Sharir, and Toledo (1994) for some of the applications.

A natural approach for solving the above point location problem is to use a divide-and-conquer paradigm. The main idea is as follows: If $|\Gamma|$ is bounded by some fixed constant, simply store the set Γ. Otherwise, decompose $\mathbb{R}^d$ into elementary cells so that each cell intersects at most $|\Gamma|/r$ surfaces of Γ, where r is some sufficiently large constant parameter. At each cell c, store auxiliary information (depending on the specific problem that we wish to solve) for surfaces that do not intersect c, and recursively construct the data structure for surfaces that intersect c. The resulting structure is a tree data structure with $O(\log n)$ height. A point location query is answered by following a path of the tree in a top-down fashion starting from the root; see Section 8.3.3 for details.

The size of the data structure depends on the number of cells (as a function of r) into which $\mathbb{R}^d$ has to be decomposed. We apply the theory of ε-nets (Haussler and Welzl (1987) and Clarkson (1987b); see Appendix 7.2 for a brief overview), which has been used in geometry quite extensively in the last few years. This theory implies that we can choose a $1/r$-net $R \subseteq \Gamma$ of size $ar \log r$ (for some suitable constant a that depends on d and on the maximum surface degree b), so that, if we decompose $\mathcal{A}(R)$ into elementary cells, then each cell intersects at most $|\Gamma|/r$ surfaces of Γ. (This property crucially depends on the cells having constant description complexity; as mentioned in Appendix 7.2, the property just stated may fail to hold without this assumption.) Thus the point-location problem reduces to the problem of decomposing an arrangement of surfaces into a small number of elementary cells.

In the plane, the vertical decomposition technique discussed in Chapter 6 gives a decomposition of $\mathcal{A}(\Gamma)$ into $O(n^2)$ elementary cells. The problem becomes much harder for $d \geq 3$. The so-called *cylindrical algebraic decomposition*, due to Collins (1975), yields a decomposition of $\mathcal{A}(\Gamma)$ into $(bn)^{2^{O(d)}}$ elementary cells, but this bound is quite far from the known lower bound of $\Omega(n^d)$. Here we will describe a scheme that decomposes $\mathcal{A}(\Gamma)$ into roughly n^{2d-3} elementary cells. Since the general scheme is quite technical, we will first describe it in detail for arrangements of spheres in $\mathbb{R}^3$, and then briefly sketch how to extend it to general surfaces and to higher dimensions. A more comprehensive description of the method is given by Chazelle et al. (1989a, 1991).

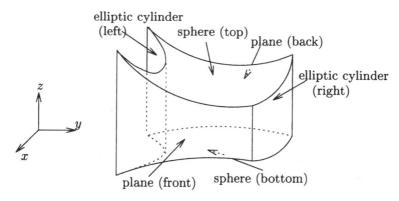

FIGURE 8.10. An elementary cell in an arrangement of spheres.

8.3.1 Decomposing arrangements of spheres

Let Γ be a collection of n spheres in $\mathbb{R}^3$. The arrangement $\mathcal{A}(\Gamma)$ has $O(n^3)$ vertices, edges, faces, and (three-dimensional) cells. We want to decompose $\mathcal{A}(\Gamma)$ into a roughly cubic number of elementary cells. The scheme described below constructs elementary cells whose combinatorial structure is similar to that of a box, that is, it has six sides—front, back, top, bottom, left, and right; see Figure 8.10. The front and back faces are portions of planes normal to the x-axis. The top and bottom faces lie on two hemispheres[2] of Γ, and the left and right faces are portions of vertical elliptic cylinders.[3] See Figure 8.10

---

[2]The points of vertical tangencies on a sphere (that is, the points at which the normal vectors lie parallel to the xy-plane) form a great circle, called the *equator*, which partitions the sphere into two *hemispheres*, one lying above and the other lying below the equator.

[3]By this we mean a cylinder whose axis is parallel to the z-axis and whose intersection with the xy-plane is an ellipse. The tangent planes normal to the x-axis meet the cylinder in two lines that partition it into its left and right portions.

for an example. Degenerate cells, where some of the faces are empty or unbounded, are also allowed. We now describe the decomposition scheme.

Step I. For each sphere γ_i, we draw a maximal vertical (relatively) open segment, which does not meet any other sphere, from each point of the equator of γ_i. The union of all line segments drawn from a single equator forms a portion of a vertical circular cylinder.

After the first step, the intersection of each cell with any vertical line is a single connected segment.

Step II. For each pair γ_i, γ_j of spheres, for $1 \leq i < j \leq n$, do the following: Draw a maximal vertical line segment from each point p on the intersection circle $\delta_{ij} = \gamma_i \cap \gamma_j$, which avoids all spheres except that it intersects γ_i and γ_j at p. Since the vertical projection of a circle in $\mathbb{R}^3$ is an ellipse, the union of all segments drawn from a single intersection circle is a portion of a vertical elliptic cylinder.

After this step, each cell has a unique top face and a unique bottom face, each lying in a hemisphere. (Step I ensures that the top and bottom faces do not intersect the equator of any sphere.) However, a cell may still have a large number of vertical faces.

The fact that the intersection of each vertical line with a cell is a single connected interval implies that the projection of a cell onto the xy-plane is equal to the projection of its top (or bottom) face, that is, it is a connected (but not necessarily simply connected) region, whose edges are portions of circles and ellipses.

Step III. Consider the vertical projection τ^* of a cell τ onto the xy-plane. A point $p = (a, b)$ of an edge of τ^* is called x-extreme if the circle or ellipse containing the edge is contained in one of the (closed) half-planes bounded by the line $x = a$.

Draw a maximal line segment e parallel to the y-axis from each x-extreme point, so that e lies in τ^* (see Figure 8.11). Erect a vertical wall on e that lies within τ, that is, for each point $q \in e$, draw the vertical segment that is the intersection of τ with the vertical line passing through q.

After Step III, each cell has unique top, bottom, front, and back faces.

Step IV. Finally, for each vertex v of τ^*, draw from v a maximal segment parallel to the y-axis within τ^* (see Figure 8.11). Again, erect a vertical wall within τ from each such segment.

After this step, each cell has unique top, bottom, front, back, left, and right faces. Before analyzing the number of cells in the above decomposition, let us make a few remarks.

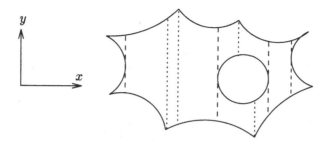

FIGURE 8.11. The xy-projection of a cell after Step II. Dashed edges are added in Step III and dotted edges are added in Step IV.

Remark 8.17 (i) The resulting decomposition is not a cell complex, because the boundaries of elementary cells may not glue together properly. For example, a two-dimensional face of one cell may contain an edge or a vertex of another adjacent cell.

(ii) The scheme does not produce a partition of the entire three-dimensional space, because we have assumed cells to be open. If we allow cells to overlap, we can either take the closure of each cell, or include lower-dimensional faces of each cell in the decomposition. However, if we want to ensure that cells remain pairwise disjoint, we cannot simply include these faces of all the cells in our decomposition, since the faces are not always glued properly. We omit here the details on the way in which this issue can be handled; they can be found in Chazelle et al. (1989a, 1991).

8.3.2 Analyzing the number of elementary cells

Initially, $\mathcal{A}(\Gamma)$ has $O(n^3)$ cells. We will count the number of new cells created in each of the four steps of the above decomposition scheme. Step I can be regarded as a special case of Step II, so we will bound the number of new cells created in both steps simultaneously. Step III creates four new cells for each equator or circle δ_{ij}, because the projection of each equator and circle (which is either a circle or an ellipse) has two x-extreme points; we draw a vertical segment from both of them in the positive y-direction and another in the negative y-direction; and a vertical wall is raised from each of the four line segments. Since there are $\binom{n}{2} + n$ such circles and ellipses, Step III creates at most $O(n^2)$ new cells. Finally, Step IV gives rise to two vertical walls for each vertical edge created in Steps I and II and for each original vertex of the arrangement, so the number of such walls is proportional to the number of these vertical edges plus $O(n^3)$.

Hence, we only have to bound the number of vertical edges created in

Steps I and II. A vertical edge is an intersection of two vertical walls. Consider a circle $\delta = \gamma_1 \cap \gamma_2$ and the vertical cylinder C_δ erected on δ (the case where δ is the equator of a sphere is handled in essentially the same manner). For $i \geq 3$, define $\omega_i = \gamma_i \cap C_\delta$. Assuming that the spheres are in general position, ω_i is either a simple closed curve or consists of two simple closed curves (see Figure 8.12).

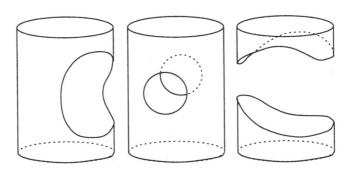

FIGURE 8.12. Different intersection patterns of a sphere and a vertical elliptic cylinder.

It is easily verified that a vertical edge is created in C_δ, whenever the intersection of two spheres, or the equator of a sphere, meets C_δ (that is, at an intersection point of two ω_i's, or at a point of vertical tangency along some ω_i) at a point that is *vertically visible*[4] from δ, or whenever a sphere γ_i intersects δ (that is, at an intersection point of ω_i and δ).

Lemma 8.18 *If $\delta \not\subset \omega_i$, then, for $3 \leq i \leq n$, ω_i intersects δ in at most two points.*

Proof. Since $\delta = \gamma_1 \cap \gamma_2$ and $\omega_i \subseteq \gamma_i$, every point of $\delta \cap \omega_i$ is also in $\gamma_1 \cap \gamma_2 \cap \gamma_i$. Unless the three spheres intersect in a common circle, the intersection consists of at most two points. □

Lemma 8.19 *If $\gamma_i \neq \gamma_j$ and the intersection circle $\gamma_i \cap \gamma_j \not\subseteq C_\delta$, then ω_i intersects ω_j in at most four points.*

Proof. We have $\omega_i \cap \omega_j \subseteq \gamma_i \cap \gamma_j$, which is a circle in $\mathbb{R}^3$. The vertical projection of $\gamma_i \cap \gamma_j$ onto the xy-plane is an ellipse and so is the intersection of C_δ with the xy-plane. Unless the two ellipses are equal, they intersect in at most four points. Those points are the projections of the points of $\omega_i \cap \omega_j$. □

---

[4]Two points are vertically visible from each other if the line segment connecting them is vertical and its relative interior meets no sphere of Γ.

Since the equator of γ_i intersects C_δ in at most four points (a circle and an ellipse in the plane intersect in at most four points), ω_i has at most four points of vertical tangency. We remove from ω_i these points of vertical tangency and the intersection points of ω_i and δ. This partitions ω_i into at most six connected components (arcs), which satisfy the following properties:

(i) each arc intersects any vertical line in C_δ in at most one point;

(ii) each arc lies either fully above δ or fully below δ; and

(iii) any two arcs intersect in at most four points.

By (i), for each arc ξ we can define a partially defined function $f_\xi : \delta \to \mathbb{R}$ as follows. For a point $p \in \delta$, let q be the intersection point of ξ and the vertical line passing through p. If q is not defined, then f_ξ is also not defined. Otherwise, $f_\xi(p) = z(q) - z(p)$, where $z(\cdot)$ is the z-coordinate of a point in $\mathbb{R}^3$. By property (ii), f_ξ is either always positive, or always negative. Let F^+ be the set of functions with positive values, and let F^- be the set of functions with negative values. By construction, each vertical edge created in Step I or Step II corresponds to a breakpoint in the lower envelope of F^+ or in the upper envelope of F^-. Since $|F^+| + |F^-| \leq 6n$, and the graphs of any pair of functions intersect in at most four points, the total number of breakpoints is $O(\lambda_6(n))$. Repeating the same argument for all pairs of spheres and for the equators of all spheres, we obtain that Steps I and II increase the number of cells by at most $O(n^2 \lambda_6(n))$. Since the total number of cells in the overall decomposition is proportional to $O(n^3)$ plus the number of cells created in Steps I and II, we can conclude:

Theorem 8.20 *An arrangement Γ of n spheres in $\mathbb{R}^3$ can be decomposed into $O(n^3 2^{O(\alpha^2(n))})$ elementary cells.*

The above scheme can be extended to general algebraic surfaces of constant maximum degree in $\mathbb{R}^3$, except that the technical details of the decomposition scheme become more complicated. Steps III and IV are performed on planar regions, and are trivial to extend to the general case. Steps I and II are technically more challenging to extend. In Step I, for each surface γ_i one has to draw a maximal vertical segment from each singular point on γ_i, for example, points of vertical tangency, self-intersections, cusps, etc.; see also Section 7.3.1. If the maximum degree of a surface in Γ is b, then all singular points of γ_i lie on an algebraic curve of degree at most b^2. Similarly, the intersection curve δ_{ij} of any pair of surfaces, γ_i, γ_j, of Γ is an algebraic curve of degree at most b^2. These properties, which we have already exploited in Chapter 7, follow from standard algebraic elimination theory, which is based on Sylvester's resultants and subresultants; see van der Waerden (1970) and also Chazelle et al. (1989a, 1991). These observations imply that if we define the curves δ and ω_i in analogy with the definitions given above, then any pair of curves, ω_i and ω_j, intersect in at most $s = O(b^4)$ points. Hence, following the same argument as above, the number of cells created can easily be shown to be $O(n^2 \lambda_{s+2}(n))$.

Chazelle et al. (1989a, 1991) also describe a decomposition scheme for arrangements of n algebraic surfaces (of constant maximal degree) in $\mathbb{R}^d$, for any $d > 3$. Their construction is inductive in d, and uses the three-dimensional decomposition scheme described above as the basis of the induction. Since their technique uses Davenport–Schinzel sequences only in the three-dimensional case (in the manner outlined above), we will review it here only briefly.

The method fixes a pair of surfaces, $\gamma_i, \gamma_j \in \Gamma$, and considers the collection Γ_{ij} of the vertical projections (on the hyperplane $x_d = 0$) of the surfaces $\gamma_i \cap \gamma_k$ (for $k \neq i$), $\gamma_j \cap \gamma_k$ (for $k \neq j$), and γ_k^s (for all k), where γ_k^s is the locus of singular points on γ_k. Thus $|\Gamma_{ij}| \leq 3n$. We obtain, recursively, an elementary cell decomposition of the arrangement of Γ_{ij} in $\mathbb{R}^{d-1}$. For each cell τ of that decomposition, we consider the vertical cylinder $C_\tau = \tau \times \mathbb{R}$ and intersect it with γ_i and γ_j. It is easily seen that this divides C_τ into a constant number of relatively open cells. Each of these cells has the property that every vertical line cuts the cell in a connected segment (which might be empty or a singleton), each of whose endpoints lies on a fixed surface (γ_i or γ_j). We call each of the resulting cells an *elementary cell*—it is 'elementary' in the x_d-direction, and its vertical projection τ is elementary by recursion. Now we examine every resulting elementary cell: if it is not intersected by any surface $\gamma_k \neq \gamma_i, \gamma_j$ and if it has not already been constructed earlier, we add it to an output collection of elementary cells; otherwise we discard it. We repeat this procedure to each pair of surfaces γ_i, γ_j, and the overall output list yields the desired elementary cell decomposition of $\mathcal{A}(\Gamma)$, as is shown in Chazelle et al. (1989a, 1991). A simple inductive argument shows that the number of cells in such a decomposition grows by a factor of $O(n^2)$ for each added dimension, which leads to a bound of $O(n^{2d-3}\beta(n))$ on the number of cells; here $\beta(n)$ is $\lambda_s(n)/n$, where s depends on the degree of the curves that arise when the recursion winds down to $d = 3$. Each recursive step of the algorithm roughly squares the degree of the resulting surfaces, and hence s is bounded by a doubly exponential function of d. (It is therefore important to emphasize that this analysis is useful only if we regard d, as well as the maximum degree of the surfaces in Γ, to be constant; otherwise the factor $\beta(n)$ is rather large.)

We note that each elementary cell is defined in terms of at most $2d$ surfaces of Γ. In fact, an alternative way to obtain the same decomposition is as follows. For each subset $\Gamma_0 \subseteq \Gamma$ of $2d$ surfaces, construct an elementary cell decomposition of $\mathcal{A}(\Gamma_0)$, using, for example, the technique just described, and collect all elementary cells of $\mathcal{A}(\Gamma_0)$ that are not crossed by any surface of Γ. The resulting collection of cells, over all subsets Γ_0 of Γ as above, yields the same elementary cell decomposition of $\mathcal{A}(\Gamma)$ obtained by the above recursive process, a fact that follows from the analysis of Chazelle et al. (1989a, 1991). Since the number of elementary cells of each $\mathcal{A}(\Gamma_0)$ is bounded by a constant (depending on b and d), it follows that the complexity of the elementary cell decomposition of $\mathcal{A}(\Gamma)$ is $O(n^{2d})$; the more refined argument given above thus demonstrates the improvement that can be achieved by using Davenport–Schinzel sequences in the analysis of the decomposition in $\mathbb{R}^3$.

We summarize the result in the following theorem:

Theorem 8.21 *Given a set Γ of n real algebraic surfaces in $\mathbb{R}^d$, of constant maximum degree b, the arrangement $\mathcal{A}(\Gamma)$ can be decomposed into $O(n^{2d-3}\beta(n))$ relatively open elementary cells, each defined by at most $2d$ surfaces of Γ; here $\beta(n) = \lambda_s(n)/n$, where s is some constant depending on b and d.*

Remark 8.22 (i) A challenging open problem is whether the bound on the number of elementary cells can be improved. The only lower bound we are aware of is the trivial bound $\Omega(n^d)$. A recent modest progress on this problem, by Guibas et al. (1993), shows that the vertical decomposition scheme defined above, when applied to an arrangement of n hyperplanes in $\mathbb{R}^4$, yields only $O(n^4 \log n)$ elementary cells. Of course, for arrangement of hyperplanes, there exist better decomposition schemes, like the triangulation described in Section 7.2. Another interesting open problem is whether $\mathcal{A}(\Gamma)$ can be decomposed into $n^{d^{O(1)}}$ elementary cells that form a cell complex. The cylindrical algebraic decomposition of Collins (1975) produces a cell complex, but the number of elementary cells created is about $n^{2^{O(d)}}$.

(ii) Many applications require a sharp bound on the number of cells in the vertical decomposition of a portion of the arrangement. For example, a sharp bound on the size of the vertical decomposition of the region lying below the lower envelope of a set of functions (this decomposition is equivalent to a vertical decomposition of the minimization diagram) will yield an efficient algorithm for computing their minimization diagram, and the same holds for the vertical decomposition of a single cell (or of a set of marked cells) in an arrangement of surfaces; see Section 7.2.2 and Remark 7.48. For $d \geq 3$, it is not known whether the number of cells in the vertical decomposition of the minimization diagram of a set $\mathcal{F}$ of d-variate functions, satisfying Assumptions 7.2, is $O(n^{d+\varepsilon})$. Sharir (1994b) has shown that if $\mathcal{F}$ is a collection of n partially defined trivariate functions of constant maximum degree, with the additional property that the intersection surface $f(x, y, z) = f'(x, y, z)$, for any $f, f' \in \mathcal{F}$, is xy-monotone, then the complexity of the vertical decomposition of the minimization diagram of $\mathcal{F}$ is $O(n^{3+\varepsilon})$, for any $\varepsilon > 0$.

8.3.3 Point location among surfaces

We now show how the above analysis can be applied to solve the point location problem mentioned at the beginning of the section. Let Γ be a collection of n (real) algebraic surfaces in $\mathbb{R}^d$; that is, each $\gamma_i \in \Gamma$ is the zero set $f_i = 0$

of some real polynomial f_i. We assume that the degree of each f_i is at most some constant integer b. The goal is to preprocess Γ for efficient *point location queries*. For the sake of definiteness, we assume that, for a query point x, we want to count the number of surfaces γ_i for which $f_i(x) > 0$. We give here an overview of the technique, and omit most of the technical details, which can be found in Chazelle and Sharir (1990) and in Chazelle et al. (1989a, 1991).

We construct a tree data structure T, each of whose nodes is associated with a 'canonical' subset of surfaces. The root u is associated with the whole set Γ. Let $\Psi(d, t)$ denote the set of all semialgebraic sets obtained by a boolean combination of at most $2d$ $(d-1)$-variate polynomial equalities and inequalities, each of degree at most t, where $t = t(b, d)$ is the maximum degree of surfaces defining the cells in the vertical decomposition in an arrangement of surfaces in $\mathbb{R}^d$ of maximum degree b. Consider the range space

$$\mathcal{F}_{d,t} = (\Gamma, \ \{\{\gamma \in \Gamma \mid \gamma \text{ intersects } \tau\} \mid \tau \in \Psi(d, t)\}).$$

Let r be some sufficiently large constant. By Corollary 7.72 and Theorem 7.64, we can compute a $1/r$-net $R \subseteq \Gamma$ of size $O(r \log r)$ for $\mathcal{F}_{d,t}$ in $O(n)$ time. We decompose the arrangement of R into $k = O((r \log r)^{2d-3}\beta(r))$ elementary cells, $\tau_1, \ldots, \tau_k$, as described above; each cell τ_i is defined by at most $2d$ surfaces. For each τ_i, determine the set of surfaces in Γ that intersect τ_i. Since τ_i does not intersect any surface of R, it intersects at most n/r surfaces of Γ. We create k children, $v_1, \ldots, v_k$, of u, and associate with v_i the cell τ_i and the surfaces intersecting τ_i. If a surface γ_j does not intersect τ_i, then either $f_j(x) > 0$ for all $x \in \tau_i$, or $f_j(x) < 0$ for all $x \in \tau_i$. We count the number $\mu(v_i)$ of surfaces of the former type, and store it at the node v_i of T. Next, for each cell τ_i, we recursively construct a similar structure on the subset of surfaces intersecting τ_i. The recursion stops when the number of surfaces within a cell falls below some prespecified constant. The resulting tree has depth $O(\log n)$ and the degree of each node is $O((r \log r)^{2d-3}\beta(r))$.

Let x be a query point. We trace a path in T in a top-down fashion, starting from the root. We maintain a global count, which, at the end of the query procedure, gives us the number of surfaces satisfying $f_i(x) > 0$. Initially, the count is set to zero. At each visited node v, if v is a leaf then we explicitly compare x with each surface γ_i associated with v, count the number of these surfaces for which $f_i(x) > 0$, add this number to the global count, and stop. Otherwise, we add $\mu(v)$ to the global count and find (by brute force) the child w_i of v such that τ_i contains x. We descend to w_i and recursively search in the subtree rooted at w_i. Since $r = O(1)$, the time spent at each node is bounded by a constant. The overall query time is thus $O(\log n)$.

Let $S(n)$ be the maximum storage required by the data structure; then $S(n)$ satisfies the following recurrence:

$$S(n) \leq \begin{cases} c & \text{for } n \leq n_0, \\ c_1(r \log r)^{2d-3}\beta(r) \cdot S\left(\frac{n}{r}\right) + c_2(r \log r)^{2d-3}\beta(r) & \text{for } n > n_0, \end{cases}$$

where n_0, c, c_1, c_2 are appropriate constants. We claim that the solution of the above recurrence is $An^{2d-3+\varepsilon}$, for any $\varepsilon > 0$ and for an appropriate constant A that depends on ε. Indeed, the claim is obviously true for $n \leq n_0$ if A is sufficiently large. For larger values of n we have, using induction,

$$
\begin{aligned}
S(n) &\leq c_1(r \log r)^{2d-3} \beta(r) A \left(\frac{n}{r}\right)^{2d-3+\varepsilon} + c_2(r \log r)^{2d-3} \beta(r) \\
&\leq An^{2d-3+\varepsilon} \left(\frac{c_1(\log r)^{2d-3} \beta(r)}{r^\varepsilon} + \frac{c_2(r \log r)^{2d-3} \beta(r)}{An_0^{2d-3+\varepsilon}} \right) \\
&\leq An^{2d-3+\varepsilon},
\end{aligned}
$$

provided that r and A are chosen sufficiently large. Since the decomposition of $\mathcal{A}(R)$ can be computed in time $r^{O(1)}$, a similar analysis shows that the preprocessing time is also $O(n^{2d-3+\varepsilon})$.

Theorem 8.23 *Given a collection Γ of n (real) algebraic surfaces of constant maximum degree b in $\mathbb{R}^d$, one can preprocess it, in time $O(n^{2d-3+\varepsilon})$, for any $\varepsilon > 0$, into a data structure of size $O(n^{2d-3+\varepsilon})$, so that a point location query in $\mathcal{A}(\Gamma)$ can be answered in time $O(\log n)$. The constants of proportionality depend on ε, d, and b.*

Remark 8.24 (i) The technique just presented has numerous applications to other problems in computational geometry, including counting intersection points among a collection of circular arcs, finding the longest segment that can be placed inside a simple polygon, and finding the width of a set of points in $\mathbb{R}^3$. The latter application is presented in more detail in Section 8.5. For additional details concerning these and other related problems, see Chazelle et al. (1989a, 1991), Agarwal, Sharir, and Toledo (1994), Agarwal, Aronov, and Sharir (1994), Chazelle et al. (1993), and Sharir (1994b).

(ii) If Γ is a set of n hyperplanes in $\mathbb{R}^d$, then a point location query in $\mathcal{A}(\Gamma)$ can be answered in time $O(\log n)$ using only $O(n^d / \log^{d-1} n)$ storage and preprocessing time; see Chazelle and Friedman (1994) and Matoušek (1993b).

8.4 Visibility problems for polyhedral terrains

In this section we consider various visibility problems related to polyhedral terrains. A *polyhedral terrain* is a piecewise linear surface in $\mathbb{R}^3$ having exactly one intersection point with every vertical line, that is, it is the graph of a piecewise linear function defined over the entire xy-plane. Let Σ be such a terrain with n edges. The xy-projection of Σ is a planar map with n edges, so Σ has $O(n)$ vertices and faces as well. Let a be a fixed point, which, without loss of generality, we assume to be the origin. A point p of Σ is *visible* from a

if the relative interior of the segment ap does not intersect Σ. In other words, p is the first point on Σ hit by the ray emanating from a toward p. Each ray r emanating from a can be represented by a point $\bar{r} = (\theta, \phi)$ on the unit sphere $\mathbb{S}^2$, where ϕ is the angle between r and the positive z-direction (the *azimuth* of r), and θ is the horizontal planar orientation of the vertical projection of r (simply referred to as the *orientation* of r). The *visibility map* of Σ from a, denoted $M(a)$, is the decomposition of $\mathbb{S}^2$ into maximal connected regions so that, for each region R and for all points $\bar{r} \in R$, either the first intersection point of the corresponding rays r and Σ lie in the same face of Σ (which depends on R), or none of these rays meet Σ. $M(a)$ is called the *perspective view* of Σ from a. Intuitively, $M(a)$ represents the portion of Σ visible from a. For a point $p \in \mathbb{R}^3$, the intersection point of $\mathbb{S}^2$ and the ray emanating from a in direction $\vec{ap}$ is called the *(spherical) projection* of p. Each edge of $M(a)$ is a portion of the projection of an edge in Σ, and each vertex of $M(a)$ is either the projection of a vertex of Σ or the intersection point of the projections of two edges in Σ. If a lies at infinity, then all rays emanating from a are parallel. In this case the view of Σ, called the *orthographic view* of Σ in direction $b = -a$, is defined as follows. Let Π be a plane at infinity orthogonal to the direction b. The orthographic view of Σ in direction b is the decomposition of Π into maximal regions so that the rays emerging in direction b from all points in such a region hit the same face of Σ, or none of them hit Σ.

We study various problems related to the visibility map of Σ. The first problem that we consider is the following: Assuming a to be fixed, preprocess Σ into a data structure so that the first intersection point of Σ and a query ray emanating from a can be determined efficiently, that is, the point of Σ visible from a in a query direction can be computed efficiently.

As the view point a varies, the projection of each edge and vertex of Σ varies continuously with a. Therefore, the combinatorial structure of the visibility map $M(a)$ remains the same as a moves slightly (that is, the planar graphs induced by $M(a')$ are isomorphic to the graph induced by $M(a)$, for all points a' in a sufficiently small neighborhood of a), except at certain critical locations of a. A natural problem that arises is to obtain a bound on the number of distinct combinatorial structures that the visibility map of Σ can assume as a varies. We prove upper bounds on this quantity for the cases when the view point moves along a vertical line, when the view point moves along a sphere at infinity, and when the view point varies over the entire $\mathbb{R}^3$. Davenport–Schinzel sequences and envelopes in higher dimensions play a crucial role in the solution of all these problems.

8.4.1   View from a fixed point

Let Σ and a be as defined above. We wish to preprocess them into a data structure that supports fast *ray-shooting queries* from a, where each query seeks the first intersection (if any) with Σ of a ray emerging from a in some specified direction. An obvious approach is to compute the visibility map $M(a)$ and preprocess it for planar (or, rather, spherical) point-location queries. Unfortunately, $M(a)$ may have $\Omega(n^2)$ features in the worst case; see Figure 8.13 for an example. Our goal is thus to obtain an implicit and more efficient representation of $M(a)$. In this section we present an algorithm requiring $O(n\alpha(n)\log n)$ preprocessing time and storage, which supports $O(\log n)$ time ray-shooting queries. Note that, if the viewing point is at $z = +\infty$, then $M(a)$ is the vertical projection of the terrain, so it has linear complexity, and our ray-shooting problem degenerates to a point location in that map, for which optimal solutions are well-known (e.g., the one of Edelsbrunner, Guibas, and Stolfi (1986), or of Sarnak and Tarjan (1986)).

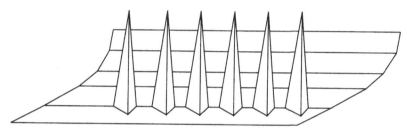

FIGURE 8.13. A polyhedral terrain whose visibility map, as shown, has quadratic complexity.

This result has potential applications to computer graphics and can be regarded as a special case of the hidden surface removal problem (see de Berg (1993) and Mulmuley (1993)). It can be used to provide compact representation of an image of a polyhedral terrain Σ as viewed from some point, from which the actual pixel-by-pixel image can be quickly generated, or the portion of Σ appearing at certain "query pixels" can be determined efficiently without having to generate the entire image.

Our solution proceeds as follows. For any geometric object u in $\mathbb{R}^3$, denote by $u^\star$ its vertical projection onto the xy-plane. The projection $\Sigma^\star$ of Σ can be regarded as a planar map whose vertices, edges, and faces are projections of corresponding vertices, edges, and faces of Σ. We define a partial order on the edges of $\Sigma^\star$ so that, for any pair u, v of edges of $\Sigma^\star$, $u < v$ if there exists a (horizontal) ray emerging from $a^\star$ that intersects both u and v such that its intersection with u is nearer to $a^\star$ than its intersection with v; see Figure 8.14 (i). To make this into a partial order, we need to ensure that there is some orientation ($\theta = 0$, say) that no edge crosses; this is easily achieved by replacing each edge that does cross $\theta = 0$ with its two subsegments clockwise and counterclockwise from $\theta = 0$. (If we do not have this property there could be a circular sequence of edges, $e_1, e_2, \ldots, e_k$, such that $e_i < e_{i+1}$, for $1 \le i < k$, and $e_k < e_1$; see Figure 8.14 (ii); with this extra property, it is easy to check that $<$ is indeed a partial order.) Moreover, it is easy to calculate this partial order by a standard ray-sweeping procedure in time $O(n \log n)$, and to complete this order into a total linear order in additional $O(n)$ time, using a well-known topological sorting procedure (see, e.g., Coreman, Leiserson, and Rivest (1990)). Let this linear order be $\mathcal{E} = \langle e_1 < e_2 < \cdots < e_n \rangle$.

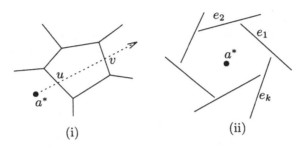

FIGURE 8.14. (i) Partial order on the projected terrain edges; (ii) a possible cycle.

Next, for each edge e_i, we define a partial function $h_i : \mathbb{S} \to [0, 2\pi)$ as follows (here $\mathbb{S}$ is the unit circle of orientations). For each $\theta \in \mathbb{S}$, if the ray r_θ^* in the xy-plane emanating from a^* in direction θ does not intersect e_i^*, then $h_i(\theta)$ is undefined. Otherwise, let p^* be the intersection point of r_θ^* and e_i^*. We define $h_i(\theta)$ to be the azimuth angle of the ray emanating from a and passing through p, where $p \in e_i$ is the point whose projection is p^*. For each subset $E \subseteq \mathcal{E}$, we define

$$h_E(\theta) = \min_{e_i \in E} h_i(\theta)$$

to be the lower envelope of the h_i's. We call the graph of h_E the *upper rim* of E. Intuitively, the upper rim of E corresponds to the 'skyline' of E seen from a; see Figure 8.15. Clearly, the upper rim consists of a finite number of smooth connected portions, such that for each such portion γ, all the rays $r_\theta = (\theta, h_E(\theta))$ in γ pass through the same edge e_γ of E. Here we use the convention that if, in such a smooth portion, all rays emanating from a pass through two segments, say e, e', which can happen if e, e', and a are coplanar, then we take e_γ to be the further of these two segments. The endpoints of these smooth portions of h_E are at orientations θ at which either r_θ passes through an endpoint of some edge of E, or r_θ passes simultaneously through two segments of E. We will also use the term "upper rim" to refer to the (not necessarily connected) locus of points on the edges of E touched by the rays r_θ, for $\theta \in \mathbb{S}$.

Lemma 8.25 *Let $E = \{e_1, e_2, \ldots, e_n\}$ be a collection of n (nonintersecting) segments in $\mathbb{R}^3$. Then the upper rim of E has $O(n\alpha(n))$ breakpoints, and this bound is tight in the worst case, and can actually be realized by a collection of edges of some polyhedral terrain.*

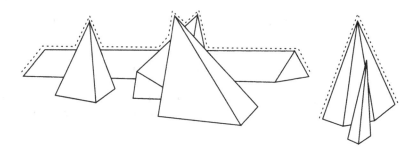

FIGURE 8.15. Upper rim.

Proof. Let h_i be the functions defined above. Then two functions h_i, h_j $(i \neq j)$ intersect in at most one point or in a single connected interval. Indeed, if they intersect at two points, say at orientations θ_1 and θ_2, then the rays $r_{\theta_1} = (\theta_1, h_i(\theta_1))$ and $r_{\theta_2} = (\theta_2, h_i(\theta_2))$ pass through both e_i and e_j. This implies that e_i, e_j, and a are coplanar, in which case $h_i(\theta) = h_j(\theta)$ for all θ between θ_1 and θ_2. It follows that if we form the sequence of edges e_γ that represent the smooth portions of h_E, as defined above, we obtain a $DS(n, 3)$-sequence. The lemma now follows from Corollary 2.16.

A lower bound of $\Omega(n\alpha(n))$ on the worst-case complexity of the upper rim of n segments follows from the constructions of Chapter 4. Indeed, let $e_1, \ldots, e_n$ be n segments in the plane whose upper envelope consists of $\Omega(n\alpha(n))$ sub-segments. Assume that all these segments are drawn in the upper half of the xz-plane. We can construct from these segments a polyhedral terrain as follows. Shift each segment e_i in the y-direction to the plane $y = i$, and associate with each shifted segment $\hat{e}_i$ a sharp wedge having $\hat{e}_i$ as its upper edge. The terrain Σ is then defined as the upper envelope of all these wedges and of the xy-plane. Plainly, Σ has $O(n)$ faces. If we view Σ from a point a lying on the y-axis sufficiently far away from these segments, then it is easily checked that the complexity of the resulting upper rim (of the entire collection of edges of Σ) is also $\Omega(n\alpha(n))$. $\qquad\square$

We now describe the overall data structure. Let T be a minimum-height binary search tree whose i-th leftmost leaf is associated with $e_i \in \mathcal{E}$. Each internal node v of T is associated with the subset $\mathcal{E}_v$ of edges stored at the leaves of the subtree rooted at v; the root is associated with the entire set $\mathcal{E}$. At each internal node v of T, we compute the upper rim of the edges associated with its left child. We store the orientations of breakpoints of this upper rim in a list L_v, stored in counterclockwise order, and we also store, for each breakpoint of the rim, the edge that appears on the rim on its counterclockwise side. Lemma 8.25 implies that each node v of T, associated with n_v edges, requires $O(n_v \alpha(n_v))$ storage. Since an edge $e \in \mathcal{E}$ is associated with only one node at each level of T, the total storage required is $O(n\alpha(n)\log n)$. The upper rim at v can be computed in $O(n_v \log n_v)$ time, using the algorithm described in Section 6.2 (see Theorem 6.5), which implies an overall $O(n\log^2 n)$ preprocessing time. However, if we compute the upper rims of the full set $\mathcal{E}_v$ at all the nodes v of T in a bottom-up fashion, then the upper rim at a node v can be computed in $O(n_v \alpha(n_v))$ time by merging the upper rims computed at its children (see Section 6.2). Thus the overall preprocessing time now becomes $O(n\alpha(n)\log n)$. Each list L_v can be directly obtained from the upper rim computed at the left child of v.

Next, we describe how a ray-shooting query is answered. Let r be a query ray emerging from a, and let (θ, ϕ) be its spherical coordinates. We perform a binary search through T by first comparing r with the topmost upper rim h, stored at the root u of T. To compute $h(\theta)$, we perform an auxiliary binary search with θ in L_u to find the orientation θ' immediately preceding θ in L_u; the edge of the upper rim stored along with θ' contains the point $(\theta, h(\theta))$. We compare (in constant time) ϕ with $h(\theta)$; if $\phi < h(\theta)$ then r lies above all the edges of $\mathcal{E}_{v_1}$, where v_1 is the left child of u, and we continue the search through T at the right child v_2 of u; otherwise r must hit some face of Σ bounded on its far side by an edge of $\mathcal{E}_{v_1}$, and we continue the search through T at the left child v_1 of u (the linear order of the edges of Σ guarantees that the first intersection of r with Σ must indeed occur at such a face). When this search is completed, we will have found two edges $e_i < e_j$, necessarily bounding the same face f of Σ, such that the vertical projection r^* of r intersects both e_i^*, e_j^* and r lies above e_i (actually above all edges of Σ preceding e_i, whose projections intersect r^*) and below e_j. Hence the first intersection of r with Σ lies in f, and can now be calculated in constant time. The whole search takes $O(\log^2 n)$ time.

We can reduce the search time to $O(\log n)$, with only a constant increase in the storage requirement, by using the following simple variant of the *fractional cascading* technique, proposed by Chazelle and Guibas (1986). We store an extended list $L'_v \supseteq L_v$ at each node v of T, defined in the following bottom-up manner. If v is a leaf, then $L'_v = L_v = \emptyset$. Otherwise, let w and z be the left and right children of v. Suppose $L'_w = (x_1, x_2, x_3, \ldots)$, and define $L''_w = (x_1, x_3, \ldots)$ to be the sublist of L'_w consisting of every other element of L'_w. Construct L''_z in a similar manner. L'_v is then obtained by merging L_v, L''_w, and L''_z. For each element x in L'_v we store three pointers, $top(x)$, $left(x)$, $right(x)$, where $top(x)$ (respectively, $left(x)$, $right(x)$) points to the largest element of L_v (respectively, L''_w, L''_z) smaller than or equal to x; if there is no such element then the pointer is null. These pointers can be obtained as an immediate by-product of the merging process of L_v, L''_w, and L''_z.

In order to answer a query, we proceed as described above, except that we perform the auxiliary search with θ only in the list L'_u at the root u. That is, given a query ray $r = (\theta, \phi)$, we find the element x of L'_u immediately preceding θ. The pointer $top(x)$ gives us the element of L_u immediately preceding θ, from which we can obtain $h(\theta)$ and proceed as above. If we decide to descend to the left child w of u, we follow the pointer $left(x)$, which gives us the largest element y of L_w'' not exceeding x. Then the largest element of L_w' not exceeding θ is either y or its successor, which we can thus compute in constant time. Descending to the right child of u is completely symmetric. Since we visit only $O(\log n)$ nodes of T, and spend $O(\log n)$ time at the root and $O(1)$ time at any other node, the overall query time is $O(\log n)$.

The total storage required by the data structure is now $\sum_v |L_v'|$. Let us assume that $|L_v| \leq cn_v\alpha(n_v)$ for some constant $c > 0$. We claim that $|L_v'| \leq 2cn_v\alpha(n_v)$. The claim follows by a bottom-up induction on the nodes of T. It is obviously true for the leaves of T. If v is an internal node, with children w, z, then, by the induction hypothesis,

$$
\begin{aligned}
|L_v'| &= |L_v| + \frac{1}{2}\left(|L_w'| + |L_z'|\right) \\
&\leq cn_v\alpha(n_v) + c(n_w\alpha(n_w) + n_z\alpha(n_z)) \\
&\leq 2c_v n_v\alpha(n_v),
\end{aligned}
$$

where the last inequality follows from the fact that $n_v = n_w + n_z$. Hence, we can conclude:

Theorem 8.26 *Given a polyhedral terrain Σ having n edges and a fixed view point a, one can preprocess a and Σ in $O(n\alpha(n)\log n)$ time and storage, so as to support ray-shooting queries from a in $O(\log n)$ time per query.*

8.4.2   Views along a vertical line

In this subsection we obtain a sharp upper bound on the number of topologically different perspective views of Σ as the view point varies along a fixed *vertical* line L. Without loss of generality, assume that L is the z-axis, and so a point on L can be specified by its z-coordinate. We can also assume, with no loss of generality, that L meets Σ at the origin, so we will consider only those viewing points that lie in the positive half of L. As mentioned in the beginning of the section, the combinatorial structure of the visibility map of Σ remains unchanged as a varies, except when a passes through certain *critical points*. We will obtain a sharp bound on the number of those critical points. The following lemma gives necessary conditions for a point $a \in L$ to be a critical point.

Lemma 8.27 *A point $a \in L$ is a critical point only if there is a ray ρ emanating from a that satisfies one of the following two conditions:*

P1. *ρ intersects an edge e of Σ and passes through a vertex v of Σ before crossing Σ (see Figure 8.16 (i)); ρ may cross Σ at v or at e, whichever is farther from a.*

P2. ρ *touches two edges* e_1, e_2 *of* Σ *and then meets another edge* e_3 *before crossing* Σ *(see Figure 8.16 (ii))*; ρ *may cross* Σ *at* e_3.

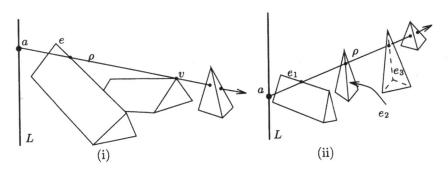

FIGURE 8.16. Critical points on L: (i) ρ passes through an edge e and a vertex v; (ii) ρ passes through three edges e_1, e_2, and e_3.

Proof. A combinatorial change in $M(a)$, which is a planar (or, rather, spherical) map, must involve the appearance of a new vertex v or the disappearance of an old vertex v from $M(a)$. (The other possibility, of a face of $M(a)$ newly appearing or disappearing, must also, in our case, be accompanied by such a vertex change, as is easily verified.) If v corresponds to a ray passing through a vertex of Σ, then, as is easily verified, v must lie on an edge of $M(a)$ induced by a visible edge of Σ not incident to v. This implies condition P1. If v arises as the intersection in the sphere of directions of two projected terrain edges, then (as again is easily verified) v must also lie on the projection of a third visible edge of Σ, which implies condition P2. $\square$

In view of the above lemma, it suffices to bound the number of points on L that satisfy condition P1 or P2. Let us first consider condition P1. Let v be a vertex of Σ. For any edge e such that $e < v$ or $e > v$,[5] let p be the intersection point of L and the plane spanned by e and v (i.e., the affine hull of e and v). Clearly, condition P1 can occur for v and e only at p, if it occurs at all. Hence, the number of points on L that satisfy P1 is at most $O(n^2)$.

For each edge $e \in \Sigma$ (to play the role of e_3 in condition P2), let $e(\theta)$ be the point on e whose horizontal orientation (as seen from L) is θ; if e does not intersect the vertical plane containing L whose orientation is θ, then $e(\theta)$ is undefined. For each edge $e_i < e$, we define a function $g_i : \mathbb{S} \to \mathbb{R}$ as follows. If $e(\theta)$ or $e_i(\theta)$ is undefined, then $g_i(\theta)$ is also undefined; otherwise $g_i(\theta)$ is the z-coordinate of the intersection point of L and the line passing through $e_i(\theta)$

---

[5]Since L is vertical, the order of edges of Σ, as defined in the previous subsection, is the same for all points $a \in L$.

and $e(\theta)$. It is easily seen that $g_i(\theta)$ is defined over some connected angular interval. Let

$$F_e(\theta) = \max \left\{ \max_{e_i < e} g_i(\theta),\ 0 \right\}$$

(where the maximum is taken over all $e_i < e$ for which $g_i(\theta)$ is defined). If $F_e(\theta)$ is attained by some g_i (i.e., $F_e(\theta) > 0$), then the ray ρ emanating from $(0, 0, F_e(\theta))$ with horizontal orientation θ and passing through e touches e_i before intersecting e, and ρ does not cross Σ before intersecting e. Conversely, for any ray ρ that emanates from L, passes through e and another edge preceding e, and does not cross Σ before e, there is an orientation θ such that ρ emanates from $(0, 0, F_e(\theta))$ in direction θ. Thus the point $\xi = (0, 0, F_e(\theta_0))$ is a critical point of type P2, with e being the third edge intersected by the critical ray of condition P2, if and only if F_e has a breakpoint at θ_0 (which is not an endpoint of the graph of one of the g_i's).

Lemma 8.28 *Let $e_i, e_j < e$ be a pair of distinct edges of Σ. If e_i, e_j, e are all coplanar, then $g_i(\theta) \equiv g_j(\theta)$ throughout its domain of definition; otherwise $g_i(\theta)$, $g_j(\theta)$ intersect in at most two points θ. Similarly, if e_i, e, and $a^\star$ are coplanar, then $g_i(\theta) \equiv 0$ throughout its domain of definition; otherwise $g_i(\theta) = 0$ in at most one point θ.*

Proof. The first claim is a special case of a well-known property, asserting that, in general position, there are at most two lines that pass through four given lines in $\mathbb{R}^3$ (see Sommerville (1951)). Nevertheless, for the sake of completeness, we include an explicit proof. We need to estimate the number of orientations θ at which the three points $e_i(\theta)$, $e_j(\theta)$, and $e(\theta)$ are collinear. Consider the point $e(\theta)$. Let d be the distance from the origin to the line containing the projection $e^\star$ of e. It is straightforward to check that the cylindrical coordinates of $e(\theta)$ are

$$\left(\frac{d}{\alpha \cos\theta + \beta \sin\theta},\ \theta,\ \frac{\gamma \cos\theta + \delta \sin\theta}{\alpha \cos\theta + \beta \sin\theta} \right)$$

for appropriate constants α, β, γ, δ. Similar expressions represent $e_i(\theta)$, $e_j(\theta)$, allowing us to express the collinearity of these three points by an equation of the form

$$\det \begin{bmatrix} 1 & \dfrac{d}{\alpha \cos\theta + \beta \sin\theta} & \dfrac{\gamma \cos\theta + \delta \sin\theta}{\alpha \cos\theta + \beta \sin\theta} \\[2mm] 1 & \dfrac{d_i}{\alpha_i \cos\theta + \beta_i \sin\theta} & \dfrac{\gamma_i \cos\theta + \delta_i \sin\theta}{\alpha_i \cos\theta + \beta_i \sin\theta} \\[2mm] 1 & \dfrac{d_j}{\alpha_j \cos\theta + \beta_j \sin\theta} & \dfrac{\gamma_j \cos\theta + \delta_j \sin\theta}{\alpha_j \cos\theta + \beta_j \sin\theta} \end{bmatrix} = 0. \qquad (8.1)$$

It is easy to check that this equation can be rewritten as a quadratic homogeneous equation in $\cos\theta$, $\sin\theta$, or rather as a quadratic equation in $\tan\theta$

(the denominators do not vanish over the common domain of definition of $e(\theta)$, $e_i(\theta)$, and $e_j(\theta)$). Moreover, it can be easily checked that, unless e_i, e_j, and e are coplanar, (8.1) does not vanish identically. We thus obtain at most two values of $\tan\theta$, each yielding at most one value of θ in the angular interval where these functions are defined (whose length is clearly less than π), at which (8.1) vanishes. This implies that the equation $g_i(\theta) = g_j(\theta)$ has at most two roots. The analysis of equations of the form $g_i(\theta) = 0$ is the same, except that the last row of the above determinant is $[1, 0, 0]$ (since $a^\star$ lies at the origin). This leads to a linear homogeneous equation in $\cos\theta$, $\sin\theta$ (which does not vanish identically unless e_i, e, and $a^\star$ are coplanar), and thus has at most one root within our range.   □

It follows from Lemma 1.4 (and from Theorem 3.12) that the maximum number of breakpoints in F_e is at most $\lambda_4(n) = O(n \cdot 2^{\alpha(n)})$. Repeating this argument for each edge e of Σ we conclude that the total number of critical orientations of the second type is $O(n\lambda_4(n))$. Hence we have:

Theorem 8.29 *Let Σ be a polyhedral terrain with n edges. Then the number of points on a fixed vertical line, at which the combinatorial structure of the visibility map of Σ changes, is $O(n^2 \cdot 2^{\alpha(n)})$.*

Remark 8.30 (i) We do not know whether the bound $O(n\lambda_4(n))$ is tight in the worst case, but the following example shows that the number of changes in the visibility map can be $\Omega(n\lambda_3(n)) = \Omega(n^2\alpha(n))$. In this example, we first take, as in the preceding subsection, k segments whose upper rim, as viewed from $a^\star$, consists of $\Omega(k\alpha(k))$ subsegments. Each of these segments lies in a vertical plane, and these planes are all parallel and sufficiently close to one another, so that the combinatorial structure of their upper rim remains unchanged as a varies along L from $a^\star$ to a sufficiently high point $a^{\star\star}$. Moreover, by scaling down the y-coordinate in the lower bound construction of Chapter 4 (e.g., in Section 4.3), we can assume that all the breakpoints in the upper rim of these segments correspond to rays passing sufficiently near some fixed horizontal line h that passes close to those k segments. We can now complete Σ by k additional long horizontal parallel segments, lying beyond the first k edges, such that the faces they bound form a convex surface (bending upward), and such that, as a varies along L from $a^\star$ to $a^{\star\star}$, the rays emanating from a and passing through h will encounter each of the latter k edges. See Figure 8.17 for an illustration of such a terrain. It is now clear that for such a terrain Σ, which has $n = O(k)$ edges, the number of changes in the visibility structure along L is $\Omega(n^2\alpha(n))$. In particular, L contains $\Omega(n^2\alpha(n))$ points from which there emerge rays that pass through three visible edges of Σ simultaneously.

(ii) The requirement that the viewing line L be vertical is rather crucial to the analysis. Of course, it can be trivially relaxed by requiring only that each line parallel to L intersects Σ in precisely one point. In other words, the above

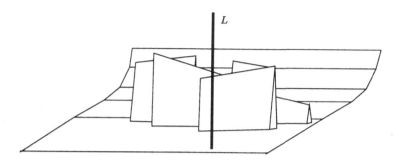

FIGURE 8.17. Lower bound construction.

analysis will continue to apply for nonvertical lines L, provided that when the coordinate system is rotated so as to make L vertical, Σ remains the graph of a single-valued piecewise linear function. However, if L is an arbitrary line, then it is easy to construct examples in which the visibility map changes $\Theta(n^3)$ times as we move along L.

8.4.3 Orthographic views

We next consider the case when the view point can vary along a sphere at infinity, that is, consider all orthographic views of a terrain. We consider the space of all spatial orientations, represented by points on the unit sphere $\mathbb{S}^2$ about the origin. As mentioned at the beginning of this section, each spatial orientation $\omega \in \mathbb{S}^2$ is parametrized by its spherical coordinates (θ, ϕ), where θ is the *horizontal orientation* of the xy-projection of ω, and ϕ is the *azimuth* of ω. We wish to partition $\mathbb{S}^2$ into maximal connected regions, so that the topological and combinatorial structure of the view from infinity of Σ in all directions within each region remains the same. Let $\Psi(\Sigma)$ denote the resulting subdivision of $\mathbb{S}^2$.

Theorem 8.31 *The number of topologically different orthographic views of a polyhedral terrain Σ with n edges is $O(n^{5+\varepsilon})$, for any $\varepsilon > 0$, where the constant of proportionality depends on ε.*

Proof. By Lemma 8.27, appropriately modified to the case at hand, the topological structure of the orthographic view of Σ changes at a direction ω if there is a ray ρ in direction ω coming from infinity and satisfying at least one of the conditions P1, P2. Therefore, for each direction ω lying on an edge of $\Psi(\Sigma)$, there is a ray in direction ω that satisfies one of the conditions P1, P2. Moreover, a vertex of $\Psi(\Sigma)$ corresponds to a direction ω such that there are two parallel rays coming from infinity in direction ω, each of which satisfies one of these two conditions (or a single ray satisfying a combination of two such conditions). To bound the number of different topological views of Σ, we will obtain a bound on the number of vertices of $\Psi(\Sigma)$; the number of all other features of $\Psi(\Sigma)$ can be shown to be proportional to the number of vertices.

It is easily checked that there are only $O(n^2) \cdot O(n^3) = O(n^5)$ pairs of parallel rays for which at least one of the rays satisfies P1 (and the other ray satisfies either P1 or P2). Hence, it suffices to bound the number of pairs of parallel rays both satisfying P2, that is, each of them passes through three edges of Σ before intersecting the open region lying below Σ. Let ρ be such a ray, and let e be the third edge of Σ intersected by ρ. Then the ray emanating from the intersection point of e and ρ in the direction opposite to that of ρ passes through three edges of Σ (including e) and is disjoint from the open region below Σ.

Suppose ρ_1 and ρ_2 are two such parallel (reversed) rays, and suppose that ρ_i passes through the edges a_i, b_i, and c_i of Σ in this order, for $i = 1, 2$ (note that the corresponding orthographic view is seen in the direction $(\theta + \pi, \pi - \phi)$ opposite to the orientation (θ, ϕ) of these rays). Let us consider the fixed pair a_1, a_2 of edges of the terrain, and define the following collection $\mathcal{F}_{a_1 a_2}$ of tri-variate partial functions. The three independent variables are (s_1, s_2, θ), and each such triple represents the vertical projection of a pair of parallel rays, as follows: s_1 (respectively, s_2) parametrizes a point on a_1 (respectively, a_2) that we denote by $p(s_1)$ (respectively, $p(s_2)$) (e.g., s_1 is the distance from the left endpoint of a_1 (respectively, a_2) to $p(s_1)$ (respectively, $p(s_2)$)), and θ is the common horizontal orientation of the two rays, one of which emanates from the point $p(s_1)$ on a_1 and the other emanates from the point $p(s_2)$ on a_2 (the only variable degree of freedom available for these rays is their common azimuth ϕ).

For each edge e of Σ we define a function $F_e(s_1, s_2, \theta) \in \mathcal{F}_{a_1 a_2}$ as follows. For $i = 1, 2$, let ϕ_i denote the azimuth angle of the ray emanating from s_i at horizontal orientation θ and passing through e. We set $F_e(s_1, s_2, \theta)$ to $\min\{\phi_1, \phi_2\}$. If only one of these rays exists, $F_e(s_1, s_2, \theta)$ is equal to the azimuth of that ray, and if none of these rays exist, $F_e(s_1, s_2, \theta)$ is undefined.

Let $E_{\mathcal{F}_{a_1 a_2}}$ denote the lower envelope of the collection $\mathcal{F}_{a_1 a_2}$. For each triple (s_1, s_2, θ) the following is easily seen to hold: let $\phi = E_{\mathcal{F}_{a_1 a_2}}(s_1, s_2, \theta)$ (assuming that it is defined); then there exist two parallel rays, with common orientation (θ, ϕ), emanating respectively from $p(s_1) \in a_1$ and from $p(s_2) \in a_2$, so that both rays are disjoint from the open region lying below Σ and at least one of them passes through another edge of Σ. (Some care must be exercised to handle the unbounded faces over which these rays pass, to ensure that they do not pierce through such a face. This can be enforced by adding extra functions to the collection $\mathcal{F}_{a_1 a_2}$ that constrain the behavior of these rays at infinity; we leave it to the reader to work out the easy details.) Moreover, if (s_1, s_2, θ, ϕ) is a vertex of $E_{\mathcal{F}_{a_1 a_2}}$, where four surfaces of $\mathcal{F}_{a_1 a_2}$ meet, then the two corresponding rays collectively pass through four edges of Σ (in addition to a_1 and a_2). Conversely, any pair of rays with these properties appear as a vertex of $E_{\mathcal{F}_{a_1 a_2}}$, so, in particular, each critical orthographic view that is a vertex of $\Psi(\Sigma)$ must give rise to such a vertex of the envelope.

Hence, by Theorem 7.17 (using an appropriate parametrization that makes the functions of $\mathcal{F}_{a_1 a_2}$ algebraic of constant maximum degree), the number of such critical pairs of rays is $O(n^{3+\varepsilon})$, where the constant of proportionality depends on ε. Multiplying this bound by the $O(n^2)$ pairs of edges a_1, a_2, we obtain that the overall number of such critical pairs of rays, and thus also the number of topologically different orthographic views of Σ, is $O(n^{5+\varepsilon})$, for any $\varepsilon > 0$. $\qquad\square$

Remark 8.32 (i) Using a more careful analysis, exploiting the fact that each quadruple of functions in $\mathcal{F}_{a_1 a_2}$ intersect in at most two points (as in Lemma 8.28), Halperin and Sharir (1994c) have obtained a slightly improved bound of $O(n^5 2^{c\sqrt{\log n}})$ on the number of orthographic views of a polyhedral terrain with n edges, where c is some small constant.

(ii) de Berg et al. (1992) have given a lower bound of $\Omega(n^5 \alpha(n))$ for the number of topologically different orthographic views of a polyhedral terrain with n edges. Hence, the above upper bound is close to optimal in the worst case.

(iii) Theorem 8.31 can be extended to more general terrains. For example, Theorem 8.31 holds even if each face of Σ is a portion of a sphere (or of any constant-degree algebraic surface). In this case it suffices to bound the number of pairs of parallel rays, each of which is tangent to three faces of Σ and is disjoint from the open region lying below Σ. Following a similar approach it can be shown that the number of such pairs of parallel rays, and thus the number of topologically different orthographic views of such a terrain, is also $O(n^{5+\varepsilon})$, for any $\varepsilon > 0$.

8.4.4 Perspective views

Next, we prove an upper bound on the number of toplogically different perspective views of a terrain Σ, obtained by allowing the view point to be anywhere in $\mathbb{R}^3$ (above Σ).

Theorem 8.33 *The number of topologically different perspective views of a polyhedral terrain with n edges is $O(n^{8+\varepsilon})$, for any $\varepsilon > 0$, where the constant of proportionality depends on ε.*

Proof. The proof is very similar to that of Theorem 8.31. Specifically, an appropriate variant of the proof of Theorem 8.31 implies that it suffices to bound the number of points (x, y, z) for which there exist three segments emanating from (x, y, z), each of which passes through three edges of Σ and is disjoint from the open region lying below Σ. (Such a point (x, y, z) is an intersection of three surfaces of critical viewpoints in 3-space, where each surface is the locus of viewpoints at which some specific combinatorial change in the perspective view takes place.) Suppose that ρ_1, ρ_2, and ρ_3 are these segments, and suppose that ρ_i passes through the edges a_i, b_i, and c_i of Σ in this order when directed *toward* (x, y, z), for $i = 1, 2, 3$. Let us consider the fixed triple a_1, a_2, a_3 of edges of Σ, and define the following collection $\mathcal{F}_{a_1 a_2 a_3}$ of 5-variate partial functions. The five independent variables are (s_1, s_2, s_3, x, y), and each such 5-tuple represents the vertical projection of a triple of concurrent segments, as follows: s_i parametrizes, as above, a point on a_i, for $i = 1, 2, 3$, which we denote by $p(s_i)$, and (x, y) is the vertical projection of the common endpoint w of the three segments $p(s_i)w$, for $i = 1, 2, 3$, that this 5-tuple defines.

For each edge e of Σ we define a function $F_e \in \mathcal{F}_{a_1 a_2 a_3}$ so that, for a point $(s_1, s_2, s_3, x, y) \in \mathbb{R}^5$, $F_e(s_1, s_2, s_3, x, y)$ is the largest z-coordinate of a point $q = (x, y, z)$ with the property that at least one of the three segments connecting q to $p(s_1)$, $p(s_2)$, $p(s_3)$ passes through e (if none of these segments exist, $F_e(s_1, s_2, s_3, x, y)$ is undefined).

Let $E_{\mathcal{F}_{a_1 a_2 a_3}}$ denote the upper envelope of the collection $\mathcal{F}_{a_1 a_2 a_3}$. For each 5-tuple (s_1, s_2, s_3, x, y) the following is easily seen to hold: let $z = E_{\mathcal{F}_{a_1 a_2 a_3}}(s_1, s_2, s_3, x, y)$ (assuming that it is defined); then the three segments connecting (x, y, z) to $p(s_1)$, $p(s_2)$, $p(s_3)$ are disjoint from the open region lying below Σ and at least one of them touches another edge of Σ (again, we need to modify the collection of functions so as to handle properly the unbounded faces of Σ; we omit the straightforward details). Moreover, if (s_1, s_2, s_3, x, y, z) is a vertex of $E_{\mathcal{F}_{a_1 a_2 a_3}}$, where six surfaces of $\mathcal{F}_{a_1 a_2 a_3}$ meet, then the three corresponding segments collectively pass through six edges of Σ (in addition to a_1, a_2, and a_3). Conversely, any triple of segments with these properties corresponds to a vertex of $E_{\mathcal{F}_{a_1 a_2 a_3}}$.

Hence, by Theorem 7.17, the number of such critical triples of segments is $O(n^{5+\varepsilon})$, where the constant of proportionality depends on ε. Multiplying this bound by the $O(n^3)$ triples of edges a_1, a_2, a_3, we obtain that the overall number of such critical triples of segments, and thus also the number of topologically different perspective views of Σ, is $O(n^{8+\varepsilon})$, for any $\varepsilon > 0$. $\square$

Remark 8.34 (i) de Berg et al. (1992) have given a lower bound of $\Omega(n^8 \alpha(n))$ for the number of topologically different perspective views of a terrain with n edges. Thus our bound is close to optimal in the worst case.

(ii) It is worth noting that all the upper bounds that we have obtained in Theorems 8.29, 8.31, and 8.33 are smaller roughly by a factor of n from their counterparts obtained when viewing an arbitrary polyhedral scene. See Plantinga and Dyer (1990), and also Remark 8.30(ii).

8.5   Width in 3-space

Let S be a set of n points in $\mathbb{R}^3$. The *width* of S is the smallest distance between a pair of parallel planes so that the closed slab between the planes contains S. In two dimensions, it is well-known (and easy to show) that the width of a set S of n points (the smallest distance between a pair of lines that enclose S between them) can be easily obtained in $O(n \log n)$ time, by computing and processing the convex hull of S. In this section, we present a randomized algorithm for computing the width of a set of n points in $\mathbb{R}^3$ whose expected running time is $O(n^{5/3+\varepsilon})$.

Clearly, it suffices to compute the width of the convex hull of S, so assume that the points of S are in convex position, and that the convex hull $\mathcal{P}$ of S is known. It is easily seen that any two planes defining the width of S are such that either

(i) one of the planes contains a face of $\mathcal{P}$ and the other touches a vertex of $\mathcal{P}$, or

(ii) each of the planes contains an edge of $\mathcal{P}$;

see Houle and Toussaint (1988).

Let $\mathcal{G}$ denote the *Gaussian diagram* (or *normal diagram*) of $\mathcal{P}$, which is a spherical map on the unit sphere $\mathbb{S}^2 \subset \mathbb{R}^3$. The vertices of $\mathcal{G}$ are points on $\mathbb{S}^2$, each being the outward normal direction of a face of $\mathcal{P}$, the edges of $\mathcal{G}$ are great circular arcs, each being the locus of the outward normal directions of all planes supporting $\mathcal{P}$ at a fixed edge, and the faces of $\mathcal{G}$ are regions, each being the locus of the outward normal directions of all planes supporting $\mathcal{P}$ at a vertex. The map $\mathcal{G}$ can be computed in linear time from $\mathcal{P}$. Let $\mathcal{G}'$ denote the spherical map $\mathcal{G}$ reflected through the origin. By preprocessing $\mathcal{G}'$, in $O(n \log n)$ time, for fast point location queries (as given in Edelsbrunner (1987) or Sarnak and Tarjan (1986)), and by locating the vertices of $\mathcal{G}$ in $\mathcal{G}'$, we can determine all parallel supporting planes of type (i), in time $O(n \log n)$. (If a vertex v of $\mathcal{G}$ lies in a face φ of $\mathcal{G}'$, such that v corresponds to a face f of $\mathcal{P}$ and φ corresponds to a vertex w of $\mathcal{P}$, then the plane containing f and the parallel plane passing through w are a pair of planes of type (i), and vice versa.)

Next, we compute the minimum distance between pairs of parallel supporting planes of type (ii). Consider the superposition of $\mathcal{G}$ and $\mathcal{G}'$. It suffices to consider the top parts of $\mathcal{G}$ and $\mathcal{G}'$, that is, their portions within the hemisphere $z \geq 0$, because the overlay of the two maps is centrally symmetric. Each intersection point between an edge of $\mathcal{G}$ and an edge of $\mathcal{G}'$ gives us a direction $\mathbf{u}$ for which there exist two parallel planes orthogonal to $\mathbf{u}$ and supporting $\mathcal{P}$ at two so-called antipodal edges (corresponding to these edges of $\mathcal{G}$ and $\mathcal{G}'$), and vice versa. Thus the problem reduces to finding an intersection point between an edge of $\mathcal{G}$ and an edge of $\mathcal{G}'$ for which the distance between the corresponding parallel supporting planes is minimum. The number of such intersection points is $\Omega(n^2)$ in the worst case, so it may be too expensive to compute all of them explicitly. Instead, we use the following approach:

We centrally project the edges of (the top portions of) $\mathcal{G}$ and $\mathcal{G}'$ onto the plane $z = 1$. Each edge projects to a line segment or a ray. Let $\mathcal{E}$ and $\mathcal{E}'$ be the resulting sets of segments (or rays) in that plane. Using the algorithm described by Chazelle, Edelsbrunner, Guibas, and Sharir (1993, 1994), we can decompose $\mathcal{E} \times \mathcal{E}'$ into a family of 'canonical subsets'

$$\mathcal{C} = \{(\mathcal{E}_1, \mathcal{E}_1'), (\mathcal{E}_2, \mathcal{E}_2'), \ldots, (\mathcal{E}_t, \mathcal{E}_t')\}, \tag{8.2}$$

such that

(i) $\mathcal{E}_i \subseteq \mathcal{E}$ and $\mathcal{E}_i' \subseteq \mathcal{E}'$ for each i,

(ii) $\displaystyle\sum_{i=1}^{t}(|\mathcal{E}_i| + |\mathcal{E}_i'|) = O(n \log^2 n)$,

(iii) each segment in $\mathcal{E}_i$ intersects every segment of $\mathcal{E}_i'$, and

(iv) for every pair, e, e', of intersecting segments in $\mathcal{E} \times \mathcal{E}'$, there is an i such that $e \in \mathcal{E}_i$ and $e' \in \mathcal{E}_i'$.

By property (iv), it suffices to consider each pair $(\mathcal{E}_i, \mathcal{E}_i')$ separately. Let $\mathcal{L}_i$ (respectively, $\mathcal{L}_i'$) denote the sets of lines containing the edges of $\mathcal{P}$ corresponding to the edges of $\mathcal{E}_i$ (respectively, $\mathcal{E}_i'$). It is easily seen from the construction that all lines of $\mathcal{L}_i$ lie above all lines of $\mathcal{L}_i'$. It is also easily seen that the distance between a line $\ell \in \mathcal{L}_i$ and a line $\ell' \in \mathcal{L}_i'$ is equal to the distance between the pair of parallel planes supporting $\mathcal{P}$ at the corrresponding edges. Hence, the problem reduces to a collection of t subproblems, each of the following form: Given a set $\mathcal{L} = \mathcal{L}_i$ of m 'red' lines and another set $\mathcal{L}' = \mathcal{L}_i'$ of n 'blue' lines in $\mathbb{R}^3$, such that all red lines lie above all blue lines, compute the closest pair of lines in $\mathcal{L} \times \mathcal{L}'$. The minimum distance, over all subproblems, gives us the smallest distance between a pair of planes of type (ii). For two lines ℓ, ℓ' in $\mathbb{R}^3$, let $d(\ell, \ell')$ be the Euclidean distance between ℓ and ℓ', and let $d(\mathcal{L}, \mathcal{L}') = \min_{\ell \in \mathcal{L}, \ell' \in \mathcal{L}'} d(\ell, \ell')$.

We first present a simple randomized divide-and-conquer algorithm for computing $d(\mathcal{L}, \mathcal{L}')$, whose expected running time is $O(n^{3+\varepsilon} + m \log^2 n)$, for any $\varepsilon > 0$. If $m = O(1)$, we compute $d(\ell, \ell')$ for all pairs $\ell \in \mathcal{L}, \ell' \in \mathcal{L}'$, and choose the minimum distance. Otherwise, the algorithm consists of the following steps:

(a) Choose a random subset $R_1 \subseteq \mathcal{L}$ of $m/2$ red lines; each subset of size $m/2$ is chosen with equal probability.

(b) Solve the problem recursively for $(R_1, \mathcal{L}')$. Let $\delta_1 = d(R_1, \mathcal{L}')$.

(c) Compute the subset $R_2 \subseteq \mathcal{L} \setminus R_1 = \{\ell \in \mathcal{L} \mid d(\ell, \mathcal{L}') < \delta_1\}$.

(d) Compute $d(\ell, \ell')$ for all pairs $\ell \in R_2, \ell' \in \mathcal{L}'$, and output the minimum distance. (If $R_2 = \emptyset$, output δ_1.)

For a line $\ell' \in \mathcal{L}'$, let

$$R^{(\ell')} = \{\ell \in \mathcal{L} \mid d(\ell, \ell') < \delta_1\},$$

so that $R_2 = \bigcup_{\ell' \in \mathcal{L}'} R^{(\ell')}$. Using a standard probabilistic argument, as in Clarkson and Shor (1989), one can show that the expected size of $R^{(\ell')}$ is $O(1)$, for each $\ell' \in \mathcal{L}'$. Therefore the expected size of R_2 is $O(n)$. Consequently, the expected running time of Step (d) is $O(n^2)$, much below our target bound.

The only nontrivial step in the above algorithm is Step (c). We compute R_2 as follows. We map each line $\ell \in \mathcal{L}$ to a point $\psi(\ell) = (a_1, a_2, a_3, a_4)$ in $\mathbb{R}^4$, where $y = a_1 x + a_2$ is the equation of the xy-projection of ℓ, and $z = a_3 u + a_4$ is the equation of ℓ in the vertical plane $y = a_1 x + a_2$ (where u denotes the axis orthogonal to the z-axis). This representation excludes lines parallel to the yz-plane; these lines can be handled separately, using a simpler procedure, whose description is omitted here. Let $P = \{\psi(\ell) \mid \ell \in \mathcal{L} \setminus R_1\}$. We can also map a line ℓ' to a surface $\gamma = \gamma(\ell')$, which is the locus of all points $\psi(\ell)$ such that $d(\ell, \ell') = \delta_1$ and ℓ lies above ℓ'. Removal of γ partitions $\mathbb{R}^4$ into two subsets, one, denoted by γ^-, consisting of points for which the corresponding lines either lie below ℓ' or lie above ℓ' and $d(\ell, \ell') < \delta_1$, and the other subset, γ^+, consisting of points whose corresponding lines lie above ℓ' and $d(\ell, \ell') > \delta_1$. Our choice of parameters ensures that γ is $x_1 x_2 x_3$-monotone, that is, any line parallel to the x_4-axis intersects γ in at most one point. Hence, $\gamma(\ell')$ is the graph of a function $x_4 = f_{\ell'}(x_1, x_2, x_3)$. Let $\mathcal{F} = \{f_{\ell'} \mid \ell' \in \mathcal{L}'\}$ be the resulting set of trivariate functions, and let $E_{\mathcal{F}}^*$ denote the upper envelope of $\mathcal{F}$. For a line $\ell \in \mathcal{L}$ with $\psi(\ell) = (a_1, a_2, a_3, a_4)$, we have $a_4 \geq E_{\mathcal{F}}^*(a_1, a_2, a_3)$ if and only if $d(\ell, \mathcal{L}') \geq \delta_1$. The problem of computing R_2 thus reduces to computing the set of points $\psi(\ell) = (a_1, a_2, a_3, a_4) \in P$ such that $E_{\mathcal{F}}^*(a_1, a_2, a_3) > a_4$. By Theorem 7.25, this can be accomplished in time $O(n^{3+\varepsilon} + m \log^2 n)$, for any $\varepsilon > 0$. Hence, the expected time spent in Steps (c) and (d) is $O(n^{3+\varepsilon} + m \log^2 n)$. Let $T(m, n)$ denote the maximum expected time of the algorithm. Then we have the following recurrence

$$T(m, n) \leq \begin{cases} c_1 n & \text{for } m \leq m_0, \\ T\left(\frac{m}{2}, n\right) + c_2(n^{3+\varepsilon} + m \log^2 n) & \text{for } m > m_0, \end{cases}$$

where c_1, c_2, m_0 are appropriate constants, and c_2 depends on ε. The solution to the above recurrence is easily seen to be

$$T(m, n) = O(n^{3+\varepsilon} \log m + m \log^2 n).$$

The expected running time can be improved to $O(nm^{2/3+\varepsilon} + m^{1+\varepsilon})$ by using the following batching technique: Partition $\mathcal{L}'$ into $\mu = \lceil n/m^{1/3} \rceil$ subsets,

$\mathcal{L}'_1, \ldots, \mathcal{L}'_\mu$, each of size at most $\lceil m^{1/3} \rceil$. Clearly,

$$d(\mathcal{L}, \mathcal{L}') = \min_{1 \le i \le \mu} d(\mathcal{L}, \mathcal{L}'_i).$$

Therefore, we compute $d(\mathcal{L}, \mathcal{L}'_i)$ for each $i \le \mu$ separately, and then output the minimum of these distances. The expected time is thus

$$\lceil n/m^{1/3} \rceil \cdot O(m^{1+\varepsilon}) = O(nm^{2/3+\varepsilon} + m^{1+\varepsilon}),$$

for any $\varepsilon > 0$.

Returning to the problem of computing the width, we compute $d(\mathcal{L}, \mathcal{L}')$ for all pairs $(\mathcal{L}, \mathcal{L}')$ corresponding to all canonical pairs of $\mathcal{C}$ (see (8.2)), and then output the minimum of these values. By property (ii) of $\mathcal{C}$, the total expected time spent is

$$\sum_{i=1}^{t} O\left(|\mathcal{E}_i| \cdot |\mathcal{E}'_i|^{2/3+\varepsilon} + |\mathcal{E}'_i|^{1+\varepsilon}\right) = O(n^{5/3+\varepsilon'}),$$

where $\varepsilon' > \varepsilon$ is another, but still arbitrarily small, constant. Hence, we can conclude:

Theorem 8.35 *The width of any set of n points in $\mathbb{R}^3$ can be computed in randomized expected time $O(n^{5/3+\varepsilon})$, for any $\varepsilon > 0$.*

Remark 8.36 The best known algorithm for computing the width of a point set in $\mathbb{R}^3$, due to Sharir (1994b), runs in time $O(n^{3/2+\varepsilon})$, for any $\varepsilon > 0$; see also Agarwal, Aronov, and Sharir (1994). This algorithm is based on the ε-net theory and on the parametric search technique of Megiddo (1979, 1983) (see Section 8.8.2.4), and combines these tools with a more efficient procedure for computing the minimum distance between two sets of lines in $\mathbb{R}^3$ (where all the lines in one set lie above all the lines of the other set), similar to the one described above. This procedure exploits the fact, also established in Sharir (1994b), that there exists a vertical decomposition of small size of the region below the upper envelope $E^*_{\mathcal{F}}$, for the collection $\mathcal{F}$ of trivariate functions used above. See also Remark 8.22. Agarwal (1994) has presented a different (randomized) approach for computing the minimum distance between two sets of lines, which does not use the parametric search technique. The expected running time of his algorithm is also $O(n^{3/2+\varepsilon})$.

8.6   Dynamic geometry

In this section we consider various problems related to a set of points in the plane, each moving along some predefined trajectory. We assume that we are given a collection $P = \{p_1, \ldots, p_n\}$ of n points in the plane such that the coordinates of each p_i are functions of time. Let $p_i(t) = (x_i(t), y_i(t))$ denote the position of the point p_i at time t, and let $P(t)$ denote the configuration of P at time t. We assume that $x_i(t), y_i(t)$, for $1 \leq i \leq n$, are polynomials of maximum degree s, for some constant s. For the sake of convenience, we also assume that the points of P never collide with each other.

The goal of this section is to study how various geometric structures defined by P change with time. We consider three basic structures: convex hulls, nearest neighbors, and Voronoi diagrams. Similar techniques can be applied to analyze the dynamic behavior of other structures as well.

8.6.1 Convex hulls

Let $C(t)$ denote the convex hull of P at time t, and let $\partial C(t)$ denote its boundary. $C(t)$ can be described combinatorially by specifying the circular sequence of points of P that appear, say in counterclockwise order, on $\partial C(t)$. Although $C(t)$ changes continuously, its combinatorial structure can change only at critical values of t—when a new point is added to the sequence, or a point is deleted from the sequence. We wish to obtain a bound on the number of these events.

Clearly, if at time t a point of P newly appears on $\partial C(t)$, or a point is about to disappear from $\partial C(t)$, then, since the points are moving continuously, there must be three collinear points of $P(t)$ on $\partial C(t)$. It thus suffices to bound the number of values of t at which there exist three such collinear points. For a pair of points $p_i, p_j \in P$, let $-\pi < \theta_{ij}(t) \leq \pi$ denote the angle that the directed segment $p_i(t)p_j(t)$ makes with the positive x-axis; see Figure 8.18. We define $\theta_{ij}^+(t)$ (respectively, $\theta_{ij}^-(t)$) to be $\theta_{ij}(t)$ if it is positive (respectively, negative) and undefined otherwise. Note that $\theta_{ij}(t) = 0$ if and only if $y_j(t) - y_i(t) = 0$. Since each of $y_i(t), y_j(t)$ is a polynomial of degree at most s, $\theta_{ij}(t)$ has at most s roots. This implies that θ_{ij}^+ and θ_{ij}^- have at most s points of discontinuity. Moreover, $\theta_{ij}(t) = \theta_{ik}(t)$ only if p_i, p_j, and p_k are collinear, that is,

$$\det \begin{vmatrix} x_i(t) & y_i(t) & 1 \\ x_j(t) & y_j(t) & 1 \\ x_k(t) & y_k(t) & 1 \end{vmatrix} = 0.$$

The above determinant is a polynomial of degree at most $2s$, so $\theta_{ij}(t) - \theta_{ik}(t)$ has at most $2s$ roots. For a point $p_i \in P$, let

$$A_i(t) = \min_{j \neq i} \theta_{ij}^+(t),$$

$$B_i(t) = \max_{j \neq i} \theta_{ij}^+(t),$$

$$C_i(t) = \min_{j \neq i} \theta_{ij}^-(t),$$

$$D_i(t) = \max_{j \neq i} \theta_{ij}^-(t).$$

By the above discussion, each of the functions A_i, B_i, C_i, and D_i has at most $O(\lambda_{2s+2}(n))$ breakpoints.

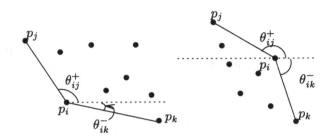

FIGURE 8.18. (i) $\theta_{ij}^+(t) - \theta_{ik}^-(t) < \pi$; (ii) $\theta_{ij}^+(t) - \theta_{ik}^-(t) > \pi$.

Lemma 8.37 *A point p_i is on $\partial C(t)$ if and only if one of the following four conditions is satisfied:*

(i) $A_i(t) - D_i(t) \geq \pi$;

(ii) $B_i(t) - C_i(t) \leq \pi$;

(iii) both A_i and B_i are undefined; or

(iv) both C_i and D_i are undefined.

Proof. We will prove the 'only if' part of the lemma. Let $p_i(t)$ be a point on $\partial C(t)$, and let $p_j(t)$ and $p_k(t)$ be the points adjacent to $p_i(t)$ along $\partial C(t)$. If $p_i(t)$ is the topmost vertex of $\partial C(t)$, then $\theta_{ij}(t) < 0$ for all $j \neq i$, so $A_i(t)$ and $B_i(t)$ are undefined. Similarly if $p_i(t)$ is the bottommost vertex of $\partial C(t)$, then both $C_i(t)$ and $D_i(t)$ are undefined.

Otherwise, one of the two neighbors, $p_j(t)$ and $p_k(t)$, of $p_i(t)$ must lie above $p_i(t)$ and the other must lie below it. Without loss of generality, assume that $\theta_{ij}(t) \geq 0$ and $\theta_{ik}(t) < 0$. Since $p_i(t)$ lies on $\partial C(t)$, all points of $P(t)$ lie in one of the cones whose apex is $p_i(t)$ and that is bounded by the rays emanating from $p_i(t)$ in directions $\overrightarrow{p_i(t)p_j(t)}$ and $\overrightarrow{p_i(t)p_k(t)}$. Let $W(t)$ denote this cone. If $W(t)$ contains the horizontal ray emanating from p_i in the positive x-direction (see Figure 8.18 (i)), then it is easily seen that $\theta_{ij}(t) = B_i(t)$ and $\theta_{ik}(t) = C_i(t)$. Since $C(t)$ is a convex polygon, $W(t)$ spans an angle of at most π, which implies that condition (ii) holds. Similarly, if $W(t)$ contains the horizontal ray emanating in the negative x-direction (see Figure 8.18 (ii)), then condition (i) holds.

A similar argument can be used to prove the 'if' part of the lemma. □

In view of the above lemma, the combinatorial structure of the convex hull changes at $t = t_0$ if, for some point p_i, one of the conditions of Lemma 8.37 changes from being true to being false or vice versa. Conditions (iii) and (iv) can change only at some of the breakpoints of the functions A_i, B_i, C_i, or D_i. As for condition (i), merge the lists of breakpoints of A_i and D_i (the length of the merged list is $O(\lambda_{2s+2}(n))$), and let t_u, t_{u+1} be two consecutive breakpoints of the merged list. Then A_i, D_i are realized by a fixed pair of functions, say, $\theta_{ij}^+(t), \theta_{ik}^-(t)$, respectively, over all $t \in (t_u, t_{u+1})$. Hence, within (t_u, t_{u+1}), condition (i) becomes an equality when $\theta_{ij}^+(t) - \theta_{ik}^-(t) = \pi$, and this can occur at most $2s$ times. Hence, for any fixed point p_i, condition (i) changes from being true to being false, or vice versa, at most $O(\lambda_{2s+2}(n))$ times. A similar argument implies that condition (ii) also changes $O(\lambda_{2s+2}(n))$ times for any fixed p_i. Summing these bounds over all points in P, we obtain the following result:

Theorem 8.38 *Let P be a set of points in the plane, each moving along a trajectory defined by a pair of polynomials of maximum degree s, for some constant s; then the combinatorial structure of the convex hull of P changes at most $O(n\lambda_{2s+2}(n))$ times.*

Remark 8.39 It is easy to give an example where the combinatorial structure of the convex hull of a set P of n moving points in the plane changes $\Omega(n^2)$ times. For instance, take $\lfloor n/2 \rfloor$ stationary points with coordinates $(-2i/n, -4i^2/n^2)$, for $1 \le i \le \lfloor n/2 \rfloor$; all these points lie on the parabolic arc

$$\gamma_0 : \quad y = -x^2, \quad -1 \le x \le 0.$$

For $i > \lfloor n/2 \rfloor$, the i-th point p_i of P moves so that

$$p_i(t) = (t - 3i, 1 - (t - 3i)^2)$$

all these points move along the parabola $\gamma_1 : y = 1 - x^2$. It is easily checked that, for any $1 \le i \le \lfloor n/2 \rfloor < j \le n$, the segment $p_i(t_{ij})p_j(t_{ij})$ is an edge of $\partial C(t_{ij})$, for $t_{ij} = 3j + 1 - \frac{2i}{n}$. This establishes the asserted lower bound.

8.6.2 Nearest neighbors

Let P be a set of n moving points in the plane, as defined above. For a point $p_i(t) \in P(t)$, let $q_i(t)$ denote its *nearest neighbor* in $P(t)$, that is,

$$d(p_i(t), q_i(t)) = \min_{j \ne i} \, d(p_i(t), p_j(t)),$$

where $d(\cdot, \cdot)$ is the Euclidean distance between two points. For the sake of simplicity, assume that the nearest neighbor of each point of P is unique, except for finitely many values of t (this will be the case under an appropriate general position assumption). We wish to bound the number of times the nearest neighbor of some point of P changes.

Fix a point $p_i \in P$. For every $j \neq i$, let

$$g_{ij}(t) = d^2(p_i(t), p_j(t)) = (x_i(t) - x_j(t))^2 + (y_i(t) - y_j(t))^2.$$

Let

$$G_i(t) = \min_{j \neq i} g_{ij}(t).$$

By definition, the nearest neighbor of $p_i(t)$ changes only at breakpoints of G_i. Since each g_{ij} is a polynomial of degree at most $2s$, G_i has at most $\lambda_{2s}(n)$ breakpoints.

This simple technique can also be used to bound the number of times at which the closest pair of points in $P(t)$ changes. For this, consider the function

$$G(t) = \min_{i < j} g_{ij}(t).$$

Again, by definition, the closest pair in $P(t)$ changes only at breakpoints of $G(t)$, and $G(t)$ has at most $\lambda_{2s}(\binom{n}{2}) \leq n\lambda_{2s}(n)$ breakpoints. We thus have:

Theorem 8.40 *Let P be a set of points in the plane, each moving along a trajectory defined by a pair of polynomials of maximum degree s, for some constant s; then the nearest neighbor of any point p_i in P changes at most $\lambda_{2s}(n)$ times. Moreover, the closest pair in $P(t)$ changes at most $\lambda_{2s}(\binom{n}{2}) \leq n\lambda_{2s}(n)$ times. The same bounds hold for the farthest neighbors of the points of P and for the diameter (farthest pair) of P.*

Remark 8.41 It is easy to show that there exists a set P of n points, each moving along some line at constant speed, such that the nearest neighbor of each point of P changes $\Omega(n)$ times, and the closest pair of P changes $\Omega(n^2)$ times. This shows that for $s = 1$ the bounds of Theorem 8.40 are asymptotically tight in the worst case. Let $A = \{a_1, \ldots, a_{\lceil n/2 \rceil}\}$ be a set of $\lceil n/2 \rceil$ points, each moving along the x-axis in the negative x-direction with unit speed. The initial position of a_i is $(2i, 0)$, for $i = 0, \ldots, \lceil n/2 \rceil$. Since all points in A are moving with unit speed in the same direction, the distance between any two points of A does not change with time. Let $B = \{b_1, \ldots, b_{\lfloor n/2 \rfloor}\}$ be another set of $\lfloor n/2 \rfloor$ points moving along the line $y = 1$ in the positive x-direction with unit speed. The initial position of b_i is $(-(2 - \varepsilon)i, 1)$, for $i = 0, \ldots, \lfloor n/2 \rfloor$. where $\varepsilon > 0$ is some sufficiently small parameter so that there exist no four indices i, j, k, l such that $d(a_i, a_j) = d(b_k, b_l) > 0$. Let $P = A \cup B$. It is easily seen that each a_i becomes co-vertical at some time with each b_j, and if a_i and b_j lie on the same vertical line at time t then, by construction, b_j is the nearest neighbor of a_i at that time and (a_i, b_j) is the unique closest pair of $P(t)$. This implies that the nearest neighbor of each a_i changes at least $\lfloor n/2 \rfloor$ times, and that the closest pair of P changes $\Omega(n^2)$ times.

8.6.3 Voronoi diagrams and Delaunay triangulations

Let $P = \{p_1, \ldots, p_n\}$ be a set of n points in the plane, each moving along some given trajectory $p_i = p_i(t)$ satisfying the assumptions made above. Let $Vor(P(t))$ denote the Voronoi diagram of the set P at time t; see Appendix 7.1 for the definition of Voronoi diagrams and related notation. The dual graph of $Vor(P)$ (whose nodes are the points of P and whose edges connect pairs of points with adjacent Voronoi cells) is called the *Delaunay triangulation* of P, and is denoted as $DT(P)$. If P is in general position—no three points are collinear and no four points are cocircular—then each edge of $DT(P)$ corresponds to an edge of $Vor(P)$ and $DT(P)$ is a triangulation of the convex hull of P. A well-known property of $DT(P)$ is that it contains an edge between a pair of points p_i and p_j if and only if there is a circle passing through p_i and p_j that does not contain any point of P in its interior; see, for example, Preparata and Shamos (1985). An immediate consequence of this property is that a triangle $\triangle p_i p_j p_k$ is in $DT(P)$ if and only if the circumscribing circle of the triangle does not contain any point of P in its interior.

If the points of P move continuously with t, then the Voronoi diagram also changes continuously, but its Delaunay triangulation, viewed as an abstract graph, changes only at certain critical values of t, at which there is a change in the combinatorial structure of $Vor(P)$ (because there is a one-to-one correspondence between the edges of $DT(P)$ and those of $Vor(P)$). We will give an upper bound on the number of changes in the Delaunay triangulation of P as the points in P vary with time in the manner assumed above.

It follows from the definition of $DT(P)$ that it changes at time t if and only if one of the following two events occurs:

(i) The combinatorial structure of the convex hull of P changes at time t.

(ii) There is a circle passing through four points $p_i(t), p_j(t), p_k(t), p_l(t)$ that does not contain any point of $P(t)$ in its interior.

Indeed, condition (ii) is obvious from the definition of $DT(P)$. Condition (i) corresponds to cases where the vertices p_i, p_j, p_k of a Delaunay triangle become collinear. Then the circumscribing disk of $\triangle p_i p_j p_k$ approaches a half-plane bounded by the line $p_i p_j p_k$; since this half-plane has to contain no points of P, such shrinkages of Delaunay triangles must occur along the convex hull boundary. By Theorem 8.38, there are only $O(n\lambda_{2s+2}(n))$ combinatorial changes in the convex hull of P.

In order to bound the number of events of type (ii), fix a pair of points p_i, p_j. Let $\vec{\ell}_{ij}(t)$ denote the directed line passing through $p_i(t)$ and $p_j(t)$ and oriented from $p_i(t)$ to $p_j(t)$, and let $\xi_{ij}(t)$ denote the midpoint of the segment $p_i(t)p_j(t)$. The center of any circle passing through $p_i(t), p_j(t)$ lies on the perpendicular bisector, $b_{ij}(t)$, of $p_i(t), p_j(t)$ (which passes through $\xi_{ij}(t)$). For $k \neq i, j$, let $c_{ijk}(t)$ denote the circumcenter of $p_i(t), p_j(t)$, and $p_k(t)$, and let $g_{ijk}(t)$ be the distance along $b_{ij}(t)$ between $\xi_{ij}(t)$ and $c_{ijk}(t)$; the sign of $g_{ijk}(t)$

is positive (respectively, negative) if c_{ijk} lies to the left (respectively, to the right) of $\vec{\ell}_{ij}(t)$. See Figure 8.19 for an illustration. For $k \neq l$, $g_{ijk}(t) = g_{ijl}(t)$ if $p_i(t), p_j(t), p_k(t)$, and $p_l(t)$ are cocircular, which is equivalent to

$$\det \begin{vmatrix} x_i(t) & y_i(t) & x_i^2(t) + y_i^2(t) & 1 \\ x_j(t) & y_j(t) & x_j^2(t) + y_j^2(t) & 1 \\ x_k(t) & y_k(t) & x_k^2(t) + y_k^2(t) & 1 \\ x_l(t) & y_l(t) & x_l^2(t) + y_l^2(t) & 1 \end{vmatrix} = 0.$$

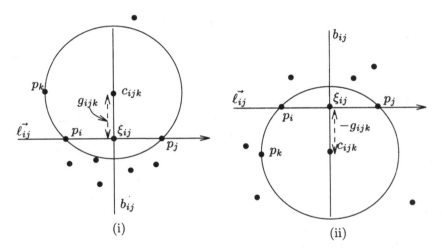

FIGURE 8.19. Definition of the functions $g_{ijk}(t)$: (i) $g_{ijk}(t)$ is positive; (ii) $g_{ijk}(t)$ is negative.

Since the above determinant is a polynomial of degree at most $4s$, the function $g_{ijk} - g_{ijl}$ has at most $4s$ roots. We define $g_{ijk}^+(t)$ (respectively, $g_{ijk}^-(t)$) to be $g_{ijk}(t)$ if p_k lies to the left (respectively, to the right) of $\vec{\ell}_{ij}$, and undefined otherwise. As shown in Section 8.6.1, p_i, p_j, and p_k become collinear for at most $2s$ values of t, so each of g_{ijk}^+ and g_{ijk}^- has at most $2s$ points of discontinuity (it is easily checked that these functions are continuous at any other point where they are defined). Define

$$A_{ij}(t) = \min_{k \neq i,j} g_{ijk}^+(t),$$
$$B_{ij}(t) = \max_{k \neq i,j} g_{ijk}^-(t).$$

In view of the above discussion, each of the envelopes A_{ij}, B_{ij} has at most $O(\lambda_{4s+2}(n))$ breakpoints.

Lemma 8.42 *A combinatorial change of $DT(P)$ of type (ii), involving p_i, p_j and two other points of P that lie on the same side of $\vec{\ell}_{ij}(t)$, occurs at time t only if one of the envelopes $A_{ij}(t), B_{ij}(t)$ has a breakpoint at t.*

Proof. Let the other two points involved in the critical event be p_k, p_l. If p_k, p_l lie on the left side of $\vec{\ell}_j(t)$, then $g_{ijk}^+(t) = g_{ijl}^+(t) = A_{ij}(t)$, because, for any other point $p_m \in P$ that lies to the left of $\vec{\ell}_{ij}(t)$, we must have $g_{ijm}^+(t) \geq g_{ijk}^+(t)$, as is easily verified. A symmetric argument applies if p_k, p_l lie on the right side of $\vec{\ell}_{ij}(t)$. □

Hence, repeating this argument for all pairs $p_i, p_j \in P$, and observing that each combinatorial change of type (ii) is counted in this manner at least once, we easily conclude that the number of critical events of type (ii) is $O(n^2 \lambda_{4s+2}(n))$. We thus have:

Theorem 8.43 *Let P be a set of n points in the plane, each moving along a trajectory defined by polynomials of maximum degree s, for some constant s; then the combinatorial structure of the Voronoi diagram (and the Delaunay triangulation) of P changes at most $O(n^2 \lambda_{4s+2}(n))$ times.*

Remark 8.44 The best known lower bound on the number of changes in $Vor(P)$ is a trivial $\Omega(n^2)$ bound. The example described in Remark 8.41 gives such a bound. It is conjectured that the actual number of changes is indeed close to quadratic, perhaps $O(n\lambda_r(n))$ for some appropriate constant r.

If each point in P moves along a line with unit speed, then we can obtain a slightly improved bound on the number of combinatorial changes in $Vor(P)$. In this case, if the point p_i moves with velocity $(a_i, \sqrt{1 - a_i^2})$ and has initial position (u_i, v_i), for some $0 \leq a_i \leq 1$ and $u_i, v_i \in \mathbb{R}$, then the position of p_i at time t is

$$p_i(t) = \left(u_i + a_i \cdot t, \ v_i + \sqrt{1 - a_i^2} \cdot t \right).$$

Let $\mathcal{F} = \{f_1, \ldots, f_n\}$ be the collection of the following n trivariate functions: for each $i = 1, \ldots, n$

$$f_i(x, y, t) = (u_i + a_i t - x)^2 + \left(v_i + \sqrt{1 - a_i^2} \cdot t - y \right)^2, \text{ for } i = 1, \ldots, n. \quad (8.3)$$

Then the Voronoi diagram of P at time $t = t_0$ is the intersection of the minimization diagram $M_{\mathcal{F}}$ with the plane $t = t_0$ (see also Appendix 7.1). This is easily seen to imply that the number of combinatorial changes in $Vor(P)$ is bounded by the complexity of the lower envelope of $\mathcal{F}$. Since each f_i is of the form (7.17), Corollary 7.37 implies:

Theorem 8.45 *Let P be a set of n points in the plane, each moving along some line with unit speed. Then the number of combinatorial changes in the Voronoi diagram of P is $O(n^3)$.*

Remark 8.46 The problems studied in this section can be solved in a much simpler manner, if one is willing to accept bounds that are only slightly worse than those obtained above. This is done by applying the results of Chapter 7 concerning lower envelopes in higher dimensions. For example, in the dynamic convex hull problem, define, for each point $p_i \in P$, the bivariate function

$$F_i(\theta, t) = x_i(t) \cos \theta + y_i(t) \sin \theta,$$

which gives the signed distance from the origin to the line passing through $p_i(t)$ and having normal direction θ. It is easily verified that the upper envelope

$$E(\theta, t) \equiv \max_{1 \le i \le n} F_i(\theta, t)$$

gives the signed distance from the origin to the line supporting $C(t)$ and having outward normal direction θ. Hence, the combinatorial complexity of E gives an upper bound on the number of combinatorial changes of $C(t)$ over time. By an appropriate parametrization, one can easily verify that the functions F_i satisfy Assumptions 7.1, so Theorem 7.7 implies that the complexity of E is $O(n^{2+\varepsilon})$, for any $\varepsilon > 0$. In fact, one can prove an upper bound of $O(n\lambda_q(n))$, for some $q > 0$, on the complexity of E by applying Theorem 7.32, because, for any fixed $t = t_0$, the equation

$$F_i(\theta, t_0) = F_j(\theta, t_0)$$

has at most two solutions.

Similarly, as also follows from the discussion in Appendix 7.1, the dynamic Voronoi diagram problem can be expressed in terms of the lower envelope of n trivariate functions $F_i(x, y, t)$, each expressing the distance from a point (x, y) to $p_i(t)$, for $i = 1, \ldots, n$ (similar to those given in (8.3)). Again, the results of Section 7.4 easily imply that the number of combinatorial changes in the dynamic Voronoi diagram is $O(n^{3+\varepsilon})$, for any $\varepsilon > 0$.

We also note that this approach can be extended to more complex situations, replacing the moving points by more complex objects, replacing the Euclidean distance by another metric, and so on.

8.7   Hausdorff distance and Voronoi surfaces

In this section we analyze the combinatorial complexity of the upper envelope of so-called *Voronoi surfaces*, show how this envelope is related to the problem of computing the minimum Hausdorff distance between point sets under translation, and give an efficient algorithm for computing the envelope. The minimum Hausdorff distance between two point sets under translation has been proposed as a measure of the degree to which the two sets resemble each other, and is thus a useful construct in pattern recognition.

The *Hausdorff distance* between two point sets A and B in $\mathbb{R}^d$ is defined as

$$H(A, B) = \max\{h(A, B), h(B, A)\},$$

where

$$h(A, B) = \max_{a \in A} \min_{b \in B} \rho(a, b)$$

and $\rho(\cdot, \cdot)$ is the distance function in the underlying metric. In what follows we assume that ρ is an L_p metric, for some $1 \leq p \leq \infty$.[6] Suppose we fix the set A and allow B to translate; then we define the *minimum Hausdorff distance under translation* between A and B, denoted by $D(A, B)$, to be

$$D(A, B) = \min_x H(A, B \oplus x),$$

where $B \oplus x = \{b + x \mid b \in B\}$. It is shown by Huttenlocher and Kedem (1990) that D is a metric. The value of x minimizing D gives us the translation of B under which it most resembles A, in the sense that for each point of $B \oplus x$ there is a sufficiently close point of A and vice versa.

We will shortly show that the computation of $D(A, B)$ can be reduced to the problem of constructing the upper envelope of so-called *Voronoi surfaces*. We first study this construct, which is interesting in its own right, and then show the connection to the minimum Hausdorff distance problem.

Let S be a set of points in $\mathbb{R}^d$. The *Voronoi surface* of S is defined as

$$d(x) = \min_{q \in S} \rho(q, x),$$

where $\rho(\cdot, \cdot)$ is the distance function in $\mathbb{R}^d$ under some fixed L_p metric. By definition, and as noted in Appendix 7.1, the orthogonal projection of the graph of $d(x)$ onto the hyperplane $x_{d+1} = 0$ is the Voronoi diagram of S in the L_p-metric, which we denote by $Vor(S)$. It is a partitioning of $\mathbb{R}^d$ into cells, one for each $q \in S$, so that the cell of q contains all points of $\mathbb{R}^d$ that are nearest to q than to any other point of S. It is well known that each cell of the Voronoi diagram is star-shaped with respect to its associated point. In $\mathbb{R}^2$ this implies, by Euler's formula, that the number of vertices, edges, and faces of $Vor(S)$ is linear in the size of S (see Lee (1980)).

Let $S_1, \ldots, S_m$ be a family of pairwise-disjoint point sets in $\mathbb{R}^d$, with $|S_i| = n_i$ and $\sum_{i=1}^{m} n_i = n$, and let $d_i(x)$ denote the Voronoi surface of S_i. The upper

---

[6]The distance between two points $a, b \in \mathbb{R}^d$ under an L_p metric is defined as $\max_i |a_i - b_i|$ if $p = \infty$ and as $\left(\sum_{i=1}^{d} |a_i - b_i|^p\right)^{1/p}$ otherwise, where $(a_1, \ldots, a_d)$ and $(b_1, \ldots, b_d)$ are the coordinates of a and b, respectively.

envelope of these surfaces is the (graph of the) function

$$E^*(x) = \max_{1 \le i \le m} d_i(x).$$

Thus $E^*(x)$ gives the largest L_p-distance from x to its m nearest neighbors, one from each set S_i. We will use $d_i(x)$ and $E^*(x)$ to denote both the corresponding function and its graph in $\mathbb{R}^{d+1}$. The combinatorial complexity of the upper envelope $E^*(x)$ is defined as in Chapter 7.

We analyze the combinatorial complexity of $E^*(x)$ for the case of planar point sets. Let us first derive an easy (but not sharp) upper bound on that complexity. Notice that the Voronoi surface of a planar set of points under the L_1 or L_∞ metric is piecewise linear. Since each Voronoi surface $d_i(x)$ has $O(n_i)$ vertices, it follows by Theorem 7.1 that $E^*(x)$ has complexity $O(n^2\alpha(n))$ for the L_1 or L_∞ metric. The distance function $\rho(q, x)$, under the L_2 metric in $\mathbb{R}^2$, for points $q = (q_1, q_2), x = (x_1, x_2)$, is

$$d(q, x) = \sqrt{x_1^2 + x_2^2 - 2q_1 x_1 - 2q_2 x_2 + q_1^2 + q_2^2}.$$

As noted in Appendix 7.1, the combinatorial structure of the Voronoi surface of S_i under the L_2 metric is the same as that of

$$\delta_i(x) = \min_{(q_1, q_2) \in S_i} -2q_1 x_1 - 2q_2 x_2 + q_1^2 + q_2^2.$$

This implies that the combinatorial structure of $E^*(x)$, under the L_2 metric, is the same as that of the function

$$E_0^*(x) = \max_i \delta_i(x).$$

But $\delta_i(x)$ is a piecewise-linear function—it is the lower envelope of n_i planes in $\mathbb{R}^3$; thus, as above, we can regard $E_0^*(x)$ as the upper envelope of $O(n)$ triangles in $\mathbb{R}^3$, which implies, by Theorem 7.1, that the combinatorial complexity of $E^*(x)$, under the L_2 metric, is also $O(n^2\alpha(n))$. We also note that this argument can be combined with the results of Section 7.3 to obtain $O(n^{2+\varepsilon})$ bounds for this complexity under any L_p distance, and also for more general distance functions. However, in what follows we will improve and extend these results, showing that, for any L_p metric, the complexity of $E^*(x)$ is $O(mn\alpha(n))$, and that it can be computed in time $O(mn \log n)$.

Fix one set S_i. Let $\tau(q)$ be the Voronoi cell of a point $q \in S_i$ in the Voronoi diagram $Vor(S_i)$. Now consider the Voronoi diagrams $Vor(S_i \cup S_j)$, for all $j \ne i$. For each $j \ne i$, denote by $\sigma_j(q)$ the Voronoi cell of q in $Vor(S_i \cup S_j)$. It is easily seen that $\sigma_j(q) \subseteq \tau(q)$. Let $\sigma(q) = \bigcup_{j \ne i} \sigma_j(q)$; see Figure 8.20.

Lemma 8.47 *For a point $x \in \tau(q)$, the upper envelope $E^*(x)$ is equal to $d_i(x)$ if and only if $x \in \tau(q) - \sigma(q)$.*

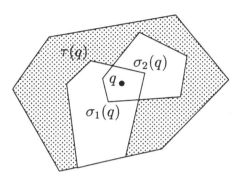

FIGURE 8.20. The cells $\sigma_j(q)$ within the Voronoi cell $\tau(q)$ of a given point $q \in S_i$.

Proof. For a point $x \in \tau(q)$ we have $d_i(x) = d(x, q)$. If $x \in \sigma(q)$, then there is a set S_j such that $x \in \sigma_j(q)$, so q is the nearest neighbor of x in $S_i \cup S_j$. Hence,

$$d_i(x) = d(x, q) < \min_{q' \in S_j} d(x, q') = d_j(x) \le E^*(x).$$

Conversely, if $x \notin \sigma(q)$, then, for all $j \ne i$, $x \notin \sigma_j(q)$, which implies

$$d_j(x) = \min_{q' \in S_j} d(x, q') \le d(x, q) = d_i(x);$$

hence $E^*(x) = d_i(x)$. $\square$

Lemma 8.48 *For any $p \ne 1, \infty$, the Voronoi diagram of a set $\{p_1, p_2, p_3\}$ of three points in $\mathbb{R}^2$, under the L_p metric, has at most one vertex.*

Proof. If p_1, p_2, and p_3 are collinear, with, say, p_2 lying between p_1 and p_3, then, since the L_p-distance ρ is a strictly convex function, it follows that $\rho(x, p_2) < \max\{\rho(x, p_1), \rho(x, p_3)\}$, so the Voronoi diagram of these points cannot contain any vertex. Thus assume that p_1, p_2, p_3 are not collinear.

Suppose to the contrary that $Vor(\{p_1, p_2, p_3\})$ has two vertices x, y. Since, as mentioned above, each cell of the diagram is star-shaped with respect to its defining point, it follows that the relative interiors of the six straight segments $p_i x, p_i y$, for $i = 1, 2, 3$, are pairwise disjoint. At least one of x, y must lie outside the convex hull of p_1, p_2, p_3, for otherwise we can find a point z outside the hull for which the segments $p_1 z, p_2 z, p_3 z$ all lie outside the hull, and this leads to an impossible plane embedding of the graph $K_{3,3}$; see Figure 8.21(i).

Suppose, with no loss of generality, that x lies outside the hull. The convex hull of $\{x, p_1, p_2, p_3\}$ is either a triangle or a quadrangle. Suppose first that it is a triangle, say, $x p_1 p_3$. Then there is a line ℓ through p_2 that separates x from p_1, p_3, and then p_2 lies on ℓ between $q_1 = \ell \cap x p_1$ and $q_3 = \ell \cap$

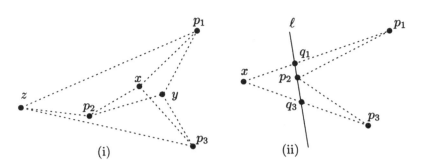

FIGURE 8.21. Illustration of the proof of Lemma 8.48.

xp_3 (see Figure 8.21(ii)). If the hull of $\{x, p_1, p_2, p_3\}$ is a convex quadrangle Q, say, $xp_1p_2p_3$, then two cases can arise: If y lies inside Q, then we get an impossible plane embedding of $K_{3,3}$, by choosing another point z in an appropriate location outside the hull of p_1, p_2, p_3, and by connecting each of x, y, z to the three points p_i. Otherwise, y lies outside Q, which is easily seen to imply that the configuration of Figure 8.21(ii) must then hold for y instead of x. Thus, in the setting of Figure 8.21(ii), we obtain

$$\rho(x, p_2) < \max\{\rho(x, q_1), \rho(x, q_3)\} < \max\{\rho(x, p_1), \rho(x, p_3)\},$$

a contradiction that completes the proof of the lemma.   □

Theorem 8.49 *The combinatorial complexity of the upper envelope of Voronoi surfaces of m point sets in the plane, with a total of n points, is $O(mn)$ for the L_1 or L_∞ metric, and $O(mn\alpha(mn))$ for all other L_p metrics.*

Proof. Let $S_1, \ldots, S_m$ be the given sets, and let $|S_i| = n_i$, so that $n = \sum_{i=1}^{m} n_i$. Fix one of the sets S_i. For $j \neq i$, let $\mu_j(q)$ denote the number of edges in the Voronoi cell $\sigma_j(q)$ of $q \in S_i$ in $Vor(S_i \cup S_j)$. Let $\mu(q) = \sum_j \mu_j(q)$.

As mentioned above, each cell of a Voronoi diagram in the L_p metric is star-shaped, so, if we introduce polar coordinates with q as the origin, the boundary of each $\sigma_j(q)$ can be regarded as the graph of a function $r = \gamma_j(\theta)$. Thus the boundary of $\sigma(q) = \bigcup_{j \neq i} \sigma_j(q)$ can be regarded as the graph of the upper envelope of these functions. For the L_1 and L_∞ metrics, the Voronoi edges are segments with orientations $0, \pi/4, \pi/2$, and $3\pi/4$. We partition the edges of all Voronoi cells $\sigma_j(q)$, for $j \neq i$, into four subsets, so that all edges within each subset have the same orientation. The upper envelope of the edges (each of which is a partially defined function in polar coordinates) within each subset has obviously linear complexity. We combine the four families of upper envelopes, by merging in pairs three times, to obtain the overall upper envelope. The same argument as in Section 6.2.1 implies that the complexity of the resulting envelope is also linear in $\mu(q)$.

For $p \neq 1, \infty$, we note that any pair of Voronoi edges bounding two Voronoi cells, $\sigma_k(q), \sigma_l(q)$, can intersect at most once. Indeed, let $e_k \subseteq \partial\sigma_k(q)$ and $e_l \subseteq \partial\sigma_l(q)$ be two such Voronoi edges. Let q_k, q_l denote the respective points in S_k, S_l that, together with q, induce the edges e_k, e_l in $Vor(S_i \cup S_k), Vor(S_i \cup S_l)$, respectively (we assume here that e_k and e_l are both interior to $\tau(q)$; a similar argument applies if one of them does not lie in the interior of $\tau(q)$). Any intersection of e_k, e_l is thus a vertex of the Voronoi diagram $Vor(\{q, q_k, q_l\})$ common to its three cells. By Lemma 8.48, $Vor(\{q, q_k, q_l\})$ has at most one vertex, so e_k and e_l can intersect in at most one point. This implies that $\partial\sigma(q)$, as the upper envelope of these edges, has $O(\mu(q)\alpha(\mu(q)))$ vertices.

Lemma 8.47 implies that the complexity of the entire upper envelope $E^*(x)$ is bounded by the sum of the complexities of the regions $\sigma(q)$, over all $q \in S_i$ and over all $i = 1, \ldots, m$, plus the sum of complexities of the individual Voronoi diagrams $Vor(S_i)$. If we put

$$t = \sum_{i=1}^{m} \sum_{q \in S_i} \mu(q),$$

then the overall complexity of all the regions $\sigma(q)$ is $O(t)$ for $p = 1, \infty$ and $O(t\alpha(t))$ for $p \neq 1, \infty$. We have

$$
\begin{aligned}
t &= \sum_{i=1}^{m} \sum_{q \in S_i} \mu(q) = \sum_{i=1}^{m} \sum_{j \neq i} \left(\sum_{q \in S_i} \mu_j(q) \right) \\
&= \sum_{i=1}^{m} \sum_{j \neq i} O(n_i + n_j) \\
&= \sum_{i=1}^{m} O((m-1)n_i + (n - n_i)) \\
&= O(mn).
\end{aligned}
$$

This completes the proof of the theorem. $\qquad\qquad\qquad\qquad\qquad\qquad$ □

Next, we prove a lower bound that implies that the bounds in Theorem 8.49 are asymptotically tight for the L_1, L_∞ metrics and almost tight for all other L_p metrics.

Theorem 8.50 *For any given integers $m < n$, there is a family of m point sets with n points in total, so that the upper envelope of their Voronoi surfaces, under any L_p metric, has $\Omega(mn)$ edges.*

Proof. We will describe the construction for the L_∞ metric, but the same construction works for any L_p metric. Assume, with no loss of generality, that $2m$ divides n. Each S_i consists of $n_i = n/m$ points, and we construct these

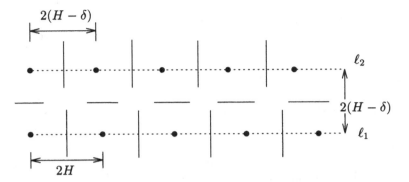

FIGURE 8.22. The set S_1 in the lower bound construction.

sets as follows. We fix two parameters, $H \gg \delta > 0$. We first construct S_1, placing its points on two horizontal lines $\ell_1 : y = 0$ and $\ell_2 : y = 2(H - \delta)$ (see Figure 8.22). The coordinates of the first $n_1/2$ points of S_1, lying on ℓ_1, are $(2Hi, 0)$ for $0 \le i < n_1/2$, and the coordinates of the next $n_1/2$ points, lying on ℓ_2, are $(2i(H - \delta), 2(H - \delta))$ for $0 \le i < n_1/2$. The diagram $Vor(S_1)$ thus consists of two sets of parallel vertical edges (each having $n_1/2 - 1$ edges), of a set of $n_1/2$ horizontal Voronoi edges, and of other edges that are not important for the construction (and are not shown in Figure 8.22). Moreover, the Voronoi surface $d_1(x)$ has constant height over each of the vertical and horizontal Voronoi edges. For the vertical edges separating points on ℓ_1, we have $d_1(x) \equiv H$. For the vertical edges separating points on ℓ_2, we have $d_1(x) \equiv H - \delta$. For the horizontal Voronoi edges, $d_1(x)$ is also $H - \delta$.

We now create m translated copies of S_1, so that, for $1 \le i \le m/2$, we have $S_i = S_1 \oplus z_i$, where $z_i = ((i - 1)\varepsilon, 0)$, and $S_{m/2+i} = S_1 \oplus w_i$, where $w_i = ((H - \delta), -i\varepsilon)$; here $\varepsilon > 2\delta$ and $\varepsilon \cdot m/2 < 2H$.

The upper envelope $E^*(x)$ of these surfaces is depicted in Figure 8.23. There are $O((n/m) \cdot m)$ vertical edges over which the height of $E^*(x)$ is H. In addition, the surfaces $d_i(x)$ have $O(n)$ slightly lower horizontal edges (at height $H - \delta$), arranged along m horizontal lines. Since $\varepsilon > 2\delta$, the lines disappear from the upper envelope $E^*(x)$ below the vertical edges and reappear on the upper envelope at small intervals between them. This produces $\Omega(mn)$ edges on $E^*(x)$.

Although the value of $d_i(x)$ on the vertical and horizontal edges is not constant for other L_p metrics, the same construction of points, with an appropriate choice of parameters, leads to a similar lower bound for these metrics as well. $\square$

We next describe an algorithm for computing the upper envelope $E^*(x)$ of

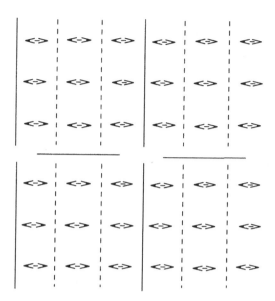

FIGURE 8.23. The upper envelope of the Voronoi surfaces in the lower-bound construction.

Voronoi surfaces of a family of m point sets, $S_1, \ldots, S_m$, in the plane with a total of n points. We first compute, in time $O((n_i + n_j)\log(n_i + n_j))$, the Voronoi diagrams $Vor(S_i \cup S_j)$, for each $1 \le i < j \le m$; see, for example, Preparata and Shamos (1985), and Lee (1980). Then, for each point $q \in S_i$, $1 \le i \le m$, we compute the region $\sigma(q) = \bigcup_{j \ne i} \sigma_j(q)$, where $\sigma_j(q)$ is the cell of q in $Vor(S_i \cup S_j)$. In view of Lemma 8.47, $\partial\sigma(q)$ is the upper envelope, in polar coordinates about q, of the boundaries $\partial\sigma_j(q)$, for $j \ne i$, so it can be computed in time $O(\mu(q)\log\mu(q))$ (since each pair of the partial functions participating in the envelope intersects at most once; see Theorem 6.5). Summing up all these costs, and using the same analysis as in the proof of Theorem 8.49, we obtain:

Theorem 8.51 *The upper envelope of Voronoi surfaces of m point sets in the plane, with a total of n points, under any L_p metric, can be computed in $O(mn\log n)$ time.*

We now return to the problem of computing the minimum Hausdorff distance $D(A, B)$, under translation, between two planar point sets A, B. We now show, as promised, a reduction from the problem of computing $D(A, B)$ to the construction of the upper envelope of Voronoi surfaces. Let $A = \{a_1, \ldots, a_u\}$ and $B = \{b_1, \ldots, b_v\}$ be the two given sets of points in the plane. For each point $a_i \in A$, let $S_i = \{a_i - b \mid b \in B\}$, and, for each point $b_i \in B$, let

$S_{u+i} = \{a - b_i \mid a \in A\}$. Finally, let $d_i(x)$ denote the Voronoi surface of S_i, for $i = 1, \ldots, u + v$.

Lemma 8.52 *Let $E^*(x)$ denote the upper envelope of the Voronoi surfaces $d_1(x), \ldots, d_{u+v}(x)$, as defined above; then*

$$D(A, B) = \min_x E^*(x).$$

Proof. Recall that

$$
\begin{aligned}
h(A, B \oplus x) &= \max_{a_i \in A} \min_{b_j \in B} \rho(a_i, b_j + x) \\
&= \max_{a_i \in A} \min_{b_j \in B} \rho(a_i - b_j, x) \\
&= \max_{1 \leq i \leq u} \min_{q \in S_i} \rho(q, x) \\
&= \max_{1 \leq i \leq u} d_i(x).
\end{aligned}
$$

Similarly, one can show that

$$h(B \oplus x, A) = \max_{u < i \leq u+v} d_i(x).$$

Hence,

$$
\begin{aligned}
D(A, B) &= \min_x H(A, B \oplus x) \\
&= \min_x \max \left\{ \max_{1 \leq i \leq u} d_i(x), \ \max_{u < i \leq u+v} d_i(x) \right\} \\
&= \min_x E^*(x). \qquad \square
\end{aligned}
$$

Since there are $u + v$ different point sets S_i, and the total number of points in them is $2uv$, the upper envelope of the Voronoi surfaces of the S_i's, under any L_p metric, can be computed in time $O(uv(u + v) \log uv)$. After having computed the upper envelope, we find the global minimum of $E^*(x)$. It is easily checked that the global minimum of $E^*(x)$ occurs at one of its vertices, if the underlying metric is L_1, L_2, or L_∞. Thus, in these cases, $\min_x E^*(x)$ can be computed without any additional overhead. For all other L_p metrics, the global minimum of $E^*(x)$ occurs either at one of its vertices or at one of its edges. Indeed, observe that the function $d_i(x)$ is unimodal for $x \in \tau(q)$, with the minimum $d_i(x) = 0$ at $x = q$. Thus the local minima of $d(x)$ for $x \in \tau(q) - \sigma(q)$ must occur as close to q as possible. Since $\sigma(q)$ is star-shaped, such a closest point must lie on the boundary of $\sigma(q)$. We therefore compute the local minima of $E^*(x)$ over each edge of $E^*(x)$ (in constant time per edge), and choose the overall minimum. We thus obtain:

Theorem 8.53 *Let A and B be two sets of points in the plane with $|A| = u$ and $|B| = v$. Then the minimum Hausdorff distance between A and B under translation, under any L_p metric, can be computed in time $O(uv(u+v) \log uv)$.*

8.8   Polygon placement

In this section we study several applications of Davenport–Schinzel sequences to polygon placement problems. Let B be a *convex* polygonal object with k sides, which can be placed in the plane amid a collection of polygonal obstacles with a total of n edges, which B must avoid. We denote by V the closure of the free space available for B, and by V^c its complement (the union of the interiors of the obstacles). Each placement of B can be parametrized by three real parameters, (x, y, θ), where (x, y) are the coordinates of some fixed reference point on B, and θ is the angle between the positive x-axis and some fixed reference axis rigidly attached to B (see Figure 8.24). Thus we can represent the space of all placements of B by the three-dimensional space $\mathbb{R}^2 \times \mathbb{S}$, where $\mathbb{S}$ is the unit circle. This parametric space is called the *configuration space* of B. A placement $Z = (x, y, \theta)$ of B is called a *free placement* (or a *free configuration*) if at this placement B does not intersect any obstacle. We say that a placement is *semi-free* if at this placement B makes contact with one or more obstacles but does not intersect the interior of any obstacle. The subset of all free and semi-free placements of B is known as the *free configuration space* of B, and we denote it by *FP*.

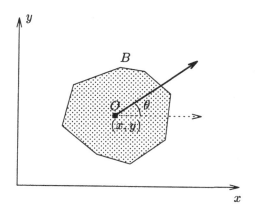

FIGURE 8.24. A placement of B.

Our goal is to construct *FP* and represent it in some appropriate discrete combinatorial fashion. This construction facilitates the solution of various problems involving placements of B, such as:

Polygon placement: Determine whether there exists a free or semi-free placement of B, that is, whether *FP* is nonempty.

Extremal polygon placement: Find the largest similar copy of B that admits a semi-free placement.

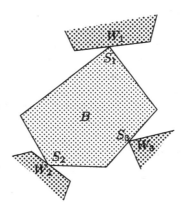

FIGURE 8.25. A critical placement of B.

Motion planning: Given two free placements of B, determine whether there exists a continuous obstacle-avoiding motion of B from the initial to the final placement.

The first two applications are discussed in this section, while the motion-planning application is described in Section 8.9.

8.8.1   The number of critical semi-free placements

We will focus here only on the problem of estimating the combinatorial complexity of FP, which will suffice to highlight the way in which Davenport–Schinzel sequences are applied to these problems. We will discuss the algorithmic aspects of the problem, only briefly, in the following subsection. To measure the complexity of FP, we first introduce the following definition:

Definition 8.54   A placement of B is called *critical* if it is semi-free and makes simultaneously three contacts with the obstacle edges (we refer to them as *walls*). Hence a critical placement Z is one for which there exist three distinct pairs (W_1, S_1), (W_2, S_2), (W_3, S_3), such that, for each $i = 1, 2, 3$, either W_i is a wall edge and S_i is a corner of B, or W_i is a wall corner and S_i is a side of B, and such that, at placement Z, S_i touches W_i. See Figure 8.25 for an illustration of such a critical contact.

Note that this somewhat 'liberal' definition also regards as critical placements at which a corner of B touches a wall corner and another corner/side of B touches another wall edge/corner (including also placements at which a side of B overlaps a wall segment with an endpoint in common).

The importance of critical placements comes from the following result:

Lemma 8.55 *If there exists a free placement of B, then there also exists a critical placement of B (assuming there is at least one obstacle).*

Proof. Start at a free placement of B, and move B until contact is made between some vertex or edge S_1 of B and some obstacle edge or vertex W_1, respectively. With no loss of generality, assume that S_1 is a vertex and that W_1 is an edge—the other case can be analyzed in much the same way. Translate B without rotation so that it maintains contact between S_1 and W_1, until either the contact is about to cease to exist (meaning that S_1 is touching an endpoint Q_1 of W_1) or a contact is made between another feature of B and another obstacle feature (whichever occurs first). In the former case, rotate B around the endpoint Q_1 until either W_1 overlaps an edge of B adjacent to S_1 or another contact is made; in either of these events, we reach a critical placement. In the latter case, we have two distinct points of contact, between S_1 and W_1, and between another pair of polygon and obstacle features S_2, W_2. If S_2 and W_2 are both corners, we again have a critical placement. Otherwise, we move B so that it maintains contact between S_1 and W_1 and between S_2 and W_2 (this 'gliding' motion has one remaining degree of freedom).

If during this motion a third contact is made, or one of the contacts (W_1, S_1), (W_2, S_2) degenerates into a corner-corner contact, we again reach a critical placement. We claim that one of these cases must indeed arise during the motion. This is in fact a simple exercise in analytic geometry, which we include here for the sake of completeness. As long as no third contact occurs, we may ignore the rest of B and consider only the pair of features, S_1, S_2, of B as moving rigidly together while maintaining contact with W_1, W_2, respectively. Suppose both S_1 and S_2 are corners, so that W_1 and W_2 are wall edges. If these edges are parallel, we simply translate the segment $S_1 S_2$ until an endpoint of either W_1 or W_2 is reached. If W_1 and W_2 are not parallel, extend them to full lines that meet at some point O (see Figure 8.26(i)). Since obstacle edges are disjoint, at least one of them, say, W_1, must end before O. One can easily verify that S_1 can move toward O while touching W_1 so that S_2 keeps contact with W_2. Eventually this motion will get S_1 to an endpoint of W_1 (or S_2 to an endpoint of W_2, whichever occurs first), as claimed.

The case where S_1 and S_2 are both edges is symmetric—interchange the roles of polygon and obstacles in the above analysis.

The case where S_1 is a corner and S_2 is an edge (or vice versa) is different (see Figure 8.26(ii)). Here we claim that we can always translate B so that S_1 moves slightly along W_1, and then compensate for the move by rotating B around S_1 so as to bring it back into contact between S_2 and W_2. A simple calculation shows that this is indeed always possible, except for the case where the segment $S_1 W_2$ is perpendicular to S_2, and we move B in a direction that makes S_1 get too close to W_2; see Figure 8.26(iii). In this case we simply move S_1 in the opposite direction along W_1, and observe that this degenerate configuration cannot arise again. This one-way motion of S_1 must eventually reach a corner-corner contact.

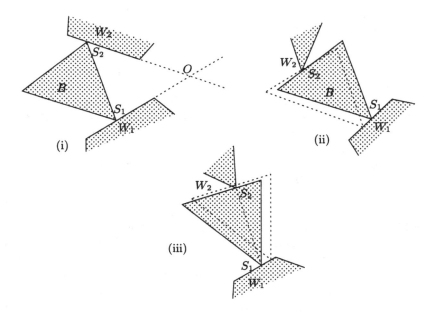

FIGURE 8.26. Illustrating the proof of the existence of critical placements.

Thus in all cases we reach a critical placement, thereby completing the proof of the lemma.   □

Remark 8.56 (i) The proof of the lemma actually shows that each connected component of FP contains a critical placement.

(ii) The double-contact motions analyzed in the proof of the lemma can be represented by curves that describe the motion of the reference point on B, and are known as *glissettes*. An easy exercise in analytic geometry shows that these are algebraic curves of degree ≤ 4. For example, when S_1 and S_2 are both corners we get an ellipse, and when S_1 is a corner, S_2 is an edge incident to S_1, and the reference point is the other endpoint of S_2, we get a quartic curve known as the *conchoid of Nicomedes*. We refer the reader to Lockwood (1961) for more details concerning these glissettes.

Hence, in a certain sense, it suffices to compute only critical placements of B. (For example, for the polygon placement problem we just need to decide whether there exists at least one critical placement.) The main problem that we consider in this section is to obtain a sharp upper bound on the number of critical placements. This will be achieved by reducing the three-dimensional problem of finding critical placements to a collection of two-dimensional problems involving lower envelopes of certain univariate functions. This reduction, however, is fairly involved and is among the more complex geometric applications of Davenport–Schinzel sequences. We will nevertheless describe it in detail, because of its significance in polygonal placement and motion-planning problems.

We assume that B and the set of obstacles are in *general position*. By this we mean that the shape of B and the locations of the obstacles are such that there does not exist a placement of B at which it satisfies four *algebraically independent* constraints imposed on B by its possible contacts with obstacles. Each constraint of this form requires a specific corner of B to touch a specific wall edge, a specific side of B to touch a specific wall corner, or that the segment connecting two points of contact be perpendicular to the wall edge or to the side of B involved in one of these contacts (see Figure 8.26(iii) for an illustration of the latter type of constraint). We refer the reader to Leven and Sharir (1987b) for more details concerning the issue of general position.

We begin the analysis by introducing a few notations.

Definition 8.57

(a) A (potential) *contact pair* O is a pair (W, S) such that either W is a (closed) wall edge and S is a corner of B, or W is a wall corner and S is a (closed) side of B. The contact pair is said to be of type I in the first case, and of type II in the second case.

(b) An actual *obstacle contact* (i.e., a contact of B with an obstacle) is said to *involve* the contact pair $O = (W, S)$ if this contact is of a point on S against a point of W, and furthermore if this contact is *locally free*, that is, the inner angle of B at S lies entirely on the exterior side of W if S is a corner of B, and the entire angle within the wall region V^c at W lies exterior to B if W is a wall corner.

(c) The *tangent line* T of a contact pair $O = (W, S)$ is either the line passing through W if W is a wall edge or the line passing through W and parallel to S if S is a side of B (in the second case T depends of course on the orientation of B).

It is clear from the above definition that there are $O(kn)$ possible contact pairs. Throughout this section we will use the same index i to refer to a contact pair O_i, to its corresponding wall feature W_i and boundary feature S_i of B, and to its tangent line T_i. Let Z be a free placement of B at which it makes two simultaneous obstacle contacts involving the contact pairs O_i, O_j for which T_i, T_j are not parallel. Then we denote by $z_{ij} = z_{ji}$ the intersection point of T_i and T_j, by x_{ij} (respectively, x_{ji}) the contact point of W_i with S_i (respectively, of W_j with S_j) at placement Z, and by ℓ_{ij} the line passing through x_{ij} and x_{ji}. Also u_{ij}, v_{ij} denote the endpoints of W_i if O_i is of type I or the endpoints of S_i when B is placed at Z if O_i is of type II, such that u_{ij}

and z_{ij} lie on the same side of x_{ij} on T_i, and v_{ij} lies on the other side of x_{ij} (u_{ji}, v_{ji} are defined similarly for O_j); see Figure 8.27.

An extreme situation arises when $x_{ij} = z_{ij}$, which is the case when W_i is a wall edge, W_j is a wall corner, and S_i is an endpoint of the side S_j of B. In this case u_{ij}, v_{ij} are not well-defined, although u_{ji} and v_{ji} are. We will refer to this case by calling O_i, O_j *adjacent* contact pairs. Another extreme situation arises when a corner S of B touches a wall corner W; formally speaking (see also the discussion earlier in this section), this can be regarded as a double contact (e.g., of S against the two wall edges meeting at W). In this case we have $x_{ij} = x_{ji} = z_{ij}$, so that all four points u_{ij}, v_{ij}, u_{ji}, v_{ji}, as well as the line ℓ_{ij}, are not well-defined. We will ignore such singular contacts in our upper bound analysis (as justified in Remark 8.63 below).

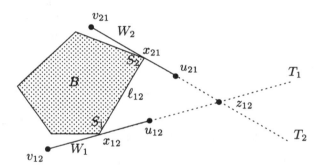

FIGURE 8.27. A double contact of B.

Definition 8.58   Let O_1, O_2 be two contact pairs. We say that O_2 *bounds* O_1 at the orientation θ if there exists a (not necessarily free) placement $Z = (X, \theta)$ of B at which it makes two simultaneous obstacle contacts involving O_1, O_2, respectively, such that $B^\star = \text{conv}(S_1 \cup S_2)$ always intersects W_2 as we translate B from Z (without changing the orientation θ) along the tangent T_1 in the direction of z_{12}, until the last placement at which S_1 still touches W_1.

In case of adjacent contact pairs O_1, O_2, with O_1 of type I and O_2 of type II, we have $z_{12} = x_{12}$ so that the direction of motion of B in this definition is not defined; moreover, in this case $B^\star$ is simply the segment S_2, which stops intersecting W_2 immediately as we move it toward either endpoint of W_1. In this ill-defined case we prefer to regard O_2 as not bounding O_1 (note, however, that in this case O_1 does bound O_2 in accordance with the above definition).

The following lemma, which is based, in a rather strong manner, on the fact that B is convex, is crucial to our analysis:

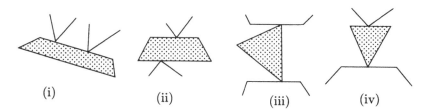

FIGURE 8.28. Degenerate double contacts.

Lemma 8.59 *Let O_1, O_2 be two contact pairs for which there exists a placement $Z = (X, \theta)$ of B at which it makes two simultaneous obstacle contacts involving O_1, O_2, respectively. Then either O_1 bounds O_2 at θ or O_2 bounds O_1 at θ, except when the corresponding tangents T_1, T_2 are coincident or parallel. Typical degenerate cases of this kind, depicted in Figure 8.28, are:*

(a) W_1, W_2 are both wall corners and $S_1 = S_2$;

(b) W_1, W_2 are both wall corners and S_1, S_2 are parallel sides of B;

(c) W_1, W_2 are parallel wall edges;

(d) W_1 is a wall edge and S_2 is a side of B parallel to W_1.

Proof. In the nondegenerate case, the tangents T_1, T_2 must intersect at a single point. Using the terminology introduced above, we consider separately three possible subcases (see Figure 8.29).

(i) W_1, W_2 are both wall edges (see Figure 8.29(i)). Consider the line ℓ_1 (respectively, ℓ_2) parallel to ℓ_{12} and passing through u_{12} (respectively, u_{21}). Obviously either ℓ_1 intersects W_2 or ℓ_2 intersects W_1. Suppose, without loss of generality, that ℓ_1 intersects W_2. But then, as we move B along W_1 from x_{12} until $S_1 S_2$ reaches ℓ_1, the segment $B^\star = S_1 S_2$ will always intersect W_2. Thus O_2 bounds O_1 at θ.

(ii) W_1, W_2 are both wall corners (see Figure 8.29(ii)). Let ℓ_1 (respectively, ℓ_2) be the line parallel to ℓ_{12} that passes through v_{12} (respectively, v_{21}). Obviously, either ℓ_1 intersects S_2 or ℓ_2 intersects S_1. Suppose, without loss of generality, that ℓ_1 intersects S_2. Then, since $B^\star$ is convex, the entire trapezoid Δ, bounded by ℓ_{12}, ℓ_1, S_1, and S_2, is contained in $B^\star$ (in this placement of simultaneous contact with W_1 and W_2). Thus, as we move B along T_1 toward z_{12} until the endpoint v_{12} of S_1 coincides with W_1, then, throughout this motion, W_2 will intersect Δ, hence $B^\star$, again showing that O_2 bounds O_1.

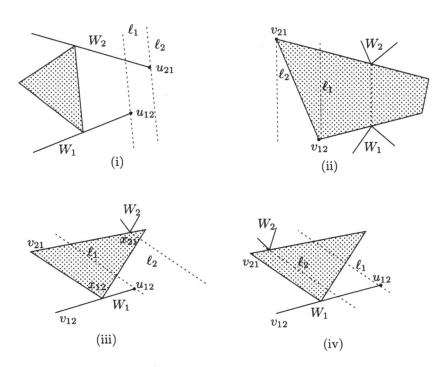

FIGURE 8.29. Illustrating the proof of Lemma 8.59.

(iii) W_1 is a wall edge and W_2 is a wall corner (or the other way around); see Figure 8.29(iii,iv). If O_1 and O_2 are adjacent contact pairs, then O_1 bounds O_2 (see a comment following Definition 8.59). Assume that this is not the case, and let ℓ_1 (respectively, ℓ_2) be the line parallel to $S_1 v_{21}$ passing through u_{12} (respectively, through $x_{21} = W_2$). Obviously, either ℓ_1 intersects the line segment $x_{21} v_{21}$ or ℓ_2 intersects the line segment $x_{12} u_{12}$. In the former case (Figure 8.29(iii)), observe that, at the placement of mutual contact, the triangle $x_{12} x_{21} v_{21}$ is contained in $B^\star$; thus if we move B along W_1 until S_1 meets u_{12}, then, throughout this motion, W_2 must intersect this triangle, hence $B^\star$, so in this case O_2 bounds O_1. In the latter case (Figure 8.29(iv)), if we translate B along T_2 until v_{21} meets W_2, then, throughout this motion, the line segment $S_1 v_{21}$ (and hence also $B^\star$) will intersect W_1, so in this case O_1 bounds O_2. □

Remark 8.60 The proof of Lemma 8.59 actually implies that, for each double contact of B involving contact pairs O_1, O_2, there exists a delimiting orientation $\theta_{O_1 O_2}$ of B (for which the lines ℓ_1 and ℓ_2 coincide) such that, at orientations greater than $\theta_{O_1 O_2}$, one of the contact pairs, say, O_1, bounds O_2

but O_2 does not bound O_1, and, at orientations smaller than $\theta_{O_1 O_2}$, the contact pair O_2 bounds O_1 but O_1 does not bound O_2. Such a delimiting orientation is depicted in Figure 8.30. If O_1, O_2 are adjacent, then on one side of $\theta_{O_1 O_2}$ one of these contact pairs, say, O_1, always bounds O_2, whereas on the other side of $\theta_{O_1 O_2}$ no such double contact of B is possible.

Definition 8.61 Let O_1 be any contact pair and consider all contact pairs that bound O_1 (at any orientation θ). For each such pair O_2 we define the *bounding function* $F_{O_1 O_2}(\theta)$, over the domain $\Pi = \Pi_{O_1 O_2}$ of orientations θ of B at which O_2 bounds O_1, to be the distance of x_{12} from v_{12} or from u_{12}, at the placement $Z = (X, \theta)$ in which B simultaneously makes two obstacle contacts involving O_1 and O_2. The distance is measured to v_{12} if S_1 is a corner of B, and to u_{12} if S_1 is a side of B (see Figure 8.30; note that v_{12} and u_{12} are always well-defined in this situation).

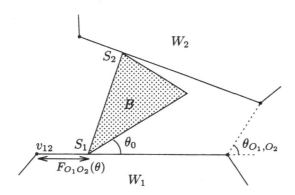

FIGURE 8.30. The definition of $F_{O_1 O_2}(\theta)$.

Note that, in general, Π need not be connected but may consist of several subintervals, such that, for orientations θ outside these intervals, either two obstacle contacts, involving O_1, O_2, respectively, cannot occur simultaneously, or O_2 does not bound O_1. Nevertheless, we claim that $\Pi_{O_1 O_2}$ consists of at most a constant number of intervals. This follows from the fact that O_2 bounds O_1 at an orientation θ of B if and only if the following four conditions hold:

1. θ lies on the appropriate side of the delimiting orientation $\theta_{O_1 O_2}$ that separates between the domain in which O_2 bounds O_1 and the domain in which O_1 bounds O_2 (see Remark 8.60).

2. There exists, at orientation θ, a placement of B at which S_1 touches W_1 and S_2 touches W_2 simultaneously.

3. Suppose S_1 is a corner of B and W_1 is a wall edge. Then, at this placement of double contact, the inner angle of B at S_1 lies entirely on the exterior side of W_1; if S_1 is a side of B and W_1 is a wall corner, then, again, the entire angle within the wall region V^c at W_1 should lie exterior to B. Similar conditions should hold for the contact of S_2 against W_2.

4. The tangents T_1, T_2 of O_1, O_2, respectively, are not parallel or coincident at θ.

Clearly, these conditions involve only a constant number of polygon and obstacle features, and their constraints can be expressed as a Boolean combination of equalities and inequalities involving low-degree algebraic expressions. Hence, the number of intervals over which all these conditions hold must be constant. A more meticulous analysis, which can be found in Leven and Sharir (1987b), shows in fact that Π_{O_1,O_2} consists of at most five intervals.

If $\Pi_{O_1 O_2}$ is indeed not connected, we will consider each connected portion of the graph of $F_{O_1 O_2}$ as a separate partially defined function. Clearly, the number of such functions is still at most $O(kn)$, for each fixed contact pair O_1.

Next recall that the definition of v_{12} (and thus also of $F_{O_1 O_2}$) depends on the position of the intersection point of T_1, T_2 relative to the contact point of S_1 with W_1, and that the respective 'reference' endpoint v_{12} or u_{12} is one of the endpoints of W_1 if O_1 is of type I or one of the endpoints of S_1 if O_1 is of type II. We partition the collection of bounding functions $F_{O_1 O_2}$ for O_1 into two classes $\mathcal{F}_1$, $\mathcal{F}_2$, so that, for all functions in $\mathcal{F}_1$, the reference point v_{12} (or u_{12}) is the same endpoint of W_1 (or of S_1), whereas for all functions in $\mathcal{F}_2$ it is the other endpoint. (Thus if O_1, O_2 are contact pairs of mixed types, the domain of $F_{O_1 O_2}$ has to be split at the orientation θ^* at which the side of B involved in one contact becomes parallel to the wall edge involved in the other contact, so that on one side of θ^* the function $F_{O_1 O_2}$ is in $\mathcal{F}_1$, whereas on the other side of θ^* it belongs to $\mathcal{F}_2$.) Thus each contact pair O_1 defines two 'complementary' coordinate frames (θ, ρ) that can be used to represent placements of B at which it makes an obstacle contact involving O_1. Here θ is the orientation of B and ρ is the distance from the contact point of the contact involving O_1 to a designated reference endpoint v of either W_1 or S_1. Within each frame, let C_{O_1} denote the region representing placements of B at which a contact involving O_1 occurs (see Definition 8.57(b)). Consider one such coordinate frame for O_1 and the corresponding collection $\mathcal{F}_1$ of bounding functions (for which the reference endpoint v_{12} or u_{12} coincides with the designated endpoint v for that coordinate frame). It follows, by definition, that if $F_{O_1 O_2} \in \mathcal{F}_1$, $(\theta, \rho) \in C_{O_1}$, $\rho_0 = F_{O_1 O_2}(\theta)$ is defined, and $\rho > \rho_0$, then (θ, ρ) is a nonfree placement of B (because W_2 intersects the interior of B at this placement); in other words, the area of C_{O_1} above each bounding function in $\mathcal{F}_1$ represents nonfree placements of B. This crucial property of bounding functions is the reason for introducing this notion, and we will shortly see that critical placements arise only along the lower envelopes of the bounding functions.

Let $Z = (X, \theta)$ be a critical placement of B, and let the contact pairs involved in the three corresponding simultaneous contacts be $O_i = (W_i, S_i)$, for $i = 1, 2, 3$. For each pair $i \neq j$, either O_i bounds O_j or O_j bounds O_i at the orientation θ of B (unless one of the degenerate situations listed in Lemma 8.59 occurs). Hence, in general, the placement Z is represented by points lying on the graphs of some of the bounding functions $F_{O_i O_j}$. Suppose, without loss of generality, that it lies on the graph of $F_{O_1 O_2} \in \mathcal{F}_1$. Then, since Z is semi-free, we must have

$$F_{O_1 O_2}(\theta) = \min \{ F_{O_1 O}(\theta) \mid F_{O_1 O} \in \mathcal{F}_1 \};$$

in other words, Z is represented by a point on the lower envelope $E_{O_1 \mathcal{F}_1}$ of the functions in $\mathcal{F}_1$. (Note that the converse property does not necessarily hold, that is, a placement represented by a point lying on $E_{O_1 \mathcal{F}_1}$ may be nonfree, because B might intersect at this placement obstacles whose contacts with B involve pairs that either do not bound O_1 at θ, or bound it but are represented in the complementary collection $\mathcal{F}_2$.) Furthermore, since at Z the object B also makes an obstacle contact involving the pair O_3, we must have one of the following situations:

(i) O_3 also bounds O_1 at θ and $F_{O_1 O_3}$ (over some neighborhood of θ) also belongs to $\mathcal{F}_1$. In this case Z is represented by an intersection point of $F_{O_1 O_2}$ and $F_{O_1 O_3}$ on $E_{O_1 \mathcal{F}_1}$ (a breakpoint of $E_{O_1 \mathcal{F}_1}$); see Figure 8.31(i).

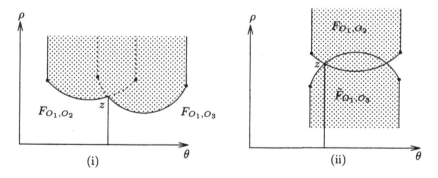

FIGURE 8.31. Schematic illustration of the representation of various types of critical contacts.

(ii) O_3 also bounds O_1 at θ, but $F_{O_1 O_3}$ (over some neighborhood of θ) belongs to $\mathcal{F}_2$. Let $\tilde{E}_{O_1 \mathcal{F}_2}$ denote the lower envelope of the functions in $\mathcal{F}_2$, reflected into the coordinate frame (θ, ρ) in which the functions in $\mathcal{F}_1$ are represented (since this transformation is a reflection of the ρ-axis, $\tilde{E}_{O_1 \mathcal{F}_2}$ will be the upper envelope of the reflections $\tilde{F}_{O_1 O}$ of the functions $F_{O_1 O}$ in $\mathcal{F}_2$). Then in this case Z is represented as an intersection point of $E_{O_1 \mathcal{F}_1}$ with $\tilde{E}_{O_1 \mathcal{F}_2}$; see Figure 8.31(ii).

(iii) O_3 does not bound O_1 at θ, and, moreover, no two of these contact pairs simultaneously bound the third pair at θ, but two of these pairs, say, O_1, O_3, have parallel or coincident associated tangents; see Figure 8.32(i).

(iv) As in (iii), no two of these contact pairs simultaneously bound the third one, and, furthermore, the degenerate cases in (iii) above do not arise at θ. In this case we can assume, without loss of generality, that O_1 does not bound O_2, O_2 does not bound O_3, and O_3 does not bound O_1 at θ. But then, by Lemma 8.59, it must be the case that O_2 bounds O_1, O_3 bounds O_2, and O_1 bounds O_3 at θ, so that Z is represented by a point on $F_{O_1 O_2}$, a point on $F_{O_2 O_3}$, and a point on $F_{O_3 O_1}$, each lying in a corresponding lower envelope; see Figure 8.32(ii).

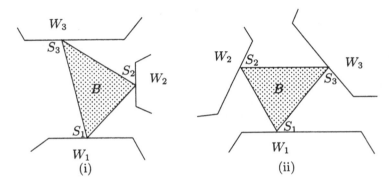

FIGURE 8.32. Critical contacts of types (iii) and (iv).

We now proceed to estimate separately the number of critical contacts of each of these four types.

Type (i) critical contacts: Let O_1 be a contact pair and consider the lower envelope $E = E_{O_1 \mathcal{F}_1}$ of one of the collections $\mathcal{F}_1$ of bounding functions for O_1. To estimate the number of breakpoints along E, it suffices to obtain a bound on the number of intersections between any pair of functions in $\mathcal{F}_1$. Note that each intersection of two functions $F_{O_1 O_2}, F_{O_1 O_3} \in \mathcal{F}_1$ represents a placement of B in which it simultaneously makes three contacts involving the pairs O_1, O_2, O_3, respectively.

Lemma 8.62 *Let O_1, O_2, O_3 be three distinct contact pairs. Then there are at most four placements of B at which it makes simultaneously three obstacle contacts involving O_1, O_2, O_3, respectively.*

Proof. By the analysis of Schwartz and Sharir (1983a), which is a rather simple exercise in analytic geometry, it follows that the curve $\gamma_{O_1 O_2}$, traced by some reference point on B as B makes simultaneously two obstacle contacts involving the pairs O_1, O_2, is a straight segment, a portion of an ellipse, or a portion of a quartic algebraic curve (see also Remark 8.56(ii)). Hence if one of the contact pairs, say, O_3, is of type I then we can take S_3 to be the reference point on B, so that the desired placements of triple contact of B correspond to the intersection points of $\gamma_{O_1 O_2}$ with the straight segment W_3. Since $\gamma_{O_1 O_2}$ is at most quartic, there are at most four such intersections, thus at most four placements of B at which this triple contact can occur. If all three contact pairs are of type II, we can consider a coordinate frame in which B is stationary and the obstacles move in a collectively rigid manner. Then the desired placements of triple contact correspond to placements in this coordinate frame of the moving triangle $W_1 W_2 W_3$ at which its vertices touch simultaneously the three segments S_1, S_2, S_3, respectively. Hence this case can be treated in much the same way as the case in which all contact pairs are of type I, and the preceding argument implies that there are at most four placements of triple contact in this case too. □

It therefore follows by Corollary 1.3 that each lower envelope $E_{O\mathcal{F}}$ has $O(\lambda_6(kn))$ breakpoints. Thus, summing the number of such critical breakpoints, over all contact pairs O_1, we conclude that there are $O(kn\lambda_6(kn))$ critical contacts of type (i).

Type (ii) critical contacts: Let O_1 be a contact pair. We wish to estimate the number of intersections of the lower envelope $E_{O_1 \mathcal{F}_1}$ with the reflected envelope $\tilde{E}_{O_1 \mathcal{F}_2}$. The discussion preceding Corollary 5.20 implies that the number of such intersection points is only $O(\lambda_6(kn))$. Summing these bounds over all contact pairs O_1, we conclude that the number of critical contacts of type (ii) is $O(kn\lambda_6(kn))$.

Type (iii) critical contacts: Let θ be an orientation of B at which it makes simultaneously three contacts involving the pairs O_1, O_2, O_3, such that no two of them bound simultaneously the third pair at θ, and such that two of these contact pairs, say, O_1, O_2, satisfy at θ one of the degenerate conditions listed in Lemma 8.59. Since we assume that B and the obstacles are in general position, it can be checked that none of these degenerate cases can arise (at θ) also for O_1, O_3 or for O_2, O_3. Since, by assumption, O_1, O_2 do not both bound O_3, it then follows that O_3 bounds one of them, say, O_1. Hence this critical contact is represented as a point on one of the envelopes for O_1. But it is easily seen that there are only $O(kn)$ orientations θ of B in which it can make a contact involving O_1 and another contact involving O_2 in one of those degenerate manners. Moreover, since the type (iii) critical contact that we consider must be represented by a point lying on an envelope for O_1, it follows that each such θ can determine only one critical contact of the above form, represented by the point at orientation θ on that envelope of O_1 that coincides with $F_{O_1 O_3}$ at θ. Hence, summing over all possible contact pairs O_1, we obtain at most $O(k^2 n^2)$ (which is also $O(kn\lambda_6(kn))$) critical contacts of type (iii).

Type (iv) critical contacts: Finally, consider the (most complex) case of type (iv) contacts. Consider first the set C of all critical orientations at which some envelope $E_{O\mathcal{F}}$ has a breakpoint. Without loss of generality, we can assume that each $\theta \in C$ is defined by a unique triple of contact pairs. (Otherwise, if some $\theta \in C$ is induced by more than one triple of contact pairs, then, applying an infinitely small perturbation to the obstacle configuration, we can split θ into several orientations, infinitely close to one another, each now induced by a unique triple of contact pairs; see Schwartz and Sharir (1983a) for details of such a perturbation technique.) By the preceding arguments, C consists of $O(kn\lambda_6(kn))$ orientations, which partition the angular range for θ into $O(kn\lambda_6(kn))$ disjoint noncritical intervals. Consider one such interval I.

For each contact pair O_1, each of the envelopes $E_{O_1\mathcal{F}_1}$, $E_{O_1\mathcal{F}_2}$ is equal, over I, to a single bounding function in $\mathcal{F}_1$, $\mathcal{F}_2$, respectively. Suppose I contains an orientation θ_0 at which a type (iv) critical contact occurs, which involves O_1 and two additional contact pairs O_2, O_3. Also, without loss of generality, assume that O_2 bounds O_1, O_3 bounds O_2, and O_1 bounds O_3 at θ_0. Then, throughout I, one of the lower envelopes for O_1 coincides with $F_{O_1O_2}$, one of the lower envelopes for O_2 coincides with $F_{O_2O_3}$, and one of the lower envelopes for O_3 coincides with $F_{O_3O_1}$. It follows that, to find all possible triples O_1, O_2, O_3 of contact pairs that include a specific contact O_1, and that can induce a type (iv) critical contact at some orientation within I, one simply has to consider the two contact pairs whose bounding functions appear on the two lower envelopes for O_1 over I, then obtain, for each of these contact pairs O_2, the two contact pairs representing the two lower envelopes for O_2 over I, and finally check that O_1 is a contact pair representing one of the envelopes for such a third contact pair O_3. Hence, there exist at most four such triples of contact pairs (involving a specific O_1), so that altogether the lower envelopes over I induce at most $O(kn)$ critical orientations at which a type (iv) contact can occur. Note that not all these induced orientations necessarily lie in I; but even if such an orientation θ lies outside I, it can still realize the corresponding type (iv) critical contact, because the functions appearing in the corresponding lower envelopes over I may still appear along these envelopes over the noncritical interval containing θ.

Now let I' be a noncritical interval adjacent to I, and let θ^* be their common endpoint. By assumption, B makes at the critical orientation θ^* a unique triple obstacle contact involving three contact pairs O_1^*, O_2^*, O_3^*. This implies that, as we cross through θ^* from I to I', only the functions appearing in the lower envelopes for O_1^*, O_2^*, O_3^* can change. But the preceding argument then implies that only $O(1)$ new critical contacts of type (iv) can be induced by the various lower envelopes over I', in addition to those that were already induced by the envelopes over I. In other words, each noncritical interval can contribute only $O(1)$ additional potential contacts of type (iv), so that altogether there can be at most $O(kn\lambda_6(kn))$ critical contacts of type (iv).

Remark 8.63 So far we have been ignoring critical contacts involving a contact pair O_1 of a corner S_1 of B against a wall corner W_1. Since O_1 involves two independent constraints on the placement of B, we seek here critical contacts involving O_1 and just one more contact pair O_2. Such double critical contacts, however, are quite easy to analyze. Indeed, for such a contact pair O_1, the only degree of freedom left for B as it makes the contact involving O_1 is rotation about the common point of contact of S_1 against W_1. During this rotation, each additional contact involving some pair O_2 can occur in at most two orientations, so that there are only $O(kn)$ potential critical orientations at which a critical contact involving O_1 can occur. Thus, altogether, there are at most $O(k^2n^2)$ critical contacts of this form.

Similar remarks apply to the case in which a side S_1 of B overlaps a wall edge W_1. Again, this condition leaves only one degree of freedom to vary (namely that of sliding S_1 along W_1), and one can show, in the same manner as above, that only $O(kn)$ critical contacts involving O_1 are possible. Thus there are at most $O(k^2n^2)$ singular contacts of this second kind.

All this gives us the following main theorem of this section:

Theorem 8.64 *The number of triple-contact critical semi-free placements of a convex k-sided polygonal object B, moving amid polygonal obstacles composed of n edges altogether, is $O(kn\lambda_6(kn))$.*

Remark 8.65 (i) We do not know whether this upper bound is tight. However, there exist instances where the number of critical placements of B is $\Omega(k^2n^2)$, thus leaving only a rather small gap between the upper and lower bounds.

(ii) Note that the preceding analysis crucially depends on the fact that the polygon B is convex (which is used in the proof of Lemma 8.59). In fact, if B is nonconvex, it is easy to construct examples where there are $\Theta(k^3n^3)$ critical semi-free placements of B, as illustrated in Figure 8.33.

8.8.2 Algorithms

In this subsection we consider several specific polygon placement and related problems, and briefly describe their algorithmic solutions.

8.8.2.1 Polygon placement

We begin with the simplest version of the original problem—given a convex k-gon B and a polygonal region V bounded by n edges, determine whether there exists at least one free or semi-free placement of B in V. By the preceding analysis, it suffices to determine whether there exists at least one semi-free

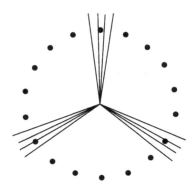

FIGURE 8.33. A nonconvex polygon with $\Omega(k^3 n^3)$ critical placements.

critical placement of B. In more generality, we want to calculate the entire collection of critical placements of B; this will also be needed in other applications, mentioned below (e.g., in motion planning).

The preceding analysis can be transformed into an efficient procedure for calculating all critical placements of B. Roughly, this procedure first calculates the two lower envelopes for each contact pair. This can be done, as described in Theorem 6.1, in time $O(kn\lambda_6(kn)\log kn)$, and yields right away all the type (i) placements. Next, the type (ii) and type (iv) critical placements can be calculated by a 'sweeping process' that iterates over the noncritical intervals of θ, and maintains a priority queue of potential critical contacts of these types. This process requires only a constant number of updates as we cross from one noncritical interval to an adjacent one, following the same steps as in the analysis given above. This process also requires $O(kn\lambda_6(kn)\log kn)$ time. Type (iii) critical contacts are even easier to calculate. Hence all the critical semi-free placements of B can be calculated in time $O(kn\lambda_6(kn)\log kn)$.

There is, however, a technical problem with this approach: The analysis given above may produce orientations θ whose corresponding critical placement of B may be nonfree. This is because the conditions that define critical orientations in terms of the lower envelopes $E_{O\mathcal{F}}$ are necessary but not sufficient; for example, as already noted, a breakpoint of such an envelope does not always correspond to a semi-free critical placement, and similarly for the other types of criticalities. (This is not just a hypothetical problem—there exist configurations where such spurious critical orientations can arise.) One possible solution is to compute (the superset of) all critical placements in the manner outlined above, and then test each of them whether it is really semi-free, by preparing certain *range searching* data structures, and by querying them with each potential critical placement. If the complexity k of B is small, this can be done fairly efficiently. We omit here further details concerning this issue, and refer the reader to Sharir and Toledo (1994), where this solution is described in detail. The running time of their solution is $O(k^2 n \lambda_6(kn) \log kn)$.

8.8.2.2 Line segment placement

It is also instructive to consider the simpler case where B is just a line segment PQ. In this case, if Z is any critical placement of B that involves three distinct points of contact, then, assuming general position of the obstacles, Z must be one of the two following types (see Figure 8.34 for an illustration):

(i) Two of the contacts at Z are of P and of Q against two respective wall edges, and the third contact is between some wall corner and an interior point of PQ (Figure 8.34(i)); or

(ii) two contacts are between two wall corners and the relative interior of PQ and one contact is between an endpoint of B and some wall edge (Figure 8.34(ii)); or

(iii) one (double) contact at Z is of P (or of Q) against a wall corner and the third contact is arbitrary (Figure 8.34(iii)).

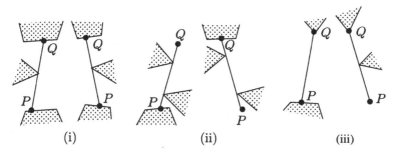

FIGURE 8.34. Critical placements of a line segment.

It is easily verified that there are only $O(n^2)$ placements of types (ii) and (iii). Concerning placements of type (i), fix the wall corner W touching the interior of PQ, and consider all placements of B where such a contact with W is made. For each orientation θ of B, consider the pair of wall edges, $W^+(\theta)$, $W^-(\theta)$, seen from W at directions θ and $\theta + \pi$, respectively. If there is a critical placement Z of B at orientation θ with W touching the interior of PQ, then the two other contacts at Z must involve the endpoints of B and the two walls $W^+(\theta)$, $W^-(\theta)$. Note that this pair of wall edges can change only at orientations θ where W sees an obstacle corner in direction θ or $\theta + \pi$. Hence, there are only $O(n)$ orientations where this pair of walls can change, which implies that there are only $O(n)$ critical placements of B of this form.

Summed over all wall corners W, this gives a total bound of $O(n^2)$ for the number of critical placements of B. Using standard algorithms for computing *visibility graphs* in the plane (see, e.g., Welzl (1985)), the above analysis can easily be transformed into an algorithm that produces all critical placements of B in time $O(n^2)$. It is easy to see that this quadratic bound on the number of critical placements of B is tight in the worst case.

8.8.2.3   Segment center

Next consider the following seemingly unrelated problem: Let S be a given set of n points in the plane, and let $a, r > 0$ be two real parameters. We wish to determine whether there exists a placement of a line segment e of length a so that all points of S are at distance at most r from the segment.[7] This is a subproblem of the following *segment center* problem: Given S and a as above, find a placement of a line segment of length a that minimizes the maximum distance from any point of S to the segment.

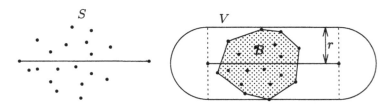

FIGURE 8.35. Transforming the segment center problem to a polygon placement problem.

We can rephrase the former problem as follows. Let V denote the locus of all points lying at distance at most r from (some standard placement of) e. Clearly, V is the union of a rectangle of sides a and $2r$ and of two half-discs of radius r attached to the rectangle; see Figure 8.35. Let B be the convex hull of S. It is easily checked that there exists a placement of e with the desired property if and only if there exists a free placement of B inside V. We thus have reduced our problem to a polygon placement problem, with the new twist that the region in which B has to be placed is not polygonal (although it has a very simple shape).

The whole mechanism of critical orientations and lower envelopes can be applied to this problem as well. One can show that the number of critical placements of B in V is at most $O(n\lambda_s(n))$, where s is some small constant. Note that here n denotes the complexity of the moving polygon, whereas the complexity of V is constant.

Nevertheless, since V is the interior of a convex region with a very simple shape, a more careful analysis, given recently by Efrat and Sharir (1994), shows

---

[7]The distance between a point p and a segment e is defined as $d(p,e) = \min_{q \in e} d(p,q)$.

that the number of critical placements in this case is only $O(n \log n)$, and that they can be computed in close to linear time. The analysis used in their proof is based on a special case of the analysis given in Section 8.10.3 concerning $\{0, 1\}$ matrices with forbidden configurations.

8.8.2.4 Extremal polygon placement

Next consider an extension of the polygon placement problem, where we wish to find the largest similar copy of a given convex polygon B, which admits a semi-free placement inside a given polygonal environment V. This problem can be handled using an ingenious algorithmic technique due to Megiddo (1979, 1983), and known as *parametric searching*. Here is a rough sketch of the technique.

Parametric searching is applied to problems that depend on a certain real parameter r, and ask for the value of r at which some extremal conditions hold. In our case, r is the expansion ratio of the copy of B, and we wish to find the largest value r^* of r for which $r^* B$ still admits a semi-free placement inside V. The parametric searching technique requires an algorithm $\mathcal{A}(r)$ that solves the problem for any fixed value of r; in our case, we require an algorithm that determines whether rB has a semi-free placement inside V. We also assume that $\mathcal{A}(r)$ can determine whether the given r is smaller than, equal to, or greater than r^* (in our case, this is trivial). The parametric searching technique then runs $\mathcal{A}(r)$ *generically*, without specifying the value of r, with the intention of simulating its execution at the unknown r^*. Every time the generic algorithm has to resolve a comparison that depends on r, it computes the few critical values of r at which the outcome of the comparison may change, and then runs the nongeneric version of $\mathcal{A}(r)$ at each of these values, to find the relative position of r^* among them, thereby determining the outcome of the comparison at r^*, which allows the generic algorithm to continue its execution. Each comparison-resolving step narrows the range of possible values for r^*, and, at the end of execution, we are left with a final interval I (usually a single point), and r^* is taken to be the larger or smaller endpoint of I (in our case, the larger one).

To make this method efficient, one has to execute as few comparison-resolving steps as possible, because they are very time consuming. To this end, the parametric searching method employs a parallel algorithm for the generic execution. Such an algorithm generates many independent comparisons at a single parallel step, and we can resolve all of them simultaneously and efficiently by computing the critical values of r for each comparison, by merging these values into a single sorted list of critical values, and by running a binary search through the list, to find the pair of critical values between which r^* lies. This usually results in only an overall polylogarithmic number of calls to the nongeneric, 'fixed-size' algorithm, which usually implies that the running time of the parametric searching technique is worse than the time of the fixed-size algorithm only by a polylogarithmic factor.

In our problem, we thus need to provide both a sequential algorithm and a parallel algorithm for the following fixed-size problem: Given B and V as above, and a parameter $r > 0$, determine whether rB has a free or semi-free placement inside V. Since rB is also a convex polygon, the fixed-size problem is just a standard polygon placement problem. We already described a (sequential) algorithm for solving the problem. This algorithm can also be easily parallelized, at least in the model of computation in which we require only that comparisons be executed in parallel, and are willing to simulate all other steps sequentially (which indeed we will do anyway). For example, the calculation of all the lower envelopes $E_{O\mathcal{F}}$ can be done in parallel, and each envelope can be computed in parallel by a simple divide-and-conquer process (much like the simpler way of computing envelopes, as given in Section 6.2.1). Some of the other steps are somewhat trickier to parallelize. We omit here further details concerning the algorithm, and refer the reader to Sharir and Toledo (1994) for a more comprehensive treatment of the problem. The running time of the resulting algorithm is $O(k^2 n \lambda_6(kn) \log^3(kn) \log\log(kn))$. A similar technique can also be used to solve efficiently the segment-center problem; see Efrat and Sharir (1994) for details.

8.9   Motion planning

Geometric algorithms for *robot motion planning* are one of the major research areas that has motivated the study of Davenport–Schinzel sequences over the past decade. In this section we will describe the strong connection between the two topics, give a few applications in some detail, and review several other results.

Although the term 'robot motion planning' covers by now many different types of problems, we focus here on the simplest type of motion planning, which can be stated in the following general manner. We are given a robot system B with k degrees of freedom and an environment filled with obstacles. The *configuration space* of B is a k-dimensional parametric space, each point of which represents a possible placement of B by a k-tuple of real numbers that gives the values of the parameters controlling the k degrees of freedom of B. An example of such a configuration space was given in the preceding section, for a rigid polygon moving in the plane. We will consider here only robot systems for which k is fairly small; typical values of k range from two (e.g., for a rigid object translating in the plane) to six (for most robot manipulator arms in $\mathbb{R}^3$, and for a rigid object translating and rotating in $\mathbb{R}^3$).

The presence of obstacles in the robot's environment causes portions of the configuration space of B to be 'forbidden' or nonfree; these consist of placements of B where it intersects some obstacle. Our goal is to compute the *free configuration space* of B, which we denote by FP, consisting of those placements of B in which it does not intersect any obstacle. As in the preceding section, we prefer to make FP a closed set, by including in it also semi-free placements, where B might touch some obstacles but does not intersect the interior of any obstacle. The motion-planning problem that we consider is to determine, for any given pair of free (or semi-free) placements, Z_1, Z_2, of B, whether there exists a continuous obstacle-avoiding motion of B from Z_1 to Z_2, and, if so, to plan such a motion.

This problem, under reasonable assumptions concerning the geometry of B and of the obstacles, can be restated as the problem of computing the connected components of FP, and of representing them in an appropriate discrete combinatorial fashion. This follows from the observation that a collision-free motion of B is a connected arc in FP, and such an arc connects Z_1 and Z_2 if and only if they lie in the same (arcwise-) connected component of FP. Thus, in general, motion-planning problems are essentially problems in computational topology, which tends to make their analysis fairly involved. Since our goal here is mainly to highlight the connection between motion planning and Davenport–Schinzel sequences, we will finesse many details concerning the topological aspects of the problem, and focus on its combinatorial and algorithmic aspects; more details can be found in the relevant literature, which will be cited below and is also listed in the bibliographic Notes at the end of the chapter.

The space FP can be defined in terms of an arrangement of surfaces within the configuration space, as follows. For each obstacle feature w (e.g., an obstacle corner, boundary edge, face, etc.) and each robot feature s, let $\sigma_{w,s}$ denote the locus of all placements of B at which s makes contact with w. Under reasonable assumptions concerning the shape of the robot and of the obstacles, the possible types of degrees of freedom of B, and an appropriate choice of the features w, s, we can assume that each locus $\sigma_{w,s}$ is a (portion of some) $(k-1)$-dimensional algebraic surface of low bounded degree (and, if $\sigma_{w,s}$ is not a full surface, its boundary is defined by an additional constant number of algebraic equalities and inequalities, all involving polynomials of low bounded degree). For example, in the case of a rigid motion of a polygon B in the plane amid a collection of polygonal obstacles, each locus $\sigma_{w,s}$ represents placements of B where a specific vertex s of B touches a specific obstacle edge w, or a specific edge s of B touches a specific obstacle corner w; using the coordinates $(x, y, \tan(\theta/2))$ for the configuration space, one easily verifies that each locus $\sigma_{w,s}$ is indeed a two-dimensional algebraic surface patch, of degree at most four, with the above properties (see also the preceding section).

Let Σ denote the resulting collection of surface patches $\sigma_{w,s}$. We refer to these surfaces as *contact surfaces*, and let n denote their number. Let $Z \in FP$ be some initial free placement of B. As we move B from Z, it will remain free as long as the corresponding path traced in the configuration space does not reach any contact surface. Moreover, ignoring certain degenerate possibilities, we can also assume that if B crosses (in configuration space) a contact surface then its placement ceases to be free (B then penetrates into some obstacle in physical space). In other words, the free configuration space of B is a collection of some of the cells of the arrangement $\mathcal{A}(\Sigma)$ of the contact surfaces. Moreover, if we only want to compute the portion of FP that consists of all free placements reachable (via a collision-free motion) from a fixed initial free placement Z of B, then this portion is the cell of $\mathcal{A}(\Sigma)$ that contains Z. This restricted version of the problem is often what is really needed in practice, because, once the robot B is 'started' at placement Z, it will never be able to move (in configuration space) out of the connected component of FP that contains Z, unless we artificially 'restart' it in a different placement.

Hence, the problem has been reduced to the problem of computing a single cell in an arrangement of a collection Σ of n algebraic surface patches, of low bounded degree, in $\mathbb{R}^k$. This immediately shows the connection between motion-planning problems and Davenport–Schinzel sequences. In particular, motion-planning problems with two degrees of freedom can be tackled, in fairly full generality, using the analysis, given in Chapters 5 and 6, concerning planar arrangements of arcs. This will be described below in more detail, and we will conclude that the results of these chapters provide a fairly satisfactory and general solution to any motion-planning problem with two degrees of freedom.

For systems with more degrees of freedom, the situation is more involved. In general, we need to compute a single cell in an arrangement of surfaces in higher dimensions. The first problem that arises is to derive sharp upper bounds on the maximum combinatorial complexity of such a cell. In three dimensions, the results reported in Chapter 7 show that, under reasonable assumptions, which usually hold for typical motion-planning problems, the complexity of a single cell in an arrangement of n contact surfaces is $O(n^{2+\varepsilon})$, for any $\varepsilon > 0$. As mentioned in Chapter 7, similar bounds, $O(n^{d-1+\varepsilon})$, probably hold for $d \geq 4$ dimensions as well. However, the results of Chapter 7 do not yet provide efficient algorithms, of comparable time complexity, for the construction of such a cell, except in several special cases, which we will review below.

We also note that there are certain motion-planning problems for which there is no need to focus on just a single cell in the arrangement of contact surfaces, because the complexity of the entire free configuration space can be shown to be small. In what follows we will also review some of these 'favorable' motion-planning instances.

8.9.1 Translational motion planning for a polygon

Let us begin by considering a fairly simple example of a motion-planning problem with two degrees of freedom. Let B be an arbitrary rigid polygonal object with k sides, and let V be a planar polygonal region, bounded by n edges, in which B is free to translate (without changing its orientation). Any placement of B can be represented by the position (x, y) of some fixed reference point P attached to B. For each obstacle edge w and each vertex v of B, let $\gamma_{w,v}$ denote the locus of all placements of B at which v touches w; clearly, this is a line segment obtained by an appropriate translation of w. Similarly, for each obstacle corner c and each side e of B, let $\gamma_{c,e}$ denote the locus of all placements of B at which e touches c; this is also an appropriately translated copy of e. Hence, in this simple instance, the contact loci are $O(kn)$ straight segments in the plane, and the set of all free placements reachable from a given initial free placement Z of B is the face containing Z in the arrangement formed by these $O(kn)$ contact segments. The analysis of Chapters 5 and 6 thus immediately implies the following result:

Theorem 8.66 *With the above notations, the combinatorial complexity of the space C of all free placements of B that are reachable from Z by a collision-free translational motion is $O(kn\alpha(kn))$. Moreover, C can be constructed in $O(kn\alpha(kn)\log kn)$ randomized expected time, or in $O(kn\alpha(kn)\log^2 kn)$ deterministic time.*

Note that, once C is available, a path that connects Z to some desired target placement (that also lies in C) can be easily computed in time $O(kn\alpha(kn))$.

Note also that in the above analysis B can be an arbitrary polygonal region. In fact, B does not even have to be connected and may consist of several disjoint pieces, all translating rigidly together. However, if B is a single *convex* polygon, better results can be obtained. Suppose in this case the obstacles consist of m convex polygons with pairwise-disjoint interiors (nonconvex obstacles are assumed to be cut into convex pieces). For each convex obstacle O, let γ_O denote the locus of all placements of B at which it touches O (but their interiors remain disjoint). As is well-known (see, e.g., Kedem et al. (1986)), γ_O is (the boundary of) a closed convex polygon, which is the Minkowski sum $O \oplus (-B_0) = \{x - y \mid x \in O, y \in B_0\}$, where B_0 is a standard placement of B at which P lies at the origin. (As is well-known, the number of edges of γ_O is at most $k + n_O$, where n_O is the number of edges bounding O.) It has been shown by Kedem et al. (1986) that, for any pair of distinct obstacles O, O' (with pairwise-disjoint interiors), the polygons γ_O, $\gamma_{O'}$ intersect in at most two points, assuming general position of B and of the obstacles. Hence, applying Theorem 5.7, we conclude that the space C of free placements of B reachable from Z has complexity at most $\lambda_2(m) = 2m - 1$. Note, however, that here we measure complexity only in terms of the number of intersections of the loci γ_O that appear along ∂C; to this we have to add the total number of vertices of the individual polygons γ_O, which is at most $\sum_O (k + n_O) = km + n$. Hence, we conclude that the boundary of the desired free component C contains at most $km + n$ *reflex* corners and at most $2m - 1$ nonreflex (convex) corners. Moreover, as shown by Kedem et al. (1986), the entire free configuration space of B in this case (which is simply the complement of the union of the polygons γ_O) has at most $6m - 12$ nonreflex corners (for $m > 2$) and at most $km + n$ reflex corners. See also Section 7.5.2.

8.9.2   Motion planning with two degrees of freedom

For robot systems B with two degrees of freedom, the configuration space is two-dimensional, and we may as well assume that it is the Euclidean plane. Under reasonable assumptions concerning the shape of B and of the obstacles, and the types of the degrees of freedom that B has, the contact loci will be algebraic arcs of some constant maximum degree, say, b. It follows that any pair of contact arcs intersect in at most $s \leq b^2$ points. Moreover, each of the primitive operations that the algorithms in Chapter 6 require can be assumed to take constant time, in a reasonable model of computation. Hence, given an initial free placement Z of B, the face f that contains Z in the arrangement of the contact arcs has combinatorial complexity $O(\lambda_{s+2}(n))$, where n is the number of contact arcs, and f can be constructed in $O(\lambda_{s+2}(n) \log n)$ randomized expected time, or in $O(\lambda_{s+2}(n) \log^2 n)$ deterministic time.

We note that the bound $s \leq b^2$ on the number of intersections between any pair of contact arcs is often too big, and various ad-hoc arguments, based on the underlying geometry of the robot and environment, are often used to obtain smaller values for s. For example, the observation of Corollary 6.9 is a useful tool in such an analysis. Another possibility is to cut each contact arc into several subarcs so as to reduce further the maximum number of intersections between any pair of subarcs.

8.9.3   General motion planning for a polygon

Let B be a polygonal object bounded by k sides, free to move (translate and rotate) in a planar polygonal region V bounded by n edges. The configuration space of B is now three-dimensional, and each placement of B can be represented by an appropriate triple $(x, y, \tan(\theta/2))$, as already mentioned above.

Consider first the case where B is convex. Observe that any vertex of the free configuration space FP of B must be a semi-free critical placement of B, and vice versa. Thus, the analysis of the polygon placement problem, as given in Section 8.8, implies that the number of vertices of the entire free configuration space, FP, is $O(kn\lambda_6(kn))$. With a few additional topological arguments, one can show that the total combinatorial complexity of FP is also $O(kn\lambda_6(kn))$.

However, turning this bound into an efficient motion-planning algorithm requires more work. We give here only a brief review of such an algorithm, as developed by Kedem and Sharir (1990), and modified by Kedem, Sharir and Toledo (1993). The algorithm constructs a network N of edges within FP and along its boundary. These edges are mostly (but not exclusively) actual edges of FP (i.e., maximal connected portions of intersection curves of pairs of the contact surfaces, which are not met by any third surface and which lie on the boundary of FP). The network N has two properties: (i) it *preserves the connectivity* of FP, in the sense that the portion of N that lies within (the closure of) a single connected component of FP is connected, and (ii) it is *reachable*, in the sense that there exists a simple procedure that, given any free placement Z of B, constructs a canonical motion that 'pushes' B to a placement on N. With the availability of such a network, motion planning is easy: Given two free placements Z_1, Z_2 of B, apply the canonical motions to get from these placements to two respective placements W_1, W_2 on N, and then check whether W_1 and W_2 lie in the same connected component of N. If so, obtain a path that connects W_1 and W_2 within N, and concatenate to that path the two canonical paths between Z_1 and W_1 and between Z_2 and W_2, to obtain the desired motion. If W_1 and W_2 do not lie in the same network component, conclude that there is no collision-free motion of B from Z_1 to Z_2. Since N is one-dimensional, testing connectedness and planning paths between points on N can be easily done by standard graph-searching techniques, in time proportional to the size of N.

We omit here the full details of the manner in which the network N is constructed. Roughly speaking, the algorithm first computes all critical placements of B, as in Section 8.8, and then determines which pairs of critical placements are adjacent along some edge of FP, and forms these edges. This is not yet sufficient to ensure the preservation of connectivity, so extra edges have to be added. These edges connect between different pieces of the boundary of the same connected component of FP, in a certain canonical manner. As shown by Kedem and Sharir (1990), adding these extra edges does not change the asymptotic complexity of the network, and their construction is actually simpler than the calculation of critical placements. The cost of calculation of the entire network is bounded by the time needed to compute all critical placements, that is, $O(k^2 n \lambda_6(kn) \log(kn))$ (see Section 8.8). This can be improved to $O(kn \lambda_6(kn) \log kn)$ if we want to compute only the connected component of FP that contains a given initial placement of B. We refer the reader to Kedem and Sharir (1990) and to Kedem, Sharir, and Toledo (1993) for more details concerning the algorithm. We also note that an alternative approach to motion-planning and placement problems for a convex polygon has been recently obtained by Chew and Kedem (1993). This approach is based on constructing the *Delaunay triangulation* (the dual of the Voronoi diagram) of the obstacles, under a convex distance function induced by B (at any fixed orientation), and analyzing the pattern in which the triangulation changes as B rotates. The running time of Chew and Kedem's algorithm is $O(k^4 n \lambda_4(kn) \log n)$.

The situation becomes considerably more difficult when B is a nonconvex polygon. It is easy to produce an example of an L-shaped robot B that moves amid n point obstacles, whose free configuration space has complexity $\Theta(n^3)$, and it actually consists of $\Theta(n^3)$ connected components; see Figure 8.36. This is in sharp contrast with the situation for a convex B, and thus calls for considerably more involved techniques to obtain near-quadratic, or even subcubic solutions. An intuitive conclusion of this difference might be that convex bodies are easier to navigate in the plane than are nonconvex bodies.

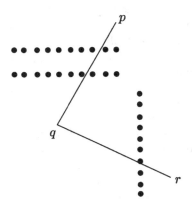

FIGURE 8.36. An L-shaped robot with $\Omega(n^3)$ critical contacts.

There have been several recent studies of this problem for nonconvex bodies B. Halperin, Overmars, and Sharir (1992) have obtained an $O(n^2 \log^2 n)$ 'reachability' algorithm for the above-mentioned case of an L-shaped robot B moving amid n point obstacles. Their algorithm determines whether two given free placements of B lie in the same connected component, but it cannot produce a collision-free path connecting between these placements, and it cannot compute the connected component containing a given free placement. This has been considerably improved subsequently, with recent results of Halperin (1992) showing that the complexity of a single cell in the corresponding three-dimensional arrangement of contact surfaces is $O(n^2 \log^2 n)$, and that it can be constructed in time $O(n^2 \log^4 n)$.

The recent results of Halperin and Sharir (1994b) concerning the complexity of a single cell, as reported in Theorem 7.53, show that the combinatorial complexity of a single connected component of FP in the case of a k-sided polygonal robot B moving in a two-dimensional polygonal environment bounded by n edges is $O((kn)^{2+\varepsilon})$, for any $\varepsilon > 0$ (with the constant of proportionality depending on ε). However, this work does not give an efficient algorithm for constructing such a connected component. Nevertheless, an earlier work by these authors (Halperin and Sharir (1993)) presents such an algorithm, assuming that the number of sides of B is constant; this algorithm runs in time $O(n^{2+\varepsilon})$, for any $\varepsilon > 0$.

8.9.4   Translational motion planning for a polyhedron

Another important case of motion planning with three degrees of freedom is that of a polyhedron B translating in an arbitrary three-dimensional polyhedral region V. Here a placement of B can be parametrized by the coordinates

(x, y, z) of some fixed reference point on B. Assume that B is bounded by k faces and V by n faces. Each contact surface is the locus of placements of B in which a vertex of B touches a face of V, an edge of B touches an edge of V, or a face of B touches a vertex of V. Hence, as is easily checked, the contact surfaces are all planar polygons, bounded by a total of $O(kn)$ edges. We can triangulate each of these surfaces and wind up with a collection of $N = O(kn)$ triangles in $\mathbb{R}^3$.

Hence, the problem we face is: Given a collection of N triangles in $\mathbb{R}^3$, and a point Z not lying on any of them, we want to bound the combinatorial complexity of the cell containing Z in the arrangement of the triangles, and to develop efficient algorithms for computing that cell. As a matter of fact, we can extend this single-cell problem to any number $k > 3$ of degrees of freedom, provided they induce only linear constraints on the possible motions of B. In this case we need to derive combinatorial bounds and efficient algorithms for computing a single cell in an arrangement of N $(k-1)$-simplices in k-space. For example, this problem arises in the case of two independent polyhedral robots, both translating in the same polyhedral environment, or in the case of a polyhedral robot with prismatic (sliding) joints, translating in a polyhedral environment, etc.

We can therefore apply the results of Section 7.6, to conclude that the complexity of a single cell in such an arrangement is $O(N^{k-1} \log N)$. For $k = 3$ we can also compute the desired cell in $O(N^{2+\varepsilon})$ randomized expected time, for any $\varepsilon > 0$.

Returning to the case of a single rigid polyhedral robot B, we next consider the problem of bounding the complexity of the entire free configuration space of B. In general, this complexity is $\Theta(N^3)$—it is never more than $O(N^3)$, as is trivially seen, and there are easy constructions showing that this bound is tight in the worst case. However, if B is *convex*, then we can apply the result of Aronov and Sharir (1994b), reported in Section 7.8, concerning the union of Minkowski sums of polyhedra, as follows. We take the space V^c (the union of all obstacles), and decompose it into a collection of convex polyhedra, $O_1, \ldots, O_q$, with pairwise-disjoint interiors. Then, as in the two-dimensional case, define the Minkowski sums $P_i = O_i \oplus (-B_0) = \{x - y \mid x \in O_i, y \in B_0\}$, for $i = 1, \ldots, q$, where B_0 is an appropriate standard placement of B. The free configuration space FP of B is easily seen to be the complement of the union of these 'expanded obstacles' P_i. By Theorem 7.58, the complexity of FP is $O(qN \log^2 q)$, and it can be constructed in randomized expected time $O(qN \log^3 q)$, where N is the total number of faces of the polyhedra P_i. A special case of this problem has recently been studied by Halperin and Yap (1993), who showed that if B is a box (and the environment is polyhedral) then the complexity in question is $O(N^2 \alpha(N))$. Curiously enough, their proof involves a variant of the analysis of the number of critical placements of a convex polygon, as given in Section 8.8.

8.9.5   Other motion-planning problems

As the preceding review of results indicates, the 'research front' on the combinatorics and algorithms of motion-planning problems is at problems involving three degrees of freedom. In view of the results of Halperin and Sharir (1993, 1994b) mentioned above, the main problems of this kind (for motion-planning instances with three degrees of freedom) that call for further study are of two major types: (i) to establish the strong version of the conjectured bound on the complexity of a single cell, namely $O(n\lambda_s(n))$ for some appropriate constant s; and (ii) to design efficient (near quadratic) algorithms for computing a single cell.

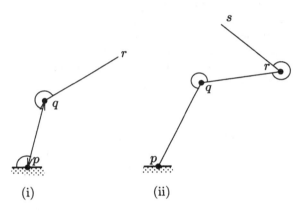

FIGURE 8.37. (i) Telescopic arm; (ii) 3-link arm.

The conjectured sharp bound on the complexity of a single cell still seems very hard to establish in the general setting. Halperin (1992) presents a few results in which sharp near-quadratic bounds are established for the complexity of a single cell in arrangements induced by several motion-planning instances. These special cases include the cases of a *telescoping arm* and of a *3-link arm* moving in certain planar polygonal regions. A telescopic arm is a 2-link arm pqr, where p is anchored at the origin, pq can rotate around p and also expand or shrink its length, and qr, which has a fixed length, is free to rotate around q. A 3-link arm has three links pq, qr, rs, of fixed lengths, where p is anchored at the origin, pq can rotate around p, qr can rotate around q, and rs can rotate around r; see Figure 8.37 for an illustration. Halperin (1992) has shown that:

(i) In the case of a telescopic arm moving amid n point obstacles in the plane, the complexity of a single free cell is $O(n^2\alpha(n))$.

(ii) In the case of a telescopic arm moving amid polygonal obstacles with a total of n edges, the complexity of a single free cell is $O(n^2\log n)$.

(iii) In the case of a 3-link arm moving amid n point obstacles in the plane, the complexity of a single free cell is $O(n^2\alpha(n)\log n)$.

Halperin (1992) also presents efficient (near-quadratic) algorithms for computing a single cell in some of these cases.

The single-cell problem can be stated for any number $k \geq 3$ of degrees of freedom, and its goal is to show that the complexity of a single cell in an arrangement of n algebraic surface patches of constant maximum degree in k-space is close to $O(n^{k-1})$, or, in sharper form, to show that this complexity is $O(n^{k-2}\lambda_s(n))$, for an appropriate constant s that depends on the given surfaces. This has indeed been established for arrangements of simplices (Section 7.6), and the recent results of Halperin and Sharir (1994b) suggest that the general form of this problem might be successfully attacked soon.

We finally remark that for practical motion-planning purposes, the conjectured single-cell bound loses some of its appeal as k increases, because this bound is still very large, and the improvement over the naive $O(n^k)$ bound looks less significant. Still, from a theoretical point of view, this is one of the most basic problems concerning arrangements of surfaces, and we hope to see soon some further progress on its general solution, in the light of the comments made above.

8.10 Other applications

In this section some other geometric applications of Davenport–Schinzel sequences are briefly sketched. We have attempted to cover in this chapter as many applications as possible, but it certainly does not encompass all the known applications of Davenport–Schinzel sequences. Several other applications are mentioned in the bibliographic notes at the end of this chapter.

8.10.1 Union of Jordan regions

Let $\Gamma = \{\gamma_1, \ldots, \gamma_n\}$ be a set of n closed or unbounded Jordan curves in the plane, and let K_i denote any one of the two regions bounded by γ_i. Let $K = \bigcup_{i=1}^{n} K_i$. We want to bound the combinatorial complexity of K, that is, the number of intersection points of Γ that appear on the boundary ∂K of K. As already mentioned in Section 7.5.2, Kedem et al. (1986) have proved that if any two curves in Γ intersect in at most two points, then ∂K contains at most $6n - 12$ intersection points (provided $n \geq 3$), and that this bound is tight in the worst case. (Incidentally, an immediate corollary of their result is that the complexity of the union of a collection of homothets of some fixed convex set is linear, because the boundaries of any two such homothetic copies in general position can intersect in at most two points, as can be easily verified.) On the other hand, if pairs of curves in Γ may intersect in four or more points, then ∂K may contain $\Omega(n^2)$ intersection points in the worst case; see Figure 7.8.

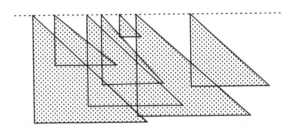

FIGURE 8.38. 'Almost-homothetic' right-angle triangles.

This raises the question of what happens if any two curves in Γ intersect in at most three points. Notice that if the curves in Γ are closed, then any two curves must intersect in an even number of points (assuming nondegenerate configurations). To make the problem interesting, let Γ be a collection of n Jordan arcs, such that both endpoints of each arc in Γ lie on the x-axis, and such that K_i is the region between γ_i and the x-axis. Using $DS(n, 3)$-sequences, Edelsbrunner et al. (1989) have shown that the maximum combinatorial complexity of the union K is $\Theta(n\alpha(n))$. The lower bound follows from the lower envelope construction described in Chapter 4, and the upper bound requires a rather sophisticated analysis of the topological structure of K.

Next, consider the case when each K_i is a triangle in the plane. If the triangles are arbitrary, then a simple modification of the configuration shown in Figure 7.8 proves that K may have quadratic complexity in the worst case. But in this example the triangles have to be 'thin,' that is, some of their angles are very small. Matoušek et al. (1994) have shown that if the given triangles are all 'fat', meaning that each of their angles is at least some fixed constant θ_0, then their union K has only a linear number of 'holes' (i.e., connected components of K^c), and that the combinatorial complexity of K is $O(n \log \log n)$; the constants of proportionality in these bounds depend on θ_0. The proof of Matoušek at al. (1994) for the bound on the combinatorial complexity is based on a divide-and-conquer approach, and uses the Combination Lemma (Lemma 6.7) to obtain a bound on the complexity of the union of two subfamilies that are merged together. This divide-and-conquer approach results (after an appropriate affine transformation) in the following subproblem at the bottom of the recursion: We are given n 'almost-homothetic' right-angle triangles, whose orthogonal sides are parallel to the x- and y-axes, whose right-angle vertex is the lowest-leftmost point of the triangle, and whose hypotenuses have orientations in the range $[\frac{3\pi}{4} - \varepsilon, \frac{3\pi}{4} + \varepsilon]$ for some small constant $\varepsilon > 0$. Moreover, we further assume that the top vertex of each triangle lies on the x-axis (see Figure 8.38).

Using $DS(n, 4)$-sequences, Matoušek et al. (1994) show that the complexity of the union of such a collection of triangles is $O(\lambda_4(n))$. This bound, combined with the Combination Lemma (Lemma 6.7) and with the fact that the overall union K has only $O(n)$ holes, yields the bound $O(n \log \log n)$ for the complexity of K in the general case. The best known lower bound for this complexity is $\Omega(n\alpha(n))$; it follows from the lower envelope construction of Chapter 4, and one can achieve this bound even with equilateral triangles.

8.10.2 Shortest paths

Computing a collision-free shortest path between two points amid a collection of polyhedral obstacles in $\mathbb{R}^3$ is a fundamental problem in robotics (it is a special case of optimal motion planning). Formally, the problem is defined as follows: Given a collection $\mathcal{O}$ of pairwise-disjoint polyhedral obstacles in $\mathbb{R}^3$ with a total of n vertices, and two points p, q, compute a 'collision-free' shortest path between p and q that does not intersect the interior of any obstacle in $\mathcal{O}$. The cost of a path π is defined as its Euclidean length. Canny and Reif (1987) showed that the problem is NP-Hard, which has motivated the study of approximate algorithms and of developing polynomial-time algorithms for special cases. The best known algorithm is due to Clarkson (1987a). In this algorithm, one constructs, for a given $\varepsilon > 0$, a graph G_ε of size

$$O \left(\frac{n^2 \lambda_s(n)}{\varepsilon^4} + n^2 \log(n\rho) \right),$$

where s is some fixed constant and ρ is the ratio of the length of the longest edge in $\mathcal{O}$ to the (straight) distance between p and q. One then reduces the problem to that of constructing a shortest path in G_ε (where the weight of an edge is the Euclidean length of the straight segment connecting the corresponding pair of points). Clarkson shows that the ratio between the length of the path obtained in this manner and the actual collision-free shortest path between p and q is at most $1 + \varepsilon$. The running time of his algorithm is

$$O \left(\frac{n^2 \lambda_s(n) \log(n/\varepsilon)}{\varepsilon^4} + n^2 \log(n\rho) \log(n \log \rho) \right).$$

A special case of shortest paths in 3-space that has been widely studied is when $\mathcal{O}$ consists of a single convex polytope or of a single polyhedral surface homeomorphic to a sphere, and p, q lie on its surface; see, for example, Sharir and Schorr (1986), Mitchell, Mount, and Papadimitriou (1987), and Chen and Han (1990). Baltsan and Sharir (1988) considered the special case where $\mathcal{O}$ consists of two disjoint convex polytopes (and p and q lie anywhere in the free space). Using Davenport–Schinzel sequences to bound the number of candidate paths that one has to consider, they presented an algorithm with running time $O(n^2 \lambda_{10}(n) \log n) = O(n^3 2^{O(\alpha(n)^4)} \log n)$ to find an exact collision-free shortest path between p and q. We describe here their construction in some detail.

With no loss of generality, one can assume that p lies on one convex polytope K_1, that q lies on the other polytope K_2, and that each of K_1, K_2 has n vertices. It is easily seen that the shortest path π from p to q is in general the concatenation of a shortest path along ∂K_1 with a single straight 'jump' from an edge of K_1 to an edge of K_2, and with a shortest path along ∂K_2. The main step in the algorithm of Baltsan and Sharir is to compute all combinatorially different 'takeoff' and 'landing' points. We call two paths on ∂K_1 *combinatorially equivalent* if they cross the same sequence of edges of K_1. For an edge $e \in K_1$, let E_e be the set of maximal connected portions of e such that the shortest path from p to all points in such a 'subedge' are combinatorially equivalent. The analysis of Mitchell et al. (1987) shows that $|E_e| = O(n)$. Let $\mathcal{E}_1 = \bigcup_{e \in K_1} E_e$. Similarly, we define a set $\mathcal{E}_2$ of subedges for K_2. For a given pair $(e_i, e_j) \in \mathcal{E}_1 \times \mathcal{E}_2$, all takeoff and landing points, lying respectively on e_i and e_j, are combinatorially equivalent, which implies that the length of a shortest path that takes off from e_i and lands at e_j can be computed in $O(1)$ time. Therefore, by considering all such pairs (e_i, e_j), a shortest path between p and q can be computed in time $O(n^4)$.

To improve upon this, Baltsan and Sharir introduce a variant of a two-dimensional Voronoi diagram, called the *peeper's Voronoi diagram* and denoted as $PV(S, W)$, in which all the input points lie in the half-plane $H^- : x < 0$, there is an interval 'window' W on the y-axis, and the diagram is defined in the half-plane $H^+ : x > 0$ under the distance function defined to be the Euclidean distance between z and p, provided z and p can see each other through W (i.e., $zp \cap W \neq \emptyset$), and to be ∞ otherwise; see Figure 8.39. Revolve $PV(S, W)$ about the line containing W to obtain a three-dimensional diagram, called the *revolved peeper's Voronoi diagram* of S with respect to W, and denoted as $RPV(S, W)$. Baltsan and Sharir (1988) show that the intersection of $RPV(S, W)$ with any segment γ consists of $O(\lambda_{10}(n))$ intervals, each fully contained in a single revolved cell of the diagram. This follows by arguing that the sequence of cells crossed by γ, each labeled by the point inducing it, does not contain an alternating subsequence of these labels of length 12.

Returning to the problem of computing a shortest path between p and q, fix an edge $e \in K_1$ and assume that e lies on the y-axis, and that a face incident to e lies on the xy-plane. It has been shown (see, e.g., Mitchell, Mount, and Papadimitriou (1987)) that the partition of e induced by E_e is the intersection of e and the Voronoi diagram of a certain set P_e of $O(n)$ points in the xy-plane. For a subedge $e_i \in E_e$, let $\varphi(e_i)$ denote the point of P_e whose Voronoi cell contains e_i. Baltsan and Sharir (1988) show that a pair $e_i \in E_e, e_j \in \mathcal{E}_2$ has to be considered for a possible jump from a point on e_i to a point on e_j only if e_j intersects the cell of $\varphi(e_i)$ in $RPV(P_e, e)$. Since $RPV(P_e, e)$ partitions each edge of K_2 into $O(\lambda_{10}(n))$ subedges, it can be shown that one has to consider only $O(n^2 \lambda_{10}(n)) = O(n^3 2^{O(\alpha(n)^4)})$ pairs of takeoff and landing points, and this leads to a near-cubic algorithm for computing the shortest path from p to q. See the original paper for more details.

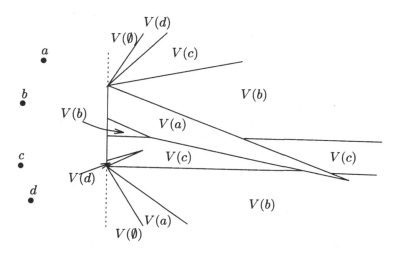

FIGURE 8.39. Peeper's Voronoi diagram.

If the moving object is not a point and the object is allowed to rotate, the problem of computing a shortest path becomes significantly more difficult, even in the planar case. In fact, even the notion of shortest path becomes much vaguer now. (Notice that if the object is allowed only to translate, the problem can be reduced to computing a shortest path for a moving point by expanding the obstacles and shrinking the moving object to a point; see Section 8.8.)

Suppose we want to compute an optimal path for moving a line segment $\gamma = pq$ (allowing both translations and rotations) amid polygonal obstacles with a total of n edges. Assume that the cost of a path is defined as the total distance traveled by one of its endpoints, say, p, and restrict the problem further by requiring that p moves only along polygonal paths that can bend only at obstacle vertices. This rather restricted version of the problem has been studied by Papadimitriou and Silverberg (1987), who gave an $O(n^4 \log n)$-time algorithm for computing a shortest path in the above setting. Their algorithm constructs a visibility graph on the obstacle vertices, in which two obstacle vertices a, b are connected by an edge if the interior of the segment ab does not intersect any obstacle. The weight of an edge e is its Euclidean length if there exists a collision-free path for γ with p moving along e, and $+\infty$ otherwise (we are finessing certain technical issues in this brief description). One can now apply the well-known Dijkstra's shortest path algorithm to that graph. The main bottleneck in the algorithm is the computation of the weights of the edges of the graph (the task is to determine which edges have finite length). Papadimitriou and Silverberg (1987) describe an $O(n^2)$ time procedure to determine the weight of an edge e, and this has been improved by Sharir (1989b), using Davenport–Schinzel sequences, as follows.

To obtain an improved bound, one observes that a placement of γ with p lying on e can be described by two parameters—the distance between p and the left endpoint of e, and the orientation of γ. With some care, the problem of determining whether there exists a collision-free path for γ along e can be reduced to that of computing a certain collection of cells in a planar arrangement of $O(n)$ Jordan arcs, where each arc is the locus of placements of γ at which p lies on e and either the other endpoint of γ touches a specific obstacle edge or the relative interior of γ touches a specific obstacle vertex (see also the analysis given in Sections 8.8 and 8.9). The cells one needs to consider are those that lie in the zone of the locus of all possible placements of γ with p at the left endpoint of e. If any of these cells contains placements of γ where p lies at the other endpoint of e, then a collision-free passage of γ along e is possible. By partitioning these contact loci into two subcollections—those that involve contact of the other endpoint of γ, and those that involve contact of the relative interior of γ, one easily verifies that a pair of curves within the same subcollection can intersect at most once. Using the observation in Corollary 6.9 and Theorem 5.11, we conclude that the combinatorial complexity of all cells in question is $O(n\alpha(n))$, and that they can all be constructed in deterministic time $O(n\alpha(n)\log^2 n)$ or in randomized expected time $O(n\alpha(n)\log n)$. Hence, the overall running time of the algorithm can be improved to $O(n^3\alpha(n)\log^2 n)$ deterministic time or $O(n^3\alpha(n)\log n)$ randomized expected time.

8.10.3   Extremal $\{0,1\}$-matrices

Let $M = \{M_{ij}\}$ be an $m \times n$ matrix such that $M_{ij} \in \{0,1\}$ for all $1 \le i \le m$ and $1 \le j \le n$; we call M a $\{0,1\}$-matrix. A configuration

$$C = \{C_{ij} \mid 1 \le i \le u, 1 \le j \le v\}$$

is a $u \times v$ matrix with 1's and blanks as its entries. We say that M does not contain C if there is no submatrix A of M that contains the 1-entries of C, that is, there are no u rows $i_1 < i_2 < \cdots < i_u$ and v columns $j_1 < j_2 < \cdots < j_v$ such that $M_{i_s j_t} = 1$ for all (s,t) for which C_{st} is 1. Let $f(m,n;C)$ be the maximum number of 1's in an $m \times n$ $\{0,1\}$-matrix not containing C. An upper bound on $f(m,n;C)$ for various C is useful in solving certain combinatorial problems in geometry, and also in bounding the time and storage complexity of certain geometric algorithms; see, for example, Füredi (1990), Bienstock and Győri (1991), Pach and Sharir (1991), and Efrat and Sharir (1994).

Let C_0 be the 2×4 configuration

$$\begin{pmatrix} 1 & & 1 & \\ & 1 & & 1 \end{pmatrix}.$$

A matrix M does not contain C_0 if there are no two rows $i_1 < i_2$ and four distinct columns $j_1 < j_2 < j_3 < j_4$ such that

$$M_{i_1 j_1} = M_{i_2 j_2} = M_{i_1 j_3} = M_{i_2 j_4} = 1. \tag{8.4}$$

Füredi and Hajnal (1992) have shown that $f(m, n, C_0) = \Theta(m\alpha(m) + n)$. The lower bound can be proved by constructing an $m \times n$ matrix using a recursive scheme similar to the one used for proving the lower bound on $\lambda_3(n)$ in Chapter 2. We briefly sketch a proof of the upper bound. Let M be an $m \times n$ $\{0, 1\}$-matrix not containing C_0. Delete the first and last 1 in each row, and keep only the columns that still have at least two 1's. Let N denote the number of 1's left in M; then the original number of 1's in M is at most $N + 2m + n$. We construct a sequence $S' = S_1 \| S_2 \| \cdots \| S_n$, as follows. For each $j = 1, \ldots, n$, let $l(j)$ denote the number of 1's left in the j-th column of M, then we define

$$S_j = \langle k_1, k_2, \ldots, k_{l(j)} \rangle,$$

where $k_1 < k_2 < \cdots < k_{l(j)}$ and $M_{k_t j} = 1$ for $1 \le t \le l(j)$. For each j, delete from S' the last element of S_j if it is the same as the first element of S_{j+1} (i.e., if the last 1 in the j-th column occurs in the same row as the first 1 in the $(j+1)$-st column). Let S denote the resulting sequence. By construction, no two consecutive elements of S are identical.

We claim that S is a $DS(m, 3)$-sequence. Suppose to the contrary that there exists a subsequence $\sigma = \langle a \ldots b \ldots a \ldots b \ldots a \rangle$ in S, for two distinct rows a, b. Then there also exists a subsequence of S of the form

$$\langle i_1 \ldots i_2 \ldots i_1 \ldots i_2 \rangle \tag{8.5}$$

with $i_1 < i_2$ (if $a < b$, discard the last occurrence of a in σ, otherwise discard the first occurrence of a in σ). In other words, there are four columns $j_1 \le j_2 < j_3 \le j_4$ such that $M_{i_1 j_1} = M_{i_2 j_2} = M_{i_1 j_3} = M_{i_2 j_4} = 1$; here $j_2 < j_3$ because otherwise the two middle entries of (8.5) occur in the same column of M, which is impossible since $i_1 < i_2$. Recall that we erased the first and last 1's from each row of M, so there exist two columns $j_0 < j_1$ and $j_5 > j_4$ such that $M_{i_1 j_0} = M_{i_2 j_5} = 1$. In other words, we have two rows $i_1 < i_2$ and four distinct columns $j_0 < j_2 < j_3 < j_5$ such that

$$M_{i_1 j_0} = M_{i_2 j_2} = M_{i_1 j_3} = M_{i_2 j_5} = 1.$$

But this contradicts the fact that M does not contain C_0 (see (8.4)), thus showing that S is a $DS(m, 3)$-sequence. We thus obtain:

Theorem 8.67 *Let $M = \{M_{ij}\}$ be an $m \times n$ $\{0, 1\}$-matrix that does not contain the configuration*

$$\begin{pmatrix} 1 & & 1 & \\ & 1 & & 1 \end{pmatrix};$$

then the maximum number of 1's in M is $O(m\alpha(m) + n)$.

Füredi and Hajnal (1992) give many other results of this type for other forbidden configurations C.

8.10.4 Ray shooting amid spheres

Let S be a given collection of n arbitrary spheres in $\mathbb{R}^3$; our goal is to pre-process S, so as to answer efficiently *ray-shooting* queries, each seeking the first sphere of S, if any, hit by a query ray. Several solutions have been given to this problem; each of them constructs a multilevel range-searching structure whose bottom level caters to the following subproblem: Given a set B of n spheres in $\mathbb{R}^3$, preprocess it into a data structure, so that, given a query line λ with the property that for each sphere $B \in B$, either λ intersects B or there is no point of B lying vertically below λ, determine whether λ intersects any sphere of B. (See Agarwal and Matoušek (1994), Agarwal et al. (1992), Mohaban and Sharir (in press), and Agarwal, Aronov, and Sharir (1994) for more details.) This subproblem can be easily reduced to point location in the region lying below the lower envelope of the following collection of trivariate functions. Parametrize lines λ in $\mathbb{R}^3$ by four parameters $(\xi_1, \xi_2, \xi_3, \xi_4)$, so that the equations defining λ are $y = x\xi_1 + \xi_2$, $z = x\xi_3 + \xi_4$ (this excludes lines parallel to the yz-plane, which have to be treated separately); see also Section 8.5. For each sphere $B \in B$, define a function $\xi_4 = f_B(\xi_1, \xi_2, \xi_3)$, so that the line $\lambda(\xi_1, \xi_2, \xi_3, \xi_4)$ is tangent to B from below (note that f_B is only partially defined). Let $\mathcal{F} = \{f_B \mid B \in B\}$ denote the resulting collection of functions. It is easily seen that $\mathcal{F}$ satisfies Assumptions 7.2. Let $E_{\mathcal{F}}$ denote the lower envelope of $\mathcal{F}$. Then a query line $\lambda(\xi_1, \xi_2, \xi_3, \xi_4)$, having the properties assumed above, misses all spheres of B if and only if $\xi_4 < E_{\mathcal{F}}(\xi_1, \xi_2, \xi_3)$. Thus, by Theorem 7.25, one can answer such queries in time $O(\log^2 n)$, using $O(n^{3+\varepsilon})$ expected preprocessing time and storage. Plugging this data structure into the structure given by Agarwal et al. (1992), it follows that the overall resulting data structure requires $O(n^{3+\varepsilon})$ preprocessing time and storage, and each ray-shooting query can be answered in time $O(\log^4 n)$. That is, we have:

Theorem 8.68 *A set S of n spheres in $\mathbb{R}^3$ can be preprocessed, for any $\varepsilon > 0$, in randomized expected time $O(n^{3+\varepsilon})$ into a data structure of size $O(n^{3+\varepsilon})$, so that any ray-shooting query can be answered in time $O(\log^4 n)$.*

8.10.5 Nearest-neighbor queries

Let $S = \{S_1, \ldots, S_n\}$ be a collection of n compact convex objects ('sites') in $\mathbb{R}^3$, each having constant description complexity (as defined in Section 8.2.3). For a point w, we define

$$d(w, S_i) = \min_{q \in S_i} d(w, q),$$

where $d(\cdot, \cdot)$ is the Euclidean distance; S_i is the *nearest neighbor* of w in S if $d(w, S_i) \leq d(w, S_j)$ for all $S_j \in S$. We wish to preprocess S for efficient *nearest-neighbor queries*, that is, for a query point $w \in \mathbb{R}^3$, we want to compute efficiently a nearest neighbor of w in S. This is a generalization of the classical *Post Office Problem* in $\mathbb{R}^3$ (see Knuth (1973)).

We follow the approach outlined in Appendix 7.1. For each $i \leq n$, let $f_i(w) = d(w, S_i)$, and let $\mathcal{F} = \{f_i\}_{i \leq n}$ be the resulting collection of trivariate functions. Let $E_{\mathcal{F}}$ denote the lower envelope of $\mathcal{F}$. Then, given a query point w, the site(s) $S \in \mathcal{S}$ nearest to w are those that attain the lower envelope $E_{\mathcal{F}}$ at w. Thus, by Theorem 7.25, $\mathcal{S}$ can be preprocessed in randomized expected time $O(n^{3+\varepsilon})$, into a data structure of size $O(n^{3+\varepsilon})$, so that a nearest-neighbor query can be answered in $O(\log^2 n)$ time. (Note that Theorem 7.25 is indeed applicable here, because the functions f_i are all (piecewise) algebraic of constant maximum degree, as is easy to verify from the conditions assumed above.) That is, we have:

Theorem 8.69 *A set $\mathcal{S}$ of n compact convex sets in $\mathbb{R}^3$, each of constant description complexity, can be preprocessed, for any $\varepsilon > 0$, in randomized expected time $O(n^{3+\varepsilon})$ into a data structure of size $O(n^{3+\varepsilon})$, so that any nearest-neighbor query can be answered in time $O(\log^2 n)$.*

This is a fairly general framework, and admits numerous generalizations, for example, we may replace the Euclidean distance by other distances, perform queries with objects other than points (as long as the location of a query object can be specified by only three real parameters; this is the case, for example, if the query objects are translates of some rigid convex object), etc. An interesting generalization is to *dynamic* nearest-neighbor queries in the plane, where each object of $\mathcal{S}$ moves along some given trajectory, and each query (x, y, t) asks for the object of $\mathcal{S}$ nearest to the point (x, y) at time t (see also Section 8.6). Using the same approach as above, this can also be done, under appropriate assumptions on the shape and motion of the objects of $\mathcal{S}$, with $O(n^{3+\varepsilon})$ randomized expected preprocessing time and storage, and $O(\log^2 n)$ query time.

Similar results can be obtained for nearest-neighbor queries in two dimensions, using the same approach as above, except that now we have a collection $\mathcal{F}$ of bivariate functions, whose lower envelope can be computed in time and storage $O(n^{2+\varepsilon})$, for any $\varepsilon > 0$, and searched with any query point in $O(\log n)$ time. The problem can also be stated in any dimension $d > 3$, but we currently do not have any efficient procedure for constructing and searching lower envelopes of d-variate functions, for $d > 3$.

8.10.6 Lines in 3-space

We conclude this section by giving an application of lower envelopes to certain problems involving lines in $\mathbb{R}^3$. Let $\mathcal{S}$ be a set of n objects in $\mathbb{R}^3$, each having constant description complexity. We say that a line ℓ in $\mathbb{R}^3$ passes *above* an object $S \in \mathcal{S}$ if the relatively open vertical half-plane bounded from below by ℓ does not intersect S. We can parametrize lines as points in projective 4-space, as in Section 8.5 (see also Section 8.10.4). It follows that in this representation, the space of all lines that pass above all the objects of S is the region of $\mathbb{R}^4$ that lies above the upper envelope of n surface patches, each representing the locus of all lines that touch an object of S (but otherwise pass above it). The combinatorial complexity of this space is defined as the complexity of this upper envelope. Theorem 7.17 is easily seen to imply:

Theorem 8.70 *The combinatorial complexity of the space of all lines that pass above all objects of S, in the setup just defined, is $O(n^{3+\varepsilon})$, for any $\varepsilon > 0$.*

The following is an immediate corollary of Theorem 8.70.

Corollary 8.71 *Let Σ be a polyhedral terrain with n edges. The combinatorial complexity of the space of all lines that pass above Σ and do not intersect Σ is $O(n^{3+\varepsilon})$, for any $\varepsilon > 0$.*

8.11   Bibliographic notes

There is by now extensive literature on applications of Davenport–Schinzel sequences. Some surveys of these applications are by Sharir et al. (1986), Sharir (1988b), Guibas and Sharir (1993), and Halperin and Sharir (1994a).

The sweep-line algorithm for computing Voronoi diagrams, described in Section 8.1.1, is due to Fortune (1987). His algorithm can be extended to compute the Voronoi diagram of a set of n nonintersecting segments in the plane in $O(n \log n)$ time. Many other optimal or near-optimal algorithms for computing Voronoi diagrams and their extensions are known by now; see Appendix 7.1, and the survey papers by Aurenhammer (1991), Leven and Sharir (1987c), and Fortune (1992) for a summary of the known results.

The close relationship between $DS(n, 2)$-sequences and triangulations of convex polygons was observed by Roselle (1974). The bound on the number of distinct $DS(n, 2)$-sequences of maximum length was first proved by Mullin and Stanton (1972). See also Edelsbrunner and Guibas (1989) and Ramos (1994) for additional applications of $DS(n, 2)$-sequences.

The material in Section 8.2 is taken from Edelsbrunner and Sharir (1990), Sharir (1991), and Agarwal, Schwarzkopf, and Sharir (1994). The notion of a geometric permutation was introduced by Katchalski, Lewis, and Zaks (1985) and by Katchalski, Lewis, and Liu (1986), who proved a quadratic upper bound on the number of geometric permutations of a set of n disjoint convex objects in the plane. This bound was first improved by Wenger (1990), and then by Edelsbrunner and Sharir (1990). The lower bound described in Section 8.2 is due to Katchalski, Lewis, and Zaks (1985). Although the problem concerning geometric permutations is completely settled in the plane, it remains open in higher dimensions. The best known upper bound on the number of geometric permutations of a set of n disjoint convex bodies in $\mathbb{R}^d$ (i.e., the order in which all these bodies can be stabbed by a line) is $O(n^{2d-2})$ (Wenger (1990)) and the best known lower bound is $\Omega(n^{d-1})$ (Katchalski, Lewis, and Liu (1992)). See also Pellegrini and Shor (1992). Atallah and Bajaj (1987) gave an algorithm for computing a line transversal of a set of polygons. They reduced the problem to that of computing the lower envelope of a set of line segments. See also Edelsbrunner, Overmars, and Wood (1983) and Edelsbrunner (1985) for earlier algorithms for computing transversals. The proof of Theorem 8.10 is due to Sharir (1991), and is based on the general random sampling technique by Clarkson and Shor (1989), as already described in earlier chapters. The material of Section 8.2.3 is taken from Agarwal, Schwarzkopf, and Sharir (1994). See the survey paper by Goodman, Pollack, and Wenger (1993) for most of the known results on transversals.

Section 8.3 is taken from Chazelle et al. (1989a, 1991) and from Clarkson et al. (1990). The cylindrical algebraic decomposition scheme by Collins (1975) gives an algorithm for decomposing an arrangement of n surfaces in $\mathbb{R}^d$ into $n^{2^{O(d)}}$ elementary cells. This bound was improved by Chazelle et al. (1989a, 1991) to a bound close to n^{2d-3}. The best known lower bound is only $\Omega(n^d)$. It remains an open problem whether there exists a decomposition scheme that partitions the arrangement of n surfaces in $\mathbb{R}^d$ into roughly $O(n^d)$ elementary cells. At present, such a bound can be attained only in some special cases, including the case of hyperplanes (see also Guibas et al. (1993) for a slightly weaker bound for the complexity of the vertical decomposition of arrangements of hyperplanes in $\mathbb{R}^4$). Some of the applications of decomposition of arrangements of surfaces can be found in Chazelle and Sharir (1990), Chazelle et al. (1989a, 1991), Agarwal, Pellegrini, and Sharir (1993), Agarwal, Sharir, and Toledo (1994), and Agarwal and Matoušek (1994).

The ray-shooting algorithm for polyhedral terrains described in Section 8.4.1, and the bound given in Section 8.4.2 on the number of different views of a terrain from a point moving along a vertical line, are due to Cole and Sharir (1989). Cole and Sharir also describe a ray-shooting algorithm for polyhedral terrains where the origin of the query ray lies on a fixed vertical line. A similar algorithm is developed by Bern et al. (1994); see also Mulmuley (1991a). Recently, Agarwal and Matoušek (1993) and Chazelle et al. (1989b) have given a ray-shooting algorithm in polyhedral terrains for the general case where the origin of the ray can lie anywhere in space. See also the recent monograph by de Berg (1993) for a comprehensive treatment of the ray-shooting problem in three dimensions.

The bound on the number of different orthographic or perspective views of a polyhedral terrain is taken from Agarwal and Sharir (1994); earlier works on this problem are by de Berg et al. (1992) and by Halperin and Sharir (1994c).

Section 8.5 is adapted from Agarwal, Aronov, and Sharir (1994). An $O(n^2)$-time algorithm for computing the width of n points in $\mathbb{R}^3$ was presented by Houle and Toussaint (1988), which was improved by Chazelle et al. (1993)

to $O(n^{8/5+\varepsilon})$. The algorithm of Agarwal, Aronov, and Sharir (1994) actually computes the width in randomized expected time $O(n^{17/11+\varepsilon})$. The version presented in Section 8.5 is a simpler (albeit less efficient) version of that algorithm. The best known algorithm for computing the width in $\mathbb{R}^3$, due to Sharir (1994b), runs in time $O(n^{3/2+\varepsilon})$; see also Agarwal (1994). Many other applications of lower envelopes of trivariate functions are presented in Agarwal, Sharir, and Toledo (1994), and in Chazelle et al. (1993). Improved solutions to some of these problems are given by Agarwal, Aronov, and Sharir (1994), Sharir (1994b), and Agarwal (1994).

Sections 8.6.1 and 8.6.2 are taken from Atallah (1985). As mentioned in Chapter 1, Atallah's paper was the first paper in computational geometry that applies Davenport–Schinzel sequences to geometric problems. Concerning Section 8.6.3, sharp upper bounds on the number of combinatorial changes in the Voronoi diagram of a set of points moving in the plane seem very difficult to obtain. The best known lower bound is quadratic, and the best known upper bound, which is close to cubic, is due to Imai, Sumino, and Imai (1989), Fu and Lee (1991), and Guibas, Mitchell, and Roos (1991). Chew (1993) showed that if the underlying metric is L_1 or L_∞, instead of the Euclidean metric, the number of combinatorial changes in the Voronoi diagram of a set of n points moving in the plane, each with a constant velocity (along some line), is only $O(n^2\alpha(n))$. Aonuma et al. (1990) have shown that, given k sets of points in the plane, each consisting of n points and moving rigidly according to some continuous function of time, the number of combinatorial changes in the Voronoi diagram of these kn points is $O(k^4 n\lambda_s(n))$, for an appropriate constant s. The bound has been improved by Huttenlocher et al. (1992a) to $O(n^2 k^2 \lambda_s(k))$, using Theorem 1.13. The more general bounds for dynamic Voronoi diagrams are given by Sharir (1994a). See Albers and Roos (1992), Roos (1993), and Roos and Albers (1992) for bounds on dynamic Voronoi diagrams in higher dimensions. See also Megiddo (1982, 1986), Ottmann and Wood (1984), Hwang, Chang, and Tu (1990), Monma and Suri (1992), Katoh, Tokuyama, and Iwano (1992), and Tamaki and Tokuyama (1995) for other studies in dynamic geometry.

The analysis given in Section 8.7 is due to Huttenlocher, Kedem, and Sharir (1993) (see also Huttenlocher and Kedem (1990)). As mentioned in Appendix 7.1, the connection between Voronoi diagrams and lower envelopes was first noted by Edelsbrunner and Seidel (1986). The algorithm of Huttenlocher et al. (1993) can be extended to compute the minimum Hausdorff distance $D(A, B)$ for sets of nonintersecting segments under the L_1 or L_∞-metric. Alt, Behrends, and Blömer (1991) have presented an algorithm for computing $D(A, B)$ for sets of nonintersecting segments under the L_2 metric, which has been improved by Agarwal, Sharir, and Toledo (1994). If we allow both translations and rotations, the problem of computing a placement that minimizes the Hausdorff distance becomes considerably more difficult. The time complexity of the best known algorithm in this case is close to n^5

(see Alt, Behrends, and Blömer (1991), Chew et al. (1993), and Huttenlocher, Kedem, and Kleinberg (1992b)).

The first study of the polygon placement problem is by Chazelle (1983). Theorem 8.64 is due to Leven and Sharir (1987b). A quadratic bound on the number of critical free placements for a moving line segment is derived by Leven and Sharir (1987d). Chew and Kedem (1993) have presented an $O(k^4 n \lambda_4(kn) \log kn)$ algorithm for finding the largest copy of a convex k-gon that can be placed amid a set of polygonal obstacles without intersecting any of the obstacles; here n is the total number of obstacle vertices. A different algorithm for this problem is presented by Sharir and Toledo (1994), and a related placement problem is studied by Aonuma et al. (1990). Using ideas similar to those of Leven and Sharir (1987b), Imai, Sumino, and Imai (1989) have developed efficient algorithms for some geometric fitting problems. The first nontrivial algorithm for the segment center problem, as described in Section 8.8.2, is due to Imai, Lee, and Yang (1992); it has been improved by Agarwal et al. (1993) and further improved by Efrat and Sharir (1994).

Motion planning is one of the most fundamental problems in robotics. Schwartz and Sharir (1983b) have presented the first algorithm for the general motion-planning problem, which is based on the cylindrical algebraic decomposition technique of Collins (1975). The time complexity of their algorithm is $O(n^{2^{O(d)}})$, where n is the total complexity of the obstacles and the robot, and d is the number of degrees of freedom of the moving robot. Canny (1987, 1988a, 1993) has improved the running time to $O(n^{O(d)})$ using a different approach. It is known that the general motion-planning problem (with arbitrarily many degrees of freedom) is PSPACE-Complete (Reif (1979), Hopcroft, Schwartz, and Sharir (1984), Canny (1988b)), and this has motivated the study of special cases with few degrees of freedom. One of the most widely studied special cases is where the moving object is a rigid body with few degrees of freedom (somewhere between two and six). See the books of Latombe (1991) and Hopcroft, Schwartz, and Sharir (1987), as well as the survey papers by Schwartz and Sharir (1988) and Sharir (1989a) for some of the main known results.

Schwartz and Sharir (1983a) gave an algorithm for moving a segment amid polygonal obstacles. Later Ó'Dúnlaing, Sharir, and Yap (1986, 1987) improved the running time to $O(n\lambda_s(n) \log n)$, for some constant $s > 0$. They define a generalized Voronoi diagram in the configuration space of the moving segment, and use Davenport–Schinzel sequences to analyze the complexity of the diagram. Simpler algorithms for this problem have been developed by Leven and Sharir (1987d), Sifrony and Sharir (1987), and Bhattacharya and Zorbas (1988). Kedem and Sharir (1985) and Leven and Sharir (1987b) have presented algorithms for translating a convex polygon amid polygonal obstacles.

A close-to-linear algorithm for the general motion-planning problem with two degrees of freedom is given by Guibas, Sharir, and Sifrony (1989); see also Pollack, Sharir, and Sifrony (1988). Halperin (1993) has shown that the complexity of a single connected component of the Minkowski sum of two simple polygons with m and n vertices, respectively, is $O(nm \log m)$, which improves Theorem 8.66 in some special cases. Moving a convex polygon with both translation and rotation is considered by Leven and Sharir (1987b), Kedem and Sharir (1990), Chew and Kedem (1993), and Kedem, Sharir, and Toledo (1993). The motion-planning problem for nonconvex polygons is studied by Halperin (1992), Halperin, Overmars, and Sharir (1992), and Halperin and Sharir (1993). See Halperin (1992, 1994) for the study of several additional cases of motion planning with three degrees of freedom. The algorithm for translational motion planning for a convex polyhedron in $\mathbb{R}^3$ is taken from Aronov and Sharir (1994b). See also Agarwal and Sharir (1990) for other applications of Davenport–Schinzel sequences to motion-planning and collision-detection problems.

Section 8.10.1 is taken from Matoušek et al. (1994). Alt et al. (1992) have shown that the boundary of the union of a set of n fat wedges has only a linear number of vertices. Further work on this topic has been done by Efrat, Rote, and Sharir (1993), van Kreveld (1993), and van der Stappen et al. (1993).

The material in Section 8.10.2 can be found in Clarkson (1987a), Baltsan and Sharir (1988), and Sharir (1989b) (see also Papadimitriou and Silverberg (1987)). Papaditmitiou (1985) and Choi, Sellen, and Yap (1994) have also given algorithms for computing approximate shortest paths in $\mathbb{R}^3$. Aurenhammer and Stöckl (1991) have shown that the complexity of the two-dimensional peeper's Voronoi diagram of a set of n points in the plane is $\Theta(n^2)$ and that it can be computed in time $O(n^2 \log n)$. Much work has been done on computing a shortest path for moving a point amid polygonal obstacles, culminating with the recent optimal $O(n \log n)$ solution by Hershberger and Suri (1993) (see also Mitchell (1993)). In contrast, very little is known about computing a collision-free shortest path for other moving objects (e.g., a segment, or a convex polygon) when the object is also allowed to rotate.

The material in Section 8.10.3 is taken from Füredi and Hajnal (1992). Related work is by Anstee (1985), Anstee and Füredi (1986), Bienstock and Győri (1991), and Füredi (1990). See also Klawe (1990) for a related result.

The material in Sections 8.10.4 and 8.10.5 are taken from Agarwal, Aronov, and Sharir (1994). Earlier solutions of the problem of ray shooting amid spheres are by Agarwal and Matoušek (1994), Agarwal (1992), and Mohaban and Sharir (in press). Additional material on the general problem of ray shooting in three dimensions can be found in de Berg's dissertation (1993) and in the references therein. Section 8.10.6 is taken from Sharir (1994a). Related results are also given in Chazelle et al. (1989b) and Pellegrini (1994).

BIBLIOGRAPHY

W. Ackermann (1928), Zum Hilbertschen Aufbau der reellen Zahlen, *Mathematical Annals* 99, 118–133.

R. Adamec, M. Klazar, and P. Valtr (1992), Generalized Davenport–Schinzel sequences with linear upper bound, *Discrete Mathematics* 108, 219–229.

P. Agarwal (1990), Partitioning arrangements of lines: II. Applications, *Discrete and Computational Geometry* 5, 533–573.

P. Agarwal (1991), Geometric partitioning and its applications, in: *Discrete and Computational Geometry: Papers from DIMACS Special Year* (J. Goodman, R. Pollack, and W. Steiger, eds.), American Mathematical Society, Providence, RI, pp. 1–37.

P. Agarwal (1992), Ray shooting and other applications of spanning trees with low stabbing number, *SIAM Journal on Computing* 22, 540–570.

P. Agarwal (1994), Randomized algorithms for some geometric optimization problems, in preparation.

P. Agarwal, B. Aronov, and M. Sharir (1994), Computing lower envelopes in four dimensions with applications, *Proceedings 10th Annual Symposium on Computational Geometry*, pp. 348–358.

P. Agarwal, M. de Berg, J. Matoušek, and O. Schwarzkopf (1994), Computing k-levels and higher order Voronoi diagrams, *Proceedings 10th Annual Symposium on Computational Geometry*, pp. 67–75.

P. Agarwal, A. Efrat, M. Sharir, and S. Toledo (1993), Computing a segment-center for a planar point set, *Journal of Algorithms* 15, 314–323.

P. Agarwal, L. Guibas, M. Pellegrini, and M. Sharir (1992), Ray shooting amidst spheres, manuscript.

P. Agarwal, M. Katz, and M. Sharir (1994), Computing depth orders and related problems, *Proceedings 4th Scandinavian Workshop on Algorithm Theory*, pp. 1–12.

P. Agarwal and J. Matoušek (1993), Ray shooting and parametric search, *SIAM Journal on Computing* 22, 794–806.

P. Agarwal and J. Matoušek (1994), Range searching with semialgebraic sets, *Discrete and Computational Geometry* 11, 393–418.

P. Agarwal, J. Matoušek, and O. Schwarzkopf (1994), Computing many faces in arrangements of lines and segments, *Proceedings 10th Annual Symposium on Computational Geometry*, pp. 76–84.

P. Agarwal, M. Pellegrini, and M. Sharir (1993), Counting circular arc intersections, *SIAM Journal on Computing* 22, 778–793.

P. Agarwal, O. Schwarzkopf, and M. Sharir (1994), Overlay of lower envelopes and its applications, Technical Report CS-1994-18, Dept. Computer Science, Duke University.

P. Agarwal and M. Sharir (1990), Red–blue intersection detection algorithms, with applications to collision detection and motion planning, *SIAM Journal on Computing* 19, 297–321.

P. Agarwal and M. Sharir (1994), On the number of views of polyhedral terrains, *Discrete and Computational Geometry* 12, 177–182.

P. Agarwal, M. Sharir, and P. Shor (1989), Sharp upper and lower bounds for the length of general Davenport–Schinzel sequences, *Journal of Combinatorial Theory, Series A* 52, 228–274.

P. Agarwal, M. Sharir, and S. Toledo (1994), New applications of parametric searching in computational geometry, *Journal of Algorithms* 17, 292–318.

G. Albers and T. Roos (1992), Voronoi diagrams of moving points in higher dimensional spaces, *Proceedings 3rd Scandinavian Workshop on Algorithm Theory*, Lecture Notes in Computer Science, vol. 621 (O. Numri and E. Ukkonen, eds.), Springer-Verlag, New York–Berlin–Heidelberg, pp. 399–409.

P. Alevizos, J. D. Boissonnat, and F. Preparata (1990), An optimal algorithm for the boundary of a cell in a union of rays, *Algorithmica* 5, 573–590.

H. Alt, B. Behrends, and J. Blömer (1991), Approximate matching of polygonal shapes, *Proceedings 7th Annual Symposium on Computational Geometry*, pp. 186–193.

H. Alt, R. Fleischer, M. Kaufmann, K. Mehlhorn, S. Näher, S. Schirra, and C. Uhrig (1992), Approximate motion planning and the complexity of the boundary of the union of simple geometric figures, *Algorithmica* 8, 391–406.

R. Anstee (1985), General forbidden configuration theorems, *Journal of Combinatorial Theory, Series A* 40, 108–124.

R. Anstee and Z. Füredi (1986), Forbidden submatrices, *Discrete Mathematics* 62, 225–243.

M. Anthony and N. Biggs (1992), *Computational Learning Theory*, Cambridge University Press, Cambridge.

H. Aonuma, H. Imai, K. Imai, and T. Tokuyama (1990), Maxmin location of convex objects in a polygon and related dynamic Voronoi diagrams, *Proceedings 6th Annual Symposium on Computational Geometry*, pp. 225–234.

B. Aronov, B. Chazelle, H. Edelsbrunner, L. Guibas, M. Sharir, and R. Wenger (1991), Points and triangles in the plane and halving planes in space, *Discrete and Computational Geometry* 6, 435–442.

B. Aronov, H. Edelsbrunner, L. Guibas, and M. Sharir (1992), Improved bounds on the complexity of many faces in arrangements of segments, *Combinatorica* 12, 261–274.

B. Aronov, J. Matoušek, and M. Sharir (1994), On the sum of squares of cell complexities in hyperplane arrangements, *Journal of Combinatorial Theory, Series A* 65, 311–321.

B. Aronov, M. Pellegrini, and M. Sharir (1993), On the zone of a surface in a hyperplane arrangement, *Discrete and Computational Geometry* 9, 177–186.

B. Aronov and M. Sharir (1990), Triangles in space, or building (and analyzing) castles in the air, *Combinatorica* 10, 137–173.

B. Aronov and M. Sharir (1993), The union of convex polyhedra in three dimensions, *Proceedings 34th Annual IEEE Symposium on Foundations of Computer Science*, pp. 518–527.

B. Aronov and M. Sharir (1994a), Castles in the air revisited, *Discrete and Computational Geometry* 12, 119–150.

B. Aronov and M. Sharir (1994b), On translational motion planning in 3-space, *Proceedings 10th Annual Symposium on Computational Geometry*, pp. 21–30.

B. Aronov and M. Sharir (1994c), The common exterior of convex polygons in the plane, manuscript.

M. Atallah (1985), Some dynamic computational geometry problems, *Computers and Mathematics with Applications* 11, 1171–1181.

M. Atallah and C. Bajaj (1987), Efficient algorithms for common transversals, *Information Processing Letters* 25, 87–91.

F. Aurenhammer (1991), Voronoi diagrams—A survey of a fundamental geometric data structure, *ACM Computing Surveys* 23, 346–405.

F. Aurenhammer and G. Stöckl (1991), On the peeper's Voronoi diagram, *SIGACT News* 22, 50–59.

A. Baltsan and M. Sharir (1988), On shortest paths between two convex polyhedra, *Journal of Association for Computing Machinery* 35, 267–287.

I. Bárány, Z. Füredi, and L. Lovász (1990), On the number of halving planes, *Combinatorica* 10, 175–183.

J. Bentley and T. Ottmann (1979), Algorithms for reporting and counting geometric intersections, *IEEE Transactions on Computers* C–28, 643–647.

M. Bern, D. Dobkin, D. Eppstein, and R. Grossman (1994), Visibility with a moving point of view, *Algorithmica* 11, 360–378.

M. Bern, D. Eppstein, P. Plassmann, and F. Yao (1991), Horizon theorems for lines and polygons, in: *Discrete and Computational Geometry: Papers from DIMACS Special Year* (J. Goodman, R. Pollack, and W. Steiger, eds.), American Mathematical Society, Providence, RI, pp. 45–66.

B. Bhattacharya and J. Zorbas (1988), Solving the two-dimensional findpath problem using a line-triangle representation of the robot, *Journal of Algorithms* 9, 449–469.

D. Bienstock and E. Győri (1991), An extremal problem on sparse 0–1 matrices, *SIAM Journal on Discrete Mathematics* 4, 17–27.

A. Björner, M. Las Vergnas, B. Sturmfels, N. White, and G. Ziegler (1993), *Oriented Matroids*, Cambridge University Press, Cambridge.

A. Blumer, A. Ehrenfeucht, D. Haussler, and M. Warmuth (1989), Classifying learnable geometric concepts with the Vapnik-Chervonenkis dimension. *Journal of Association for Computing Machinery* 36, 929–965.

J. Bochnak, M. Coste, and M. F. Roy (1987), *Géométrie Algébrique Réelle*, Springer-Verlag, New York–Berlin–Heidelberg.

J. D. Boissonnat, O. Devillers, R. Schott, M. Teillaud, and M. Yvinec (1992), Applications of random sampling to on-line algorithms in computational geometry, *Discrete and Computational Geometry* 8, 51–71.

J. D. Boissonnat and K. Dobrindt (1992), Randomized construction of the upper envelope of triangles in $\mathbb{R}^3$, *Proceedings 4th Canadian Conference on Computational Geometry*, pp. 311–315.

J. D. Boissonnat and K. Dobrindt (1993), On-line randomized construction of the upper envelope of triangles and surface patches in $\mathbf{R}^3$, Technical Report 1878, INRIA, Sophia-Antipolis, France.

H. Brönnimann, B. Chazelle, and J. Matoušek (1993), Product range spaces, sensitive sampling, and derandomization, *Proceedings 34th Annual IEEE Symposium on Foundations of Computer Science*, pp. 400–409.

A. Brøndsted (1983), *An Introduction to Convex Polytopes*, Springer-Verlag, New York–Berlin–Heidelberg.

R. Canham (1969), A theorem on arrangements of lines in the plane, *Israel Journal of Mathematics* 7, 393–397.

J. Canny (1987), A new algebraic method for robot motion planning and real geometry, *Proceedings 28th Annual IEEE Symposium on Foundations of Computer Science*, pp. 39–48.

J. Canny (1988a), *The Complexity of Robot Motion Planning*, MIT Press, Cambridge, MA.

J. Canny (1988b), Some algebraic and geometric computations in PSPACE, *Proceedings 20th Annual ACM Symposium on Theory of Computing*, pp. 460–467.

J. Canny (1993), Computing roadmaps in general semialgebraic sets, *Computer Journal*, 36, 409–418.

J. Canny and J. Reif (1987), New lower bound techniques for robot motion planning problems, *Proceedings 28th Annual IEEE Symposium on Foundations of Computer Science*, pp. 49–60.

S. Cappell, J. Goodman, J. Pach, R. Pollack, M. Sharir, and R. Wenger (1990), The combinatorial complexity of hyperplane transversals, *Proceedings 6th Annual Symposium on Computational Geometry*, pp. 83–91. (A revised version, entitled "Common tangents and common transversals," *Advances in Mathematics* 106 (1994), 198–215.)

B. Chazelle (1983), The polygon containment problem, in: *Advances in Computing Research, Vol. I: Computational Geometry* (F. Preparata, ed.), JAI Press, Greenwich, CT, pp. 1–33.

B. Chazelle (1993a), Cutting hyperplanes for divide-and-conquer, *Discrete and Computational Geometry* 10, 145–158.

B. Chazelle (1993b), An optimal convex hull algorithm in any fixed dimension, *Discrete and Computational Geometry* 10, 377–409.

B. Chazelle and H. Edelsbrunner (1992), An optimal algorithm for intersecting line segments in the plane, *Journal of Association for Computing Machinery* 39, 1–54.

B. Chazelle, H. Edelsbrunner, L. Guibas, and M. Sharir (1989a), A singly exponential stratification scheme for real semi-algebraic varieties and its applications, *Proceedings 16th International Colloquium on Automata, Languages and Programming*, Lecture Notes in Computer Science, vol. 372 (G. Ausiello, ed.), Springer-Verlag, New York–Berlin–Heidelberg, pp. 179–192.

B. Chazelle, H. Edelsbrunner, L. Guibas, and M. Sharir (1989b), Lines in space: Combinatorics, algorithms, and applications, *Proceedings 21st Annual ACM Symposium on Theory of Computing*, pp. 382–393.

B. Chazelle, H. Edelsbrunner, L. Guibas, and M. Sharir (1991), A singly exponential stratification scheme for real semi-algebraic varieties and its applications, *Theoretical Computer Science* 84, 77–105.

B. Chazelle, H. Edelsbrunner, L. Guibas, and M. Sharir (1993), Diameter, width, closest line pair, and parametric searching, *Discrete and Computational Geometry* 10, 183–196.

B. Chazelle, H. Edelsbrunner, L. Guibas, and M. Sharir (1994), Algorithms for bichromatic line segment problems and polyhedral terrains, *Algorithmica* 11, 116–132.

B. Chazelle, H. Edelsbrunner, L. Guibas, M. Sharir, and J. Snoeyink (1993), Computing a face in an arrangement of line segments and related problems, *SIAM Journal on Computing* 22, 1286–1302.

B. Chazelle and J. Friedman (1990), A deterministic view of random sampling and its use in geometry, *Combinatorica* 10, 229–249.

B. Chazelle and J. Friedman (1994), Point location among hyperplanes and unidirectional ray shooting, *Computational Geometry: Theory and Applications* 4, 53–62.

B. Chazelle and L. Guibas (1986), Fractional cascading: I. A data structuring technique, *Algorithmica* 1, 133–162.

B. Chazelle and L. Guibas (1989), Visibility and intersection problems in plane geometry, *Discrete and Computational Geometry* 4, 557–581.

B. Chazelle, L. Guibas, and D. Lee (1985), The power of geometric duality, *BIT* 25, 76–90.

B. Chazelle and D. Lee (1986), On a circle placement problem, *Computing* 36, 1–16.

B. Chazelle and M. Sharir (1990), An algorithm for generalized point location and its applications, *Journal of Symbolic Computation* 10, 281–309.

J. Chen and Y. Han (1990), Shortest paths on a polyhedron, *Proceedings 6th Annual Symposium on Computational Geometry*, pp. 360–369.

P. Chew (1993), Near-quadratic bounds for the L_1 Voronoi diagram of moving points, *Proceedings 5th Canadian Conference on Computational Geometry*, pp. 364–369.

P. Chew, M. Goodrich, D. Huttenlocher, K. Kedem, J. Kleinberg, and D. Kravets (1993), Geometric pattern matching under Euclidean motion, *Proceedings 5th Canadian Conference on Computational Geometry*, pp. 151–156.

P. Chew and K. Kedem (1993), A convex polygon among polygonal obstacles: Placement and high-clearance motion, *Computational Geometry: Theory and Applications* 3, 59–89.

P. Chew, K. Kedem, M. Sharir, B. Tagansky, and E. Welzl (1995), Voronoi diagrams of lines in 3-space under polyhedral convex distance functions, *Proceedings 6th Annual ACM-SIAM Symposium on Discrete Algorithms*, pp. 197–204.

J. Choi, J. Sellen, and C. Yap (1994), Approximate Euclidean shortest path in 3-space, *Proceedings 10th Annual Symposium on Computational Geometry*, pp. 41–48.

K. Clarkson (1987a), Approximation algorithms for shortest path motion planning, *Proceedings 19th Annual ACM Symposium on Theory of Computing*, pp. 56–65.

K. Clarkson (1987b), New applications of random sampling in computational geometry, *Discrete and Computational Geometry* 2, 195–222.

K. Clarkson (1990), Computing a single face in an arrangement of segments, manuscript.

K. Clarkson (1992), Randomized geometric algorithms, in: *Computing in Euclidean Geometry* (D.-Z. Du and F. Hwang, eds.), World Scientific, Singapore, pp. 117–162.

K. Clarkson, H. Edelsbrunner, L. Guibas, M. Sharir, and E. Welzl (1990), Combinatorial complexity bounds for arrangements of curves and spheres, *Discrete and Computational Geometry* 5, 99–160.

K. Clarkson and P. Shor (1989), Applications of random sampling in computational geometry II, *Discrete and Computational Geometry* 4, 387–421.

R. Cole and M. Sharir (1989), Visibility problems for polyhedral terrains, *Journal of Symbolic Computation* 7, 11–30.

G. Collins (1975), Quantifier elimination for real closed fields by cylindrical algebraic decomposition, *Second GI Conf. on Automata Theory and Formal Languages*, Lecture Notes in Computer Science, vol. 33 (H. Barkhage, ed.), Springer-Verlag, New York–Berlin–Heidelberg, pp. 134–183.

T. Coreman, C. Leiserson, and R. Rivest (1990), *Introduction to Algorithms*, McGraw-Hill, New York.

H. Davenport (1971), A combinatorial problem connected with differential equations II, *Acta Arithmetica* 17, 363–372.

H. Davenport and A. Schinzel (1965), A combinatorial problem connected with differential equations, *American Journal of Mathematics* 87, 684–689.

M. de Berg (1993), *Ray Shooting, Depth Orders, and Hidden Surface Removal*, Lecture Notes in Computer Science, vol. 703, Springer-Verlag, New York–Berlin–Heidelberg.

M. de Berg, K. Dobrindt, and O. Schwarzkopf (1994), On lazy randomized incremental construction, *Proceedings 26th Annual ACM Symposium on Theory of Computing*, pp. 105–114.

M. de Berg, L. Guibas, and D. Halperin (1994), Vertical decompositions for triangles in 3-space, *Proceedings 10th Annual Symposium on Computational Geometry*, pp. 1–10.

M. de Berg, D. Halperin, M. Overmars, and M. van Kreveld (1992), Sparse arrangements and the number of views of polyhedral scenes, Technical Report, Dept. Computer Science, Utrecht University, Utrecht.

T. Dey and H. Edelsbrunner (1994), Counting triangle crossings and halving planes, *Discrete and Computational Geometry* 12, 281–289.

D. Dobkin and D. Souvaine (1990), Computational geometry in a curved world, *Algorithmica* 5, 421–457.

K. Dobrindt (1994), *Algorithmes Dynamiques Randomisés pour les Arrangements: Application à la Planification de Trajectoires*, Ph.D. Dissertation, Ecole des Mines de Paris, Paris.

A. Dobson and S. Macdonald (1974), Lower bounds for lengths of Davenport–Schinzel sequences, *Utilitas Mathematica* 6, 251–257.

J. Driscoll, N. Sarnak, D. Sleator, and R. Tarjan (1989), Making data structures persistent, *Journal of Computer and Systems Sciences* 38, 86–124.

R. Dudley (1978), Central limit theorems for empirical measures, *Annals of Probability* 6, 899–929.

H. Edelsbrunner (1985), Finding transversals for sets of simple geometric figures, *Theoretical Computer Science* 35, 55–69.

H. Edelsbrunner (1987), *Algorithms in Combinatorial Geometry*, Springer-Verlag, New York–Berlin–Heidelberg.

H. Edelsbrunner (1989), The upper envelope of piecewise linear functions: Tight complexity bounds in higher dimensions, *Discrete and Computational Geometry* 4, 337–343.

H. Edelsbrunner and L. Guibas (1989), Topologically sweeping an arrangement, *Journal of Computer and Systems Sciences* 38, 165–194. (Corrigendum in vol. 42 (1991), 249–251.)

H. Edelsbrunner, L. Guibas, J. Hershberger, J. Pach, R. Pollack, R Seidel, M. Sharir, and J. Snoeyink (1989), On arrangements of Jordan arcs with three intersections per pair, *Discrete and Computational Geometry* 4, 523–539.

H. Edelsbrunner, L. Guibas, J. Pach, R. Pollack, R Seidel, and M. Sharir (1992), Arrangements of curves in the plane—topology, combinatorics, and algorithms, *Theoretical Computer Science* 92, 319–336.

H. Edelsbrunner, L. Guibas, and M. Sharir (1989), The upper envelope of piecewise linear functions: Algorithms and applications, *Discrete and Computational Geometry* 4, 311–336.

H. Edelsbrunner, L. Guibas, and M. Sharir (1990), The complexity of many faces in arrangements of lines and of segments, *Discrete and Computational Geometry* 5, 161–196.

H. Edelsbrunner, L. Guibas, and J. Stolfi (1986), Optimal point location in a monotone subdivision, *SIAM Journal on Computing* 15, 317–340.

H. Edelsbrunner, H. Maurer, F. Preparata, A. Rosenberg, E. Welzl, and D. Wood (1982), Stabbing line segments, *BIT* 22, 274–281.

H. Edelsbrunner, J. O'Rourke, and R. Seidel (1986), Constructing arrangements of lines and hyperplanes with applications, *SIAM Journal on Computing* 15, 341–363.

H. Edelsbrunner, M. Overmars, and D. Wood (1983), Graphics in flatland: A case study, in: *Advances in Computing Research* (F. Preparata, ed.), vol. 1, JAI Press, London, pp. 35–59.

H. Edelsbrunner and R. Seidel (1986), Voronoi diagrams and arrangements, *Discrete and Computational Geometry* 1, 25–44.

H. Edelsbrunner, R. Seidel, and M. Sharir (1993), On the zone theorem for hyperplane arrangements, *SIAM Journal on Computing* 22, 418–429.

H. Edelsbrunner and M. Sharir (1990), The maximum number of ways to stab n convex non-intersecting objects in the plane is $2n-2$, *Discrete and Computational Geometry* 5, 35–42.

H. Edelsbrunner and E. Welzl (1985), On the number of line separations of a finite set in the plane, *Journal of Combinatorial Theory, Series A* 38, 15–29.

A. Efrat, G. Rote, and M. Sharir (1993), On the union of fat wedges and separating a collection of segments by a line, *Computational Geometry: Theory and Applications* 3, 277–288.

A. Efrat and M. Sharir (1994), A near-linear algorithm for the planar segment center problem, *Proceedings 5th Annual ACM-SIAM Symposium on Discrete Algorithms*, pp. 87–97.

P. Erdős, L. Lovász, A. Simmons, and E. Strauss (1973), Dissection graphs of planar point sets, in: *A Survey of Combinatorial Theory* (J. Srivastava et al., eds.), North-Holland, Amsterdam, pp. 139–149.

M. Fischer (1972), Efficiency of equivalence algorithms, in: *Complexity of Computer Computations* (R. Miller and J. Thatcher, eds.), Plenum Press, New York, pp. 153–168.

S. Fortune (1987), A sweepline algorithm for Voronoi diagrams, *Algorithmica* 2, 153–174.

S. Fortune (1992), Voronoi diagrams and Delaunay triangulations, in: *Computing in Euclidean Geometry* (D.-Z. Du and F. Hwang, eds.), World Scientific, Singapore, pp. 193–233.

J. Fu and R. Lee (1991), Voronoi diagrams of moving points in the plane, *International Journal of Computational Geometry and Applications* 1, 23–32.

Z. Füredi (1990), The maximum number of unit distances in a convex n-gon, *Journal of Combinatorial Theory, Series A* 55, 316–320.

Z. Füredi and P. Hajnal (1992), Davenport–Schinzel theory of matrices, *Discrete Mathematics* 103, 233–251.

D. Gardy and D. Gouyou-Beauchamps (1990), Enumeration of some Davenport–Schinzel sequences, Technical Report 564, Université de Paris-Sud, Paris.

J. Goodman, R. Pollack, and R. Wenger (1993), Geometric transversal theory, in: *New Trends in Discrete and Computational Geometry* (J. Pach, ed.), Springer-Verlag, New York–Berlin–Heidelberg, pp. 163–198.

J. Goodman, R. Pollack, and R. Wenger (1994), Bounding the number of geometric permutations induced by k-transversals, *Proceedings 10th Annual Symposium on Computational Geometry*, pp. 198–202.

M. Goodrich (1991), Approximation algorithms to design parallel algorithms that may ignore processor allocation, *Proceedings 32nd Annual IEEE Symposium on Foundations of Computer Science*, pp. 711–722.

R. Graham, B. Rothschild, and J. Spencer (1980), *Ramsey Theory*, Wiley-Interscience, New York.

M. Greenberg (1967), *Lectures on Algebraic Topology*, Benjamin, Reading, MA.

B. Grünbaum (1967), *Convex Polytopes*, John Wiley, Chichester.

L. Guibas, D. Halperin, J. Matoušek, and M. Sharir (1993), On vertical decomposition of arrangements of hyperplanes in four dimensions, *Proceedings 5th Canadian Conference on Computational Geometry*, pp. 127–132.

L. Guibas, J. Hershberger, D. Leven, M. Sharir, and R. Tarjan (1987), Linear time algorithms for shortest path and visibility problems inside triangulated simple polygons, *Algorithmica* 2, 209–233.

L. Guibas, D. Knuth, and M. Sharir (1992), Randomized incremental construction of Delaunay and Voronoi diagrams, *Algorithmica* 7, 381–413.

L. Guibas, J. Mitchell, and T. Roos (1991), Voronoi diagrams of moving points in the plane, *Proceedings 17th International Workshop on Graph-Theoretic Concepts in Computer Science*, Lecture Notes in Computer Science, vol. 570 (G. Schmidt and R. Berghammer, eds.), Springer-Verlag, New York–Berlin–Heidelberg, pp. 113–125.

L. Guibas and M. Sharir (1993), Combinatorics and algorithms of arrangements, in: *New Trends in Discrete and Computational Geometry* (J. Pach, ed.), Springer-Verlag, New York–Berlin–Heidelberg, pp. 9–36.

L. Guibas, M. Sharir, and S. Sifrony (1989), On the general motion planning problem with two degrees of freedom, *Discrete and Computational Geometry* 4, 491–521.

D. Halperin (1992), *Algorithmic Motion Planning via Arrangements of Curves and of Surfaces,* Ph.D. Dissertation, Computer Science Department, Tel-Aviv University, Tel Aviv.

D. Halperin (1993), On the Minkowski sum of two simple polygons, manuscript.

D. Halperin (1994), On the complexity of a single cell in certain arrangements of surfaces in 3-space, *Discrete and Computational Geometry* 11, 1–33.

D. Halperin, M. Overmars, and M. Sharir (1992), Efficient motion planning for an *L*-shaped object, *SIAM Journal on Computing* 21, 1–23.

D. Halperin and M. Sharir (1993), Near-quadratic bounds for the motion planning problem for a polygon in a polygonal environment, *Proceedings 34th Annual IEEE Symposium on Foundations of Computer Science,* pp. 382–391.

D. Halperin and M. Sharir (1994a), Arrangements and their applications in robotics: Recent developments, *Proceedings of Workshop on Algorithmic Foundations of Robotics* (K. Goldberg et al., eds.), A. K. Peters, Boston, MA.

D. Halperin and M. Sharir (1994b), Almost tight upper bounds for the single cell and zone problems in three dimensions, *Proceedings 10th Annual Symposium on Computational Geometry,* pp. 11–20.

D. Halperin and M. Sharir (1994c), New bounds for lower envelopes in three dimensions, with applications to visibility in terrains, *Discrete and Computational Geometry* 12, 313–326.

D. Halperin and C. Yap (1993), Complexity of translating a box in polyhedral 3-space, *Proceedings 9th Annual Symposium on Computational Geometry,* pp. 29–38.

S. Har Peled (1993), The complexity of many cells in the overlay of many arrangements, manuscript.

S. Hart and M. Sharir (1986), Nonlinearity of Davenport–Schinzel sequences and of generalized path compression schemes, *Combinatorica* 6, 151–177.

R. Hartshorne (1977), *Algebraic Geometry,* Springer-Verlag, New York–Berlin–Heidelberg.

D. Haussler and E. Welzl (1987), ε-nets and simplex range queries, *Discrete and Computational Geometry* 2, 127–151.

J. Heintz, T. Recio, and M. F. Roy (1991), Algorithms in real algebraic geometry and applications to computational geometry, in: *Discrete and Computational Geometry: Papers from DIMACS Special Year* (J. Goodman, R. Pollack, and W. Steiger, eds.), American Mathematical Society, Providence, RI, pp. 137–163.

J. Hershberger (1989), Finding the upper envelope of n line segments in $O(n \log n)$ time, *Information Processing Letters* 33, 169–174.

J. Hershberger and S. Suri (1993), Efficient computation of Euclidean shortest paths in the plane, *Proceedings 34th Annual IEEE Symposium on Foundations of Computer Science,* pp. 508–517.

J. Hopcroft, J. Schwartz, and M. Sharir (1984), On the complexity of motion planning for multiple independent objects: PSPACE hardness of the 'warehouseman's problem,' *The International Journal of Robotics Research* 3 (4), 76–88.

J. Hopcroft, J. Schwartz, and M. Sharir (eds.) (1987), *Planning, Geometry and Complexity of Robot Motion*, Ablex Publishing, Norwood, NJ.

M. Houle and G. Toussaint (1988), Computing the width of a set, *IEEE Transactions on Pattern Analysis and Machine Intelligence* 5, 761–765.

D. Huttenlocher and K. Kedem (1990), Efficiently computing the Hausdorff distance for point sets under translation, *Proceedings 6th Annual Symposium on Computational Geometry*, pp. 340–349.

D. Huttenlocher, K. Kedem, and J. Kleinberg (1992a), Voronoi diagrams of rigidly moving sets of points, *Information Processing Letters* 43, 217–223.

D. Huttenlocher, K. Kedem, and J. Kleinberg (1992b), On dynamic Voronoi diagrams and the minimum Hausdorff distance for point sets under Euclidean motion in the plane, *Proceedings 8th Annual Symposium on Computational Geometry*, pp. 110–120.

D. Huttenlocher, K. Kedem, and M. Sharir (1993), The upper envelope of Voronoi surfaces and its applications, *Discrete and Computational Geometry* 9, 267–291.

H. Hwang, R. Chang, and H. Tu (1990), The separability problem in dynamic computational geometry, manuscript.

H. Imai, D. Lee, and C. Yang (1992), 1-Segment center covering problems, *ORSA Journal of Computing* 4, 426–434.

K. Imai, S. Sumino, and H. Imai (1989), Minmax geometric fitting of two corresponding sets of points, *Proceedings 5th Annual Symposium on Computational Geometry*, pp. 266–275.

J. Jaromczyk and M. Kowaluk (1988), Skewed projections with an application to line stabbing in $\mathbb{R}^3$, *Proceedings 4th Annual Symposium on Computational Geometry*, pp. 362–370.

M. Katchalski, T. Lewis, and A. Liu (1986), Geometric permutation and common transversals, *Discrete and Computational Geometry* 1, 371–377.

M. Katchalski, T. Lewis, and A. Liu (1987), Geometric permutations of disjoint translates of convex sets, *Discrete Mathematics* 65, 249–259.

M. Katchalski, T. Lewis, and A. Liu (1992), The different ways of stabbing disjoint convex sets, *Discrete and Computational Geometry* 7, 197–206.

M. Katchalski, T. Lewis, and J. Zaks (1985), Geometric permutations for convex sets, *Discrete Mathematics* 54, 271–284.

N. Katoh, T. Tokuyama, and K. Iwano (1992), On the minimum and maximum spanning trees of linearly moving points, *Proceedings 33rd Annual IEEE Symposium on Foundations of Computer Science*, pp. 396–405.

K. Kedem, R. Livne, J. Pach, and M. Sharir (1986), On the union of Jordan regions and collision-free translational motion amidst polygonal obstacles, *Discrete and Computational Geometry* 1, 59–71.

K. Kedem and M. Sharir (1985), An efficient algorithm for planning collision-free translational motion of a convex polygonal object in 2-dimensional space amidst polygonal obstacles, *Proceedings 1st Annual Symposium on Computational Geometry*, pp. 75–80.

K. Kedem and M. Sharir (1990), An efficient motion planning algorithm for a convex polygonal object in two-dimensional polygonal space, *Discrete and Computational Geometry* 5, 43–75.

K. Kedem, M. Sharir, and S. Toledo (1993), On critical orientations in the Kedem-Sharir motion planning algorithm for a convex polygon in the plane, *Proceedings 5th Canadian Conference on Computational Geometry*, pp. 204–209.

J. Ketonen and R. Solovay (1981), Rapidly growing Ramsey functions, *Annals of Mathematics* 113, 267–314.

M. Klawe (1990), Superlinear bounds on matrix searching, *Proceedings 1st Annual ACM-SIAM Symposium on Discrete Algorithms*, pp. 485–493.

M. Klazar (1992), A general upper bound in extremal theory of sequences, *Commentationes Mathematicae Universitatis Carolinae* 33, 737–746.

M. Klazar (1993), Two results on a partial ordering of finite sequences, *Commentationes Mathematicae Universitatis Carolinae* 34, 667–675.

M. Klazar (1994), A linear upper bound in extremal theory of sequences, *Journal of Combinatorial Theory, Series A* 68, 454–464.

M. Klazar (1995), *Combinatorial Aspects of Davenport–Schinzel Sequences*, Ph.D. Dissertation, Department of Applied Mathematics, Charles University, Prague.

M. Klazar and P. Valtr (1994), Generalized Davenport–Schinzel sequences, *Combinatorica* 14, 463–476.

D. Knuth (1973), *The Art of Computer Programming, Vol. 3: Sorting and Searching*, Addison-Wesley, Reading, MA.

P. Komjáth (1988), A simplified construction of nonlinear Davenport–Schinzel sequences, *Journal of Combinatorial Theory, Series A* 49, 262–267.

J. Komlós, J. Pach, and G. Woeginger (1992), Almost tight bounds for epsilon–nets, *Discrete and Computational Geometry* 7, 163–173.

G. Kreisel (1952), On the interpretation of nonfinitistic proofs, II, *Journal of Symbolic Logic* 17, 43–58.

M. van Kreveld (1993), On fat partitioning, fat covering, and the union size of polygons, *Proceedings 3rd Workshop on Algorithms and Data Structures*, Lecture Notes in Computer Science, vol. 709 (F. Dehne et al., eds.), pp. 452–463.

J. Latombe (1991), *Robot Motion Planning*, Kluwer Academic Publishers, Boston, MA.

D. Lee (1980), Two-dimensional Voronoi diagrams in the L_p-metric, *Journal of Association for Computing Machinery* 27, 604–618.

D. Leven and M. Sharir (1987a), Planning a purely translational motion for a convex object in two-dimensional space using generalized Voronoi diagrams, *Discrete and Computational Geometry* 2, 9–31.

D. Leven and M. Sharir (1987b), On the number of critical free contacts of a convex polygonal object moving in two-dimensional polygonal space, *Discrete and Computational Geometry* 2, 255–270.

D. Leven and M. Sharir (1987c), Intersection and proximity problems and Voronoi diagrams, in: *Algorithmic and Geometric Aspects of Robotics* vol. 1 (J. Schwartz and C. Yap, eds.), LEA Publishers, Hillsdale, NJ, pp. 187–228.

D. Leven and M. Sharir (1987d), An efficient and simple motion planning algorithm for a ladder amidst polygonal obstacles, *Journal of Algorithms* 8, 192–215.

R. Livne and M. Sharir (1985), On maxima of functions, intersection patterns of curves, and Davenport–Schinzel sequences, *Proceedings 26th Annual IEEE Symposium on Foundations of Computer Science*, pp. 312–320.

E. Lockwood (1961), *A Book of Curves*, Cambridge University Press, Cambridge.

M. Loebl and J. Nešetřil (1988), Linearity and unprovability of set union problems, *Proceedings 20th Annual ACM Symposium on Theory of Computing*, pp. 367–376.

L. Lovász (1971), On the number of halving lines, *Annales Universitatis Scientiarum Budapesttimensis de Rolando Eötvös Nominatae, Sectio Mathematica* 14, 107–108.

A. Mandel (1981), *Topology of Oriented Matroids*, Ph.D. Dissertation, University of Waterloo, Waterloo.

J. Matoušek (1991), Approximations and optimal geometric divide-and-conquer, *Proceedings 23rd Annual ACM Symposium on Theory of Computing*, pp. 506–511.

J. Matoušek (1993a), Epsilon-nets and computational geometry, in: *New Trends in Discrete and Computational Geometry* (J. Pach, ed.), Springer-Verlag, New York–Berlin–Heidelberg, pp. 69–89.

J. Matoušek (1993b), On vertical ray shooting in arrangements, *Computational Geometry: Theory and Applications* 2, 279–285.

J. Matoušek, J. Pach, M. Sharir, S. Sifrony, and E. Welzl (1994), Fat triangles determine linearly many holes, *SIAM Journal on Computing* 23, 154–169.

M. McKenna and J. O'Rourke (1988), Arrangements of lines in 3-space: A data structure with applications, *Proceedings 4th Annual Symposium on Computational Geometry*, pp. 371–380.

P. McMullen and G. Shepard (1971), *Convex Polytopes and the Upper Bound Conjecture*, London Mathematical Society Lecture Note Series, vol. 3, Cambridge University Press, Cambridge.

N. Megiddo (1979), Combinatorial optimization with rational objective functions, *Mathematical Operations Research* 4, 414–424.

N. Megiddo (1982), Poly-log parallel algorithms for LP with an application to exploding flying objects, manuscript.

N. Megiddo (1983), Applying parallel computation algorithms in the design of serial algorithms, *Journal of Association for Computing Machinery* 30, 852–865.

N. Megiddo (1986), Dynamic location problems, *Annals of Operations Research* 6, 313–319.

K. Mehlhorn (1984), *Data Structures and Algorithms 3: Multi-dimensional Searching and Computational Geometry*, Springer-Verlag, Berlin–Heidelberg–New York.

K. Mehlhorn, M. Sharir, and E. Welzl (1993), Tail estimates for the efficiency of randomized incremental algorithms for line segment intersection, *Computational Geometry: Theory and Applications* 3, 235–246.

N. Miller and M. Sharir (1991), Efficient randomized algorithms for constructing the union of fat triangles and of pseudodiscs, manuscript.

W. Mills (1973), Some Davenport–Schinzel sequences, *Congressus Numerantium IX: Proceedings 3rd Manitoba Conference on Numerical Mathematics and Computing* (R. Thomas and H. Williams, eds.), pp. 307–313.

J. Mitchell (1992), L_1 shortest paths among polygonal obstacles in the plane, *Algorithmica* 8, 55–88.

J. Mitchell (1993), Shortest paths among obstacles in the plane, *Proceedings 9th Annual Symposium on Computational Geometry*, pp. 308–317.

J. Mitchell, D. Mount, and C. Papadimitriou (1987), The discrete geodesic problem, *SIAM Journal on Computing* 16, 647–668.

J. Mitchell, G. Rote, and G. Woeginger (1992), Minimum-link paths among obstacles in the plane, *Algorithmica* 8, 431–459.

S. Mohaban and M. Sharir (in press), Ray shooting amidst spheres in 3 dimensions and related problems, *SIAM Journal on Computing*.

C. Monma and S. Suri (1992), Transitions in geometric minimum spanning trees, *Discrete and Computational Geometry* 8, 265–293.

R. Mullin and R. Stanton (1972), A map-theoretic approach to Davenport–Schinzel sequences, *Pacific Journal of Mathematics* 40, 167–172.

K. Mulmuley (1990), A fast planar partition algorithm, I, *Journal of Symbolic Computation* 10, 253–280.

K. Mulmuley (1991a), Hidden surface removal with respect to a moving point of view, *Proceedings 23rd Annual ACM Symposium on Theory of Computing*, pp. 512–522.

K. Mulmuley (1991b), A fast planar partition algorithm, II, *Journal of Association for Computing Machinery* 38, 74–103.

K. Mulmuley (1991c), On levels in arrangements and Voronoi diagrams, *Discrete and Computational Geometry* 6, 307–338.

K. Mulmuley (1993), *Computational Geometry: An Introduction Through Randomized Algorithms*, Prentice Hall, Englewood Cliffs, NJ.

C. Ó'Dúnlaing, M. Sharir, and C. Yap (1986), Generalized Voronoi diagrams for a ladder. I: Topological analysis, *Communications on Pure and Applied Mathematics* 34, 423–483.

C. Ó'Dúnlaing, M. Sharir, and C. Yap (1987), Generalized Voronoi diagrams for a ladder: II. Efficient construction of the diagram, *Algorithmica* 2, 27–59.

J. O'Rourke (1987), *Art Gallery Theorems and Algorithms*, Oxford University Press, New York, NY.

T. Ottmann and D. Wood (1984), Dynamical sets of points, *Computer Vision, Graphics and Image Processing* 27, 157–166.

J. Pach and M. Sharir (1989), The upper envelope of piecewise linear functions and the boundary of a region enclosed by convex plates: Combinatorial analysis, *Discrete and Computational Geometry* 4, 291–309.

J. Pach and M. Sharir (1991), On vertical visibility in arrangements of segments and the queue size in the Bentley–Ottmann line sweeping algorithm: Combinatorial analysis, *SIAM Journal on Computing* 20, 460–470.

J. Pach, W. Steiger, and E. Szemerédi (1992), An upper bound on the number of planar k-sets, *Discrete and Computational Geometry* 7, 109–123.

C. Papadimitriou (1985), An algorithm for shortest path motion in three dimensions, *Information Processing Letters* 20, 259–263.

C. Papadimitriou and E. Silverberg (1987), Optimal piecewise linear motion of an object among obstacles, *Algorithmica* 2, 523–539.

J. Paris and L. Harrington (1977), A mathematical incompleteness in Peano arithmetic, in: *Handbook of Mathematical Logic* (J. Barwise, ed.), North-Holland, Amsterdam, pp. 1133–1142.

M. Pellegrini (1994), On lines missing polyhedral sets in 3-space, *Discrete and Computational Geometry* 12, 203–221.

M. Pellegrini and P. Shor (1992), Finding stabbing lines in 3-Space, *Discrete and Computational Geometry* 8, 191–208.

C. Peterkin (1973), Some results on Davenport–Schinzel sequences, *Congressus Numerantium IX: Proceedings 3rd Manitoba Conference on Numerical Mathematics and Computing* (R. Thomas and H. Williams, eds.), pp. 337–344.

H. Plantinga and C. Dyer (1990), Visibility, occlusion, and the aspect graph, *International J. Computer Vision* 5, 137–160.

R. Pollack and M. F. Roy (1993), On the number of cells defined by a set of polynomials, *C.R. Acad. Sci. Paris*, t. 316, Série I, 573–577.

R. Pollack, M. Sharir, and S. Sifrony (1988), Separating two simple polygons by a sequence of translations, *Discrete and Computational Geometry* 3, 123–136.

G. Polya (1956), On picture writing, *American Mathematical Monthly* 63, 689–697.

F. Preparata and M. Shamos (1985), *Computational Geometry: An Introduction*, Springer-Verlag, New York–Berlin–Heidelberg.

F. Preparata and R. Tamassia (1992), Efficient point location in a convex spatial cell-complex, *SIAM Journal on Computing* 21, 267–280.

E. Ramos (1994), Intersection of unit-balls and diameter of a point set in $\mathbb{R}^3$, manuscript.

J. Reif (1979), Complexity of the mover's problem and generalizations, *Proceedings 20th Annual IEEE Symposium on Foundations of Computer Science*, pp. 421–427. (Also in: *Planning, Geometry and Complexity of Robot Motion* (J. Hopcroft, J. Schwartz, and M. Sharir, eds.), 1987, pp. 267–281.)

B. Rennie and A. Dobson (1975), Upper bounds for the lengths of Davenport–Schinzel sequences, *Utilitas Mathematica* 8, 181–185.

H. Rogers (1967), *Theory of Recursive Functions and Effective Computability*, McGraw-Hill, New York.

T. Roos (1993), Tighter bounds on Voronoi diagrams of moving points, *Proceedings 5th Canadian Conference on Computational Geometry*, pp. 358–363.

T. Roos and G. Albers (1992), Maintaining proximity in higher dimensional spaces, *Proceedings 17th Symposium on Mathematical Foundations of Computer Science*, Lecture Notes in Computer Science, vol. 629 (I. Havel and V. Koubek, eds.), Springer-Verlag, New York–Berlin–Heidelberg, pp. 483–493.

D. Roselle (1974), An algorithmic approach to Davenport–Schinzel sequences, *Utilitas Mathematica* 6, 91–93.

D. Roselle and R. Stanton (1970), Results on Davenport–Schinzel sequences, *Congressus Numerantium I, Proceedings Louisiana Conference on Combinatorics, Graph Theory, and Computing* (R. Mullin et al., eds.), pp. 249–267.

D. Roselle and R. Stanton (1971), Some properties of Davenport–Schinzel sequences, *Acta Arithmetica* 17, 355–362.

N. Sarnak and R. Tarjan (1986), Planar point location using persistent search trees, *Communications of the ACM* 29, 609–679.

J. Schwartz and M. Sharir (1983a), On the piano mover's problem: I. The case of a two-dimensional rigid polygonal body moving amidst polygonal barriers, *Communications on Pure and Applied Mathematics* 36, 345–398.

J. Schwartz and M. Sharir (1983b), On the piano mover's problem: II. General techniques for computing topological properties of real algebraic manifolds, *Advances in Applied Mathematics* 4, 298–351.

J. Schwartz and M. Sharir (1988), A survey of motion planning and related geometric algorithms, *Artificial Intelligence* 37, 157–169.

J. Schwartz and M. Sharir (1990), On the two-dimensional Davenport–Schinzel problem, *Journal of Symbolic Computation* 10, 371–393.

R. Seidel (1991), Small-dimensional linear programming and convex hulls made easy, *Discrete and Computational Geometry* 6, 423–434.

R. Seidel (1993), Backward analysis of randomized incremental geometric algorithms, in: *New Trends in Discrete and Computational Geometry* (J. Pach, ed.), Springer-Verlag, New York–Berlin–Heidelberg, pp. 37–67.

M. Sharir (1987), Almost linear upper bounds on the length of general Davenport–Schinzel sequences, *Combinatorica* 7, 131–143.

M. Sharir (1988a), Improved lower bounds on the length of Davenport–Schinzel sequences, *Combinatorica* 8, 117–124.

M. Sharir (1988b), Davenport–Schinzel sequences and their geometric applications, in: *Theoretical Foundations of Computer Graphics and CAD* (R. Earnshaw, ed.), NATO ASI Series, F40, Springer-Verlag, New York–Berlin–Heidelberg, pp. 253–278.

M. Sharir (1989a), Algorithmic motion planning in robotics, *IEEE Computer* 22, 9–20.

M. Sharir (1989b), A note on the Papadimitriou-Silverberg algorithm for planning optimal piecewise linear motion of a ladder, *Information Processing Letters* 32, 187–190.

M. Sharir (1991), On k-sets in arrangements of curves and surfaces, *Discrete and Computational Geometry* 6, 593–613.

M. Sharir (1994a), Almost tight upper bounds for lower envelopes in higher dimensions, *Discrete and Computational Geometry* 12, 327–345.

M. Sharir (1994b), Vertical decomposition of lower envelopes in four dimensions and its applications, manuscript.

M. Sharir, R. Cole, K. Kedem, D. Leven, R. Pollack, and S. Sifrony (1986), Geometric applications of Davenport–Schinzel sequences, *Proceedings 27th Annual IEEE Symposium on Foundations of Computer Science*, pp. 77–86.

M. Sharir and A. Schorr (1986), On shortest paths in polyhedral spaces, *SIAM Journal on Computing* 15, 193–215.

M. Sharir and S. Toledo (1994), Extremal polygon containment problems, *Computational Geometry: Theory and Applications* 4, 99–118. (See also S. Toledo, Extremal polygon containment problems, *Proceedings 7th Annual Symposium on Computational Geometry*, 1991, pp. 176–185.)

P. Shor (1990), Geometric realization of superlinear Davenport–Schinzel sequences I: Line segments, manuscript.

P. Shor (1994), Geometric realization of superlinear Davenport–Schinzel sequences I: Fourth degree polynomials, in preparation.

S. Sifrony (1989), *Efficient Algorithms for Motion Planning Problems in Robotics*, Ph.D. Dissertation, Computer Science Department, Tel Aviv University, Tel Aviv.

S. Sifrony and M. Sharir (1987), A new efficient motion-planning algorithm for a rod in two-dimensional polygonal space, *Algorithmica* 2, 367–402.

D. Sommerville (1951), *Analytical Geometry in Three Dimensions*, Cambridge University Press, Cambridge.

R. Stanton and P. Dirksen (1976), Davenport–Schinzel sequences, *Ars Combinatorica* 1, 43–51.

R. Stanton and D. Roselle (1969), A result on Davenport–Schinzel sequences, in: *Combinatorial Theory and Its Applications, Colloq. Mathematical Society János Bolyai* vol. 4 (P. Erdős et al., eds.), North-Holland, Amsterdam, pp. 1023–1027.

E. Szemerédi (1974), On a problem of Davenport and Schinzel, *Acta Arithmetica* 25, 213–224.

E. Szemerédi and W. Trotter Jr. (1983), Extremal problems in discrete geometry, *Combinatorica* 3, 381–392.

H. Tamaki and T. Tokuyama (1995), How to cut pseudo-parabolas into segments, *Proceedings 11th Annual Symposium on Computational Geometry*.

A. Tamir (1988), Improved complexity bounds for center location problems on networks by using dynamic data structures, *SIAM Journal on Discrete Mathematics* 1, 377–396.

R. Tarjan (1975), Efficiency of a good but not linear set-union algorithm, *Journal of Association for Computing Machinery* 22, 215–225.

A. F. van der Stappen, D. Halperin, and M. Overmars (1993), The complexity of the free space of a robot moving amidst fat obstacles, *Computational Geometry: Theory and Applications* 3, 353–373.

B. van der Waerden (1970), *Algebra*, vol. 2, Fredrick Unger Publishing Co., New York, NY.

V. Vapnik and A. Chervonenkis (1971), On the uniform convergence of relative frequencies of events to their probabilities, *Theory of Probability and Its Applications* 16, 264–280.

G. Voronoi (1907), Nouvelles applications des paramètres continus à la théorie des formes quadratiques. Premier Mémoire: Sur quelques propriétés des formes quadratiques positives parfaites, *Journal für die Reine und Angewwandte Mathematik* 133, 97–178.

G. Voronoi (1908), Nouvelles applications des paramètres continus à la théorie des formes quadratiques. Deuxiéme Mémoire: Recherches sur les parallélloédres primitifs, *Journal für die Reine und Angewwandte Mathematik* 134, 198–207.

H. Warren (1968), Lower bounds for approximation of nonlinear manifolds, *Transactions American Mathematical Society* 133, 167–178.

E. Welzl (1985), Constructing the visibility graph for n line segments in $O(n^2)$ time, *Information Processing Letters* 20, 167–171.

R. Wenger (1990), Upper bounds on geometric permutations, *Discrete and Computational Geometry* 5, 27–33.

R. Wenocur and R. Dudley (1981), Some Vapnik-Chervonenkis classes, *Discrete Mathematics* 33, 313–318.

A. Wiernik and M. Sharir (1988), Planar realization of nonlinear Davenport–Schinzel sequences by segments, *Discrete and Computational Geometry* 3, 15–47.

F. Yao and A. Yao (1985), A general approach to geometric queries, *Proceedings 17th Annual ACM Symposium on Theory of Computing*, pp. 163–168.

R. Živaljević and S. Vrećica (1992), The colored Tverberg's problem and complexes of injective functions, *Journal of Combinatorial Theory, Series A* 61, 309–318.

INDEX